COUNSELING
A COMPREHENSIVE PROFESSION

FOURTH EDITION

Samuel T. Gladding
Wake Forest University

Merrill
an imprint of Prentice Hall
Upper Saddle River, New Jersey   *Columbus, Ohio*

Library of Congress Cataloging-in-Publication Data
Gladding, Samuel T.
    Counseling : a comprehensive profession / Samuel T. Gladding.—4th ed.
        p.   cm.
    Includes bibliographical references and index.
    ISBN 0-13-080333-2
    1. Counseling.   I. Title.
BF637.C6G53   2000
158'.3—dc21   99-25440
                                                                 CIP

Cover art: © Super Stock
Editor: Kevin M. Davis
Assistant Editor: Heather Doyle Fraser
Editorial Assistant: Holly Jennings
Production Editor: Linda Hillis Bayma
Copyeditor: Laura Larson
Design Coordinator: Diane C. Lorenzo
Cover Designer: Dan Eckel
Photo Coordinator: Nancy Ritz
Production Manager: Laura Messerly
Electronic Text Management: Marilyn Wilson Phelps, Karen L. Bretz, Melanie N. King
Illustrations: Jane Lopez
Director of Marketing: Kevin Flanagan
Marketing Manager: Meghan Shepherd-McCauley
Marketing Coordinator: Krista Groshong

This book was set in Garamond by Prentice Hall and was printed and bound by R.R. Donnelley & Sons Company. The cover was printed by Phoenix Color Corp.

© 2000, 1996 by Prentice-Hall, Inc.
Pearson Education
Upper Saddle River, New Jersey 07458

Earlier editions © 1992 and 1988 by Macmillan Publishing.

Photo credits: Scott Cunningham/Merrill, pp. 50, 78, 140, 182, 232, 258, 290, 320, 348, 380, 410, 478; John Deeks, Photo Researcher, p. 28; Mary Hagler/Merrill, p. 502; Photo Disc, Inc., pp. 2, 114, 164, 432; Simon & Schuster/PH College, pp. 208, 458.

Printed in the United States of America

10 9 8 7 6

ISBN: 0-13-080333-2

Prentice-Hall International (UK) Limited, *London*
Prentice-Hall of Australia Pty. Limited, *Sydney*
Prentice-Hall of Canada, Inc., *Toronto*
Prentice-Hall Hispanoamericana, S. A., *Mexico*
Prentice-Hall of India Private Limited, *New Delhi*
Prentice-Hall of Japan, Inc., *Tokyo*
Prentice-Hall (Singapore) Pte. Ltd., *Singapore*
Editora Prentice-Hall do Brasil, Ltda., *Rio de Janeiro*

To Thomas M. Elmore, who first instructed me in the art and science of counseling and who patiently taught me by example how to make the process personal

DISCOVER COMPANION WEBSITES: A VIRTUAL LEARNING ENVIRONMENT

Technology is a constantly growing and changing aspect of our field that is creating a need for content and resources. To address this emerging need, we have developed an online learning environment for students and professors alike—Companion Websites—to support our textbooks.

In creating a Companion Website, our goal is to build on and enhance what the textbook already offers. For this reason, the content for each user-friendly website is organized by topic and provides the professor and student with a variety of meaningful resources. Common features of a Companion Website include:

For the Professor—

Every Companion Website integrates Syllabus Manager™, an online syllabus creation and management utility.

- Syllabus Manager™ provides you, the instructor, with an easy, step-by-step process to create and revise syllabi, with direct links into Companion Website and other online content without having to learn HTML.
- Students may logon to your syllabus during any study session. All they need to know is the web address for the Companion Website and the password you've assigned to your syllabus.
- After you have created a syllabus using Syllabus Manager™, students may enter the syllabus for their course section from any point in the Companion Website.
- Class dates are highlighted in white and assignment due dates appear in blue. Clicking on a date, the student is shown the list of activities for the assignment. The activities for each assignment are linked directly to actual content, saving time for students.
- Adding assignments consists of clicking on the desired due date, then filling in the details of the assignment—name of the assignment, instructions, and whether or not it is a one-time or repeating assignment.
- In addition, links to other activities can be created easily. If the activity is online, a URL can be entered in the space provided, and it will be linked automatically in the final syllabus.
- Your completed syllabus is hosted on our servers, allowing convenient updates from any computer on the Internet. Changes you make to your syllabus are immediately available to your students at their next logon.

For the Student—

- **Topic Overviews**—outline key concepts in topic areas
- **Electronic Blue Book**—send homework or essays directly to your instructor's email with this paperless form
- **Message Board**—serves as a virtual bulletin board to post—or respond to—questions or comments to/from a national audience
- **Web Destinations**—links to www sites that relate to each topic area
- **Professional Organizations**—links to organizations that relate to topic areas
- **Additional Resources**—access to topic specific content that enhances material found in the text

To take advantage of these resources, please visit the Companion Website for *Counseling: A Comprehensive Profession,* Fourth Edition, at www.prenhall.com/gladding.

PREFACE

Counseling is a dynamic, ever-evolving, and exciting profession that deals with human tragedy and possibility in an intensive, personal, and caring way. It is a profession dedicated to prevention, development, exploration, empowerment, change, and remediation in an increasingly complex and chaotic world. In the past, counseling emphasized guidance by helping people make wise choices. Now guidance is but one part of this multidimensional profession.

This text presents counseling in a broad manner covering its history, theories, processes, issues, specialties, and trends. In addition, this book concentrates on the importance of the personhood of counselors and of the multicultural, ethical, and legal environments in which counselors operate. By focusing on the context and process of counseling, this book provides you with a better idea of what counselors do and how they do it.

Materials in *Counseling: A Comprehensive Profession,* Fourth Edition, have been divided into three main sections. Part I contains four chapters dealing with the history and foundation on which counseling rest. Specific chapters that will orient you to the counseling profession are

- A Definition and History of Counseling,
- The Effective Counselor,
- Ethical and Legal Aspects of Counseling, and
- Counseling in a Multicultural and Pluralistic Society.

Part II highlights the process, stages, and theories of the counseling profession. This section addresses the universal aspects of popular counseling approaches and hones in on specific theories and ways of dealing with client concerns. The seven chapters are

- Building a Counseling Relationship,
- Working in a Counseling Relationship,
- Termination of Counseling Relationships,
- Psychoanalytic and Adlerian Approaches to Counseling,
- Person-Centered, Existential, and Gestalt Approaches to Counseling,
- Rational Emotive Behavior Therapy and Transactional Analysis, and
- Behavioral, Cognitive-Behavioral, and Reality Therapy Approaches.

Part III emphasizes the skills and specialties required in counseling. Counselors may function as generalists or experts, practicing in various areas or concentrating in one or two areas. Particular areas addressed in this section are

- Marriage and Family Counseling: Systems Theory;
- Groups in Counseling;
- Career Counseling over the Life Span;
- Elementary, Middle, and Secondary School Counseling;
- College Counseling and Student Life Services;
- Mental Health, Substance Abuse, and Rehabilitation Counseling;
- Consultation;
- Evaluation and Research; and
- Testing, Assessment, and Diagnosis in Counseling.

A common theme woven throughout this book is that counseling is both a generic and specialized part of the helping field. Although it is a profession that has come of age, it is also still growing. It is best represented in professional organizations such as the American Counseling Association (ACA) and Division 17 (counseling psychology) of the American Psychological Association (APA). There are also numerous other professional groups—social workers, psychiatric nurses, psychiatrists, marriage and family therapists, and pastoral counselors—that use and practice counseling procedures and theories on a daily basis. In essence, no one profession owns the helping process.

In this text is the result of a lifetime of effort on my part to understand the counseling profession as it was, as it is, and as it will be. My journey has included a wide variety of experiences—working with clients of all ages and stages of life in clinical settings and with students who are interested in learning more about the essence of how counseling works. Research, observation, dialogue, assimilation, and study have contributed to the growth of the content contained in these pages.

Acknowledgments

I am particularly indebted to input from my original mentors Thomas M. Elmore and Wesley D. Hood (Wake Forest University) and W. Larry Osborne (University of North Carolina, Greensboro). Other significant colleagues who have contributed to my outlook and perception of counseling include C. W. Yonce, Peg Carroll, Allen Wilcoxon, Jim Cotton, Robin McInturff, Miriam Cosper, Charles Alexander, Michael Hammonds, Chuck Kormanski, Rosie Morganett, Jane Myers, Diana Hulse-Killacky, Ted Remley, Jerry Donigian, Art Lerner, and Thomas Sweeney. Then, of course, there have been graduate students who have contributed significantly to this endeavor, especially Shirley Ratliff, Jennifer Doris, Marianne Dreyspring, Hank Paine, Don Norman, Reina Braisher, Tom McClure, Paul Myers, Virginia Perry, Pamela Karr, Jim Weiss, Tim Rambo, and Sheryl Harper.

I am also grateful to the reviewers of the current edition's manuscript for their significant contributions: James S. DeLo (West Virginia University), Michael Duffy (Texas A&M University), Stephen Feit (Idaho State University), Roger L. Hutchinson (Ball State University),

Simeon Schlossberg (Western Maryland College), and Scott Young (Mississippi State University). Also appreciated is the valuable input of the reviewers of the third edition: Thomas M. Elmore (Wake Forest University), David L. Fenell (University of Colorado–Colorado Springs), Janice Holden (University of North Texas), Robert Levison (California Polytechnic State University–San Luis Obispo), Michael Forrest Maher (Sam Houston University), A. Scott McGowan (Long Island University), Holly A. Stadler (University of Missouri–Kansas City), Arthur Thomas (University of Kansas), JoAnna White (Georgia State University), and Mark E. Young (Stetson University). Their feedback and excellent ideas on how to improve this book were invaluable. I also owe a debt of gratitude to my past and present editors at Merrill/Prentice Hall, including Vicki Knight, Linda Sullivan, and Kevin Davis.

Finally, I am grateful to my parents, Russell and Gertrude Gladding, who gave me the opportunities and support to obtain a good education and who called my attention to the importance of serving people. Their influence continues to be a part of my life. Likewise, I am indebted to my wife, Claire, who has given me support over the years in writing and refining this text. She has been patient, understanding, encouraging, and humorous about this book even in the midst of three pregnancies and three moves. She exemplifies what an ally in marriage should be. Her presence has brightened my days and made all the hard work a joy.

Samuel T. Gladding

CONTENTS

PART I

HISTORICAL AND PROFESSIONAL FOUNDATIONS OF COUNSELING

Counseling is a distinct profession that has developed in a variety of ways during the 20th century. In chapter 1, I define counseling, examine its history decade by decade, and look at trends in the profession. Chapter 2 explores qualities of effective counselors, especially in regard to their personal and educational backgrounds, and discusses ways of promoting practitioners' competency from a theoretical and systemic perspective. Chapter 3 focuses on the ethical and legal domain of counseling, especially counselor responsibilities to clients and society. Finally, chapter 4 highlights counseling's importance in a multicultural and pluralistic world. Counselors discriminate against clients if they treat them all the same. Because counselors must work hard to be sensitive to and responsible for all their clients, I emphasize ways of working with culturally distinct persons and groups, the aged, and women and men.

As you read these four chapters, I hope you will recognize both overt and subtle aspects of counseling, including ways in which it differs from other mental health disciplines and some of the major events in its historical evolution. This section should help you understand the importance of a counselor's personhood and education as well as emphasize the knowledge necessary to work ethically and legally with diverse clients.

1

HISTORY OF AND TRENDS IN COUNSELING

There is a quietness that comes

in the awareness of presenting names

and recalling places

in the history of persons

who come seeking help.

Confusion and direction are a part of the process

where in trying to sort out tracks

that parallel into life

a person's past is traveled.

Counseling is a complex riddle

where the mind's lines are joined

with scrambling and precision

to make sense out of nonsense,

a tedious process

like piecing fragments of a puzzle together

until a picture is formed.

From "In the Midst of the Puzzles and Counseling Journey," by S. T. Gladding, 1978, Personnel and Guidance Journal, 57, p. 148. © ACA. *Reprinted with permission. No further reproduction authorized without written permission of the American Counseling Association.*

Counseling is distinguished from other mental health disciplines by both its emphasis and its history. Counseling emphasizes growth as well as remediation. Counselors work with persons, groups, families, and systems who are experiencing situational and long-term problems. Counseling's emphasis on development, prevention, and treatment make it attractive to those seeking healthy life-stage transitions and productive lives free from disorders (Romano, 1992).

Counseling has not always been an encompassing and comprehensive profession. It has evolved over the years. Many people, unaware of its evolution, associate counseling with schools or equate the word guidance *with counseling. As a consequence, old ideas linger in their minds in contrast to reality. Therefore, they sometimes misunderstand the profession. Even among counselors themselves, those who fail to keep up in their professional development may become confused. As C. H. Patterson, a pioneer in counseling, once observed, some writers in counseling journals seem "ignorant of the history of the counseling profession . . . [and thus] go over the same ground covered in publications of the 1950s and 1960s" (Goodyear & Watkins, 1983, p. 594).*

Therefore, it is important to examine the history of counseling because a counselor who is informed about the evolution of the profession is more likely to have a strong professional identity and make real contributions to the field. This chapter covers the people, events, and circumstances that have been prominent and have shaped modern counseling as well as current directions (Paisley, 1997). By understanding the past, you may better appreciate present and future trends of the profession.

Definition of Counseling

There have always been "counselors"—people who listen to others and helped them resolve difficulties—but the word *counselor* has been misused over the years by connecting it with descriptive adjectives to promote products. Thus, one hears of carpet counselors, color coordination counselors, pest control counselors, financial counselors, and so on. These counselors are most often glorified salespersons or advice givers. They are to professional counseling what furniture doctors are to medicine (see Figure 1.1).

Counseling as a profession grew out of the guidance movement, in opposition to traditional psychotherapy. Yet, today professional counseling encompasses within its practice clinicians who focus on both growth and lifestyle issues as well as the remediation of mental disorders. To understand what counseling is now, it is important first to understand the concepts of guidance and psychotherapy and the history of the profession.

Guidance

Guidance is the process of helping people make important choices that affect their lives, such as choosing a preferred lifestyle. While the decision-making aspect of guidance has

"Essentially, what I hear you saying is, you've resolved your sugar/saccharin conflict, but you're still not secure with your role as a decaf drinker."

Figure 1.1
The coffee counselor
Source: From a cartoon by J. Millard, 1987, *Chronicle of Higher Education, 33,* p. 49. Reprinted with permission.

long played an important role in the counseling process, the concept itself, as an often used word in counseling, "has gone the way of 'consumption' in medicine" (Tyler, 1986, p. 153). It has more historical significance than present-day usage. Nevertheless, it sometimes distinguishes a way of helping that differs from the more encompassing word *counseling,* and it is still a useful term.

One distinction between guidance and counseling is that whereas guidance focuses on helping individuals choose what they value most, counseling focuses on helping them make changes. Much of the early work in guidance occurred in schools: an adult would help a student make decisions, such as deciding on a vocation or course of study. That relationship was between unequals, teacher and pupil, and was beneficial in helping the less experienced person find direction in life. Similarly, children have long received "guidance" from parents, ministers, scout leaders, and coaches. In the process they have gained an understanding of themselves and their world (Shertzer & Stone, 1981). This type of guidance will never become passé; no matter what the age or stage of life, a person often needs help in making choices. Yet such guidance is only one part of the overall service provided by professional counseling.

Psychotherapy

Psychotherapy (or *therapy*) traditionally focuses on serious problems associated with intrapsychic, internal, and personal issues and conflicts. It deals with the "recovery of adequacy" (Casey, 1996, p. 175). Characteristically, psychotherapy traditionally has emphasized the following issues (Corsini, 1995; Super, 1993): (a) the past more than the present, (b) insight more than change, (c) the detachment of the therapist, and (d) the therapist's role as an expert.

Psychiatrists and clinical psychologists generally use the term *psychotherapy* to describe their work. The professionals who provide the service, however, often determine whether clients receive counseling or psychotherapy. Some counseling theories are commonly referred to as therapies and can be used in either a counseling or therapy setting. There are other similarities in the counseling and psychotherapy processes, as Figure 1.2 shows.

Generally, when making a distinction between psychotherapy and counseling, you should consider two criteria. First, psychotherapy usually involves a *long-term relationship* (20 to 40 sessions over a period of 6 months to 2 years) that focuses on reconstructive change. Counseling, on the other hand, tends to usually be a more *short-term relationship* (8 to 12 sessions spread over a period of less than 6 months) and focuses on the resolution of developmental and situational problems. Second, counseling is usually provided in *outpatient settings* (nonresidential buildings such as schools or community agen-

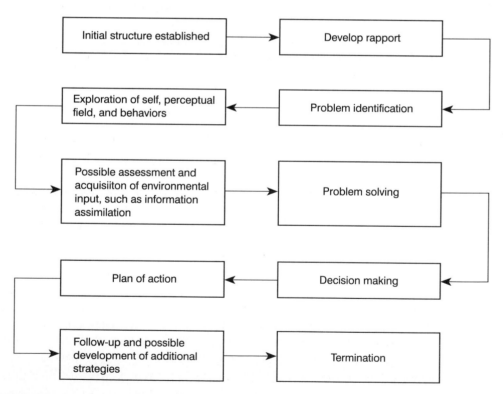

Figure 1.2
The work of counselors and psychotherapists has similar processes.
Source: From *Counseling: An introduction* by J. J. Pietrofesa, A. Hoffman, & H. H. Splete, 1984, Boston: Houghton Mifflin. © 1982 by Houghton Mifflin. Reprinted with permission.

cies), whereas therapy is provided in both outpatient and *inpatient settings* (residential treatment facilities such as mental hospitals).

Counseling

Although attempts have been made through the years to define counseling, there has been disagreement as well. The Governing Council of the American Counseling Association (ACA) in October 1997 accepted a *definition of the practice of professional counseling* that appears to satisfy the different constituencies in the counseling profession and that gives a clear picture of counseling practices to the public (H. Smith, personal communication, June 6, 1998). According to the ACA, the practice of professional counseling is "the application of mental health, psychological or human development principles, through cognitive, affective, behavioral or systemic interventions, strategies that address wellness, personal growth, or career development, as well as pathology" (www.counseling.org/consumers media).This definition contains a number of implicit and explicit points that are important for counselors as well as consumers to realize.

- *Counseling is a profession.*   Counselor practitioners complete a prescribed course of study leading eventually to a master's or a doctorate degree. Counselors are members of organizations that set professional and ethical standards and promote state licensing and certification by national associations (Glosoff & Rockwell, 1997). The processes of certification and licensing and the adherence to ethical codes assure the public that the counselor meets minimal educational and professional standards. Overall, counseling is active and proactive in dealing with different life problems.
- *Counseling deals with wellness, personal growth, career, and pathological concerns.*   In other words, counselors work in areas that involve relationships (Casey, 1996). These areas include intra- and interpersonal concerns related to finding meaning and adjustment in such settings as schools, families, and careers.
- *Counseling is conducted with persons who are considered to be functioning well and those who are having more serious problems.*   Counseling meets the needs of a wide spectrum of people. Clients seen by counselors have developmental or situational concerns that require help in regard to adjustment or remediation. Their problems often require short-term intervention, but occasionally treatment may be extended to encompass disorders included in the *Diagnostic and Statistical Manual of Mental Disorders* (1994) of the American Psychiatric Association.
- *Counseling is theory based.*   Counselors draw from a number of theoretical approaches, including those that are cognitive, affective, behavioral, and systemic. These theories may be applied to individuals, groups, and families.
- *Counseling is a process that may be developmental or intervening.*   Counselors focus on their clients' goals. Thus, counseling involves both choice and change. In some cases, "counseling is a rehearsal for action" (Casey, 1996, p. 176).
- *Counseling includes various specialties.*   According to the ACA definition of *professional counseling,* "a specialty is narrowly focused, requiring advanced knowledge in the field" of counseling (www.counseling.org/consumers media). Specialties include

aspects of counseling that focus on the application of mental health or human development principles. Among the specialties within counseling as a whole are school or college counseling, marriage and family counseling, mental health counseling, gerontological counseling, rehabilitation counseling, addiction and offender counseling, and career counseling. Each has specific educational and experiential requirements for practitioners. Becoming a specialist according to the American Counseling Association is founded on the premise that "all professional counselors must first meet the requirements for the general practice of professional counseling" (www.counseling.org/consumers media).

History of Counseling

Before 1900

Counseling is a relatively new profession (Aubrey, 1977, 1982). Its basis was and is interdisciplinary. "Some of the functions of counselors were and are shared by persons in other professions" (Herr & Fabian, 1993, p. 3). Before the 1900s, most counseling was in the form of advice or information. In the United States, counseling developed out of a humanitarian concern to improve the lives of those adversely affected by the Industrial Revolution of the mid- to late 1800s (Aubrey, 1983). The social welfare reform movement, the spread of public education, and various changes in population makeup (e.g., the enormous influx of immigrants) also influenced the growth of the emerging profession (Aubrey, 1977; Goodyear, 1984).

Most of the pioneers in counseling identified themselves as teachers and social reformers. They focused on teaching children and young adults about themselves, others, and the world of work. Initially, these helpers were involved primarily in child welfare, educational or vocational guidance, and legal reform. Their work was built on specific information and lessons, such as moral instruction on being good and doing right, a concentrated effort to deal with intra- and interpersonal relations (Nugent, 1994). They saw needs in American society and took steps to fulfill them. Nevertheless, "no mention of counseling was made in the professional literature until 1931" (Aubrey, 1983, p. 78). Classroom teachers and administrators were the main practitioners.

One way to chart the evolution of counseling is to trace important events and personal influences through the 20th century. Keep in mind that the development of professional counseling, like the activity itself, was and is a process. Therefore, some names and events do not fit neatly into a rigid chronology.

1900–1909

Counseling was an infant profession in the early 1900s, a time when the helping process was dominated by Sigmund Freud's psychoanalytic theory. During this decade, however, three persons emerged as leaders in counseling's development: Jesse B. Davis, Frank Parsons, and Clifford Beers.

Jesse B. Davis was the first person to set up a systematized guidance program in the public schools (Aubrey, 1977). As superintendent of the Grand Rapids, Michigan, school system, he suggested in 1907 that classroom teachers of English composition teach their students a lesson in guidance once a week, with the goal of building character and preventing problems. Influenced by progressive American educators such as Horace Mann and John Dewey, Davis believed that proper guidance would help cure the ills of American society. What he and other progressive educators advocated was not counseling in the modern sense but a forerunner of counseling: *school guidance* (a preventive educational means of teaching students how to deal effectively with life events).

Like Davis, Frank Parsons focused his work on growth and prevention, but his influence was greater. Parsons has been characterized as a broad scholar, a persuasive writer, a tireless activist, and a great intellect (Davis, 1988; Zytowski, 1985). Often called the "Father of Guidance," he is best known for founding Boston's Vocational Bureau in 1908, a major step in the institutionalization of vocational guidance.

Parsons worked with young people who were in the process of making career decisions. He theorized that choosing a vocation was a matter of relating three factors: a knowledge of work, a knowledge of self, and a matching of the two (Drummond & Ryan, 1995). Parsons devised a number of procedures to help his clients learn more about themselves and the world of work. One of his devices was an extensive questionnaire that asked about experiences ("How did you spend each evening last week?"), preferences ("At a World's Fair, what would you want to see first? second? third?"), and morals ("When have you sacrificed advantage for the right?") (Gummere, 1988, p. 404).

Parsons's book *Choosing a Vocation* (1909), published 1 year after his death, was quite influential, especially in Boston. For example, the superintendent of Boston schools, Stratton Brooks, designated 117 elementary and secondary teachers as vocational counselors (Nugent, 1994). The "Boston example" soon spread to other major cities as school personnel recognized the need for vocational planning. By 1910, 35 cities were emulating Boston (Lee, 1966).

Clifford Beers, a former Yale student, was hospitalized for mental illness several times during his life. He found conditions in mental institutions deplorable and exposed them in his book, *A Mind That Found Itself* (1908), which became a popular best-seller. Beers advocated better mental health facilities and reform in the treatment of the mentally ill. His work had an especially powerful influence on the fields of psychiatry and clinical psychology, in which "many people in these fields referred to what they were doing as counseling," which was seen "as a means of helping people adjust to themselves and society" (Hansen, Rossberg, & Cramer, 1994, p. 5). Beers was the impetus for the mental health movement in the United States, and his work was a forerunner of mental health counseling.

1910s

Three events had a profound impact on the development of counseling during this decade. The first was the 1913 founding of the National Vocational Guidance Association (NVGA), which began publishing a bulletin in 1915 (Goodyear, 1984). In 1921, the *National Vocational Guidance Bulletin* started regular publication. It evolved in later years to become the *National Vocational Guidance Magazine* (1924–1933), *Occupations: The Vocational Guidance Magazine* (1933–1944), *Occupations: The Vocational Guidance Journal* (1944–1952), *Personnel and Guidance Journal* (1952–1984), and, finally, the *Journal of Counseling and Development* (1984 to the present). NVGA was important because it established an association offering guidance literature and united those with an interest in vocational counseling for the first time.

Complementing the founding of NVGA was congressional passage of the Smith-Hughes Act of 1917. This legislation provided funding for public schools to support vocational education.

World War I was the third important event of the decade. To screen its personnel, the U.S. Army commissioned the development of numerous psychological instruments, among them the Army Alpha and Army Beta intelligence tests. Several of the army's screening devices were employed in civilian populations after the war, and *psychometrics* (psychological testing) became a popular movement.

Aubrey (1977) observes that, because the vocational guidance movement developed without an explicit philosophy, it quickly embraced psychometrics to gain a legitimate foundation in psychology. Reliance on psychometrics had both positive and negative effects. On the positive side, it gave vocational guidance specialists a stronger and more "scientific" identity. On the negative side, it distracted many specialists from examining developments in other behavioral sciences, such as sociology, biology, and anthropology.

1920s

The 1920s were relatively quiet for the developing counseling profession. This was a period of consolidation. Education courses for counselors, which had begun at Harvard University in 1911, almost exclusively emphasized vocational guidance during the 1920s. The dominant influences on the emerging profession were the progressive theories of education and the federal government's use of guidance services with war veterans.

A notable event was the certification of counselors in Boston and New York in the mid-1920s (Lee, 1966). Another turning point was the development of the first standards for the preparation and evaluation of occupational materials (Lee, 1966). Along with these standards came the publication of new psychological instruments such as Edward Strong's Strong Vocational Interest Inventory (SVII) in 1927. The publication of this instrument set the stage for future directions for assessment in counseling (Strong, 1943).

A final noteworthy event was Abraham and Hannah Stone's 1929 establishment of the first marriage and family counseling center in New York City. This center was followed by others across the nation, marking the beginning of the specialty of marriage and family counseling.

Throughout the decade, the guidance movement gained acceptance within American society. At the same time, the movement's narrow emphasis on vocational interests began to be challenged. Counselors were broadening their focus to include issues of personality and development, such as those that concerned the family.

1930s

The 1930s were not as quiet as the 1920s, in part because the Great Depression influenced researchers and practitioners, especially in university and vocational settings, to emphasize helping strategies and counseling methods that related to employment (Ohlsen, 1983). A highlight of the decade was the development of the first theory of counseling, which was formulated by E. G. Williamson and his colleagues (including John Darley and Donald Paterson) at the University of Minnesota. Williamson modified Parsons's theory and used it to work with students and the unemployed. His emphasis on a directive, counselor-centered approach came to be known by several names—for example, as the Minnesota point of view and trait-factor counseling. His pragmatic approach emphasized the counselor's teaching, mentoring, and influencing skills (Williamson, 1939).

One premise of Williamson's theory was that persons had *traits* (e.g., aptitudes, interests, personalities, achievements) that could be integrated in a variety of ways to form *factors* (constellations of individual characteristics). Counseling was based on a scientific, problem-solving, empirical method that was individually tailored to each client to help him or her stop nonproductive thinking and become an effective decision maker (Lynch & Maki, 1981). Williamson's influence dominated counseling for the next 2 decades, and he continued to write about his theory into the 1970s (Williamson & Biggs, 1979).

Another major occurrence was the broadening of counseling beyond occupational concerns. The seeds of this development were sown in the 1920s, when Edward Thorndike and other psychologists began to challenge the vocational orientation of the guidance movement (Lee, 1966). The work of John Brewer completed this change in emphasis. Brewer published a book titled *Education as Guidance* in 1932. He proposed that every teacher be a counselor and that guidance be incorporated into the school curriculum as a subject. Brewer believed that all education should focus on preparing students to live outside the school environment. His emphasis made counselors see vocational decisions as just one part of their responsibilities.

During the 1930s the U.S. government became more involved in counseling, especially by establishing the U.S. Employment Service. This agency published the first edition of the *Dictionary of Occupational Titles* (DOT) in 1939. The DOT, which became a major source of career information for guidance specialists working with students and the unemployed, described known occupations in the United States and coded them according to job titles.

1940s

Three major events in the 1940s radically shaped the practice of counseling: the theory of Carl Rogers, World War II, and government's involvement in counseling after the war.

Carl Rogers rose to prominence in 1942 with the publication of his book *Counseling and Psychotherapy*, which challenged the counselor-centered approach of Williamson as well as major tenets of Freudian psychoanalysis. Rogers emphasized the importance of the client, espousing a nondirective approach to counseling. His ideas were both widely accepted and harshly criticized. Rogers advocated giving clients responsibility for their own growth. He thought that if clients had an opportunity to be accepted and listened to, then they would begin to know themselves better and become more congruent (genuine). He described the role of the professional helper as being nonjudgmental and accepting. Thus, the helper served as a mirror, reflecting the verbal and emotional manifestations of the client.

Aubrey (1977, p. 292) has noted that, before Rogers, the literature in guidance and counseling was very practical, dealing with testing, cumulative records, orientation procedures, vocations, placement functions, and so on. In addition, this early literature dealt extensively with the goals and purpose of guidance. With Rogers, there was a new emphasis on the techniques and methods of counseling, research, refinement of counseling technique, selection and training of future counselors, and the goals and objectives of counseling. Guidance, for all intents and purposes, suddenly disappeared as a major consideration in the bulk of the literature and was replaced by a decade or more of concentration on counseling. The Rogers revolution had a major impact on both counseling and psychology. Each still identifies Rogers as a central figure in its professional history.

With the advent of World War II, the U.S. government needed counselors and psychologists to help select and train specialists for the military and industry (Ohlsen, 1983). The war also brought about a new way of looking at vocations for men and women. Many women worked outside the home during the war, and that situation made a lasting impact. Traditional occupational sex roles began to be questioned, and greater emphasis was placed on personal freedom.

After the war, the U.S. Veterans Administration (VA) funded the training of counselors and psychologists by granting stipends and paid internships for students engaged in graduate study. The VA also "rewrote specifications for vocational counselors and coined the term 'counseling psychologist'" (Nugent, 1981, p. 25). Money made available through the VA and the GI bill (benefits for veterans) influenced teaching professionals in graduate education to define their curriculum offerings more precisely. Counseling psychology, as a profession, began to move farther away from its historical alliance with vocational guidance.

1950s

"If one decade in history had to be singled out for the most profound impact on counselors, it would be the 1950s" (Aubrey, 1977, p. 292). Indeed, the decade produced at least four major events that dramatically changed the history of counseling:

- the establishment of the American Personnel and Guidance Association (APGA),
- the establishment of Division 17 (Counseling Psychology) within the American Psychological Association (APA),
- the passing of the National Defense Education Act (NDEA), and
- the introduction of new guidance and counseling theories.

American Personnel and Guidance Association.   APGA grew out of the American Council of Guidance and Personnel Associations (ACGPA), a loose confederation of organizations "concerned with educational and vocational guidance and other personnel activities" (Harold, 1985, p. 4). ACGPA operated from 1935 to 1951, but its major drawback was a lack of power to commit its members to any course of action. APGA was formed in 1952 with the purpose of formally organizing groups interested in guidance, counseling, and personnel matters. Its original four divisions were the American College Personnel Association (Division 1), the National Association of Guidance Supervisors and Counselor Trainers (Division 2), the NVGA (Division 3), and the Student Personnel Association for Teacher Education (Division 4) (Harold, 1985). In 1953, the American School Counselor Association joined APGA, bringing the total membership of the umbrella organization to 6,089 (Romano, 1992). During its early history, APGA was an interest group rather than a professional organization because it did not originate or enforce standards for membership (Super, 1955).

Division 17.   In 1952, the Division of Counseling Psychology (Division 17) of APA was formally established. Its formation required dropping the term *guidance* from what had formerly been the association's Counseling and Guidance Division. Part of the impetus for the division's creation came from the Veterans Administration, but the main impetus came from APA members interested in working with a more "normal" population than the one seen by clinical psychologists (Whiteley, 1984).

Once created, Division 17 became more fully defined. Super (1955), for instance, distinguished between counseling psychology and clinical psychology, holding that counseling psychology was more concerned with normal human growth and development and was influenced in its approach by both vocational counseling and humanistic psychotherapy. Despite Super's work, counseling psychology had a difficult time establishing a clear identity within the APA (Whiteley, 1984). Yet the division's existence has had a major impact on the growth and development of counseling as a profession.

National Defense Education Act.   A third major event was the passage in 1958 of the National Defense Education Act (NDEA), which was enacted following the Soviet Union's launching of its first space satellite, *Sputnik I.* The act's primary purpose was to identify scientifically and academically talented students and promote their development. It provided funds through Title V-A for upgrading school counseling programs. It established counseling and guidance institutes and offered funds and stipends through Title V-B to train counselors. In 1964, the NDEA was extended to include elementary counseling. By 1965, the number of school counselors exceeded 30,000 (Armour, 1969). Indeed, the end of the 1950s began a boom in school counseling that lasted through the 1960s thanks to the cold war and the coming of school age of the baby boom generation (Baker, 1996).

New Theories.   The last major event during this decade was the emergence of new guidance and counseling theories. Before 1950, four main theories influenced the work of counselors: (a) psychoanalysis and insight theory (e.g., Sigmund Freud); (b) trait-factor or directive theories (e.g., E. G. Williamson); (c) humanistic and client-centered theories (e.g., Carl Rogers); and, to a lesser extent, (d) behavioral theories (e.g., B. F. Skinner). Debates among counselors usually centered on whether directive or nondirective counseling was most effective, and almost all counselors assumed that certain tenets of psychoanalysis (e.g., defense mechanisms) were true.

During the 1950s, debate gradually shifted away from this focus as new theories of helping began to emerge. Applied behavioral theories, such as Joseph Wolpe's systematic desensitization, began to gain influence. Cognitive theories also made an appearance, as witnessed by the growth of Albert Ellis's rational-emotive therapy and Eric Berne's transactional analysis. Learning theory, self-concept theory, Donald Super's work in career development, and advances in developmental psychology made an impact as well (Aubrey, 1977). By the end of the decade, the number and complexity of theories associated with counseling had grown considerably.

1960s

The initial focus of the 1960s was on counseling as a developmental profession. Gilbert Wrenn set the tone for the decade in his widely influential book, *The Counselor in a Changing World* (1962). His emphasis, reinforced by other prominent professionals such as Leona Tyler and Donald Blocher, was on working with others to resolve developmental needs. Wrenn's book had influence throughout the 1960s, and he, along with Tyler, became one of the strongest counseling advocates in the United States.

The impact of the developmental model lessened, however, as the decade continued, primarily because of three events: the Vietnam War, the civil rights movement, and the women's movement. Each event stirred up passions and pointed out needs within society. Many counselors attempted to address these issues by concentrating their attention on special needs created by the events and focusing on crisis counseling and other short-term intervention strategies.

Other powerful influences that emerged during the decade were the humanistic counseling theories of Dugald Arbuckle, Abraham Maslow, and Sidney Jourard. Also important was the phenomenal growth of the group movement (Gladding, 1999). The emphasis of counseling shifted from a one-on-one encounter to small-group interaction. Behavioral counseling grew in importance with the appearance of John Krumboltz's *Revolution in Counseling* (1966), in which learning (beyond insight) was promoted as the root of change. Thus, the decade's initial focus on development became sidetracked. As Aubrey notes, "the cornucopia of competing counseling methodologies presented to counselors reached an all-time high in the late 1960s" (1977, p. 293).

Another noteworthy occurrence was the passage of the 1963 Community Mental Health Centers Act, which authorized the establishment of community mental health centers. These centers opened up opportunities for counselor employment outside educational settings.

Professionalism within the APGA and the continued professional movement within Division 17 of the APA also increased during the 1960s. In 1961, the APGA published a "sound code of ethics for counselors" (Nugent, 1981, p. 28). Also during the 1960s, Loughary, Stripling, and Fitzgerald (1965) edited an APGA report that summarized role definitions and training standards for school counselors. Division 17, which had further clarified the definition of a counseling psychologist at the 1964 Greyston Conference, began in 1969 to publish a professional journal, *The Counseling Psychologist,* with Gilbert Wrenn as its first editor.

A final noteworthy milestone was the establishment of the ERIC Clearinghouse on Counseling and Personnel Services (CAPS) at the University of Michigan. Founded in 1966 by Garry Walz and funded by the Office of Educational Research and Improvement at the U.S. Department of Education, ERIC/CAPS was another example of the impact of government on the development of counseling. Through the years ERIC/CAPS (now ERIC/CASS; http://www.uncg.edu/~ericcas2) would become one of the largest and most used resources on counseling activities and trends in the United States and throughout the world. It also sponsored conferences on leading topics in counseling that brought national leaders together.

1970s

The 1970s saw the emergence of several trends. Among the more important were the rapid growth of counseling outside educational settings, the formation of helping skills programs, the beginning of licensure for counselors, and the further development of the APGA as a professional organization for counselors.

Diversification in Counseling Settings. The rapid growth of counseling outside educational institutions began in the 1970s when mental health centers and community agencies began to employ counselors. Before this time, almost all counselors had been employed in educational settings, usually public schools. But the demand for school counselors decreased as the economy underwent several recessions and the number of school-age children began to decline. The rate of growth for school counselors was 1% to 3% each year from 1970 through the mid-1980s, compared with an increase of 6% to 10% during the 1960s (Shertzer & Stone, 1981). In addition, the number of counselor education programs increased from 327 in 1964 to about 475 by 1980 (Hollis & Wantz, 1980). This dramatic rise in the number of programs meant that more counselors were competing for available jobs (Steinhauser, 1985).

The diversification of counseling meant that specialized training began to be offered in counselor education programs. It also meant the development of new concepts of counseling. For example, Lewis and Lewis (1977) coined the term *community counselor* for a new type of counselor who could function in multidimensional roles regardless of employment setting. Many community counseling programs were established, and counselors became more common in agencies such as mental health clinics, hospices, employee assistance programs, psychiatric hospitals, and substance abuse centers. Equally as striking, and more dramatic in growth, was the formation of the American Mental Health Counselor Association (AMHCA) within APGA. Founded in 1976, AMHCA quickly became one of the largest divisions within APGA and united mental health counselors into a professional organization where they defined their roles and goals.

Helping Skills Programs. The 1970s saw the development of helping skills programs that concentrated on relationship and communication skills. Begun by Truax and Carkhuff (1967) and Ivey (1971), these programs taught basic counseling skills to professionals and nonprofessionals alike. The emphasis was humanistic and eclectic. It was assumed that certain fundamental skills should be mastered to establish satisfactory personal interaction. A bonus for counselors who received this type of training was that they could teach it to others rather easily. Thus, counselors could now consult by teaching some of their skills to those with whom they worked, mainly teachers and paraprofessionals. In many ways, this trend was a new version of Brewer's concept of education as guidance.

State Licensure. By the mid-1970s, state boards of examiners for psychologists had become restrictive. Some of their restrictions, such as barring graduates of education department counseling programs from taking the psychology licensure exam, caused considerable tension, not only between APA and APGA but also within the APA membership itself (Ohlsen, 1983). The result was APGA's move toward state and national licensure for counselors. Virginia was the first state to adopt a professional counselor licensure law, doing so in 1976, although it should be noted that California passed a marriage, family, and child counselor law in 1962. The problem with the California law was it defined *counselor* broadly and later replaced the term with the word *therapist*, which was strictly defined.

A Strong APGA.   During the 1970s, APGA emerged as an even stronger professional organization. Several changes altered its image and function, one of which was the building of its own headquarters in Alexandria, Virginia. APGA also began to question its professional identification because guidance and personnel seemed to be outmoded ways of defining the organization's emphases.

In 1973, the Association of Counselor Educators and Supervisors (ACES), a division of APGA, outlined the standards for a master's degree in counseling. In 1977, ACES approved guidelines for doctoral preparation in counseling (Stripling, 1978). During the decade, APGA membership increased to almost 40,000. Four new divisions (in addition to AMHCA) were chartered, also: the Association for Religious and Value Issues in Counseling, the Association for Specialists in Group Work, the Association for Non-white Concerns in Personnel and Guidance, and the Public Offender Counselor Association.

1980s

The 1980s saw the continued growth of counseling as a profession, exemplified by proactive initiatives from counselors associated with APGA and Division 17. Among the most noteworthy events of the decade were those that standardized the training and certification of counselors, recognized counseling as a distinct profession, increased the diversification of counselor specialties, and emphasized human growth and development.

Standardization of Training and Certification.   The move toward standardized training and certification was one that began early in the decade and grew stronger yearly. In 1981, the Council for Accreditation of Counseling and Related Educational Programs (CACREP) was formed as an affiliate organization of APGA. It refined the standards first proposed by ACES in the late 1970s and initially accredited four programs and grandparented programs already recognized as accredited by the California state counselor association and ACES (Steinhauser & Bradley, 1983). In 1987, the CACREP achieved membership in the Council on Postsecondary Accreditation (COPA), bringing it "into a position of accreditation power parallel to" such specialty accreditation bodies as the APA (Herr, 1985, p. 399). The CACREP standardized counselor education programs for master's and doctoral programs in the areas of school, community, mental health, and marriage and family counseling, as well as for personnel services for college students.

Complementary to the work of CACREP, the National Board for Certified Counselors (NBCC), which was formed in 1983, began to certify counselors on a national level. It developed a standardized test and defined eight major subject areas in which counselors should be knowledgeable: (a) human growth and development, (b) social and cultural foundations, (c) helping relationships, (d) groups, (e) lifestyle and career development, (f) appraisal, (g) research and evaluation, and (h) professional orientation. To become a national certified counselor (NCC), examinees have to pass a standardized test and meet experiential and character reference qualifications. In 1984, NBCC also set up standards for certifying career counselors; as a result, many individuals became national certified career counselors (NCCCs) (Herr, 1985). By the end of the decade, there were approximately 17,000 NCC and NCCC professionals.

Finally, in collaboration with the CACREP, the National Academy of Certified Clinical Mental Health Counselors (NACCMHC), an affiliate of the American Mental Health Counselor Association (AMHCA), continued to define training standards and certify counselors in mental health counseling, a process it had begun in the late 1970s (Seiler, Brooks, & Beck, 1987; Wilmarth, 1985). It also began training supervisors of mental health counselors in 1988. Both programs attracted thousands of new professionals into counseling and upgraded the credentials of those already in the field.

Counseling as a Distinct Profession.   A profession is characterized by its "role statements, codes of ethics, accreditation guidelines, competency standards, licensure, certification and other standards of excellence" (VanZandt, 1990, p. 243). The evolution of counseling in the 1980s as a distinct mental health profession came as a result of events, issues, and forces, both inside and outside APGA (Heppner, 1990). Inside APGA was a growing awareness among its leaders that the words *personnel* and *guidance* no longer described the work of its members. In 1983, after considerable debate, the APGA changed its name to the American Association for Counseling and Development (AACD) to "reflect the changing demographics of its membership and the settings in which they worked" (Herr, 1985, p. 395). The name change was symbolic of the rapid transformation in identity that APGA members had been experiencing through the implementation of policies regarding training, certification, and standards. External events that influenced APGA to change its name and ultimately its focus included legislation, especially on the federal level, that recognized mental health providers and actions by other mental health services associations.

Moreover, there was a newness in professional commitment among AACD members. Chi Sigma Iota, an international academic and professional honor society, was formed in 1985 to promote excellence in the counseling profession. It grew to more than 100 chapters and 5,000 members by the end of the decade (Sweeney, 1989). Furthermore, liability insurance policies, new counseling specialty publications, legal defense funds, legislative initiatives, and a variety of other membership services were made available to AACD members by its national headquarters (Myers, 1990). By 1989, over 58,000 individuals had become members of AACD, an increase of more than 18,000 members in 10 years.

Division 17 also continued to grow at a steady rate (Woody, Hansen, & Rossberg, 1989). In 1987, a professional standards conference was assembled by its president, George Gazda, to define further the uniqueness of counseling psychology and counseling in general.

Diversification of Counseling.   During the 1980s, counselors became more diversified. Large numbers of counselors continued to be employed in primary and secondary schools and in higher education in a variety of student personnel services. Mental health counselors and community/agency counselors were the two largest blocks of professionals outside formal educational environments. In addition, the number of counselors swelled in mental health settings for business employees, the aging, and married persons and families. Symbolic of that growth, the Association for Adult Development and Aging (AADA) and the International Association for Marriage and Family Counselors (IAMFC) were organized and chartered as divisions of AACD in 1987 and 1990, respectively.

Strong membership in AACD divisions dedicated to group work, counselor education, humanistic education, measurement and development, religious and value issues, employment and career development, rehabilitation, multicultural concerns, addiction and offender work, and military personnel further exemplified the diversity of counseling during the 1980s. Special issues of AACD journals focused on topics such as violence (*Journal of Counseling and Development,* March 1987), the gifted and talented (*Journal of Counseling and Development,* May 1986), the arts (*Journal of Mental Health Counseling,* January 1985), and prevention (*Elementary School Guidance and Counseling,* October 1989). These publications helped broaden the scope of counseling services and counselor awareness.

Increased Emphasis on Human Growth and Development.   Counseling's emphasis on human growth and development during the 1980s took several forms. For example, a new spotlight was placed on developmental counseling across the life span (Gladstein & Apfel, 1987). New behavioral expressions associated with Erik Erikson's first five stages of life development were formulated, too (Hamachek, 1988), and an increased emphasis on the development of adults and the elderly resulted in the formation of the Association for Adult Aging and Development (AAAD).

A second way that human growth and development was stressed was through increased attention to gender issues and sexual preferences (see, for example, O'Neil & Carroll, 1988; Pearson, 1988; Weinrach, 1987). Carol Gilligan's (1982) landmark study on the development of moral values in females, which helped introduce feminist theory into the counseling arena, forced human growth specialists to examine the differences between genders.

An emphasis on moral development was the third way in which human growth issues were highlighted (Colangelo, 1985; Lapsley & Quintana, 1985). There was a renewed emphasis on models of moral development, such as Lawrence Kohlberg's theory (1969), and increased research in the area of enhancing moral development. In counselor education, it was found that moral development was closely related to both cognitive ability and empathy (Bowman & Reeves, 1987).

Finally, the challenges of working with different ethnic and cultural groups received more discussion (Ponterotto & Casas, 1987). In focusing on multicultural issues, the Association for Multicultural Counseling and Development (AMCD) took the lead, but multicultural themes, such as the importance of diversity, became a central issue among all groups, especially in light of the renewed racism that developed in the 1980s (Carter, 1990).

1990s

The 1990s continued to see changes in the evolution of the counseling profession, some of them symbolic and others structural. One change that was both symbolic and substantial was the 1992 decision by the American Association for Counseling and Development to modify its name and become the American Counseling Association (ACA). The new name better reflected the membership and mission of the organization. The following 17 divisions operated in 1999 under ACA's reorganized structure:

1. *National Career Development Association* (NCDA)—founded in 1913; formerly the National Vocational Guidance Association
2. *Association for Humanistic Education and Development* (AHEAD)—founded in 1931; formerly the Student Personnel Association for Teacher Education
3. *Association for Counselor Education and Supervision* (ACES)—founded in 1938; formerly the National Association of Guidance Supervisors and Counselor Trainers
4. *American School Counselor Association* (ASCA)—founded in 1953
5. *American Rehabilitation Counseling Association* (ARCA)—founded in 1958; formerly the Division of Rehabilitation Counseling
6. *Association for Assessment in Counseling* (AAC)—founded in 1965; formerly the Association for Measurement and Evaluation in Guidance
7. *National Employment Counselors Association* (NECA)—founded in 1966
8. *Association for Multicultural Counseling and Development* (AMCD)—founded in 1972; formerly the Association for Non-white Concerns in Personnel and Guidance
9. *International Association of Addictions and Offender Counselors* (IAAOC)—founded in 1972; formerly the Public Offender Counselor Association
10. *Association for Specialists in Group Work* (ASGW)—founded in 1973
11. *Association for Spiritual, Ethical, and Religious Values in Counseling* (ASERVIC)—founded in 1974; formerly the National Catholic Guidance Conference
12. *American Mental Health Counselors Association* (AMHCA)—founded in 1976
13. *Association for Counselors and Educators in Government* (ACEG)—founded in 1984
14. *Association for Adult Development and Aging* (AADA)—founded in 1986
15. *International Association of Marriage and Family Counselors* (IAMFC)—founded in 1989
16. *American College Counseling Association* (ACCA)—founded in 1991
17. *Association for Gay, Lesbian, and Bisexual Issues in Counseling*—founded in 1996

A second noteworthy event in the 1990s occurred in 1992, too, when counseling, as a primary mental health profession, was included for the first time in the health care human resource statistics compiled by the Center for Mental Health Services and the National Institute of Mental Health (Manderscheid & Sonnenschein, 1992). This type of recognition put counseling on par with other mental health specialties such as psychology, social work, and psychiatry. In the middle of the decade, it was estimated that between 50,000 and 67,000 certified or licensed counselors were practicing in the United States (Wedding, 1995).

A third event in counseling that also originated in 1992 was the writing of the multicultural counseling competencies and standards that were published by Sue, Arredondo, and McDavis (1992). Although these competencies mainly applied to counseling with people of color, they set the stage for a larger debate about the nature of multicultural counseling—for instance, the inclusion within the definition of other groups, such as people with disabilities. Thus, a lively discussion occurred during the decade about what diversity and counseling within a pluralistic society entailed (Weinrach & Thomas, 1998).

A fourth issue in the 1990s was a focus on health care and an increase in managed health care organizations. Conglomerates emerged, and many counselors became providers under these new organized ways of providing services. As a result, the number of independent counselor practitioners decreased as did the number of sessions a counselor could offer under managed health care plans. A new emphasis on legislation connected with these organizations forced counselors to become increasingly informed and active as legislative proponents (Barstow, 1998).

In addition, there was a renewed focus within the decade on counseling issues related to the whole person. Counselors became more aware of social factors important to the development and maintenance of mental disorders and health including the importance of organism-context interaction (i.e., contextualism) (Thomas, 1996). These factors include spirituality, family environment, socioeconomic considerations, the impact of groups and group work, and prevention (Bemak, 1998).

Other developments in the 1990s included the following:

* The merger of the National Academy of Clinical Mental Health Counselors with NBCC to credential over 22,000 counselors
* The growth of CACREP- and APA-accredited programs in counselor education and counseling psychology on both the doctoral and master's levels (Hollis, 1997)
* An increase in the number of publications by ACA, APA, commercial publishers, and ERIC/CASS (Counseling and Student Services Clearinghouse) on counseling
* The growth of Chi Sigma Iota to over 185 chapters and 22,000 members.

Current Trends in the New Millennium

Counseling is an ever-changing profession that emphasizes certain topics, issues, and developmental concerns in accordance with the needs of its clients and society. Various aspects of counseling have moved to the forefront during its relatively brief history. Current concerns of professional counselors will take on added significance in the future because of unforeseen crises, new developments, and continuing dysfunctional patterns in people and systems. Increases in pollution, decreases in the Earth's resources, changing roles of women, innovations in media and technology, poverty, homelessness, loneliness, and aging will all capture counseling's attention (Hackney & Wrenn, 1990; Lee & Walz, 1998). Although counselors will face a myriad of issues in the 21st century, three of the most pervasive topics are the challenges of dealing with managed care, the effective use of computers and technology, and the growth of leadership.

The Challenge of Managed Care

"Managed care involves a contractual arrangement between a mental health professional and a third party, the managed care company, regarding the care and treatment of the first party, the client" (Murphy, 1998, p. 3). Managed care is and will be a major concern to counselors during the 21st century. There are only a few dominant companies in the managed care business, but their influence is tremendous. They determine how health care providers, including counselors, deliver services and what rights and recourses consumers have to receive regarding treatment. Managed care arrangements require clients first to see a gatekeeper physician before they can be referred to a specialist such as a counselor. This restriction, along with limited financial reimbursement, and the limitation of sessions allowed under managed care has had mixed results.

Managed care has advanced the counseling profession by including counselors on both managed care boards and as providers of services (Goetz, 1998). However, as a group, counselors have not been well compensated under managed care arrangements, and client consumers have often been limited in getting the services they need. Likewise, counselors have been frustrated in being able to offer adequate treatment.

The challenge for counselors in the near future is to find ways to either work more effectively with managed care companies or work outside such companies and still be major players in the mental health arena.

The Effective Use of Computers and Technology

Computer use has grown rapidly in counseling and elsewhere. What once was considered a promising technology has now became reality. Much of the use of computers in counseling has focused on record keeping, manipulating data, and word processing. More attention is now being placed on factors affecting computer and client interaction. For instance, clients who are high in maturity and low in direction may especially benefit from computer programs such as SIGI-PLUS in career counseling (Kivlighan, Johnston, Hogan, & Mauer, 1994). "The number of network-based computer applications in counseling has been increasing rapidly," too (Sampson, Kolodinsky, & Greeno, 1997, p. 203). List servers and bulletin board systems (BBSs) have become especially popular for posting messages and encouraging dialogue between counselors. E-mail is also used in counselor-to-counselor interactions as well as counselor-to-client conversations. Web sites are maintained by counseling organizations, counselor education programs, and individual counselors.

The similarities between working with computers and working with clients are notable (e.g., establishing a relationship, learning a client's language, learning a client's thought process, setting goals, and taking steps to achieve them). Although the practice is controversial, a number of counselors and helping specialists offer services across the Internet. "In addition, the general public is already making use of the internet for assistance with career choice and job placement" (Sampson et al., 1997, p. 204). Furthermore, the general public surfs the Internet for mental health and pharmacology information, such as "Dr. Bob's Psychopharmacology Tips" (http://uhs.bsd.uchicago.edu/dr-bob/tips/tips.html) (Ingram, 1998). Thus, counselors can use the Internet to access a world of information on counseling-related subjects (Wilson, 1994). They are also being bombarded with a host of new computer programs, especially in the area of testing.

In the future, counselors will have to decide how collectively they will use computers and technology to enhance the services they offer to meet clients' needs. Technical competencies for counselor education students have been developed under the leadership of Thomas Hohenshil of Virginia Tech for the Association for Counselor Education and Development. These competencies include skills counselors should master such as being able to use word processing programs, audiovisual equipment, E-mail, the Internet, listservs, and CD-ROM databases. Counselors should also be aware of ethical and legal codes related to the Internet and the strengths and weaknesses of offering counseling services via the Internet.

The Growth of Leadership

With the rapid changes in society and counseling, there is an increased need for counselors to develop their leadership skills and become a more positive force in society. "Counselors are now challenged by the opportunity to assume leadership roles as visionaries and guides" (Stephenson, 1996, p. 91). Professional counseling associations are engaged in leadership activities, as are their divisions. Chi Sigma Iota (an international academic and professional counseling honor society) is especially strong in providing leadership training and services to counselors.

One area of leadership, strategic planning, involves envisioning the future and making preparations to meet anticipated needs. Similar to the counseling skill of leading, it is usually accomplished in a group and involves hard data as well as anticipations and expectations (C. Kormanski, personal interview, June 20, 1994). This skill is greatly needed in advocacy and in promoting the profession of counseling.

In addition to envisioning the future and knowing how to plan, leadership includes delegating, motivating, and using the collective talents of people to the fullest. Leadership style is also important (Gardner, 1990). In the 21st century, counselors must learn how to become better leaders and how to promote the leadership talents within the profession if counseling and the clients who use counseling services are going to do well.

Summary and Conclusion

Counseling is a profession distinguished from guidance and psychotherapy. It is concerned with wellness, development, and situational difficulties as well as with helping dysfunctional persons. It is based on principles and a definition that has evolved over the years. It contains within it a number of specialties.

An examination of the history of counseling shows that the profession has an interdisciplinary base. It began with the almost simultaneous concern and activity of Frank Parsons, Jesse B. Davis, and Clifford Beers to provide, reform, and improve services in vocational guidance, character development of schoolchildren, and mental health treatment. Counseling became interlinked early in its history with psychometrics, psychology, and sociology. Other important events include the involvement of the government in counseling during and after World War I, the Great Depression, World War II, and the launching of *Sputnik*.

Ideas from innovators such as John Brewer, E. G. Williamson, Carl Rogers, Gilbert Wrenn, Leona Tyler, John Krumboltz, Allen Ivey, Carol Gilligan, and Derald Wing Sue have shaped the development of the profession and broadened its horizon. The emergence and growth of the American Counseling Association (rooted in the establishment of the National Vocational Guidance Association in 1913) and Division 17 (Counseling Psychology) of the American Psychological Association have been major factors in the growth of the counseling profession. Challenges for the profession in the 21st century include interacting positively with managed care organizations, using computer technology wisely and effectively, and providing leaders.

SUMMARY TABLE
Highlights in the History of Counseling

1900s

Jesse B. Davis sets up first systematic guidance program in the public schools (Grand Rapids, Michigan)

Frank Parsons, the "Father of Guidance," establishes the Boston Vocational Bureau to help young people make career decisions; writes *Choosing a Vocation*.

Clifford Beers, a former mental patient, advocates for better treatment of the mentally ill; publishes influential book: *A Mind That Found Itself*.

Sigmund Freud's psychoanalytic theory becomes the basis for treating the mentally disturbed.

1910s

National Vocational Guidance Association (NVGA) established; forerunner of American Counseling Association (ACA).

Passage of the Smith-Hughes Act, which provided funding for public schools to support vocational education.

Psychometrics embraced by vocational guidance movement after World War I.

1920s

First certification of counselors in Boston and New York.

Publication of the Strong Vocational Interest Inventory (SVII).

Abraham and Hannah Stone establish the first marriage and family counseling center in New York City.

Counselors begin broadening focus beyond vocational interests.

1930s

E. G. Williamson and colleagues develop a counselor-centered trait-factor approach to work with students and the unemployed. It is the first theory of counseling, often called the Minnesota point of view.

John Brewer advocates education as guidance with vocational decision making as a part of the process.

Publication of the *Dictionary of Occupational Titles*, the first government effort to code job titles systematically.

1940s

Carl Rogers develops client-centered approach to counseling; publishes *Counseling and Psychotherapy*.

With advent of World War II, traditional occupational roles are questioned publicly; personal freedom is emphasized over authority.

U.S. Veterans Administration (VA) funds the training of counselors and psychologists; coins the term *counseling psychology*, which begins as a profession.

1950s

American Personnel and Guidance Association (APGA) founded; forerunner of the American Counseling Association.

Division 17 (Counseling Psychology) of American Psychological Association created.

National Defense Education Act (NDEA) enacted. Title V-B provides training for counselors.

New theories (e.g., transactional analysis, rational-emotive therapy) are formulated. They challenge older theories (psychoanalysis, behaviorism, trait-factor, and client centered).

1960s

Emphasis in counseling on developmental issues. Gilbert Wrenn publishes *The Counselor in a Changing World*.

Leona Tyler writes extensively about counseling and counseling psychology.

Behavioral counseling emerges as a strong counseling theory; led by John Krumboltz's *Revolution in Counseling*.

Upheaval created by civil rights and women's movements and Vietnam War. Counseling sidetracked from a developmental emphasis; counselors increasingly concerned with addressing social and crisis issues.

Community Mental Health Centers Act passed; establishes community mental health centers.

Groups gain popularity as a way of resolving personal issues.

APGA publishes its first code of ethics.

ERIC/CAPS founded; begins building database of research in counseling.

Role definitions and training standards for school counselors formulated.

Greyston Conference helps define counseling psychology.

First publication of *The Counseling Psychologist* journal.

1970s

Diversification of counseling outside educational settings. Term *community counseling* coined to describe this type of multifaceted counselor.

Derald Sue, editor of the *Personnel and Guidance Journal*, focuses attention on multicultural issues.

American Mental Health Counseling Association formed.

Basic helping skills programs begun by Robert Carkhuff, Allen Ivey, and colleagues.

State licensure of counselors begins; Virginia is first.

APGA emerges as a strong professional association.

1980s

Council for Accreditation of Counseling and Related Educational Programs (CACREP) formed.

National Board of Certified Counselors (NBCC) established.

Chi Sigma Iota (international academic and professional honor society) begun.

Atlanta Conference on professional standards for counseling psychology held.

Growing membership continues in counseling associations. New headquarters buildings for AACD.

Human growth and development highlighted as an emphasis of counseling. *In a Different Voice* by Carol Gilligan focuses attention on the importance of studying women and women's issues in counseling.

1990s

AACD changes name to American Counseling Association (ACA).

Diversity and multicultural issues in counseling stressed.

Spiritual issues in counseling addressed more openly.

Increased focus on regulations and accountability for counselors.

National Academy for Clinical Mental Health Counselors merges with NBCC.

Counselors seek to be recognized as core providers when national health care reform is discussed and enacted.

CLASSROOM ACTIVITIES

1. How do you distinguish between the terms *counseling, psychotherapy,* and *guidance?* Working in groups of three, choose one spokesperson to argue that the terms are similar and another to argue that the terms are distinctive. The third person should give feedback to both persons.
2. What decade do you consider the most important for the development of counseling? Is there a decade you consider least important? Be sure to give reasons for your position.
3. What do you know about counseling now that you have read this chapter? Discuss how it is similar to or different from what you expected. Explain your answer fully.
4. Investigate in more detail the life and influence of a historical figure in counseling. You may choose one of the innovators mentioned in this chapter or a person suggested by your instructor. Share your information with the class.
5. Besides managed care, technology, and leadership, what do you consider pressing future issues for the profession of counseling? How do you think counselors should address these concerns? See whether there is a consensus of topics and ways to address them within your class.

REFERENCES

American Psychiatric Association. (1994). *Diagnostic and statistical manual of mental disorders* (4th ed.). Washington, DC: Author.

Armour, D. J. (1969). *The American counselor.* New York: Sage.

Aubrey, R. F. (1977). Historical development of guidance and counseling and implications for the future. *Personnel and Guidance Journal, 55,* 288–295.

Aubrey, R. F. (1982). A house divided: Guidance and counseling in twentieth-century America. *Personnel and Guidance Journal, 60,* 198–204.

Aubrey, R. F. (1983). The odyssey of counseling and images of the future. *Personnel and Guidance Journal, 61,* 78–82.

Baker, S. (1996). Recollections of the boom era in school counseling. *The School Counselor, 43,* 163–164.

Barstow, S. (1998, June). Managed care debate heats up in Congress. *Counseling Today,* 1, 26.

Beers, C. (1908). *A mind that found itself.* New York: Longman Green.

Bemak, F. (1998, February 13). *Counseling at-risk students.* Presentation at Wake Forest University Institute for Ethics and Leadership in Counseling, Winston-Salem, NC.

Bowman, J. T., & Reeves, T. G. (1987). Moral development and empathy in counseling. *Counselor Education and Supervision, 26,* 293–298.

Brewer, J. M. (1932). *Education as guidance.* New York: Macmillan.

Carter, R. T. (1990). The relationship between racism and racial identity among white Americans: An exploratory investigation. *Journal of Counseling and Development, 69,* 46–50.

Casey, J. M. (1996). Gail F. Farwell: A developmentalist who lives his ideas. *The School Counselor, 43,* 174–180.

Colangelo, N. (1985). Overview. *Elementary School Guidance and Counseling, 19,* 244–245.

Corsini, R. J. (1995). Introduction. In R. J. Corsini & D. Wedding (Eds.), *Current psychotherapies* (5th ed., pp. 1–14). Itasca, IL: Peacock.

Davis, H. V. (1988). *Frank Parsons: Prophet, innovator, counselor.* Carbondale: University of Southern Illinois Press.

Drummond, R. J., & Ryan, C. W. (1995). *Career counseling: A developmental approach.* Upper Saddle River, NJ: Merrill/Prentice Hall.

Gardner, G. W. (1990). *On leadership.* New York: Free Press.

Gilligan, C. (1982). *In a different voice.* Cambridge, MA: Harvard University Press.

Gladding, S. T. (1999). *Group work: A counseling specialty* (3rd ed.). Upper Saddle River, NJ: Merrill/Prentice Hall.

Gladstein, G. A., & Apfel, F. S. (1987). A theoretically based adult career counseling center. *Career Development Quarterly, 36,* 178–185.

Glosoff, H. L., & Rockwell, P. J., Jr. (1997). The counseling profession: A historical perspective. In D. Capuzzi & D. R. Gross (Eds.), *Introduction to the counseling profession* (2nd ed., pp. 3–47). Boston: Allyn & Bacon.

Goetz, B. (1998, May 27). *An inside/outsider's view of the counseling profession today.* Paper presented at the Chi Sigma Iota Invitational Counselor Advocacy Conference, Greensboro, NC.

Goodyear, R. K. (1984). On our journal's evolution: Historical developments, transitions, and future directions. *Journal of Counseling and Development, 63,* 3–9.

Goodyear, R. K., & Watkins, C. E., Jr. (1983). C. H. Patterson: The counselor's counselor. *Personnel and Guidance Journal, 61,* 592–597.

Gummere, R. M., Jr. (1988). The counselor as prophet: Frank Parsons, 1854–1908. *Journal of Counseling and Development, 66,* 402–405.

Hackney, H., & Wrenn, C. G. (1990). The contemporary counselor in a changed world. In H. Hackney (Ed.), *Changing contexts for counselor preparation in the 1990s* (pp. 1–20). Alexandria, VA: Association for Counselor Education and Supervision.

Hamachek, D. E. (1988). Evaluating self-concept and ego development within Erikson's psychosocial framework: A formulation. *Journal of Counseling and Development, 66,* 354–360.

Hansen, J. C., Rossberg, R. H., & Cramer, S. H.. (1994). Counseling: Theory and process (5th ed.). Boston: Allyn & Bacon.

Harold, M. (1985). Council's history examined after 50 years. *Guidepost, 27*(10), 4.

Heppner, P. P. (1990). Life lines: Institutional perspectives [Feature editor's introduction]. *Journal of Counseling and Development, 68,* 246.

Herr, E. L. (1985). AACD: An association committed to unity through diversity. *Journal of Counseling and Development, 63,* 395–404.

Herr, E. L., & Fabian, E. S. (1993). The *Journal of Counseling and Development:* Its legacy and its aspirations. *Journal of Counseling and Development, 72,* 3–4.

Hollis, J. W. (1997). *Counselor preparation 1996–1998.* Muncie, IN: Accelerated Development.

Hollis, J. W., & Wantz, R. A. (1980). *Counselor preparation.* Muncie, IN: Accelerated Development.

Ingram, J. (1998, Spring/Summer). Psychopharmacology questions? *WACES Wire, 36,* 4.

Ivey, A. E. (1971). *Microcounseling: Innovations in interviewing training.* Springfield, IL: Thomas.

Kivlighan, D. M., Jr., Johnston, G. A., Hogan, R. S., & Mauer, E. (1994). Who benefits from computerized career counseling? *Journal of Counseling and Development, 72,* 289–292.

Kohlberg, L. (1969). *Stages in the development of moral thought and action.* New York: Holt, Rinehart, & Winston.

Krumboltz, J. D. (Ed.) (1966). *Revolution in counseling.* Boston: Houghton Mifflin.

Lapsley, D. K., & Quintana, S. M. (1985). Recent approaches to the moral and social education of children. *Elementary School Guidance and Counseling, 19,* 246–259.

Lee, C. C., & Walz, G. R. (1998). *Social action: A mandate for counselors.* Alexandria, VA: American Counseling Association.

Lee, J. M. (1966). Issues and emphases in guidance: A historical perspective. In J. M. Lee & N. J. Pallone (Eds.), *Readings in guidance and counseling.* New York: Sheed & Ward.

Lewis, J., & Lewis, M. (1977). *Community counseling: A human services approach.* New York: Wiley.

Loughary, J. W., Stripling, R. O., & Fitzgerald, P. W. (Eds.). (1965). *Counseling: A growing profession.* Washington, DC: American Personnel and Guidance Association.

Lynch, R. K., & Maki, D. (1981). Searching for structure: A trait-factor approach to vocational rehabilitation. *Vocational Guidance Quarterly, 30,* 61–68.

Manderscheid, R. W., & Sonnenschein, M. A. (1992). *Mental health in the United States, 1992* (DHHS Publication No. [SMA] 92-1942). Washington, DC: U.S. Government Printing Office.

Murphy, K. E. (1998). Is managed care unethical? *IAMFC Family Digest, 11*(1), 3.

Myers, J. (1990). Personal interview. Greensboro, NC.

Nugent, F. A. (1981). *Professional counseling.* Pacific Grove, CA: Brooks/Cole.

Nugent, F. A. (1994). *An introduction to the profession of counseling* (2nd ed.). Upper Saddle River, NJ: Merrill/Prentice Hall.

Ohlsen, M. M. (1983). *Introduction to counseling.* Itasca, IL: Peacock.

O'Neil, J. M., & Carroll, M. R. (1988). A gender role workshop focused on sexism, gender role conflict, and the gender role journey. *Journal of Counseling and Development, 67,* 193–197.

Paisley, P. O. (1997). Personalizing our history: Profiles of theorists, researchers, practitioners, and issues. *Journal of Counseling and Development, 76,* 4–5.

Parsons, F. (1909). *Choosing a vocation.* Boston: Houghton Mifflin.

Pearson, J. E. (1988). A support group for women with relationship dependency. *Journal of Counseling and Development, 66,* 394–396.

Ponterotto, J. G., & Casas, J. M. (1987). In search of multicultural competence within counselor education programs. *Journal of Counseling and Development, 65,* 430–434.

Rogers, C. R. (1942). *Counseling and psychotherapy.* Boston: Houghton Mifflin.

Romano, G. (1992, Spring). AACD's 40th anniversary. *American Counselor, 1,* 18–26.

Sampson, J. P., Kolodinsky, R. W., & Greeno, B. P. (1997). Counseling on the information highway: Future possibilities and potential problems. *Journal of Counseling & Development, 75,* 203–212.

Seiler, G., Brooks, D. K., Jr., & Beck, E. S. (1987). Training standards of the American Mental Health Counselors Association: History, rationale, and implications. *Journal of Mental Health Counseling, 9,* 199–209.

Shertzer, B., & Stone, S. C. (1981). *Fundamentals of guidance.* Boston: Houghton Mifflin.

Steinhauser, L. (1985). A new PhD's search for work: A case study. *Journal of Counseling and Development, 63,* 300–303.

Steinhauser, L., & Bradley, R. (1983). Accreditation of counselor education programs. *Counselor Education and Supervision, 25,* 98–108.

Stephenson, J. B. (1996). Changing families, changing systems: Counseling implications for the twenty-first century. *School Counselor, 44*, 85–99.

Stripling, R. O. (1978). ACES guidelines for doctoral preparation in counselor education. *Counselor Education and Supervision, 17,* 163–166.

Strong, E. K., Jr. (1943). *Vocational interests of men and women.* Stanford, CA: Stanford University Press.

Sue, D. W., Arredondo, P., & McDavis, R. J. (1992). Multicultural counseling competencies and standards: A call to the profession. *Journal of Multicultural Counseling and Development, 20,* 64–88.

Super, D. E. (1955). Transition: From vocational guidance to counseling psychology. *Journal of Counseling Psychology, 2,* 3–9.

Super, D. E. (1993). The two faces of counseling: Or is it three? *Career Development Quarterly, 42,* 132–136.

Sweeney, T. (1989). Excellence vs. elitism. *Newsletter of Chi Sigma Iota, 5,* 1, 11.

Thomas, S. C. (1996). A sociological perspective on contextualism. *Journal of Counseling & Development, 74,* 529–536.

Truax, C. B., & Carkhuff, R. R. (1967). *Toward effective counseling and psychotherapy: Training and practice.* Chicago: Aldine.

Tyler, L. E. (1986). Farewell to guidance. *Journal of Counseling and Human Service Professions, 1,* 152–155.

U.S. Employment Service. (1939). *Dictionary of occupational titles.* Washington, DC: Author.

VanZandt, C. E. (1990). Professionalism: A matter of personal initiatives. *Journal of Counseling and Development, 68,* 243–245.

Wedding, D. (1995). Current issues in psychotherapy. In R. J. Corsini & D. Wedding (Eds.), *Current psychotherapies* (5th ed., pp. 419–432). Itasca, IL: Peacock.

Weinrach, S. G. (1987). Microcounseling and beyond: A dialogue with Allen Ivey. *Journal of Counseling and Development, 65,* 532–537.

Weinrach, S. G., & Thomas, K. R. (1998). Diversity-sensitive counseling today: A postmodern clash of values. *Journal of Counseling & Development, 76,* 115–122.

Whiteley, J. M. (1984). Counseling psychology: A historical perspective. *Counseling Psychologist, 12,* 2–109.

Williamson, E. G. (1939). *How to counsel students: A manual of techniques for clinical counselors.* New York: McGraw-Hill.

Williamson, E. G., & Biggs, D. A. (1979). Trait-factor theory and individual differences. In H. M. Burks, Jr., & B. Stefflre (Eds.), *Theories of counseling* (3rd ed., pp. 91–131). New York: McGraw-Hill.

Wilmarth, R. R. (1985, Summer). Historical perspective, part two. *AMHCA News, 8,* 21.

Wilson, F. R. (1994, Spring). Assessment and counseling information: Access via Internet. *AAC Newsnotes, 29,* 6–8.

Woody, R. H., Hansen, J. C., & Rossberg, R. H. (1989). *Counseling psychology.* Pacific Grove, CA: Brooks/Cole.

Wrenn, C. G. (1962). *The counselor in a changing world.* Washington, DC: American Personnel and Guidance Association.

Zytowski, D. (1985). Frank! Frank! Where are you now that we need you? *Counseling Psychologist, 13,* 129–135.

2

THE EFFECTIVE COUNSELOR

♦

In the midst of a day

that has brought only gray skies, hard rain,

and two cups of lukewarm coffee,

You come to me with Disney World wishes

Waiting for me to change into:

a Houdini figure with Daniel Boone's style

Prince Charming's grace and Abe Lincoln's wisdom

Who with magic words, a wand,

frontier spirit, and perhaps a smile

Can cure all troubles in a flash.

But reality sits in a green-cushioned chair,

lightning has struck a nearby tree,

Yesterday ended another month,

I'm uncomfortable sometimes in silence,

And unlike fantasy figures

I can't always be

what you see in your mind.

From "Reality Sits in a Green-Cushioned Chair," by S. T. Gladding, 1973, Personnel and Guidance Journal, 54, p. 222. © ACA. Reprinted with permission. No further reproduction authorized without written permission of the American Counseling Association.

Counseling is "an altruistic and noble profession." For the most part, "it attracts caring, warm, friendly and sensitive people" (Myrick, 1997, p. 4). Yet, individuals aspire to become counselors for many reasons. Some motivators, like the people involved, are healthier than others are, just as some educational programs, theories, and systems of counseling are stronger than others are. It is important that persons who wish to be counselors examine themselves before committing their lives to the profession. Whether they choose counseling as a career or not, people can be helped by studying themselves as well as counseling. They may gain insight into their lives, learn how to relate to others, and understand how the counseling process works (Cavanagh, 1990). They may also further develop their moral reasoning and empathetic abilities (Bowman & Reeves, 1987).

The effectiveness of a counselor and of counseling depends on numerous variables, including

- *the personality and background of the counselor;*
- *the formal education of the counselor;*
- *the theoretical and systemic frameworks of the counselor; and*
- *the ability of the counselor to engage in professional counseling-related activities, such as continuing education, supervision, and advocacy.*

The counselor and the counseling process have a dynamic effect on others, if not beneficial then most likely harmful (Carkhuff, 1969; Ellis, 1984; Mays & Franks, 1980). In this chapter, personal, educational, theoretical/systemic, and related counseling factors that influence counselors, the counseling process, and the counseling profession are examined.

The Personality and Background of the Counselor

A counselor's personality is at times a crucial ingredient in determining the effectiveness of counseling. Counselors should possess personal qualities of maturity, empathy, and warmth. They should be altruistic in spirit and not easily upset or frustrated. Unfortunately, such is not always the case.

Negative Motivators for Becoming a Counselor

Not everyone who wants to be a counselor or applies to a counselor education program should enter the field. The reason has to do with the motivation behind the pursuit of the profession and the incongruent personality match between the would-be counselor and the demands of counseling.

A number of students "attracted to professional counseling . . . appear to have serious personality and adjustment problems" (Witmer & Young, 1996, p. 142). Most are weeded out or decide to pursue other careers before they finish a counselor preparation program.

However, some entry-level students who matriculate into graduate counseling programs enter the profession for the wrong reasons. According to Guy (1987), dysfunctional motivators for becoming a counselor include the following:

Emotional distress—individuals who have unresolved personal traumas

Vicarious coping—persons who live their lives through others rather than have meaningful lives of their own

Loneliness and isolation—individuals who do not have friends and seek them through counseling experiences

A *desire for power*—people who feel frightened and impotent in their lives and seek to control others

A *need for love*—individuals who are narcissistic and grandiose and believe that all problems are resolved through the expression of love and tenderness

Vicarious rebellion—persons who have unresolved anger and act out their thoughts and feelings through their clients' defiant behaviors

Fortunately, most people who eventually become counselors and remain in the profession have healthy reasons for pursuing the profession, and a number even consider it to be a "calling" (Foster, 1996). Counselors and counselors-in-training should always assess themselves in regard to who they are and what they are doing. Such questions may include those that examine their development histories, their best and worst qualities, and personal/professional goals and objectives (Faiver, Eisengart, & Colonna, 1995).

Personal Qualities of an Effective Counselor

Among the functional and positive factors that motivate individuals to pursue careers in counseling and make them well suited for the profession are the following qualities as delineated by Foster (1996) and Guy (1987). Although this list is not exhaustive, it highlights aspects of one's personal life that make him or her more or less suited to function as a counselor.

* *Curiosity and inquisitiveness*—a natural interest in people
* *Ability to listen*—the ability to find listening stimulating
* *Comfort with conversation*—enjoyment of verbal exchanges
* *Empathy and understanding*—the ability to put oneself in another's place, even if that person is a different gender or from a different culture
* *Emotional insightfulness*—comfort dealing with a wide range of feelings, from anger to joy
* *Introspection*—the ability to see or feel from within
* *Capacity for self-denial*—the ability to set aside personal needs to listen and take care of others' needs first
* *Tolerance of intimacy*—the ability to sustain emotional closeness
* *Comfort with power*—the acceptance of power with a certain degree of detachment
* *Ability to laugh*—the capability of seeing the bittersweet quality of life events and the humor in them

In addition to personal qualities associated with entering the counseling profession, a number of personal characteristics are associated with being an effective counselor over time (Patterson & Welfel, 1994). They include stability, harmony, constancy, and purposefulness. Overall, the potency of counseling is related to counselors' personal togetherness (Carkhuff & Berenson, 1967; Kottler, 1993). The personhood or personality of counselors is as important, if not more crucial, than their mastery of knowledge, skills, or techniques (Cavanagh, 1990; Rogers, 1961). Education cannot change a person's basic characteristics. Effective counselors are growing as persons and are helping others do the same both personally and globally (Lee & Sirch, 1994). In other words, effective counselors are sensitive to themselves and others. They monitor their own biases, listen, ask for clarification, and explore racial and cultural differences in an open and positive way (Ford, Harris, & Schuerger, 1993).

Related to this sensitive and growth-enhancing quality of effective counselors are their appropriate use of themselves and their use of themselves as instruments (Brammer & MacDonald, 1996; Combs, 1982). Effective counselors are able to be spontaneous, creative, and empathetic. "There is a certain art to the choice and timing of counseling interventions" (Wilcox-Matthew, Ottens, & Minor, 1997, p. 288). Effective counselors choose and time their moves intuitively and according to what research has verified works best. It is helpful if counselors' lives have been tempered by multiple life experiences that have enabled them to realize some of what their clients are going through and therefore be both aware and appropriate.

The ability to work from a perspective of resolved emotional experience that has sensitized a person to self and others in a helpful way is what Rollo May characterizes as being a *wounded healer* (May, Remen, Young, & Berland, 1985). It is a paradoxical phenomenon. Individuals who have been hurt and have been able to transcend their pain and gain insight into themselves and the world can be helpful to others who struggle to overcome emotional problems (Miller, Wagner, Britton, & Gridley, 1998). They have been where their clients are now. Thus, "counselors who have experienced painful life events and have adjusted positively can usually connect and be authentic with clients in distress" (Foster, 1996, p. 21).

Effective counselors are also people who have successfully integrated scientific knowledge and skills into their lives. That is, they have achieved a balance of interpersonal and technical competence (Cormier & Cormier, 1998). Qualities of effective counselors over time other than those already mentioned include the following:

- *Intellectual competence*—the desire and ability to learn as well as think fast and creatively
- *Energy*—the ability to be active in sessions and sustain that activity even when one sees a number of clients in a row
- *Flexibility*—the ability to adapt what one does to meet clients' needs
- *Support*—the capacity to encourage clients in making their own decisions while helping engender hope
- *Goodwill*—the desire to work on behalf of clients in a constructive way that ethically promotes independence
- *Self-awareness*—a knowledge of self, including attitudes, values, and feelings and the ability to recognize how and what factors affect oneself

According to Holland (1997), specific personality types are attracted to and work best in certain vocational environments. The environment in which counselors work well is primarily social and problem oriented. It calls for skill in interpersonal relationships and creativity. The act of creativity requires courage (May, 1975) and involves a selling of new ideas and ways of working that promote intra- as well as interpersonal relations (Gladding, 1998). The more aligned counselors' personalities are to their environments, the more effective and satisfied they will be.

Wiggins and Weslander (1979) found empirical support for Holland's hypothesis. They studied the personality traits and rated the job performance of 320 counselors in four states. In general, those counselors who were rated "highly effective" scored highest on the social (social, service oriented) and artistic (creative, imaginative) scales of the Vocational Preference Inventory (Holland, 1977). Counselors who were rated "ineffective" generally scored highest on the realistic (concrete, technical) and conventional (organized, practical) scales. Other factors, such as gender, age, and level of education, were not found to be statistically significant in predicting effectiveness. The results of this research affirm that the personality of counselors is related to their effectiveness in the profession. Nevertheless, the relationship of persons and environments is complex: individuals with many different personality types manage to find places within the broad field of counseling and make significant contributions to the profession.

Maintaining Effectiveness as a Counselor

Persons who become counselors experience the same difficulties as everyone else. They must deal with aging, illness, death, marriage, parenting, job changes, divorce, and a host of other common problems. Some of these life events, such as marrying for the first time late in life or experiencing the death of a child, are considered developmentally "off time," or out of sequence and even tragic (Skovholt & McCarthy, 1988). Other events consist of unintended but fortuitous chance encounters, such as meeting a person with whom one develops a lifelong friendship (Bandura, 1982).

Both traumatic and fortunate experiences are problematic because of the stress they naturally create. A critical issue is how counselors handle these life events. As Roehlke (1988) points out, Carl Jung's idea of *synchronicity*, "which he [Jung] defined as two simultaneous events that occur coincidentally [and that] result in a meaningful connection," is perhaps the most productive way for counselors to perceive and deal with unexpected life experiences (p. 133).

Besides finding meaning in potentially problematic areas, other strategies counselors use for coping with crisis situations include remaining objective, accepting and confronting situations, asserting their own wishes, participating in a wellness lifestyle, and grieving (Lenhardt, 1997; Witmer & Young, 1996). Counselors who have healthy personal lives and learn from both their mistakes and their successes are more likely than others to grow therapeutically and be able to concentrate fully and sensitively on clients' problems (Cormier, 1988). Therefore, counselors and those who wish to enter the profession need to adapt to losses as well as gains and remain relatively free from destructive triangling patterns with persons, especially parents, in their families of origin. Such a stance enables them to foster and maintain intimate yet autonomous relationships in the present as desired (Gaushell & Lawson, 1994).

Other ways effective counselors maintain their health and well-being include taking preventive measures to avoid problematic behaviors, such as burnout (Grosch & Olsen, 1994). *Burnout* is the state of becoming emotionally or physically drained to the point that one cannot perform functions meaningfully. It is the single most common personal consequence of working as a counselor (Emerson & Markos, 1996; Kottler, 1993). People cannot function adequately if they never step out of their professional roles. Counselors must develop interests outside counseling and avoid taking their work home, either mentally or physically. They also must take responsibility for rejuvenating themselves through such small but significant steps as refurbishing their offices every few years; purging, condensing, and creating new files; evaluating new materials; and contributing to the counseling profession through writing or presenting material on which they are comfortable (McCormick, 1998). A number of researchers suggest other ways in which counselors can avoid or treat burnout (Boy & Pine, 1980; Pines & Aronson, 1981; Savicki & Cooley, 1982; Watkins, 1983):

- Associate with healthy individuals.
- Work with committed colleagues and organizations that have a sense of mission.
- Be reasonably committed to a theory of counseling.
- Use stress reduction exercises.
- Modify environmental stressors.
- Engage in self-assessment (i.e., identify stressors and relaxers).
- Periodically examine and clarify counseling roles, expectations, and beliefs (i.e., work smarter, not necessarily longer).
- Obtain personal therapy.
- Set aside free and private time (i.e., balance one's lifestyle).
- Maintain an attitude of detached concern when working with clients.
- Retain an attitude of hope.

In summing up previous research about the personalities, qualities, and interests of counselors, Auvenshine and Noffsinger (1984) concluded, "Effective counselors must be emotionally mature, stable, and objective. They must have self-awareness and be secure in that awareness, incorporating their own strengths and weaknesses realistically" (p. 151).

The Formal Education of Counselors

Few, if any, people have the ability to work effectively as counselors without formal education in human development and counseling (Kurpius, 1986). The level of education needed is directly related to the intensity, expertise, and emphasis of work in which one engages. Before examining the education necessary for a professional counselor, we will first explore three levels of helping and the educational emphases of several other helping professions.

Levels of Helping

There are three levels of helping relationships: nonprofessional, paraprofessional, and professional. To practice at a certain level requires that helpers acquire the skills necessary for the task (see Figure 2.1).

Figure 2.1 Kinds of helping relationships

Source: From *Effective Helping: Interviewing and Counseling Techniques*, by Barbara F. Okun. © 1997, 1992, 1987, 1982, 1976 by Brooks/Cole Publishing Company, Pacific Grove, CA 93950, a division of Thomson Publishing, Inc. By permission of the publisher.

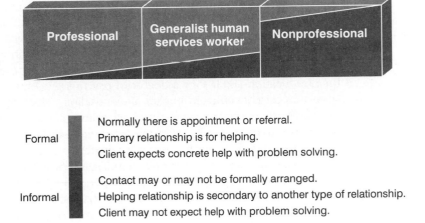

Formal — Normally there is appointment or referral.
Primary relationship is for helping.
Client expects concrete help with problem solving.

Informal — Contact may or may not be formally arranged.
Helping relationship is secondary to another type of relationship.
Client may not expect help with problem solving.

The first level of helping involves *nonprofessional helpers.* These helpers may be friends, colleagues, untrained volunteers, or supervisors who try to assist those in need in whatever ways they can. Nonprofessional helpers possess varying degrees of wisdom and skill. No specific educational requirements are involved, and the level of helping varies greatly among people in this group.

A second and higher level of helping encompasses what is known as *generalist human services workers.* These individuals are usually human service workers who have received some formal training in human relations skills but work as part of a team rather than as individuals. People on this level often work as mental health technicians, child care workers, probation personnel, and youth counselors. When properly trained and supervised, generalist human services workers such as residence hall assistants can have a major impact on facilitating positive relationships that promote mental health throughout a social environment (Waldo, 1989).

Finally, there are *professional helpers.* These persons are educated to provide assistance on both a preventive and a remedial level. People in this group include counselors, psychologists, psychiatrists, social workers, psychiatric nurses, and marriage and family therapists. Workers on this level have a specialized advanced degree and have had supervised internships to help them prepare to deal with a plethora of situations.

In regard to the education of helpers on the last two levels, Robinson and Kinnier (1988) have found that self-instructional and traditional classroom training are equally effective at teaching skills.

Professional Helping Specialties

Each helping profession has its own educational and practice requirements. Counselors need to know the educational backgrounds of other professions in order to use their services, communicate with them in an informed manner, and collaborate with them on matters of mutual concern. Three helping professions with which counselors frequently interact are psychiatrists, psychologists, and social workers.

Psychiatrists earn a medical degree (M.D.) and complete a residency in psychiatry. They are specialists in working with people who have major psychological disorders. They frequently prescribe medicines and take a biopsychological approach in treatment. Their clients are called *patients.* They must pass both national and state examinations to practice.

Psychologists earn one of the following degrees: a doctor of philosophy (Ph.D.), a doctor of education (Ed.D.), or a doctor of psychology (Psy.D.). Their coursework and internships may be concentrated in clinical, counseling, or school-related areas. All states license psychologists, but the requirements for licensure differ from state to state. Most clinically oriented psychologists are listed in the *National Register of Health Service Providers,* which has uniform standards for inclusion. Graduates of counseling psychology programs follow a curriculum that includes courses in scientific and professional ethics and standards, research design and methodology, statistics and psychological measurement, biological bases of behavior, cognitive-affective bases of behavior, social bases of behavior, individual behavior, and courses in specialty areas. Counseling psychology and counselor education share many common roots, concerns, and significant persons in their histories (Elmore, 1984).

Social workers usually earn a master's of social work degree (M.S.W.), although some universities award a bachelor's degree in social work. Regardless of their educational background, social workers on all levels have completed internships in social agency settings. Social workers vary in regard to how they function. Some administer government programs for the underprivileged and disenfranchised. Others engage in counseling activities. The National Association of Social Workers (NASW) offers credentials for members who demonstrate advanced clinical and educational competencies.

The Education of Professional Counselors

Professional *counselors* obtain either a master's or a doctorate in counseling from a counselor education or related program and complete internships in specialty areas such as school counseling, community/agency counseling, mental health counseling, career counseling, gerontological counseling, addiction counseling, or marriage and family counseling. They are usually certified by the National Board of Certified Counselors or are licensed to practice by individual states, or both.

An *accredited counselor education program* is one recognized at either the master's or doctoral level. The accrediting body for these programs is the Council for Accreditation of Counseling and Related Educational Programs (CACREP). This independent body evolved from the efforts of the Association for Counselor Education and Supervision (ACES) and the American Counseling Association (ACA) to establish standards and guidelines for counseling independent of the National Council for Accreditation of Teacher Education (NCATE).

On the master's level, CACREP accredits programs in community counseling, mental health counseling, school counseling, marriage and family counseling/therapy, and student affairs practice in higher education with two emphases: college counseling and professional practice. Graduates from accredited masters' programs have an advantage over graduates from nonaccredited programs in (a) obtaining admittance to accredited counselor education doctoral programs, (b) meeting the educational requirements for counselor licensure and certification, and (c) obtaining employment as a counselor.

The following broad standards must be met in an accredited counselor education master's degree program (CACREP, 1994):

- The entry-level program must be a minimum of 2 full academic years in length, with a minimum of 48 semester hours required of all students. The entry-level program in mental health counseling must be 60 semester hours long, and the entry-level program in marriage and family counseling must also be 60 semester hours.
- Curricular experiences and demonstrated knowledge and skill competence is required of all students in each of eight common core areas: (a) human growth and development, (b) social and cultural foundations, (c) helping relationships, (d) groups, (e) lifestyles and career development, (f) appraisal, (g) research and evaluation, and (h) professional orientation.
- Clinical experiences are required under the direction of supervisors with specific qualifications. The student must complete 100 clock hours of a supervised practicum with 1 hour per week of individual supervision and 1½ hours per week of group supervision with other students in similar practice.
- The program must require that each student complete 600 clock hours of a supervised internship, which is to begin only after successful completion of the student's practicum.
- Three full-time faculty members must be assigned to the academic unit in counselor education.

CACREP accredits programs on the doctoral level (Ed.D. and Ph.D.). In 1996 there were 52 doctoral programs in counselor education, with 34 of them accredited by CACREP (Hollis, 1997). Standards at this level assume that an individual has completed an entry-level master's degree in counseling. Doctoral-level programs require more in-depth research, supervised field experiences, and specialization. A growing number of graduate schools are applying for CACREP accreditation because of the benefits and recognition such accreditation brings to themselves and to their students.

Hollis (1997) mentions several trends in the accreditation of counseling programs. Two of the most noteworthy are that the number of counselor preparation programs becoming accredited is increasing, and nationally recognized accreditation of counselor preparation programs is becoming more important. Graduating from an accredited counseling program enhances the ease at which students can proceed with their professional lives. Faculty and administrators understand that accreditation standards are associated with good programs, and standards are a way of determining program priorities. Overall, counselor education programs have become deeper in course offerings and broader developmentally as a result of accreditation trends.

Theoretical and Systematic Framework of the Counselor

The theoretical and systematic framework of counselors makes a difference in what they do and how effectively they do it. A *theory* is a model or explanation that counselors use as a guide to hypothesize about the formation of problems and possible solutions. Effective counselors decide which theory or theories and methods to use on the basis of their educational background, philosophy, and the needs of clients. Not all approaches are appropriate for all counselors or clients, but a theoretical base is usually necessary to be effective. Likewise, a systematic approach to the profession of counseling is essential. A *system* is a unified and organized set of ideas, principles, and behaviors. Systems associated with counseling are concerned with how the counselor approaches clients and are interrelated to theories. Two systems, one based on developmental issues and one based on the diagnosis of disorders, will be examined here because it is from these two perspectives (and the places in between) that counselors work.

Theory

The Basis of Theory.   Exceptional practitioners who formulated their ideas on the basis of their experiences and observations have developed most counseling theories. Yet most theorists are somewhat tentative about their positions, realizing that no one theory fits all situations. Indeed, one theory may not be adequate for the same client over an extended period. Counselors must choose their theoretical positions carefully and regularly reassess them.

Some theoretical models are more comprehensive than others are, and effective counselors are aware of which theories are most comprehensive and for what reasons. Hansen, Stevic, and Warner (1986) list five requirements of good theory:

1. *Clear, easily understood, and communicable.* It is coherent and not contradictory.
2. *Comprehensive.* It encompasses explanations for a wide variety of phenomena.
3. *Explicit and heuristic.* It generates research because of its design.
4. *Specific in relating means to desired outcomes.* It contains a way of achieving a desired end product.
5. *Useful to its intended practitioners.* It provides guidelines for research and practice.

In addition to these five qualities, a good theory for counselors is one that matches their personal philosophies of helping. Shertzer and Stone (1974) suggest that a counseling theory must fit counselors like a suit of clothes. Some theories, like some suits, need tailoring. Therefore, effective counselors realize the importance of alterations. Counselors who wish to be versatile and effective should learn a wide variety of counseling theories and know how to apply each without violating its internal consistency (Auvenshine & Noffsinger, 1984).

Importance of Theory.   Theory is the foundation of good counseling. It challenges counselors to be caring and creative within the confines of a highly personal relationship that is structured for growth and insight (Gladding, 1990). Theory has an impact on how client communication is conceptualized, how interpersonal relationships develop, how professional ethics are implemented, and how counselors view themselves as professionals (Carey, Neukrug, McAuliffe, Pratt, & Lovell, 1990). Without theoretical backing, counselors operate haphazardly in a trial-and-error manner and risk being both ineffective and harmful. Brammer, Abrego, and Shostrom (1993) stress the pragmatic value of a solidly formulated theory for counselors. Theory helps explain what happens in a counseling relationship and assists the counselor in predicting, evaluating, and improving results. Theory provides a framework for making scientific observations about counseling. Theorizing encourages the coherence of ideas about counseling and the production of new ideas. Hence, counseling theory can be practical by helping to make sense out of the counselor's observations.

Boy and Pine (1983) elaborate on the practical value of theory by suggesting that theory is the *why* behind the *how* of counselors' roles, providing a framework within which counselors can operate. Counselors guided by theory can meet the demands of their roles because they have reasons for what they do. Boy and Pine point out six functions of theory that help counselors in a practical way:

1. Theory helps counselors find unity and relatedness within the diversity of existence.
2. Theory compels counselors to examine relationships they would otherwise overlook.
3. Theory gives counselors operational guidelines by which to work and helps them evaluate their development as professionals.
4. Theory helps counselors focus on relevant data and tells them what to look for.
5. Theory helps counselors assist clients in the effective modification of their behavior.
6. Theory helps counselors evaluate both old and new approaches to the process of counseling. It is the base from which new counseling approaches are constructed.

"The ultimate criterion for all counseling theories is how well they provide explanations of what occurs in counseling" (Kelly, 1988, pp. 212–213). Their value as ways of organizing information "hinges on the degree to which they are grounded in the reality of people's lives" (Young, 1988, p. 336).

Theoretical Purity and Eclecticism.   In its infancy, counseling was a profession in which *theoretical purity* (allegiance to and practice of one theory) was expected and actually necessary for counselors seeking employment. It was important that counselors be able to identify their practices as stemming from one of fewer than half a dozen available choices (psychoanalysis, behaviorism, client centered, and so forth). But with the flood of new theories—cognitive, behavioral, and affective—that were formulated during the 1960s, allegiance to a specific theory began to wane in popularity and importance. The development of *microskills training* (training in human relations skills common to all theories of helping) hastened the demise of theoretical positions stemming from one specific source. In its place came eclectic counseling.

Many professional counselors (approximately 60% to 70%) identify themselves as *eclectic* in the use of theory and techniques (Lazarus & Beutler, 1993). That is, they use various theories and techniques to match their clients' needs. As needs change, counselors depart from a theory they are using to another approach (a phenomenon called *style-shift counseling*). Changes counselors make are related to the client's developmental level (Ivey & Goncalves, 1988). To be effective, counselors must consider how far their clients have progressed in their structural development, as described by Jean Piaget. For example, a client who is not developmentally aware of his or her environment may need a therapeutic approach that focuses on "emotions, the body, and experience in the here and now"; whereas a client who is at a more advanced level of development may respond best to a "consulting-formal operations" approach, in which the emphasis is on thinking about actions (Ivey & Goncalves, 1988, p. 410). The point is that counselors and theories must start with where their clients are, helping them develop in a holistic manner.

An eclectic approach can be hazardous to the counseling process if the counselor is not thoroughly familiar with all the processes involved. The unexamined approach of undereducated counselors is sometimes sarcastically referred to as "electric"; that is, such counselors try any and all methods that "turn them on." The problem with an electric orientation is that counselors often do more harm than good if they have little or no understanding about what is helping the client.

To combat this problem, McBride and Martin (1990) advocate a hierarchy of eclectic practices and discuss the importance of having a sound theoretical base as a guide. The lowest or first level of eclecticism is really *syncretism*—a sloppy, unsystematic process of putting unrelated clinical concepts together. It is encouraged when graduate students are urged to formulate their own theories of counseling without first having experienced how tested models work. The second level of eclecticism is *traditional*. It incorporates "an orderly combination of compatible features from diverse sources [into a] harmonious whole" (English & English, 1956, p. 168). It is more thought out than syncretism, and theories are examined in greater depth.

On a third level, eclecticism is described as professional or theoretical or as *theoretical integrationism* (Lazarus & Beutler, 1993; Simon, 1989). This type of eclecticism requires that counselors master at least two theories before trying to make any combinations. The trouble with this approach is that it assumes a degree of equality between theories (which may not be true) and the existence of criteria "to determine what portions or pieces of each theory to preserve or expunge" (Lazarus & Beutler, 1993, p. 382). It differs from the traditional model in that no mastery of theory is expected in the traditional approach.

A final level of eclecticism is called *technical eclecticism*, exemplified in the work of Arnold Lazarus (1967). In this approach, procedures from different theories are selected and used in treatment "without necessarily subscribing to the theories that spawned them" (Lazarus & Beutler, 1993, p. 384). The idea is that techniques, not theories, are actually used in treating clients. Therefore, after properly assessing clients, counselors may use behavioral methods (such as assertiveness training) with existential techniques (such as confronting persons about the meaning in their lives) if the situations warrant.

This final approach is in line with what Cavanagh (1990) proposes as a healthy eclectic approach to counseling. It requires counselors to have (a) a sound knowledge and understanding of the counseling theories used, (b) a basic integrative philosophy of human behavior that brings disparate parts of differing theories into a meaningful collage, and (c) a flexible means of fitting the approach to the client, not vice versa. Counselors who follow this model may operate pragmatically and effectively within an eclectic framework. The critical variables in being a healthy eclectic counselor are a mastery of theory and an acute sensitivity to knowing what approach to use when, where, and how (Harman, 1977).

Systems of Counseling

Effective counselors adhere to certain systems of counseling as well as theories of counseling. Indeed, the strength of counseling ultimately depends on a continuation of that process. This section explores two systems of counseling: one based on a developmental perspective that includes wellness, the other based on a disorders and dysfunctional view of human nature.

Unsystematic Beginnings.   That counseling is not governed by one dominant system approach is hardly surprising considering its historical development. Counseling started like a person who mounted a horse and rode off in all directions; that is, the person had no focus or planned direction (Ungersma, 1961).

As far back as the late 1940s, professionals noticed the lack of a system for counseling. Robert Mathewson (1949) observed that counseling was in "a search for a system . . . to win free from inadequate frames borrowed from traditional philosophy and education, from psychology, from political formulations underlying democratic government, from the concepts of physical science, etc." (p. 73).

Until the late 1940s, counseling used a variety of systems. Because the profession was without an organizational base, different factions defined what they did according to the system that suited them best. Competition among points of view, especially those connected with theories, was often spirited. Some counselors recognized the need for a unifying systematic approach to their discipline, but the unplanned growth of the profession proved an obstacle. However, by the 1990s several systems of counseling had emerged, the two most dominant (as stated previously) being the developmental/wellness approach and the medical/pathological approach.

The Developmental/Wellness Approach.   The developmental/wellness perspective to counseling is based on stages that various personality theorists have outlined that people go through as a normal part of human growth. Counseling from this perspective is based on whether a problem a client is having is based on a developmental task of life. Behaviors that are appropriate at one stage of life may not be seen as healthy at another stage of life.

Allen Ivey (1990) was not the first to suggest that counseling systems be based on a developmental perspective, but his integration of developmental growth with counseling strategies stands out as one of the most unique expressions of this approach. Basically, Ivey suggests applying Piagetian concepts of cognitive levels (i.e., sensorimotor, concrete, formal, and postformal) to clinical interviews with adults and children. Therefore, if clients do not initially recognize their feelings, counselors will work from a sensorimotor level to bring out emotions. In a similar way, clients who are interested in planning strategies for change will be helped using a formal pattern of thought. *Developmental counseling and therapy* (DCT) "specifically addresses the sequence and process of development as it occurs in the natural language of the interview" (Ivey & Ivey, 1990, p. 299).

Wellness goes even further than development in emphasizing the positive nature and health of human beings (Myers, 1992). "Counselors have historically been in the business of helping their clients identify their strengths and build on their strengths" (Rak & Patterson, 1996, p. 368). In this perspective, individuals are seen as having the resources to solve their own problems in a practical, immediate way. "Problems are not evidence of an underlying pathology" (Mostert, Johnson, & Mostert, 1997, p. 21). Indeed, as Rak and Patterson (1996) point out, even most at-risk children show resilience and become coping adults.

An example of a counseling approach based on the wellness model is *solution-focused theory*. *Stress inoculation training* (SIT) (Meichenbaum, 1993), a proactive, psychoeducational intervention that can be used in schools and with adults, is another example of a present and future wellness emphasis approach (Israelashvili, 1998). In this model individuals are helped to understand their problematic situations, acquire skills for coping with them, and apply this knowledge to present and even future events through the use of imagery or simulated rehearsal.

A cornerstone of the developmental/wellness approach is an emphasis on prevention and education (Kleist & White, 1997). Counselors and clients function best when they are informed about the mental, physical, and social spheres of human life. Through such a process they recognize how they can focus on avoiding or minimizing disruptive forces that are either internal or external in nature.

The Medical/Pathology Model.   In contrast to the developmental view of counseling is the *medical/pathological model* of human nature represented by those who base treatment plans in accordance with the *Diagnostic and Statistical Manual* (DSM) (American Psychiatric Association, 1994). The DSM is compatible with the *International Classification of Diseases* manual (ICD-10), published by the World Health Organization, in codifying psychiatric disorders. The fourth edition of this manual (DSM-IV) contains 400 different categorical classifications of defined disorders and is culturally more sensitive than its predecessors. For example, "14 of the 16 major diagnostic classes (e.g., mood disorder, anxiety disorder) include some discussion of cultural issues" (Smart & Smart, 1997, p. 393).

A unique feature of the DSM system since 1980 is the use of five axes to describe client diagnoses. *Axis I* includes "clinical syndromes and other conditions that may be a focus of clinical attention" and is usually thought of as the axis on which a client's presenting problem and principal diagnosis appear (Hinkle, 1994, p. 38). *Axis II* contains diagnostic information only on personality disorders and mental limitations. *Axis III* describes information about general medical conditions of the client, such as chronic pain. *Axis IV* contains information on psychosocial and environmental problems that may affect the diagnosis, treatment, and prognosis of mental disorders, such as a lack of friends and inadequate housing. *Axis V* gives a global assessment of functioning for the client on a scale from 0 to 100. (Higher numbers on the scale indicate a better level of functioning.) The assessment can be in relationship to the past or the present. When all of the axes are combined, the result might look like the following:

> Axis I: 305.00; alcohol abuse, moderate
> Axis II: 317.00; mild mental retardation
> Axis III: chronic pain
> Axis IV: divorced, unemployed, no friends
> Axis V: GAF = 30 (present)

Overall, the DSM is an extremely interesting but controversial systemic model (Denton, 1990; Hinkle, 1994). It is atheoretical and does not substantially deal with anything but individual diagnoses, many of which are severe. Therefore, it is of limited value to group workers, marriage and family counselors, and counseling professionals who are not working with highly disturbed populations or who work from a humanistic orientation. On the other hand, the DSM-IV contains information related to multicultural considerations, gender, and age in diagnoses and treatment of persons. In addition, it is logically organized and includes a good network of decision trees. (See Appendix C for DSM-IV classifications.)

Counselors should master DSM terminology regardless of their setting or specialty for the following reasons (Geroski, Rodgers, & Breen, 1997; Seligman, 1997):

1. The DSM system is universally used in other helping professions and forms the basis for a common dialogue between counselors and other mental health specialists.
2. The DSM system helps counselors recognize patterns of mental distress in clients who need to be referred to other mental health professionals or treated in a certain way.
3. By learning the DSM system, counselors establish accountability, credibility, uniform record keeping, informed treatment plans, research, and quality assurance.

Engaging in Professional Counseling-Related Activities

Becoming a counselor is a lifelong process. It continues well past the formal education of obtaining a master's or doctorate degree and includes participation in professional counseling–related activities. Counselors must obtain continuing education units (CEUs) to stay up-to-date, get needed supervision to ensure excellence in treatment, and advocate for both their clients and the profession of counseling.

Continuing Education

There is a need for continuing education of all counselors, even after graduation from a well-planned counselor education program. The reason is that new ideas in the treatment and practice of clients are always evolving and must be evaluated, incorporated, and, if necessary, mastered. Counselors who stop reading professional publications or stop attending in-service workshops and conventions quickly become dated in the delivery of skills. Therefore, counselors must obtain a certain number of CEUs annually to stay abreast of the latest and best methods of working.

CEUs are offered by approved professional counseling organizations on the local, state, regional, and national levels. It is possible to earn CEUs through correspondence courses as well as attending workshops. Counselors who are licensed or certified have to earn a certain number of CEUs to retain their credentials (Dingman, 1990). Engaging in such continuous efforts is sometimes expensive in terms of time and money, but the cost of not keeping up professionally (i.e., becoming incompetent or outdated) is much higher.

Supervision

Supervision is another way of improving professional counseling skills. *Supervision* is an interactive and evaluative process in which someone with more proficiency oversees the work of someone with less knowledge and skill to enhance the professional functioning of the junior member (Bernard & Goodyear, 1998). At its best, supervision is a facilitative experience that combines didactic and experiential learning in the context of a developmental relationship. It allows the acquiring of expertise in theory and practice that is not possible to gain in any other way (Borders & Leddick, 1988).

Supervision is a required area of instruction in all CACREP-accredited doctoral programs (CACREP, 1994). In addition, counselors may undergo supervision from members of the profession who have received advanced training and in the process obtain approved supervisor status. Standards for counseling supervisors have been developed for counselors, and the National Board of Certified Counselors now offers a specialty credential in supervision. Often, those already licensed as counselors can count supervised experiences toward CEUs.

To be effective, supervision must be given on a counselor's developmental level. For beginning graduate students who have a noticeable gap between their knowledge of theory and practice, supervisors are most potent if they assume a highly structured teaching role (Ronnestad & Skovholt, 1993). For example, supervisors may be more authoritarian, didactic, and supportive than they would be with advanced graduate students or experienced counselors. In the latter cases, supervisors might be more confrontive and consultative. Although supervision, like counseling, may increase one's self-awareness, this process is focused on professional rather than personal growth (Ronnestad & Skovholt, 1993).

In setting up supervisory situations, one must address several myths and many realities. Myths are made up of extreme views: for example, "one supervisor can perform all supervisory roles," "individual supervision is best," or "individuals do not need training to supervise" (McCarthy, DeBell, Kanuha, & McLeod, 1988). Realities include the following facts:

- There is not just one theoretical model of supervision but several (e.g., behavioral, facilitative, dynamic, systemic) (Landis & Young, 1994).
- Before a productive supervisory relationship can be established, the developmental level of the supervisee must be verified and a written plan of realistic goals must be completed (Borders & Leddick, 1987).
- There is a significant relationship between a supervisor's credibility, such as trustworthiness, and a supervisee's performance (Carey, Williams, & Wells, 1988).

Overall, the literature and the sophistication of supervisory techniques in counseling are growing (Dye & Borders, 1990). For example, the *reflective team model* is a recent innovative way of providing group supervision, especially in working with couples and families (Landis & Young, 1994). In this model graduate students are asked to collaborate, brainstorm, and take their clients' perspectives as they advance hypotheses about client behaviors, view situations from the clients' framework, and work cooperatively.

Counselors who take advantage of supervisory opportunities, especially opportunities for *peer supervision* (supervision among equals), can both gain and give information about themselves and their clinical abilities. This increased awareness is the bedrock on which other positive professional experiences can be built.

Advocacy

In addition to other characteristics and qualities connected with themselves and the counseling process, effective counselors engage in advocacy. "Advocacy can be defined simply as promoting an idea or a cause through public relations. It involves networking and education" (Tysl, 1997, p. 16). Counselors need to support and actively espouse client concerns and the profession of counseling. By doing so they correct injustices and improve conditions for an individual or group (Osborne et al., 1998). This process can be achieved in a number of ways, such as making presentations to clubs and civic groups, writing articles for newspapers, and focusing on community issues through giving one's time and effort. It is especially important to make others aware of social concerns of needy populations, since such groups do not usually have a voice or recognition. At times advocacy involves speaking on the behalf of such people and promoting ways of ensuring that their rights are respected and that their needs are taken care of through social action (McClure & Russo, 1996).

Another form of advocacy is working through the political process. Not only must counselors be knowledgeable about social matters, but they must also influence the passage of laws when conditions adversely affect either their clients or the profession of counseling. Counselors can make a difference by writing letters or visiting with legislators. Advocating for the passage of socially enhancing bills, such as school-to-work legislation, or the reauthorization of initiatives, such as rehabilitation acts, is vital for the health of counselors and their constituents.

Advocacy occurs at multiple levels, such as the county, state, or federal (Goetz, 1998). Counselors can work to positively impact the passage of laws in a number of ways. The first is to stay informed and know what bills are being considered. The American Counseling Association's Office of Public Policy and Information is an excellent resource for federal legislative initiatives and can be accessed through the ACA Web site.

A second way to advocate is to know the rules for effective communication with legislators. The use of jargon, exaggeration, or rambling hurts a counselor's presentation. Therefore, it is important to be organized, concise, and concrete in advocating for certain actions. Flexibility and anticipation of opposite points of view are crucial to being successful.

Finally, be persistent. As in counseling, follow-up is essential in dealing with legislative situations. Initiatives may require years of lobbying before they are enacted. For instance, counselor licensure was passed in Maryland in 1998, but only after a 20-year effort!

Summary and Conclusion

The qualities necessary to become an effective counselor will probably increase as counseling evolves as a profession. Yet there will always be some basic qualities that all counselors must embody to become effective.

One such quality is the core personality of counselors. Persons feel comfortable working in counseling environments because of their interests, backgrounds, and abilities. The majority of effective counselors have social and artistic interests and enjoy working with people in a variety of problem-solving and developmental ways. Effective counselors are generally characterized as warm, friendly, open, sensitive, patient, and creative. They are consistently working on their own mental health and strive to avoid becoming burned out and ineffective.

Education is a second quality related to the effectiveness of counselors. Effective counselors have gone through an accredited counseling program or its equivalent on either a doctoral or master's level. Many have also achieved the skills and experience necessary to work in counseling specialty areas.

A third area related to effectiveness in counseling is theory and systems. Effective counselors know that theory is the *why* behind the *how* of technique and practice and that nothing is more practical than mastering major theoretical approaches to counseling. These counselors are not unsystematic and capricious in using theories and methods in their practice. Many use a healthy type of eclecticism in their work. They operate systemically from a developmental/wellness approach, a medical/pathology model, or some place in between. Regardless, effective counselors know how individuals develop over the life span and also know the terminology and uses of the latest edition of the *Diagnostic and Statistical Manual*.

Finally, effective counselors are active in counseling-related activities. They realize the importance of keeping their knowledge up-to-date by participating in continuing education programs and supervisory activities. Furthermore, they advocate for both the needs of their clients and the profession of counseling.

CLASSROOM ACTIVITIES

1. Research indicates that some personality types are more suited to be counselors than others are. Suppose you do not possess the ideal personality for this profession (i.e., social, artistic, and enterprising). What are some ways in which you could compensate? In groups of three, discuss your reaction to the qualities of personality associated with effective counseling.

2. Review the personal, theoretical, and educational qualities that ideal counselors possess. Discuss how you think these qualities might differ if you were counseling outside the United States—for example, in India, Sweden, Israel, Australia, or Argentina. Share your opinions with the class.

3. Discuss with another classmate how you might help each other grow professionally if you were unequal in ability as counselors. After you have made your list, share it with another group of two and then with the class as a whole. As a class, discuss how the strategies you have formulated might be helpful in your lifetime development as counselors.

4. With another classmate, discuss how you would approach clients differently and similarly if you were coming from a developmental/wellness perspective as opposed to a medical/pathology model. Report your results to the class.

5. Investigate how counseling associations or counselors have advocated for their clients' needs and for the profession of counseling itself. A good place to begin is to consult the Public Policy section of the American Counseling Association homepage.

REFERENCES

American Psychiatric Association. (1994). *Diagnostic and statistical manual of mental disorders* (4th ed.). Washington, DC: Author.

Auvenshine, D., & Noffsinger, A. L. (1984). *Counseling: An introduction for the health and human services.* Baltimore: University Park Press.

Bandura, A. (1982). The psychology of chance encounters and life paths. *American Psychologist, 37,* 747–755.

Bernard, J. M., & Goodyear, R. K. (1998). *Fundamentals of clinical supervision* (2nd ed.). Boston: Allyn & Bacon.

Borders, L. D., & Leddick, G. R. (1987). *Handbook of counseling supervision.* Alexandria, VA: Association for Counselor Education and Supervision.

Borders, L. D., & Leddick, G. R. (1988). A nationwide survey of supervision training. *Counselor Education and Supervision, 27,* 271–283.

Bowman, J. T., & Reeves, T. G. (1987). Moral development and empathy in counseling. *Counselor Education and Supervision, 26,* 293–298.

Boy, A. V., & Pine, G. J. (1980). Avoiding counselor burnout through role renewal. *Personnel and Guidance Journal, 59,* 161–163.

Boy, A. V., & Pine, G. J. (1983). Counseling: Fundamentals of theoretical renewal. *Counseling and Values, 27,* 248–255.

Brammer, L. M., Abrego, P., & Shostrom, E. (1993). *Therapeutic counseling and psychotherapy* (6th ed.). Upper Saddle River, NJ: Prentice Hall.

Brammer, L. M., & MacDonald, G. (1996) *The helping relationship: Process and skills* (6th ed.). Boston: Allyn & Bacon.

Carey, J., Neukrug, E., McAuliffe, G., Pratt, L., & Lovell, C. (1990, November). *Developmentalizing the process of counselor education and supervision: What does the research tell us?* Paper presented at the Southern Association for Counselor Education and Supervision Conference, Norfolk, VA.

Carey, J. C., Williams, K. S., & Wells, M. (1988). Relationships between dimensions of supervisors' influence and counselor trainees' performance. *Counselor Education and Supervision, 28,* 130–139.

Carkhuff, R. R. (1969). *Helping and human relations* (Vols. 1 & 2). New York: Holt, Rinehart, & Winston.

Carkhuff, R. R., & Berenson, B. G. (1967). *Beyond counseling and psychotherapy.* New York: Holt, Rinehart, & Winston.

Cavanagh, M. E. (1990). *The counseling experience.* Prospect Heights, IL: Waveland.

Combs, A. (1982). *A personal approach to teaching: Beliefs that make a difference.* Boston: Allyn & Bacon.

Cormier, L. S. (1988). Critical incidents in counselor development: Themes and patterns. *Journal of Counseling and Development, 67,* 131–132.

Cormier, L. S., & Cormier, W. H. (1998). *Fundamental skills and cognitive behavioral interventions* (4th ed.). Pacific Grove, CA: Brooks/Cole.

Council for Accreditation of Counseling and Related Educational Programs (CACREP). (1994). *Accreditation procedures manual and application.* Alexandria, VA: Author.

Denton, W. (1990). A family systems analysis of DSM-III-R. *Journal of Marital and Family Therapy, 16,* 113–126.

Dingman, R. L. (1990, November). *Counselor credentialing laws.* Paper presented at the Southern Association for Counselor Education and Supervision Conference, Norfolk, VA.

Dye, H. A., & Borders, L. D. (1990). Counseling supervisors: Standards for preparation and practice. *Journal of Counseling and Development, 69,* 27–29.

Ellis, A. (1984). Must most psychotherapists remain as incompetent as they are now? In J. Hariman (Ed.), *Does psychotherapy really help people?* Springfield, IL: Thomas.

Elmore, T. M. (1984). Counselor education and counseling psychology: A house divided? *ACES Newsletter, 44,* 4, 6.

Emerson, S., & Markos, P. A. (1996). Signs and symptoms of the impaired counselor. *Journal of Humanistic Education and Development, 34,* 108–117.

English, H. B., & English, A. C. (1956). *A comprehensive dictionary of psychological and psychoanalytical terms.* New York: Longman Green.

Ford, D. Y., Harris, J. J., III, & Schuerger, J. M. (1993). Racial identity development among gifted black students. *Journal of Counseling & Development, 71,* 409–417.

Foster, S. (1996, December). Characteristics of an effective counselor. *Counseling Today,* 21.

Gaushell, H., & Lawson, D. (1994, November). *Counselor trainee family-of-origin structure and current intergenerational family relationships: Implications for counselor training.* Paper presented at the Southern Association of Counselor Education and Supervision Convention, Charlotte, NC.

Geroski, A. M., Rodgers, K. A., & Breen, D. T. (1997). Using the DSM-IV to enhance collaboration among school counselors, clinical counselors, and primary care physicians. *Journal of Counseling & Development, 75,* 231–239.

Gladding, S. T. (1990). Let us not grow weary of theory. *Journal for Specialists in Group Work, 15,* 194.

Gladding, S. T. (1998). *Counseling as an art: The creative arts in counseling* (2nd ed.). Alexandria, VA: American Counseling Association.

Goetz, B. (1998, May 27). *An inside/outsider's view of the counseling profession today.* Paper presented at the Chi Sigma Iota Invitational Counselor Advocacy Conference, Greensboro, NC.

Grosch, W. N., & Olsen, D. C. (1994). *When helping starts to hurt.* New York: Norton.

Guy, J. D. (1987). *The personal life of the psychotherapist.* New York: Wiley.

Hansen, J. C., Stevic, R. R., & Warner, R. W. (1986). *Counseling: Theory and process* (4th ed.). Boston: Allyn & Bacon.

Harman, R. L. (1977). Beyond techniques. *Counselor Education and Supervision, 17,* 157–158.

Hinkle, J. S. (1994). *Psychodiagnosis and treatment planning using the DSM-IV.* Greensboro, NC: Author.

Holland, J. L. (1977). *The self-directed search.* Palo Alto, CA: Consulting Psychologists Press.

Holland, J. L. (1997). *Making vocational choices* (3rd ed.). Odessa, FL: Psychological Assessment Resources.

Hollis, J. W. (1997). Counselor preparation, 1996–1998. Muncie, IN: Accelerated Development.

Israelashvili, M. (1998). Preventive school counseling: A stress inoculation perspective. *Professional School Counseling, 1,* 21–25.

Ivey, A. (1990). *Developmental counseling and therapy.* Pacific Grove, CA: Brooks/Cole.

Ivey, A. E., & Goncalves, O. F. (1988). Developmental therapy: Integrating developmental processes into the clinical practice. *Journal of Counseling and Development, 66,* 406–413.

Ivey, A., & Ivey, M. B. (1990). Assessing and facilitating children's cognitive development: Developmental counseling and therapy in a case of child abuse. *Journal of Counseling and Development, 68,* 299–305.

Kelly, K. R. (1988). Defending eclecticism: The utility of informed choice. *Journal of Mental Health Counseling, 10,* 210–213.

Kleist, D. M., & White, L. J. (1997). The values of counseling: A disparity between a philosophy of prevention in counseling and counselor practice and training. *Counseling and Values, 41,* 128–140.

Kottler, J. A. (1993). *On being a therapist.* San Francisco: Jossey-Bass.

Kurpius, D. J. (1986). The helping relationship. In M. D. Lewis, R. L. Hayes, & J. A. Lewis (Eds.), *The counseling profession* (pp. 96–129). Itasca, IL: Peacock.

Landis, L. L., & Young, M. E. (1994). The reflective team in counselor education. *Counselor Education and Supervision, 33,* 210–218.

Lazarus, A. A. (1967). In support of technical eclecticism. *Psychological Reports, 21,* 415–416.

Lazarus, A. A., & Beutler, L. E. (993). On technical eclecticism. *Journal of Counseling and Development, 71,* 381–385.

Lee, C. C., & Sirch, M. L. (1994). Counseling in an enlightened society: Values for a new millennium. *Counseling and Values, 38,* 90–97.

Lenhardt, A. M. C. (1997). Grieving disenfranchised losses: Background and strategies for counselors. *Journal of Humanistic Education and Development, 35,* 208–218.

Mathewson, R. H. (1949). *Guidance policy and practice.* New York: Harper.

May, R. (1975). *The courage to create.* New York: Norton.

May, R., Remen, N., Young, D., & Berland, W. (1985). The wounded healer. *Saybrook Review, 5,* 84–93.

Mays, D. T., & Franks, C. M. (1980). Getting worse: Psychotherapy or no treatment: The jury should still be out. *Professional Psychology, 2,* 78–92.

McBride, M. C., & Martin, G. E. (1990). A framework for eclecticism: The importance of theory to mental health counseling. *Journal of Mental Health Counseling, 12,* 495–505.

McCarthy, P., DeBell, C., Kanuha, V., & McLeod, J. (1988). Myths of supervision: Identifying the gaps between theory and practice. *Counselor Education and Supervision, 28,* 22–28.

McClure, B. A., & Russo, T. R. (1996). The politics of counseling: Looking back and forward. *Counseling and Values, 40,* 162–174.

McCormick, J. F. (1998). Ten summer rejuvenators for school counselors. *Professional School Counseling, 1,* 61–63.

Meichenbaum, D. (1993). Changing conceptions of cognitive behavior modification: Retrospect and prospect. *Journal of Consulting and Clinical Psychology, 61,* 202–204.

Miller, G. A., Wagner, A., Britton, T. P., & Gridley, B. E. (1998). A framework for understanding the wounding of healers. *Counseling and Values, 42,* 124–132.

Mostert, D. L., Johnson, E., & Mostert, M. P. (1997). The utility of solution-focused, brief counseling in schools: Potential from an initial study. *Professional School Counseling, 1,* 21–24.

Myers, J. E. (1992). Wellness, prevention, development: The cornerstone of the profession. *Journal of Counseling & Development, 71,* 136–138.

Myrick, R. D. (1997). Traveling together on the road ahead. *Professional School Counseling, 1,* 4–8.

Osborne, J. L., Collison, B. B., House, R. M., Gray, L. A., Firth, J., & Lou, M. (1998). Developing a social advocacy model for counselor education. *Counselor Education and Supervision, 37,* 190–202.

Patterson, L. E., & Welfel, E. R. (1994). *Counseling process* (4th ed.). Pacific Grove, CA: Brooks/Cole.

Pines, A., & Aronson, E. (1981). *Burnout: From tedium to personal growth.* New York: Free Press.

Rak, C. F., & Patterson, L. E. (1996). Promoting resilience in at-risk children. *Journal of Counseling & Development, 74,* 368–373.

Robinson, S. E., & Kinnier, R. T. (1988). Self-instructional versus traditional training for teaching basic counseling skills. *Counselor Education and Supervision, 28,* 140–145.

Roehlke, H. J. (1988). Critical incidents in counselor development: Examples of Jung's concept of synchronicity. *Journal of Counseling and Development, 67,* 133–134.

Rogers, C. R. (1961). *On becoming a person.* Boston: Houghton Mifflin.

Ronnestad, M. H., & Skovholt, T. M. (1993). Supervision of beginning and advanced graduate students of counseling and psychotherapy. *Journal of Counseling & Development, 71,* 396–405.

Savicki, V., & Cooley, E. J. (1982). Implications of burnout research and theory for counselor educators. *Personnel and Guidance Journal, 60,* 415–419.

Seligman, L. (1997). *Diagnosis and treatment planning in counseling* (2nd ed.). New York: Plenum.

Shertzer, B., & Stone, S. C. (1974). *Fundamentals of counseling.* Boston: Houghton Mifflin.

Simon, G. M. (1989). An alternative defense of eclecticism: Responding to Kelly and Ginter. *Journal of Mental Health Counseling, 2,* 280–288.

Skovholt, T. M., & McCarthy, P. R. (1988). Critical incidents: Catalysts for counselor development. *Journal of Counseling and Development, 67,* 69–72.

Smart, D. W., & Smart, J. F. (1997). DSM-IV and culturally sensitive diagnosis: Some observations for counselors. *Journal of Counseling & Development, 75,* 392–398.

Tysl, L. (1997, January). Counselors have a responsibility to promote the counseling profession. *Counseling Today,* 16.

Ungersma, A. J. (1961). *The search for meaning.* Philadelphia: Westminster.

Waldo, M. (1989). Primary prevention in university residence halls: Paraprofessional-led relationship enhancement groups for college roommates. *Journal of Counseling and Development, 67,* 465–471.

Watkins, C. E., Jr. (1983). Burnout in counseling practice: Some potential professional and personal hazards of becoming a counselor. *Personnel and Guidance Journal, 61,* 304–308.

Wiggins, J., & Weslander, D. (1979). Personality characteristics of counselors rated as effective or ineffective. *Journal of Vocational Behavior, 15,* 175–185.

Wilcox-Matthew, L., Ottens, A., & Minor, C. W. (1997). An analysis of significant events in counseling. *Journal of Counseling & Development, 75,* 282–291.

Witmer, J. M., & Young, M. E. (1996). Preventing counselor impairment: A wellness model. *Journal of Humanistic Education and Development, 34,* 141–155.

Young, R. A. (1988). Ordinary explanations and career theories. *Journal of Counseling and Development, 66,* 336–339.

3

ETHICAL AND LEGAL ASPECTS OF COUNSELING

◆
_____

In the cool grey dawn of early September,

I place the final suitcase into my Mustang

And silently say "good-bye"

to the quiet beauty of North Carolina.

Hesitantly, I head for the blue ocean-lined coast

of Connecticut.

Bound for a new position and the unknown.

Traveling with me are a sheltie named "Eli"

and the still fresh memories of our last counseling session.

You, who wrestled so long with fears

that I kiddingly started calling you "Jacob,"

are as much a part of me as my luggage.

Moving in life is bittersweet

like giving up friends and fears.

The taste is like smooth, orange, fall persimmons,

deceptively delicious but tart.

From "Bittersweet," by S. T. Gladding, 1984, Counseling and Values, 28, *p. 146. © ACA. Reprinted with permission. No further reproduction authorized without written permission of the ACA.*

Counseling is not a value-free or neutral activity (Cottone & Tarvydas, 1998; Schulte, 1990). Rather, it is an active profession based on values, which are "orienting beliefs about what is good . . . and how that good should be achieved" (Bergin, 1985, p. 99). Values are at the core of counseling relationships. All goals in counseling, "whether they are goals for symptom relief or goals to modify a lifestyle, are subtended by value systems" (Bergin, 1992, p. 9). In addition, because counseling is such a complex and multifaceted profession, counselors, by necessity, must be dependent on codes of ethics and also external codes of law (DePauw, 1986; McGovern, 1994).

Counselors who are not clear about their values, ethics, and legal responsibilities, as well as those of their clients, can cause harm despite their best intentions (Huber, 1994; Remley, 1991). Therefore, it is vital for counselors to be knowledgeable about themselves in addition to the ethics of and laws pertaining to the profession of counseling.

In this chapter, ethical standards, legal constraints, and mandates under which counselors operate are explored. Both ethics and the law are crucial in the work and well-being of counselors and the counseling process. In some cases, but not all, ethical and legal considerations overlap (Wilcoxon, 1993).

Definitions: Ethics, Morality, and Law

Ethics involves "making decisions of a moral nature about people and their interaction in society" (Kitchener, 1986, p. 306). The term is often used synonymously with *morality*, and in some cases the two terms overlap. Both deal with "what is good and bad or the study of human conduct and values" (Van Hoose & Kottler, 1985, p. 2). Yet each has a different meaning.

"Ethics is generally defined as a philosophical discipline that is concerned with human conduct and moral decision making" (Van Hoose & Kottler, 1985, p. 3). Ethics are normative in nature and focus on principles and standards that govern relationships between individuals, such as those between counselors and clients. *Morality,* on the other hand, involves judgment or evaluation of action. It is associated with such words as *good, bad, right, wrong, ought,* and *should* (Brandt, 1959; Grant, 1992). Counselors have morals, and the theories counselors employ have embedded within them moral presuppositions about human nature that explicitly and implicitly question first "what is a person and second, what should a person be or become?" (Christopher, 1996, p. 18).

Law is the precise codification of governing standards that are established to ensure legal and moral justice (Hummell, Talbutt, & Alexander, 1985). Law is created by legislation, court decision, and tradition, as in English common law (Anderson, 1996). The law does not dictate what is ethical in a given situation but what is legal. Sometimes what is legal at a given time (e.g., matters pertaining to race, age, or sex) is considered unethical or immoral by some significant segments of society. An example is the controversy between law and ethics in the 1994 Helms/Smith Amendment to the Elementary and Secondary Education Act (ESEA), an attempt to cut off funds to schools that provide counseling for gay and lesbian students.

Conflicts between the legal and the ethical/moral system of a society can occur on many levels (see Table 3.1). Some of these conflicts are resolved in the courts. Indeed, many counselors treat ethical complaints with the same seriousness that they treat lawsuits (Chauvin & Remley, 1996). Laws are more objective and specific than most ethical or moral codes; they are changed as a result of challenges from individuals and groups.

Ethics and Counseling

As a group professional counselors are concerned with ethics and values. However, some counselors are better informed or more attuned to these issues. Patterson (1971) has observed that counselors' professional identity is related to their knowledge and practice of ethics. Welfel (1998) has added that the effectiveness of counselors is connected to their ethical knowledge and behavior as well.

Unethical behavior in counseling can take many forms. The temptations common to people everywhere exist for counselors. They include "physical intimacy, the titillation of gossip, or the opportunity (if the gamble pays off) to advance one's career" (Welfel & Lipsitz, 1983b, p. 328). Some forms of unethical behavior are obvious and willful, whereas others are more subtle and unintentional. Regardless, the harmful outcome is the same. The following are some of the most prevalent forms of unethical behaviors in counseling (Levenson, 1986; Pope & Vetter, 1992; Swanson 1983a):

Table 3.1 Interactions between ethics and the law

			Example
1.	Ethical & Legal	Following a just law	Keeping a client's confidences that are also protected by law from disclosure
2.	Ethical & Illegal	Disobeying an unjust law	Refusing to breach promised confidentiality even though ordered to by court
3.	Ethical & Alegal	Doing good where no law applies	Offering free service to poor clients
4.	Unethical & Legal	Following an unjust law	Following the Federal Trade Commission's edict that ethical codes cannot prohibit the use of testimonials in ads for counseling services
5.	Unethical & Illegal	Breaking a just law	Disclosing confidential information protected by law from disclosure
6.	Unethical & Alegal	Doing harm that no law prohibits	Promoting client dependency to enhance one's own feeling of power

Source: Adapted from *Ethical and Professional Issues in Counseling* (p. 86), by R. R. Cottone and V. M. Tarvydas, 1998, Upper Saddle River, NJ: Prentice Hall; and *Guide to Ethical Practice in Psychotherapy* by A. Thompson, 1990, New York: John Wiley & Sons. Copyright 1990 by John Wiley & Sons. Adapted by permission.

Violation of confidentiality
Exceeding one's level of professional competence
Negligent practice
Claiming expertise one does not possess
Imposing one's values on a client
Creating dependency in a client
Sexual activity with a client
Certain conflicts of interest, such as dual relationships
Questionable financial arrangements, such as charging excessive fees
Improper advertising

A division within the American Counseling Association (ACA)—the Association for Spiritual, Ethical, and Religious Values in Counseling (ASERVIC)—is especially concerned with the values and ethics of counseling professionals (Bartlett, Lee, & Doyle, 1985). This division, which regularly deals with ethical concerns, addressed issues such as counseling the aged, values education, and feminism long before they were concerns of counselors in general. ASERVIC has even published ethical guidelines for leaders in professional counseling organizations. In addition to the vanguard work on ethics and values that ASERVIC has done, it also publishes a journal, *Counseling and Values*, that contains articles on ethical situations.

Professional Codes of Ethics and Standards

To address ethical situations, counselors have developed professional codes of ethics and standards of conduct "based upon an agreed-on set of values" (Hansen, Rossberg, & Cramer, 1994, p. 362). Professionals in counseling voluntarily abide by such codes for many reasons. "Among its many purposes, a code of ethical conduct is designed to offer formal statements for ensuring protection of clients' rights while identifying expectations of practitioners" (Wilcoxon, 1987, p. 510). Another reason for ethical codes is that "without a code of established ethics, a group of people with similar interests cannot be considered a professional organization" (Allen, 1986, p. 293). Ethics not only help professionalize an association on a general level but "are designed to provide some guidelines for the professional behavior of members" on a personal level (Swanson, 1983a, p. 53). Three other reasons for the existence of ethical codes according to Van Hoose and Kottler (1985) are as follows:

- Ethical codes protect the profession from government. They allow the profession to regulate itself and function autonomously instead of being controlled by legislation.
- Ethical codes help control internal disagreements and bickering, thus promoting stability within the profession.
- Ethical codes protect practitioners from the public, especially in regard to malpractice suits. If counseling professionals behave according to ethical guidelines, the behavior is judged to be in compliance with accepted standards.

In addition, ethical codes provide clients with some protection from charlatans and incompetent counselors (Swanson, 1983a). Like counselors, clients can use codes of ethics and standards as a guide in evaluating questionable treatment.

The Development of Codes of Ethics for Counselors

The first counseling code of ethics was developed by the American Counseling Association (ACA)(then the American Personnel and Guidance Association, or APGA) based on the original American Psychological Association code of ethics (Allen, 1986). The initial ACA code was initiated by Donald Super and approved in 1961 (Callis, Pope, & DePauw, 1982). It has been revised periodically since that time (in 1974, 1981, 1988, and 1995). The ACA also produces *A Practitioner's Guide to Ethical Decision Making* (Forester-Miller & Davis, 1996), video conferences on resolving leading-edge ethical dilemmas (Salo, Forester-Miller, & Hamilton, 1997), and an *Ethical Standards Casebook* (Herlihy & Corey, 1996).

The ACA's latest ethics code is entitled a *Code of Ethics and Standards of Practice*. This code is one of the major signs that counseling has developed into a mature discipline because professions are characterized by a claim to specialized knowledge and a code of ethics.

In the ACA, ethical standards are arranged under eight topical sectional headings. They contain material similar to that found in many other ethical codes (Allen, Sampson, & Herlihy, 1988), yet they are unique to the profession of counseling. Section 1 deals with the nature of the counseling relationship, including counselors' professional responsibilities to clients and their welfare (e.g., respecting diversity and client rights). The section also discusses counselors' personal needs and how to handle troublesome subjects such as dual relationships, fees, and termination. For example, in this section the ACA clearly states that sexual intimacies between counselors and clients are unethical. It also addresses professional competencies with clients, such as computer use in counseling.

Section 2 covers confidentiality in counseling, including the right to privacy, records, minor or incompetent clients, consultation, and research and training. Section 3 focuses on issues related to professional responsibility, such as professional competence, advertising and solicitation, credentials, and public responsibility. Section 4 covers relationships with other professionals, including employers and employees, referral fees (which are unethical), and subcontractor arrangements.

Section 5 deals with evaluation, assessment, and interpretation. In addition to general information, it includes material on competence to use and interpret tests, informed consent, release of information to competent professionals, proper diagnosis of mental disorders, testing conditions, test security, and test scoring and interpretation. Section 6 focuses on issues related to teaching, training, and supervision, including expectations of counselor educators and trainers, counselor education programs, and students and supervisees. Section 7 deals with research and publications and delineates research responsibilities, informed consent practices, and reporting of research results (including publications). Finally, section 8 addresses ways to resolve ethical issues, including how to handle suspected violations and cooperate with ethics committees.

Limitations of Ethical Codes

Remley (1985) notes that ethical codes are general and idealistic; they seldom answer specific questions. Furthermore, he points out that such documents do not address "foreseeable professional dilemmas" (Remley, 1985, p. 181). Rather, they provide guidelines, based on experiences and values, of how counselors should behave. In many ways, ethical standards represent the collected wisdom of a profession at a particular time.

A number of specific limitations exists in any code of ethics. Here are some of the limitations most frequently mentioned (Beymer, 1971; Corey, Corey, & Callanan, 1998; Mabe & Rollin, 1986; Talbutt, 1981):

> Some issues cannot be resolved by a code of ethics.
> Enforcing ethical codes is difficult.
> There may be conflicts within the standards delineated by the code.
> Some legal and ethical issues are not covered in codes.
> Ethical codes are historical documents. Thus, what may be acceptable practice at one time may be considered unethical later.
> Sometimes conflicts arise between ethical and legal codes.
> Ethical codes do not address cross-cultural issues.
> Ethical codes do not address every possible situation.
> There is often difficulty in bringing the interest of all parties involved in an ethical dispute together systematically.
> Ethical codes are not proactive documents for helping counselors decide what to do in new situations.

Thus, ethical codes are useful in many ways, but they do have their limitations. Counselors need to be aware that they will not always find all the guidance they want when consulting these documents. Nevertheless, whenever an ethical issue arises in counseling, the counselor should first consult ethical standards to see whether the situation is addressed.

Conflicts Within and Among Ethical Codes

The adoption of ethical codes and the emphasis placed on them have paralleled the increased professionalism of counseling (Stude & McKelvey, 1979). But the presence of such standards poses a potential dilemma for many counselors, for three reasons. First, as Stadler (1986) points out, to act ethically counselors must be aware of ethical codes and be able to differentiate an ethical dilemma from other types of dilemmas, a differentiation that is not always easy. For example, a person may take a stand on a controversial issue, such as homosexuality, that he or she seemingly supports with ethical principles but in reality supports only with personal beliefs or biases.

Second, often different ethical principles in a code offer conflicting guidelines about what to do in a given situation (Stadler, 1986). An example is the potential conflict over confidentiality and acting in the client's best interest. A client may reveal an attempt to harass someone else or harm him- or herself. In such a situation, the counselor who keeps this information confidential may actually act against the best interests of the client and the community in which the client resides.

Third, conflicts may occur when counselors belong to two or more professional organizations whose codes of ethics differ, such as the codes of the APA and the ACA. Such counselors may become involved in situations in which ethical action is unclear. Mabe and Rollin (1986) note, for instance, that APA's code of ethics has only six paragraphs dealing with assessment, whereas ACA's ethical standards on this topic are much more elaborate.

If a professional belongs to both organizations and is dealing with assessment instruments, which code of ethics should he or she follow?

Making Ethical Decisions

Ethical decision making is often not easy yet is a part of being a counselor. It requires "virtues such as character, integrity, and moral courage" as well as knowledge (Welfel, 1998, p. 9). Some counselors operate from personal ethical standards without regard to the ethical guidelines developed by professional counseling associations. They usually function well until faced with a dilemma "for which there is no apparent good or best solution" (Swanson, 1983a, p. 57). At such times, ethical issues arise and these counselors experience anxiety, doubt, hesitation, and confusion in determining their conduct. Unfortunately, when they act, their behavior may turn out to be unethical because it is not grounded in any ethical code.

This fact is illustrated by a study conducted in western New York state (Hayman & Covert, 1986). Researchers found five types of ethical dilemmas most prevalent among the university counselors they surveyed there: confidentiality, role conflict, counselor competence, conflicts with employer or institution, and degree of dangerousness. The situational dilemmas that involved danger were the least difficult to resolve, and those that dealt with counselor competence and confidentiality were the most difficult. The surprising finding of this study, however, was that less than one-third of the respondents indicated that they relied on published professional codes of ethics in resolving dilemmas. Instead, most used "common sense," a strategy that at times may be professionally unethical and at best unwise.

It is in such types of situations that counselors need to be aware of resources for ethical decision making, especially when questions arise over controversial behaviors such as setting or collecting fees or conducting dual relationships (Gibson & Pope, 1993). *Ethical reasoning,* "the process of determining which ethical principles are involved and then prioritizing them based on the professional requirements and beliefs," is also crucial (Lanning, 1992, p. 21).

In making ethical decisions, counselors should take actions "based on careful, reflective thought" about responses they think are professionally right in particular situations (Tennyson & Strom, 1986, p. 298). Several ethical principles relate to the activities and ethical choices of counselors:

- *beneficence* (doing good and preventing harm),
- *nonmaleficence* (not inflicting harm),
- *autonomy* (respecting freedom of choice and self-determination),
- *justice* (fairness), and
- *fidelity* (faithfulness or honoring commitments) (Herlihy, 1996; Stadler, 1986).

All these principles involve conscious decision making by counselors throughout the counseling process. Of these principles, some experts identify nonmaleficence as the primary ethical responsibility in the field of counseling. Nonmaleficence not only involves the "removal of present harm" but the "prevention of future harm, and passive avoidance of harm" (Thompson, 1990, p. 105). It is the basis on which counselors respond to clients who may endanger themselves or others and why they respond to colleagues' unethical behavior (Daniluk & Haverkamp, 1993).

Other Guidelines for Acting Ethically

Swanson (1983a) also lists guidelines for assessing whether counselors act in ethically responsible ways. The first is *personal and professional honesty.* Counselors need to operate openly with themselves and those with whom they work. Hidden agendas or unacknowledged feelings hinder relationships and place counselors on shaky ethical ground. One way to overcome personal or professional honesty problems that may get in the way of acting ethically is to receive supervision (Kitchener, 1994).

A second guideline is *acting in the best interest of clients.* This ideal is easier to discuss than achieve. At times, a counselor may impose personal values on clients and ignore what they really want (Gladding & Hood, 1974). At other times, a counselor may fail to recognize an emergency and too readily accept the idea that the client's best interest is served by doing nothing.

A third guideline is that counselors *act without malice or personal gain.* Some clients are difficult to like or deal with, and it is with these individuals that counselors must be especially careful. On the other hand, counselors must be careful to avoid relationships with likable clients either on a personal or professional basis. Errors in judgment are most likely to occur when the counselor's self-interest becomes a part of the relationship with a client (St. Germaine, 1993).

A final guideline is whether counselors can *justify an action* "as the best judgment of what should be done based upon the current state of the profession" (Swanson, 1983a, p. 59). To make such a decision, counselors must keep up with current trends by reading the professional literature; attending in-service workshops and conventions; and becoming actively involved in local, state, and national counseling activities.

The *ACA Ethical Standards Casebook* (Herlihy & Corey, 1996) contains examples in which counselors are presented with issues and case studies of questionable ethical situations and given both guidelines and questions to reflect on in deciding what an ethical response would be. Each situation involves a standard of the ethical code.

As helpful as the casebook may be, in many counseling situations the proper behavior is not obvious (Huber, 1994). For example, the question of confidentiality in balancing the individual rights of a person with AIDS and society's right to be protected from the spread of the disease is one with which some counselors struggle (Harding, Gray, & Neal, 1993). Likewise, there are multiple ethical dilemmas in counseling adult survivors of incest, including those of confidentiality and the consequences of making decisions about reporting abuse (Daniluk & Haverkamp, 1993). Therefore, when they are in doubt about what to do in a given situation, it is crucial for counselors to consult and talk over situations with colleagues, in addition to using principles, guidelines, casebooks, and professional codes of ethics.

Educating Counselors in Ethical Decision Making

Ethical decision making in counseling can be promoted in many ways, but one of the best is through course offerings that are now required in most graduate counseling programs and available also for continuing education credit. Such courses can bring about significant attitudinal changes in students and practicing professionals, including increased knowledge about the ethical areas of self-awareness, dual relationships, impairment, and multi-culturalism (Coll, 1993). Because ethical attitudinal changes are related to ethical behavioral changes, courses in ethics on any level are extremely valuable.

Van Hoose and Paradise (1979) conceptualize the ethical behavior of counselors in terms of a five-stage developmental continuum of reasoning:

1. *Punishment orientation.* At this stage the counselor believes external social standards are the basis for judging behavior. If clients or counselors violate a societal rule, they should be punished.
2. *Institutional orientation.* Counselors who operate at this stage believe in and abide by the rules of the institutions for which they work. They do not question the rules and base their decisions on them.
3. *Societal orientation.* Counselors at this stage base decisions on societal standards. If a question arises about whether the needs of society or an individual should come first, the needs of society are always given priority.
4. *Individual orientation.* The individual's needs receive top priority at this stage. Counselors are aware of societal needs and are concerned about the law, but they focus on what is best for the individual.
5. *Principle (conscience) orientation.* In this stage concern for the individual is primary. Ethical decisions are based on internalized ethical standards, not external considerations.

As Welfel and Lipsitz (1983a) point out, the work of Van Hoose and Paradise is especially important because it "is the first conceptual model in the literature that attempts to explain how counselors reason about ethical issues" (p. 36). It is *heuristic* (i.e., researchable or open to research) and can form the basis for empirical studies of the promotion of ethical behavior.

Several other models have been proposed for educating counselors in ethical decision making. Gumaer and Scott (1985), for instance, offer a method for training group workers based on the ethical guidelines of the Association for Specialists in Group Work (ASGW). Their method uses case vignettes and Carkhuff's three-goal model of helping: self-exploration, self-understanding, and action. Kitchener (1986) proposes an integrated model of goals and components for an ethics education curriculum based on research on the psychological processes underlying moral behavior and current thinking in applied ethics. Her curriculum includes "sensitizing . . . counselors to ethical issues, improving their abilities to make ethical judgments, encouraging responsible ethical actions, and tolerating the ambiguity of ethical decision making" (Kitchener, 1986, p. 306). Her model and one proposed by Pelsma and Borgers (1986) are process oriented and assume that counselors do not learn to make ethical decisions on their own. Pelsma and Borgers particularly emphasize the *how* as opposed to the *what* of ethics—that is, how to reason ethically in a constantly changing field. Other practitioner guides for making ethical decisions are a seven-step decision-making model based on a synthesis of the professional literature (Forester-Miller & Davis, 1996) and a nine-step ethical decision-making model based on critical-evaluative judgements (Welfel, 1998; see Figure 3.1).

Figure 3.1   A model for ethical decision making
Source: From *Ethics in Counseling and Psychotherapy* (p. 24), by E. R. Welfel. © 1998 Brooks/Cole Publishing Company, Pacific Grove, CA 93950, a division of Thomson Publishing Inc. By permission of the publisher.

Step 1: Develop ethical sensitivity.
Step 2: Define dilemma and options.
Step 3: Refer to professional standards.
Step 4: Search out ethics scholarship.
Step 5: Apply ethical principles to situation.
Step 6: Consult with supervisor and respected colleagues.
Step 7: Deliberate and decide.
Step 8: Inform supervisor; implement and document actions.
Step 9: Reflect on the experience.

Ethics in Specific Counseling Situations

Ethical behavior is greatly influenced by the prevalent attitudes in the setting in which one works, by one's colleagues, and by the task the counselor is performing (e.g., diagnosing). Therefore, implementing ethical decisions and actions in counseling sometimes involves "substantial personal and professional risk or discomfort" (Faiver, Eisengart, & Colonna, 1995, p. 121). The reasons are multiple, but as Ladd (1971) observes, the difficulty in making ethical decisions can sometimes be attributed to the environments in which counselors work. "Most organizations that employ counselors are organized not collegially or professionally, as is in part the case with universities and hospitals, but hierarchically. In a hierarchical organization, the administrator or executive decides which prerogatives are administrative and which are professional" (Ladd, 1971, p. 262). Counselors should check thoroughly the general policies and principles of an institution before accepting employment because employment in a specific setting implies that the counselor agrees with its policies, principles, and ethics. When counselors find themselves in institutions that misuse their services and do not act in the best interests of their clients, they must act either to change the institution through educational or persuasive means or find other employment.

School Counseling and Ethics

The potential for major ethical crises between a counselor and his or her employer exists in many school settings (Davis & Ritchie, 1993). School counselors are often used as tools by school administrators (Boy & Pine, 1968). When the possibility of conflict exists between a counselor's loyalty to the employer and the client, "the counselor should always attempt to find a resolution that protects the rights of the client; the ethical responsibility is to the client first and the school [or other setting] second" (Huey, 1986, p. 321).

Computers, Counseling, and Ethics

The use of computers and technology in counseling is another area of potential ethical difficulty. The possibility exists for a breach of client information when computers are used to transmit information among professional counselors. Other ethically sensitive areas include client or counselor misuse and even the validity of data offered over computer links (Sampson, Kolodinsky, & Greeno, 1997). In addition, the problem of *cyber counseling*—that is, counseling over the Internet in which the counselor may be hundreds of miles away—is fraught with ethical dilemmas. Thus, the National Board of Certified Counselors has issued ethical guidelines regarding such conduct.

Marriage/Family Counseling and Ethics

Another counseling situation in which ethical crises are common is marriage and family counseling (Corey et al., 1993; Huber, 1994; Margolin, 1982). The reason is that counselors are treating a number of individuals together as a system, and it is unlikely that all members of the system have the same goals (Wilcoxon, 1986). To overcome potential problems, Thomas (1994) has developed a dynamic, process-oriented framework for counselors to use when working with families. This model discusses six values that affect counselors, clients, and the counseling process: (a) responsibility, (b) integrity, (c) commitment, (d) freedom of choice, (e) empowerment, and (f) right to grieve.

Other Settings and Ethics

Other counseling settings or situations with significant potential for ethical dilemmas include counseling the elderly (Myers, 1998), multicultural counseling (Sue, Ivey, & Pedersen, 1996), working in managed care (Murphy, 1998), diagnosis of clients (Rueth, Demmitt, & Burger, 1998), and counseling research (Jencius & Rotter, 1998). In all of these areas, counselors must take care not to stereotype or otherwise be insensitive to clients with whom they are working. For instance, "a primary emphasis of research ethics is, appropriately, on the protection of human subjects in research" (Parker & Szymanski, 1996, p. 182). In the area of research in particular, there are four main ethical issues that must be resolved: "(1) informed consent, (2) coercion and deception, (3) confidentiality and privacy, and (4) reporting the results" (Robinson & Gross, 1986, p. 331).

Dual Relationships

The matter of dual relationships as an ethical consideration is relatively new, emerging from debates in the 1970s on the ethical nature of counselor-client sexual relations. When professional groups concluded that sexual relationships between counselors and clients were unethical, questions were raised about the formation of other types of relationships between counselors and clients, such as business deals or friendship. Such relationships are not built on mutuality because of the past therapeutic nature of the people involved. In other words, one (the client) was more vulnerable than another (the counselor).

Discussions among professional groups concluded that nonsexual dual relationships should be avoided. The reason is "that no matter how harmless a dual relationship seems, a conflict of interest almost always exists, and any professional counselor's judgment is likely to be affected" (St. Germaine, 1993, p. 27). What follows is usually harmful because counselors lose their objectivity and clients may be placed in situation in which they cannot be assertive and take care of themselves. For example, if a business transaction takes place between a counselor and a client at the same time that counseling is occurring, either party may be negatively affected if the product involved does not work well or work as well as expected. The thought and emotion that take place as a result will most likely have an impact on the therapeutic relationship. Therefore, as a matter of ethics, counselors should remove themselves from socializing or doing business with present or former clients; accepting gifts from them; or entering into a counseling relationship with a close friend, family member, student, lover, or employee.

Although the principles underlying the ethics of dual relationships seem clear, implementing them is sometimes difficult. For instance, many substance abuse counselors are in recovery. "For these individuals, existing ethical codes do not specifically or adequately address the unique circumstances in which they periodically find themselves" (Doyle, 1997, p. 428). Among the issues that are problematic and require thoughtful consideration are those involving confidentiality and anonymity, attending self-help groups with clients, social relationships among self-help group members, employment, and sponsorship in self-help programs.

Working with Counselors Who May Act Unethically

Although most counselors are ethical, occasional situations arise in which such is not the case. In these circumstances, counselors must take some action. Otherwise, by condoning or ignoring a situation they risk eroding their own sense of moral selfhood and find it easier to condone future ethical breaches, a phenomenon known as the "slippery slope effect." Herlihy (1996) suggests several steps to take in working through potential ethical dilemmas, especially with impaired professionals. The first is to identify the problem as objectively as possible and the counselor's relationship to it. Such a process is best done on paper to clarify thinking.

The second step in the process is for a counselor to apply the current ACA Code of Ethics to the matter. In such cases, clear guidance as to a course of action may emerge. Next, a counselor should consider moral principles of the helping profession discussed earlier in this chapter, such as beneficence, justice, and autonomy. Consultation with a colleague is an option, also.

If action is warranted, the colleague in question should first be approached informally. This approach involves confrontation in a caring context, which hopefully will lead to the counselor in question seeking help. If it does not, the confronting counselor should consider the potential consequences of all other options and then define a course of action.

In examining courses of action, a counselor must evaluate where each potential action might lead. Criteria for judgment include one's comfort surrounding (a) "publicity" (i.e., if the actions of the confronting counselor were reported in the press), (b) "justice" (i.e., fairness), (c) "moral traces" (i.e., lingering feelings of doubt), and (d)
"universality" (i.e., is this a course I would recommend others take in this situation?).

Finally, a course of action is chosen and implemented. In such a case, the counselor must realize that not everyone will agree. Therefore, he or she needs to be prepared to take criticism as well as credit for what has been done.

The Law and Counseling

The profession of counseling is also governed by legal standards. *Legal* refers to "law or the state of being lawful," and *law* refers to "a body of rules recognized by a state or community as binding on its members" (Shertzer & Stone, 1980, p. 386). Contrary to popular opinion, "law is not cut and dried, definite and certain, or clear and precise" (Van Hoose & Kottler, 1985, p. 44). Rather, it always seeks compromise between individuals and parties. It offers few definite answers, and there are always notable exceptions to any legal precedent.

There is "no general body of law covering the helping professions" (Van Hoose & Kottler, 1985, p. 45). But there are a number of court decisions and statutes that influence legal opinion on counseling, and counselors need to keep updated. The 1993 Napa County, California, case involving Gary Ramona is one such legal decision. In this widely publicized trial, Ramona sued his daughter's therapists, "charging that by implanting false memories of sexual abuse in her mind they had destroyed his life" (Butler, 1994, p. 10). Ramona was awarded $475,000 after the jury "found the therapists had negligently reinforced false memories" (Butler, 1994, p. 11). The legal opinion on which the case was decided was *duty to care*—health providers' legal obligation not to act negligently.

Another important legal case in recent years was the 1996 U.S. Supreme Court decision in *Jaffee v. Redmond* that held that communications between licensed psychotherapists and their patients are privileged and do not have to be disclosed in cases held in federal court (Remley, Herlihy, & Herlihy, 1997). The importance of the case for counseling is that a legal precedent was set regarding confidentiality between a master's-level clinician (in this case a social worker) and her client. The case also brought positive attention to mental health services, including counseling.

In most cases, the law is "generally supportive or neutral" toward professional codes of ethics and counseling in general (Stude & McKelvey, 1979, p. 454). It supports licensure or certification of counselors as a means of ensuring that those who enter the profession attain at least minimal standards. It also supports the general "confidentiality of statements and records provided by clients during therapy" (p. 454). In addition, the law is neutral "in that it allows the profession to police itself and govern counselors' relations with their clients and fellow counselors" (p. 454). The only time the law overrides a professional code of ethics is when it is necessary "to protect the public health, safety, and welfare" (p. 454). This necessity is most likely in situations concerning confidentiality, when disclosure of information is necessary to prevent harm. In such cases, counselors have a duty to warn potential victims about the possibility of a client's violent behavior (Costa & Altekruse, 1994).

Legal Recognition of Counseling

Swanson (1983b) points out that, in part, counseling gained professional recognition and acceptance through the legal system. As recently as 1960, counseling did not have a strong enough identity as a profession to be recognized legally. In that year, a judge ruled in the case of *Bogust v. Iverson* that a counselor with a doctoral degree could not be held liable for the suicide of one of his clients because counselors were "mere teachers" who received training in a department of education.

It was not until 1971, in an *Iowa Law Review Note,* that counselors were legally recognized as professionals who provided personal as well as vocational and educational counseling. The profession was even more clearly defined in 1974 in *Weldon v. Virginia State Board of Psychologists Examiners.* The judgment rendered stated that counseling was a profession distinct from psychology. The U.S. House of Representatives further refined the definition of counseling and recognized the profession in H.R. 3270 (94th Congress, 1976), stating that counseling is "the process through which a trained counselor assists an individual or group to make satisfactory and responsible decisions concerning personal, educational and career development."

Swanson (1983b) notes that state laws regulating counseling, such as the first one passed in Virginia in 1976 exclusively recognizing counseling as a profession, saw counseling as a "generic profession" with specialties such as career counseling (p. 29). Further impetus for defining counseling as a profession came with the adoption and implementation of minimum preparation standards, such as those adopted by CACREP in the late 1970s.

Professional Credentialing

With the recognition of counseling as a separate professional entity, a need has arisen to regulate it through credentialing procedures. Obtaining certification, licensure, or both is becoming increasingly important in the counseling profession (Glosoff, 1992; Romano, 1992). "Credentialed counselors possess enhanced visibility and credibility" (Clawson & Wildermuth, 1992, p. 1).

There are basically four types of professional credentials, two of which, certification and licensure, have considerable prestige. In the past, most credentials were awarded by states, but now certification is also the function of professional organizations, such as the National Board of Certified Counselors (NBCC). Before deciding on what credentials to pursue, counselors need to know which are legally required for their practice and will enhance their credibility and development (Anderson & Swanson, 1994).

Credentialing procedures have four levels (Swanson, 1983b):

1. **Inspection.** In this process "a state agency periodically examines the activities of a profession's practitioners to ascertain whether they are practicing the profession in a fashion consistent with the public safety, health, and welfare" (Swanson, 1983b, p. 28). Many state agencies that employ counselors, such as mental health centers, are subject to having their personnel and programs regularly inspected. Such an inspection may include a review of case notes on treatment during a specific period, a review of agency procedures, and personal interviews.

2. **Registration.** This plan requires practitioners to submit information to the state concerning the nature of their practice. Usually a professional organization, such as a state division of the ACA, assumes the responsibility for setting standards necessary to qualify as a registrant and maintains a list of names of those who voluntarily meet those standards. This method is employed in Kansas, for instance, as a way to gain legal recognition for counselors who used the title "registered professional counselor."

3. **Certification.** *Certification* is a professional, statutory, or nonstatutory process "by which an agency or association grants recognition to an individual for having met certain predetermined professional qualifications. Stated succinctly, certification . . . is a 'limited license, that is, the protection of title only" (Fretz & Mills, 1980, p. 7). In this case, a state or national board or department issues a certificate to an individual in a specialty. Certification basically implies that the person meets the minimum skills necessary to engage in that profession and has no known character defects that would interfere with such a practice. Often states require candidates for certification to pass a competency test and submit letters of reference before a certificate is issued. School counselors were among the first counselors to be certified.

The National Board for Certified Counselors (NBCC) is the leading national organization that certifies counselors (see Figure 3.2). Certification specialties are available from the NBCC in school counseling, mental health counseling, career counseling, substance abuse counseling, and gerontological counseling. Counselors who wish to become a national certified counselor (NCC) must have a minimum of 48 semester or 72 quarter hours of graduate study in counseling or a related field, including a master's degree in counseling from a regionally accredited institution of higher education. They must include courses in their program of study that cover human growth and development, group work, research and program evaluation, counseling theories/helping relationships, professional orientation, career and lifestyle development, ethics, social/cultural foundations, and appraisal. They must also have a minimum of two academic terms of supervised field experience in a counseling setting. In addition, they must pass the National Counselor Examination (NCE). In the case of individuals graduating from a non-CACREP program, 2 years of postmaster's field experience with 3,000 client contact hours and 100 hours of weekly face-to-face supervision with an NCC or equivalent is also required.

Counselors should obtain both NBCC certification and state licensure for four reasons (Clawson & Wildermuth, 1992). First, national certification is broader than state licensure and based on a larger population. Second, licensure is more susceptible than national certification to state politics. Third, national certification more readily provides referral sources and networking across state lines. Finally, most state counseling licenses do not recognize specialty areas, whereas national certification does.

4. **Licensure.** Fretz and Mills (1980) define *licensure* as "the statutory process by which an agency of government, usually a state, grants permission to a person meeting predetermined qualifications to engage in a given occupation and/or use a particular title and to perform specified functions" (p. 7). Licensure differs in purpose from certification but requires similar procedures in terms of education and testing for competence (Shimberg, 1981). Once licensure requirements are established, individuals cannot practice a profession legally without obtaining a license (Anderson & Swanson, 1994). Licensure is almost exclusively a state-governed process, and those states that have licensure have established boards to oversee the issuing of licenses.

In general, the licensing of professional helpers is always under scrutiny from the public, other professions, and state legislatures. The licensing of counselors gained momentum in the 1970s and 1980s, just as the licensing of psychologists did in the 1960s and 1970s. In 1999, 46 states and the District of Columbia legally regulated the practice of counseling (see Figure 3.3).

What Is the National Board for Certified Counselors?

The National Board for Certified Counselors (NBCC) is a nonprofit, independent organization that establishes and monitors a national counselor certification process. NBCC was created in 1982 through the efforts of the American Counseling Association to promote professional credentialing standards for counselors.

The NBCC grants six professional certifications:
- National Certified Counselor
- National Certified Career Counselor
- National Certified Gerontological Counselor
- National Certified School Counselor
- Certified Clinical Mental Health Counselor
- Master Addictions Counselor

Counselors who meet the NBCC's standards and obtain certification are required to maintain and renew certification through continuing education. Through its certification programs, the NBCC provides a national standard in the counseling profession that can be used as a measure of professionalism.

Who Are National Certified Counselors?

Counselors certified by the NBCC are authorized to identify themselves as national certified counselors (NCCs). These counselors meet the professional standards for general practice established by the NBCC and agree to abide by the NBCC Code of Ethics.

NCCs work in a variety of educational and social service settings such as schools, private practice, mental health agencies, correctional facilities, community agencies, rehabilitation agencies, and business and industry. NCCs are trained in many areas including aging, vocational development, adolescence, and family and marriage concerns.

Individual NCCs may limit practice to special areas of interest or expertise (e.g., career development, ethnic groups) or age group (adolescents, older adults, etc.). In addition to being certified by the NBCC, many NCCs are licensed by their state or hold a specialty certification in mental health, career, school, gerontological, addictions, or rehabilitation counseling.

Figure 3.2   The National Board of Certified Counselors

To coordinate efforts at uniformity and growth, the American Association of State Counseling Boards (AASCB) was formed in 1986 (Dingman, 1990).

Legal Aspects of the Counseling Relationship

Counselors must follow specific legal guidelines in working with certain populations. For example, PL 94-142 (the Education of All Handicapped Children Act of 1975) provides that schools must make provisions for the free, appropriate public education of all children in the least restrictive environment possible. Part of this process is the development of an individual education plan (IEP) for each child as well as the provision for due-process pro-

How Does a Counselor Become a National Certified Counselor?

Candidates for NCC must meet both the minimum education and professional counseling experience.

- NCCs hold a master's degree or doctorate in counseling or a closely related field from a regionally accredited institution.
- NCCs have at least 2 years' professional counseling experience and must document supervised experience.
- All NCCs must pass the NBCC National Counselor Examination for Licensure and Certification (NCE).

NCCs are certified for a period of 5 years during which the NCC must participate in approved continuing education activities to be eligible for recertification. This continuing education requirement ensures that NCCs stay current with developments in the counseling field.

What Are the NBCC Ethical Standards for Practice?

All national certified counselors agree to abide by the NBCC Code of Ethics. This code states that NCCs only offer services for which they are professionally qualified, that they respect the integrity and promote the welfare of the client, and that they commit themselves to establishing appropriate fees.

Before you begin working with an NCC, you may want to ask the NCC for a copy of the NBCC Code of Ethics. Also, request a detailed explanation of the services offered as well as your financial and time commitments. You should be fully informed and comfortable with all arrangements before counseling begins.

How Many Counselors Are Certified by NBCC?

More than 20,000 counselors have successfully completed the NBCC certification process, and approximately 3,500 of these NCCs hold NBCC specialty certifications.

Figure 3.2   *continued*
Source: © NBCC, 3 Terrace Way, Suite D, Greensboro, NC 27403-3660. Used with permission.

cedures and identifying and keeping records on every disabled child (Humes, 1978). School counselors who work with disabled children have specific tasks to complete under the terms of this act.

Similarly, counselors have a legal obligation under all child abuse laws to report suspected cases of abuse to proper authorities, usually specific personnel in a state social welfare office (Henderson & Fall, 1998). Such situations may be especially difficult when counselors are working directly with families in which the abuse is suspected (Stevens-Smith & Hughes, 1993). Furthermore, the legal obligations of counselors are well defined under the Family Educational Rights and Privacy Act (FERPA) of 1974, known as the Buckley Amendment. This statute gives students access to certain records that educational institutions have kept on them.

Counselors have considerable trouble in situations in which the law is not clear or a conflict exists between the law and professional counseling ethics. Nevertheless, it is

Figure 3.3   States (shaded) that legally regulate counselors, 1999

important that providers of mental health services be fully informed about what they can or cannot do legally. Such situations often involve the sharing of information among clients, counselors, and the court system.

Sharing may be broken down into confidentiality, privacy, and privileged communication. *Confidentiality* is "the ethical duty to fulfill a contract or promise to clients that the information revealed during therapy will be protected from unauthorized disclosure" (Arthur & Swanson, 1993, p. 7). Confidentiality becomes a legal as well as an ethical concern if it is broken, whether intentionally or not.

"*Privacy* is an evolving legal concept that recognizes individuals' rights to choose the time, circumstances, and extent to which they wish to share or withhold personal information" (Herlihy & Sheeley, 1987, p. 479; emphasis added). Clients who think they have been coerced into revealing information they would not normally disclose may seek legal recourse against a counselor.

Privileged communication, a narrower concept, regulates privacy protection and confidentiality by protecting clients from having their confidential communications disclosed in court without their permission. It is defined as "a client's legal right, guaranteed by statute, that confidences originating in a therapeutic relationship will be safeguarded" (Arthur & Swanson, 1993, p. 7). "The legal concept of privileged communication generally does not apply in group and family counseling" (Anderson, 1996, p. 35). However, counselors should consider certain ethical concerns in protecting the confidentiality of group and family members.

One major difficulty with any law governing client and counselor communication is that laws vary from state to state. It is essential that counselors know and communicate to their clients potential situations in which confidentiality may be broken (Woody, 1988).

A landmark court case that reflects the importance of limiting confidentiality is *Tarasoff v. Board of Regents of the University of California* (1976). In this case, Prosenjit Poddar, a student who was a voluntary outpatient at the student health services on the Berkeley campus of the University of California, informed the psychologist who was counseling him that he intended to kill his former girlfriend, Tatiana Tarasoff, when she arrived back on campus. The psychologist notified the campus police, who detained and questioned the student about his proposed activities. The student denied any intention of killing Tarasoff, acted rationally, and was released. Poddar refused further treatment from the psychologist, and no additional steps were taken to deter him from his intended action. Two months later, he killed Tarasoff. Her parents sued the Regents of the University of California for failing to notify the intended victim of a threat against her. The California Supreme Court ruled in their favor, holding, in effect, that a therapist has a duty to protect the public that overrides any obligation to maintain client confidentiality.

Thus, there is a limit to how much confidentiality a counselor can or should maintain. When it appears that a client is dangerous to him- or herself or to others, state laws specify that this information must be reported to proper authorities. Knapp and Vandecreek (1982) note, however, that state laws vary, and reporting such information is often difficult. They suggest that when client violence is at risk, a counselor should try to defuse the danger while also satisfying any legal duty. They recommend consulting with professional colleagues who have expertise in working with violent individuals and documenting the steps taken.

Civil and Criminal Liability

The *Tarasoff* case raises the problem of counselor liability and malpractice. Basically, *liability* in counseling involves issues concerned with whether counselors have caused harm to clients (Wittmer & Loesch, 1986). The concept of liability is directly connected with malpractice. *Malpractice* in counseling is defined "as harm to a client resulting from professional negligence, with *negligence* defined as the departure from acceptable professional standards" (Hummell et al., 1985, p. 70; emphasis added). Until recently, there were relatively few counselor malpractice lawsuits. But with the increased number of licensed, certified, and practicing counselors, malpractice suits have become more common. Therefore, professional counselors need to make sure they protect themselves from such possibilities.

Two ways to protect oneself from malpractice are (a) to follow professional codes of ethics and (b) to follow normal practice standards (Hopkins & Anderson, 1990). Regardless of how careful counselors are, however, malpractice lawsuits can still occur. Therefore, carrying liability insurance is a must (Bullis, 1993). *Avoiding Counselor Malpractice* (Crawford, 1994) is an excellent book explaining the nature and scope of malpractice and ways to take reasonable precautions to avoid being implicated in lawsuits.

Liability can be classified under two main headings: civil and criminal. *Civil liability* "means that one can be sued for acting wrongly toward another or for failing to act when there [is] a recognized duty to do so" (Hopkins & Anderson, 1990, p. 21). *Criminal liability,* on the other hand, involves a counselor's working with a client in a way the law does not allow (Burgum & Anderson, 1975).

The concept of civil liability rests on the concept of *tort,* "a wrong that legal action is designed to set right" (Hopkins & Anderson, 1990, p. 21). The legal wrong can be against a person, property, or even someone's reputation and may be unintentional or direct. Counselors are most likely to face civil liability suits for malpractice in the following situations: (a) malpractice in particular situations (birth control, abortion, prescribing and administering drugs, treatment), (b) illegal search, (c) defamation, (d) invasion of privacy, and (e) breach of contract (Hopkins and Anderson, 1990). Three situations in which counselors risk criminal liability are (a) accessory to a crime, (b) civil disobedience, and (c) contribution to the delinquency of a minor (Burgum & Anderson, 1975; Hopkins & Anderson, 1990).

Client Rights and Records

Clients have a number of legal as well as ethical rights in counseling, but they frequently do not know about them. One of a counselor's first tasks is to learn what rights clients have and to inform clients of them. This process is not as simple as it might seem. For instance, for minors, the "consent to enter counseling or to release information about counseling services resides in the custodial parent or guardian as a matter of common law and state statues" (Kaplan, 1996, p. 167).

There are two main types of client rights: implied and explicit (Hansen et al., 1994). Both relate to due process. *Implied rights* are linked to substantive due process. When a rule is made that arbitrarily limits an individual (i.e., deprives the person of his or her constitutional rights), he or she has been denied substantive due process. *Explicit rights* focus on procedural due process (the steps necessary to initiate or complete an action when an explicit rule is broken). An individual's procedural due process is violated when an explicit rule is broken and the person is not informed about how to remedy the matter. A client has a right to know what recourse he or she has when either of these two types of rights is violated. Legally, as noted in the last paragraph, the issue of rights is clearer in dealing with adults than with children. Remley (1985) notes "that children under the age of majority do not have the capacity or right to make decisions for themselves" (p. 182). Nevertheless, children have rights and are legally protected from any arbitrary professional actions.

The records of all clients are legally protected except under special circumstances. For example, in some instances, such as those provided by the Buckley Amendment, an individual has the right legally to inspect his or her record. There are also some cases (cited by Hummell et al., 1985) in which third parties have access to student information without the consent of the student or parent. In the vast majority of cases, counselors are legally required to protect clients of all ages by keeping records under lock and key, separate from any required business records, and not disclosing any information about a client without that person's written permission. The best method to use in meeting a request for disclosing information is a release-of-information form, which can be drawn up by an attorney (Rosenthal, 1998). Counselors should not release client information they have not obtained firsthand.

Because record keeping is one of the top five areas pertaining to legal liability of counselors (Snider, 1987), the question often arises about what should go into records. Basically, records should contain "all information about the client necessary for his or her treatment" (Piazza & Baruth, 1990, p. 313). The number and types of forms in a client record vary with the agency and practitioner, but six categories of documents are usually included:

1. *Identifying or intake information:* name, address, telephone number(s), date of birth, sex, occupation, and so on
2. *Assessment information:* psychological evaluation(s), social/family history, health history, and so on
3. *Treatment plan:* presenting problem, plan of action, steps to be taken to reach targeted behavior, and so on
4. *Case notes:* for example, documentation of progress in each session toward the stated goal
5. *Termination summary:* outcome of treatment, final diagnosis (if any), after-care plan, and so on
6. *Other data:* client's signed consent for treatment, copies of correspondence, notations about rationale for any unusual client interventions, administrative problems, and so on

It is vital for counselors to check their state legal codes for exact guidelines about record keeping. It is critical for counselors who receive third-party reimbursement to make sure that their client records refer to progress in terms of a treatment plan and a diagnosis (if required) (Hinkle, 1994). In no case, however, should confidential information about a client be given over the telephone. Counselors are also ethically and legally bound to ensure that a client's rights are protected by not discussing counseling cases in public.

The Counselor in Court

The court system in the United States is divided into federal and state courts. Each is similarly patterned with "trial courts, a middle-level appellate court, and a supreme court" (Anderson, 1996, p. 7). Most counselors who appear in court do so on the state level because the federal courts deal with cases arising primarily under the laws of the United States or those involving citizens of different states where the amount of controversy exceeds $50,000.

Most counselors wind up in court in two main ways. One is voluntary and professional: when the counselor serves as an *expert witness*. "An expert witness is an objective and unbiased person with specialized knowledge, skills, or information, who can assist a judge or jury in reaching an appropriate legal decision" (Remley, 1992, p. 33). A counselor who serves as an expert witness is compensated financially for his or her time.

The other way in which a counselor may appear in court is through a *court order* (a subpoena to appear in court at a certain time in regard to a specific case). Such a summons is issued with the intent of having the counselor testify on behalf of or against a present or former client. Because the legal system is adversarial, counselors are wise to seek the advice of attorneys before responding to court orders (Remley, 1991). By so doing, counselors may come to understand law, court proceedings, and options they have in response to legal requests. Role-playing possible situations before appearing in court may also help counselors function better in such situations.

Overall, in preparing for legal encounters, counselors should read some or all of the 12 volumes in the American Counseling Association Legal Series. These volumes, edited by Theodore P. Remley, Jr., are written by experts in the field of counseling who have either legal degrees or expert knowledge on important legal issues such as preparing for court appearances, documenting counseling records, counseling minors, understanding confidentiality and privileged communication, receiving third-party payments, and managing a counseling agency.

Summary and Conclusion

Counselors are like other professionals in having established codes of ethics to guide them in the practice of helping others. The ethical standards of the ACA and the APA are two of the main documents counselors consult when they face ethical dilemmas. Acting ethically is not always easy, comfortable, or clear.

In making an ethical decision, counselors rely on personal values as well as ethical standards and legal precedents. They also consult with professional colleagues, casebooks, and principles. It is imperative that counselors become well informed in the area of ethics for the sake of their own well-being and that of their clients. It is not enough that counselors have an academic knowledge of ethical standards; they must have a working knowledge and be able to assess at what developmental level they and their colleagues are operating.

In addition, counselors must be informed about state and national legislation and legal decisions. These will affect the ways in which counselors work. Counselors are liable for civil and criminal malpractice suits if they violate client rights or societal rules. One way for counselors to protect themselves legally is to follow the ethical standards of the professional organizations with which they are affiliated and operate according to recognized normal practices. It is imperative that counselors be able to justify what they do.

Ethical standards and legal codes reflect current conditions and are ever-evolving documents. They do not cover all situations, but they do offer help beyond that contained in counselors' personal beliefs and values. As counseling continues to develop as a profession, its ethical and legal aspects will probably become more complicated, and enforcement procedures will become stricter. Ignorance of ethics and law is no excuse for any practicing counselor.

CLASSROOM ACTIVITIES

1. Obtain copies of early ethical codes for the ACA. Compare these guidelines to the most recently published ACA ethical standards. What differences do you notice? Discuss your observations with fellow class members.

2. In groups of four, use the ACA ethical standards casebook as a guide to enact specific ethical dilemmas before your classmates. Have the other groups write down at least two courses of action they would pursue in

solving your enacted situation. Have them justify the personal and professional reasons for their actions. Discuss each of these situations with the class as whole and with your instructor.

3. Invite three or four professional counselors to your class to discuss specific ethical and legal concerns they have encountered. Ask about what areas they find the most difficult to deal with. After their presentations, question them about the role of ethics and law in the future of counseling.

4. Obtain as many copies as you can of counseling laws in states where counselors are licensed. Compare these laws for similarities and differences. What areas do you think the laws need to address that are not being covered?

5. Write down ways that you, as a professional counselor, can influence the development of counseling ethics and law. Be specific. Share your thoughts with fellow classmates.

REFERENCES

Allen, V. B. (1986). A historical perspective of the AACD ethics committee. *Journal of Counseling and Development, 64,* 293.

Allen, V. B., Sampson, J. P., Jr., & Herlihy, B. (1988). Details of the 1988 AACD ethical standards. *Journal of Counseling and Development, 67,* 157–158.

American Counseling Association (ACA). (1995). *Ethical standards of the American Counseling Association.* Alexandria, VA: Author.

Anderson, B. S. (1996). *The counselor and the law* (4th ed.). Alexandria, VA: American Counseling Association.

Anderson, D., & Swanson, C. (1994). *Legal issues in licensure.* Alexandria, VA: American Counseling Association.

Arthur, G. L., & Swanson, C. D. (1993). *Confidentiality and privileged communication.* Alexandria, VA: American Counseling Association.

Bartlett, W. E., Lee, J. L., & Doyle, R. E. (1985). Historical development of the Association for Religious and Values Issues in Counseling. *Journal of Counseling and Development, 63,* 448–451.

Bergin, A. E. (1985). Proposed values for guiding and evaluating counseling and psychotherapy. *Counseling and Values, 29,* 99–115.

Bergin, A. E. (1992). Three contributions of a spiritual perspective to counseling, psychotherapy, and behavior change. In M. T. Burke & J. G. Miranti (Eds.), *Ethical and spiritual values in counseling* (pp. 5–15). Alexandria, VA: American Counseling Association.

Beymer, L. (1971). Who killed George Washington? *Personnel and Guidance Journal, 50,* 249–253.

Boy, A. V., & Pine, G. J. (1968). *The counselor in the schools: A reconceptualization.* Boston: Houghton Mifflin.

Brandt, R. (1959). *Ethical theory.* Upper Saddle River, NJ: Prentice Hall.

Bullis, R. K. (1993). *Law and the management of a counseling agency or private practice.* Alexandria, VA: American Counseling Association.

Burgum, T., & Anderson, S. (1975). *The counselor and the law.* Washington, DC: APGA Press.

Butler, K. (1994, July/August). Duty of care. *Family Therapy Networker, 18,* 10–11.

Callis, R., Pope, S., & DePauw, M. (1982). *Ethical standards casebook* (3rd ed.). Alexandria, VA: American Counseling Association.

Chauvin, J. C., & Remley, T. P., Jr. (1996). Responding to allegations of unethical conduct. *Journal of Counseling & Development, 74,* 563–568.

Christopher, J. C. (1996). Counseling's inescapable moral visions. *Journal of Counseling & Development, 75,* 17–25.

Clawson, T. W., & Wildermuth, V. (1992, December). The counselor and NBCC. *CAPS Digest,* EDO-CG-92-14.

Coll, K. M. (1993). Student attitudinal changes in a counseling ethics course. *Counseling and Values, 37,* 165–170.

Corey, G., Corey, M. S., & Callanan, P. (1998). *Issues and ethics in the helping professions* (5th ed.). Pacific Grove, CA: Brooks/Cole.

Costa, L., & Altekruse, M. (1994). Duty-to-warn guidelines for mental health counselors. *Journal of Counseling and Development, 72,* 346–350.

Cottone, R. R., & Tarvydas, V. M. (1998). *Ethical and professional issues in counseling.* Upper Saddle River, NJ: Merrill/Prentice Hall.

Crawford, R. L. (1994). *Avoiding counselor malpractice.* Alexandria, VA: American Counseling Association.

Daniluk, J. C., & Haverkamp, B. E. (1993). Ethical issues in counseling adult survivors of incest. *Journal of Counseling and Development, 72,* 16–22.

Davis, T., & Ritchie, M. (1993). Confidentiality and the school counselor: A challenge for the 1990s. *School Counselor, 41,* 23–30.

DePauw, M. E. (1986). Avoiding ethical violations: A timeline perspective for individual counseling. *Journal of Counseling and Development, 64,* 303–305.

Dingman, R. L. (1990, November). *Counselor credentialing laws.* Paper presented at the Southern Association for Counselor Education and Supervision, Norfolk, VA.

Doyle, K. (1997). Substance abuse counselors in recovery: Implications for the ethical issue of dual relationships. *Journal of Counseling & Development, 75,* 428–432.

Faiver, C., Eisengart, S., & Colonna, R. (1995). *The counselor intern's handbook.* Pacific Grove, CA: Brooks/Cole.

Forester-Miller, H., & Davis, T. E. (1996). *A practitioner's guide to ethical decision making.* Alexandria, VA: American Counseling Association.

Fretz, B. R., & Mills, D. H. (1980). *Licensing and certification of psychologists and counselors.* San Francisco: Jossey-Bass.

Gibson, W. T., & Pope, K. S. (1993). The ethics of counseling: A national survey of certified counselors. *Journal of Counseling and Development, 71,* 330–336.

Gladding, S. T., & Hood, W. D. (1974). Five cents, please. *School Counselor, 21,* 40–43.

Glosoff, H. (1992). Accrediting and certifying professional counselors. *Guidepost, 34*(12), 6–8.

Grant, B. (1992). The moral nature of psychotherapy. In M. T. Burke & J. G. Miranti (Eds.), *Ethical and spiritual values in counseling* (pp. 27–35). Alexandria, VA: American Counseling Association.

Gumaer, J., & Scott, L. (1985). Training group leaders in ethical decision making. *Journal for Specialists in Group Work, 10,* 198–204.

Hansen, J. C., Rossberg, R. H., & Cramer, S. H. (1994). *Counseling: Theory and process* (5th ed.). Boston: Allyn & Bacon.

Harding, A. K., Gray, L. A., & Neal, M. (1993). Confidentiality limits with clients who have HIV: A review of ethical and legal guidelines and professional policies. *Journal of Counseling and Development, 71,* 297–304.

Hayman, P. M., & Covert, J. A. (1986). Ethical dilemmas in college counseling centers. *Journal of Counseling and Development, 64,* 318–320.

Henderson, D. A., & Fall, M. (1998). School counseling. In R. R. Cottone & V. M. Tarvydas (Eds.), *Ethical and professional issues in counseling* (pp. 263–294). Upper Saddle River, NJ: Prentice Hall.

Herlihy, B. (1996). When a colleague is impaired: The individual counselor's response. *Journal of Humanistic Education and Development, 34,* 118–127.

Herlihy, B., & Corey, C. (1996). *ACA ethical standards casebook* (5th ed.). Alexandria, VA: American Counseling Association.

Herlihy, B., & Sheeley, V. L. (1987). Privileged communication in selected helping professions: A comparison among statutes. *Journal of Counseling and Development, 64,* 479–483.

Hinkle, J. S. (1994, September). *Psychodiagnosis and treatment planning under the DSM-IV.* Workshop presentation of the North Carolina Counseling Association, Greensboro.

Hopkins, B. R., & Anderson, B. S. (1990). *The counselor and the law* (3rd ed.). Alexandria, VA: American Counseling Association.

Huber, C. H. (1994). *Ethical, legal and professional issues in the practice of marriage and family therapy* (2nd ed.). Upper Saddle River, NJ: Merrill/Prentice Hall.

Huey, W. C. (1986). Ethical concerns in school counseling. *Journal of Counseling and Development, 64,* 321–322.

Humes, C. W., II. (1978). School counselors and P.L. 94-142. *School Counselor, 25,* 192–195.

Hummell, D. L., Talbutt, L. C., & Alexander, M. D. (1985). *Law and ethics in counseling.* New York: Van Nostrand Reinhold.

Jencius, M., & Rotter, J. C. (1998, March). *Applying naturalistic studies in counseling.* Paper presented at the American Counseling Association World Conference, Indianapolis, IN.

Kaplan, L. S. (1996). Outrageous or legitimate concerns: What some parents are saying about school counseling. *School Counselor, 43,* 165–170.

Kitchener, K. S. (1986). Teaching applied ethics in counselor education: An integration of psychological processes and philosophical analysis. *Journal of Counseling and Development, 64,* 306–310.

Kitchener, K. S. (1994, May). Doing good well: The wisdom behind ethical supervision. *Counseling and Human Development,* 1–8.

Knapp, S., & Vandecreek, L. (1982). *Tarasoff*: Five years later. *Professional Psychology, 13,* 511–516.

Ladd, E. T. (1971). Counselors, confidences, and the civil liberties of clients. *Personnel and Guidance Journal, 50,* 261–268.

Lanning, W. (1992, December). Ethical codes and responsible decision-making. *ACA Guidepost, 35,* 21.

Levenson, J. L. (1986). When a colleague practices unethically: Guidelines for intervention. *Journal of Counseling and Development, 64,* 315–317.

Mabe, A. R., & Rollin, S. A. (1986). The role of a code of ethical standards in counseling. *Journal of Counseling and Development, 64,* 294–297.

Margolin, G. (1982). Ethical and legal considerations in marital and family therapy. *American Psychologist, 37,* 788–801.

McGovern, T. F. (1994, May/June). Being good and doing good: An ethical reflection around alcoholism and drug abuse counseling. *The Counselor,* 14–18.

Murphy, K. E. (1998). Is managed care unethical? *IAMFC Family Digest, 11*(1), 3.

Myers, J. E. (1998). Combatting agesim: The rights of older persons. In C. C. Lee & G. Walz (Eds.), *Social action for counselors.* Alexandria, VA: American Counseling Association.

Parker, R. M., & Szymanski, E. M. (1996). Ethics and publications. *Rehabilitation Counseling Bulletin, 39,* 162–163.

Patterson, C. H. (1971). Are ethics different in different settings? *Personnel and Guidance Journal, 50,* 254–259.

Pelsma, D. M., & Borgers, S. B. (1986). Experience-based ethics: A developmental model of learning ethical reasoning. *Journal of Counseling and Development, 64,* 311–314.

Piazza, N. J., & Baruth, N. E. (1990). Client record guidelines. *Journal of Counseling and Development, 68,* 313–316.

Pope, K. S., & Vetter, V. A. (1992). Ethical dilemmas encountered by members of the American Psychological Association. *American Psychologist, 47,* 397–411.

Remley, T. P., Jr. (1985). The law and ethical practices in elementary and middle schools. *Elementary School Guidance and Counseling, 19,* 181–189.

Remley, T. P., Jr. (1991). *Preparing for court appearances.* Alexandria, VA: American Counseling Association.

Remley, T. P., Jr. (1992, Spring). You and the law. *American Counselor, 1,* 33.

Remley, T. P., Jr., Herlihy, B., & Herlihy, S. B. (1997). The U.S. Supreme Court decision in *Jaffee v. Redmond*: Implications for counselors. *Journal of Counseling & Development, 75,* 213–218.

Robinson, S. E., & Gross, D. R. (1986). Counseling research: Ethics and issues. *Journal of Counseling and Development, 64,* 331–333.

Romano, G. (1992). The power and pain of professionalization. *American Counselor, 1,* 17–23.

Rosenthal, H. (1998). *Before you see your first client.* Holmes Beach, FL: Learning Publications.

Rueth, T., Demmitt, A., & Burger, S. (1998, March). *Counselors and the DSM-IV: Intentional and unintentional consequences of diagnosis.* Paper presented at the American Counseling Association World Conference, Indianapolis, IN.

Salo, M., Forester-Miller, H., & Hamilton, W. M. (1996). Report of the ACA ethics committee: 1995–1996. *Journal of Counseling and Development, 75,* 174–175.

Sampson, J. P., Kolodinsky, R. W., & Greeno, B. P. (1997). Counseling on the information highway: Future possibilities and potential problems. *Journal of Counseling & Development, 75,* 203–212.

Schulte, J. M. (1990). The morality of influencing in counseling. *Counseling and Values, 34,* 103–118.

Shertzer, B., & Stone, S. (1980). *Fundamentals of counseling* (3rd ed.). Boston: Houghton Mifflin.

Shimberg, B. (1981). Testing for licensure and certification. *American Psychologist, 36,* 1138–1146.

Snider, P. D. (1987). Client records: Inexpensive liability protection for mental health counselors. *Journal of Mental Health Counseling, 9,* 134–141.

St. Germaine, J. (1993). Dual relationships: What's wrong with them? *American Counselor, 2,* 25–30.

Stadler, H. (1986). Preface to the special issue. *Journal of Counseling and Development, 64,* 291.

Stevens-Smith, P., & Hughes, M. M. (1993). *Legal issues in marriage and family counseling.* Alexandria, VA: American Counseling Association.

Stude, E. W., & McKelvey, J. (1979). Ethics and the law: Friend or foe? *Personnel and Guidance Journal, 57,* 453–456.

Sue, D. W., Ivey, A. E., & Pedersen, P. B. (1996). *A theory of multicultural counseling and therapy.* Pacific Grove, CA: Brooks/Cole.

Swanson, C. D. (1983a). Ethics and the counselor. In J. A. Brown & R. H. Pate, Jr. (Eds.), *Being a counselor* (pp. 47–65). Pacific Grove, CA: Brooks/Cole.

Swanson, C. D. (1983b). The law and the counselor. In J. A. Brown & R. H. Pate, Jr. (Eds.), *Being a counselor* (pp. 26–46). Pacific Grove, CA: Brooks/Cole.

Talbutt, L. C. (1981). Ethical standards: Assets and limitations. *Personnel and Guidance Journal, 60,* 110–112.

Tennyson, W. W., & Strom, S. M. (1986). Beyond professional standards: Developing responsibleness. *Journal of Counseling and Development, 64,* 298–302.

Thomas, V. (1994). Value analysis: A model of personal and professional ethics in marriage and family counseling. *Counseling and Values, 38,* 193–203.

Thompson, A. (1990). *Guide to ethical practice in psychotherapy.* New York: Wiley.

Van Hoose, W. H., & Kottler, J. (1985). *Ethical and legal issues in counseling and psychotherapy* (2nd ed.). San Francisco: Jossey-Bass.

Van Hoose, W. H., & Paradise, L. V. (1979). *Ethics in counseling and psychotherapy.* Cranston, RI: Carroll.

Welfel, E. R. (1998). *Ethics in counseling and psychotherapy.* Pacific Grove, CA: Brooks/Cole.

Welfel, E. R., & Lipsitz, N. E. (1983a). Ethical orientation of counselors: Its relationship to moral reasoning and level of training. *Counselor Education and Supervision, 23,* 35–45.

Welfel, E. R., & Lipsitz, N. E. (1983b). Wanted: A comprehensive approach to ethics research and education. *Counselor Education and Supervision, 22,* 320–332.

Wilcoxon, S. A. (1986). Engaging nonattending family members in marital and family counseling: Ethical issues. *Journal of Counseling and Development, 64,* 323–324.

Wilcoxon, S. A. (1987). Ethical standards: A study of application and utility. *Journal of Counseling and Development, 65,* 510–511.

Wilcoxon, S. A. (1993, March/April). Ethical issues in marital and family counseling: A framework for examining unique ethical concerns. *Family Counseling and Therapy, 1,* 1–15.

Wittmer, J. P., & Loesch, L. C. (1986). Professional orientation. In M. D. Lewis, R. L. Hays, & J. A. Lewis (Eds.), *The counseling profession* (pp. 301–330). Itasca, IL: Peacock.

Woody, R. H. (1988). *Fifty ways to avoid malpractice.* Sarasota, FL: Professional Resource Exchange.

4

COUNSELING IN A MULTICULTURAL AND PLURALISTIC SOCIETY

◆

An old black man in downtown Atlanta

is clubfooted, blind, and bends like the willows.

He sits by his papers near Peachtree Street

passing the time by tapping his crutches.

I flow by him in the five o'clock stream

of white-collared, blue suited, turbulent people

rushing for MARTA trains to neighboring suburbs

and the prospects of quiet in the flood-tide of life.

Spring rains now enrich the earth . . .

But where do the willows and waters meet?

The effectiveness of counseling depends on many factors, but among the most important is for the counselor and client to be able to understand and relate to each other. Such a relationship is usually easier to achieve if the client and counselor are similar in such diverse factors as age, culture, disability, educational level, ethnicity, gender, language, physique, race, religion, sexual orientation, and socioeconomic background (Weinrach & Thomas, 1996). Because similarities in all these categories at any one time is rare, it is imperative that counselors be acutely sensitive to their clients' backgrounds and special needs and equally attuned to their own values, biases, and abilities (Brinson, 1996; Holiday, Leach, & Davidson, 1994). Understanding and dealing positively with differences is a matter of developing self-awareness (from the inside out) as well as developing an awareness of others (from the outside in) (Okun, Fried, & Okun, 1999). Differences between counselors and clients should never be allowed to influence the counseling process negatively.

This chapter considers distinct populations and issues that impact counseling in a culturally diverse world. "Culturally neutral counseling does not exist" (Coleman, 1998, p. 153). Topics covered here include working with culturally and ethnically distinct clients, the aged, women/men, gays/lesbians, and spirituality. The variety of clients that counselors encounter in their work is almost endless. Methods that work best with one concern or population may be irrelevant or even inappropriate for others. Therefore, counselors must be constant lifelong learners and implementers of new and effective methods of working.

Counseling Across Culture and Ethnicity

Many distinct cultural and ethnic groups live in the United States. European Americans make up the largest group (approximately 75%), with four other distinct groups—African Americans, Native American Indians, Asian Americans, and Hispanics—composing the majority of the rest of population (approximately 25%) (Baruth & Manning, 1999). However, minority cultural and ethnic groups are expected to grow rapidly in number and as a percentage of the population into the 21st century (Pope-Davis & Ottavi, 1994).

Several factors influence the counseling of cultural and ethnic groups, such as understanding a client's identity, education, age, religion, socioeconomic status, and experiences with racism (Brinson, 1996). An understanding of these factors is especially important if the assistance being offered is by someone outside a client's tradition. One way to systematically consider complex cultural influences in counseling is the ADRESSING model (Hayes, 1996; see Table 4.1). Letters of this model stand for "Age and generational influences, Disability, Religion, Ethnicity (which may include race), Social status, Sexual orientation, Indigenous heritage, National origin, and Gender" (p. 332). This model is transcultural-specific and "places a high value on culture-specific expertise regarding minority groups" but also considers a wide range of issues that cross many cultures (p. 334).

Table 4.1 The ADRESSING model: Nine cultural factors, related minority groups, and forms of oppression

Cultural Factor	Minority Group	Biases with Power
Age/generational	Older adults	Ageism
Disability	People with disabilities	—[a]
Religion	Religious minorities	—[b]
Ethnicity/race	Ethnic minorities	Racism
Social status	People of lower status	Classism
Sexual orientation	Sexual minorities	Heterosexism
Indigenous heritage	Native peoples	Racism
National origin	Refugees, immigrants, and international students	Racism and colonialism
Gender	Women	Sexism

[a] Prejudice and discrimination against people with disabilities.
[b] Religious intolerance includes anti-Semitism (i.e., against both Jewish and Muslim people) and oppression of other religious minorities (e.g., Buddhists, Hindus, Mormons).

Source: From "Addressing the Complexities of Culture and Gender in Counseling," by P. A. Hayes, 1996, *Journal of Counseling and Development, 74*, p. 334. © ACA. Reprinted with permission. No further reproduction authorized without written permission of the American Counseling Association.

About a quarter of those who initially use mental health facilities are from minority cultural and ethnic group populations (Cheung, 1991). Yet researchers have consistently found that these groups in the United States are collectively not as well satisfied with the services they receive. Some 50% of minority–culture group members who begin counseling terminate after one session, as compared with about 30% of majority-culture clients (Sue & Sue, 1990). This statistic suggests that, as a rule, minority-culture clients have negative experiences in counseling. As a group, ethnic minorities underuse counseling services because of the treatment they receive or fail to have provided. The results work against such clients, their families, and society in general.

Defining Culture and Multicultural Counseling

Culture may be defined in several ways. They include "*ethnographic variables* such as ethnicity, nationality, religion, and language, as well as *demographic variables* of age, gender, place of residence, etc., *status variables* such as social, economic, and educational background and a wide range of formal or informal memberships and affiliations" (Pedersen, 1990, p. 550; emphasis added). A culture "structures our behavior, thoughts, perceptions, values, goals, morals, and cognitive processes" (Cohen, 1998, p. B4). It may do so on an unconscious or a conscious level.

A broad definition of *culture* that is inclusive as well as accurate is "any group of people who identify or associate with one another on the basis of some common purpose, need, or similarity of background" (Axelson, 1993, p. 2). Shared elements of a culture include learned experiences, beliefs, and values. These aspects of a culture are "webs of significance" that give coherence and meaning to life (Geertz, 1973). Whereas some cultures may define themselves partially in regard to similar physical features, others do so more in terms of a common history and philosophy, and still others combine the two. What people claim as a part of their culture and heritage is not usually apparent on first sight.

Just as the word *culture* is multidimensional, the term *multicultural* has been conceptualized in a number of different ways. There is no universal agreement as to what it includes, although accrediting groups such as the CACREP have defined the term broadly. "The lack of a concrete definition for multiculturalism has been a continuing problem" (Middleton, Flowers, & Zawaiza, 1996, p. 19). The most prominent foci of multiculturalism are distinct group uniquenesses and concepts that facilitate attention to individual differences (Locke, 1998).

Therefore, *multicultural counseling* may be viewed generally as counseling "in which the counselor and client differ" (Locke, 1990, p. 18). The differences may be the result of socialization in a unique cultural way, developmental or traumatic life events, or the product of being raised in a particular ethnic environment. The debate in the multicultural counseling field is how broad should differences be defined. On the one hand, some proponents advocate what is known as an *etic perspective,* stating universal qualities exist in counseling that are culturally generalizable. The opposite approach is the *emic perspective* that assumes counseling approaches must be designed to be culturally specific.

"The etic approach can be criticized for not taking important cultural differences into account. The emic approach can be criticized for placing too much emphasis on specific techniques as the vehicle for client change" (Fisher, Jome, & Atkinson, 1998, p. 578). Some professionals have tried to find common elements shared by these two approaches. For example, Fisher et al. (1998) have proposed four conditions common to any type of counseling treatment: "the therapeutic relationship, a shared worldview between client and counselor, client expectations for positive change, and interventions believed by both client and counselor to be a means of healing" (p. 531). However, this proposal has received only limited support. Thus, in the 21st century, the definition of multicultural counseling continues to be argued.

History of Multicultural Counseling

The history of offering counseling services for culturally distinct populations in the United States is rather brief and uneven (Arredondo, 1998). For example, in a survey of experts in the field, Ponterotto and Sabnani (1989) found "only 8.5% of the most frequently cited books in the field [were published] before 1970" (p. 35). Indeed, the focus of multicultural counseling has shifted in its short history from an emphasis on the client (1950s), to the counselor (1960s), to the total counseling process itself (1970s to the present). In the late 1980s, multicultural counseling was described as "the hottest topic in the profession" (Lee, 1989, p. 165), and throughout the 1990s it remained so.

Although a number of scholars had already pointed out the cultural limits of counseling, Gilbert Wrenn (1962) was the first prominent professional to call attention to the unique aspects of counseling people from different cultures (Ivey, 1990). In a landmark work, he described the *culturally encapsulated counselor* as one who disregards cultural differences and works under the mistaken assumption that theories and techniques are equally applicable to all people. Such a counselor is insensitive to the actual experiences of clients from different cultural, racial, and ethnic backgrounds and therefore may discriminate against some persons by treating everyone the same. Clemmont Vontress (1966, 1967, 1996) was also an early active pioneer in defining culture and showing how it influences counseling relationships. In 1973, Paul Pedersen chaired a panel on multicultural counseling at the APA's annual convention and with his colleagues later published the first book specifically on the subject, *Counseling across Cultures* (Pedersen, Lonner, & Draguns, 1976). Since that time, numerous publications and workshops have highlighted different aspects of multicultural counseling.

The Association for Multicultural Counseling and Development (AMCD), a division within the American Counseling Association (ACA), is dedicated primarily to defining and dealing with issues and concerns related to counseling across cultures within the United States. Originally known as the Association for Non-white Concerns in Personnel and Guidance (ANWC), the division became part of the ACA in 1972 (McFadden & Lipscomb, 1985). It publishes a quarterly periodical, the *Journal of Multicultural Counseling and Development*, which addresses issues related to counseling in a culturally pluralistic society. The AMCD has also sponsored an attempt to help counselors understand competencies needed in working with clients from non-European backgrounds and to promote standards in this area (Sue, Arredondo, & McDavis, 1992).

The AMCD, in cooperation with the ACA, regularly sponsors conferences to address real or perceived problems related to counseling relationships involving clients and counselors from different cultural groups. The focus of such training is to help counselors obtain *cultural expertise* (effectiveness in more than one culture) and *cultural intentionality* (awareness of individual differences within each culture) (Ivey, 1977, 1987). The need for such educational efforts continues to be great because many professionals have reported receiving only a minimal amount of training in multicultural counseling in their graduate programs (Allison, Crawford, Echemendia, Robinson, & Knepp, 1994).

Difficulties in Multicultural Counseling

Smith and Vasquez (1985) caution that it is important to distinguish differences that arise from cultural backgrounds from those that are the result of poverty or deprived status. A failure to make this distinction can lead to *overculturalizing*—that is, "mistaking people's reactions to poverty and discrimination for their cultural pattern" (p. 533). In the United States, many members of minority culture groups live in poverty (Hodgkinson, 1992). This problem is compounded by persistent second-language patterns in which the primary language of the client is not English. Nonverbal behaviors, especially in immigrant populations, are another problematic area in that they may not be understood or accepted by counselors from other than the client's own culture.

Racism is a third problematic area in working across cultures. *Racism* is prejudice displayed in blatant or subtle ways due to recognized or perceived differences in the physical and psychological backgrounds of people. It demeans all who participate in it and is a form of projection usually displayed out of fear or ignorance. Another difficulty in multicultural counseling involves *acculturation,* "the process by which a group of people give up old ways and adopt new ones" (Romero, Silva, & Romero, 1989, p. 499). It is crucial to know where clients are located on a continuum of acculturation in order to provide them with appropriate services (Weinrach & Thomas, 1998). Each of these difficulties in multicultural counseling must be recognized, understood, and empathetically resolved if counselors are to be effective with clients who are different from them.

Issues in Multicultural Counseling

A primary issue of concern for some multicultural counselors in the United States, especially those with an emic perspective, is the dominance of theories based on European/North American cultural values (Katz, 1985). Some of the predominant beliefs of European/North Americans are the value of individuals, an action-oriented approach to problem solving, the work ethic, the scientific method, and an emphasis on rigid time schedules (Axelson, 1993). A liability of these values in counseling is that theories built around them may not always be applicable to clients from other cultural traditions (Lee, 1997; Nwachuka & Ivey, 1991; Sue, 1992). If this fact is not recognized and dealt with, bias and a breakdown in counselor-client relationships may occur (Pedersen, 1987).

A second issue in multicultural counseling is sensitivity to cultures in general and in particular. Pedersen (1982) believes that it is essential for counselors to be sensitive to cultures in three areas: knowledge, awareness, and skills. Such sensitivity is derived from one's understanding of cultures on many levels. To help counselors achieve a deeper understanding of cultures in general, Pedersen (1977, 1978) developed a triad model for helping. The four areas in the model are "articulating the problem from the client's cultural perspective; anticipating resistance from a culturally different client; diminishing defensiveness by studying the trainee's own defensive responses; and learning recovery skills for getting out of trouble when counseling the culturally different" (1978, p. 481). In this model, an anticounselor, who functions like an alter ego and deliberately tries to be subversive, works with a counselor and a client in a videotaped session. The interaction and feedback generated through this process help break down barriers and foster greater understanding and sensitivity in counselors (Parker, Archer, & Scott, 1992).

Another model for understanding specific cultures has been devised by Nwachuka and Ivey (1991). They propose that counselors first study a culture and its values before trying to adapt a theory to fit a particular client. A starting point in achieving this goal is to view popular diversity-focused films about specific cultures. Pinterits and Atkinson (1998) list some films that can help counselors understand different cultures and experience the issues within these cultures vicariously (see Figure 4.1).

A third issue in multicultural counseling is understanding how cultural systems operate and influence behaviors. Counselors who have gained knowledge and awareness from within the cultural system are more likely to be skilled in helping members from a specific cultural group. These counselors are able to share a particular worldview with clients, make skillful and appropriate interventions, and yet maintain a sense of personal integrity. This type of cultural sensitivity requires "active participation on the part of the practitioner" including self-awareness (Brinson, 1996, p. 201).

African American

Autobiography of Miss Jane Pittman
Boyz 'n the Hood
The Color Purple
Colors
Do the Right Thing
Driving Miss Daisy
Eye on the Prize
Guess Who's Coming to Dinner
I Know Why the Caged Bird Sings
Jungle Fever
Long Walk Home
Malcolm X
Matewan
Mississippi Masala
Mo' Better Blues
Raisin in the Sun
Roots I & II
Sounder
To Kill a Mockingbird
White Man's Burden

Asian American

Come See the Paradise
Dim Sum
Double Happiness
Farewell to Manzanar
Joy Luck Club
The Wash
Wedding Banquet

Latino/Latina

American Me
Ballad of Gregorio Cortez
Born in East L.A.
El Norte
Like Water for Chocolate
Mi Familia
Milagro Bean Field War
Romero
Stand and Deliver

People with Disabilities

Born on the Fourth of July
Children of a Lesser God
Coming Home
Frankie Starlight
If You Can See What I Can Hear
Miracle Worker
My Left Foot
One Flew over the Cuckoo's Nest
The Other Side of the Mountain
A Patch of Blue
Waterdance
What's Eating Gilbert Grape

Gay, Lesbian, and Bisexual

And the Band Played On
Long Time Companion
Personal Best
Philadelphia
Priest
Strawberries and Chocolate
Torch Song Trilogy

Native American

Dances with Wolves
The Last of the Mohicans
The Mission
Never Cry Wolf
Pow Wow Highway
Thunderheart

Asian Indian

Mississippi Masala

Elderly

Cocoon
Driving Miss Daisy
Foxfire
Fried Green Tomatoes
Nobody's Fool
On Golden Pond

Figure 4.1   Sample list of films focusing on diverse populations

Source: From "The Diversity Video Forum: An Adjunct to Diversity Sensitive Training in the Classroom," by E. J. Pinterits and D. R. Atkinson, 1998, *Counselor Education and Supervision, 37*, pp. 213–214. © 1998 by ACA. Reprinted with permission. No further reproduction authorized without written permission of the American Counseling Association.

A fourth issue in multicultural counseling is providing effective counseling services across cultures. Sue (1978) established five guidelines for effectively counseling across cultures:

1. Counselors recognize the values and beliefs they hold in regard to acceptable and desirable human behavior. They are then able to integrate this understanding into appropriate feelings and behaviors.
2. Counselors are aware of the cultural and generic qualities of counseling theories and traditions. No method of counseling is completely culture-free.
3. Counselors understand the sociopolitical environment that has influenced the lives of members of minority groups. Persons are products of the milieus in which they live.
4. Counselors are able to share the worldview of clients and do not question its legitimacy.
5. Counselors are truly eclectic in counseling practice. They are able to use a wide variety of counseling skills and apply particular counseling techniques to specific lifestyles and experiences.

Sue (1978) further suggests a framework for multicultural counseling based on a two-dimensional concept, with locus of control on the horizontal axis and locus of responsibility on the vertical axis (Figure 4.2). The four quadrants represent the kinds and degrees of possible interactions among these variables with clients from different cultures.

A final issue in multicultural counseling is the development and employment of counseling theories. Cultural bias is present in majority and minority counselors (Wendel, 1997) and in the past has spilled over into counseling theories. To deal with culturally limited counseling theories, bias, and help transcend cultural limitations, McFadden (1993) and a number of leading counselor educators have devised ways to overcome ideas and methods developed before there was any awareness of the need for multicultural counseling. McFadden's model is a transcultural perspective that focuses on three primary dimensions counselors must master: cultural-historical, psychosocial, and scientific-ideological. In the cultural-historical dimension, counselors must possess knowledge of a client's culture. In the psychosocial dimension it is crucial that counselors understand the client's ethnic, racial, and social group's performance, speeches, or behaviors to communicate meaningfully. Finally, in the scientific-ideological dimension, counselors must use counseling approaches to deal with problems related to regional, national, and international environments.

Explanations of existing theories and their applicability to certain populations and problems are also becoming popular (e.g., Corsini & Wedding, 1995; Sue, Ivey, & Pedersen, 1996; Vontress, 1996). Existential counseling is one such approach that, like McFadden's transcultural perspective, is holistic and applicable across "all cultures and socioeconomic groups" (Epp, 1998, p. 7). As a theoretical approach it deals with meaning and human relationships and with the ultimate issues of life and death.

Another exciting development in multicultural counseling is the renewed emphasis on theories specifically designed for different cultures (Lee, 1997). For example, traditional Asian psychotherapies, which have existed for more than 3,000 years, have recently become more popular in the West (Walsh, 1995). Many of these traditions stress existential and transpersonal health and development over pathology, employing such techniques as

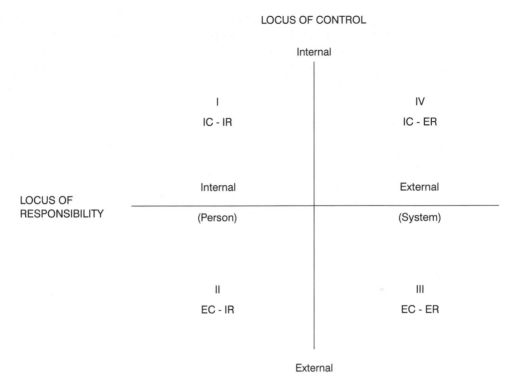

Figure 4.2 Graphic representation of worldviews
Source: From "Counseling across Cultures," by D. W. Sue, 1978, *Personnel and Guidance Journal, 56,* p. 460. © ACA. Reprinted with permission. No further reproduction authorized without written permission of the American Counseling Association.

meditation and yoga. They have a beneficial effect on wellness and psychological growth whether used alone or in concert with other approaches.

Counseling Considerations with Specific Cultural Groups

In addition to general guidelines for working with culturally different clients, counselors should keep in mind some general considerations when working with specific cultural groups. In reviewing these considerations, it is crucial that counselors remind themselves that *each individual, like each counseling session, is unique.* There are *probably more within-group differences than between-group differences in counseling people from specific cultural traditions.* Therefore, knowing a cultural tradition is only a part of the information counselors need to be effective. They must work to know their clients, problems, and themselves equally well.

In examining themselves, counselors who are from minority cultures need to be aware that they may harbor "historical hostility" at either a conscious or unconscious level toward members of majority cultures (Wendel, 1997). On the opposite side, counselors from majority cultures may carry attitudes of superiority and privilege. Neither attitude is healthy or productive.

European Americans

As a group, European Americans are a diverse population. Although Europe is the most common ancestral homeland, there are large differences between the cultural heritages of people from Sweden, Italy, France, England, Poland, Germany, Russia, Hungary, and Austria. (In addition, many people from Spain or from Spanish ancestry consider their heritage distinct from other Europeans in general.) Europeans who have recently arrived in the United States differ widely from those whose families settled in North America generations ago. Therefore, there is no typical European American.

Nevertheless, European Americans have a long and dominant history in the United States that has some common threads (Baruth & Manning, 1999). As a group, European Americans have blended together more than most other cultural groups. Reasons include a history of intergroup marriages and relationships that have simultaneously influenced the group as a whole and made it more homogeneous. European Americans are more likely than not to espouse a worldview that "values linear, analytical, empirical, and task solutions" and stresses that "rugged individualism should be valued, and that autonomy of the parts and independence of action are more significant than group conformance" (Sue, 1992, p. 8).

Because of their shared experiences, European Americans are usually quick to embrace counseling theories that stress their common values. Many European Americans gravitate toward rational or logical methods in understanding themselves and others. Therefore, cognitive and cognitive-behavioral approaches may work well with this group as a whole. However, existential, psychoanalytic, Adlerian, and affective counseling theories may be appropriate for some. Just as there is no typical European American, there is no one counseling theory or approach that will work with all members of this group.

African Americans

When counseling African Americans, counselors must understand African-American history, cultural values, and conflicts and be aware of their own attitudes and prejudices about this group (Garretson, 1993; Vontress & Epp, 1997). It is possible for counselors from different cultural backgrounds to be effective with African-American clients if they understand the nature of racism and stereotypical thinking and have successfully resolved these issues. Such a process involves perceiving African Americans as a diverse group that displays a broad range of behaviors (Harper, 1994; Smith, 1977).

"Counseling is frequently perceived by African Americans as a process that requires the client to relinquish his or her independence by first having to 'tell your business to a stranger' and then having to 'heed the unsolicited advice of that stranger'" (Priest, 1991, p. 215). Therefore, many African Americans are unwilling to voluntarily commit themselves to a counseling relationship. Another factor that influences African-American participation in counseling is the perception that the relationship takes place among unequals. Given the history of slavery in America and the common misdiagnosis of African Americans in mental health centers, members of this group who enter into an unequal relationship do so with great reluctance (Garretson, 1993). A third factor that affects African Americans in counseling is the emphasis on the collective in most of their community tradition. "In historical times the collective was the clan or tribe" (Priest, 1991, p. 213). Today, it is the family and those who live, work, or worship nearby. This emphasis on the collective is the antithesis of individual responsibility for resolving difficulties. Spirituality and the role of the minister in African-American culture are factors influencing members of this group, too. Rather than a counselor, a minister is usually sought out as a "source of mental and emotional sustenance" (Priest, 1991, p. 214).

Hispanics

The term *Hispanic* refers to people of Spanish origin in the Americas. The common denominator for Hispanic is the Spanish language, but Hispanics are a very diverse group. Most Hispanics in the United States are bicultural, but they vary in degree of acculturation (Baruth & Manning, 1999). Their ethnic histories and cultures play a major part in influencing their worldviews and behaviors, and many within-group differences exist among Hispanics (Romero et al., 1989).

As a group, Hispanics are usually reluctant to use counseling services. Part of this hesitancy is cultural tradition (e.g., pride), and part is cultural heritage (e.g., reliance on extended family ties). More practical reasons are the distance to service agencies (as in the Southwest), inadequate transportation, a lack of health insurance, and the absence of counseling professionals fluent in Spanish and familiar with Hispanic cultures (Gonzalez, 1997; Ruiz, 1981).

In addition, many Hispanics perceive psychological problems as similar to physical problems (Ruiz & Padilla, 1977). Therefore, they expect the counselor to be active, concrete, and goal directed. This perception is especially true for clients who are "very" Hispanic (Ruiz, 1981).

Overall, counselors of Hispanics must address numerous topics and work within cultural concepts and beliefs. It is often helpful if the counselor is bilingual because many Hispanics prefer Spanish to English. Lower socioeconomic status, racism, and discrimination are some of the universal difficulties affecting members of this population that directly or indirectly may come up in counseling (Baruth & Manning, 1999).

Asian and Pacific Islander Americans

Asian and Pacific Islander Americans (referred to here as Asian Americans) include Chinese, Japanese, Filipinos, Indochinese, Indians, and Koreans, among others. They vary widely in cultural background (Axelson, 1993; Morrissey, 1997), and "the demographic profile of Asian and Pacific Islander Americans includes an array of more than 40 disparate cultural groups" (Sandhu, 1997, p. 7). Historically, they have faced strong discrimination in the United States and have been the subject of many myths (Sue & Sue, 1972, 1990). A combination of factors has promoted stereotypes of Asian Americans.

Because of bias and misunderstandings, Asian Americans have "been denied the rights of citizenship, forbidden to own land, locked in concentration camps, maligned, mistreated, and massacred" (Sue & Sue, 1973, p. 387). Ironically, a combination of factors has also promoted a positive image of them. They are collectively described as hardworking and successful and not prone to mental or emotional disturbances. Sometimes they are referred to as the "model minority" (Bell, 1985). Like all stereotypes, there are kernels of truth in this descriptor, but it is still not realistic or accurate. Until counselors see Asian Americans in the context of their cultural heritage, they will be unable to offer them help in mentally healthy ways (Henkin, 1985).

There are many subtleties in Asian American cultures, as there are in all cultures. For example, religious traditions (such as Islamic, Hindu, and Buddhist) play a strong role in some of their views of mental health and mental illness. For some Asian Americans "psychological distress and disorders are explained within a religious framework in terms of either spirit possession or violation of some religious or moral principle. Healing may take the form of invoking the help of some supernatural power or restoring the sufferer to a state of well being through prescribing right conduct and belief" (Das, 1987, p. 25). Another important subtlety, which may have a major impact on career counselors, is that many Asian Americans typically eschew occupations that call for forceful self-expression (Watanabe, 1973). Genteel ways of communicating stem from cultural traditions and must be dealt with positively if a strong counseling relationship is to be established.

It is critical that counselors appreciate the history and unique characteristics of select Asian-American groups in the United States, such as the Chinese, Japanese, and Vietnamese (Axelson, 1993; Sandhu, 1997). This sensitivity often enables counselors to facilitate the counseling process in ways not otherwise possible. For example, counselors may promote self-disclosure with Chinese Americans through educational or career counseling rather than direct, confrontational psychotherapeutic approaches.

Native American Indians

Native American Indians, mistakenly called Indians by the first European settlers in America, are made up of "478 tribes recognized by the U.S. Bureau of Indian Affairs, plus another 52 tribes without official status" (Heinrich, Corbin, & Thomas, 1990, p. 128). Tremendous diversity prevails among Native American Indians, including 149 languages, but they also have a common identity that stresses values such as harmony with nature, cooperation, holism, a concern with the present, and a reliance on one's extended family (Heinrich et al., 1990). In general, Native American Indians have strong feelings about the loss of ancestral lands, a desire for self-determination, conflicts with the values of mainstream American culture, and a confused self-image resulting from past stereotyping (Axelson, 1993). Anger from or about past transgressions of people from other cultures is a theme that must be handled appropriately (Hammerschlag, 1988). Native American Indians, as a group, have high suicide, unemployment, and alcoholism rates and a low life expectancy. "American Indians continue to have the highest dropout rate of any ethnic group at the high school level, regardless of region or tribal affiliation" (Sanders, 1987, p. 81). In short, as a group "Native Americans face enormous problems" (Heinrich et al., 1990, p. 128).

A number of counseling approaches, from existentialism to directed counseling, have been tried with Native American Indians. Effective counseling, however, depends in part on whether they live on a reservation; whether other Native Americans help facilitate the counseling process; and whether their acculturation is traditional, bicultural, or assimilated (Avasthi, 1990; Valle, 1986). Regardless, it is crucial that counselors understand Native American Indian cultures and avoid imposing culturally inappropriate theories on them (Herring, 1996, 1997; Ivey, 1990).

According to Richardson (1981), four ideas to be considered when counseling Native American Indians are silence, acceptance, restatement, and general lead. Richardson has used vignettes to model ways of using these techniques. The use of the *vision quest,* a rite of passage and religious renewal for adult men, is recommended in some cases (Heinrich et al., 1990). The use of the creative arts is also an approach that has considerable merit because emotional, religious, and artistic expression is "an inalienable aspect of Native culture" (Herring, 1997, p. 105). The creative arts do not require verbal disclosure. In addition, they may focus on rituals and wellness in Native American culture. Using multiple counseling approaches in a synergetic way, such as network therapy, home-based therapy, indigenous-structural therapy, and traditional native activities such as "the talking circle," "the talking stick," and storytelling, are also recommended (Herring, 1996).

More important than specific ways of working is the crucial nature of a sense of "realness" when in a counseling relationship with a Native American. Being willing to be a learner and to admit one's mistakes can help a counselor and a Native American bond.

International Counseling

The cultural perspective of the United States is just one among the many in the world. Super (1983) questions whether counseling, as practiced in North America, is adaptable to other countries. His analysis of culture and counseling concludes that prosperous and secure countries view counseling as a way of promoting individual interests and abilities. Economically less fortunate countries and those under threat of foreign domination view counseling services as a way of channeling individuals into areas necessary for cultural survival (Super, 1954). Knowledge about such cultural differences must be considered in international counseling.

Such knowledge is crucial in counseling internationally. For instance, in Poland career counseling is more highly prized than other forms of counseling because of the developing nature of the country (Richard Lamb, personal communication, June 7, 1997). In other countries, such as China, counseling as practiced in the United States is basically a foreign concept to the majority of the population. Therefore, students from such countries who attend colleges and universities in the United States may be reluctant to initiate a counseling relationship. Instead, as Boyer and Sedlacek (1989) explain, many international students to the United States experience psychological problems in physical terms, rely on networks of family and friends, and fear being seen as a failure and sent home. International students who do use counseling services differ from other internationals in their understanding and ability to deal with racism, their preference for working on long-term rather than short-term goals, their immediate needs, and their nontraditional ways of acquiring knowledge.

Henkin (1985) proposes a number of practical guidelines for counselors interacting with Japanese Americans, and his advice is appropriate for use on an international level as well:

- Establish a clear-cut structure for the counseling process.
- Explain the process to the client.
- Allow clients to ask questions about you as a counselor and about the process itself.
- Refrain from making an assessment as long as possible.
- Educate yourself about the culture of your clients, especially about the importance of their family and community.

Aged Populations

Development is traditionally defined as any kind of systematic change that is lifelong and cumulative (Papalia & Olds, 1998). Throughout their lives individuals develop on a number of levels: cognitively, emotionally, and physically. When development occurs within an expected time dimension, such as physical growth during childhood, individuals generally have only minor transitional or adjustment problems, if they have any difficulties at all. But if life events are accelerated or delayed or fail to materialize, the well-being of persons and their associates is negatively affected (Schlossberg, 1984). For instance, if individuals do not develop a positive self-esteem by young adulthood, they may act out in delinquent and inappropriate ways. Theorists such as Jean Piaget, Lawrence Kohlberg, Erik Erikson, Carol Gilligan, and Nancy Schlossberg have addressed issues associated with developmental stages from infancy to old age. The Association for Adult Development and Aging (AADA) is the division within the ACA that particularly focuses on chronological life-span growth after adolescence.

The *aged* are defined here as persons over age 65. Since 1935 age 65 has been seen as the beginning of old age. The Social Security Act of that year designated 65 as the time when people could retire from work and collect retirement funds. When the United States was founded, only 2% of its population was 65 years or older, by 2000 it was 13%, and by 2030 it will be approximately 21% (Cavanaugh, 1997). Reasons for this segment's remarkable growth include high birthrate during the 20th century, immigration policies that favored the admittance of persons who are now growing older, improved health care, better nutrition, and the reduction of infectious diseases (Lefrancois, 1996). Therefore, counselor attention needs to focus on this group.

Historically, counseling older adults has been a misunderstood and neglected area of the profession. For instance, as a group, members of this population receive only 6% of all mental health services (less than half of what might be expected since approximately 15% of the elderly population in the United States manifest at least moderate emotional problems) (Hashimi, 1991; Turner & Helms, 1994). In part, this situation stems from the group's unique developmental concerns, especially those involving financial, social, and physical losses.

In the mid-1970s, Blake (1975) and Salisbury (1975) raised counselor awareness about counseling older adults by respectively noting a lack of articles on this population in the counseling literature and a dearth of counselor education programs offering an elective course on the aged and their special needs. By the mid-1980s, the situation had changed.

Based on a national survey, Myers (1983) reported that 36% of all counseling programs offered one or more courses on working with older people. That percentage has continued to increase along with new studies on the aged (Hollis, 1997; Myers, Poidevant, & Dean, 1991). In 1992, gerontological counseling became a specialty area regulated by the National Board of Certified Counselors (NBCC) (Myers, 1995).

Old Age

Several prominent theories of aging, many of them multidimensional, have been proposed. For instance, Birren, Schaie, and Gatz (1996) view aging from a biological, psychological, and social perspective, recognizing that the multidimensional process may be uneven. Aging is a natural part of development (DeLaszlo, 1994; Erikson, 1963; Friedan, 1993; Havighurst, 1959). People have specific tasks to accomplish as they grow older. For example, Erikson views middle and late adulthood as a time when the individual must develop a sense of generativity and ego integrity or become stagnant and despairing. Jung believes spirituality is a domain that those over 40 are uniquely qualified to explore.

Neugarten (1978), stressing development, sees two major periods of old age. The *young-old* are those between ages 55 and 75 who are still active physically, mentally, and socially, whether they are retired or not. The *old-old* are individuals beyond age 75 whose physical activity is far more limited. The effects of decline with age are usually more apparent in the old-old population, although patterns of aging are clearly unique.

Despite an increased understanding of aging and an ever-growing number of older adults, the elderly have to deal with age-based expectations and prejudices. For instance, "older people often are tagged with uncomplimentary labels such as senile, absentminded, and helpless" (McCracken, Hayes, & Dell, 1997, p. 385). These negative attitudes and stereotypes, which are known as *ageism,* prevent intimate encounters with people in different age groups and sometimes lead to outright discrimination (Butler, 1988, 1998; Kimmel, 1988; Levenson, 1981). Unfortunately, individuals who are growing older often deny and dread the process, a phenomenon that Friedan (1993) calls "the age mystique." Even counselors are not immune to ageist attitudes (Blake, 1982).

Needs of the Aged

Older adults in the United States must deal with a wide variety of complex issues in their transition from midlife to senior citizen status, including changes in physical abilities, social roles, and relationships (Cox, 1995). Many of these changes have the potential to spark an identity crisis within the person. Pulvino and Colangelo (1980) state that the developmental demands of older adults are probably second only to those of young children. According to Havighurst (1959), older adults must learn to cope successfully with (a) the death of friends and spouses, (b) reduced physical vigor, (c) retirement and the reduction of income, (d) more leisure time and the process of making new friends, (e) the development of new social roles, (f) dealing with grown children, and (g) changing living arrangements or making satisfactory ones.

Some of the required changes associated with aging are gradual, such as the loss of physical strength. Others are abrupt, such as death. Overall, aging is a time of both "positive and negative transitions and transformations" (Myers, 1990a, p. 249). Positive transitions for older adults involve a gain for the individual, such as becoming a grandparent or receiving a discount on purchases. Transitions that involve a high level of stress are those connected with major loss, such as the death of a spouse, the loss of a job, or the contraction of a major illness. In these situations many older adults struggle because they lack a peer support group through which to voice their grief and work through emotions (Morgan, 1994).

Major problems of the aged include loneliness, physical illness, retirement, idleness, bereavement, and abuse (Morrissey, 1998; Shanks, 1982). In addition, members of this group suffer more depression and psychosis as they grow older, with approximately 30% of the beds in mental hospitals being occupied by the elderly. About 25% of all reported suicides are committed by persons over age 60, with white males being especially susceptible. *Domestic elder abuse*—"any form of maltreatment by someone who has a special relationship with the elder," including neglect—is problematic, too (Morrissey, 1998, p. 14).

Counseling the Aged

Most counselors interested in working with the aged need additional professional training in this specialty (Myers, 1990b; Schlossberg, 1990; Sinick, 1979). Many simply do not understand older adults and therefore do not work with them. Such may be especially true in regard to new phenomena regarding older adults, such as grandparents raising grandchildren (Pinson-Milburn, Fabian, Schlossberg, & Pyle, 1996). In such situations, counseling-related services may need to be offered on multiple levels such as direct outreach interventions like teaching new coping strategies and skill training. In addition, indirect or supportive interventions may be needed, such as grandparent support groups, family support groups, and the sponsoring of events such as "Grandparents Day" at school.

Another reason that older people do not receive more attention from mental health specialists is the *investment syndrome* described by Colangelo and Pulvino (1980). According to these authors, some counselors feel their time and energy are better spent working with younger people "who may eventually contribute to society" (p. 69). Professionals who display this attitude are banking on future payoffs from the young and may well be misinformed about the possibilities for change in older adults.

A third reason that older adults may not receive attention from counselors and mental health specialists is the irrational fear of aging and the psychological distancing from older persons that this fear generates (Neugarten, 1971).

One broad and important approach to working successfully with the aged is to treat them as adults (Cox & Waller, 1991). Old age is a unique life stage and involves continuous growth. When the aged are treated with respect and empathy, they are likely to respond appropriately.

Another strategy for promoting change in the aged is to modify the attitudes of people within the systems in which they live (Colangelo & Pulvino, 1980; Ponzo, 1978; Sinick, 1980). Many societal attitudes negatively influence older people's attitudes about themselves. Often, older adults act old because their environments encourage and support such behavior. Hansen and Prather (1980) point out that American society "equates age with obsolescence and orders its priorities accordingly" (p. 74). Therefore, counselors must become educators and advocates for change in societal attitudes if destructive age restrictions and stereotypes are to be overcome. "We need to develop a society that encourages people to stop acting their age and start being themselves" (Ponzo, 1978, pp. 143–144).

In addition to treating the aged with respect and working for changes in systems, counselors can help older adults deal with specific and immediate problems. Tomine (1986) asserts that counseling services for the elderly are most helpful if they are portable and practical, such as being educational and focused on problem solving. For example, Hitchcock (1984) reviewed successful programs to help the elderly obtain employment. A particularly successful program was a job club for older job seekers, where participants at regular meetings shared information on obtaining employment. For older adults with Alzheimer's disease, counseling based on Rogers's theories and Carkhuff's practical application is beneficial in the early stages of the disease. Group counseling, based on Yalom's existential writings, may be productive in helping family members cope as the disease progresses (LaBarge, 1981). A structured life-review process has also proven beneficial in working with the elderly (Beaver, 1991; Westcott, 1983). This approach helps them integrate the past and prepare themselves for the future. Short-term rational emotive behavioral exercises have been used successfully with some older adults in increasing rational thinking and decreasing anxiety about aging (Keller, Corake, & Brooking, 1975).

The following groups are among the most popular for adults age 65 and older (Gladding, 1999):

- *Reality-oriented groups,* which help orient confused group members to their surroundings
- *Remotivation therapy groups,* which are aimed at helping older clients become more invested in the present and the future
- *Reminiscing groups,* which conduct life reviews to help members become more personally integrated
- *Psychotherapy groups,* which are geared toward specific problems of the aging, such as loss
- *Topic-specific groups,* which center on relevant areas of interest to the aging, such as health or the arts
- *Member-specific groups,* which focus on particular transition concerns of individual members, such as hospitalization or dealing with in-laws

In working with the aged, counselors often become students of life and older persons become their teachers (Kemp, 1984). When this type of open attitude is achieved, clients are more likely to deal with the most important events in their lives, and counselors are more prone to learn about a different dimension of life and be helpful in the process.

Gender-Based Counseling

The third population considered in this chapter focuses on counseling based according to gender and sexual orientation. Clients have distinct needs and concerns that are determined in part by the cultural climates and social groups in which they live and develop (Cook, 1993; Moore & Leafgren, 1990). Women and men are "basically cultural-social beings" (McFadden, 1996, p. 234). Counselors who are not fully aware of the influence of societal discrimination, stereotypes, and role expectations based on gender are not likely to succeed in helping their clients in counseling. Effective counseling requires special knowledge and insight that focuses on one's sex and sexual orientation issues.

There is no longer any debate over the question of whether counselors need to possess specialized knowledge and skill in counseling women and men as separate groups. Both genders have much in common, but because women and men "experience different developmental challenges," they may need different styles of interaction from professionals (Nelson, 1996, p. 343). Furthermore, counselors who work more with one gender or another may need in-depth training and experience in particular areas. For example, women in the United States suffer from major depression at twice the rate of men (7 million compared with 3.5 million) (McGrath, Keita, Strickland, & Russo, 1990). This finding holds true across cultures and countries, even when definitions of depression change (Shea, 1998). At least part of the reason may be that women are more prone to focus inwardly and passively on their emotions, a phenomenon known as *ruminative coping*.

Counseling Women

Women are the primary consumers of counseling services (Wastell, 1996). They have special needs related to biological differences and socialization patterns that make many of their counseling concerns different from men's (Cook, 1993). Women still lack the degree of freedom, status, access, and acceptance that men possess, although their social roles and career opportunities have expanded considerably since the 1960s when the women's movement influenced substantial changes. As a group, women have quite different concerns about fundamental issues such as intimacy, career options, and life development (Bradley, Gould, & Hayes, 1992). Among the group's major concerns are development and growth, depression, eating disorders, sexual victimization, widowhood, and multiple roles.

Counseling women "is not a simple matter of picking a counseling theory or approach and commencing treatment" (Hanna, Hanna, Giordano, & Tollerud, 1998, p. 181). Rather, counselors' attitudes, values, and knowledge may either facilitate or impede the potential development of women clients. Women are basically relational beings, and counselors' approaches should be geared toward that fact (Davenport & Yurich, 1991; Nelson, 1996). An examination of the literature indicates that professionals who counsel women should be "highly empathic, warm, understanding, and sufficiently well developed as a person to appreciate the predicament in which women find themselves" (Hanna et al., 1998, p. 167).

Unfortunately, evidence indicates that some counselors and health professionals still hold sex-role stereotypes of women (Simon, Gaul, Friedlander, & Heatherington, 1992), and some counselors are simply uninformed about particular difficulties that women face in general or at different stages of their lives. For example, on a developmental level, there is "a noticeable gap in the literature with respect to studies on women in midlife who are childless, single, disabled, lesbian, ethnic minorities, or members of extended family networks" (Lippert, 1997, p. 17). False assumptions, inaccurate beliefs, and a lack of counselor understanding may all contribute to the problems of women clients. It is important that counselors consider sociopolitical as well as other factors when counseling members of this population.

Committees and task forces within professional counseling organizations have been formed to address issues related to counseling women. For instance, there is a national Commission on Women within ACA, and APA has devoted its Division 35 exclusively to the psychology of women. In addition, APA's Division 17 (Counseling Psychology) sponsors an active Committee on Women.

Concerns in Counseling Women.

One of the major concerns in counseling women revolves around the issue of adequate information about their lives. Many early theories of the nature and development of women, especially those based on psychoanalytic principles, tended to characterize women as innately "passive, dependent, and morally inferior to men" (Hare-Mustin, 1983, p. 594). Those theories promoted the status quo in regard to women and limited their available options (Garfield, 1981; Lewis, Hayes, & Bradley, 1992). The general standard of healthy adult behavior came to be identified with men, and a double standard of mental health evolved with regard to adult females (Lawler, 1990; Nicholas, Gobble, Crose, & Frank, 1992). This double standard basically depicted adult female behavior as less socially desirable and healthy, a perception that lowered expectations for women's behavior and set up barriers against their advancement in nontraditional roles (Broverman, Broverman, Clarkson, Rosenkrantz, & Vogel, 1970).

However, the literature in the field of women's studies and female psychology has grown from only three textbooks in the early 1970s to a plethora of texts and articles today. Many of these publications have been written by women to correct some older theoretical views generated by men without firsthand knowledge of women's issues (Axelson, 1993; Enns, 1993; Lerner, 1988). For example, some theorists have proposed that women's development is in marked contrast to Erikson's psychosocial stages of development. These theorists stress the uniqueness of women and connectedness rather than separation.

A second major concern in counseling women involves sexism, which Goldman (1972) describes as "more deep rooted than racism" (p. 84). *Sexism* is the belief (and the behavior resulting from that belief) that females should be treated on the basis of their sex without regard to other criteria, such as interests and abilities. Such treatment is arbitrary, illogical, counterproductive, and self-serving. In the past, sexism has been blatant, such as limiting women's access to certain professions and encouraging them to pursue so-called pink-collar jobs that primarily employ women, such as nursing. Today, sexism is much more subtle, involving acts more of "omission rather than commission" (Leonard & Collins, 1979, p. 6). Many acts of omission result from lack of information or a failure to change beliefs in light of new facts. In either case, sexism hurts not only women but society in general.

Issues and Theories of Counseling Women.

One of the main issues in counseling women involves the counselor's response to them as individuals and as a group. Women are diverse, and it is important for counselors to react to women in regard to their uniqueness as well as their similarity (Cook, 1993; Van Buren, 1992). Counselors should recognize that specialized knowledge is required for counseling women at various stages of life, such as childhood and adolescence (Bradley et al., 1992), midlife (Lippert, 1997), and old age (Myers, 1992). Counselors must also understand the dynamics of working with females under various conditions, such as eating disorders (Marino, 1994), sexual abuse and rape (Enns, 1996), suicide (Rogers, 1990), and career development (Scott & Hatalla, 1990).

Johnson and Scarato (1979) have presented a model that outlines major areas of knowledge about the psychology of women. It proposes seven areas in which counselors should increase their knowledge of women and thereby decrease prejudice: (a) history and sociology of sex-role stereotyping, (b) psychophysiology of women and men, (c) theories of personality and sex-role development, (d) life-span development, (e) special populations, (f) career development, and (g) counseling/psychotherapy. In the last area, the authors focus on alternatives to traditional counseling approaches as well as specific problems of women.

Thames and Hill (1979) assert that, beyond the issue of basic knowledge, effective counselors of women need to be skilled in four areas of counseling: verbal, nonverbal, process, and techniques. They must also be able to apply appropriate intervention skills for special populations of women. Finally, counselors must be aware of personal difficulties they may have in dealing with female clients.

A major approach to working with women in counseling is *feminist theory*. Feminist views of counseling sprang from the eruption of the women's movement in the 1960s. Initially, this movement was a challenge to patriarchal power; but as it grew, its focus centered on the development of females as persons with common and unique qualities (Okun, 1990). Beginning with the publication of Carol Gilligan's *In a Different Voice* (1982), there has been an increased integration of feminist theory into counseling. This approach encourages individuals to become more aware of socialization patterns and personal options in altering traditional gender roles as they make changes and encourages clients to become involved in social change activities that stress equality as a way of bringing about change (Enns & Hackett, 1993).

In many respects, feminist theory is more an approach to counseling rather than a well-formulated set of constructs. It is assertive in challenging and questioning attitudes of traditional counseling theories because these models often advocate the maintenance of the status quo of a male-dominated, hierarchical society. Two main emphases in the feminist position distinguish it from other forms of helping:

- Its emphasis on equality in the helping relationship, which stems from a belief that women's problems are inseparable from society's oppression of women (Okun, 1997)
- Its emphasis on valuing social, political, and economic action as a major part of the process of treatment

Androgyny, the importance of relationships, the acceptance of one's body "as is," and nonsexist career development are also stressed in feminist thought (Boyce, 1988). Overall, "feminist theory starts with the experience of women and uses women's values and beliefs as the assumptive framework" (Nwachuku & Ivey, 1991, p. 106).

Counseling Men

An outgrowth of the focus on counseling women and eliminating sexism is new attention to the unique concerns and needs of men. "Although research on men and masculinity has a long history " within the past 20 years, there has been increasing research interest in men, masculinity, and the male experience" (Wade, 1998, p. 349). In the early 1980s, Collison (1981) pointed out that "there seem to be fewer counseling procedures tailored to men than to women " (p. 220). That situation has since changed, and "the burgeoning interest in men's psychology has led to a greater demand for clinical services tailored explicitly for men" (Johnson & Hayes, 1997, p. 302).

Concerns in Counseling Men.
Concerns related to counseling men often stem from their socialization. Part of men's general social behavior can be explained by the fact that men's traditional sex roles are more narrowly defined than women's. For example, during childhood, girls are rewarded for being emotionally or behaviorally expressive; boys are reinforced primarily for nonemotional physical actions. Thus, many men internalize their emotional reactions and seek to be autonomous, aggressive, and competitive (Scher & Stevens, 1987). They are oriented to display fighterlike rather than nurturing behavior, and they often "perceive themselves as losing power and status by changing in the direction of androgyny," especially in young adulthood (Brown, 1990, p. 11). Thus, as a group men operate primarily from a cognitive perspective (Pollack & Levant, 1998; Scher, 1979). Affective expression is usually eschewed because of a lack of experience in dealing with it and the anxiety it creates.

In such constrictive roles, an insensitivity to the needs of others and self often develops, and a denial of mental and physical problems becomes lethal in the form of shorter life spans (Jourard, 1971). In addition, "men find psychological safety in independence and fear closeness" (Davenport & Yurich, 1991, p. 65). Therefore, counselors who work with men need to be aware that many of them will be loners and reticent to talk. Because of this isolation, they may well minimize their behaviors and others' actions. Most times they are not being obstinate but simply displaying behaviors they have been reinforced for. Many men incorporate in childhood social taboos about self-disclosure, especially before other men.

Scher (1981) provides guidelines to assist counselors in understanding the realities of men's situations, including (a) an emphasis on the difficulty of change for most men, (b) the constraints imposed by sex-role stereotypes, (c) the importance of asking for assistance and dealing with affective issues, and (d) the need to distinguish between differences of roles and rules in one's personal and work lives.

As a group, men are more reluctant than women to seek counseling (Worth, 1983). Most men enter counseling only in crisis situations because they are generally expected to be self-sufficient, deny needs, and take care of others (Moore & Leafgren, 1990). Men have unique concerns at different age and stage levels (Moore & Leafgren, 1990). Thus, when working with men, it is important to consult developmental models, such as those by Erikson (1968) and Levinson (1978), that underscore developmental themes.

Issues and Theories in Counseling Men.
Many myths as well as realities exist about counseling men (Kelly & Hall, 1994). When males are able to break through traditional restrictions, they usually work hard in counseling and see it as if it were another competition. They have high expectations of the process and want productive sessions. Thus, as a group, they are likely to be clear and sincere in the process and express themselves directly and honestly.

The dominance of cognitive functioning in men creates special challenges for counselors. Marino (1979) advises counselors to stay away from the cognitive domain in working with men and explore with them the feeling tones of their voices, the inconsistencies of their behaviors and feelings, and their ambivalence about control and nurturance. Scher (1979) also advises moving the client from the cognitive to the affective realm and recommends that the process be started by explaining to men clients the importance of owning feelings in overcoming personal difficulties and then working patiently with men to uncover hidden affect.

In contrast to eschewing the cognitive domain, Burch and Skovholt (1982) suggest that Holland's (1979) model of person-environment interaction may serve as the framework for understanding and counseling men. In this model, men are most likely to operate in the realistic dimension of functioning. Such individuals usually lack social skills but possess mechanical-technical skills; therefore, the authors recommend that counselors adopt a cognitive-behavioral approach to establish rapport and facilitate counseling. Giles (1983) disagrees with this idea, pointing out that no conclusive research supports it. He believes that counselors are not necessarily effective when they alter the counseling approach to fit the personal typology of clients.

Given the emphasis on interpersonal learning in groups, working with men in this way may be an effective intervention strategy (Andronica, 1997; Jolliff, 1994). The goals of men's groups are to increase personal awareness of sex-role conditioning, practice new desired behaviors, and promote a lifestyle based on the individual's needs. Three types of men—male sex offenders, gay men, and homeless men—may especially benefit from group work (DeAngelis, 1992). Men who do not do well in groups are those who are manic, very depressed, in severe crisis, addicted, inebriated, or paranoid (Horne & Mason, 1991).

Group work for men in general can be powerful in cutting through defenses, such as denial, and building a sense of community. To be effective, the counselor must publicize the availability of such a group, screen potential candidates carefully, identify specific behaviors on which to focus, institute opening and closing rituals, and develop intervention strategies aimed at resolving deep psychological issues such as conflict management (Hetzel, Barton, & Davenport, 1994; Horne & Mason, 1991).

In working with men in groups, Moore and Haverkamp (1989) found, in a well-controlled study, that "men age 30 to 50 are able to increase their level of affective expression, as measured by both self-report and behavioral tests" (p. 513). During this developmental stage of life, many men are seeking to become more intimate, deepen their relationships, and deal directly with their emotions. Thus, a group for men at this level of maturity can be very effective in producing change, especially, as the authors state, when it follows a social-learning paradigm in which other men serve as models and reinforcers for new behaviors. The impact of Robert Bly and the *mythopoetic movement* (the use of myths and poetry with men in groups) is one example of the power of such a paradigm for change (Erkel, 1990).

While promoting change and an exploration of affective issues, it is crucial that counselors be aware that rules within most men's world of work differ from those within the personal domain. Counselors must caution men not to naively and automatically introduce newly discovered behaviors that work in their personal lives into what may be a hostile environment—that is, the world of work.

Counseling with men, as with all groups, is a complex phenomenon; but the potential benefits are enormous. They include helping men develop productive strategies for dealing with expectations and changing roles (Moore & Leafgren, 1990). Through counseling, men may also develop new skills applicable to "marital communication, stress-related health problems, career and life decision making, and family interaction" (Moore & Haverkamp, 1989, p. 516). A particularly powerful procedure that may be employed with select men involves having them interview their fathers. Using a series of structured, open-ended questions about family traditions, these men make discoveries about themselves by understanding their fathers more clearly. This new understanding can serve as a catalyst for implementing different behaviors within their own families.

Counseling and Sexual Orientation

In ending this section on gender, it is important to address sexual orientation because not all men and women are heterosexual. Whether one approves or not, individuals have different lifestyles and distinct social and sexual orientations (Dworkin & Gutierrez, 1989). At least 10% of the population in the United States is composed of gays, lesbians, and bisexuals. These individuals are often stereotyped and discriminated against. A number of myths and stereotypes have grown up around them over the years, such as that members of this population are child molesters and that same-sex relationships never last (Chen-Hayes, 1997). Within the American Counseling Association, the Association for Gay, Lesbian, and Bisexual Issues in Counseling (AGLBIC) deals with concerns specifically related to these populations.

Difficulties usually begin for gays, lesbians, and bisexuals early in life. Children who are oriented toward any of these lifestyles frequently have trouble growing up in regard to their identity. They often have feelings of isolation and stigmatization, and trouble with peer relationships, as well as family disruptions (Marinoble, 1998). Even some counselors are less accepting of members of these population than one might expect. As Rudolph (1989) states, "ministering to the psychotherapy needs of homosexuals [and bisexuals] has historically been an exercise in dissatisfaction and discomfort for many clients and counselors" (p. 96).

The majority culture, which professional helpers represent, has a predominantly negative view of persons who do not have a heterosexual orientation. When these views are voiced in strong, dogmatic ways, they can have a detrimental impact on the mental health and well-being of gays, lesbians, and bisexuals and may severely disrupt their total development. For example, in career decision making, gay men often lack role models and are directed often into socially stereotyped occupations (Hetherington, Hillerbrand, & Etringer, 1989).

In any minority culture that is treated with prejudice, people suffer and the overall culture is negatively affected. Similar to the growth in other areas of multicultural counseling, a current movement is working to sensitize counselors to issues faced by gays, lesbians, and bisexuals, such as "coming out," forming community organizations, following religious practices, and coping with AIDS, anger, and relationships (House & Miller, 1997). Now that conservative politics have become stronger in American society and AIDS cases have risen, working with gays, lesbians, and bisexuals is bound to be an unpopular activity in many locales but one that can do much good if conducted properly.

Counseling and Spirituality

A final area that we will address in this multicultural and diversity chapter is spirituality, a complex, multidimensional construct. "At present, there is no generally agreed on definition of spirituality" (Ganje-Fling & McCarthy, 1996, p. 253). However, the importance of spirituality in counseling has been voiced by such luminaries as Carl Jung, Victor Frankl, Abraham Maslow, and Rollo May. *Spirituality* usually refers to a unique, personally meaningful experience of a transcendent dimension that is associated with wholeness and wellness (Hinterkopf, 1997; Westgate, 1996).

In a comprehensive overview of spirituality, religion, and counseling, Ingersoll (1994) points out the importance of defining spirituality and lists dimensions that describe it:

A concept of the divine or a force greater than oneself
A sense of meaning
A relationship with the divine
Openness to mystery
A sense of playfulness
Engagement in spiritually enhancing activities
Systematic use of spiritual forces as an integrator of life

Thus, one's spiritual journey often involves an active search toward overcoming one's current centricity to becoming more connected with the meaning of life, including a oneness of ultimate Being (Chandler, Holden, & Kolander, 1992; Kelly, 1995).

Within counseling is an increased emphasis on spirituality and its importance in the well-being of those seeking help and wishing to maintain their own health (Burke & Miranti, 1995; Hudson, 1998). "Spiritual competencies for counselors have been proposed and distributed nationally and are beginning to be assimilated into counselor training programs" (Myers & Truluck, 1998, p. 120). Three events of recent years have profoundly affected the attitude on spirituality in America at large and indirectly in counseling. One has been the "informal spirituality promulgated by Alcoholics Anonymous, Adult Children of Alcoholics, and other 12-step programs" (Butler, 1990, p. 30). Another has been the writings of Scott Peck, whose books, especially *The Road Less Traveled* (1978), bridge the gap between traditional psychotherapy and religion. The final event has been the film series featuring Joseph Campbell, as interviewed by Bill Moyers, in which Campbell gives "respectability to the spiritual-psychological quest itself, even in modern-times" (Butler, 1990, p. 30).

It is impossible to determine the reasons behind the mass attraction of these three events. However, the Association for Spiritual, Ethical, and Religious Values in Counseling (ASERVIC), a division within the ACA, rapidly grew in the 1990s. There were also renewed emphases on the counselor as a spiritual person (Goud, 1990; Kottler, 1986) and the use of clients' values to aid progress in counseling (Aust, 1990; Goldberg, 1994).

Ingersoll (1994) states that counselors interested in working well with clients committed to a particular spiritual view can best do so by affirming the importance of spirituality in the client's life, using language and imagery in problem solving and treatment that is congruent with the client's worldview, and consulting with other "healers" in the client's life such as ministers. This process calls for cultural sensitivity as well as ethical practices of the highest standard. Thus, asking about a client's spirituality or spiritual resources has become more of a fundamental intake question in many counseling practices, as counselors address the total person of the client.

Sometimes spirituality is manifested in a particular philosophy or religious belief, such as Zen, Buddhism, or Christianity. At other times, it is more nebulous. Regardless of the form spirituality takes, spiritual aspects of clients' lives can be enhanced through creating rituals or other ways for clients to focus on their lives that help them appreciate life rather than depreciate themselves. For example, one ritual distraught clients might be invited to engage in is writing down five things for which they grateful (Hudson, 1998). Such an assignment can help them move away from bitterness and transcend the adversity of the moment.

In addition to helping clients, forms of spirituality, such as meditation and prayer, may be important aspects of counselors' lives as well. Kelly (1995) found in a nationally representative sample of ACA-affiliated counselors that the majority of respondents valued spirituality in their lives (even more than institutionalized religion). In many cases, a "counselor's personal spirituality/religiousness may prove a value base for being attuned to clients' spiritual and religious issues" (Kelly, 1995, p. 43). Therefore, counselors should assess their own spirituality as well as that of their clients.

Summary and Conclusion

In this chapter we have examined counseling issues related to special areas: the culturally different, the aged, women and men (including sexual orientation), and spirituality. There is a wealth of material in the professional literature on the general concerns of each group and on the counseling theories and techniques most appropriate for working with these populations and topics. Indeed, specialty courses and counseling concentrations that focus on one or more of these groups are offered in many graduate counselor education programs.

Although information on a special population may appear unrelated to other populations, it is not. A common theme is that counselors who work with a variety of clients must be knowledgeable about them collectively and individually be able to deal effectively with their common and unique concerns. Stereotypes and prescribed roles are assigned to members of distinct cultural groups, the aged, members of genders (including gays, lesbians, and bisexuals), and even the spiritually oriented. Cultural limitations on these restrict not only the growth of the people involved in them but the larger society as well. Overcoming traditions, prejudices, fears, and anxieties and learning new skills based on accurate information and sensitivity are major parts of counseling in a multicultural and pluralistic society.

When working with specific groups, counselors need to be aware of uniqueness and common concerns. They must also realize the limitations and appropriateness of counseling theories they employ. Talking and self-disclosure are not valued in many cultures, especially with someone outside one's own tradition. Likewise, gender and sexual orientation are factors in displaying feelings and revealing personal weaknesses. Age and one's spiritual development also play a part in the counseling process. The aged need to express emotions and resolve past conflicts in their own unique ways if they are to benefit from counseling. Similarly, the spiritually oriented may wish to resolve difficulties or focus on issues in nontraditional ways.

Counselors must constantly ask themselves how each of their clients is similar to and different from others. What are within- and between-group universals and uniquenesses?

They must concentrate on increasing their sensitivity to global issues as well as individual concerns. When clients differ significantly from counselors, extra attention and skill must be devoted to establishing and cultivating the counseling relationship.

CLASSROOM ACTIVITIES

1. Talk with a person from a different cultural background, and discuss the difficulties that he or she faces. How many of these problems are culturally related? How many are unique to the person? Present your findings to the class. What similarities do you and your classmates find in the results? Discuss your personal interviews as they relate to the material presented in this chapter.

2. Research counseling approaches offered in other countries. How do the theories and techniques generated in these cultures fit the needs of individuals in their societies? How do you think the counseling approach you have researched would work in the United States?

3. Role-play the following situation with another class member. Imagine that you have reached age 65. What are you doing at this age? What are your needs and expectations? How might a counselor help you? Do you find your life perspective different from your present outlook? Discuss these questions in relation to Ponzo's (1978) advice that individuals need to be themselves, not act their age.

4. Divide the class according to gender. Have the males in the class assume traditional female roles and vice versa. Then discuss making decisions about a career and marriage. Talk about what feelings each side of the class has in relation to the decision-making process. Discuss how these feelings would differ if one had a gay, lesbian, or bisexual orientation.

5. Discuss the following question in groups of three. What is the place of spirituality in counseling? Share your opinions with the class.

REFERENCES

Allison, K. W., Crawford, I., Echemendia, R., Robinson, L., & Knepp, D. (1994). Human diversity and professional competence. *American Psychologist, 49,* 792–796.

Andronico, M. P. (Ed.). (1997). *Men in groups: Insights, interventions, and psychoeducational work.* Washington, DC: American Psychological Association.

Arredondo, P. (1998). Integrating multicultural counseling competencies and universal helping conditions in culture-specific contexts. *Counseling Psychologist*, 26, 592–601.

Aust, C. F. (1990). Using client's religious values to aid progress in therapy. *Counseling and Values, 34,* 125–129.

Avasthi, S. (1990). Native American students targeted for math and sciences. *Guidepost, 33*(6), 1, 6, 8.

Axelson, J. A. (1993). *Counseling and development in a multicultural society* (2nd ed.). Pacific Grove, CA: Brooks/Cole.

Baruth, L. G., & Manning, M. L. (1999). *Multicultural counseling and psychotherapy* (2nd ed.). Upper Saddle River, NJ: Merrill/Prentice Hall.

Beaver, M. L. (1991). Life review/reminiscent therapy. In P. K. H. Kim (Ed.), *Serving the elderly: Skills for practice* (pp. 67–89). New York: Aldine de Gruyter.

Bell, D. A. (1985, July 15 and 22). America's great success story: The triumph of Asian Americans. *The New Republic, 3678/3679,* 24–31.

Birren, J. E., Schaie, K. W., & Gatz, M. (Eds.). (1996). *Handbook of the psychology of aging* (4th ed.). San Diego: Academic Press.

Blake, R. (1975). Counseling in gerontology. *Personnel and Guidance Journal, 53,* 733–737.

Blake, R. (1982). Assessing the counseling needs of older persons. *Measurement and Evaluation in Guidance, 15,* 188–193.

Boyer, S. P., & Sedlacek, W. E. (1989). Noncognitive predictors of counseling center use by international students. *Journal of Counseling and Development, 67,* 404–407.

Bradley, L. J., Gould, L. J., & Hayes, B. A. (1992). The impact of gender social role socialization. In J. A. Lewis, B. A. Hayes, & L. J. Bradley (Eds.), *Counseling women over the life span* (pp. 55–76). Denver: Love.

Brinson, J. A. (1996). Cultural sensitivity for counselors: Our challenge for the twenty-first century. *Journal of Humanistic Education and Development, 34,* 195–206.

Broverman, I., Broverman, D., Clarkson, F., Rosenkrantz, P., & Vogel, S. (1970). Sexrole stereotypes and clinical judgments of mental health. *Journal of Consulting and Clinical Psychology, 34,* 1–7.

Brown, N. M. (1990). Men nurturing men. *Family Therapy Networker, 14,* 11.

Burch, M. A., & Skovholt, T. M (1982). Counseling services and men in need: A problem in person-environment matching. *AMHCA Journal, 4,* 89–96.

Burke, M. T., and Miranti, J. G. (1995). *Counseling: The spiritual dimension.* Alexandria, VA: American Counseling Association.

Butler, K. (1990). Spirituality reconsidered. *Family Therapy Networker, 14,* 26–37.

Butler, R. N. (1988). Ageism. In G. L. Maddox (Ed.), *Encyclopedia of aging* (pp. 22–23). New York: Springer.

Butler, R. N. (1998). *Aging and mental health: Positive psychosocial and biomedical approaches* (5th ed.). Boston: Allyn & Bacon.

Cavanaugh, J. C. (1997). *Adult development and aging.* Pacific Grove, CA: Brooks/Cole.

Chandler, C. K., Holden, J. M., & Kolander, C. A. (1992). Counseling for spiritual wellness: Theory and practice. *Journal of Counseling and Development, 71,* 168–175.

Chen-Hayes, S. F. (1997). Counseling lesbian, bisexual, and gay persons in couple and family relationships: Overcoming the stereotypes. *Family Journal, 5,* 236–240.

Cheung, F. K. (1991). The use of mental health services by ethnic minorities. In H. F. Myers, P. Wholford, L. P. Guzman, & R. J. Echemendia (Eds.), *Ethnic minority perspectives on clinical training and services in psychology* (pp. 23–31). Washington, DC: American Psychological Association.

Cohen, M. N. (1998, April 17). Culture, not race, explains human diversity. *Chronicle of Higher Education,* B4–B5.

Colangelo, N., & Pulvino, C. J. (1980). Some basic concerns in counseling the elderly. *Counseling and Values, 24,* 68–73.

Coleman, H. L. K. (1998). General and multicultural counseling competency: Apples and oranges? *Journal of Multicultural Counseling and Development, 26,* 147–156.

Collison, B. B. (1981). Counseling adult males. *Personnel and Guidance Journal, 60,* 219–222.

Cook, E. P. (Ed.). (1993). *Women, relationships, and power: Implications for counseling.* Alexandria, VA: American Counseling Association.

Corsini, R. J., & Wedding, D. (Eds.). (1995). *Current psychotherapies* (5th ed.). Itasca, IL: Peacock.

Cox, B. J., & Waller, L. L. (1991). *Bridging the communication gap with the elderly.* Chicago: American Hospital Association.

Cox, H. G. (1995). *Later life: The realities of aging* (5th ed.). Upper Saddle River, NJ: Prentice Hall.

Das, A. K. (1987). Indigenous models of therapy in traditional Asian societies. *Journal of Multicultural Counseling and Development, 15,* 25–37.

Davenport, D. S., & Yurich, J. M. (1991). Multicultural gender issues. *Journal of Counseling & Development, 70,* 64–71.

DeAngelis, T. (1992, November). Best psychological treatment for many men: Group therapy. *APA Monitor, 23,* 31.

DeLaszlo, V. S. (1994). *The basic writings of C. G. Jung.* New York: Modern Library.

Dworkin, S. H., & Gutierrez, F. (1989). Special issue: Gay, lesbian, and bisexual issues in counseling. *Journal of Counseling and Development, 68,* 6–8.

Enns, C. Z. (1993). Twenty years of feminist counseling and therapy. *Counseling Psychologist, 21,* 3–87.

Enns, C. Z. (1996). Counselors and the backlash: "Rape hype" and "false-memory syndrome." *Journal of Counseling & Development, 74*, 358–367.

Enns, C. Z., & Hackett, G. (1993). A comparison of feminist and nonfeminist women's and men's reactions to nonsexist and feminist counseling: A replication and extension. *Journal of Counseling and Development, 71*, 499–509.

Epp, L. R. (1998). The courage to be an existential counselor: An interview with Clemmont E. Vontress. *Journal of Mental Health Counseling, 20*, 1–12.

Erikson, E. H. (1963). *Childhood and society* (2nd ed.). New York: Norton.

Erikson, E. H. (1968). *Identity, youth and crisis.* New York: Norton.

Erkel, R. T. (1990, May/June). The birth of a movement. *Family Therapy Networker, 14*, 26–35.

Friedan, B. (1994). *The fountain of age.* New York: Touchstone.

Ganje-Fling, M. A., & McCarthy, P. (1996). Impact of childhood sexual abuse on client spiritual development: Counseling implications. *Journal of Counseling and Development, 74*, 253–258.

Garfield, S. L. (1981). Psychotherapy: A forty year appraisal. *American Psychologist, 36*, 174–183.

Garretson, D. J. (1993). Psychological misdiagnosis of African Americans. *Journal of Multicultural Counseling and Development, 21*, 119–126.

Geertz, C. (1973). *The interpretation of cultures.* New York: Basic Books.

Giles, T. A. (1983). Counseling services and men in need: A response to Burch and Skovholt. *AMHCA Journal, 5*, 39–43.

Gilligan, C. (1982). *In a different voice: Psychological theory and women's development.* Cambridge, MA: Harvard University Press.

Gladding, S. T. (1999). *Group work: A counseling specialty* (3rd ed.). Upper Saddle River, NJ: Merrill/Prentice Hall.

Goldberg, J. R. (1994, June). Spirituality, religion and secular values: What role in psychotherapy? *Family Therapy News, 25*, 9, 16–17.

Goldman, L. (1972). Introduction. *Personnel and Guidance Journal, 51*, 85.

Gonzalez, G. M. (1997). The emergence of Chicanos in the twenty-first century: Implications for counseling, research, and policy. *Journal of Multicultural Counseling and Development, 25*, 94–106.

Goud, N. (1990). Spiritual and ethical beliefs of humanists in the counseling profession. *Journal of Counseling and Development, 68*, 571–574.

Hammerschlag, C. A. (1988). *The dancing healers.* San Francisco: Harper & Row.

Hanna, C. A., Hanna, F. J., Giordano, F. G., & Tollerud, T. (1998). Meeting the needs of women in counseling: Implications of a review of the literature. *Journal of Humanistic Education and Development, 36*, 160–170.

Hansen, J. C., & Prather, F. (1980). The impact of values and attitudes in counseling the aged. *Counseling and Values, 24*, 74–85.

Hare-Mustin, R. T. (1983). An appraisal of the relationship between women and psychotherapy. *American Psychologist, 38*, 593–599.

Harper, F. D. (1994). Afrinesians of the Americas: A new concept of ethnic identity. *Journal of Multicultural Counseling and Development, 22*, 3–6.

Hashimi, J. (1991). Counseling older adults. In P. K. H. Kim (Ed.), *Serving the elderly: Skills for practice* (pp. 33–51). New York: Aldine de Gruyter.

Havighurst, R. J. (1959). Social and psychological needs of the aging. In L. Gorlow & W. Katkovsky (Eds.), *Reading in the psychology of adjustment* (pp. 443–447). New York: McGraw-Hill.

Hayes, P. A. (1996). Addressing the complexities of culture and gender in counseling. *Journal of Counseling and Development, 74*, 332–338.

Heinrich, R. K., Corbin, J. L., & Thomas, K. R. (1990). Counseling native Americans. *Journal of Counseling and Development, 69*, 128–133.

Henkin, W. A. (1985). Toward counseling the Japanese in America: A cross-cultural primer. *Journal of Counseling and Development, 63*, 500–503.

Herring, R. D. (1996). Synergetic counseling and Native American Indian students. *Journal of Counseling & Development, 74*, 542–547.

Herring, R. D. (1997). The creative arts: An avenue to wellness among Native American Indians. *Journal of Humanistic Education and Development, 36*, 106–113.

Hetherington, C., Hillerbrand, E., & Etringer, B. D. (1989). Career counseling with gay men: Issues and recommendations for research. *Journal of Counseling and Development, 67*, 452–453.

Hetzel, R. D., Barton, D. A., & Davenport, D. S. (1994). Helping men change: A group counseling model for male clients. *Journal for Specialists in Group Work, 19,* 52–64.

Hinterkopf, E. (1998). *Integrating spirituality in counseling: A manual for using the experiential focusing method.* Alexandria, VA: American Counseling Association.

Hitchcock, A. A. (1984). Work, aging, and counseling. *Journal of Counseling and Development, 63,* 258–259.

Hodgkinson, H. L. (1992). *A demographic look at tomorrow.* Washington, DC: Institute for Educational Leadership.

Holiday, M., Leach, M. M., & Davidson, M. (1994). Multicultural counseling and intrapersonal value conflict: A case study. *Counseling and Values, 38,* 136–142.

Holland, J. L. (1979). *The self-directed search: Professional manual.* Palo Alto, CA: Consulting Psychologists Press.

Hollis, J. W. (1997). *Counselor preparation 1996–1998* (9th ed.). Muncie, IN: Accelerated Development.

Horne, A. M., & Mason, J. (1991, August). *Counseling men.* Paper presented at the Annual Convention of the American Psychological Association, San Francisco.

House, R. M., & Miller, J. L. (1997). Counseling gay, lesbian, and bisexual clients. In D. Capuzzi & D. R. Gross (Eds.), *Introduction to the counseling profession* (2nd ed., pp. 397–432). Boston: Allyn & Bacon.

Hudson, P. (1998, April/May). Spirituality: A growing resource. *Family Therapy News, 29*(2), 10–11.

Ingersoll, R. E. (1994). Spirituality, religion, and counseling: Dimensions and relationships. *Counseling and Values, 38,* 98–111.

Ivey, A. E. (1977). Cultural expertise: Toward systematic outcome criteria in counseling and psychological education. *Personnel and Guidance Journal, 55,* 296–302.

Ivey, A. E. (1987). Cultural intentionality: The core of effective helping. *Counselor Education and Supervision, 25,* 168–172.

Ivey, A. E. (1990). Prejudice in the profession. *Guidepost, 33*(6), 2.

Johnson, M., & Scarato, A. M. (1979). A knowledge base for counselors of women. *Counseling Psychologist, 8,* 14–16.

Johnson, W. B., & Hayes, D. N. (1997). An identity-focused counseling group for men. *Journal of Mental Health Counseling, 19,* 295–303.

Jolliff, D. (1994). Group work with men. *Journal for Specialists in Group Work, 19,* 50–51.

Jourard, S. (1971). *The transparent self.* Princeton, NJ: Van Nostrand.

Katz, J. H. (1985). The sociopolitical nature of counseling. *Counseling Psychologist, 13,* 615–624.

Keller, J. F., Corake, J. W., & Brooking, J. Y. (1975). Effects of a program in rational thinking on anxieties in older persons. *Journal of Counseling Psychology, 22,* 54–57.

Kelly, E. W., Jr. (1995). *Spirituality and religion in counseling and psychotherapy.* Alexandria, VA: American Counseling Association.

Kelly, K. R., & Hall, A. S. (1994). Affirming the assumptions of the developmental model for counseling men. *Journal of Mental Health Counseling, 16,* 475–482.

Kemp, J. T. (1984). Learning from clients: Counseling the frail and dying elderly. *Personnel and Guidance Journal, 62,* 270–272.

Kimmel, D. C. (1988). Ageism, psychology, and public policy. *American Psychologist, 43,* 175–178.

Kottler, J. A. (1986). *On being a therapist.* San Francisco: Jossey-Bass.

LaBarge, E. (1981). Counseling patients with senile dementia of the Alzheimer type and their families. *Personnel and Guidance Journal, 60,* 139–142.

Lawler, A. C. (1990). The healthy self: Variations on a theme. *Journal of Counseling and Development, 68,* 652–654.

Lee, C. C. (1989). AMCD: The next generation. *Journal of Multicultural Counseling and Development, 17,* 165–170.

Lee, C. C. (Ed.). (1997). *Multicultural issues in counseling* (2nd ed.). Alexandria, VA: American Counseling Association.

Lefrancois, G. R. (1996). *The lifespan* (5th ed.). Belmont, CA: Wadsworth.

Leonard, M. M., & Collins, A. M. (1979). Woman as footnote. *Counseling Psychologist, 8,* 6–7.

Lerner, H. G. (1988). *Women in therapy.* Northvale, NJ: Aronson.

Levenson, A. J. (1981). Ageism: A major deterrent to the introduction of curricula in aging. *Gerontology and Geriatrics Education, 1,* 161–162.

Levinson, D. (1978). *The seasons of a man's life.* New York: Knopf.

Lewis, J. A., Hayes, B. A., & Bradley, L. J. (Eds.). (1992). *Counseling women over the life span.* Denver: Love.

Lippert, L. (1997). Women at midlife: Implications for theories of women's adult development. *Journal of Counseling and Development, 76,* 16–22.

Locke, D. C. (1990). A not so provincial view of multicultural counseling. *Counselor Education and Supervision, 30,* 18–25.

Locke, D. C. (1998, Spring). Beyond U.S. borders. *American Counselor, 1,* 13–16.

Marino, T. M. (1979). Resensitizing men: A male perspective. *Personnel and Guidance Journal, 58,* 102–105.

Marino, T. M. (1994, December). Starving for acceptance. *Counseling Today, 37,* 1, 4.

Marinoble, R. M. (1998). Homosexuality: A blind spot in the school mirror. *Professional School Counseling, 1,* 4–7.

McCracken, J. E., Hayes, J. A., & Dell, D. (1997). Attributions of responsibility for memory problems in older and younger adults. *Journal of Counseling and Development, 75,* 385–391.

McFadden, J. (Ed.) (1993). *Transcultural counseling.* Alexandria, VA: American Counseling Association.

McFadden, J., & Lipscomb, W. D. (1985). History of the Association for Non-white Concerns in Personnel and Guidance. *Journal of Counseling and Development, 63,* 444–447.

McGrath, E., Keita, G. F., Strickland, N. R., & Russo, N. (1990). *Women and depression.* Washington, DC: American Psychological Association.

Middleton, R. A., Flowers, C., & Zawaiza, T. (1996). Multiculturalism, affirmative action, and section 21 of the 1992 Rehabilitation Act amendments: Fact or fiction? *Rehabilitation Counseling Bulletin, 40,* 11–30.

Moore, D., & Haverkamp, B. E. (1989). Measured increases in male emotional expressiveness following a structured group intervention. *Journal of Counseling and Development, 67,* 513–517.

Moore, D., & Leafgren, F. (Eds.). (1990). *Problem solving strategies and interventions for men in conflict.* Alexandria, VA: American Counseling Association.

Morgan, J. P., Jr. (1994). Bereavement in older adults. *Journal of Mental Health Counseling, 16,* 318–326.

Morrissey, M. (1997, October). The invisible minority: Counseling Asian Americans. *Counseling Today,* 1, 21.

Morrissey, M. (1998, January). The growing problem of elder abuse. *Counseling Today,* 14.

Myers, J. E. (1983). A national survey of geriatric mental health services. *AMHCA Journal, 5,* 69–74.

Myers, J. E. (1990a). Aging: An overview for mental health counselors. *Journal of Mental Health Counseling, 12,* 245–259.

Myers, J. E. (Ed.). (1990b). Techniques for counseling older persons. *Journal of Mental Health Counseling, 12,* 245–394.

Myers, J. E. (1992). Mature women: Confronting the social stereotypes. In J. A. Lewis, B. A. Hayes, & L. J. Bradley (Eds.), *Counseling women over the life span* (pp. 211–240). Denver: Love.

Myers, J. E. (1995). From "forgotten and ignored" to standards and certification: Gerontological counseling comes of age. *Journal of Counseling and Development, 74,* 143.

Myers, J. E., Poidevant, J. M., & Dean, L. A. (1991). Groups for older persons and their caregivers: A review of the literature. *Journal for Specialists in Group Work, 16,* 197–205.

Myers, J. E., & Truluck, M. (1998). Human beliefs, religious values, and the counseling process: A comparison of counselors and other mental health professionals. *Counseling and Values, 42,* 106–123.

Nelson, M. L. (1996). Separation versus connection: The gender controversy: Implications for counseling women. *Journal of Counseling and Development, 74,* 339–344.

Neugarten, B. (1971, December). Grow old along with me! The best is yet to be. *Psychology Today,* pp. 48–56.

Neugarten, B. L. (1978). The rise of the young-old. In R. Gross, B. Gross, & S. Seidman (Eds.), *The new old: Struggling for decent aging* (pp. 47–49). New York: Doubleday.

Nicholas, D. R., Gobble, D. C., Crose, R. G., & Frank, B. (1992). A systems view of health, wellness, and gender: Implications for mental health counseling. *Journal of Mental Health Counseling, 14,* 8–19.

Nwachuka, U., & Ivey, A. (1991). Culture-specific counseling: An alternative model. *Journal of Counseling & Development, 70,* 106–111.

Okun, B. F. (1990). *Seeking connections in psychotherapy*. San Francisco: Jossey-Bass.

Okun, B. F. (1997). *Effective helping* (5th ed.). Pacific Grove, CA: Brooks/Cole.

Okun, B. F., Fried, J., & Okun, M. L. (1999). *Understanding diversity: A learning-as-practice primer*. Pacific Grove, CA: Brooks/Cole.

Papalia, D. E., & Olds, S. W. (1998). *Human development* (7th ed.). New York: McGraw-Hill.

Parker, W. M., Archer, J., & Scott, J. (1992). *Multicultural relations on campus*. Muncie, IN: Accelerated Development.

Peck, M. S. (1978). *The road less traveled*. New York: Simon & Schuster.

Pedersen, P. (1987). Ten frequent assumptions of cultural bias in counseling. *Journal of Multicultural Counseling and Development, 15,* 16–22.

Pedersen, P. (1990). The constructs of complexity and balance in multicultural counseling theory and practice. *Journal of Counseling and Development, 68,* 550–554.

Pedersen, P. B. (1977). The triad model of cross-cultural counselor training. *Personnel and Guidance Journal, 56,* 94–100.

Pedersen, P. B. (1978). Four dimensions of cross-cultural skill in counselor training. *Personnel and Guidance Journal, 56,* 480–484.

Pedersen, P. B. (1982). Cross-cultural training for counselors and therapists. In E. Marshall & D. Kurtz (Eds.), *Interpersonal helping skills: A guide to training methods, programs, and resources*. San Francisco: Jossey-Bass.

Pedersen, P., Lonner, W. J., & Draguns, J. G. (Eds.). (1976). *Counseling across cultures*. Honolulu: University Press of Hawaii.

Pinson-Milburn, N. M., Fabian, E. S., Schlossberg, N. K., & Pyle, M. (1996). Grandparents raising grandchildren. *Journal of Counseling & Development, 74,* 548–554.

Pinterits, E. J., & Atkinson, D. R. (1998). The diversity video forum: An adjunct to diversity sensitive training in the classroom. *Counselor Education and Supervision, 37,* 203–216.

Pollack, W. S., & Levant, R. F. (Eds.). (1998). *New psychotherapies for men*. New York: Wiley.

Ponterotto, J. G., & Sabnani, H. B. (1989). "Classics" in multicultural counseling: A systematic five-year content analysis. *Journal of Multicultural Counseling and Development, 17,* 23–37.

Ponzo, Z. (1978). Age prejudice of "act your age." *Personnel and Guidance Journal, 57,* 140–144.

Pope-Davis, D. B., & Ottavi, T. M. (1994). The relationships between racism and racial identity among white Americans. *Journal of Counseling and Development, 72,* 293–297.

Priest, R. (1991). Racism and prejudice as negative impacts on African American clients in therapy. *Journal of Counseling and Development, 70,* 213–215.

Pulvino, C. J., & Colangelo, N. (1980). Counseling the elderly: A developmental perspective. *Counseling and Values, 24,* 139–147.

Richardson, E. H. (1981). Cultural and historical perspectives in counseling American Indians. In D. W. Sue (Ed.), *Counseling the culturally different* (pp. 216–249). New York: Wiley.

Rogers, J. R. (1990). Female suicide: The trend toward increased lethality in method of choice and its implications. *Journal of Counseling and Development, 69,* 37–38.

Romero, D., Silva, S. M., & Romero, P. S. (1989). In memory: Rene A. Ruiz. *Journal of Counseling and Development, 67,* 498–505.

Rudolph, J. (1989). The impact of contemporary ideology and AIDS on the counseling of gay clients. *Counseling and Values, 33,* 96–108.

Ruiz, R. A. (1981). Cultural and historical perspectives in counseling Hispanics. In D. W. Sue (Ed.), *Counseling the culturally different* (pp. 186–215). New York: Wiley.

Ruiz, R. A., & Padilla, A. M. (1977). Counseling Latinos. *Personnel and Guidance Journal, 55,* 401–408.

Salisbury, A. (1975). Counseling older persons: A neglected area in counselor education and supervision. *Counselor Education and Supervision, 4,* 237–238.

Sanders, D. (1987). Cultural conflicts: An important factor in the academic failures of American Indian students. *Journal of Multicultural Counseling and Development, 15,* 81–90.

Sandhu, D. S. (1997). Psychocultural profiles of Asian and Pacific Islander Americans: Implications for counseling and psychotherapy. *Journal of Multicultural Counseling and Development, 25,* 7–22.

Scher, M. (1979). On counseling men. *Personnel and Guidance Journal, 57,* 252–254.

Scher, M. (1981). Men in hiding: A challenge for the counselor. *Personnel and Guidance Journal, 60,* 199–202.

Scher, M., & Stevens, M. (1987). Men and violence. *Journal of Counseling and Development, 65,* 351–355.

Schlossberg, N. K. (1984). *Counseling adults in transition: Linking practice with theory.* New York: Springer.

Schlossberg, N. K. (1990). Training counselors to work with older adults. *Generations, 15,* 7–10.

Scott, J., & Hatalla, J. (1990). The influence of chance and contingency factors on career patterns of college-educated women. *Career Development Quarterly, 39,* 18–30.

Shanks, J. L. (1982). Expanding treatment for the elderly: Counseling in a private medical practice. *Personnel and Guidance Journal, 61,* 553–555.

Shea, C. (1998, January 30). Why depression strikes more women than men: "Ruminative coping" may provide answers. *Chronicle of Higher Education, 44,* A14.

Simon, L., Gaul, R., Friedlander, M. L., & Heatherington, L. (1992). Client gender and sex role: Predictors of counselors' impressions and expectations. *Journal of Counseling and Development, 71,* 48–52.

Sinick, D. (1979). Professional development in counseling older persons. *Counselor Education and Supervision, 19,* 4–12.

Sinick, D. (1980). Attitudes and values in aging. *Counseling and Values, 24,* 148–154.

Smith, E. J. (1977). Counseling black individuals: Some stereotypes. *Personnel and Guidance Journal, 55,* 390–396.

Smith, E. M. J., & Vasquez, M. J. T. (1985). Introduction. *Counseling Psychologist, 13,* 531–536.

Sue, D. W. (1978). Counseling across cultures. *Personnel and Guidance Journal, 56,* 451.

Sue, D. W. (1992, Winter). The challenge of multiculturalism. *American Counselor, 1,* 6–14.

Sue, D. W., Arredondo, P., & McDavis, R. J. (1992). Multicultural counseling competencies and standards: A call to the profession. *Journal of Counseling & Development, 70,* 477–486.

Sue, D. W., Ivey, A. E., & Pedersen, P. (1996). *A theory of multicultural counseling and therapy.* Pacific Grove, CA: Brooks/Cole.

Sue, D. W., & Sue, D. (1973). Understanding Asian-Americans: The neglected minority: An overview. *Personnel and Guidance Journal, 51,* 387–389.

Sue, D. W., & Sue, D. (1990). *Counseling the culturally different: Theory and practice* (2nd ed.). New York: Wiley.

Sue, D. W., & Sue, S. (1972). Counseling Chinese-Americans. *Personnel and Guidance Journal, 50,* 637–644.

Super, D. E. (1954). Guidance: Manpower utilization or human development? *Personnel and Guidance Journal, 33,* 8–14.

Super, D. E. (1983). Synthesis: Or is it distillation? *Personnel and Guidance Journal, 61,* 511–514.

Thames, T. B., & Hill, C. E. (1979). Are special skills necessary for counseling women? *Counseling Psychologist, 8,* 17–18.

Tomine, S. (1986). Private practice in gerontological counseling. *Journal of Counseling and Development, 64,* 406–409.

Turner, J., & Helms, D. (1994). *Lifespan development* (5th ed.). Chicago: Holt, Rinehart.

Valle, R. (1986). Cross-cultural competence in minority communities: A curriculum implementation strategy. In M. R. Miranda & H. H. L. Kitano (Eds.), *Mental health research and practice in minority communities: Development of culturally sensitive training programs* (pp. 29–49). Rockville, MD: National Institute of Mental Health. (ERIC Document Reproduction Service No. ED 278 754)

Van Buren, J. (1992). Gender-fair counseling. In J. A. Lewis, B. Hayes, & L. J. Bradley (Eds.), *Counseling women over the life span* (pp. 271–289). Denver: Love.

Vontress, C. E. (1966). Counseling the culturally different adolescent: A school-community approach. In J. C. Gowan & G. Demos (Eds.), *The disadvantaged and potential dropout* (pp. 357–366). Springfield, IL: Thomas.

Vontress, C. E. (1967). The culturally different. *Employment Service Review, 4,* 35–36.

Vontress, C. E. (1996). A personal retrospective on cross-cultural counseling. *Journal of Multicultural Counseling and Development, 16,* 73–83.

Vontress, C. E., & Epp, L. R. (1997). Historical hostility in the African client: Implications for counseling. *Journal of Multicultural Counseling and Development, 25,* 170–184.

Wade, J. C. (1998). Male reference group identity dependence: A theory of male identity. *Counseling Psychologist, 26,* 349–383.

Walsh, R. (1995). Asian psychotherapies. In R. J. Corsini & D. Wedding (Eds.), *Current psychotherapies* (5th ed., pp. 387–398). Itasca, IL: Peacock.

Wastell, C. A. (1996). Feminist development theory: Implications for counseling. *Journal of Counseling & Development, 74,* 575–581.

Watanabe, C. (1973). Self-expression and the Asian American experience. *Personnel and Guidance Journal, 51,* 390–396.

Weinrach, S. G., & Thomas, K. R. (1996). The counseling profession's commitment to diversity-sensitive counseling: A critical reassessment. *Journal of Counseling & Development, 73,* 472–477.

Weinrach, S. G., & Thomas, K. R. (1998). Diversity-sensitive counseling today: A postmodern clash of values. *Journal of Counseling & Development, 76,* 115–122.

Wendel, P. (1997, October). Cultural bias among minority counselors. *Counseling Today,* 1, 20.

Westcott, N. A. (1983). Application of the structured life-review technique in counseling elders. *Personnel and Guidance Journal, 62,* 180–181.

Westgate, C. E. (1996). Spiritual wellness and depression. *Journal of Counseling and Development, 75,* 26–35.

Worth, M. R. (1983). Adults. In J. A. Brown & R. H. Pate, Jr., (Eds.), *Being a counselor* (pp. 230–252). Pacific Grove, CA: Brooks/Cole.

Wrenn, C. G. (1962). The culturally encapsulated counselor. *Harvard Educational Review, 32,* 444–449.

PART II

COUNSELING PROCESS AND THEORY

Counseling is a process guided by theory. Chapters 5 through 7 discuss three major stages of the process: building, working in, and terminating a relationship. For each stage, the universal qualities and problems associated with it are outlined. Regardless of their theoretical orientation, counselors must be aware of the process of counseling.

Chapters 8 through 11 describe and discuss major theories of individual counseling. The theories included are among the most popular in the profession. They have been modified for work with families and groups, and other theories have evolved from them. Because the majority of counselors are eclectic as practitioners, counseling from an eclectic viewpoint is emphasized early in Chapter 8. Systems theory is the only major theoretical perspective not covered in this section. It is discussed in Chapter 12, which focuses on marriage and family counseling—a specialty that theoretically views the world from a connected and interrelated perspective.

5

BUILDING A COUNSELING RELATIONSHIP

◆

Your words splash heavily upon my mind

like early cold October rain

falling on my roof at dusk.

The patterns change like an autumn storm

from violently rumbling thundering sounds

to clear, soft steady streams of expression.

Through it all I look at you

soaked in past fears and turmoil;

Then patiently I watch with you in the darkness

for the breaking of black clouds

that linger in your turbulent mind

And the dawning of your smile

that comes in the light of new beginnings.

From "Autumn Storm," by S. T. Gladding, 1975, Personnel and Guidance Journal, 54, p. 149. © 1975 by ACA. Reprinted with permission. No further reproduction authorized without written permission of the American Counseling Association.

The process of counseling develops in definable stages with recognizable transitions. The first stage involves building a relationship and focuses on engaging clients to explore issues that directly affect them. Two struggles take place at this time (Napier & Whitaker, 1978). One is the battle for structure, *which involves issues of administrative control (e.g., scheduling, fees, participation in sessions). The other is the* battle for initiative, *which concerns motivation for change and client responsibility. It is essential that counselors win the first battle and clients win the second. If there are failures at these points, the counseling effort will be prematurely terminated, and both the counselor and client may feel worse for the experience.*

Other factors that influence the progress and direction of counseling are the physical setting, the client's background, the counselor's skill, and the quality of the relationship established. They will be examined here as well as the nature of the first interview and the exploration stage of counseling. Carkhuff (1969) and Ivey (1971, 1994) have demonstrated that some counseling responses cut across theoretical lines in helping build a client-counselor relationship. These responses are sometimes known as microskills *and include atheoretical and social-learning behaviors such as attending, encouraging, reflecting, and listening. When mastered, these abilities allow counselors to be with their clients more fully, "act in a culturally appropriate manner, and find positives in life experience" (Weinrach, 1987, p. 533). Thus, part of this chapter will focus on microskills.*

Factors That Influence the Counseling Process

A number of factors affect the counseling process for better or worse. Those covered here are structure, initiative, physical setting, client qualities, and counselor qualities.

Structure

Clients and counselors sometimes have different perceptions about the purpose and nature of counseling. Clients often do not know what to expect from the process or how to act (Riordan, Matheny, & Harris, 1978). Seeing a counselor is a last resort for many individuals. They are likely to have already sought help from more familiar sources, such as friends, family members, ministers, or teachers (Hinson & Swanson, 1993). Therefore, many clients enter counseling reluctantly and hesitantly. This uncertainty can inhibit the counseling process unless some structure is provided (Ritchie, 1986). *Structure* in counseling is defined as "a joint understanding between the counselor and client regarding the characteristics, conditions, procedures, and parameters of counseling" (Day & Sparacio, 1980, p. 246). Structure helps clarify the counselor-client relationship and give it direction; protect the rights, roles, and obligations of both counselors and clients; and ensure the success of counseling (Brammer, Abrego, & Shostrom, 1993; Day & Sparacio, 1980).

Practical guidelines are part of building structure. They include time limits (such as a 50-minute session), action limits (for the prevention of destructive behavior), role limits (what will be expected of each participant), and procedural limits (in which the client is given the responsibility to work on specific goals or needs) (Brammer & MacDonald, 1996; Goodyear & Bradley, 1980; Kelly & Stone, 1982). Guidelines also provide information on fee schedules and other important concerns of clients. In general, structure promotes the development of counseling by providing a framework in which the process can take place. "It is therapeutic in and of itself" (Day & Sparacio, 1980, p. 246).

Structure is provided throughout all stages of counseling but is especially important at the beginning. Dorn (1984) states that "clients usually seek counseling because they are in a static behavior state" (p. 342). That is, clients feel stuck and out of control to change behavior. To help clients gain new directions in their lives, counselors provide constructive guidelines. Their decisions on how to establish this structure are based on their theoretical orientation to counseling, the personalities of their clients, and the major problem areas with which they will deal. Too much structure can be just as detrimental as not enough (Patterson & Welfel, 1994). Therefore, counselors need to stay flexible and continually negotiate the nature of the structure with their clients.

The importance of structure is most obvious when clients arrive for counseling with unrealistic expectations (Patterson & Welfel, 1994). Counselors need to move quickly to establish structure at such times. One way is for counselors to provide information about the counseling process and themselves with professional disclosure statements such as the counselor-client contract depicted in Figure 5.1 (Gill, 1982). These statements often define a counselor's philosophy of human nature as well as the purposes, expectations, responsibilities, methods, and ethics of counseling.

Initiative

Initiative can be thought of as the motivation to change. Ritchie (1986) notes that most counselors and counseling theories assume that clients will be cooperative. Indeed, many clients come to counseling on a voluntary or self-referred basis. They experience tension and concern about themselves or others, but they are willing to work hard in counseling sessions. Other clients, however, are more reserved about participating in counseling. Vriend and Dyer (1973) estimate that the majority of clients who visit counselors are reluctant to some degree. When counselors meet clients who seem to lack initiative, they often do not know what to do with them, much less how to go about doing it. Therefore, some counselors are impatient, irritated, and may ultimately give up trying to work with such persons (Doyle, 1998). The result is not only termination of the relationship but also *scapegoating*, blaming a person when the problem was not entirely his or her fault. Many counselors end up blaming themselves or their clients if counseling is not successful (West, 1975). Such recriminations need not occur if counselors understand the dynamics involved in working with difficult clients. Part of this understanding involves assuming the role of an involuntary client and imagining how it would feel to come for counseling. A role-reversal exercise can promote counselor empathy in dealing with reluctant and resistant clients.

A *reluctant client* is one who has been referred by a third party and is frequently "unmotivated to seek help" (Ritchie, 1986, p. 516). Many schoolchildren and court-

A COUNSELOR-CLIENT CONTRACT

By Joseph Wittmer, Ph.D., NCC, and Theodore P. Remley, J.D., Ph.D., NCC

The following statement was written by Joe Wittmer, Ph.D., NCC, and Theodore P. Remley, J.D., Ph.D., NCC. Wittmer is Distinguished Service Professor and Department Chair, Department of Counselor Education, at the University of Florida, Gainesville. Remley holds both a law degree and a Ph.D. in Counselor Education. He is chairperson of the Counselor Education Department at the University of New Orleans.

Our profession is becoming more attuned to client rights as well as to counselor accountability. The client-counselor contract given here addresses both of these important issues. Please feel free to change and use the contract as you deem appropriate. However, be aware of the laws in your state, the uniqueness of your own setting, and your own competencies in your use of the contract. NBCC considers this document particularly helpful to those formulating state mandated disclosure statements used in most licensure states.

INFORMATION AND CONSENT

Qualification/Experience:

I am pleased you have selected me as your counselor. This document is designed to inform you about my background and to insure that you understand our professional relationship.

I am licensed by (your state) as a Professional Counselor. In addition, I am certified by the National Board for Certified Counselors, a private national counselor certifying agency. My counseling practice is limited to (types of clients, i.e. adolescents, personal, career, marriage, etc.).

Nature of Counseling:

I hold a (your post graduate degree or degrees relevant to counseling) from (name of institution[s]) and have been a professional counselor since (year of your master's degree in counseling or related field).

I accept only clients who I believe have the capacity to resolve their own problems with my assistance. I believe that as people become more accepting of themselves, they are more capable of finding happiness and contentment in their lives. However, self-awareness and self-acceptance are goals that sometimes take a long time to achieve. Some clients need only a few counseling sessions to achieve these goals, while others may require months or even years of counseling relationship at any point. I will be supportive of that decision. If counseling is successful, you should feel that you are able to face life's challenges in the future without my support or intervention.

Although our sessions may be very intimate emotionally and psychologically, it is important for you to realize that we have a professional relationship rather than a personal one. Our contact will be limited to the paid sessions you have with me. Please do not invite me to social gatherings, offer gifts, or ask me to relate to you in any way other than in the professional context of our counseling sessions. You will be best served if our relationship remains strictly professional and if our sessions concentrate exclusively on your concerns. You will learn a great deal about

Figure 5.1 A counselor-client contract

me as we work together during your counseling experience. However, it is important for you to remember that you are experiencing me only in my professional role.

Referrals:

If at any time for any reason you are dissatisfied with my services, please let me know. If I am not able to resolve your concerns, you may report your complaints to the Board for Professional Counselors in (your state) at (phone number) or the National Board for Certified Counselors in Greensboro, NC, at 336-547-0607.

Fees, Cancellation and Insurance Reimbursement:

In return for a fee of $_____ per individual session, $_____ per couple/family session, and/or $_____ per group session, I agree to provide services for you. The fee for each session will be due and must be paid at the conclusion of each session. Cash or personal checks are acceptable for payment. In the event that you will not be able to keep an appointment, you must notify me 24 hours in advance. If I do not receive such advance notice, you will be responsible for paying for the session that you missed.

Some health insurance companies will reimburse clients for my counseling services and some will not. In addition, most will require that I diagnose your mental health condition and indicate that you have an "illness" before they will agree to reimburse you. Some conditions for which people seek counseling do not qualify for reimbursement. If a qualifying diagnosis is appropriate in your case, I will inform you of the diagnosis I plan to render before I submit it to the health insurance company. Any diagnosis made will become part of your permanent insurance records.

If you wish to seek reimbursement for my services from your health insurance company, I will be happy to complete any forms related to your reimbursement provided by you or the insurance company. Because you will be paying me each session for my services, any later reimbursement from the insurance company should be sent directly to you. Please do not assign any payments to me.

Those insurance companies that do reimburse for counselors usually require that a standard amount be paid (a "deductible") by you before reimbursement is allowed, and then usually only a percentage of my fee is reimbursable. You should contact a company representative to determine whether your insurance company will reimburse you and what schedule of reimbursement is used.

Records and Confidentiality:

All of our communication becomes part of the clinical record, which is accessible to you on request. I will keep confidential anything you say to me, with the following exceptions: a) you direct me to tell someone else, b) I determine that you are a danger to yourself or others, or c) I am ordered by a court to disclose information.

By your signature below (please sign both copies, keep one for your files and return the other copy to me), you are indicating that you have read and understood this statement, and/or that any questions you have had about this statement have been answered to your satisfaction.

_____   _____
(Counselor's Name and Signature)   (Client's Name and Signature)

Date: _____   Date: _____

Figure 5.1   *continued*

Source: From "A Counselor-Client Contract," by J. Wittmer and T. P. Remley, 1994, *NBCC News Notes, 2,* pp. 12–13. Reprinted with permission of J. Wittmer and T. P. Remley.

referred clients are good examples. They do not wish to be in counseling, let alone talk about themselves. Many reluctant clients terminate counseling prematurely and report dissatisfaction with the process (Paradise & Wilder, 1979).

A *resistant client* is a person in counseling who is unwilling or opposed to change (Otani, 1989; Ritchie, 1986). Such an individual may actively seek counseling but does not wish to go through the pain that change demands. Instead, the client clings to the certainty of present behavior, even when such action is counterproductive and dysfunctional. Some resistant clients refuse to make decisions, are superficial in dealing with problems, and take any action to resolve a problem (i.e., do anything a counselor says). According to Sack (1988), "the most common form of resistance is the simple statement 'I don't know'" (p. 180). Such a response makes the counselor's next move difficult.

Otani (1989) has proposed four broad categories of resistance: "amount of verbalization; content of message; style of communication; and attitude toward counselors and counseling sessions" (p. 459). The 22 forms of resistance included in these categories are shown in Figure 5.2.

Counselors can help clients win the battle for initiative and achieve success in counseling in several ways. One is to anticipate the anger, frustration, and defensiveness that some clients display (Ritchie, 1986). Counselors who realize that a percentage of their clients are reluctant or resistant can work with these individuals because they are not surprised by them or their behaviors.

A second way to deal with a lack of initiative is to show acceptance, patience, and understanding as well as a general nonjudgmental attitude. This stance promotes trust. Nonjudgmental behavior also helps clients better understand their thoughts and feelings about counseling. It opens them up to themselves and the counseling process (Doyle, 1998).

A third way to win the battle for initiative is for counselors to use persuasion (Kerr, Claiborn, & Dixon, 1982; Senour, 1982). All counselors have some influence on clients, and vice versa (Dorn, 1984; Strong, 1982). How a counselor responds to the client, directly or indirectly, can make a significant difference in whether the client takes the initiative in working to produce change. Roloff and Miller (1980) mention two direct persuasion techniques employed in counseling: the "*foot in the door*" and the "*door in the face*." In the first technique, the counselor asks the client to comply with a minor request and then later follows with a larger request. In the second technique, the counselor asks the client to do a seemingly impossible task and then follows by requesting the client to do a more reasonable task.

A fourth way a counselor can assist clients in gaining initiative is through *confrontation*. In this procedure the counselor simply points out to the client exactly what the client is doing, such as being inconsistent. The client then takes responsibility for responding to the confrontation. The three primary ways of responding are denying the behavior, accepting all or part of the confrontation as true, or developing a middle position that synthesizes the first two (Young, 1998). Doing something differently or gaining a new perception on a problem can be a beneficial result of confrontation, especially if what has previously been tried has not worked.

Counselors can also use language, especially metaphors, to soften resistance or reluctance. "Metaphors can be used to teach and reduce threat levels by providing stories, by painting images, by offering fresh insights, by challenging rigid thinking, by permitting tol-

Figure 5.2 Twenty-two forms of resistance

Category A: Response quantity resistance

Definition: The client limits the amount of information to be communicated to the counselor.

Forms
Silence
Minimum talk
Verbosity

Category B: Response content resistance

Definition: The client restricts the type of information to be communicated to the counselor.

Forms
Intellectual talk
Symptom preoccupation
Small talk
Emotional display
Future/past preoccupation
Rhetorical question

Category C: Response style resistance

Definition: The client manipulates the manner of communicating information to the counselor.

Forms
Discounting
Thought censoring/editing
Second-guessing
Seductiveness
Last-minute disclosure
Limit setting
Externalization
Counselor focusing/stroking
Forgetting
False promising

Category D: Logistic management resistance

Definition: The client violates basic rules of counseling.

Forms
Poor appointment keeping
Payment delay/refusal
Personal favor-asking

erance for new beliefs, and by overcoming the tension often present between a counselor and the resistant [or reluctant] client" (James & Hazler, 1998, p. 122). For instance, in addressing a client who keeps repeating the same mistake over again, the counselor might say, "What does a fighter do when he gets badly beaten up every time he fights?" (James & Hazler, 1998, p. 127).

Finally, Sack (1988) recommends the use of pragmatic techniques, such as silence (or pause), reflection (or empathy), questioning, describing, assessing, pretending, and sharing the counselor's perspective, as ways to overcome client resistance. These techniques are especially helpful with individuals who respond to counselor initiatives with "I don't know."

The Physical Setting

Counseling can occur almost anywhere, but some physical settings promote the process better than others. Benjamin (1987) and Shertzer and Stone (1980) address external conditions involved in counseling. Among the most important factors that help or hurt the process is the place where the counseling occurs. Most counseling occurs in a room, although Benjamin (1987) tells of counseling in a tent. He says that there is no universal quality that a room should have "except [that] it should not be overwhelming, noisy, or distracting" (p. 3). Shertzer and Stone (1980) implicitly agree: "The room should be comfortable and attractive" (p. 252). Certain features of a counseling office will improve its general appearance and probably facilitate counseling by not distracting the client. These features include soft lighting, quiet colors, an absence of clutter, harmonious, comfortable furniture, and diverse cultural artifacts. When working with families who have children or with children apart from families, counselors need to have furniture that is child size (Erdman & Lampe, 1996).

The distance between counselor and client (the spatial features of the environment, or *proxemics*) can also affect the relationship. Individuals differ about the level of comfort experienced in interactions with others. Among other things, comfort level is influenced by cultural background, gender, and the nature of the relationship (Shertzer & Stone, 1980; Sielski, 1979). A distance of 30 to 39 inches has been found to be the average range of comfort between counselors and clients of both genders in the United States (Haase, 1970). This optimum distance may vary because of room size and furniture arrangement (Haase & DiMattia, 1976).

How the furniture is arranged depends on the counselor. Some counselors prefer to sit behind a desk during sessions, but most do not. The reason desks are generally eschewed by counselors is that a desk can be a physical and symbolic barrier against the development of a close relationship. Benjamin (1987) suggests that counselors include two chairs and a nearby table in the setting. The chairs should be set at a 90-degree angle from one another so that clients can look either at their counselors or straight ahead. The table can be used for many purposes, such as a place for a box of tissues. Benjamin's ideas are strictly his own; each counselor must find a physical arrangement that is comfortable for him or her.

Regardless of the arrangement within the room, counselors should not be interrupted when conducting sessions. All phone calls should be held. If necessary, counselors should put "do not disturb" signs on the door to keep others from entering. Auditory and visual privacy are mandated by professional codes of ethics and assure maximum client self-disclosure.

Client Qualities

Counseling relationships start with first impressions. The way that counselor and client perceive one another is vital to the establishment of a productive relationship. Warnath (1977) points out that "clients come in all shapes and sizes, personality characteristics, and degrees of attractiveness" (p. 85). Some clients are more likely to be successful in counseling than others. The most successful candidates for traditional approaches tend to be YAVIS: young, attractive, verbal, intelligent, and successful (Schofield, 1964). Less successful candidates are seen as HOUNDs (homely, old, unintelligent, nonverbal, and disadvantaged) or DUDs (dumb, unintelligent, and disadvantaged) (Allen, 1977). These acronyms are cruel (Lichtenberg, 1986), but counselors are influenced by the appearance and sophistication of the people with whom they work. According to Brown (1970), counselors most enjoy working with clients who they think have the potential to change.

Ponzo (1985) notes that a number of stereotypes have been built around the physical attractiveness of individuals (and these stereotypes generalize to clients). The physically attractive are perceived as healthiest and are responded to more positively than others. Goldstein (1973), for instance, found that clients who were seen by their counselors as most attractive talked more and were more spontaneous when compared with other clients. Most likely counselors were more encouraging to and engaged with the attractive clients. Therefore, aging clients and those with physical disabilities may face invisible but powerful barriers in certain counseling situations. Ponzo (1985) suggests that counselors become aware of the importance of physical attractiveness in their own lives and monitor their behavioral reactions when working with attractive clients. Otherwise, stereotypes and unfounded assumptions may "lead to self-fulfilling prophecies" (p. 485).

The nonverbal behaviors of clients are also very important. Clients constantly send counselors unspoken messages about how they think or feel. Mehrabian (1971) and his associates found that expressed like and dislike between individuals could be explained as follows:

> Total liking equals 7% verbal liking plus 38% vocal liking plus 55% facial liking. The impact of facial expression is greatest, then the impact of the tone of voice (or vocal expression), and finally that of the words. If the facial expression is inconsistent with the words, the degree of liking conveyed by the facial expression will dominate and determine the impact of the total message. (p. 43)

Thus, a client who reports that all is going well but who looks down at the ground and frowns while doing so is probably indicating just the opposite. A counselor must consider a client's body gestures, eye contact, facial expression, and vocal quality to be as important as verbal communication in a counseling relationship. It is also crucial to consider the cultural background of the person whose body language is being evaluated and interpret nonverbal messages cautiously (Gazda, Asbury, Balzer, Childers, & Phelps, 1994; Sielski, 1979).

Counselor Qualities

The personal and professional qualities of counselors are very important in facilitating any helping relationship. Okun (1997) notes that it is hard to separate the helper's personality characteristics from his or her levels and styles of functioning, as both are interrelated. She then lists five important characteristics that helpers should possess: self-awareness, honesty, congruence, ability to communicate, and knowledge.

Counselors who continually develop their self-awareness skills are in touch with their values, thoughts, and feelings. They are likely to have a clear perception of their own and their clients' needs and accurately assess both. Such awareness can help them be honest with themselves and others. They are able to be more congruent and build trust simultaneously. Counselors who possess this type of knowledge are most likely to communicate clearly and accurately.

Three other characteristics that make counselors initially more influential are perceived expertness, attractiveness, and trustworthiness (Strong, 1968). *Expertness* is the degree to which a counselor is perceived as knowledgeable and informed about his or her specialty. Counselors who display evidential cues in their offices, such as certificates and diplomas, are usually perceived as more credible than those who do not and, as a result, are likely to be effective (Loesch, 1984; Siegal & Sell, 1978). Clients want to work with counselors who appear to know the profession well.

Attractiveness is a function of perceived similarity between a client and counselor as well as physical features. Counselors can make themselves attractive by speaking in clear, simple, jargon-free sentences and offering appropriate self-disclosure (Watkins & Schneider, 1989). The manner in which a counselor greets the client and maintains eye contact can also increase the attractiveness rating. Counselors who use nonverbal cues in responding to clients, such as head nodding and eye contact, are seen as more attractive than those who do not (Claiborn, 1979; LaCross, 1975). The attire of the counselor also makes a difference (Hubble & Gelso, 1978). Clothes should be clean, neat, and professional looking but not call attention to themselves. Physical features make a difference, too, in that under controlled conditions, research suggests individuals are more willing to self-disclose to an attractive counselor than to an unattractive one (Harris & Busby, 1998).

Trustworthiness is related to the sincerity and consistency of the counselor. The counselor is genuinely concerned about the client and shows it over time by establishing a close relationship. "There is and can be no such thing as instant intimacy" or trustworthiness (Patterson, 1985, p. 124). Rather, both are generated through patterns of behavior that demonstrate care and concern. Most clients are neither completely distrusting nor given to blind trust. But, as Fong and Cox (1983) note, many clients test the trustworthiness of the counselor by requesting information, telling a secret, asking a favor, inconveniencing the counselor, deprecating themselves, or questioning the motives and dedication of the counselor. It is essential, therefore, that the counselor respond to the question of trust rather than the verbal content of the client in order to facilitate the counseling relationship.

Many beginning counselors make the mistake of dealing with surface issues instead of real concerns. For example, if a client asks a counselor, "Can I tell you anything?" a novice counselor might respond, "What do you mean by anything?" An experienced counselor might say, "It sounds as if you are uncertain about whether you can really trust me and this relationship. Tell me more." Trust with children, like adults, is built by listening first and allowing children the freedom to express themselves openly on a verbal or nonverbal level before the counselor responds (Erdman & Lampe, 1996).

Types of Initial Interviews

The counseling process begins with the initial session. Levine (1983) points out that authorities in the profession have observed that "the goals of counseling change over time and change according to the intimacy and effectiveness of the counseling relationship" (p. 431). How much change happens or whether there is a second session is usually determined by the results of the first session.

In the first session, both counselors and clients work to decide whether they want to or can continue the relationship. Counselors should quickly assess whether they are capable of handling and managing clients' problems through being honest, open, and appropriately confrontive (Okun, 1997). On the other hand, clients must ask themselves whether they feel comfortable with and trust the counselor before they can enter the relationship wholeheartedly.

Client- versus Counselor-Initiated Interviews

Benjamin (1987) distinguishes between two types of first interviews: those initiated by clients and those initiated by counselors. When the initial interview is requested by a client, the counselor is often unsure of the client's purpose. This uncertainty may create anxiety in the counselor, especially if background information is not gathered before the session. Benjamin (1987) recommends that counselors work to overcome these feelings by listening as hard as possible to what clients have to say. In such situations, as with counseling in general, listening "requires a submersion of the self and immersion in the other" (Nichols, 1998, p. 1). There is no formula for beginning the session. The helping interview is as much an art as a science, and every counselor must work out a style based on experience, stimulation, and reflection. The counselor is probably prudent not to inquire initially about any problem the client may have because the client may not have a problem in the traditional sense of the word and may just be seeking information.

When the first session is requested by the counselor, Benjamin (1987) believes that the counselor should immediately state his or her reason for wanting to see the client. In the case of a school counselor, for instance, a session might be requested so that the counselor can introduce him- or herself to the client. If the counselor does not immediately give a reason for requesting the session, the client is kept guessing and tension is created.

Patterson and Welfel (1994) think that all clients enter counseling with some anxiety and resistance regardless of prior preparation. Benjamin (1987) hypothesizes that most counselors are also a bit frightened and uncertain when conducting a first interview. Uncertain feelings in both clients and counselors may result in behaviors such as seduction or aggression (Watkins, 1983). Counselors can prevent such occurrences by exchanging information with clients. Manthei (1983) advocates that counselors' presentations about themselves and their functioning be *multimodal*: visual, auditory, written, spoken, and descriptive. Although such presentations may be difficult, they pay off by creating good counselor-client relationships. Overall, early exchanges of information increase the likelihood that clients and counselors will make meaningful choices and participate more fully in the counseling process.

Information-Oriented First Interview

Hackney and Cormier (1994) point out that the initial counseling interview can fulfill two functions: (a) it can be an intake interview to collect needed information about the client, or (b) it can signal the beginning of a relationship. Either type of interview is appropriate, and certain tasks are common to both, though the skills emphasized in each differ.

If the purpose of the first interview is to gather information, the structure of the session will be counselor focused: the counselor wants the client to talk about certain subjects. The counselor will respond to the client predominantly through the use of probes, accents, closed questions, and requests for clarification (Hackney & Cormier, 1994). These responses are aimed at eliciting facts.

The *probe* is a question that usually begins with who, what, where, or how. It requires more than a one- or two-word response: for example, "What do you plan to do about getting a job?" Few probes ever begin with the word *why*, which usually connotes disapproval and places a client on the defensive (e.g., "Why are you doing that?") (Benjamin, 1987).

An *accent* is highlighting the last few words of the client. For example:

CLIENT: The situation I'm in now is driving me crazy!
COUNSELOR: Driving you crazy?

A *closed question* is one that requires a specific and limited response, such as yes or no. It often begins with the word *is, do,* or *are* (Galvin & Ivey, 1981):

COUNSELOR: Do you enjoy meeting other people?
CLIENT: Yes.

The closed question is quite effective in eliciting a good deal of information in a short period of time. But it does not encourage elaboration that might also be helpful.

In contrast to the closed question is the *open question,* which typically begins with *what, how,* or *could* and allows the client more latitude to respond. Examples are "How does this affect you?" "Could you give me more information?" and "Tell me more about it." The major difference between a closed and open question "is whether or not the question encourages more client talk" (Galvin & Ivey, 1981, p. 539). It is the difference between a multiple-choice inquiry that checks the facts and an essay in which a deeper level of understanding and explanation is encouraged (Young, 1998).

Finally, a *request for clarification* is a response the counselor uses to be sure he or she understands what the client is saying. These requests require the client to repeat or elaborate on material just covered. For example, a counselor might say, "Please help me understand this relationship" or "I don't see the connection here."

Counselors wish to obtain several facts in an information-oriented first interview. They often assume this information may be used as a part of a psychological, vocational, or psychosocial assessment. Counselors employed by medical, mental health, correctional, rehabilitation, and social agencies are particularly likely to conduct these types of interviews. Hackney and Cormier (1994) outline some of the data counselors gather in these initial sessions (see Figure 5.3).

I. **Identifying data**
   A. Client's name, address, telephone number through which client can be reached. This information is important in the event the counselor needs to contact the client between sessions. The client's address also gives some hint about the conditions under which the client lives (e.g., large apartment complex, student dormitory, private home, etc.).
   B. Age, sex, marital status, occupation (or school class and year). Again, this is information that can be important. It lets you know when the client is still legally a minor and provides a basis for understanding information that will come out in later sessions.

II. **Presenting problems, both primary and secondary**
   It is best when these are presented in exactly the way the client reported them. If the problem has behavioral components, these should be recorded as well. Questions that help reveal this type of information include
   A. How much does the problem interfere with the client's everyday functioning?
   B. How does the problem manifest itself? What are the thoughts, feelings, etc., that are associated with it? What observable behavior is associated with it?
   C. How often does the problem arise? How long has the problem existed?
   D. Can the client identify a pattern of events that surround the problem? When does it occur? With whom? What happens before and after its occurrence?
   E. What caused the client to decide to enter counseling at this time?

III. **Client's current life setting**
   How does the client spend a typical day or week? What social and religious activities, recreational activities, etc., are present? What is the nature of the client's vocational and/or educational situation?

IV. **Family history**
   A. Father's and mother's ages, occupations, descriptions of their personalities, relationships of each to the other and each to the client and other siblings.
   B. Names, ages, and order of brothers and sisters; relationship between client and siblings.
   C. Is there any history of mental disturbance in the family?
   D. Descriptions of family stability, including number of jobs held, number of family moves, etc. (This information provides insights in later sessions when issues related to client stability and/or relationships emerge.)

Figure 5.3 An information-oriented first interview

Relationship-Oriented First Interview

Interviews that focus on feelings or relationship dynamics differ markedly from information-oriented first sessions. They concentrate more on the client's attitudes and emotions. Common counselor responses include restatement, reflection of feeling, summary of feelings, request for clarification, and acknowledgment of nonverbal behavior (Hackney & Cormier, 1994).

V. Personal history

A. Medical history: any unusual or relevant illness or injury from prenatal period to present.

B. Educational history: academic progress through grade school, high school, and post-high school. This includes extracurricular interests and relationships with peers.

C. Military service record.

D. Vocational history: Where has the client worked, at what types of jobs, for what duration, and what were the relationships with fellow workers?

E. Sexual and marital history: Where did the client receive sexual information? What was the client's dating history? Any engagements and/or marriages? Other serious emotional involvements prior to the present? Reasons that previous relationships terminated? What was the courtship like with present spouse? What were the reasons (spouse's characteristics, personal thoughts) that led to marriage? What has been the relationship with spouse since marriage? Are there any children?

F. What experience has the client had with counseling, and what were the client's reactions?

G. What are the client's personal goals in life?

VI. Description of the client during the interview

Here you might want to indicate the client's physical appearance, including dress, posture, gestures, facial expressions, voice quality, tensions; how the client seemed to relate to you in the session; client's readiness of response, motivation, warmth, distance, passivity, etc. Did there appear to be any perceptual or sensory functions that intruded upon the interaction? (Document with your observations.) What was the general level of information, vocabulary, judgment, abstraction abilities displayed by the client? What was the stream of thought, regularity, and rate of talking? Were the client's remarks logical? Connected to one another?

VII. Summary and recommendations

In this section you will want to acknowledge any connections that appear to exist between the client's statement of a problem and other information collected in this session. What type of counselor do you think would best fit this client? If you are to be this client's counselor, which of your characteristics might be particularly helpful? Which might be particularly unhelpful? How realistic are the client's goals for counseling? How long do you think counseling might continue?

Figure 5.3 *continued*

Source: From *Counseling Strategies and Interventions* (pp. 66–68), by H. Hackney and L. S. Cormier, Boston: Allyn & Bacon, 1994. All rights reserved. Reprinted by permission of Allyn & Bacon.

A *restatement* is a simple mirror response to a client that lets the client know the counselor is actively listening. Used alone, it is relatively sterile and ineffective:

CLIENT: I'm not sure if I'll ever find a suitable mate. My job keeps me on the road and isolated.

COUNSELOR: You don't know if you will ever find a spouse because of the nature of your job.

Reflection of feeling is similar to a restatement, but it deals with verbal and nonverbal expression. Reflections may be on several levels; some convey more empathy than others. An example is this counselor response to a client who is silently sobbing over the loss of a parent: "You're still really feeling the pain."

Summary of feelings is the act of paraphrasing a number of feelings that the client has conveyed. For example, a counselor might say to a client, "John, if I understand you correctly, you are feeling depressed over the death of your father and discouraged that your friends have not helped you work through your grief. In addition, you feel your work is boring and that your wife is emotionally distant from you."

Acknowledgment of nonverbal behavior differs from the previous examples. For instance, acknowledgment comes when the counselor says to a client, "I notice that your arms are folded across your chest and you're looking at the floor." This type of response does not interpret the meaning of the behavior.

Conducting the Initial Interview

There is no one place to begin an initial interview, but experts recommend that counselors start by trying to make their clients feel comfortable (Hackney & Cormier, 1994). Counselors should set aside their own agendas and focus on the person of the client, including listening to the client's story and presenting issues (Wilcox-Matthew, Ottens, & Minor, 1997). This type of behavior, in which there is a genuine interest in and accepting of a client, is known as *rapport*.

Ivey (1994) states that the two most important microskills for rapport building are basic attending behavior and client-observation skills. A counselor needs to tune in to what the client is thinking and feeling and how he or she is behaving. Establishing and maintaining rapport is vital for the disclosure of information and the ultimate success of counseling.

One way in which counselors initiate rapport is by inviting clients to focus on reasons for seeking help. Such noncoercive invitations to talk are called *door openers* and contrast with judgmental or evaluative responses known as *door closers* (Bolton, 1979). Appropriate door openers include inquiries and observations such as "What brings you to see me?" "What would you like to talk about?" and "You look like you are in a lot of pain. Tell me about it." These unstructured, open-ended invitations allow clients to take the initiative (Hackney & Cormier, 1994; Young, 1998). In such situations, clients are most likely to talk about priority topics.

The amount of talking that clients engage in and the insight and benefits derived from the initial interview can be enhanced by the counselor who appropriately conveys empathy, encouragement, support, caring, attentiveness, acceptance, and genuineness. Of all of these qualities, empathy is the most important.

Empathy

Rogers (1961) describes *empathy* as the counselor's ability to "enter the client's phenomenal world, to experience the client's world as if it were your own without ever losing the 'as if' quality" (p. 284). Empathy involves two specific skills: perception and communication (Patterson & Welfel, 1994).

An effective counselor perceives the cultural frame of reference from which his or her client operates, including the client's perceptual and cognitive process (Weinrach, 1987). Nevertheless, a counselor who can accurately perceive what it is like to be the client but cannot communicate that experience is a limited helper. Such a counselor may be aware of client dynamics, but no one, including the client, knows of the counselor's awareness. The ability to communicate clearly plays a vital role in any counseling relationship (Okun, 1997).

In the initial interview, counselors must be able to convey primary empathy (Patterson & Welfel, 1994). *Primary empathy* is the ability to respond in such a way that it is apparent to both client and counselor that the counselor has understood the client's major themes. Primary empathy is conveyed through nonverbal communication and various verbal responses. For example, the counselor, leaning forward and speaking in a soft, understanding voice, may say to the client, "I hear that your life has been defined by a series of serious losses." *Advanced empathy* (discussed further in Chapter 6) is a process of helping a client explore themes, issues, and emotions new to his or her awareness (Patterson & Welfel, 1994). This second level of empathy is usually inappropriate for an initial interview because it examines too much material too quickly. Clients must be developmentally ready for counseling to be beneficial.

Verbal and Nonverbal Behavior

Whatever its form, empathy may be fostered by *attentiveness* (the amount of verbal and nonverbal behavior shown to the client). Verbal behaviors include communications that show a desire to comprehend or discuss what is important to the client (Cormier & Cormier, 1998). These behaviors (which include probing, requesting clarification, restating, and summarizing feelings) indicate that the counselor is focusing on the person of the client. Equally important are the counselor's nonverbal behaviors. According to Mehrabian (1970), physically attending behaviors such as smiling, leaning forward, making eye contact, gesturing, and nodding one's head are effective nonverbal ways of conveying to clients that the counselor is interested in and open to them.

Egan (1998) summarizes five nonverbal skills involved in initial attending. They are best remembered in the acronym SOLER. The *S* is a reminder to face the client *squarely,* which can be understood literally or metaphorically depending on the situation. The important thing is that the counselor shows involvement and interest in the client. The *O* is a reminder to adopt an *open* posture, free from crossed arms and legs and showing nondefensiveness. The *L* reminds the counselor to *lean* toward the client. Leaning too far forward and being too close may be frightening, but leaning too far away indicates disinterest. The counselor needs to find a middle distance that is comfortable for both parties. The *E* represents *eye* contact. Good eye contact with most clients is a sign that the counselor is attuned to the client. For other clients, less eye contact is appropriate. The *R* is a reminder to the counselor to *relax.* A counselor needs to be comfortable.

Okun (1997) lists supportive verbal and nonverbal behavioral aids that counselors often display throughout counseling (see Table 5.1).

The last nonverbal behavior on Okun's list, occasional touching, is politically sensitive and somewhat controversial. Although Willison and Masson (1986) (in agreement with Okun) point out that human touch may be therapeutic in counseling, Alyn (1988) emphasizes that "the wide range of individual motivations for, interpretations of, and responses to touch make it an extremely unclear and possibly a dangerous means of communication in therapy" (p. 433). As a general counseling principle, Young (1998) suggests that touch should be appropriately employed, applied briefly and sparingly, and used to communicate concern. Applying the "Touch Test," which simply asks, "Would you do this with a stranger?" is one way to implement Young's suggestions (Del Prete, 1998, p. 63). Thus, counselors who use touch in their work should do so cautiously and with the understanding that what they are doing can have adverse effects. This same critical scrutiny is suggested when using any verbal or nonverbal technique.

Table 5.1   Helpful behaviors

Verbal	Nonverbal
Uses understandable words	Tone of voice similar to helpee's
Reflects back and clarifies helpee's statements	Maintains good eye contact
Appropriately interprets	Occasional head nodding
Summarizes for helpee	Facial animation
Responds to primary message	Occasional smiling
Uses verbal reinforcers (for example, "Mm-mm," "I see," "Yes")	Occasional hand gesturing
Calls helpee by first name or "you"	Close physical proximity to helpee
Appropriately gives information	Moderate rate of speech
Answers questions about self	Body leans toward helpee
Uses humor occasionally to reduce tension	Occasional touching
Is nonjudgmental and respectful	Relaxed, open posture
Adds greater understanding to helpee's statement	Confident vocal tone
Phrases interpretations tentatively so as to elicit genuine feedback from helpee	

Source: From *Effective Helping: Interviewing and Counseling Techniques* (p. 24) by Barbara F. Okun. Copyright © by Brooks/Cole Publishing Company. Reprinted by permission of Wadsworth Publishing Company.

Nonhelpful Interview Behavior

When building a relationship, counselors must also realize what they should *not* do. Otherwise, nonhelpful behaviors may be included in their counseling repertoire. Patterson and Welfel (1994) list four major actions that usually block counselor-client communication and should be generally avoided: advice giving, lecturing, excessive questioning, and storytelling by the counselor.

Advice giving is the most controversial of these four behaviors. Knowles (1979) found that 70% to 90% of all responses from volunteer helpers on a crisis line consisted of giving advice. When a counselor gives advice, especially in the first session, it may in effect deny a client the chance to work through personal thoughts and feelings about a subject and ultimately curtail his or her ability to make difficult decisions. A response meant to be helpful ends up being hurtful by disempowering the client. For example, if a client is advised to break off a relationship he or she is ambivalent about, the client is denied the opportunity to become aware and work through the thoughts and feelings that initially led to the ambivalence.

Sack (1985) suggests that advice giving need not always be destructive. He notes that there are emergency situations (as in crisis counseling) when, for the client's immediate welfare and safety, some direct action must be taken, which includes giving advice. He cautions counselors, however, to listen carefully to make sure the client is really asking for advice or simply being reflective through self-questions. There is a big difference between "What should I do?" and "I wonder what I should do." In addition, Sack advocates the responses developed by Carkhuff (1969) as ways in which counselors can answer direct requests for advice. In this model, counselors respond using one of seven approaches: respect, empathy, genuineness, concreteness, self-disclosure, confrontation, and immediacy. Sack (1985) concludes that counselors must examine their roles in counseling to "free themselves of the limitations and pitfalls of giving advice and move toward employing a variety of responses that can more appropriately address their clients' needs" (p. 131).

Lecturing, or preaching, is really a disguised form of advice giving (Patterson & Welfel, 1994). It sets up a power struggle between the counselor and client that neither individual can win. For example, if a sexually active girl is told "Don't get involved with boys anymore," she may do just the opposite to assert her independence. In such a case, both the counselor and client fail in their desire to change behaviors. Counselors are probably lecturing when they say more than three consecutive sentences in a row to their clients. Instead of lecturing, counselors can be effective by following the client's lead (Evans, Hearn, Uhlemann, & Ivey, 1998).

Excessive questioning is a common mistake of many counselors. Verbal interaction with clients needs to include statements, observations, and encouragers as well as questions. When excessive questioning is used, the client feels as though he or she is being interrogated rather than counseled. The client has little chance to take the initiative and may become guarded. Children may especially respond in this way or make a game out of answering a question, waiting for the next one, answering it, waiting, and so on (Erdman & Lampe, 1996). Counseling relationships are more productive when counselors avoid asking more than two questions in a row and keep their questions open rather than closed.

Storytelling by the counselor is the final nonhelpful behavior. There *are* a few prominent professionals who can use stories to benefit clients. Milton Erickson, a legendary pioneer in family counseling, was one. His stories were always metaphorically tailored to his clients' situations. They were beneficial because they directed clients to think about their own situations in light of the stories he told. Most counselors, however, should stay away from storytelling because the story usually focuses attention on the counselor instead of the client and distracts from problem solving.

Okun (1997) lists other nonhelpful verbal and nonverbal behaviors (see Table 5.2). Some of these behaviors, such as yawning, clearly show the counselor's disinterest. Others, such as advice giving, appear to be helpful only at select times, for example, when the client is interested or there is a crisis. As you examine this list, think of when you last experienced the behaviors it mentions.

Exploration and the Identification of Goals

In the final part of building a counseling relationship, the counselor helps the client explore specific areas and begin to identify goals that the client wants to achieve. Hill (1975) emphasizes that establishing goals is crucial in providing direction. Egan (1998) observes that exploring and ultimately identifying goals often occur when a client is given the opportunity to talk about situations, to tell personal stories. The counselor reinforces

Table 5.2   Nonhelpful behaviors

Verbal	Nonverbal
Interrupting	Looking away from helpee
Advice giving	Sitting far away or turned away from helpee
Preaching	Sneering
Placating	Frowning
Blaming	Scowling
Cajoling	Tight mouth
Exhorting	Shaking pointed finger
Extensive probing and questioning, especially "why" questions	Distracting gestures
Directing, demanding	Yawning
Patronizing attitude	Closing eyes
Overinterpretation	Unpleasant tone of voice
Using words or jargon helpee doesn't understand	Rate of speech too slow or too fast
Straying from topic	Acting rushed
Intellectualizing	
Overanalyzing	
Talking about self too much	
Minimizing or disbelieving	

Source: From *Effective Helping: Interviewing and Counseling Techniques* (p. 25) by Barbara F. Okun. Copyright © by Brooks/Cole Publishing Company. Reprinted by permission of Wadsworth Publishing Company.

the client's focus on self by providing structure, actively listening (hearing both content and feelings), and helping identify and clarify goals.

Rule (1982) states that goals "are the energizing fabric of daily living" but are often elusive (p. 195). He describes some goals as unfocused, unrealistic, and uncoordinated. *Unfocused goals* are not identified, too broad, or not prioritized. Sometimes counselors and clients may leave unfocused goals alone because the time and expense of chasing them is not as productive as changing unwanted behaviors. In most cases, however, it is helpful to identify a client's goals, put them into a workable form, and decide which goals to pursue first.

Unrealistic goals, as defined by either counselor or client, include happiness, perfection, progress, being number one, and self-actualization. They have merit but are not easily obtained or sustained. For example, the client who has worked hard and is happy about being promoted will soon have to settle into the duties of the new job and the reality of future job progress. Unrealistic goals may best be dealt with by putting them into the context of broader life goals. Then the counselor may encourage the client to devise exploratory and homework strategies for dealing with them.

Uncoordinated goals, according to Rule (1982), are generally divided "into two groups: those probably really uncoordinated and those seemingly uncoordinated" (p. 196). In the first group are goals that may be incompatible with one another or with the personality of the client. A person who seeks counseling but really does not wish to work on changing exemplifies an individual with incompatible goals. These clients are often labeled resistant. Into the second group, Rule places the goals of clients who appear to have uncoordinated goals but really do not. These individuals may be afraid to take personal responsibility and engage any helper in a "yes, but . . . " dialogue.

Dyer and Vriend (1977) emphasize seven specific criteria for judging effective goals in counseling:

1. *Goals are mutually agreed on by client and counselor.* Without mutuality neither party will invest much energy in working on the goals.
2. *Goals are specific.* If goals are too broad, they will never be met.
3. *Goals are relevant to self-defeating behavior.* There are many possible goals for clients to work on, but only those that are relevant to changing self-defeating action should be pursued.
4. *Goals are achievement and success oriented.* Counseling goals need to be realistic and have both intrinsic and extrinsic payoffs for clients.
5. *Goals are quantifiable and measurable.* It is important that both client and counselor know when goals are achieved. When goals are defined quantitatively, achievement is most easily recognized.
6. *Goals are behavioral and observable.* This criterion relates to the previous one: an effective goal is one that can be seen when achieved.
7. *Goals are understandable and can be restated clearly.* It is vital that client and counselor communicate clearly about goals. One way to assess how well this process is achieved is through restating goals in one's own words.

Egan (1998) cautions that in the exploratory and goal-setting stage of counseling, several problems may inhibit the building of a solid client-counselor relationship. The most notable include moving too fast, moving too slow, fear of intensity, client rambling, and excessive time and energy devoted to probing the past. Counselors who are forewarned about such potential problems are in a much better position to address them effectively. It is vital that counselors work with clients to build a mutually satisfying relationship from the start. When this process occurs, a more active working stage of counseling begins.

Summary and Conclusion

Building a relationship, the first stage in counseling, is a continuous process. It begins by having the counselor win the battle for structure and the client win the battle for initiative. In such situations, both parties are winners. The client wins by becoming more informed about the nature of counseling and learning what to expect. The counselor wins by creating an atmosphere in which the client is comfortable about sharing thoughts and feelings.

Counseling may occur in any setting, but some circumstances are more likely than others to promote its development. Counselors need to be aware of the physical setting in which the counseling takes place. Clients may adjust to any room, but certain qualities about an environment, such as the seating arrangement, make counseling more conducive. Other less apparent qualities also affect the building of a relationship. For example, the perception that clients and counselors have about one another is important. Attractive clients who are young, verbal, intelligent, and social may be treated in a more positive way than clients who are older, less intelligent, and seemingly unmotivated. Clients are likely to work best with counselors they perceive as trustworthy, attractive, and knowledgeable.

Regardless of the external circumstances and the initial perceptions, a counselor who attends to the verbal and nonverbal expressions of a client is more likely to establish rapport. The relationship may be further enhanced by the counselor's conveying of empathy and the use of other helpful skills such as restatement and reflection that cut across counseling theory. When counselors are attuned to their own values and feelings, they are able to become even more effective. The initial counseling interview can be counselor or client initiated and can center on the gathering of information or on relationship dynamics. In any situation, it is vital for the counselor to explore with the client the reasons for the possibilities of counseling. Such disclosures can encourage clients to define goals and facilitate the setting of a mutually agreed-upon agenda in counseling. When this step is accomplished, the work of reaching goals begins.

CLASSROOM ACTIVITIES

1. Imagine that you are about to conduct your first counseling session in an environment of your own choosing. How would you furnish this setting, and how would you spend your first 10 minutes with an ideal client? Make notes and drawings of this experience and share it with another class member.

2. What type of people most appeal to you? With what kind of individuals do you have the most difficulty? In groups of three, role-play a 15-minute session with an imagined difficult client. Notice your verbal and nonverbal behaviors. Give your client and observer feedback on what you noticed

about yourself, and then listen to their feedback on what they observed.

3. What are some things that you can do to make yourself more attractive (likable) to your client? Share your list with fellow classmates in an open discussion. Does your combined list of behaviors differ from Okun's list? How? Which items do you consider most crucial in becoming an effective counselor?

4. In groups of four, discuss strategies you could employ to help an unrealistic client become realistic about counseling. In your discussion, have each member of the group play a different type of unrealistic client. Notice how your responses differ in particular situations.

5. What are your feelings about being a counselor now that you have some idea about what the initial process is like? Discuss your feelings and the thoughts behind them with other members of the class. Do those feelings and thoughts differ substantially from what they were at the beginning of the course? How?

REFERENCES

Allen, G. (1977). *Understanding psychotherapy: Comparative perspectives.* Champaign, IL: Research Press.

Alyn, J. H. (1988). The politics of touch in therapy: A response to Willison and Masson. *Journal of Counseling and Development, 66,* 432–433.

Benjamin, A. (1987). *The helping interview* (4th ed.). Boston: Houghton Mifflin.

Bolton, R. (1979). *People skills: How to assert yourself, listen to others, and resolve conflicts.* Upper Saddle River, NJ: Prentice Hall.

Brammer, L. M., Abrego, P., & Shostrom, E.. (1993). *Therapeutic counseling and psychotherapy* (6th ed.). Upper Saddle River, NJ: Merrill/Prentice Hall.

Brammer, L. M. & MacDonald, G. (1996). *The helping relationship* (6th ed.). Boston: Allyn & Bacon.

Brown, R. D. (1970). Experienced and inexperienced counselors' first impressions of clients and case outcomes: Are first impressions lasting? *Journal of Counseling Psychology, 17,* 550–558.

Carkhuff, R. R. (1969). *Helping and human relations.* New York: Holt, Rinehart, & Winston.

Claiborn, C. D. (1979). Counselor verbal intervention, non-verbal behavior and social power. *Journal of Counseling Psychology, 26,* 378–383.

Cormier, W. H., & Cormier, L. S. (1998). *Interviewing strategies for helpers* (4th ed.). Pacific Grove, CA: Brooks/Cole.

Day, R. W., & Sparacio, R. T. (1980). Structuring the counseling process. *Personnel and Guidance Journal, 59,* 246–249.

Del Prete, T. (1998). Getting back in touch with students: Should we risk it? *Professional School Counseling, 1(4),* 62–65.

Dorn, F. J. (1984). The social influence model: A social psychological approach to counseling. *Personnel and Guidance Journal, 62,* 342–345.

Doyle, R. E. (1998). *Essential skills & strategies in the helping process* (2nd ed.). Pacific Grove, CA: Brooks/Cole.

Dyer, W. W., & Vriend, J. (1977). A goal-setting checklist for counselors. *Personnel and Guidance Journal, 55,* 469–471.

Egan, G. (1998). *The skilled helper* (6th ed.). Pacific Grove, CA: Brooks/Cole.

Erdman, P., & Lampe, R. (1996). Adapting basic skills to counsel children. *Journal of Counseling and Development, 74,* 374–377.

Evans, D. R., Hearn, M. T., Uhlemann, M. R., & Ivey, A. E. (1998). *Essential interviewing* (5th ed.). Pacific Grove, CA: Brooks/Cole.

Fong, M. L., & Cox, B. G. (1983). Trust as an underlying dynamic in the counseling process: How clients test trust. *Personnel and Guidance Journal, 62,* 163–166.

Galvin, M., & Ivey, A. E. (1981). Researching one's own interviewing style: Does your theory of choice match your actual practice? *Personnel and Guidance Journal, 59,* 536–542.

Gazda, G. M., Asbury, F. R., Balzer, F. J., Childers, W. C., & Phelps, R. E. (1994). *Human relations development: A manual for educators* (5th ed.). Boston: Allyn & Bacon.

Gill, S. J. (1982). Professional disclosure and consumer protection in counseling. *Personnel and Guidance Journal, 60,* 443–446.

Goldstein, A. P. (1973). *Structural learning therapy: Toward a psychotherapy for the poor.* New York: Academic Press.

Goodyear, R. K., & Bradley, F. O. (1980). The helping process as contractual. *Personnel and Guidance Journal, 58,* 512–515.

Haase, R. F. (1970). The relationship of sex and instructional set to the regulation of interpersonal interaction distance in a counseling analogue. *Journal of Counseling Psychology, 17,* 233–236.

Haase, R. F., & DiMattia, D. J. (1976). Spatial environments and verbal conditioning in a quasi-counseling interview. *Journal of Counseling Psychology, 23,* 414–421.

Hackney, H., & Cormier, L. S. (1994). *Counseling strategies and interventions* (4th ed.). Boston: Allyn & Bacon.

Harris, S. M., & Busby, D. M. (1998). Therapist physical attractiveness: An unexplored influence on client disclosure. *Journal of Marital and Family Therapy, 24,* 251–257.

Hill, C. (1975). A process approach for establishing counseling goals and outcomes. *Personnel and Guidance Journal, 53,* 571–576.

Hinson, J. A., & Swanson, J. L. (1993). Willingness to seek help as a function of self-disclosure and problem severity. *Journal of Counseling and Development, 71,* 465–470.

Hubble, M. A., & Gelso, C. J. (1978). Effects of counselor attire in an initial interview. *Journal of Counseling Psychology, 25,* 581–584.

Ivey, A. E. (1971). *Microcounseling.* Springfield, IL: Thomas.

Ivey, A. E. (1994). *Intentional interviewing and counseling* (3rd ed.). Pacific Grove, CA: Brooks/Cole.

James, M. D., & Hazler, R. J. (1998). Using metaphors to soften resistance in chemically dependent clients. *Journal of Humanistic Education and Development, 36,* 122–133.

Kelly, K. R., & Stone, G. L. (1982). Effects of time limits on the interview behavior of type A and B persons within a brief counseling analog. *Journal of Counseling Psychology, 29,* 454–459.

Kerr, B. A., Claiborn, C. D., & Dixon, D. N. (1982). Training counselors in persuasion. *Counselor Education and Supervision, 22,* 138–147.

Knowles, D. (1979). On the tendency of volunteer helpers to give advice. *Journal of Counseling Psychology, 26,* 352–354.

LaCross, M. B. (1975). Non-verbal behavior and perceived counselor attractiveness and persuasiveness. *Journal of Counseling Psychology, 22,* 563–566.

Levine, E. (1983). A training model that stresses the dynamic dimensions of counseling. *Personnel and Guidance Journal, 61,* 431–433.

Lichtenberg, J. W. (1986). Counseling research: Irrelevant or ignored? *Journal of Counseling and Development, 64,* 365–366.

Loesch, L. (1984). Professional credentialing in counseling: 1984. *Counseling and Human Development, 17,* 1–11.

Manthei, R. J. (1983). Client choice of therapist or therapy. *Personnel and Guidance Journal, 61,* 334–340.

Mehrabian, A. (1970). Some determinants of affiliation and conformity. *Psychological Reports, 27,* 19–29.

Mehrabian, A. (1971). *Silent messages.* Belmont, CA: Wadsworth.

Napier, A., & Whitaker, C. (1978). *The family crucible.* New York: Harper & Row.

Nichols, M. P. (1998). The lost art of listening. *IAMFC Family Digest, 11*(1), 1–2, 4, 11.

Okun, B. F. (1997). *Effective helping* (5th ed.). Pacific Grove, CA: Brooks/Cole.

Otani, A. (1989). Client resistance in counseling: Its theoretical rationale and taxonomic classification. *Journal of Counseling and Development, 67,* 458–461.

Paradise, L. V., & Wilder, D. H. (1979). The relationship between client reluctance and counseling effectiveness. *Counselor Education and Supervision, 19,* 35–41.

Patterson, C. H. (1985). *The therapeutic relationship.* Pacific Grove, CA: Brooks/Cole.

Patterson, L. E., & Welfel, E. R. (1994). *Counseling process* (4th ed.). Pacific Grove, CA: Brooks/Cole.

Ponzo, Z. (1985). The counselor and physical attractiveness. *Journal of Counseling and Development, 63,* 482–485.

Riordan, R., Matheny, K., & Harris, C. (1978). Helping counselors minimize client resistance. *Counselor Education and Supervision, 18,* 6–13.

Ritchie, M. H. (1986). Counseling the involuntary client. *Journal of Counseling and Development, 64,* 516–518.

Rogers, C. R. (1961). *On becoming a person.* Boston: Houghton Mifflin.

Roloff, M. E., & Miller, G. R. (Eds.). (1980). *Persuasion: New directions in theory and research.* Beverly Hills, CA: Sage.

Rule, W. R. (1982). Pursuing the horizon: Striving for elusive goals. *Personnel and Guidance Journal, 61,* 195–197.

Sack, R. T. (1985). On giving advice. *AMHCA Journal, 7,* 127–132.

Sack, R. T. (1988). Counseling responses when clients say "I don't know." *Journal of Mental Health Counseling, 10,* 179–187.

Schofield, W. (1964). *Psychotherapy: The purchase of friendship.* Upper Saddle River, NJ: Prentice Hall.

Senour, M. N. (1982). How counselors influence clients. *Personnel and Guidance Journal, 60,* 345–349.

Shertzer, B., & Stone, S. C. (1980). *Fundamentals of counseling* (3rd ed.). Boston: Houghton Mifflin.

Siegal, J. C., & Sell, J. M. (1978). Effects of objective evidence of expertness and nonverbal behavior on client perceived expertness. *Journal of Counseling Psychology, 25,* 188–192.

Sielski, L. M. (1979). Understanding body language. *Personnel and Guidance Journal, 57,* 238–242.

Strong, S. R. (1968). Counseling: An interpersonal influence process. *Journal of Counseling Psychology, 15,* 215–224.

Strong, S. R. (1982). Emerging integrations of clinical and social psychology: A clinician's perspective. In G. Weary & H. Mirels (Eds.), *Integrations of clinical and social psychology* (pp. 181–213). New York: Oxford University Press.

Vriend, J., & Dyer, W. W. (1973). Counseling the reluctant client. *Journal of Counseling Psychology, 20,* 240-246.

Warnath, C. F. (1977). Relationship and growth theories and agency counseling. *Counselor Education and Supervision, 17,* 84–91.

Watkins, C. E., Jr. (1983). Counselor acting out in the counseling situation: An exploratory analysis. *Personnel and Guidance Journal, 61,* 417–423.

Watkins, C. E., Jr., & Schneider, L. J. (1989). Self-involving versus self-disclosing counselor statements during an initial interview. *Journal of Counseling and Development, 67,* 345–349.

Weinrach, S. G. (1987). Microcounseling and beyond: A dialogue with Allen Ivey. *Journal of Counseling and Development, 65,* 532–537.

West, M. (1975). Building a relationship with the unmotivated client. *Psychotherapy, 12,* 48–51.

Wilcox-Matthew, L., Ottens, A., & Minor, C. W. (1997). An analysis of significant events in counseling. *Journal of Counseling & Development, 75,* 282–291.

Willison, B., & Masson, R. (1986). The role of touch in therapy: An adjunct to communications. *Journal of Counseling and Development, 65,* 497–500.

Young, M. E. (1998). *Learning the art of helping.* Upper Saddle River, NJ: Merrill/Prentice Hall.

6

WORKING IN A COUNSELING RELATIONSHIP

I listen and you tell me how

the feelings rage and toss within you.

A mother died, a child deserted,

and you, that child, have not forgotten

what it is to be alone.

I nod my head, your words continue

rich in anger from early memories,

Feelings that you tap with care

after years of shaky storage.

As you drink their bitter flavor,

which you declined to taste at seven,

I mentally wince while watching you

open your life to the dark overflow

of pain that has grown strong with age.

From "Memory Traces," by S. T. Gladding, 1977, North Carolina Personnel and Guidance Journal, 6, *p. 50. © 1977 by S. T. Gladding. Reprinted with permission.*

The successful outcome of any counseling effort depends on a working alliance between counselor and client (Kottler, Sexton, & Whiston, 1994; Okun, 1997). Building this relationship is a developmental process that involves exploring the situation that has motivated the client to seek help. According to Carkhuff and Anthony (1979), the involvement and exploration phases of helping should occur at this time. (See Chapter 5 for a review of how to become involved and build a counseling relationship.) After these phases have been completed, the counselor works with the client to move into the understanding and action phases. Initially, the client's concerns may be stated broadly and in general terms; as the counseling process continues, specific objectives are defined or refined.

Clients arrive in counseling with certain areas of their lives open or understood and other areas hidden or suppressed. The Johari window, shown in Figure 6.1, is a conceptual device used to represent the way in which most individuals enter the counseling relationship (Luft, 1970).

The objectives of the first two phases of counseling are to help clients relax enough to tell their story and discover information located in blind areas of themselves, regions about which they have been unaware (see Figure 6.1). Once they obtain a better understanding of these areas (either verbally or nonverbally), informed clients can decide how to proceed. If they are successful in their work, they extend the dimensions of the area of free activity as represented in the Johari Window while shrinking the dimensions of the more restrictive areas (see Figure 6.2).

It may appear that the counseling process described in this book and represented in the Johari window is linear, but such is not the case. Counseling is systemic, with various factors impacting each other continuously. Therefore, procedures overlap considerably (Egan, 1998), and some techniques used in the involvement and exploration phases are

	Known to Self	**Not Known to Self**
Known to Others	I. Area of Free Activity	III. Blind Area—Blind to self, seen by others
Not Known to Others	II. Avoided or Hidden Area—Self hidden from others	IV. Area of Unknown Activity

Figure 6.1   The Johari window of the client

Source: From *Of Human Interaction* (p. 13), by J. Luft, Palo Alto, CA: National Press Books, 1969 and *Group Processes: An Introduction to Group Dynamics* (3rd ed.) by J. Luft, Mountain View, CA: Mayfield Publishing Co., 1984. Copyright 1969 by Joseph Luft. Reprinted by permission of the author.

Relationship Initiated

Close Relationship

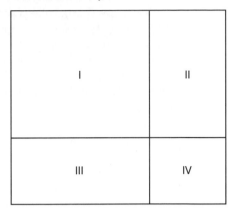

Figure 6.2   Johari window as modified through the relationship with the counselor
Source: From *Of Human Interaction* (p. 14), by J. Luft, 1969, Palo Alto, CA: National Press Books, 1969 and *Group Processes: An Introduction to Group Dynamics* (3rd ed.) by J. Luft, Mountain View, CA: Mayfield Publishing Co., 1984. Copyright 1969 by Joseph Luft. Reprinted by permission of the author.

also employed in the understanding and action phases. Yet as counseling progresses, new and different skills are regularly incorporated. Counseling requires constant sensitivity to the status of the relationship and the client's developmental nature. The counselor must be alert to new needs and demands as they develop.

In this chapter, we explore the skills commonly associated with the understanding and action phases of counseling. These phases involve a number of counselor skills, including changing perceptions, leading, multifocused responding, accurate empathy, self-disclosure, immediacy, confrontation, contracting, and rehearsal. In addition, clients and counselors must work through any transference or countertransference issues that arise out of earlier situations or present circumstances (Gelso & Carter, 1985). There is, of course, a constant need to uncover real aspects of the counselor-client relationship (i.e., those not overlaid with defense mechanisms such as denial or projection) and use them therapeutically.

Counselor Skills in the Understanding and Action Phases

Counselors must be active in helping clients change. After rapport has been established, counselors need to employ skills that result in clients' viewing their lives differently and thinking, feeling, and behaving accordingly.

Changing Perceptions

Clients often come to counseling as a last resort, when they perceive that the situation is not only serious but hopeless (Watzlawick, 1983). People think their perceptions and interpretations are accurate. When they communicate their view of reality to others, it is commonly accepted as factual (Cavanagh, 1990). This phenomenon is called *functional fixity* and is seeing things in only one way or from one perspective or being fixated on the idea that this particular situation or attribute is the issue (Cormier & Cormier, 1998).

For example, a middle-aged man is concerned about taking care of his elderly mother. He realizes that personal attention to this task will take him away from his family and put a strain on them and him. Furthermore, he is aware that his energy will be drained from his business and he might not receive the promotion he wants. He is torn between caring for two families and sees his situation as an either-or problem. Appropriate and realistic counseling objectives would include finding community and family resources the man could use to help take care of his mother, his family, and himself. In the process the man would discover what he needs to do to relieve himself of sole responsibility in this case and uncover concrete ways he can increase his work efficiency but not his stress. The focus on taking care of self and others as well as using community and family resources gives the man a different perspective about his situation and may help him deal with it in a healthy manner.

Counselors can help clients change distorted or unrealistic objectives by offering them the opportunity to explore thoughts and desires within a safe, accepting, and nonjudgmental environment. Goals are refined or altered using cognitive, behavioral, or cognitive-behavioral strategies, such as redefining the problem, altering behavior in certain situations, or perceiving the problem in a more manageable way and acting accordingly (Okun, 1997).

Perceptions commonly change through the process of *reframing,* a technique that offers the client another probable and positive viewpoint or perspective on a situation. Such a changed point of view gives a client a different way of responding (Young, 1998). Effective counselors consistently reframe life experiences for both themselves and their clients. For instance, a person's rude behavior may be explained as the result of pressure from trying to complete a task quickly rather than dislike for the rudely treated person.

Reframing is used in almost all forms of counseling. For example, in family counseling reframing helps families change their focus from viewing one member of the family as the source of all their problems (i.e., the scapegoat) to seeing the whole family as responsible. In employment counseling, Amundson (1996) has developed 12 reframing strategies that deal with looking back, looking at the present, and looking ahead to help clients widen their perspective of themselves and the labor market. In cases concerning individuals, Cormier and Cormier (1998) point out that reframing can reduce resistance and mobilize the client's energy to do something differently by changing his or her perception of the problem. In short, reframing helps clients become more aware of situational factors associated with behavior. It shifts the focus from a simplistic attribution of traits, such as "I'm a bum," to a more complex and accurate view, such as "I have some days when things don't go very well and I feel worthless" (Ellis, 1971). Through reframing, clients see themselves and their environments with greater accuracy and insight.

Leading

Changing client perceptions requires a high degree of persuasive skill and some direction from the counselor. Such input is known as *leading.* The term was coined by Francis Robinson (1950) to describe certain deliberate behaviors counselors engage in for the benefit of their clients. Leads vary in length, and some are more appropriate at one stage of counseling than another. Robinson used the analogy of a football quarterback and receiver to describe a lead. A good quarterback anticipates where the receiver will be on the field and throws the ball to that spot. The same is true of counselors and clients. Counselors anticipate where their clients are and where they are likely to go. Counselors then respond accordingly. If there is misjudgment and the lead is either too far ahead (i.e., too persuasive or direct) or not far enough (too uninvolved and nondirect), the counseling relationship suffers.

Patterson and Welfel (1994) list a number of leads that counselors can use with their clients (Figure 6.3). Some, such as silence, acceptance, and paraphrasing, are most appropriate at the beginning of the counseling process. Others, such as persuasion, are directive and more appropriate in the understanding and action phases.

The type of lead counselors use is determined in part by the theoretical approach they embrace and the current phase of counseling. *Minimal leads* (sometimes referred to as *minimal encouragers*) such as "hmmm," "yes," or "I hear you" are best used in the building phase of a relationship because they are low risk (Young, 1998). *Maximum leads*, on the other hand, such as confrontation, are more challenging and should be employed only after a solid relationship has been established.

Multifocused Responding

People have preferences for the way they process information through their senses. Counselors can enhance their effectiveness by remembering that individuals receive input from their worlds differently and that preferred styles influence perceptions and behaviors. Some clients experience the world visually: they see what is happening. Others are primarily auditory: they hear the world around them. Still others are kinesthetically oriented: they feel situations as though physically in touch with them. (Two of my three children are olfactory; they judge much of their environment through smell.) Regardless, Ivey (1994) and Lazarus (1995) think that tuning into clients' major modes of perceiving and learning is crucial to bringing about change. Because many clients have multiple ways of knowing the world, counselors should vary their responses and incorporate words that reflect an understanding of clients' worlds. For example, the counselor might say to a multimodal sensory person, "I see your point and hear your concern. I feel that you are really upset."

The importance of responding in a client's own language can be powerful, too. Counselors need to distinguish between the predominantly affective, behavioral, and cognitive nature of speech. *Affective responses* focus on a client's feelings, *behavioral responses* focus on actions, and *cognitive responses* focus on thought. Thus, counselors working with affectively oriented individuals select words accordingly. Table 6.1 shows some of the most common of these words, as identified by Carkuff and Anthony (1979).

Accurate Empathy

There is near-universal agreement among practitioners and theorists that the use of empathy is one of the most vital elements in counseling, one that transcends counseling stages (Fiedler, 1950; Gladstein, 1983; Hackney, 1978; Rogers, 1975; Truax & Mitchell, 1971). In

Least leading response

Silence	When the counselor makes no verbal response at all, the client will ordinarily feel some pressure to continue and will choose how to continue with minimum input from the counselor.
Acceptance	The counselor simply acknowledges the client's previous statement with a response such as "yes" or "uhuh." The client is verbally encouraged to continue, but without content stimulus from the counselor.
Restatement (paraphrase)	The counselor restates the client's verbalization, including both content and affect, using nearly the same wording. The client is prompted to reexamine what has been said.
Clarification	The counselor states the meaning of the client's statement in his or her own words, seeking to clarify the client's meaning. Sometimes elements of several of the client's statements are brought into a single response. The counselor's ability to perceive accurately and communicate correctly is important, and the client must test the "fit" of the counselor's lead.
Approval (affirmation)	The counselor affirms the correctness of information or encourages the client's efforts at self-determination. "That's good new information," or "You seem to be gaining more control." The client may follow up with further exploration as he or she sees fit.
General leads	The counselor directs the client to talk more about a specific subject with statements such as "Tell me what you mean," or "Please say some more about that." The client is expected to follow the counselor's suggestion.
Interpretation	The counselor uses psychodiagnostic principles to suggest sources of the client's stress or explanations for the client's motivation and behavior. The counselor's statements are presented as hypotheses, and the client is confronted with potentially new ways of seeing self.
Rejection (persuasion)	The counselor tries to reverse the client's behavior or perceptions by actively advising different behavior or suggesting different interpretations of life events than those presented by the client.
Reassurance	The counselor states that, in his or her *judgment*, the client's concern is not unusual and that people with similar problems have succeeded in overcoming them. The client may feel that the reassurance is supportive but may also feel that his or her problem is discounted by the counselor as unimportant.
Introducing new information or a new idea	The counselor moves away from the client's last statement and prompts the client to consider new material.

Most leading response

Figure 6.3 Continuum of leads

Source: From *The Counseling Process* (3rd ed., pp. 126–127), by L. E. Patterson and S. Eisenberg, 1983, Boston: Houghton Mifflin. Copyright 1983 by Houghton Mifflin. Reprinted by permission of S. Eisenberg. All rights reserved.

Table 6.1 Commonly used affect words

Level of Intensity	Category of Feeling						
	Happiness	Sadness	Fear	Uncertainty	Anger	Strength, Potency	Weakness, Inadequacy
Strong	Excited Thrilled Delighted Overjoyed Ecstatic Elated Jubilant	Despairing Hopeless Depressed Crushed Miserable Abandoned Defeated Desolate	Panicked Terrified Afraid Frightened Scared Overwhelmed	Bewildered Disoriented Mistrustful Confused	Outraged Hostile Furious Angry Harsh Hateful Mean Vindictive	Powerful Authoritative Forceful Potent	Ashamed Powerless Vulnerable Cowardly Exhausted Impotent
Moderate	"Up" Good Happy Optimistic Cheerful Enthusiastic Joyful "Turned on"	Dejected Dismayed Disillusioned Lonely Bad Unhappy Pessimistic Sad Hurt Lost	Worried Shaky Tense Anxious Threatened Agitated	Doubtful Mixed up Insecure Skeptical Puzzled	Aggravated Irritated Offended Mad Frustrated Resentful "Sore" Upset Impatient Obstinate	Tough Important Confident Fearless Energetic Brave Courageous Daring Assured Adequate Self-confident Skillful	Embarrassed Useless Demoralized Helpless Worn out Inept Incapable Incompetent Inadequate Shaken
Weak	Pleased Glad Content Relaxed Satisfied Calm	"Down" Discouraged Disappointed "Blue" Alone Left out	Jittery Jumpy Nervous Uncomfortable Uptight Uneasy Defensive Apprehensive Hesitant Edgy	Unsure Surprised Uncertain Undecided Bothered	Perturbed Annoyed Grouchy Hassled Bothered Disagreeable	Determined Firm Able Strong	Frail Meek Unable Weak

Source: Reprinted from *The Skills of Helping* written by Carkhuff, R. R. & Anthony, W. A., copyright 1979. Reprinted by permission of the publisher, HRD Press, Amherst Road, Amherst, MA, (413) 253-3488.

Chapter 5, two types of empathy were briefly noted. The basic type is called *primary empathy*; the second level is known as *advanced empathy* (Carkhuff, 1969). Accurate empathy on both levels is achieved when counselors see clients' worlds from the clients' point of view and are able to communicate this understanding back (Egan, 1998). Two factors that make empathy possible are (a) realizing that "an infinite number of feelings" does not exist and (b) having a personal security so that "you can let yourself go into the world of this other person and still know that you can return to your own world. Everything you are feeling is 'as if'" (Rogers, 1987, pp. 45–46).

Primary accurate empathy involves communicating a basic understanding of what the client is feeling and the experiences and behaviors underlying these feelings. It helps establish the counseling relationship, gather data, and clarify problems. For example, a client might say, "I'm really feeling like I can't do anything for myself." The counselor replies, "You're feeling helpless."

Advanced accurate empathy reflects not only what clients state overtly but also what they imply or state incompletely. For example, a counselor notes that a client says, " . . . and I hope everything will work out" while looking off into space. The counselor responds, "For if it doesn't, you're not sure what you will do next."

Empathy involves three elements: perceptiveness, know-how, and assertiveness (Egan, 1998). Several levels of responses reflect different aspects of counselor empathy. A scale formulated by Carkhuff (1969), called Empathic Understanding in Interpersonal Process, is a measure of these levels. Each of the five levels either adds to or subtracts from the meaning and feeling tone of a client's statement.

1. The verbal and behavioral expressions of the counselor either do not attend to or detract significantly from the verbal and behavioral expressions of the client.
2. Although the counselor responds to the expressed feelings of the client, he or she does so in a way that subtracts noticeable affect from the communications of the client.
3. The expressions of the counselor in response to the expressions of the client are essentially interchangeable.
4. The responses of the counselor add noticeably to the expressions of the client in a way that expresses feelings a level deeper than the client was able to express.
5. The counselor's responses add significantly to the feeling and meaning of the expressions of the client in a way that accurately expresses feeling levels below what the client is able to express.

Responses at the first two levels are not considered empathic; in fact, they inhibit the creation of an empathic environment. For example, if a client reveals that she is heartbroken over the loss of a lover, a counselor operating on either of the first two levels might reply, "Well, you want your former love to be happy, don't you?" Such a response misses the pain that the client is feeling.

At level 3 on the Carkhuff scale, a counselor's response is rated as "interchangeable" with that of a client. The cartoon in Figure 6.4 depicts the essence of such an interchange.

On levels 4 and 5, a counselor either "adds noticeably" or "adds significantly" to what a client has said. This ability to go beyond what clients say distinguishes counseling from conversation or other less helpful forms of behavior (Carkhuff, 1972). The following interchange is an example of a higher-level empathetic response:

> CLIENT: I have been running around from activity to activity until I am so tired I feel like I could drop.
>
> COUNSELOR: Your life has been a merry-go-round of activity, and you'd like to slow it down before you collapse. You'd like to be more in charge of your own life.

Figure 6.4   Interchangeable client and counselor reactions

Source: N. Goud [cartoon], 1983, *Personnel and Guidance Journal, 61*, p. 635. © 1983 by ACA. Reprinted with permission. No further reproduction authorized without written permission of the American Counseling Association.

Means (1973) elaborates on levels 4 and 5 to show how counselors can add noticeably and significantly to their clients' perceptions of an emotional experience, an environmental stimulus, a behavior pattern, a self-evaluation, a self-expectation, and beliefs about self. Clients' statements are extremely varied, and counselors must therefore be flexible in responding to them (Hackney, 1978). Whether a counselor's response contains accurate empathy is determined by the reaction of clients (Turock, 1978). Regardless, in the understanding and action phases of counseling, it is important that counselors integrate the two levels of empathy they use in responding to clients seeking help.

Self-Disclosure

Self-disclosure is a complex, multifaceted phenomenon that has generated more than 200 studies (Watkins, 1990). It may be succinctly defined as "a conscious, intentional technique in which clinicians share information about their lives outside the counseling relationship" (Simone, McCarthy, & Skay, 1998, p. 174). The original work in this area was done by Sidney Jourard (1958, 1964). For him, self-disclosure referred to making oneself known to another person by revealing personal information. Jourard discovered that self-disclosure helped establish trust and facilitated the counseling relationship. He labeled reciprocal self-disclosure the *dyadic effect* (Jourard, 1968).

Client self-disclosure is necessary for successful counseling to occur. Yet it is not always necessary for counselors to be self-disclosing. "Each counselor-client relationship must be evaluated individually in regard to disclosure," and when it occurs, care must be taken to match disclosure "to the client's needs" (Hendrick, 1988, p. 423).

Clients are more likely to trust counselors who disclose personal information (up to a point) and are prone to make reciprocal disclosures (Curtis, 1981; Kottler et al., 1994). Adolescents especially seem to be more comfortable with counselors who are "fairly unguarded and personally available" (Simone et al., 1998, p. 174). Counselors employ self-disclosure on a formal basis at the initial interview by giving clients written statements about the counselor and the counseling process (the professional disclosure statement illustrated in Figure 5.1). They also use self-disclosure spontaneously in counseling sessions to reveal pertinent personal facts to their clients, especially during the understanding and action phases. Spontaneous self-disclosure is important in facilitating client movement (Doster & Nesbitt, 1979; Watkins, 1990).

According to Egan (1998), counselor self-disclosure serves two principal functions: modeling and developing a new perspective. Clients learn to be more open by observing counselors who are open. Counselor self-disclosure can help clients see that counselors are not free of problems or devoid of feelings (Hackney & Cormier, 1994). Thus, while hearing about select aspects of counselors' personal lives, clients may examine aspects of their own lives, such as stubbornness or fear, and realize that some difficulties or experiences are universal and manageable. Egan (1998) stresses that counselor self-disclosure should be brief and focused, should not add to the clients' problems, and should not be used frequently. The process is not linear, and more self-disclosure is not necessarily better. Before self-disclosing, counselors should ask themselves such questions as "Have I thought through why I am disclosing?" "Are there other more effective and less risky ways to reach the same goal?" and "Is my timing right?" (Simone et al., 1998, pp. 181–182).

Kline (1986) observes that clients perceive self-disclosure as risky and may be hesitant to take such a risk. Hesitancy may take the form of refusing to discuss issues, changing the subject, being silent, and talking excessively. Kline suggests that counselors help clients overcome these fears by not only modeling and inviting self-disclosure but also exploring negative feelings that clients have about the counseling process, contracting with clients to talk about a certain subject area, and confronting clients with the avoidance of a specific issue.

Immediacy

"*Immediacy* involves a counselor's understanding and communicating of what is going on between the counselor and client within the helping relationship, particularly the client's feelings, impressions, and expectations, as well as the wants of the counselor" (Turock, 1980, p. 169; emphasis added). There are basically three kinds of immediacy:

- overall relationship immediacy—"How are you and I doing?"
- "immediacy that focuses on some particular event in a session—'What's going on between you and me right now?'" and
- self-involving statements (i.e., present-tense, personal responses to a client that are sometimes challenging)—"I like the way you took charge of your life in that situation" (Egan, 1998, pp. 180–181).

Egan (1998) believes that immediacy is difficult and demanding. It requires more courage or assertiveness than almost any other interpersonal communication skill.

Turock (1980) lists three fears many counselors have about immediacy. First, they may be afraid that clients will misinterpret their messages. Immediacy requires counselors to make a tentative guess or interpretation of what their clients are thinking or feeling, and a wrong guess can cause counselors to lose credibility with their clients.

Second, immediacy may produce an unexpected outcome. Many counseling skills, such as reflection, have predictable outcomes; immediacy does not. Its use may break down a familiar pattern between counselors and clients. In the process, relationships may suffer.

Third, immediacy may influence clients' decisions to terminate counseling sessions because they can no longer control or manipulate relationships. Some clients play games, such as "ain't it awful," and expect their counselors to respond accordingly (Berne, 1964). When clients receive an unexpected payoff, they may decide not to stay in the relationship. Egan (1998) states that immediacy is best used in the following situations:

In a directionless relationship
Where there is tension
Where there is a question of trust
When there is considerable social distance between counselor and client, such as in diversity
Where there is client dependency
Where there is counterdependency
When there is an attraction between counselor and client

Humor

Humor involves giving a funny, unexpected response to a question or situation. It requires both sensitivity and timing on the part of the counselor. Humor in counseling should never be aimed at demeaning anyone. Instead, it should be used to build bridges between counselors and clients. If used properly, it is "a clinical tool that has many therapeutic applications" (Ness, 1989, p. 35). Humor can circumvent clients' resistance, dispel tension, and help clients distance themselves from psychological pain. "Ha-ha" often leads to an awareness of "ah-ha" and a clearer perception of a situation (i.e., insight) (Kottler, 1991). For instance, when a counselor is working with a client who is unsure whether he or she wants to be in counseling, the counselor might initiate the following exchange:

COUNSELOR:	Joan, how many counselors does it take to change a lightbulb?
CLIENT:	(hesitantly) I'm not sure.
COUNSELOR:	Just one, but the lightbulb has got to really want to be changed.
CLIENT:	(smiling) I guess I'm a lightbulb that's undecided.
COUNSELOR:	It's OK to be undecided. We can work on that. Our sessions will probably be more fruitful, however, if you can turn on to what you'd like to see different in your life and what it is we could jointly work on. That way we can focus more clearly.

Overall, humor can contribute to creative thinking; help keep things in perspective; and make it easier to explore difficult, awkward, or nonsensical aspects of life (Bergman,

1985; Piercy & Lobsenz, 1994). However, "counselors must remember that to use humor effectively they must understand what is humorous and under what circumstances it is humorous" (Erdman & Lampe, 1996, p. 376).

Confrontation

Confrontation, like immediacy, is often misunderstood. Uninformed counselors sometimes think confrontation involves an attack on clients, a kind of "in your face" approach that is berating. Instead, confrontation is invitational. At its best, confrontation challenges a client to examine, modify, or control an aspect of behavior that is currently nonexistent or improperly used. Sometimes confrontation involves giving metacommunication feedback that is at variance with what the client wants or expects. This type of response may be inconsistent with a client's perception of self or circumstances (Wilcox-Matthew, Ottens, & Minor, 1997).

Confrontation can help "people see more clearly what is happening, what the consequences are, and how they can assume responsibility for taking action to change in ways that can lead to a more effective life and better and fairer relationships with others" (Tamminen & Smaby, 1981, p. 42). A good, responsible, caring, and appropriate confrontation produces growth and encourages an honest examination of oneself. Sometimes it may actually be detrimental to the client if the counselor fails to confront. Avoiding confrontation of the client's behavior is known as the MUM effect and results in the counselor's being less effective than he or she otherwise would be (Rosen & Tesser, 1970).

However, there are certain boundaries to confrontation (Leaman, 1978). The counselor needs to be sure that the relationship with the client is strong enough to sustain a confrontation. The counselor also must time a confrontation appropriately and remain true to the motives that have led to the act of confronting (Cavanagh, 1990). It is more productive in the long run to confront a client's strengths than a client's weaknesses (Berenson & Mitchell, 1974). The counselor should challenge the client to use resources he or she is failing to employ.

Regardless of whether confrontation involves strengths or weaknesses, counselors use a "you said . . . but look" structure to implement the confrontation process (Hackney & Cormier, 1994). For example, in the first part of the confrontation, a counselor might say, "You said you wanted to get out more and meet people." In the second part, the counselor highlights the discrepancy or contradiction in the client's words and actions—for instance, "But you are now watching television four to six hours a night."

Contracting

There are two aspects of contracting: one focuses on the processes involved in reaching a goal, the other concentrates on the final outcome. In goal setting, the counselor operates from a theoretical base that directs his or her actions. The client learns to change ways of thinking, feeling, and behaving to obtain goals. It is natural for counselors and clients to engage in contractual behavior. Goodyear and Bradley (1980) point out that all interpersonal relationships are contractual, but some are more explicit than others are. Because the median number of counseling sessions may be as few as five to six (Lorion, 1974), it is useful and time saving for counselors and clients to work on goals through a contract system. Such a system lets both parties participate in determining direction in counseling and evaluating change. It helps them be more specific (Brammer, 1993).

Thomas and Ezell (1972) list several other advantages to using contracts in counseling. First, a contract provides a written record of goals the counselor and client have agreed to pursue and the course of action to be taken. Second, the formal nature of a contract and its time limits may act as motivators for a client who tends to procrastinate. Third, if the contract is broken down into definable sections, a client may get a clear feeling that problems can be solved. Fourth, a contract puts the responsibility for any change on the client and thereby has the potential to empower the client and make him or her more responsive to the environment and more responsible for his or her behaviors. Finally, the contract system, by specifically outlining the number of sessions to be held, assures that clients will return to counseling regularly.

There are several approaches to setting up contracts. Goodyear and Bradley (1980) offer recommendations for promoting maximum effectiveness:

- It is essential that counselors indicate to their clients that the purpose of counseling is to work. It is important to begin by asking the client, "What would you like to work on?" as opposed to "What would you like to talk about?"
- It is vital that the contract for counseling concern change in the client rather than a person not present at the sessions. The counselor acts as a consultant when the client wishes to examine the behavior of another person, such as a child who throws temper tantrums, but work of this type is limited.
- The counselor must insist on setting up contracts that avoid the inclusion of client con words such as *try* or *maybe*, which are not specific. Such words usually result in the client's failing to achieve a goal.
- The counselor must be wary of client goals that are directed toward pleasing others and include words such as *should* or *must*. Such statements embody externally driven goals. For instance, a client who sets an initial goal that includes the statement "I should please my spouse more" may do so only temporarily because in the long run the goal is not internally driven. To avoid this kind of contract goal, the counselor needs to ask what the client really wants.
- It is vital to define concretely what clients wish to achieve through counseling. There is a great deal of difference between clients who state that they wish to be happy and clients who explain that they want to lose 10 pounds or talk to at least three new people a day. The latter goals are more concrete, and both counselors and clients are usually aware when they are achieved.
- The counselor must insist that contracts focus on change. Clients may wish to understand why they do something, but insight alone rarely produces action. Therefore, counselors must emphasize contracts that promote change in a client's behaviors, thoughts, or feelings.

Even though contracts are an important part of helping clients define, understand, and work on specific aspects of their lives, a contract system does have disadvantages. Okun (1997) stresses that contracts need to be open for renegotiating by both parties.

This process is often time-consuming and personally taxing. Thomas and Ezell (1972) list several other weaknesses of a contract system. First, a counselor cannot hold a client to a contract. The agreement has no external rewards or punishments that the counselor can use to force the client to fulfill the agreement. Second, some client problems may not lend themselves to the contract system. For example, the client who wants to make new friends may contract to visit places where there is good opportunity to encounter the types of people with whom he or she wishes to be associated. There is no way, however, that a contract can ensure that the client will make new friends. Third, a contractual way of dealing with problems focuses on outward behavior. Even if the contract is fulfilled successfully, the client may not have achieved insight or altered perception. Finally, the initial appeal of a contract is limited. Clients who are motivated to change and who find the idea fresh and appealing may become bored with such a system in time.

In determining the formality of the contract, a counselor must consider the client's background and motivational levels, the nature of the presenting problems, and what resources are available to the client to assure the successful completion of the contract. Goodyear and Bradley (1980) suggest that the counselor ask how the client might sabotage the contract. This question helps make the client aware of any resistance he or she harbors to fulfillment of the agreement.

Rehearsal

Once a contract is set up, the counselor can help the client maximize the chance of fulfilling it by getting him or her to rehearse or practice designated behavior. The old adage that practice makes perfect is as true for clients who wish to reach a goal as it is for athletes or artists. Clients can rehearse in two ways: overtly and covertly (Cormier & Cormier, 1998). Overt rehearsal requires the client to verbalize or act out what he or she is going to do. For example, if a woman is going to ask a man out for a date, she will want to rehearse what she is going to say and how she is going to act before she actually encounters the man. Covert rehearsal is imagining or reflecting on the desired goal. For instance, a student giving a speech can first imagine the conditions under which he will perform and then reflect about how to organize the subject matter that he will present. Imagining the situation beforehand can alleviate unnecessary anxiety and help the student perform better.

Sometimes a client needs counselor coaching during the rehearsal period. Such coaching may take the form of providing temporary aids to help the client remember what to do next (Bandura, 1976). It may simply involve giving feedback to the client on how he or she is doing. Feedback means helping the client recognize and correct any problem areas that he or she has in mastering a behavior, such as overexaggerating a movement. Feedback works well as long as it is not overdone (Geis & Chapman, 1971). To maximize its effectiveness, feedback should be given both orally and in writing.

Counselors can also assign clients *homework* (sometimes called "empowering assignments" or "between-session tasks") to help them practice the skills learned in the counseling sessions and generalize such skills to relevant areas of their lives. Homework involves additional work on a particular skill or skills outside the counseling session. It has numerous advantages, such as:

keeping clients focused on relevant behavior between sessions,
helping them see clearly what kind of progress they are making,
motivating clients to change behaviors,
helping them evaluate and modify their activities,
making clients more responsible for control of themselves, and
celebrating a breakthrough achieved in counseling (Hay & Kinnier, 1998; Hutchins &
   Vaught, 1997).

Cognitive-behavioral counselors are most likely to emphasize homework assignments. For instance, counselors with this theoretical background may have clients use workbooks to augment cognitive-behavioral in-session work. Workbooks require active participation and provide a tangible record of what clients have done. Two excellent cognitive-behavioral workbook exercises geared toward children are Vernon's (1989) "Decisions and Consequences," which focuses on cause and effect by having the counselor do such things as drop an egg into a bowl, and Kendall's (1990) *Coping Cat Workbook*, which concentrates on the connections between thoughts and feelings by having children engage in such activities as viewing life from a cat's perspective.

However, counselors from all theoretical perspectives can use homework if they wish to help clients help themselves. For homework to be most effective, it needs to be specifically tied to some measurable behavior change (Okun, 1997). It must also be relevant to clients' situations if it is to be meaningful and helpful (Cormier & Cormier, 1998; Young, 1998). Furthermore, clients need to complete homework assignments if they are to benefit from using a homework method.

"The kinds of homework that can be assigned are limited only by the creativity of the counselor and the client" (Hay & Kinnier, 1998, p. 126). Types of homework that are frequently given include those that are paradoxical (an attempt to create the opposite effect), behavioral (practicing a new skill), risk-taking (doing something that is feared), thinking (mulling over select thoughts), written (keeping a log or journal), bibliotherapeutic (reading, listening or viewing literature), and not doing anything (taking a break from one's usual habits) (Hay & Kinnier, 1998).

Transference and Countertransference

Counselor skills that help promote development during the counseling process are essential if the counselor is to avoid *circular counseling*, in which the same ground is covered over and over again. There is an equally important aspect of counseling, however, that influences the quality of the outcome: the relationship between counselor and client. The ability of the counselor and client to work effectively with each other is influenced largely by the relationship they develop. Counseling can be an intensely emotional experience (Cormier & Cormier, 1998; Sexton & Whiston, 1994). In a few instances, counselors and clients genuinely dislike each other or have incompatible personalities (Patterson & Welfel, 1994). Usually, however, they can and must work through transference and countertransference phenomena that result from the thoughts and emotions they think, feel, and express to one another. Although some counseling theories emphasize transference and countertransference more than others, these two concepts occur to some extent in almost all counseling relationships.

Transference.   *Transference* is the client's projection of past or present feelings, attitudes, or desires onto the counselor (Brammer & MacDonald, 1996; Brammer, Abrego, & Shostrom, 1993). The concept, from the literature of psychoanalysis, originally emphasized the transference of earlier life emotions. Today, however, transference is not restricted to psychoanalytic therapy and may be based on current experiences (Corey, Corey, & Callanan, 1998).

All counselors have what Gelso and Carter (1985) describe as a *transference pull,* an image generated through the use of personality and a particular theoretical approach. A client reacts to the image of the counselor in terms of the client's personal background and current conditions. The way the counselor sits, speaks, gestures, or looks may trigger a client reaction. An example of such an occurrence is a client's saying to a counselor, "You sound just like my mother." The statement in and of itself may be observational. But if the client starts behaving as if the counselor were the client's mother, transference has occurred.

Five patterns of transference behavior frequently appear in counseling: the client may perceive the counselor as ideal, seer, nurturer, frustrator, or nonentity (Watkins, 1983, p. 207). The counselor may at first enjoy transference phenomena that hold him or her in a positive light. Such enjoyment soon wears thin. To overcome any of the effects associated with transference experiences, Watkins (1983) advocates the specific approaches shown in Table 6.2.

Cavanagh (1990) notes that transference can be either direct or indirect. Direct transference is well represented by the example of the client who thinks of the counselor as his or her mother. Indirect transference is harder to recognize. It is usually revealed in client statements or actions that are not obviously directly related to the counselor (e.g., "Talk is cheap and ineffective" or "I think counseling is the experience I've always wanted").

Regardless of its degree of directness, transference is either negative or positive. Negative transference is when the client accuses the counselor of neglecting or acting negatively toward him or her. Although painful to handle initially, negative transference must be worked through for the counseling relationship to get back to reality and ultimately be productive. It has a direct impact on the quality of the relationship. Positive transference, especially a mild form, such as client admiration for the counselor, may not be readily acknowledged because it appears at first to add something to the relationship (Watkins, 1983). Indirect or mild forms of positive transference are least harmful to the work of the counselor and client.

Cavanagh (1990) holds that both negative and positive transference are forms of resistance. As long as the client keeps the attention of the counselor on transference issues, little progress is made in setting or achieving goals. To resolve transference issues, the counselor may work directly and interpersonally rather than analytically. For example, if the client complains that counselors only care about being admired, the counselor can respond, "I agree that some counselors may have this need, and it is not very helpful. On the other hand, we have been focusing on your goals. Let's go back to them. If the needs of counselors, as you observe them, become relevant to your goals, we will explore that issue."

Corey and associates (1998) see a therapeutic value in working through transference. They believe that the counselor-client relationship improves once the client resolves dis-

Table 6.2 Conceptualizing and intervening in transference patterns

Transference Pattern	Client Attitudes/Behaviors	Counselor Experience	Intervention Approach
Counselor as ideal	Profuse complimenting, agreements Bragging about counselor to others Imitating counselor's behaviors Wearing similar clothing Hungering for counselor's presence General idealization	Pride, satisfaction, strength Feelings of being all-competent Tension, anxiety, confusion Frustration, anger	Focus on: client's expectations, effects of these expectations Intra-punitive expressions trend toward self-negation tendency to give up oneself
Counselor as seer	Ascribes omniscience, power to counselor Views counselor as "the expert" Requests answers, solutions Solicits advice	Feelings of being all-knowing Expertness, "God-complex" Self-doubt, questioning of self Self-disillusionment Sense of incompetence	Focus on: client's need for advice lack of decision lack of self-trust opening up of options
Counselor as nurturer	Profuse emotion, crying Dependence and helplessness Indecision, solicitation of advice Desire for physical touch, to be held Sense of fragility	Feeling of sorrow, sympathy Urge to soothe, coddle, touch Experiences of frustration, ineptitude Depression and despair Depletion	Focus on: client's need for dependence feeling of independence unwillingness to take responsibility for self behavior-attitudinal alternatives
Counselor as frustrator	Defensive, cautious, guarded Suspicious and distrustful "Enter-exit" phenomenon Testing of counselor	Uneasiness, on edge, tension "Walking on eggshells" experience Increased monitoring of responses Withdrawal and unavailability Dislike for client Feelings of hostility, hate	Focus on: trust building, relationship enhancement purpose of transference pattern consequences of trusting others reworking of early experience
Counselor as nonentity	"Topic shifting," lack of focus Volubility, thought pressure Desultory, aimless meanderings	Overwhelmed, subdued Taken aback Feelings of being used, discounted Lack of recognition Sense of being a "nonperson" Feelings of resentment, frustration Experience of uselessness	Focus on: establishing contact getting behind the client's verbal barrier effects of quietness-reflection on client distancing effects of the transference

Source: From "Countertransference: Its Impact on the Counseling Situation," by C. E. Watkins, Jr., 1983, *Journal of Counseling and Development 64*, p. 208. © 1983 by ACA. Reprinted with permission. No further reproduction authorized without written permission of the American Counseling Association.

torted perceptions about the counselor. If the situation is handled sensitively, the improved relationship is reflected in the client's increased trust and confidence in the counselor. Furthermore, by resolving feelings of transference, a client may gain insight into the past and become free to act differently in the present and future.

Countertransference.   *Countertransference* refers to the counselor's projected emotional reaction to or behavior toward the client (Hansen, Rossberg, & Cramer, 1994). For example, a counselor might manifest behaviors toward her client as she did toward her sister when they were growing up. Such interaction can destroy the counselor's ability to be therapeutic, let alone objective. Unless resolved adequately, countertransference can be detrimental to the counseling relationship.

Kernberg (1975) takes two major approaches to the problem of conceptualizing countertransference. In the classic approach, countertransference is seen negatively and viewed as the direct or indirect unconscious reaction of the counselor to the client. The total approach sees countertransference as more positive. From this perspective, countertransference is a diagnostic tool for understanding aspects of the client's unconscious motivations. A third approach has been described by Blanck and Blanck (1979). It sees countertransference as both positive and negative. Watkins (1985) considers this third approach more realistic than the first two.

The manifestation of countertransference takes several forms (Corey et al., 1998). The most prevalent are (a) feeling a constant desire to please the client, (b) identifying with the problems of the client so much that one loses objectivity, (c) developing sexual or romantic feelings toward the client, (d) giving advice compulsively, and (e) wanting to develop a social relationship with the client.

Watkins (1985) thinks that countertransference can be expressed in a myriad of ways. He views four forms as particularly noteworthy: overprotective, benign, rejecting, and hostile. The first two forms are examples of *overidentification,* in which the counselor loses his or her ability to remain emotionally distant from the client. The latter two forms are examples of *disidentification,* in which the counselor becomes emotionally removed from the client. Disidentification may express itself in counselor behavior that is aloof, nonempathetic, hostile, cold, or antagonistic.

It is vital that counselors work through any negative or nonproductive countertransference. Otherwise, the progress of the client will lessen, and both counselor and client will be hurt in the process (Brammer & MacDonald, 1996; Watkins, 1985). It is also important that a counselor recognize that he or she is experiencing countertransference feelings. Once aware of these feelings, a counselor needs to discover the reasons behind them. It is critical to develop some consistent way of monitoring this self-understanding, and one way is to undergo supervision. Counselors, like clients, have blind spots, hidden areas, and aspects of their lives that are unknown to them. *Supervision* involves working in a professional relationship with a more experienced counselor so that the counselor being supervised can simultaneously monitor and enhance the services he or she offers to clients (Bernard & Goodyear, 1998). Among the procedures used in supervision are observing counselor-client interactions behind one-way mirrors, monitoring audiotapes of counseling sessions, and critiquing videotapes of counseling sessions (Borders, 1994). Analyzing the roles a counselor plays in sessions is a crucial component of supervision.

The Real Relationship

This chapter has emphasized the skills and interpersonal qualities that contribute to a working alliance between counselors and clients and ultimately result in clients' self-understanding and goal achievement. Using leads, levels of empathy, confrontation, encouragement, and contracts; recognizing transference and countertransference; and working through personal issues in professional ways all contribute to the counseling process. According to Gelso and Carter (1985), if helping skills have been used well, a *real relationship* (one that is reality oriented, appropriate, and undistorted) will emerge. The real relationship begins as a two-way experience between counselors and clients from their first encounter. Counselors are real by being genuine (owning their thoughts and feelings), trying to facilitate genuineness in their clients, and attempting to see and understand clients in a realistic manner. Clients contribute to the realness of the relationship by being genuine and perceiving their own situations realistically.

The real relationship that exists in counseling has been written about mostly from counselors' viewpoints and has been misunderstood or incompletely defined. According to Gelso and Carter (1985), there are specific propositions about the nature of a real relationship. One is that the relationship increases and deepens during the counseling process. Another is that counselors and clients have different expectations and actualizations of what a real relationship is like.

The work of Gelso and Carter has been evaluated by Sexton and Whiston (1994), who have reviewed the clinical literature on counselor-client relationships. Among other results, they have found that "the alliance between the client and counselor is a complex interactional phenomenon" (p. 45). Counseling is a dynamic, interactional process, and the strength of relationships between counselors and clients varies over time.

Study of the real relationship has headed in a promising direction: toward the *social construction perspective*—that is, "the process by which people come to describe, explain, or otherwise account for the world (including themselves) in which they live" (Sexton & Whiston, 1994, p. 60). Realness and growth, although not precisely defined at present, appear to be an important part of counseling relationships that will continue to attract attention and be important.

Summary and Conclusion

This chapter has emphasized the understanding and action phases of counseling, which occur after clients and counselors have established a relationship and explored possible goals toward which to work. These phases are facilitated by mutual interaction between the individuals involved. The counselor can help the client by appropriate leads, challenges to perception, multifocused responding, accurate empathy, self-disclosure, immediacy, confrontation, contracts, and rehearsal. These skills are focused on the client, but they also help the counselor gain self-insight.

Client and counselor must work through transference and countertransference, which can occur in several forms in a counseling relationship. Some clients and counselors will encounter less transference and countertransference than others, but it is important that each person recognize when he or she is engaged in such modes of communication. The more aware people are about these ways of relating, the less damage they are likely to do in their relationships with significant others and the more self-insight they are likely to achieve. A successful resolution of these issues promotes realness, and at the root of growth and goal attainment is the ability to experience the world realistically.

CLASSROOM ACTIVITIES

1. In groups of three, discuss ways of using the counseling skills that you learned about in this chapter. For example, how will you know when to be silent and when to confront?
2. In this chapter as well as previous ones, persuasion has been mentioned as an appropriate counselor skill. In groups of three, role-play the following situations in which persuasion might be employed: (a) a small boy is afraid of all dogs, (b) a student has high test anxiety, (c) an elderly person is withdrawn, and (d) a marriage partner will not fight fairly with his or her spouse. How do you experience persuasion differently in these situations? How effective are the persuasive techniques that you used? Discuss your feelings with the class as a whole.
3. In groups of four, two people should role-play a counselor and client and two should observe. Enact situations in which the counselor demonstrates that he or she knows

how to display the different levels of empathy. After the counselor has demonstrated these skills, he or she should receive feedback from the client and the observers about their impressions of each enactment.
4. In the same groups that were formed for activity 3, practice confrontation and immediacy skills. Discuss among yourselves and then with the class as a whole the differences and similarities between these two counseling skills.
5. Transference and countertransference are still hotly debated issues in counseling. Divide the class into two teams. One team should take the position that these phenomena do occur in counseling, while the other should argue that only real relationships are manifested between counselors and clients. Select a three-member panel from the class to judge the debate and give the class feedback on the points made by each side.

REFERENCES

Amundson, N. E. (1996). Supporting clients through a change in perspective. *Journal of Employment Counseling, 33*, 155–162.

Bandura, A. (1976). Effecting change through participant modeling. In J. D. Krumboltz & C. E. Thoresen (Eds.), *Counseling methods* (pp. 248–265). New York: Holt, Rinehart, & Winston.

Berenson, B. G., & Mitchell, K. M. (1974). *Confrontation: For better or worse.* Amherst, MA: Human Resource Development Press.

Bergman, J. S. (1985). *Fishing for barracuda.* New York: Norton.

Bernard, J. M., & Goodyear, R. K. (1998). *Fundamentals of clinical supervision* (2nd ed.). Boston: Allyn & Bacon.

Berne, E. (1964). *Games people play.* New York: Grove.

Blanck, G., & Blanck, R. (1979). *Egopsychology II: Psychoanalytic developmental psychology.* New York: Columbia University Press.

Borders, L. D. (Ed.), (1994). *Supervision: Exploring the effective components.* Greensboro, NC: ERIC/CASS.

Brammer, L. M., Abrego, P. J., & Shostrom, E. (1993). *Therapeutic counseling and psychotherapy* (6th ed.). Upper Saddle River, NJ: Merrill/Prentice Hall.

Brammer, L. M., & MacDonald, G. (1996). *The helping relationship* (6th ed.). Boston: Allyn & Bacon.

Carkhuff, R. R. (1969). *Helping and human relations: Selection and training* (Vol. 1). New York: Holt, Rinehart, & Winston.

Carkhuff, R. R. (1972). *The art of helping.* Amherst, MA: Human Resource Development Press.

Carkhuff, R. R., & Anthony, W. A. (1979). *The skills of helping.* Amherst, MA: Human Resource Development Press.

Cavanagh, M. E. (1990). *The counseling experience.* Prospect Heights, IL: Waveland.

Corey, G., Corey, M. S., & Callanan, P. (1998). *Issues and ethics in the helping professions* (5th ed.). Pacific Grove, CA: Brooks/Cole.

Cormier, W. H., & Cormier, L. S. (1998). *Interviewing strategies for helpers* (4th ed.). Pacific Grove, CA: Brooks/Cole.

Curtis, J. M. (1981). Indications and contraindications in the use of therapist's self disclosure. *Psychological Reports, 49,* 449–507.

Doster, J. A., & Nesbitt, J. G. (1979). Psychotherapy and self- disclosure. In G. J. Chelune (Ed.), *Self-disclosure: Origins, patterns, and implications and openness in interpersonal relationships* (pp. 177–224). San Francisco: Jossey-Bass.

Egan, G. (1998). *The skilled helper* (6th ed.). Pacific Grove, CA: Brooks/Cole.

Ellis, A. (1971). *Growth through reason.* Palo Alto, CA: Science and Behavior Books.

Erdman, P., & Lampe, R. (1996). Adapting basic skills to counsel children. *Journal of Counseling & Development, 74,* 374–377.

Fiedler, F. (1950). The concept of the ideal therapeutic relationship. *Journal of Consulting Psychology, 45,* 659–666.

Geis, G. L., & Chapman, R. (1971). Knowledge of results and other possible reinforcers in self-instructional systems. *Educational Technology, 2,* 38–50.

Gelso, C. J., & Carter, J. A. (1985). The relationship in counseling and psychotherapy: Components, consequences, and theoretical antecedents. *Counseling Psychologist, 13,* 155–243.

Gladstein, G. A. (1983). Understanding empathy: Integrating counseling, developmental, and social psychology perspectives. *Journal of Counseling Psychology, 30,* 467–482.

Goodyear, R. K., & Bradley, F. O. (1980). The helping process as contractual. *Personnel and Guidance Journal, 58,* 512–515.

Hackney, H. (1978). The evolution of empathy. *Personnel and Guidance Journal, 57,* 35–38.

Hackney, H., & Cormier, L. S. (1994). *Counseling strategies and objectives* (4th ed.). Boston: Allyn & Bacon.

Hansen, J. C., Rossberg, R. H., & Cramer, S. H. (1994). *Counseling: Theory and process* (5th ed.). Boston: Allyn & Bacon.

Hay, C. E., & Kinnier, R. T. (1998). Homework in counseling. *Journal of Mental Health Counseling, 20,* 122–132.

Hendrick, S. S. (1988). Counselor self-disclosure. *Journal of Counseling and Development, 66,* 419–424.

Hutchins, D. E., & Vaught, C. G. (1997). *Helping relationships and strategies* (3rd ed.). Pacific Grove, CA: Brooks/Cole.

Ivey, A. E. (1994). *Intentional interviewing and counseling* (3rd ed.). Pacific Grove, CA: Brooks/Cole.

Jourard, S. M. (1958). *Personal adjustment: An approach through the study of healthy personality.* New York: Macmillan.

Jourard, S. M. (1964). *The transparent self: Self-disclosure and well-being.* Princeton, NJ: Van Nostrand.

Jourard, S. M. (1968). *Disclosing man to himself.* Princeton, NJ: Van Nostrand.

Kendall, P. C. (1990). *Coping cat workbook.* Philadelphia: Temple University.

Kernberg, O. (1975). *Borderline conditions and pathological narcissism.* New York: Aronson.

Kline, W. B. (1986). The risks of client self-disclosure. *AMHCA Journal, 8,* 94–99.

Kottler, J. A. (1991). *The compleat therapist.* San Francisco: Jossey-Bass.

Kottler, J. A., Sexton, T. L., & Whiston, S. C. (1994). *The heart of healing.* San Francisco: Jossey-Bass.

Lazarus, A. A. (1995). *Multimodal therapy.* In R. J. Corsini & D. Wedding (Eds.), *Current psychotherapies* (5th ed., pp. 322–355). Itasca, IL: Peacock.

Leaman, D. R. (1978). Confrontation in counseling. *Personnel and Guidance Journal, 56,* 630–633.

Lorion, R. P. (1974). Patient and therapist variables in the treatment of low-income patients. *Psychological Bulletin, 81,* 344–354.

Luft, J. (1970). *Group process: An introduction to group dynamics.* Palo Alto, CA: National Press Books.

Means, B. L. (1973). Levels of empathic response. *Personnel and Guidance Journal, 52,* 23–28.

Ness, M. E. (1989). The use of humorous journal articles in counselor training. *Counselor Education and Supervision, 29,* 35–43.

Okun, B. F. (1997). *Effective helping: Interviewing and counseling techniques* (5th ed.). Pacific Grove, CA: Brooks/Cole.

Patterson, L. E., & Welfel, E. R. (1994). *Counseling process* (4th ed.). Pacific Grove, CA: Brooks/Cole.

Piercy, F. P., & Lobsenz, N. M. (1994). *Stop marital fights before they start.* New York: Berkeley.

Robinson, F. P. (1950). *Principles and procedures of student counseling.* New York: Harper.

Rogers, C. R. (1975). Empathic: An unappreciated way of being. *Counseling Psychologist, 5,* 2–10.

Rogers, C. R. (1987). The underlying theory: Drawn from experience with individuals and groups. *Counseling and Values, 32,* 38–46.

Rosen, S., & Tesser, A. (1970). On the reluctance to communicate undesirable information: The MUM effect. *Sociometry, 33,* 253–263.

Sexton, T. L., & Whiston, S. C. (1994). The status of the counseling relationship: An empirical review, theoretical implications, and research directions. *Counseling Psychology, 22,* 6–78.

Simone, D. H., McCarthy, P., & Skay, C. L. (1998). An investigation of client and counselor variables that influence the likelihood of counselor self-disclosure. *Journal of Counseling & Development, 76,* 174–182.

Tamminen, A. W., & Smaby, M. H. (1981). Helping counselors learn to confront. *Personnel and Guidance Journal, 60,* 41–45.

Thomas, G. P., & Ezell, B. (1972). The contract as counseling technique. *Personnel and Guidance Journal, 51,* 27–31.

Truax, C., & Mitchell, K. (1971). Research on certain therapist interpersonal skills in relation to process and outcome. In A. E. Bergin & S. L. Garfield (Eds.), *Handbook of psychotherapy and behavior change: An empirical analysis.* New York: Wiley.

Turock, A. (1978). Effective challenging through additive empathy. *Personnel and Guidance Journal, 57,* 144–149.

Turock, A. (1980). Immediacy in counseling: Recognizing clients' unspoken messages. *Personnel and Guidance Journal, 59,* 168–172.

Vernon, A. (1989). *Thinking, feeling, and behaving: An emotional education curriculum for children (Grades 1–6).* Champaign, IL: Research Press.

Watkins, C. E., Jr. (1983). Transference phenomena in the counseling situation. *Personnel and Guidance Journal, 62,* 206–210.

Watkins, C. E., Jr. (1985). Countertransference: Its impact on the counseling situation. *Journal of Counseling and Development, 63,* 356–359.

Watkins, C. E., Jr. (1990). The effects of counselor self- disclosure: A research review. *Counseling Psychologist, 18,* 477–500.

Watzlawick, P. (1983). *The situation is hopeless, but not serious.* New York: Norton.

Wilcox-Matthew, L., Ottens, A., & Minor, C. W. (1997). An analysis of significant events in counseling. *Journal of Counseling & Development, 75,* 282–291.

Young, M. E. (1998). *Learning the art of helping.* Upper Saddle River, NJ: Merrill/Prentice Hall.

7

TERMINATION OF COUNSELING RELATIONSHIPS

◆

Active as I am in sessions

going with you to the marrow of emotions

our shared journey has an end.

Tonight, as you hesitantly leave my office

to the early darkness of winter days

and the coldness of December nights,

you do so on your own.

Yet, this season of crystallized rain

changes, if however slowly,

and our time and words together

can be a memory from which may grow

a new seed of life within you,

Not without knowledge of past years' traumas

but rather in the sobering realization

that in being heard a chance is created

to fill a time with different feelings,

And savor them in the silent hours

when you stand by yourself alone.

From "Memory Traces," by S. T. Gladding, 1977, North Carolina Personnel and Guidance Journal, 6, *51. © 1977 by S. T. Gladding. Reprinted with permission.*

Termination *"refers to the decision, one-sided or mutual, to stop counseling" (Burke, 1989, p. 47). It is probably the least researched, most neglected aspect of counseling. Many theorists and counselors assume that termination will occur naturally and leave both clients and counselors pleased and satisfied with the results. Goodyear (1981) states that "it is almost as though we operate from a myth that termination is a process from which the counselor remains aloof and to which the client alone is responsive" (p. 347).*

But the termination of a counseling relationship has an impact on all involved, and it is often complex and difficult. Termination may well produce mixed feelings on the part of both the counselor and the client (Cowger, 1994; Kottler, Sexton, & Whiston, 1994). For example, a client may be both appreciative and regretful about a particular counseling experience. A client may also be ambivalent, anxious, fearful, confused, and sad about ending counseling. Unless it is handled properly, termination has the power to harm as well as heal (Doyle, 1998).

This chapter addresses termination as a multidimensional process that can take any of several forms. Specifically, we will examine the general function of termination as well as termination of individual sessions and counseling relationships. Termination strategies, resistance to termination, premature termination, counselor-initiated termination, and the importance of terminating a relationship on a positive note will also be discussed. The related areas of follow-up, referral, and recycling in counseling will be covered, too.

Function of Termination

Historically, addressing the process of termination directly has been avoided for several reasons. Ward (1984) has suggested two of the most prominent. First, termination is associated with loss, a traditionally taboo subject in all parts of society. Even though Hayes (1993) points out that loss may be associated with re-creation, transcendence, greater self-understanding, and new discoveries, counseling is generally viewed as emphasizing growth and development unrelated to endings. Second, termination is not directly related to the microskills that facilitate counseling relationships (Ivey, 1994). Therefore, termination is not a process usually highlighted in counselor education. Its significance has begun to emerge, however, because of societal trends, such as the aging of the American population (Hodgkinson, 1992), the wide acceptance of the concept of life stages (Sheehy, 1976), and an increased attention to death as a part of the life span (Kubler-Ross, 1969).

Termination serves several important functions. First, termination signals that something is finished. Life is a series of hellos and good-byes (Goldberg, 1975; Maholick & Turner, 1979). Hellos begin at birth, and good-byes end at death. Between birth and death, individuals enter into and leave a succession of experiences, including jobs, relationships, and life stages. Growth and adjustment depend on an ability to make the most of these experiences and learn from them. To begin something new, a former experience must be completed and resolved (Perls, 1969). Termination is the opportunity to end a learning experience properly, whether on a personal or professional level (Hulse-Killacky, 1993). In counseling, termination is more than an act signifying the end of therapy; it is also a motivator (Yalom, 1995).

Both client and counselor are motivated by the knowledge that the counseling experience is limited in time (Young, 1998). This awareness is similar to that of a young adult who realizes that he or she cannot remain a promising young person forever—an event that often occurs on one's 30th birthday. Such a realization may spur one on to hard work while there is still time to do something significant. Some counselors, such as those associated with strategic, systemic, and solution-focused family therapy, purposely limit the number of counseling sessions so that clients and counselors are more aware of time constraints and make the most of sessions (Gladding, 1998). Limiting the number of sessions in individual counseling is also effective (Munro & Bach, 1975).

Second, termination is a means of maintaining changes already achieved and generalizing problem-solving skills acquired in counseling (Dixon & Glover, 1984; Doyle, 1998). Successful counseling results in significant changes in the way the client thinks, feels, or acts. These changes are rehearsed in counseling, but they must be practiced in the real world. Termination provides an opportunity for such practice. The client can always go back to the counselor for any needed follow-up, but termination is the natural point for the practice of independence to begin. It is a potentially empowering experience for the client and enables him or her to address the present in an entirely new or modified way. At termination, the opportunity to put "insights into actions" is created (Gladding, 1990, p. 130). In other words, what seems like an exit becomes an entrance.

Third, termination serves as a reminder that the client has matured (Vickio, 1990). Besides offering the client new skills or different ways of thinking about him or herself, effective counseling termination marks a time in the client's life when he or she is less absorbed by and preoccupied with personal problems and more able to deal with outside people and events. This ability to handle external situations may result in more interdependent relationships that are mutually supportive and consequently lead toward a "more independent and satisfying life" (Burke, 1989, p. 47). Having achieved a successful resolution to a problem, a client now has new insights and abilities that are stored in memory and may be recalled and used on occasions.

Timing of Termination

When to terminate a relationship is a question that has no definite answer. If the relationship is ended too soon, clients may lose the ground they gained in counseling and regress to earlier behaviors. On the other hand, if termination is never addressed, clients can become dependent on the counselor and fail to resolve difficulties and grow as persons. There are, however, several pragmatic considerations in the timing of termination (Hackney & Cormier, 1994; Young, 1998).

- *Have clients achieved behavioral, cognitive, or affective contract goals?*   When both clients and counselors have a clear idea about whether particular goals have been reached, the timing of termination is easier to figure out. The key to this consideration is setting up a mutually agreed-on contract before counseling begins.

- *Can clients concretely show where they have made progress in what they wanted to accomplish?*   In this situation, specific progress may be the basis for making a decision about termination.
- *Is the counseling relationship helpful?*   If either the client or the counselor senses that what is occurring in the counseling sessions is not helpful, termination is appropriate.
- *Has the context of the initial counseling arrangement changed?*   In cases where there is a move or a prolonged illness, termination (as well as a referral) should be considered.

Overall, there is no one right time to terminate a counseling relationship. The "when" of termination must be figured out in accordance with the uniqueness of the situation and overall ethical and professional guidelines.

Issues of Termination

Termination of Individual Sessions

Termination is an issue during individual counseling sessions. Initial sessions should have clearly defined time limits (Brammer & MacDonald, 1996; Hackney & Cormier, 1994). A range of 45 to 50 minutes is generally considered adequate for an individual counseling session. It usually takes a counselor 5 to 10 minutes to adjust to the client and the client's concerns. Counseling sessions that terminate too quickly may be as unproductive as ones that last too long.

Benjamin (1987) proposes two important factors in closing an interview. First, both client and counselor should be aware that the session is ending. Second, no new material should be introduced or discussed during this ending. If the client introduces new material, the counselor needs to work to make it the anticipated focus of the next session. On rare occasions, the counselor has to deal with new material on an emergency basis.

A counselor can close an interview effectively in several ways. One is simply to make a brief statement indicating that time is up (Benjamin, 1987; Hackney & Cormier, 1994). For example, he or she might say, "It looks like our time is up for today." The simpler the statement, the better. If a client is discussing a number of subjects in an open-ended manner near the end of a session, the counselor should remind the client that there are only 5 or 10 minutes left. The client can then focus attention on important matters. As an alternative or in addition to the direct statement, the counselor can use nonverbal gestures to indicate that the session is ending. These include looking at his or her watch or standing up. Nonverbal gestures are probably best used with verbal indicators. Each reinforces the other.

Toward the end of the interview, it is usually helpful to summarize what has happened in the session. Either the counselor or the client may initiate this summation. A good summary ties together the main points of the session and "should be brief, to the point, and without interpretation" (Hackney & Cormier, 1994, p. 71). If both the counselor and client summarize, they may gain insight into what each has gotten out of the session. Such a process provides a means for clearing up any misunderstandings.

An important part of terminating any individual session is setting up the next appointment (Hansen, Rossberg, & Cramer, 1994). Most problems are resolved over time. Clients and counselors need to know when they will meet again to continue the work in progress. It is easier and more efficient to set up a next appointment at the end of a session than to do it later by phone.

Termination of a Counseling Relationship

Counseling relationships vary in length and purpose. It is vital to the health and well-being of everyone that the subject of termination be brought up early so that counselor and client can make the most of their time together (Cavanagh, 1990). Individuals need time to prepare for the end of a meaningful relationship. There may be some sadness, even if the relationship ends in a positive way. Thus, termination should not necessarily be presented as the zenith of the counseling experience. Hackney and Cormier (1994) stress that it is better to play down the importance of termination rather than play it up.

The counselor and client must agree on when termination of the relationship is appropriate and helpful (Young, 1998). Generally, they give each other verbal messages about a readiness to terminate. For example, a client may say, "I really think I've made a lot of progress over the past few months." Or a counselor may state, "You appear to be well on your way to no longer needing my services." Such statements suggest the beginning of the end of the counseling relationship. They usually imply recognition of growth or resolution. A number of other behaviors may also signal the end of counseling. These include a decrease in the intensity of work; more humor; consistent reports of improved abilities to cope, verbal commitments to the future, and less denial, withdrawal, anger, mourning, or dependence (McGee, Schuman, & Racusen, 1972; Patterson & Welfel, 1994; Shulman, 1999).

Hackney and Cormier (1994) believe that, in a relationship that has lasted more than 3 months, the final 3 or 4 weeks should be spent discussing the impact of termination. For instance, counselors may inquire how their clients will cope without the support of the relationship. Counselors may also ask clients to talk about the meaning of the counseling relationship and how they will use what they have learned in the future. Shulman (1999) suggests that, as a general rule of thumb, one-sixth of the time spent in a counseling relationship should be devoted to focusing on termination.

Maholick and Turner (1979) discuss specific areas of concern when deciding whether to terminate counseling:

- An examination of whether the client's initial problem or symptoms have been reduced or eliminated
- A determination of whether the stress-producing feelings that led to counseling have been eliminated
- An assessment of the client's coping ability and degree of understanding of self and others
- A determination of whether the client can relate better to others and is able to love and be loved
- An examination of whether the client has acquired abilities to plan and work productively
- An evaluation of whether the client can better play and enjoy life

These areas are not equally important for all clients, but it is essential that, before termination of counseling, clients feel confident to live effectively without the relationship (Huber, 1989; Ward, 1984; Young, 1998).

There are at least two other ways to facilitate the ending of a counselor-client relationship. One involves the use of fading. Dixon and Glover (1984) define *fading* as "a gradual decrease in the unnatural structures developed to create desired changes" (p. 165). In other words, clients gradually stop receiving reinforcement from counselors for behaving in certain ways, and appointments are spread out. A desired goal of all counseling is to help clients become less dependent on the counselor and the counseling sessions and more dependent on themselves and interdependent with others. From counseling, clients should also learn the positive reinforcement of natural contingencies. To promote fading, counseling sessions can be simply shortened as well as spaced further apart (Cormier & Cormier, 1998).

Another way to promote termination is to help clients develop successful problem-solving skills (Dixon & Glover, 1984). Clients, like everyone else, are constantly faced with problems. If counselors can help their clients learn more effective ways to cope with these difficulties, clients will no longer need the counseling relationship. This is a process of generalization from counseling experience to life. At its best, this process includes an emphasis on education and prevention as well as decision-making skills for everyday life and crisis situations.

Resistance to Termination

Resistance to termination may come from either the counselor or client. Patterson and Welfel (1994) note that resistance is especially likely when the counseling relationship has lasted for a long time or has involved a high level of intimacy. Other factors that may promote resistance include the pain of earlier losses, loneliness, unresolved grief, need gratification, fear of rejection, and fear of having to be self-reliant. Some of these factors are more prevalent with clients, whereas others are more likely to characterize counselors.

Client Resistance

Clients resist termination in many ways. Two easily recognized expressions of resistance are (a) asking for more time at the end of a session and (b) asking for more appointments once a goal has been reached. Another more troublesome form of client resistance is the development of new problems that were not part of his or her original concerns, such as depression or anxiety. The manifestation of these symptoms makes termination more difficult; in such situations, a client may convince the counselor that only he or she can help. Thus, the counselor may feel obligated to continue working with the person for either personal or ethical reasons.

Regardless of the strategy employed, the termination process is best carried out gradually and slowly (Cormier & Cormier, 1998). Sessions can become less frequent over time, and client skills, abilities, and resources can be highlighted simultaneously. Sometimes when clients are especially hesitant to terminate, the counselor can "prescribe" a limited number of future sessions or concentrate with clients on how they will set themselves up for relapse (Anderson & Stewart, 1983). These procedures make the covert more overt and help counselors and clients identify what issues are involved in leaving a helping relationship.

Vickio (1990) has developed a unique way of implementing a concrete strategy for college students who are dealing with loss and termination. In *The Goodbye Brochure,* he describes what it means to say good-bye and why good-byes should be carried out. He then discusses five *D*s for successfully dealing with departure and loss and an equal number of *D*s for unsuccessfully dealing with them (Vickio, 1990, p. 576).

SUCCESSFULLY DEALING WITH LOSS
- Determine ways to make your transition a gradual process.
- Discover the significance that different activities have had in your life.
- Describe this significance to others.
- Delight in what you have gained and in what lies ahead of you.
- Define areas of continuity in your life.

UNSUCCESSFULLY DEALING WITH LOSS
- Deny the loss.
- Distort your experience by overglorifying it.
- Denigrate your activities and relationships.
- Distract yourself from thinking about departure.
- Detach yourself abruptly from your activities and relationships.

Lerner and Lerner (1983) believe that client resistance often results from a fear of change. If clients come to value a counseling relationship, they may fear that they cannot function well without it. For example, people who have grown up in unstable or chaotic environments involving alcoholism or divorce may be especially prone to hold on to the stability of counseling and the relationship with the counselor. It is vital that the counselor recognize the special needs of these individuals and the difficulties they have in coping with loneliness and intimacy (Loewenstein, 1979; Weiss, 1973). It is even more critical that the counselor take steps to help such clients help themselves by exploring with them the advantages of working in other therapeutic settings, such as support or self-help groups. For such clients, counseling is potentially addictive. If they are to function in healthy ways, they must find alternative sources of support.

Counselor Resistance

Although the "ultimate goal in counseling is for counselors to become obsolete and unnecessary to their clients," some counselors are reluctant to say good-bye at the appropriate time (Nystul, 1993, p. 36). Clients who have special or unusual needs or those who are very productive may be especially attractive to counselors. Goodyear (1981) lists eight conditions in which termination may be particularly difficult for counselors:

1. When termination signals the end of a significant relationship
2. When termination arouses the counselor's anxieties about the client's ability to function independently

3. When termination arouses guilt in the counselor about not having been more effective with the client
4. When the counselor's professional self-concept is threatened by the client who leaves abruptly and angrily
5. When termination signals the end of a learning experience for the counselor (for example, the counselor may have been relying on the client to learn more about the dynamics of a disorder or a particular culture)
6. When termination signals the end of a particularly exciting experience of living vicariously through the adventures of the client
7. When termination becomes a symbolic recapitulation of other (especially unresolved) farewells in the counselor's life
8. When termination arouses in the counselor conflicts about his or her own individuation (p. 348)

It is important that counselors recognize any difficulties they have in letting go of certain clients. A counselor may seek consultation with colleagues in dealing with this problem or undergo counseling to resolve the problem. The latter option is quite valuable if the counselor has a personal history of detachment, isolation, and excessive fear of intimacy. Kovacs (1965, 1976) and Guy (1987) report that some persons who enter the helping professions possess just such characteristics.

Premature Termination

The question of whether a client terminates counseling prematurely is not one that can be measured by the number of sessions the client has completed. Rather, premature termination has to do with how well the client has achieved the personal goals established in the beginning and how well he or she is functioning generally (Ward, 1984).

Some clients show little, if any, commitment or motivation to change their present circumstances and request that counseling be terminated after the first session. Other clients express this desire after realizing the work necessary for change. Still others make this wish known more indirectly by missing or being late for appointments. Regardless of how clients express a wish for premature termination, it is likely to trigger thoughts and feelings within the counselor that must be dealt with. Hansen, Warner, and Smith (1980) suggest that the topic of premature termination be discussed openly between a counselor and client if the client expresses a desire to terminate before specified goals have been met or if the counselor suspects that premature termination may occur. With discussion, thoughts and feelings of both the client and counselor can be examined and a premature ending prevented.

Sometimes a client fails to keep an appointment and does not call to reschedule. In such cases, the counselor should attempt to reach the client by phone or mail. If the counselor finds that the client wishes to quit, an exit interview should be set up. Ward (1984) reports four possible benefits from such an interview:

1. An exit interview may help the client resolve any negative feelings resulting from the counseling experience.

2. An exit interview serves as a way to invite the client to continue in counseling if he or she so wishes.
3. Another form of treatment or a different counselor can be considered in an exit interview if the client so desires.
4. An exit interview may increase the chance that the next time the client needs help, he or she will seek counseling.

Cavanagh (1990) believes that, in premature termination, counselors often make one of two mistakes. One is to blame either him- or herself or the client for what is happening. A counselor is more likely to blame the client, but in either case, someone is berated and the problem is compounded. It may be more productive for the counselor to think of the situation as one in which no one is at fault. Such a strategy is premised on the idea that some matches between clients and counselors work better than others do.

A second mistake on the counselor's part is to act in a cavalier manner about the situation. An example is the counselor who says, "It's too bad this client has chosen not to continue counseling, but I've got others." To avoid making either mistake, Cavanagh (1990) recommends that counselors find out why a client terminated prematurely. Possible reasons include the following:

To see whether the counselor really cares
To try to elicit positive feelings from the counselor
To punish or try to hurt the counselor
To eliminate anxiety
To show the counselor that the client has found a cure elsewhere
To express to the counselor that the client does not feel understood

Cavanagh (1990) believes that counselors need to understand that, regardless of what they do, some clients terminate counseling prematurely. Such a realization allows counselors to feel that they do not have to be perfect and frees them to be more authentic in the therapeutic relationship. It also enables them to acknowledge overtly that, no matter how talented and skillful they are, some clients find other counselors more helpful. Ideally, counselors are aware of the anatomy of termination (see Figure 7.1). With such knowledge, they become empowered to deal realistically with situations concerning client termination.

Not all people who seek counseling are equally ready to work in such a relationship, and the readiness level may vary as the relationship continues. Some clients need to terminate prematurely for good reasons, and their action does not necessarily reflect on the counselor's competence. Counselors can control only a limited number of variables in a counseling relationship. The following list includes several of the variables most likely to be effective in preventing premature termination (Young, 1998):

- *Appointments.* The less time between appointments and the more regularly they are scheduled the better.
- *Orientation to counseling.* The more clients know about the process of counseling, the more likely they are to stay with it.

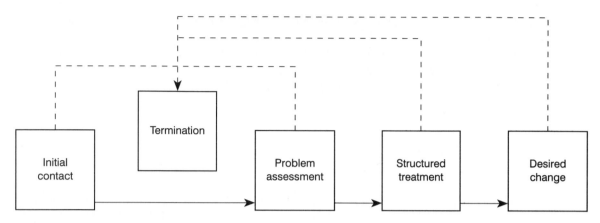

Figure 7.1   The anatomy of termination

Source: From *Contemporary Approaches to Psychotherapy and Counseling* (p. 37), by J. F. Burke, 1989, Pacific Grove, CA: Brooks/Cole. Copyright 1989 by Brooks/Cole Publishing Company, Pacific Grove, CA 93950, a division of Thomson Publishing Company Inc. Based on Gottman and Leiblum's *How to Do Psychotherapy and How to Evaluate It: A Manual for Beginners* (p. 4). Copyright by Holt, Rinehart, & Winston. Adapted by permission.

- *Consistency of counselor.*   Clients do not like to be processed from counselor to counselor. Therefore, the counselor who does the initial intake should continue counseling the client if at all possible.
- *Reminders to motivate client attendance.*   Cards, telephone calls, or E-mail can be effective reminders. Because of the sensitivity of counseling, however, a counselor should always have the client's permission to send an appointment reminder.

Counselor-Initiated Termination

Counselor-initiated termination is the opposite of premature termination. A counselor sometimes needs to end relationships with some or all clients. Reasons include illness, working through countertransference, relocation to another area, an extended trip, or the realization that client needs could be better served by someone else. These are what Cavanagh (1990) classifies as "good reasons" for the counselor to terminate.

There are also poor reasons for counselor-initiated termination. They include a counselor's feelings of anger, boredom, or anxiety. If a counselor ends a relationship because of such feelings, the client may feel rejected and even worse than he or she did in the beginning. It is one thing for a person to handle rejection from peers; it is another for that same person to handle rejection from a counselor. Cavanagh (1990) notes that, although a counselor may have some negative feelings about a client, it is possible to acknowledge and work through those feelings without behaving in an extreme or detrimental way.

Both London (1982) and Seligman (1984) present models for helping clients deal with the temporary absence of the counselor. These researchers stress that clients and counselors should prepare as far in advance as possible for temporary termination by openly discussing the impending event and working through any strong feelings about the issue of separation. Clients may actually experience benefits from counselor-initiated termination by realizing that the counselor is human and replaceable. They may also come to understand that people have choices about how to deal with interpersonal relationships. Furthermore, they may explore previous feelings and major life decisions, learning more clearly that new behaviors carry over into other life experiences (London, 1982). Refocusing may also occur during the termination process and help clients see issues on which to work more clearly.

Seligman (1984) recommends a more structured way of preparing clients for counselor-initiated termination than London does, but both models can be effective. It is important in any situation like this to make sure clients have the names and numbers of a few other counselors to contact in case of an emergency.

There is also the matter of permanent counselor-initiated termination. In today's mobile society "more frequently than before, it is counselors who leave, certain they will not return" (Pearson, 1998, p. 55). In such cases, termination is more painful for clients and presents quite a challenge for counselors. The timing expected in the counseling process is off.

In permanent counselor-initiated termination, it is still vital to review clients' progress, end the relationship at a specific time, and make postcounseling plans. A number of other tasks also must be accomplished (Pearson, 1998); among these are counselors working through their own feelings about their termination, such as sadness, grief, anger, and fear. Furthermore, counselors need to put clients' losses in perspective and plan accordingly how each client will deal with the loss of the counseling relationship. Counselors must take care of their physical needs as well and seek professional and personal support where necessary.

In the process of their own termination preparations, counselors should be open with clients about where they are going and what they will be doing. They should make such announcements in a timely manner and allow clients to respond spontaneously. "Advanced empathy is a powerful means for helping clients express and work through the range of their emotions" (Pearson, 1998, p. 61). Arranging for transfers or referrals to other counselors is critical if clients' needs are such. Finally, there is the matter of saying good-bye and ending the relationship. This process may be facilitated through the use of immediacy and/or rituals.

Ending on a Positive Note

The process of termination, like counseling itself, involves a series of checkpoints that counselors and clients can consult to evaluate the progress they are making and determine their readiness to move to another stage (Maholick & Turner, 1979). It is important that termination be mutually agreed on, if at all possible, so that all involved can move on in ways deemed most productive. Nevertheless, this is not always possible. Patterson and Welfel (1994, pp. 138–139) present eight guidelines a counselor can use to end an intense counseling relationship in a positive way:

1. "Be clearly aware of the client's needs and wants." At the end of a counseling relationship, the client may need time to talk to the counselor about the impending termination. This may require a few sessions to complete.

2. "Be clearly aware of your own needs and wants." Counseling is not a one-way street, and counselors who take care of others without taking care of themselves will most likely experience difficulty in terminating relationships. It is vital that counselors acknowledge personal feelings and needs about a counseling relationship before it ends.

3. "Be aware of your previous experiences with separation and your inner reaction to these experiences." The feelings generated from one intense relationship may be similar to those that occur in another. Counselors should be emotionally self-aware to avoid countertransference and be genuine in relationships.

4. "Invite the client to share how he or she feels about ending the experience." This guideline is similar to the first, but it focuses on the emotions, not the thoughts, of the client. Clients need to express themselves as completely as possible if closure is to be of maximum benefit.

5. "Share honestly with the client how you feel about the counseling experience." This is another aspect of the counselor's being real in the relationship. Part of this sharing includes revealing to the client what you, as a counselor, have learned from this particular experience.

6. "Review the major events of the counseling experience and bring the review into the present." The focus of this process is to help a client see where he or she is now as compared with the beginning of counseling and realize more fully the growth that has been accomplished. The procedure includes a review of significant past moments and turning points in the relationship with a focus on personalizing the summary.

7. "Supportively acknowledge the changes the client has made." At this point the counselor lets the client know that he or she recognizes the progress that has been achieved and actively encourages the client to maintain it.

8. "Invite the client to keep up to date on what is happening in his or her life." Counseling relationships eventually end, but the caring and concern the counselor has for the client are not automatically terminated at the final session. Clients need to know that the counselor continues to be interested in what is happening in their lives. Updating can be accomplished in part through follow-up sessions.

Issues Related to Termination: Follow-up and Referral

Follow-up

Follow-up entails checking to see how the client is doing, with respect to whatever the problem was, sometime after termination has occurred (Okun, 1997). In essence, it is a positive monitoring process that encourages client growth (Doyle, 1998; Egan, 1998). Follow-up is a step that some counselors neglect. It is important because it reinforces the gains clients have made in counseling and helps both counselor and client reevaluate the experience. It also emphasizes the counselor's genuine care and concern for the client.

Follow-up can be conducted on either a short- or long-term basis (Cormier & Cormier, 1998). Short-term follow-up is usually conducted 3 to 6 months after a counseling relationship terminates. Long-term follow-up is conducted at least 6 months after termination.

Follow-up may take many forms, but there are four main ways in which it is usually conducted (Cormier & Cormier, 1998). The first is to invite the client in for a session to discuss any progress he or she has continued to make in achieving desired goals. A second way is through a telephone call to the client. A call allows the client to report to the counselor, although only verbal interaction is possible. A third way is for the counselor to send the client a letter asking about the client's current status. A fourth and more impersonal way is for the counselor to mail the client a questionnaire dealing with current levels of functioning. Many public agencies use this type of follow-up as a way of showing accountability. Such procedures do not preclude the use of more personal follow-up procedures by individual counselors. Although time-consuming, a personal follow-up is probably the most effective way of evaluating past counseling experiences. It helps assure clients that they are cared about as individuals and more than just statistics.

Sometimes, regardless of the type of follow-up used, it is helpful if the client monitors his or her own progress through the use of graphs or charts. Then, when relating information to the counselor, the client can do so in a more concrete and objective way. If counselor and client agree at the end of the last session on a follow-up time, this type of self-monitoring may be especially meaningful and give the client concrete proof of progress and clearer insight into current needs.

Referral and Recycling

Counselors are not able to help everyone who seeks assistance. When a counselor realizes that a situation is unproductive, it is important to know whether to terminate the relationship or make a referral. A referral involves arranging other assistance for a client when the initial arrangement is not or cannot be helpful (Okun, 1997). There are many reasons for referring, including the following (Goldstein, 1971):

- The client has a problem the counselor does not know how to handle.
- The counselor is inexperienced in a particular area (e.g., substance abuse or mental illness) and does not have the necessary skill to help the client.
- The counselor knows of a nearby expert who would be more helpful to the client.
- The counselor and client have incompatible personalities.
- The relationship between counselor and client is stuck in an initial phase of counseling.

Referrals involve a how and a when. The *how* involves knowing how to call on a helping resource and handle the client to maximize the chances that he or she will follow through with the referral process. A client may resist a referral if the client feels rejected by the counselor. Patterson and Welfel (1994) suggest that a counselor spend at least one session with the client in preparation for the referral. Some clients will need several sessions.

The *when* of making a referral involves timing. The longer a client works with a counselor, the more reluctant the client may be to see someone else. Thus, timing is crucial. If a counselor suspects an impasse with a certain client, he or she should refer that client as soon as possible. On the other hand, if the counselor has worked with the client for a while, he or she should be sensitive about giving the client enough time to get used to the idea of working with someone else.

Recycling is an alternative when the counselor thinks the counseling process has not yet worked but can be made to do so. It means reexamining all phases of the therapeutic process. Perhaps the goals were not properly defined or an inappropriate strategy was chosen. Whatever the case, by reexamining the counseling process, counselor and client can decide how or whether to revise and reinvest in the counseling process. Counseling, like other experiences, is not always successful on the first attempt. Recycling gives both counselor and client a second chance to achieve what each wants: positive change.

Summary and Conclusion

Termination is an important but often neglected and misunderstood phase of counseling. The subjects of loss and ending are usually given less emphasis in counseling than those of growth and development. Thus, the subject of termination is frequently either ignored or taken for granted. Yet successful termination is vital to the health and well-being of both counselors and clients. It is a phase of counseling that can determine the success of all previous phases and must be handled with skill. Otherwise, everyone in the counseling relationship will become stuck in reviewing data in areas that may be of little use. In addition, termination gives clients a chance to try new behaviors and serves as a motivator.

This chapter has emphasized the procedures involved in terminating an individual counseling session as well as the extended counseling relationship. These processes can be generalized to ending group or family counseling sessions. Both clients and counselors must be prepared for these endings. One way to facilitate this preparation is through the use of structure, such as time frames, and both verbal and nonverbal signals. Clients need to learn problem-solving skills before a counseling relationship is over so that they can depend on themselves rather than their counselors when they face difficult life situations. Nevertheless, it is important that a client be given permission to contact the counselor again if needed. An open policy does much to alleviate anxiety.

At times the counselor, client, or both resist terminating the relationship. Many times this resistance is related to unresolved feelings of grief and separation (Cowger, 1994). When a client has such feelings, he or she may choose to terminate the relationship prematurely. A counselor may also initiate termination but usually does so for good reasons. Regardless of who initiates termination, it is vital that all involved know what is happening and prepare accordingly. If possible, it is best to end counseling on a positive note. Once termination is completed, it is helpful to conduct some type of follow-up within a year. Sometimes referrals or recycling procedures are indicated to ensure that the client receives the type of help needed.

CLASSROOM ACTIVITIES

1. In pairs, discuss the most significant termination experience of your life, such as the death of a loved one, graduation, or some life stage. Evaluate with your partner the positive things you learned from these experiences as well as the pain you felt.

2. In small groups, take turns role-playing different forms of counselor-client resistance to termination at the end of a session. Have one person play the part of the counselor, one person the part of the client, two persons the parts of alter egos for counselor and client,

and one person the part of an observer/evaluator. After everyone has had a chance to play the counselor, discuss the feelings you had related to resistance in yourself and others and what strategies seemed to work best in overcoming resistance.

3. Write down ways that you think you can tell whether a counselor or client is ready to end a relationship. Then silently enact two or more of your behaviors in front of your classmates and let them describe what you are doing and how they would react to it.

4. As a class, divide into two teams and debate the issue of whether counseling relationships must end on a positive note. Pay special attention to the benefits that a client or counselor might derive from terminating counseling on a negative note.

5. What are your feelings about recycling? In groups of four, discuss what you think and feel about this procedure. Also, role-play how you would refer a difficult client to another professional.

REFERENCES

Anderson, C. M., & Stewart, S. (1983). *Mastering resistance: A practical guide to family therapy.* New York: Guilford.

Benjamin, A. (1987). *The helping interview* (4th ed.). Boston: Houghton Mifflin.

Brammer, L. M., & MacDonald, G. (1996). *The helping relationship* (6th ed.). Boston: Allyn & Bacon.

Burke, J. F. (1989). *Contemporary approaches to psychotherapy and counseling.* Pacific Grove, CA: Brooks/Cole.

Cavanagh, M. E. (1990). *The counseling experience.* Prospect Heights, IL: Waveland.

Cormier, W. H., & Cormier, L. S. (1998). *Interviewing strategies for helpers* (4th ed.). Pacific Grove, CA: Brooks/Cole.

Cowger, E. (1994, November). *Dealing with grief and loss.* Presentation at the Southern Association for Counselor Education and Supervision conference, Charlotte, NC.

Dixon, D. N., & Glover, J. A. (1984). *Counseling: A problem-solving approach.* New York: Wiley.

Doyle, R. E. (1998). *Essential skills and strategies in the helping process* (2nd ed.). Pacific Grove, CA: Brooks/Cole.

Egan, G. (1998). *The skilled helper* (6th ed.). Pacific Grove, CA: Brooks/Cole.

Gladding, S. T. (1990). Coming full cycle: Reentry after the group. *Journal for Specialists in Group Work, 15,* 130–131.

Gladding, S. T. (1998). *Family therapy: History, theory, and practice* (2nd ed.). Upper Saddle River, NJ: Merrill/Prentice Hall.

Goldberg, C. (1975). Termination: a meaningful pseudo-dilemma in psychotherapy. *Psychotherapy, 12,* 341–343.

Goldstein, A. (1971). *Psychotherapeutic attraction.* New York: Pergamon.

Goodyear, R. K. (1981). Termination as a loss experience for the counselor. *Personnel and Guidance Journal, 59,* 349–350.

Guy, J. D. (1987). *The personal life of the psychotherapist.* New York: Wiley.

Hackney, H., & Cormier, L. S. (1994). *Counseling strategies and objectives* (4th ed.). Boston: Allyn & Bacon.

Hansen, J. C., Rossberg, R. H., & Cramer, S. H. (1994). *Counseling theory and process* (5th ed.). Boston: Allyn & Bacon.

Hansen, J., Warner, R., & Smith, E. (1980). *Group counseling: Theory and process* (2nd ed.). Chicago: Rand McNally.

Hayes, R. L. (1993). Life, death, and reconstructive self. *Journal of Humanistic Education and Development, 32,* 85–88.

Hodgkinson, H. L. (1992). *A demographic look at tomorrow.* Washington, DC: Institute for Educational Leadership.

Huber, C. H. (1989). Paradox-orthodox: Brief pastoral psychotherapy. *Individual Psychology, 45,* 230–237.

Hulse-Killacky, D. (1993). Personal and professional endings. *Journal of Humanistic Education and Development, 32,* 92–94.

Ivey, A. E. (1994). *Intentional interviewing and counseling* (3rd ed.). Pacific Grove, CA: Brooks/Cole.

Kottler, J. A., Sexton, T. L., & Whiston, S. C. (1994). *The heart of healing*. San Francisco: Jossey-Bass.

Kovacs, A. L. (1965). The intimate relationship: A therapeutic paradox. *Psychotherapy, 2,* 97–103.

Kovacs, A. L. (1976). The emotional hazards of teaching psychotherapy. *Psychotherapy, 13,* 321–334.

Kubler-Ross, E. (1969). *On death and dying*. New York: Macmillan.

Lerner, S., & Lerner, H. (1983). A systematic approach to resistance: Theoretical and technical considerations. *American Journal of Psychotherapy, 37,* 387–399.

Loewenstein, S. F. (1979). Helping family members cope with divorce. In S. Eisenberg & L. E. Patterson (Eds.), *Helping clients with special concerns* (pp. 193–217). Boston: Houghton Mifflin.

London, M. (1982). How do you say good-bye after you've said hello? *Personnel and Guidance Journal, 60,* 412–414.

Maholick, L. T., & Turner, D. W. (1979). Termination: The difficult farewell. *American Journal of Psychotherapy, 33,* 583–591.

McGee, T. F., Schuman, B. N., & Racusen, F. (1972). Termination in group psychotherapy. *American Journal of Psychotherapy, 26,* 521–532.

Munro, J. N., & Bach, T. R. (1975). Effect of time-limited counseling on client change. *Journal of Counseling Psychology, 22,* 395–398.

Nystul, M. S. (1993). *The art and science of counseling and psychotherapy*. Upper Saddle River, NJ: Merrill/Prentice Hall.

Okun, B. F. (1997). *Effective helping* (5th ed.). Pacific Grove, CA: Brooks/Cole.

Patterson, L. E., & Welfel, E. R. (1994). *The counseling process* (4th ed.). Pacific Grove, IL: Brooks/Cole.

Pearson, Q. M. (1998). Terminating before counseling has ended: Counseling implications and strategies for counselor relocation. *Journal of Mental Health Counseling, 20,* 55–63.

Perls, F. S. (1969). *Gestalt therapy verbation*. Lafayette, CA: Real People Press.

Seligman, L. (1984). Temporary termination. *Journal of Counseling and Development, 63,* 43–44.

Sheehy, G. (1976). *Passages: Predictable crises of adult life*. New York: Bantam.

Shulman, L. (1999). *The skills of helping individuals, families, groups, and communities* (4th ed.). Itasca, IL: Peacock.

Vickio, C. J. (1990). The goodbye brochure: Helping students to cope with transition and loss. *Journal of Counseling and Development, 68,* 575–577.

Ward, D. E. (1984). Termination of individual counseling: Concepts and strategies. *Journal of Counseling and Development, 63,* 21–25.

Weiss, R. S. (Ed.). (1973). *Loneliness*. Cambridge, MA: MIT Press.

Yalom, I. D. (1995). *The theory and practice of group psychotherapy* (4th ed.). New York: Basic Books.

Young, M. E. (1998). *Learning the art of helping*. Upper Saddle River, NJ: Merrill/Prentice Hall.

8

PSYCHOANALYTIC AND ADLERIAN APPROACHES TO COUNSELING

◆

I know how the pressure can build sometimes

In your own metallic tea-kettle world,

Sporadically you whistle to me,

At other times you explode!

Somewhere beneath that noisy facade

(In silence or stillness perhaps)

Feelings might flow with quickness and strength,

Like the Dan or the Shenandoah,

But now they incessantly boil in your mind

Steam-filling dark shadows and choking conversation.

From "Tea-Kettle Song," by S. T. Gladding, 1974, School Counselor, 21, *p. 209. © 1974 by ACA. Reprinted with permission. No further reproduction authorized without written permission of the American Counseling Association.*

Counseling, by definition, is a process that involves interpersonal relationships (Patterson, 1985). Frequently it is conducted on an individual level in which an atmosphere of trust is fostered between counselor and client that ensures communication, exploration, planning, change, and growth. In counseling, a client gains the benefit of immediate feedback from the counselor about behaviors, feelings, plans, and progress.

The following four variables determine the amount of growth and change that takes place in any type of counseling: counselor, client, setting, and theoretical orientation. We have already examined some of the universal qualities of effective counselors and the counseling process. Certain characteristics seem to distinguish these aspects of counseling. For example, effective counselors have a good understanding of themselves and others, an awareness of the importance of counseling theory, an appreciation for the influence of cultures, and a sound educational background. They understand and work with their clients on agreed-on goals and realize that the personalities of counselors and clients have a powerful impact on each other and the counseling process. The setting in which counseling is conducted is also a critical variable. Counselors respond to client needs in different ways in different settings, such as schools, rehabilitation agencies, and mental health centers. The stages of counseling relationships likewise play a role in how counseling is conducted.

Chapters 8 through 11 focus on theoretical orientations of counselors in mainly individual situations. Counseling began as a person-to-person relationship. Even though group, marriage/family, and even community counseling are now prevalent, the theories covered in these chapters are often considered the background from which other counseling approaches have evolved.

Theory into Practice

As of 1994, more than 400 systems of psychotherapy were available worldwide (Corsini, 1995). Thus, counselors have a wide variety of theories from which to choose. Effective counselors scrutinize theories for proven effectiveness and match them to personal beliefs and realities about the nature of people and change. Most counseling approaches, other than eclecticism, fall within four broad theoretical categories: psychoanalytic, affective, cognitive, and behavioral. In addition to examining these basic theoretical positions, we will study some combination of theories, such as cognitive-behavioral approaches, which have grown in scope and importance in recent years (see Chapter 11). With each theory, we will include a discussion of the background of the principal founder or founders because, as Corsini (1995) says, "there appears to be a concordance between the personality of a psychotherapy innovator and the system he or she has developed" (p. 13). After this initial discussion, we will examine the following aspects of each theory: view of human nature, role of the counselor, goals, techniques, and evaluation of uniqueness and limitations.

As you study the theories, ask yourself which would be most comfortable for you to use. Speculate about how you might employ each approach and with which types of clients.

This chapter covers Freudian (classical) psychoanalytic theory and modification of the theory, such as object-relations and psychosocial psychology. Psychoanalysis has had a direct and indirect influence on a variety of counseling approaches (Bankart, 1997). We also cover Adlerian theory in this chapter because of its close historical link to psychoanalysis and its importance in counseling.

It should be pointed out that psychoanalytic and Adlerian theory are connected only in time, not emphasis. Sigmund Freud and Alfred Adler were quite different individuals whose lives and theories varied widely. They agreed on the importance of early experiences in childhood as powerful determinants for the formation of adult personality. They also conversed and debated the merits of a number of constructs and principles. But whereas Freud stressed the importance of sexuality, instinct, and the unconscious, Adler emphasized the significance of social life, purposeful goals, and conscious experiences. In truth, Adlerian theory is multifaceted—cognitive and behavioral as well as affective. It is unique in its social emphases and pragmatic nature.

Psychoanalytic Theories

From a historical point of view alone, psychoanalytic theories are important. They were among the first to gain public recognition and acceptance. Sigmund Freud is the person primarily associated with these approaches, and his genius created the original ideas associated with psychoanalysis. Many prominent theorists of counseling (e.g., Alfred Adler, Carl Jung, Albert Ellis, Rollo May, Fritz Perls) were directly influenced by Freud's concepts, either through association with Freud himself or because they were taught his ideas. Some theorists (including Carl Rogers, B. F. Skinner, Otto Rank, and the persons just mentioned) developed theories in direct opposition to Freud's principles. Still others (e.g., Anna Freud, Erik Erikson, Harry Stack Sullivan, Karen Horney, Heinz Kohut) modified Freudian concepts in developing their own ideas and concepts. Sigmund Freud and psychoanalysis permeate counseling literature. To be uninformed about psychoanalysis and its concepts is to be an undereducated counselor.

Classical Psychoanalytic Theory

Sigmund Freud

The life of Sigmund Freud has been the focus of many books. His official biographer, Ernest Jones, wrote a definitive three-volume work (1953, 1955, 1957) on Freud's life and the development of his ideas.

Sigmund Freud was born at Freiburg, Austria, in 1856, the first son of his father's second marriage (see Figure 8.1). His mother gave him special privileges because she had higher hopes for Sigmund than for the five daughters and two sons born after him. In 1860, Freud's father moved the family to Vienna, and there Freud spent most of the remainder of his life.

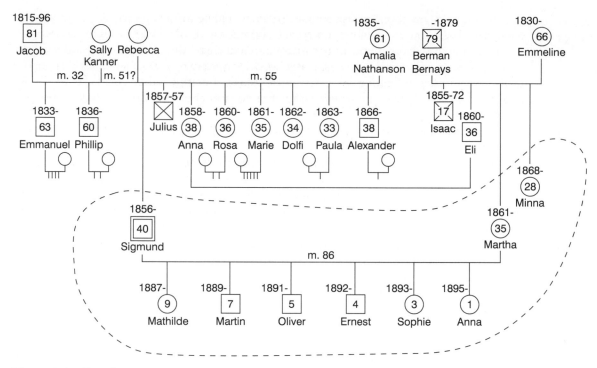

Figure 8.1   Freud's genogram

Source: Reprinted from *Genograms in Family Assessment* (p. 17), by Monica McGoldrick and Randy Gerson.
© 1985 by Monica Goldrick and Randy Gerson. Reprinted by permission of W. W. Norton & Company, Inc.

Freud, an excellent student, was limited in his occupational choices because of finances and his Jewish background. He entered the University of Vienna in 1873 after deciding to pursue medicine. He received his medical degree in 1881, mastering research methods as well as the normal course work. He married Martha Bernays in 1886 and fathered six children, the youngest of whom, Anna, became famous in her own right as a child psychoanalyst.

Freud supported his family through his private practice in psychiatry, working primarily with hysterics. Initially, he used hypnosis as his main form of treatment, a technique he had mastered in France under the tutelage of neurologist Jean Charcot. Freud was not a good hypnotist, however, and soon discovered that much of his success depended on the relationship he developed during the treatment process rather than on the hypnosis itself. This revelation led him to explore how he might use his clinical relationship with a client in combination with the client's concentration to bring about change (Freud, 1925/1959).

Freud had been impressed during medical school with Joseph Breuer's cathartic method of treating hysterics. Breuer had his patients relive painful experiences and work through emotional events suppressed for years. The method used hypnosis, but Freud added a new twist to it by pressing his hand on patients' foreheads whenever they began to block out materials verbally. In the process of touching a patient's forehead, Freud assured the patient that he or she could remember long-forgotten important events and thoughts. Freud called this method *free association.* He used it to explore the unconscious minds of his patients, and the material uncovered in the process became the stuff of interpretation and analysis. Thus, psychoanalysis was born. Freud's work with others, as well as years of self-analysis, gave him new insight into the nature of persons, and he began to stress the importance of the unconscious in the understanding of personality (Monte, 1991).

Many of Freud's colleagues, and later the general public, were outraged by his emphasis on the importance of sexuality and aggression in the etiology of personality. Nevertheless, his ideas attracted a number of followers, and in 1902 he formally organized in his home the Wednesday Psychological Society, which met to discuss personality theory. This group, which at times included Carl Jung and Alfred Adler, became known in 1908 as the Viennese Psychoanalytic Society. It acquired international prominence when Freud and some of his followers accepted an invitation in 1908 to lecture at Clark University in the United States. Despite a number of personal and professional setbacks, Freud's theory of psychoanalysis continued to grow and develop. The establishment of professional journals and international congresses devoted to the theory, as well as Freud's prolific and heuristic writings, assured the historical prominence of psychoanalysis. Freud died in London in 1939, a refugee from the Nazi occupation of Austria.

View of Human Nature

An understanding of Freud is essential to an understanding of the development of various counseling approaches. His theory, generally referred to as *psychoanalysis*, evolved throughout his lifetime; but many of its main tenets were set down in his books *The Interpretation of Dreams* (1900/1955), *New Introductory Lectures on Psychoanalysis* (1923/1933), and *The Ego and the Id* (1923/1947). The Freudian view of human nature is dynamic: that is, Freud believed in the transformation and exchange of energy within the personality (Hall, 1954). Much of what he described, however, is metaphorical because a majority of the hypotheses he proposed could not be proven scientifically at the time (Hergenhahn, 1994). Nevertheless, Freud hoped that his theories would eventually be empirically verified, and he developed techniques of working with his patients that were based on this premise.

For Freud, human nature could be explained in terms of a conscious mind, a preconscious mind, and an unconscious mind. The *conscious mind* is attuned to events in the present, to an awareness of the outside world. The *preconscious mind* is an area between the conscious and unconscious minds and contains aspects of both. Within the preconscious are hidden memories or forgotten experiences that can be remembered if a person is given the proper cues. For example, a person may recall another person's name after a long separation if enough reminders are generated. Finally, beneath the preconscious mind is the *unconscious mind*, the most powerful and least understood part of the personality. The instinctual, repressed, and powerful forces of the personality exist in the unconscious.

Id, Ego, and Superego.   According to Freud, the personality consists of three parts: id, ego, and superego. The id and the superego are confined to the unconscious; the ego operates primarily in the conscious but also in the preconscious and unconscious. The *id* comprises the basic inherited givens of the personality and is present from birth. It is amoral, impulsive, and irrational and works according to the *pleasure principle*. It pursues what it wants because it cannot tolerate tension. The id operates through drives, instincts, and images (such as dreaming, hallucinating, and fantasizing), a thought process known as *primary process*. Although primary-process thinking may bring temporary relief, it is ultimately unsatisfying. Thus, the id discharges energy to the ego, which is another way of obtaining what it wants.

If empowered and left on its own, the id would probably destroy a person or cause trouble by acting on the primitive, aggressive, and sexual drives it harbors. Those who have not grown beyond letting their ids serve as a guide for action lack insight into the consequences of what they are doing. The id contains basic life energy, collectively known as *eros,* and basic death instincts, known as *thanatos.* At first Freud associated eros with sexuality, but later he modified this idea, describing all life-preserving instincts as eros and the psychic energy that accompanies them as *libido.* The idea that each person has some sort of death wish was the result of Freud's observation of the destructiveness of World War I and his belief that, because humans are composed of inorganic matter, they ultimately have a desire to return to this state of being. The premise of thanatos was never fully developed, but Freud thought that any acts of aggression, as well as foolishly dangerous behaviors such as taking unnecessary risks, were displays of thanatos.

To keep the person from being either too self-indulgent or too morally restrained, the *ego* moderates the wishes and desires of the id and superego. It is the second system to develop, after the id and before the superego. Initially, the ego keeps the id from getting out of control. It is often called "the executive of the mind." When it is fully developed, it functions to keep the desires of the id and superego in check while realistically helping the person interact with the outside world. The ego works according to the *reality principle*, reality being what exists (Hall, 1954). As such, the ego devises ways to achieve appropriate goals, obtain energy for activities from the id (the source of all energy), and keep the person in harmony with the environment. The ego's way of thinking is known as the *secondary process.* This process is nothing more than rationally thinking through situations. A strong ego is essential to healthy functioning.

The *superego,* in contrast with the id, is the moral branch of the mind, operating according to what is ideal. The superego arises from the moral teachings of a child's parents and strives for perfection. Consequently, it is said to function according to the moral principle. Through a mechanism known as the *ego ideal,* it rewards those who follow parental and societal dictates and do what they have been taught. For example, children who have been taught by their parents that neatness is a virtue feel good when they keep a neat room. On the other hand, those who act against what they have been taught are punished through the part of the superego called the *conscience,* which induces guilt. The superego locks a person into rather rigid moral patterns if given free reign. Because its goal is perfection, the superego sometimes forces people into restrained action or no action when they face a dilemma.

Developmental Stages.   In addition to the three levels of personality, psychoanalysis is built on what Freud referred to as *psychosexual developmental stages.* Counselors who work psychoanalytically should understand at which stage a client is functioning because the stages are directly linked to the plan of treatment. Each of the four main stages focuses on a zone of pleasure that is dominant at a particular time. In the first stage, the *oral stage,* the mouth is the chief pleasure zone. Children under the age of 1 are in this stage and obtain basic gratification from sucking and biting. In the second stage, the *anal stage,* children between ages 1 and 2 delight in either withholding or eliminating feces. This stage involves the first really significant conflict between the child's internal instincts and external demands (such as toilet training).

In the third stage, the *phallic stage,* children between ages 3 and 5 attempt to resolve their sexual identities. The chief zones of pleasure are the sex organs, and members of both sexes must work through their sexual desires in a conflict of feelings known as the *Oedipus complex.* Freud thought that the conflict was clearer and more completely resolved in boys than girls. Initially, both boys and girls are attracted to the mother because she is the source of great pleasure. Both see the father as a rival for the mother's love and attention. Feelings about the mother change, however, as boys and girls discover their own sexual identities.

For a boy, there is a desire to possess the mother sexually. Yet there is a fear that if he makes his wishes known, the father, who is bigger and stronger, will become angry and castrate him. A boy assumes that his penis is the source of conflict between him and his father and that girls, because they lack a penis, have been castrated. Although the boy may feel hostile toward the father, he represses his desire for the mother and eventually comes to identify with the father, thereby gaining vicarious satisfaction through father-mother interactions.

The Oedipus complex for the girl, sometimes called the *Electra complex,* is less clearly resolved. A young girl comes to notice that she does not have a penis and that boys do. Freud says she blames her mother for the lack of this valued organ and envies her father for possessing one ("penis envy"). Thus, she has both negative and positive feelings toward each parent and is sexually ambivalent at the end of the stage. She takes some consolation from learning she has the ability to have babies because boys cannot. Therefore, she identifies with her mother and, according to Freud, hopes to receive later gratification by having children, especially boys.

The wishes of young boys and girls are not manifested directly during the phallic stage. Rather, they are disguised in dreams, fantasy, and play. Nevertheless, the wishes are real and, if not resolved, will lead to future intra- and interpersonal difficulties. Freud thought the basic ingredients of the adult personality had formed by the end of the phallic stage.

After the phallic stage, between ages 6 and 12, is a period known as *latency.* At this time there is little manifest interest in sexuality. Instead, energy is focused on peer activities and personal mastery of cognitive learning and physical skills. Around puberty, the last of the psychosexual phases occurs, the *genital stage.* If all has gone well previously, each gender takes more interest in the other and normal heterosexual patterns of interaction appear. If there were unresolved difficulties in any of the first three stages (collectively known as the *pregenital stages*), the person may have difficulty adjusting to the adult responsibilities that begin at the genital stage. Freud believed that two difficulties could arise in the pregenital stages: excessive frustration or overindulgence. In such cases, the person could become *fixated* (or arrested) at that level of development and overly dependent on the use of defense mechanisms.

Psychoanalyst Heinz Kohut (1971, 1984) proposed a much less sexually based view of childhood development. His theory is known as object-relations. An *object* is anything that satisfies a need, whether it is a person or a thing. It is used interchangeably with the term *other* to refer to an important person to whom the child and later the adult become attached. Rather than being individuals with a separate identity, others are perceived by an infant as not-me objects for gratifying basic and instinctive needs. The theory proposes that children introject what they perceive from others as good and reject and project what they perceive as bad. In this way, children form an identity with others through interactions, both real and imagined. The challenge for children "is to learn to negotiate with this outside world without trading away satisfaction of such fundamental needs as love, security, and esteem for individual autonomy and a sense of self" (Bankart, 1997, p. 179). Mature individuals are both independent and attached to others and are able to integrate all aspects of themselves and avoid *splitting* (a defense mechanism that involves keeping incompatible feelings separate) (Corey, 1996).

Erik Erikson's (1963, 1982) psychosocial theory extends Freud's developmental emphasis over the life span, focusing on the achievement of specific life-enhancing tasks. His stages of development and their accompanying ages are presented in the following table:

Stage	Age	Tasks
Trust vs. mistrust	Birth to 1	Emphasis on satisfying basic physical and emotional needs
Autonomy vs. shame/doubt	2 to 3	Emphasis on exploration and developing self-reliance
Initiative vs. guilt	4 to 5	Emphasis on achieving a sense of competence and initiative
Industry vs. inferiority	6 to 12	Emphasis on setting and attaining personal goals
Identity vs. role confusion	12 to 18	Emphasis on testing limits, achieving a self-identity
Intimacy vs. isolation	18 to 35	Emphasis on achieving intimate interpersonal relationships
Generativity vs. stagnation	35 to 65	Emphasis on helping next generation, being productive
Integrity vs. despair	65+	Emphasis on integration of life activities, feeling worthwhile

Defense Mechanisms.   *Defense mechanisms* protect a person from being overwhelmed by anxiety through adaptation to situations or through distortion or denial of events. They are normal and operate on an unconscious level. Anna Freud (1936) and other ego psychologists formulated strong ideas about defense mechanisms by elaborating on Freud's original ideas. Among the main defense mechanisms are the following:

• *Repression.*   Repression is the most basic defense mechanism, the one on which others are built. Using this mechanism, the ego involuntarily excludes from consciousness any unwanted or painful thoughts, feelings, memories, or impulses. The ego must use energy to keep excluded areas from consciousness, but sometimes the repressed thoughts slip out in dreams or verbal expressions. Repression is considered the cornerstone or foundation stone of psychoanalysis (Nye, 1996).

* *Projection.*   A person using projection attributes an unwanted emotion or characteristic to someone else. It is an effort to deny that the emotion or characteristic is part of oneself. For example, a woman may say that her boss is angry at her instead of saying that she is angry at her boss.
* *Reaction formation.*   With this mechanism, anxiety-producing thoughts, feelings, or impulses are repressed and their opposites expressed. For example, a host at a party may shower a disliked guest with attention. A reaction formation is often detected because of the intensity with which the opposite emotion is expressed.
* *Displacement.*   Displacement channels energy away from one object to an alternative— that is, to a safe target. For instance, a person who has had a hard day at the office may come home and yell at the dog. A positive form of displacement is known as *sublimation,* in which a drive that cannot be expressed directly is channeled into constructive activities. For example, those who are unable to express themselves sexually may take care of children. Freud thought sublimation was a major means of building civilization.
* *Regression.*   When regressing, a person returns to an earlier stage of development. For example, a child under stress may begin to wet the bed during early adolescence after suffering a trauma. Virtually all people regress if placed under enough pressure or stress.
* *Rationalization.*   Rationalization means that a person finds reasonable explanations for unreasonable or unacceptable behaviors to make them sound logical and acceptable. For example, a client might say, "I did it because everyone else was," or "I really didn't think it was going to be worth the time I'd have to spend, so I didn't do it."
* *Denial.*   A person in denial is not consciously acknowledging an unpleasant or traumatic event or situation. Denial protects people from having to face painful experiences. For instance, a couple may deny they are having marital problems when both are aware that the relationship is deteriorating. Denial may initially help a person cope with certain situations, such as war; but if perpetuated, it ultimately becomes destructive.
* *Identification.*   In identification a person incorporates the qualities of another. Identification removes any fear a person might have of another person and gives him or her new behavioral skills. For instance, a child might identify with a feared parent. Identification, like sublimation, differs from other defense mechanisms in that it can help a person realistically solve problems.

Freud's view of human nature stresses conflict between conscious and unconscious forces (Arlow, 1995; Monte, 1991). The theory is deterministic, holding that a person's adult personality is formed by resolving the gender-specific stages of childhood. If a person has a traumatic childhood and fails to resolve a psychosexual stage, the person will need to work through this unresolved stage later in life.

Role of the Counselor

Professionals who practice classical psychoanalysis play the role of experts. They encourage their clients to talk about whatever comes to mind, especially childhood experiences.

To create an atmosphere in which the client feels free to express difficult thoughts, psychoanalysts, after a few face-to-face sessions, often have the client lie down on a couch while the analyst remains out of view (usually seated behind the client's head). The analyst's role is to let clients gain insight by reliving and working through the unresolved past experiences that come into focus during sessions. The development of transference is encouraged to help clients deal realistically with unconscious material. Unlike some other approaches, psychoanalysis encourages the counselor to interpret for the client. Overall, the counselor employs both active and passive techniques. Psychological assessment instruments, especially projective tests such as the Rorschach Ink Blots, are sometimes employed. Psychoanalytic counselors almost always use diagnostic labels to classify clients from which they develop treatment plans.

Goals

The goals of psychoanalysis vary according to the client, but they focus mainly on personal adjustment, usually inducing a reorganization of internal forces within the person. In most cases a primary goal is to help the client become more aware of the unconscious aspects of his or her personality. The unconscious includes repressed memories and wishes too painful or threatening to have been dealt with initially. But repressing thoughts does not stop them from having influence; repression just makes identifying those thoughts more difficult. Psychoanalysis strives to help clients gain insight into themselves.

A second major goal, often tied to the first, is to help a client work through a developmental stage not previously resolved. If accomplished, clients become unstuck and are able to live more productively. Working through unresolved developmental stages may require a major reconstruction of the personality. As a consequence, psychoanalysis is often a long, intense, and expensive process (Nye, 1996).

A final goal of psychoanalysis is helping clients cope with the demands of the society in which they live. Unhappy people, according to this theory, are not in tune with themselves or society. Psychoanalysis stresses environmental adjustment, especially in the areas of work and intimacy. The focus is on strengthening the ego so that perceptions and plans become more realistic.

Techniques

Psychoanalytic techniques are most often applied within a specific setting, such as a counselor's office or a hospital's interview room. Among the most prominent of these techniques are free association, dream analysis, analysis of transference, analysis of resistance, and interpretation. Although each technique is examined separately here, in practice they are integrated.

Free Association.   Repressed material in the unconscious is always seeking release. On a daily basis, this material may be expressed in the form of sexual or aggressive jokes or through *Freudian slips*, errors of speech such as "I loathe you" instead of "I love you." In psychoanalysis, the client is encouraged to relax and freely recall early childhood memories or emotional experiences. During free association, the client abandons the normal way of censoring thoughts by consciously repressing them and instead says whatever comes to mind, even if the thoughts seem silly, irrational, suggestive, or painful. In this way, the id is requested to speak and the ego remains silent (Freud, 1936). Unconscious material enters the conscious mind, and there the counselor interprets it.

At times, clients resist free association by blocking their thoughts, denying their importance, or both. Psychoanalysts make the most of these moments by attempting to help clients work through their resistance. Often such resistance is concerned with significant earlier unresolved relationships. Regardless, the counselor assures clients that even seemingly trivial thoughts or feelings are important. Many times such assurance is enough to overcome the resistance.

Dream Analysis.   Clients regularly report dreams to counselors. Freud believed that dreams were a main avenue to understanding the unconscious, even calling them "the royal road to the unconscious." He thought dreams were an attempt to fulfill a childhood wish or express unacknowledged sexual desires. He insisted on getting at the nature of dreams by breaking them down into parts and treating them in as much detail as possible (Capuzzi & Black, 1986).

In dream analysis, clients are encouraged to dream and remember dreams. Not everything in a dream is considered important. The counselor is especially sensitive to two aspects: the *manifest content* (obvious meaning) and the *latent content* (hidden but true meaning) (Jones, 1979). The analyst helps interpret both aspects. Some dream symbols are obvious, such as hostility expressed as death or an accident (Nye, 1996). Other symbols are vague and difficult to interpret. Freud's method of dream analysis is considered the first scientific approach to the study of dreams.

Analysis of Transference.   *Transference* is the client's response to a counselor as if the counselor were some significant figure in the client's past, usually a parent figure. The analyst encourages this transference and interprets the positive or negative feelings expressed. The release of feelings is therapeutic, an emotional catharsis. But the real value of these experiences lies in the client's increased self-knowledge, which comes through the counselor's analysis of the transference. Those who experience transference and understand what is happening are then freed to move on to another developmental stage (Singer, 1970). It should be stressed that "working through" transference is a continual process that "consists of repetition, elaboration, and amplification" (Arlow, 1995, p. 32). Understanding and insight grow with each analysis of the transference experience.

Analysis of Resistance.   Sometimes clients initially make progress while undergoing psychoanalysis and then slow down or stop. Their resistance to the therapeutic process may take many forms, such as missing appointments, being late for appointments, not paying fees, persisting in transference, blocking thoughts during free association, or refusing to recall dreams or early memories. When resistance occurs in any form, it is vital that the counselor deal with it immediately. A counselor's analysis of resistance can help clients gain insight into it as well as other behaviors. If resistance is not dealt with, the therapeutic process will probably come to a halt.

Interpretation.   Interpretation should be considered part of the techniques we have already examined and complementary to them. When interpreting, the counselor helps the client understand the meaning of past and present personal events. Interpretation encompasses explanations and analysis of a client's thoughts, feelings, and actions. Counselors must carefully time the use of interpretation. If it comes too soon in the relationship, it can drive the client away. On the other hand, if it is not employed at all or used infrequently, the client may fail to develop insight. Only when the client is ready can interpretation make a significant impact on his or her growth and development.

Evaluation of Uniqueness and Limitations

Classical psychoanalysis has several unique emphases:

• The approach emphasizes the importance of sexuality and the unconscious in human behavior. Before this theory came into being, sexuality (especially childhood sexuality) was denied and little attention paid to unconscious forces. Now many theories acknowledge both the importance of the person as a sexual being and the power of the unconscious mind.

• The approach lends itself to empirical studies; it is heuristic. Freud's proposals have generated a tremendous amount of research since the early 1900s. Much of the research supporting the theory has been reported in the form of case histories and reactions in journals such as the *American Psychoanalytic Association Journal*, the *International Journal of Psychoanalysis,* and the *Psychoanalytic Review*. A good deal of the research attacking the theory has been reported as empirical studies in other reputable journals. The theory itself challenges researchers to develop sophisticated methods of inquiry so that studies about it can be made more comparable.

• The approach provides a theoretical base of support for a number of diagnostic instruments. Some psychological tests, such as the Thematic Apperception Test or the Rorschach Ink Blots, are rooted in psychoanalytic theory. Many other tests used by counselors are outgrowths of this theory or reactions to it.

• The approach reflects the complexity of human nature. Counselors of any theoretical persuasion can gain a greater appreciation of human development and various associated problems by understanding psychoanalysis (Corey, 1996; Monte, 1991).

• The approach has grown and developed through the years. Nye (1996) reports that there are some 10,000 practicing classical psychoanalysts in the United States. Undoubtedly many other professionals also engage in a modified form of psychoanalysis, such as ego psychology or object-relations. Psychoanalysis continues to evolve and most recently has emphasized adaptive processes and social relations.

• The approach appears to be effective for those who suffer from a wide variety of disorders, including hysteria, narcissism, obsessive-compulsive reactions, character disorders, anxiety, phobias, and sexual difficulties (Arlow, 1995).

• The approach stresses the importance of developmental growth stages. This emphasis has influenced a significant amount of investigation since Freud's time, especially the work of Erikson (1963) and Levinson (1978). Such knowledge is invaluable when proposing an individual treatment plan.

Despite the unique emphases of psychoanalysis, most modern professional counselors do not use the approach. The reasons are numerous, but among them are the following limiting factors:

• The approach is time-consuming and expensive. A person who undergoes psychoanalysis is usually seen three to five times a week over a period of years (Bankart, 1997; Nye, 1996). Although Corey (1996) points out the existence of psychoanalytically oriented psychotherapy (as opposed to psychoanalysis), the effectiveness of briefer versions of psychoanalysis is debatable.

• The approach does not seem to lend itself to working with older clients. Many psychoanalysts will not see any client over the age of 50.

• The approach has been claimed almost exclusively by psychiatry, despite Freud's wishes (Vandenbos, Cummings, & Deleon, 1992). Counselors and psychologists without medical degrees have had a difficult time getting extensive training in psychoanalysis (Turkington, 1985). In a 1988 settlement, the American Psychoanalytic Association, the most prestigious psychoanalytic society in the United States, "agreed that roughly 40 percent of its training slots [would] be filled by psychologists and other non-medically trained mental health professionals" (Bule, 1988, p. 1). Still, psychoanalysis tends to be a rather restricted profession. Most nonmedical mental health professionals are members of the American Academy of Psychoanalysis and the National Psychological Association for Psychoanalysis, organizations that are less prestigious than the American Psychoanalytic Association (Arlow, 1995).

• The approach is based on many concepts that are not easily communicated or understood. The id, ego, and superego, for instance, might be represented in more easily understood ways. Psychoanalytical terminology seems overly complicated.

• The approach is deterministic. For instance, Freud attributed certain limitations in women to be a result of gender—that is, of being female. This controversial side of his theory has subsided because of the influence of ego psychology and women scholars' interpretation of Freud (Winkler, 1986). Yet the appropriateness of psychoanalysis for women continues to be questioned.

• The approach does not lend itself to the needs of most individuals who seek professional counseling. The psychoanalytic model has become associated with people who have major adjustment difficulties or want or need to explore the unconscious. Yet many individuals who seek help from counselors have less disruptive developmental or situational problems or disorders.

Adlerian Counseling

Alfred Adler

Alfred Adler was born in 1870 in Penzig, Austria, a suburb of Vienna. He was the second of six children in a middle-class Jewish family (see Figure 8.2). Adler shared a close relation-

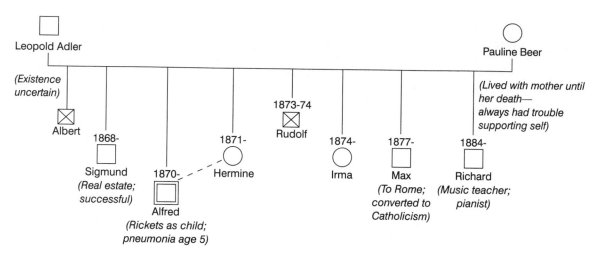

Figure 8.2   Adler's genogram

Source: Reprinted from *Genograms in Family Assessment* (p. 57), by Monica McGoldrick and Randy Gerson. © 1985 by Monica Goldrick and Randy Gerson. Reprinted by permission of W. W. Norton & Company, Inc.

ship with his mother until his younger brother was born. Because he felt abandoned at that time, he sought his father's support. Adler was also close to his older brother, Sigmund.

Adler was a sickly child and injured often. He was run over in the street, suffered from rickets, and almost died of pneumonia at age 5. At age 3, he witnessed the death of a younger brother. It is little wonder that he was later attracted to the profession of medicine.

To make up for his physical limitations, Adler spent a great deal of his childhood outside playing with other children and went out of his way to cultivate their friendship. He was not a good student at first, and he did so poorly in mathematics at the secondary level that his teacher suggested his father take him out of school and apprentice him to a shoemaker. Adler studied to overcome this deficiency and eventually became skilled in math.

In 1895, he graduated in medicine from the University of Vienna. In his first practice he worked as an ophthalmologist, but his interests turned first to neurology and finally to psychiatry. As a practicing psychiatrist, Adler was invited to join Freud's Vienna Psychoanalytic Society, where he quickly gained prominence. Adler always thought of himself as a colleague rather than a disciple of Freud. He disagreed early on with Freud's theoretical approach, especially the emphasis on biology and sexuality. Adler developed a theoretical orientation that was less deterministic and more practical and hopeful. He stressed the importance of subjective feelings rather than biological drives as the primary motivating force of life. Because of his differences with Freud, Adler resigned as president of the society in 1910 and, with about a third of the society's members, established the rival Society of Individual Psychology.

During World War I, Adler served as a physician in the Austrian army, and after the war he was instrumental in setting up child guidance clinics in the Vienna schools. He worked to refine his theory and spoke widely in Europe and the United States. Adler fled Hitler's rise to power and, in 1932, was appointed to a position in medical psychology at the Long

Island College of Medicine. He died of a heart attack in 1937 while on a lecture tour in Aberdeen, Scotland. He was survived by his wife, two daughters, and a son.

Although Adler was a popular speaker and the author of more than 300 published papers and books, he has not generally received credit for many of the concepts he formulated. Such terms as *inferiority complex, social interest, empathy*, and *lifestyle* originated with Adler and were quickly absorbed by other scholars and the public. His theory waned in popularity during the 1940s and 1950s but was revitalized during the 1960s and 1970s and has been widely used since that time.

View of Human Nature

Adler thought that people were primarily motivated by *social interest*—that is, a "feeling of being part of the social whole," an interest in others as well as a "need and willingness to contribute to the general social good" (Corsini & Wedding, 1995, p. 441). His theory holds that conscious aspects of behavior, rather than the unconscious, are central to the development of personality. A major Adlerian tenet is that people strive to become successful (i.e., the best they can be); therefore, their behavior is goal directed and purposeful. Underlying this tenet is Adler's belief that each person strives for growth and has a need for wholeness. "Adler gave his theory the name Individual Psychology to emphasize the holistic perspective, with the term *Individual* deriving from the Latin *individuum*, meaning 'indivisble'" (Mosak & Maniacci, 1998, p. 19).

People tend to try to fulfill their own unique potential, a process he called *striving for perfection* or completeness (Adler, 1964). There is also a tendency for each person initially to feel inferior to others. If this feeling is not overcome, the person develops an *inferiority complex*. Such a complex, if not changed, becomes the basis by which one's personality is defined. In contrast, a person who overcompensates for feelings of inferiority develops a *superiority complex*, which is what Adler also described as a *neurotic fiction* that is unproductive.

Adler believed that people are as influenced by future (teleological) goals as by past causes. His theory places considerable emphasis on *birth order*: those who share ordinal birth positions (e.g., firstborns) may have more in common with one another than siblings from the same family (Dreikurs, 1950). Five ordinal positions are emphasized in Adlerian literature on the family constellation: firstborns, secondborns, middle children, youngest children, and the only child (Dreikurs, 1967; Dreikurs & Soltz, 1964; Sweeney, 1998).

- *Firstborns.*   Firstborns are initially the "reigning monarchs" of a family because they receive undivided attention from parents. They are socialized to conform, achieve, behave, and please. They take responsibility when parents are absent and often act as parent substitutes in large families. All firstborns experience the loss of their unique position in the family when a second child is born. The experience of being "dethroned" may cause them to become resentful or help them better understand the significance of power and authority.
- *Secondborns.*   The position of secondborn is an enviable one, according to Adler, but does have drawbacks. Secondborns never have to worry about issues of power and authority as firstborns do because they are born into a family atmosphere in which they will never be dethroned. Usually, these individuals are more outgoing, carefree, and

creative and less concerned with rules than firstborns. They frequently pursue roles not taken by firstborns and are likely to be just the opposite of their older sibling.

- *Middle children.*   Children born in the middle positions of a family often feel "squeezed in" and treated unfairly. They do not develop the close, personal types of alliances that an oldest or a youngest child may form. But because of their position, middle children learn a great deal about family politics and the art of negotiation. These skills can prove useful for manipulating events to get what they want and choosing areas where they can be successful.
- *Youngest children.*   Youngest children in the family have difficulties and opportunities that are different from those of their older siblings. Youngest children receive a great deal of attention from others, who are likely to cater to their needs. These children may become charmers but may also have difficulty breaking out of the role of baby or family pet. They face the danger of becoming spoiled. At the same time, youngest children may make great strides in achieving because of role models provided by older siblings.
- *Only children.*   Any child born 7 or more years apart from siblings is psychologically an only child. These children, as a group, are never dethroned and are at an advantage, like oldest children, in receiving a great deal of attention. They may mature early and become high achievers. They may also develop rich imaginations because of the amount of time they spend alone. Major disadvantages are that only children may become pampered, selfish, and not well socialized.

In addition to birth order, the family environment is important to a person's development, particularly in the first 5 years of life. Adlerian theory stresses that each person creates a style of life by age 5, primarily through interacting with other family members. A negative family atmosphere might be authoritarian, rejective, suppressive, materialistic, overprotective, or pitying (Dreikurs & Soltz, 1964), whereas a positive family atmosphere might be democratic, accepting, open, and social. Nevertheless, perception of the family atmosphere, rather than any events themselves, is crucial to the development of a style of life (Adler, 1964). Individuals behave as if the world were a certain way and are guided by their *fictions*—that is, their subjective evaluations of themselves and their environments. Five basic mistakes are caused by fictions (Mosak, 1995, p. 70):

1. *Overgeneralizing*—viewing everything as the same
2. *False or impossible goals of security*—trying to please everyone
3. *Misperceptions of life and life's demands*—believing one never gets any breaks
4. *Minimization or denial of one's worth*—thinking that one will never amount to anything
5. *Faulty values*—believing in the necessity of being first no matter what needs to be done to get there

In contrast, a healthy style of life focuses on three main tasks: society, work, and sexuality. Adlerian theory places strong emphasis on developing social interest and contributing to society. His theory holds that work is essential for human survival and that we must learn to be interdependent. Furthermore, a person must define his or her sexuality in regard to self and others, in a spirit of cooperation rather than competition. He also mentions two other challenges of life, although he does not fully develop them: spirituality and coping with self (Dreikurs & Mosak, 1966). According to Adlerian theory, it is crucial to emphasize that, when facing any life task, *courage* (a willingness to take risks without knowing what the consequences may be) is required.

Role of the Counselor

Adlerian counselors function primarily as diagnosticians, teachers, and models in the egalitarian relationships they establish with their clients. They try to assess why clients are oriented to a certain way of thinking and behaving. The counselor makes an assessment by gathering information on the family constellation and a client's earliest memories. The counselor then shares interpretations, impressions, opinions, and feelings with the client and concentrates on promoting the therapeutic relationship. The client is encouraged to examine and change a faulty lifestyle by developing social interest (Adler, 1927, 1931).

Adlerians are frequently active in sharing hunches or guesses with clients and are often directive when assigning clients homework, such as to act "as if" the client were the person he or she wants to be. Adlerian counselors employ a variety of techniques, some of which are borrowed from other approaches. (Adler was not specific in detailing how counselors should operate when using his theory.) As a general rule, Adlerian counselors make little use of assessment techniques, such as psychological tests, but they usually employ life-history questionnaires to gather data. They generally avoid the types of diagnoses found in the DSM-IV but use their own language, such as "discouraged," to describe the dynamics they encounter within a person.

Goals

The goals of Adlerian counseling revolve around helping people develop healthy, holistic lifestyles. This may mean educating or reeducating clients about what such lifestyles are as well as helping them overcome feelings of inferiority. One of the major goals of Adlerian counseling is to encourage clients to cultivate social interest (Adler, 1931). According to Adler, social interest is an innate potentiality "that must be consciously developed or trained" (Watts, 1996, p. 169). A *faulty style of life* is self-centered and based on mistaken goals and incorrect assumptions associated with feelings of inferiority. These feelings might stem from being born with a physical or mental defect, being pampered by parents, or being neglected. The feelings must be corrected and inappropriate forms of behavior stopped. To do so, the counselor assumes the role of teacher and interpreter of events. Adlerian counseling deals with the whole person (Kern & Watts, 1993).

The client is ultimately in charge of deciding whether to pursue social or self-interests, but Adlerian counselors stress four goals of the therapeutic process (Dreikurs, 1967; Kottman & Warlick, 1990; Mosak, 1995):

1. Establishment and maintenance of an egalitarian counseling relationship
2. Analysis of a client's lifestyle
3. Interpretation of client's lifestyle in a way that promotes insight
4. Reorientation and reeducation of the client with accompanying behavior change

Techniques

The establishment of a counseling relationship is crucial if the goals of Adlerian counseling are to be achieved. Certain techniques help enhance this process. Adlerian counselors try to develop a warm, supportive, empathic, friendly, and egalitarian relationship with clients. Counseling is seen as a collaborative effort (Adler, 1956). Counselors actively listen and respond "in much the same way that person-centered counselors do" (Gilliland & James, 1998, p. 57). In this process they try to help their clients define specific goals and discover what prevents the achievement of these goals. A counselor also may focus on client strengths. A counselor may employ confrontation at times, pointing out client inconsistencies. The counselor's primary objective is to maintain a flexible interaction process and in so doing stress client responsibility (Dinkmeyer, Dinkmeyer, & Sperry, 1987).

After a relationship has been established, the counselor concentrates on an analysis of the client's lifestyle, including examination of the family constellation, early memories, dreams, and priorities. As previously noted, the family constellation and the atmosphere in which children grow greatly influence both self-perception and perceptions of others. No two children are born into the same environment, but a child's ordinal position and assessment of the family atmosphere have a major impact on development and behavior. Often a client is able to gain insight by recalling early memories, especially events before the age of 10. Adler (1931) contended that a person remembers childhood events that are consistent with his or her present view of self, others, and the world in general. Adlerian counselors look both for themes and specific details within these early recollections (Slavik, 1991; Statton & Wilborn, 1991; Watkins, 1985). Figures from the past are treated as prototypes rather than specific individuals: they may represent a client's attitude toward power, weakness, men, women, or almost anything else. Recent and past dreams are also a part of lifestyle analysis. Adlerian theory holds that dreams are a possible rehearsal for future courses of action. Recurrent dreams are especially important. A look at the client's priorities is also helpful in understanding his or her style of life. A client may persist in one predominant lifestyle, such as always trying to please, unless challenged to change.

Counselors next try to help clients develop insight, especially by asking open-ended questions and making interpretations. Open-ended questions allow clients to explore patterns in their lives that have gone unnoticed. Interpretation often takes the form of intuitive guesses. The ability to empathize is especially important in this process, for the counselor must be able to feel what it is like to be the client before zeroing in on the reasons for the client's present behaviors. At other times, interpretations are based on the counselor's general knowledge of ordinal position and family constellation. True to the egalitarian spirit of the process, clients are never forced to accept the counselor's point of view.

To accomplish behavioral change, the counselor uses specific techniques:

- *Confrontation.*   The counselor challenges clients to consider their own private logic. When clients examine this logic, they often realize they can change it and their behavior.
- *Asking "the question."*   The counselor asks, "What would be different if you were well?" Clients are often asked "the question" during the initial interview, but it is appropriate at any time.
- *Encouragement.*   Encouragement implies faith in a person (Dinkmeyer & Losoncy, 1980; Dreikurs & Soltz, 1964). Counselors encourage their clients by stating their

belief that behavior change is possible. Encouragement is the key to making productive lifestyle choices.

- *Acting "as if."*   Clients are instructed to act "as if" they are the persons they want to be—for instance, the ideal persons they see in their dreams (Gold, 1979). Adler originally got the idea of acting "as if" from Hans Vaihinger (1911), who wrote that people create the worlds they live in by the assumptions they make about the world.
- *Spitting in the client's soup.*   A counselor points out certain behaviors to clients and thus ruins the payoff for the behavior. For example, a mother who always acts superior to her daughter by showing her up may continue to do so after the behavior has been pointed out, but the reward for doing so is now gone.
- *Catching oneself.*   Clients learn to become aware of self-destructive behaviors or thoughts. At first, the counselor may help in the process, but eventually this responsibility is taken over by clients.
- *Task setting.*   Clients initially set short-range, attainable goals and eventually work up to long-term, realistic objectives. Once clients make behavioral changes and realize some control over their lives, counseling ends.
- *Push button.*   Clients are encouraged to realize they have choices about what stimuli in their lives they pay attention to. They are taught to create the feelings they want by concentrating on their thoughts. The technique is like pushing a button because clients can choose to remember negative or positive experiences (Mosak, 1995).

In the midst of using these techniques, counselors avoid the "tar baby"—that is, "the perceptions on life that the client carries into counseling and attempts to fit into the counselor. Anger, discouragement, seductiveness, martyrdom, and a host of other traps are set for the unwary counselor as the client resists change" (Gilliland & James, 1998, p. 63).

Evaluation of Uniqueness and Limitations

The Adlerian approach to counseling has a number of unique emphases:

- The approach fosters an egalitarian atmosphere through the positive techniques that counselors promote. Rapport and commitment are enhanced by its processes, and the chances for change are increased. Counselor encouragement and support are valued commodities. Adlerian counselors approach their clients with an educational orientation and take an optimistic outlook on life.

- The approach is versatile over the life span. "Adlerian theorists have developed counseling models for working with children, adolescents, parents, entire families, teacher groups, and other segments of society" (Purkey & Schmidt, 1987, p. 115). Play therapy for children ages 4 to 9 seems to be especially effective. It allows children to communicate through the language of play and then verbally talk about their feelings (Kottman & Warlick, 1990). On the other hand, an approach that emphasizes verbal and behavioral consequences is recommended for adolescents, especially those dealing with the typical faulty goals of this age group (e.g., power, attention, revenge, inadequacy) (Kelly & Sweeney, 1979; Sweeney, 1998). Parents may benefit from Adlerian theory by using educational support groups to understand their children better and plan effective intervention strategies

(Dinkmeyer, 1982a, 1982b; Dinkmeyer & McKay, 1976, 1983; Dinkmeyer, McKay, & Dinkmeyer, 1980). The Adlerian approach has even been successfully applied to difficulties associated with complex family interactions (Lowe, 1982).

• The approach is useful in the treatment of a variety of DSM-IV disorders, including conduct disorders, antisocial disorders, anxiety disorders of childhood and adolescence, some affective disorders, and personality disorders (Seligman, 1997).

• The approach has contributed to other helping theories and to the public's knowledge and understanding of human interactions. Many of Adler's ideas have been integrated into other counseling approaches. Concepts such as freedom, phenomenology, interpretation of events, life scripts, growth, and personal responsibility are found in existential, Gestalt, rational emotive behavioral, transactional analysis, person-centered, and reality-based counseling and therapy. Adlerian terms such as *inferiority complex* have also become part of the public's vocabulary.

• The approach can be employed selectively in different cultural contexts (Brown, 1997). For instance, the concept of "encouragement" is appropriately emphasized in working with groups that have traditionally emphasized collaboration such as Hispanics and Asian Americans, while the concept "sibling rivalry" may be highlighted with traditional European North Americans who stress competition.

Nevertheless, the Adlerian approach does have limitations:

• The approach lacks a firm, supportive research base. Relatively few empirical studies clearly outline Adlerian counseling's effectiveness (Wallace, 1986). More investigations are needed if the theory is to develop systematically. Journals devoted to the Adlerian viewpoint, such as the *Journal of Individual Psychology*, may rectify this situation.

• The approach is vague in regard to some of its terms and concepts. Corey (1996) notes that Adler emphasized practice and teaching rather than theoretical definitions and organization. Although a number of prominent educators, such as Dreikurs, Mosak, Dinkmeyer, and Sweeney, have attempted to clarify the Adlerian approach, some of its ideas remain unclear. Adler was especially nebulous about how to work with clients.

• The approach may be too optimistic about human nature. Adler, who called his theory "individual psychology," stressed social cooperation and interest. Some critics consider his view neglectful of other life dimensions, such as the power and place of the unconscious (Prochaska, 1984).

• The approach's basic principles, such as a democratic family structure, may not fit well in working with clients whose cultural context stresses the idea of a lineal social relationship, such as with traditional Arab Americans (Brown, 1997). If basic principles of Adlerian counseling cannot be followed, than the impact of the theory may be lessened.

• The approach, which "relies heavily on verbal erudition, logic, and insight," may be limited in its applicability to clients who are not intellectually bright (Gilliland & James, 1998, p. 70). This limitation is applicable to many theories and is not singularly targeted to Adlerian counseling.

Summary and Conclusion

This chapter has emphasized two important theories of individual counseling. Classical psychoanalysis is considered by many practitioners to be the grandparent of all modern theories of helping. Although Freud's ideas are controversial, his thoughts about human nature and the helping process are comprehensive. They have been elaborated on and refined since his death, and classical psychoanalysis, along with modifications to the approach, is still widely practiced, especially in psychiatry.

Alfred Adler's theory, individual psychology, has been less controversial. It has been clarified since his death, and these refinements have made the approach more understandable and popular, especially in educational environments. Ordinal family positions and the importance of socialization and encouragement are a few areas within the theory that continue to receive a good deal of attention.

Freudian and Adlerian theories differ in a number of ways even though they were developed at about the same time and in a similar environment. Psychoanalysis is biologically based and stresses causality, psychosexual development, the dynamics of the mind, and instincts. Adlerian theory, on the other hand, is socially based, interpersonal, and subjective. It emphasizes the future, holism, collaboration, and choice. Both theories focus on the importance of childhood, working through real or perceived unresolved situations, and behavioral goals.

Psychoanalysis is not used by many counselors because it is costly and time-consuming and few counselors have received the training needed to master it. The approach is also not applicable for the client populations that most counselors serve. The Adlerian approach, however, is widely practiced in school and institutional settings. Its popularity can be attributed to its hopefulness and its useful application in multiple settings. A full comparative summary of Freud and Adler appears in Table 8.1.

CLASSROOM ACTIVITIES

1. With another classmate discuss which of the two theories presented in this chapter you find most attractive. Share your reasons with one another. Speculate about how each of these approaches might be used in the following settings: a mental hospital, a public secondary school, a rehabilitation center, and a community agency.

2. Brainstorm as many examples of defense mechanisms as you can. Share your examples with a classmate and then with the class as a whole.

3. As a class, divide into five groups according to Adler's description of the five ordinal positions in a family: firstborns, second-borns, middle children, youngest children, and only children. Appoint a scribe in each group to take notes. Then discuss with other group members your perceptions of being a child in that position. After the discussions, have each scribe report back to the class as a whole.

4. Divide into groups of three. Rotating the roles of counselor, client, and observer, try to implement some of the specific ways you think a psychoanalytic or Adlerian counselor would work with clients who have the following problems: depression, anxiety, poor self-identity, and phobias. After each role-play, discuss what you observed and learned.

Table 8.1 A comparative summary of Freud and Adler

Freud	Adler
1. Objective	1. Subjective
2. Physiological substratum for theory	2. A social psychology
3. Emphasized causality	3. Emphasized teleology
4. Reductionistic. The individual is divided into "parts" that are antagonistic toward each other: e.g., id-ego-superego, Eros vs. Thanatos, conscious vs. unconscious.	4. Holistic. The individual is indivisible. He or she is a unity and all "parts" (memory, emotions, behavior) are in the service of the whole individual.
5. The study of the individual centers about the intrapersonal, the intrapsychic.	5. People can only be understood interpersonally and as social beings moving through and interacting with their environment.
6. The establishment of intrapsychic harmony constitutes the ideal goal of psychotherapy. "Where id was, there shall ego be."	6. The expansion of the individual, self-realization, and the enhancement of social interest represent the ideal goals for the individual.
7. People are basically "bad." Civilization attempts to domesticate them, for which they pay a heavy price. Through therapy the instinctual demands may be sublimated but not eliminated.	7. People are neither "good" nor "bad," but as creative, choosing human beings, they may choose to be "good" or "bad" or both, depending upon their life-style and their appraisal of the immediate situation and its payoffs. Through the medium of therapy people can choose to actualize themselves.
8. People are victims of both instinctual life and civilization.	8. People, as choosers, can shape both their internal and their external environments. Although they are not the complete masters of their fate and cannot always choose what will happen to them, they can always choose the posture they will adopt toward life's stimuli.

5. What specific aspects of psychoanalysis and Adlerian theory do you think need further research? Why? Write down your responses and share them with the class.

REFERENCES

Adler, A. (1927). *Understanding human nature.* Greenwich, CT: Fawcett.

Adler, A. (1931). *What life should mean to you.* Boston: Little, Brown.

Adler, A. (1956). *The individual psychology of Alfred Adler: A systematic presentation in selections from his writings* (H. L. Ansbacher & R. R. Ansbacher, Eds.). New York: Norton.

Adler, A. (1964). *Social interest: A challenge to mankind.* New York: Capricorn.

Arlow, J. A. (1995). Psychoanalysis. In R. J. Corsini & D. Wedding (Eds.), *Current psychotherapies* (5th ed., pp. 15–50). Itasca, IL: Peacock.

Bankart, C. P. (1997). *Talking cures.* Pacific Grove, CA: Brooks/Cole.

Brown, D. (1997). Implications of cultural values for cross-cultural consultation with families. *Journal of Counseling and Development, 76,* 29–35.

Bule, J. (1988, November). Psychoanalysis barriers tumble. *APA Monitor, 19*(1), 15.

Table 8.1 *continued*

Freud	Adler
9. Description of child development was postdictive and not based upon direct observation of children but upon the free associations of adults.	9. Children were studied directly in families, in schools, and in family education centers.
10. Emphasis upon the Oedipus situation and its resolution.	10. Emphasis upon the family constellation.
11. People are enemies. Others are our competitors, and we must protect ourselves from them. Theodore Reik quotes Nestroy, "If change brings two wolves together, . . . neither feels the least uneasy because the other is a wolf; two human beings, however, can never meet in the forest, but one must think: That fellow may be a robber" (1948, p. 477).	11. Other people are *mitmenschen*, fellow human beings. They are our equals, our collaborators, our cooperators in life.
12. Women feel inferior because they envy men their penises. Women are inferior. "Anatomy is destiny."	12. Women feel inferior because in our cultural milieu women are undervalued. Men have privileges, rights, preferred status, although in the current cultural ferment, these roles are being reevaluated.
13. Neurosis has a sexual etiology.	13. Neurosis is a failure of learning, a product of distorted perceptions.
14. Neurosis is the price we pay for civilization.	14. Neurosis is the price we pay for our lack of civilization.

Source: From "Adlerian Psychology," by H. Mosak, 1989, in R. J. Corsini & D. Wedding (Eds.), *Current Psychotherapies* (p. 70), Itasca, IL: Peacock. © 1989 by F. E. Peacock. Reprinted by permission.

Capuzzi, D., & Black, D. K. (1986). The history of dream analysis and the helping relationship: A synopsis for practitioners. *Journal of Humanistic Education and Development, 24,* 82–97.

Corey, G. (1996). *Theory and practice of counseling and psychotherapy* (4th ed.). Pacific Grove, CA: Brooks/Cole.

Corsini, R. J. (1995). Introduction. In R. J. Corsini & D. Wedding (Eds.), *Current psychotherapies* (5th ed., pp. 1–14). Itasca, IL: Peacock.

Corsini, R. J., & Wedding, D. (Eds.). *Current psychotherapies* (5th ed.). Itasca, IL: Peacock.

Dinkmeyer, D. (1982a). *Developing understanding of self and others* (DUSOD-1). Circle Pine, MN: American Guidance Service.

Dinkmeyer, D. (1982b). *Developing understanding of self and others* (DUSOD-2). Circle Pine, MN: American Guidance Service.

Dinkmeyer, D., Dinkmeyer, D., Jr., & Sperry, L. (1987). *Adlerian counseling and psychotherapy* (2nd ed.). Upper Saddle River, NJ: Merrill/Prentice Hall.

Dinkmeyer, D., & Losoncy, L. E. (1980). *The encouragement book: Becoming a positive person.* Upper Saddle River, NJ: Prentice Hall.

Dinkmeyer, D., & McKay, G. D. (1976). *Systematic training for effective parenting* (STEP). Circle Pine, MN: American Guidance Service.

Dinkmeyer, D., & McKay, G. D. (1983). *Systematic training for effective parenting/Teen* (STEP/Teen). Circle Pine, MN: American Guidance Service.

Dinkmeyer, D., McKay, G. D., & Dinkmeyer, D., Jr. (1980). *Systematic training for effective teaching* (STET) Circle Pine, MN: American Guidance Service.

Dreikurs, R. R. (1950). *Fundamentals of Adlerian psychology.* Chicago: Alfred Adler Institute.

Dreikurs, R. R. (1967). *Psychodynamics, psychotherapy, and counseling.* Chicago: Alfred Adler Institute.

Dreikurs, R. R., & Mosak, H. H. (1966). The tasks of life. I: Adler's three tests. *Individual Psychologist, 4,* 18–22.

Dreikurs, R. R., & Soltz, V. (1964). *Children: The challenge.* New York: Hawthorne.

Erikson, E. H. (1963). *Childhood and society* (2nd ed.). New York: Norton.

Erikson, E. H. (1982). *The life cycle completed.* New York: Norton.

Freud, A. (1936). *The ego and the mechanisms of defense* (J. Strachey, Trans.). New York: International Universities Press.

Freud, S. (1933). *New introductory lectures on psychoanalysis* (W. J. H. Sprott, Trans.). New York: Norton. (Original work published 1923)

Freud, S. (1947). *The ego and the id* (J. Strachey, Trans.). London: Hogarth. (Original work published 1923)

Freud, S. (1955). *The interpretation of dreams* (J. Strachey, Trans.). London: Hogarth. (Original work published 1900)

Freud, S. (1959). An autobiographical study. In J. Strachey (Ed. & Trans.), *The standard edition of the complete psychological works of Sigmund Freud* (Vol. 20, pp. 7–74). London: Hogarth. (Original work published 1925)

Gilliland, B. E., & James, R. K. (1998). *Theories and strategies in counseling and psychotherapy* (4th ed.). Boston: Allyn & Bacon.

Gold, L. (1979). Adler's theory of dreams: An holistic approach to interpretation. In B. B. Wolman (Ed.), *Handbook of dreams: Research, theories, and applications.* New York: Van Nostrand Reinhold.

Hall, C. S. (1954). *A primer of Freudian psychology.* New York: New American Library.

Hergenhahn, B. R. (1994). *An introduction to theories of personality* (4th ed.). Upper Saddle River, NJ: Prentice Hall.

Jones, E. (1953). *The life and work of Sigmund Freud* (Vol. 1). New York: Basic Books.

Jones, E. (1955). *The life and work of Sigmund Freud* (Vol. 2). New York: Basic Books.

Jones, E. (1957). *The life and work of Sigmund Freud* (Vol. 3). New York: Basic Books.

Jones, R. M. (1979). Freudian and post-Freudian theories of dreams. In B. B. Wolman (Ed.), *Handbook of dreams: Research, theories, and applications.* New York: Litton.

Kelly, E. W., Jr., & Sweeney, T. J. (1979). Typical faulty goals of adolescents: A base for counseling. *School Counselor, 26,* 236–246.

Kern, C. W., & Watts, R. E. (1993). Adlerian counseling. *Texas Counseling Association Journal, 21,* 85–95.

Kohut, H. (1971). *The analysis of the self.* New York: International Universities Press.

Kohut, H. (1984). *How does psychoanalysis cure?* Chicago: University of Chicago Press.

Kottman, T., & Warlick, J. (1990). Adlerian play therapy. *Journal of Humanistic Education and Development, 28,* 125–132.

Levinson, D. (1978). *The seasons of a man's life.* New York: Knopf.

Lowe, R. N. (1982). Adlerian/Dreikursian family counseling. In A. M. Horne & M. M. Ohlsen (Eds.), *Family counseling and therapy* (pp. 329–359). Itasca, IL: Peacock.

Monte, C. F. (1991). *Beneath the mask: An introduction to theories of personality* (4th ed.). Fort Worth, TX: Holt, Rinehart, & Winston.

Mosak, H. (1995). Adlerian psychotherapy. In R. J. Corsini & D. Wedding (Eds.), *Current psychotherapies* (5th ed., pp. 51–94). Itasca, IL: Peacock.

Mosak, H. H., & Maniacci, M. P. (1998). *Tactics in counseling and psychotherapy.* Itasca, IL: F. E. Peacock.

Nye, R. D. (1996). *Three psychologies: Perspectives from Freud, Skinner, and Rogers* (5th ed.). Pacific Grove, CA: Brooks/Cole.

Patterson, C. H. (1985). *The therapeutic relationship.* Pacific Grove, CA: Brooks/Cole.

Prochaska, J. O. (1984). *Systems of psychotherapy: A transtheoretical analysis* (2nd ed.). Homewood, IL: Dorsey.

Purkey, W. W., & Schmidt, J. J. (1987). *The inviting relationship.* Upper Saddle River, NJ: Prentice Hall.

Seligman, L. (1997). *Diagnosis and treatment planning in counseling* (2nd ed.). New York: Plenum.

Singer, E. (1970). *Key concepts in psychotherapy* (2nd ed.). New York: Basic Books.

Slavik, S. (1991). Early memories as a guide to client movement through life. *Canadian Journal of Counselling, 25,* 331–337.

Statton, J. E., & Wilborn, B. (1991). Adlerian counseling and the early recollections of children. *Individual Psychology, 47,* 338–347.

Sweeney, T. J. (1998). *Adlerian counseling* (4th ed.). Muncie, IN: Accelerated Development.

Turkington, C. (1985). Analysts sued for barring non-MDs. *APA Monitor, 16*(5), 2.

Vaihinger, H. (1911). *The philosophy of "as if."* New York: Harcourt, Brace, & World.

Vandenbos, G. R., Cummings, N., & Deleon, P. H. (1992). A century of psychotherapy: Economic and environmental influences. In D. K. Freedheim (Ed.), *History of psychotherapy: A century of change* (pp. 65–102). Washington, DC: American Psychological Association.

Wallace, W. A. (1986). *Theories of counseling and psychotherapy.* Boston: Allyn & Bacon.

Watkins, C. E., Jr. (1985). Early recollections as a projective technique in counseling: An Adlerian view. *AMHCA Journal, 7,* 32–40.

Watts, R. E. (1996). Social interest and the core conditions: Could it be that Adler influenced Rogers? *Journal of Humanistic Education and Development, 34,* 165–170.

Winkler, K. J. (1986). Scholars prescribe Freud's "talking cure" for problems. *Chronicle of Higher Education, 33*(8), 4–6.

9

PERSON-CENTERED, EXISTENTIAL, AND GESTALT APPROACHES TO COUNSELING

I feel at times that I'm wasting my mind

as we wade through your thoughts and emotions.

With my skills I could be in a world-renowned clinic

with a plush, private office, soft padded chairs,

and a sharp secretary at my command.

Instead of here in a pink cinderblock room

where it leaks when it rains

and the noise seeps under the door like water.

But in leaving, you pause for a moment

as your voice spills out in a whisper:

"Thanks for being here when I hurt."

With those words my fantasies end, as reality,

like a wellspring begins filling me

with life-giving knowledge, as it cascades through my mind,

That in meeting you, when you're flooded with pain,

I discover myself.

From "Here and Now," by S. T. Gladding, 1975, Personnel and Guidance Journal, 53, *p. 746. © 1975 by ACA.*
Reprinted with permission. No further reproduction authorized without written permission of the American
Counseling Association.

Affective theories are those that focus on making an impact on clients' emotions to bring about change. This chapter covers three prominent affective theories: person-centered counseling, existential counseling, and Gestalt therapy. According to Hackney and Cormier (1996), person-centered counseling is the most widely used affective approach, followed by Gestalt therapy and existential counseling.

Several basic characteristics are common to affective theories. First, they focus on the primacy of affect as a cause of or contributor to the development of certain human actions and reactions (Zajonc, 1984). Second, they stress helping clients cope with or change their emotions as a premise for making other life alterations. Third, they emphasize human phenomenology and how a person's views of the environment affect behavior. Fourth, they are characterized by a person-to-person relationship between counselor and client. Finally, they are humanistic in orientation, focusing on the unique growth and development within each individual. Some affective theories also share a common problem: vagueness in their descriptions of specific techniques. Among the affective approaches covered in this chapter, existential counseling is the weakest in this area, while Gestalt therapy is the strongest.

Prominent professionals associated with affective theories include Carl Rogers, Angelo Boy, Gerald Pine, Rollo May, Victor Frankl, Irvin Yalom, Sidney Jourard, Clemmont Vontress, Fritz Perls, Laura Perls, William Passons, Irma Lee Shepherd, and Joen Fagan.

Person-Centered Counseling

Carl Rogers

Carl Rogers, the person most identified with person-centered counseling, was born in 1902 in Oak Park, Illinois, a suburb of Chicago. He was the fourth of six children. His parents, who were fundamentalist Christians, discouraged Rogers from forming friendships outside the family because of the bad influence others might have on him. Rogers (1980) described his childhood as solitary, with "no close friend and only superficial personal contact" (p. 29). When he was 12, his family moved to a farm outside Chicago, and there he developed a strong interest in science and reading. Among his early scientific experiments was investigating a species of moth.

As a teenager, Rogers read everything he could get his hands on, including encyclopedias and dictionaries. But he described himself as being socially inept in high school (Rogers, 1967a). A major turning point occurred when he enrolled at the University of Wisconsin in 1919 to study agriculture. There he became involved with a YMCA group and began to develop good friendships. He also started dating and began to trust others. A major event for Rogers was a 6-month trip he took in 1922 as 1 of 10 American students attending the World Student Christian Federation conference in Peking, China. The trip exposed him to people of other cultures, religions, and ways of thinking.

After his return, Rogers broke away from his parents' domination and changed his major to history, with the goal of eventually becoming a minister. After graduation in 1924, he enrolled in New York's Union Theological Seminary, but two years later he became discouraged about the prospect of entering the ministry. He transferred to Teachers College, Columbia University, "a hotbed of radical behavioristic thinking in the 1920s" (Bankart, 1997, p. 293). There he studied clinical and educational psychology, receiving an M.A. degree in 1928 and a Ph.D. in 1931. During his time as a graduate student, Rogers studied briefly with Alfred Adler, who was a visiting instructor at the Institute for Child Guidance in New York City during 1927–1928 where Rogers was an intern (Watts, 1996).

After completing his studies, Rogers took a position with a child guidance agency in Rochester, New York. His 12-year tenure with this agency were productive and greatly influenced his later theory of counseling. He found that the psychoanalytic approach to working with troubled individuals, which was dominant in this work setting, was time-consuming and often ineffective. Insight alone produced little change, but clients with whom Rogers formed an open and permissive relationship did seem to improve. During this time, Rogers was reinforced in his clinical beliefs by the works of Otto Rank and his followers (Raskin & Rogers, 1995).

Rogers left Rochester in 1940 to accept a professorship at Ohio State University. Two years later, he published his ideas on counseling in his first book on theory, *Counseling and Psychotherapy* (1942). He refined and revised the ideas during extensive research in the 1950s and 1960s at the Universities of Chicago and Wisconsin. At Wisconsin, Rogers first examined the effectiveness of his approach with diagnosed schizophrenics in a hospital setting. In 1964, he became a resident fellow at the Western Behavioral Sciences Institute. In 1968, he helped establish the Center for the Study of Persons in La Jolla, California.

Rogers was a prolific writer and published more than 200 articles and 15 books (Heppner, Rogers, & Lee, 1990). Among his most noteworthy books are *Counseling and Psychotherapy* (1942), which laid the foundation for person-centered counseling; *Client-Centered Therapy* (1951), which thrust him and his theory into national prominence; and *On Becoming a Person* (1961), which "solidified his reputation in his chosen profession" (Whiteley, 1987, p. 8). He wrote five books after the age of 65, including *Freedom to Learn* (1969), *Carl Rogers on Encounter Groups* (1970), and *A Way of Being* (1980). Rogers considered his theory to be constantly evolving, going beyond the boundaries of individual counseling to become relevant in groups, marriages, families, and international relations, especially the peace movement of the 1980s (Goodyear, 1987; Rogers, 1987). He died unexpectedly at age 85 on February 4, 1987, from complications following hip surgery.

View of Human Nature

Implicit in person-centered counseling is a particular view of human nature: people are essentially good (Rogers, 1961). Humans are characteristically "positive, forward-moving, constructive, realistic, and trustworthy" (Rogers, 1957, p. 199). Each person is aware, inner directed, and moving toward self-actualization from infancy on. Rogers (1959) held that human infants possess the following traits:

- Whatever an infant perceives is that infant's reality. An infant's perception is an internal process that no one else can be aware of.
- All infants are born with a self-actualizing tendency that is satisfied through goal-directed behavior.
- An infant's interaction with the environment is an organized whole, and everything an infant does is interrelated.
- The experiences of an infant may be seen as positive or negative according to whether the experiences enhance the actualization tendency.
- Infants maintain experiences that are actualizing and avoid those that are not.

According to Rogers, self-actualization is the most prevalent and motivating drive of existence and encompasses actions that influence the total person. "The organism has one basic tendency and striving, to actualize, maintain, and enhance the experiencing organism" (Rogers, 1951, p. 487). Person-centered theorists believe that each person is capable of finding a personal meaning and purpose in life.

Rogers views the individual from a *phenomenological perspective*: what is important is the person's perception of reality rather than an event itself (Rogers, 1955). This way of seeing the person is similar to Adler's. The concept of self is another idea that Rogers and Adler share. But for Rogers the concept is so central to his theory that his ideas are often referred to as *self theory.* The self is an outgrowth of what a person experiences, and an awareness of self helps a person differentiate him- or herself from others (Nye, 1996).

For a healthy self to emerge, a person needs *positive regard*—love, warmth, care, respect, and acceptance. But in childhood, as well as later in life, a person often receives *conditional regard* from parents and others. Feelings of worth develop if the person behaves in certain ways because conditional acceptance teaches the person to feel valued only when conforming to others' wishes. Thus, a person may have to deny or distort a perception when someone on whom the person depends for approval sees a situation differently. An individual who is caught in such a dilemma becomes aware of incongruities between self-perception and experience. If a person does not do as others wish, he or she will not be accepted and valued. Yet if a person conforms, he or she opens up a gap between the *ideal self* (what the person is striving to become) and the *real self* (what the person is). The further the ideal self is from the real self, the more alienated and maladjusted a person becomes.

Role of the Counselor

The counselor's role is a holistic one. He or she sets up and promotes a climate in which the client is free and encouraged to explore all aspects of self (Rogers, 1951, 1980). This atmosphere focuses on the counselor-client relationship, which Rogers describes as one with a special "I-Thou" personal quality. The counselor is aware of the client's verbal and nonverbal language, and the counselor reflects back what he or she is hearing or observing (Braaten, 1986). Neither the client nor the counselor knows what direction the sessions will take or what goals will emerge in the process. Yet the counselor trusts the client to develop an agenda on which he or she wishes to work. The counselor's job is to work as a facilitator rather than a director. In the person-centered approach, the counselor is the process expert and expert learner (of the client). Patience is essential (Miller, 1996).

Person-centered counselors make limited use of psychological tests. They are usually done only at the request of the client and only after the client has had an opportunity to be reflective about his or her past decisions. If testing does take place, the counselor focuses on the test's meaning for that client rather than on test scores. One innovative test often used in evaluating clients is the Q Sort Technique (Hergenhahn, 1994). This procedure has three steps. First, the client is given 100 cards, each of which contains a self-descriptive sentence, such as "I am intelligent" or "I despise myself." Next, the client is asked to place the cards in nine piles from "most like me" to "least like me." After this self-sort, the client sorts the cards again by placing them according to how he or she would ideally like to be. The final step of the process is correlating the degree of similarity between the two sorts before, during, and after counseling.

The use of diagnosis is eschewed in person-centered counseling because diagnosis is philosophically incompatible with the objectives of the approach. Diagnosis categorizes people and implies that each person is not unique. It also puts the counselor in charge: once a diagnosis is made, a treatment plan follows.

Goals

The goals of person-centered counseling concern the client as a person, not his or her problem. Rogers (1977) emphasizes that people need to be assisted in learning how to cope with situations. One of the main ways to accomplish this is by helping a client become a fully functioning person who has no need to apply defense mechanisms to everyday experiences. Such an individual becomes increasingly willing to change and grow. He or she is more open to experience, more trusting of self-perception, and engaged in self-exploration and evaluation (Rogers, 1961). Furthermore, a fully functioning person develops a greater acceptance of self and others and becomes a better decision maker in the here and now.

Ultimately, a client is helped to identify, use, and integrate his or her own resources and potential (Boy & Pine, 1982; Miller, 1996). Rogers (1961) held that, as a result of person-centered counseling, clients should become "more realistic in their self-perceptions; more confident and self-directing; more positively valued by themselves; less likely to repress aspects of their experiences; more mature, socialized, and adaptive in their behavior; less upset by stress and quicker to recover from it; and more like the healthy integrated well functioning person in their personality structures" (p. 375). Thus, a major goal of person-centered counseling is to bring about a harmony "between the client's real self-concept and his or her perceived self-concept" (Benjamin & Looby, 1998, p. 92).

Techniques

Person-centered techniques have evolved over the years. Hart (1970) identifies three periods of evolution, each of which stressed different techniques.

- *Nondirective period (1940–1950).* During this period, person-centered counselors emphasized forming a relationship with clients by creating a permissive and noninterventive atmosphere. Their main techniques were acceptance and clarification.

• *Reflective period (1950–1957).*   This 7-year span was characterized by counselor emphasis on creating nonthreatening relationships. Main techniques included responding to clients' feelings and reflecting underlying affect back to clients. During this period, Rogers changed the language associated with his theory from nondirective to client centered to deemphasize techniques and focusing on the therapeutic relationship.

• *Experiential period (1957–1980).*   This period began when Rogers (1957) issued his statement on the necessary and sufficient (i.e., core) conditions of counseling: empathy, positive regard (acceptance), and congruence (genuineness) (Gelso & Carter, 1985; Watts, 1996). *Empathy* is the counselor's ability to feel with clients and convey this understanding back to them. It is an attempt to think with, rather than for or about, them (Brammer, Abrego, & Shostrom, 1992). Rogers (1975) noted, "The research keeps piling up and it points strongly to the conclusion that a high degree of empathy in a relationship is possibly the most potent and certainly one of the most potent factors in bringing about change and learning" (p. 3). *Positive regard,* also known as acceptance, is a deep and genuine caring for the client as a person—that is, prizing the person just for being (Rogers, 1961, 1980). *Congruence* is the condition of being transparent in the therapeutic relationship by giving up roles and facades (Rogers, 1980). This period helped make person-centered counseling more active and well defined.

Since 1980, person-centered counselors have tried a number of other procedures for working with clients, such as limited self-disclosure of feelings, thoughts, and values (Corey, 1996). Clients, however, grow by experiencing themselves and others in relationships (Cormier & Cormier, 1998). Therefore, Rogers (1967b) believed that "significant positive personality change" could not occur except in relationships (p. 73). He listed six necessary and sufficient conditions for a counseling relationship:

1. Two persons are in psychological contact.
2. The first person, the client, is in a state of incongruence and is vulnerable or anxious.
3. The second person, the counselor, is congruent, or integrated, in the relationship.
4. The counselor experiences unconditional positive regard for the client.
5. The counselor experiences an empathic understanding of the client's internal frame of reference and attempts to communicate his or her experience to the client.
6. There is at least a minimal degree of communication to the client of the counselor's understanding and unconditional positive regard.

According to Rogers (1959), these six conditions exist on a continuum. Except for the first condition, they do not exist on an all-or-nothing basis.

Methods that help promote the counselor-client relationship include, but are not limited to, the following: active and passive listening, accurate reflection of thoughts and feelings, clarification, summarization, confrontation, and general or open-ended leads (Poppen & Thompson, 1974). All these techniques have been incorporated into other counseling approaches and systematic human relations training courses. Overall, person-centered counseling places a minimum emphasis on formal techniques and a maximum focus on the therapeutic relationship. A classic example of this emphasis can be seen in

Rogers's (1965) interview with a client named "Gloria" in which he focuses on her acceptance of herself and their relationship rather than Gloria's problem.

Evaluation of Uniqueness and Limitations

Person-centered counseling can be evaluated from many perspectives. Its unique aspects include the following:

• The approach revolutionized the counseling profession by linking counseling with psychotherapy and demystifying it with the publication of an actual transcript of a counseling session (Goodyear, 1987). Basically, Rogers "turned the field of counseling upside down" (Rogers, 1974, p. 115). Furthermore, he made the person-centered approach and counseling more applicable to a wide range of human problems, including institutional changes, labor-management relationships, leadership development, career decision making, and international diplomacy. He summed up his view of the approach in this way: "I am no longer talking about psychotherapy, but about a point of view, a philosophy, an approach to life, a way of being, which fits any situation in which growth, of a person, a group, or a community is part of the goal" (Rogers, 1980, p. ix).

• The approach has generated a great deal of research and initially set the standard for doing research on counseling variables, especially those that Rogers (1957) deemed "necessary and sufficient" to bring about therapeutic change. In addition, Rogers was the first practitioner to make audiotape recordings of counseling sessions and insisted that the person-centered approach be compared only with theories that were as empirically verified (Rogers, 1986). "Above all, Rogers was the quintessential scientist practitioner. He continually put his formulations to the test of research. In fact, no model of therapy is more extensively researched than his own" (Goodyear, 1987, p. 523).

• The approach is effective. Person-centered counseling helps improve psychological adjustment, learning, and frustration tolerance and decrease defensiveness (Grummon, 1972). It is appropriate in treating mild to moderate anxiety states, adjustment disorders, and conditions not attributable to mental disorders, such as uncomplicated bereavement or interpersonal relations (Seligman, 1997).

• The approach focuses on the open relationship established by counselors and clients and the short-term nature of the process. More than most, Rogers's theory emphasizes the importance of an accepting counselor-client relationship. Specific dimensions of the relationship have been examined for their impact on the total process of counseling (Carkhuff, 1969a, 1969b).

• The basics of the approach take a relatively short time to learn. With its emphasis on mastering listening skills, person-centered counseling is a foundation for training many paraprofessional helpers.

• The approach has a positive view of human nature (Heppner et al., 1990). When it was first introduced, person-centered counseling revolutionized the field of helping because its approach was so different from the more pessimistic and deterministic views of the day. One of the strongest reasons explaining why people change is the belief that they can change. Person-centered counselors are strong believers in the change process.

The limitations of person-centered theory are also noteworthy:

• The approach initially provided few instructions for counselors on how to establish relationships with clients and bring about change. The work of Carkhuff (1969a, 1969b) and Gazda (1973) helped rectify this deficiency. Still, person-centered theory is sometimes viewed as an approach without clearly defined terms or techniques (Nye, 1996).

• The approach depends on bright, insightful, hard-working clients for best results. It has limited applicability and is seldom employed with the severely disabled or young children (Thompson & Rudolph, 1996).

• The approach ignores diagnosis, the unconscious, and innately generated sexual and aggressive drives. Many critics think it is overly optimistic. Even though Rogers compiled a great deal of data supporting his point of view, much of that research has been attacked as being simplistic and based on self-reports (Hergenhahn, 1994).

• The approach deals only with surface issues and does not challenge the client to explore deeper areas. The argument here is that only deep change is lasting; because person-centered counseling is short-term, it cannot make a permanent impact on the person.

Existential Counseling

The existential approach to counseling is unique in its diversity. There is no unanimity among existentialists about how to formulate a theory to accompany their ideas of helping others. Existentialism is represented in the writings of several prominent American theorists, including Sidney Jourard, Abraham Maslow, Irvin Yalom, Rollo May, Clemmont Vontress, and Clark Moustakas. Its philosophical roots, however, are European and lie in the writings of Soren Kierkegaard, Fyodor Dostoyevski, Jean-Paul Sartre, Albert Camus, Edmund Husserl, Friedrich Nietzsche, Martin Buber, Victor Frankl, and Martin Heidegger.

Existentialists have some beliefs in common: the importance of anxiety, values, freedom, and responsibility in human life and an emphasis on finding meaning. But they differ widely in their emphases. For example, Dostoyevski stressed the importance of consciousness, Kierkegaard concentrated on human anxiety and dread, and Buber focused on the treatment of persons and our relationships with them in an "it" or "thou" relationship. May (1961) and Frankl (1962) are probably the best-known theorists of existential counseling, and this section concentrates on them and their ideas.

Rollo May

Rollo May was born in 1909 in Ada, Ohio. Like Alfred Adler, May was the second child of six children. Unlike Adler, however, May was the oldest son in his family. His father, who worked for the YMCA, encouraged Rollo to learn self-discipline through swimming. The relationship between May's parents was discordant, and he described the home life of his boyhood as unhappy. Consequently, he became a loner and a rebel during his adolescence (Rabinowitz, Good, & Cozad, 1989).

In 1930, May graduated with a degree in English from Oberlin College and accepted a position teaching English at Anatolia College in Greece. During two of his summer vacations in Greece, he traveled to Vienna and enrolled in seminars conducted by Alfred Adler. As a result, May became interested in psychoanalysis. During his years in Greece, he was also extremely lonely and began working incessantly. The result was a breakdown, which he reflected on years later: "I had learned enough psychology at college to know that these symptoms meant that something was wrong with my whole way of life. I had to find some new goals and purposes for my living and to relinquish my moralistic, somewhat rigid way of existence" (May, 1985, p. 8).

In 1933, May returned to the United States to enter the Union Theological Seminary. There he was strongly influenced by Paul Tillich, an existential theologian. After a brief career as a Congregationalist minister, May decided to pursue a degree in clinical psychology from Columbia University. But tuberculosis interrupted his studies. He struggled with the illness for almost 2 years, during which time he was strongly impressed with the writings of the Danish existentialist Soren Kierkegaard. After his recovery, May completed his doctorate at Columbia in 1949 and joined the faculty of the William Allanson White Institute in New York City.

May's most influential book, *The Meaning of Anxiety*, was published a year later. May believed that anxiety could work for the good as well as the detriment of people. He lectured on this subject at some of the most distinguished universities in the United States, including Yale and Harvard, while continuing to practice psychotherapy and serve "as an adjunct faculty member at the New School of Social Research and New York University" (Rabinowitz et al., 1989, p. 437). May was a cofounder of the Association for Humanistic Psychology in the 1960s and later wrote two other well-known books, *Love and Will* (1969) and *The Courage to Create* (1975). In the 1980s, he retired to the San Francisco area, where he concentrated on writing about the meaning of myths for modern society and continued to promote a humanistic approach to the study of persons. He died on October 22, 1994, at the age of 85.

Victor Frankl

Victor Frankl was born in 1905 in Vienna, Austria. He received a medical degree in 1930 and a Ph.D. in 1949 from the University of Vienna. Frankl established the Youth Advisement Centers in Vienna and directed them from 1928 to 1938. He also held several hospital appointments in the city between 1930 and 1942.

Although Frankl was a student of Freud, he became interested in existentialism in the 1930s while reading philosophers such as Heidegger, Scheler, and Legan. He began formulating his ideas about an existentialist approach to counseling, using the term *logotherapy* as early as 1938. (The Greek word *logo* implies a search for meaning.)

During World War II (1942–1945), Frankl was imprisoned in Nazi concentration camps at Auschwitz and Dachau, where his parents, a brother, and his wife died. The impact of the concentration camps crystallized his thoughts about the meaning of life and suffering, and it was partly his determination to share his beliefs that kept him alive.

In 1947, Frankl joined the faculty of the University of Vienna and later became associated with the United States International University in San Diego. He lectured widely at many prestigious universities and wrote extensively. His best-known books are *Man's Search for Meaning* (1962), which has been translated into 24 languages, and *The Will to Meaning* (1969b). "According to Frankl, the *will to meaning* is the central drive of human existence" (Dollarhide, 1997, p. 181). Meaning is not attained through direct pursuit but is a by-product of discovery.

Frankl is sometimes referred to as the founder of the third school of Viennese psychotherapy (logotherapy), with Freud's psychoanalytic theory first and Adler's individual psychology second. Frankl died at the age of 92 on September 2, 1997, of heart failure in Vienna and is buried there.

View of Human Nature

As a group, existentialists believe that people form their lives by the choices they make. Even in the worst situations, such as the Nazi death camps, there is an opportunity to make important life-and-death decisions, such as whether to struggle to stay alive (Frankl, 1969b). Existentialists focus on this freedom of choice and the action that goes with it. They view people as the authors of their lives: how much one restricts his or her life depends on personal decisions. They contend that people are responsible for any choice they make and that some choices are healthier and more meaningful than others. For example, individuals who prize creativity, dedication of service to others, friendship, and self-growth within a community or family environment may, as Abraham Maslow describes, have *peak experiences:* they feel truly integrated and connected with the universe in a very emotional way (Hoffman, 1990). They are characterized as follows: "[having] a holistic perspective of the world, [having] a natural tendency toward synergy [cooperative action], [being] intrapsychic, interpersonal, intercultural and international, [being] more consciously and deliberately metamotivated" (Chandler, Holden, & Kolander, 1992, p. 168).

On the other hand, those who are self-indulgent may feel a sense of normlessness and valuelessness. They may experience what Frankl (1959) calls an *existential vacuum* (a sense that life has lost all meaning). Carried to an extreme, these individuals would develop a disorder Frankl called *noogenic neurosis* (characterized by a feeling one has nothing to live for) (Das, 1998).

According to Frankl (1962), the "meaning of life always changes but it never ceases to be" (p. 113). Meaning goes beyond self-actualization and exists at three levels: (a) ultimate meanings (e.g., there is an order to the universe); (b) meaning of the moment; and (c) common, day-to-day meaning (Das, 1998). We can discover life's meaning in three ways:

- *By doing a deed*—that is, by achieving or accomplishing something
- *By experiencing a value,* such as a work of nature, culture, or love
- *By suffering*—that is, by finding a proper attitude toward unalterable fate

Existentialists believe that psychopathology is a failure to make meaningful choices and maximize one's potential (McIllroy, 1979). Choices may be avoided and potentials not realized because of the anxiety that is involved in action. Anxiety is often associated with paralysis, but May (1977) argues that normal anxiety may be healthy and motivational and can help people change. Clients may leave existential counseling feeling more anxiety than when they began, but in such cases they are consciously aware of their anxiety and can therefore channel it toward constructive use (May, 1967). Thus, existentialism focuses on the meaning of anxiety in human life. The emphasis within this framework is on the inner person and how authentic individuals search for values in life. By being aware of feelings and the finite nature of human existence, a person comes to make healthy, life-enhancing choices.

Role of the Counselor

There are no uniform roles that existential counselors follow. Every client is considered unique. Therefore, counselors are sensitive to all aspects of their clients' character, "such as voice, posture, facial expression, even dress and apparently accidental movements of the body" (May, 1939, p. 101). Basically, counselors concentrate on being authentic with their clients and entering into deep and personal relationships with them. It is not unusual for a counselor to share personal experiences with a client to deepen the relationship and help the client realize a shared humanness and struggle. Buhler and Allen (1972) suggest that existential counselors focus on person-to-person relationships that emphasize mutuality, wholeness, and growth. Counselors who practice from a Frankl perspective are Socratic in engaging their clients in dialogue (Das, 1998). However, all existential counselors serve as a model of how to achieve individual potential and make decisions. They concentrate on helping the client experience subjective feelings, gain clearer self-understanding, and move toward the establishment of a new way of being in the world. The focus is living productively in the present, not recovering a personal past. They also "focus on ultimate human concerns (death, freedom, isolation, and meaninglessness)" (May & Yalom, 1995, p. 279).

Existential counselors do not use psychological tests, nor do they make diagnoses in accordance with the DSM-IV. Both these procedures would be antithetical to the thrust of the approach. It is interesting to note, however, that some psychological instruments (such as the Purpose of Life Test) are based on existential premises and that the DSM-IV deals with anxiety on several levels.

Goals

The goals of existentialists include helping clients realize the importance of meaning, responsibility, awareness, freedom, and potential. Existentialists hope that during the course of counseling, clients will take more responsibility for their lives. "The aim of therapy is that the patient experience his existence as real" (May, Angel, & Ellenberger, 1958, p. 85). In the process, the client is freed from being an observer of events and becomes a shaper of meaningful personal activity.

A client becomes more responsible partly because of the relationship built with the counselor. In the relationship, a client becomes aware of personal freedom. Thus, a major goal of counseling is for clients to shift from an outward to an inward frame of reference. No longer will activities depend on the judgment of others; rather, activities will be evaluated by clients first. Further goals include making the client sensitive of his or her existence, calling attention to the client's uniqueness, helping the client improve his or her encounters with others, assisting the client in establishing a will to meaning, and encouraging the client to make a decision about both present and future directions in life (Cunningham & Peters, 1973; Das, 1998; May, 1975; Reeves, 1977).

Techniques

The existential approach has fewer techniques available than almost any other model of counseling. Yet this apparent weakness is paradoxically a strength because it allows existential counselors to borrow ideas as well as use a wide range of personal and professional skills. "Approaching human beings merely in terms of techniques necessarily implies manipulating them," and manipulation is opposed to what existentialists espouse (Frankl, 1967, p. 139). Thus, existentialists are free to use techniques as widely diversified as desensitization and free association or to disassociate themselves from these practices entirely (Corey, 1996).

In any case, clients usually benefit from existential counselors who are able to address client needs in a multidimensional and highly personalized way. An example of this approach can be seen in those people coping with loss: depressed persons tend to adopt emotion-focused strategies, whereas nondepressed individuals use multiple and vying strategies (Stevens, Pfost, & Wessels, 1987). Of uppermost importance is the counselor's readiness to work with the client in an open and inquiring manner and thereby accept the truth unique to each individual (Kemp, 1976).

"Some vision of the good, the true, and the beautiful is essential to a meaningful personal life and a humanistic society" (Partenheimer, 1990, p. 44). Sometimes the process of finding one's truth requires a willingness to work through ambiguity. The most effective and powerful technique existential counselors have is the relationship with the client. Ideally, the counselor transcends his or her own needs and focuses on the client (Wallace, 1986). In the process, the counselor is open and self-revealing in an attempt to help the client become more in touch with personal feelings and experiences. The emphasis in the relationship is on authenticity, honesty, and spontaneity.

Existential counselors also make use of confrontation. Clients are confronted with the idea that everyone is responsible for his or her own life. Existential counselors borrow some techniques such as imagery exercises, awareness exercises, and goal-setting activities from other models. For example, a counselor may lead a client through a typical day in the client's life 5 years in the future. Through this process, a client is able to see the meaning in life more clearly by experiencing what choices he or she is making now.

Evaluation of Uniqueness and Limitations

The existential approach to counseling has a number of unique aspects:

• The approach emphasizes the uniqueness of each individual. It is a very humanistic way of working with others (Yalom, 1980).

• The approach recognizes that anxiety is not necessarily a negative condition. Anxiety is a part of human life and can motivate some individuals to make healthy and productive decisions.

• The approach gives counselors access to a tremendous amount of philosophy and literature that is both informative and enlightening about human nature. The philosophical base of existentialism has the potential to support a systematic counseling theory.

• The approach stresses continued human growth and development and offers hope to clients through directed readings and therapeutic encounters with the counselor. The life of Victor Frankl is a good illustration of this strength.

• The approach is effective in multicultural counseling situations because its global view of human existence allows counselors to focus on the person of the client in an "I-Thou" manner without regard to ethnic or social background (Jackson, 1987; Epp, 1998).

• The approach helps connect individuals to universal problems faced by humankind, such as the search for peace and the absence of caring (Baldwin, 1989).

• The approach may be combined with other perspectives and methods (such as those based on learning principles and behaviorism) to treat extremely difficult problems, such as alcoholism. In these cases, a major focus is on the existential values of facing "life problems and feelings through honest expression" (Wilbur, Roberts-Wilbur, & Morris, 1990, p. 157).

Professionals who embrace different and more structured approaches have noted several limitations in the existential approach:

• The approach has not produced a fully developed model of counseling. Professionals who stress developmental stages of counseling are particularly vehement in this criticism.

• The approach lacks educational and training programs. Each practitioner is unique. Although uniqueness is valued, it prohibits the systematic teaching of theory. Wallace (1986), for instance, wonders whether May's existential approach will last.

• The approach is difficult to implement beyond an individual level because of its subjective nature. Existentialism lacks the type of methodology and validation processes prevalent in most other approaches. In short, it lacks the uniformity that beginning counselors can readily understand.

• The approach is closer to existential philosophy than to other theories of counseling. This distinction limits its usefulness.

Gestalt Therapy

Gestalt therapy is associated with Gestalt psychology, a school of thought that stresses perception of completeness and wholeness. The term *gestalt* means whole figure. Gestalt psychology and therapy arose as a reaction to the reductionist emphasis in other schools of psychology and counseling, such as psychoanalysis and behaviorism. Thus, Gestalt theory emphasizes how people function in their totality. The approach was popularized in the 1960s by Fritz Perls, who focused on helping individuals become more aware of the many aspects of their personhood. Laura Perls (Fritz's wife) and Paul Goodman helped Perls develop and refine his original ideas. A number of other theorists, particularly Joen Fagan and Irma Lee Shepherd (1970), developed the model further, but the therapy rests on the work of Perls.

Fritz Perls

Frederick Salomon Perls was born in 1893 in Berlin into a middle-class Jewish family. He had a younger and an older sister. His parents fought bitterly and Perls disliked his older sister, yet he remembered his childhood as happy. He loved to read and was a top student in grade school. In secondary school, Perls encountered difficulty because of a conservative learning environment and his own rebellious spirit. He failed the 7th grade twice and as an adolescent had difficulty obeying authorities. Nevertheless, he not only completed his secondary education (once placed in a more liberal environment) but was also awarded a medical degree from Frederich Wilhelm University in 1920. His schooling was interrupted by World War I, when he served as a medic with the German army.

Perls trained as a psychoanalyst in both Vienna and Berlin. Wilhelm Reich and Karen Horney each had a part in Perls's analysis as part of his training. Later he took a position at the Institute for Brain Injured Soldiers in Frankfurt. There Perls became associated with Kurt Goldstein, from whom he learned to view humans as complete entities (i.e., holistic) rather than individuals made of separate parts.

In 1933, Perls fled Nazi Germany, first to Holland and then to Johannesburg, South Africa, where he and his wife, Laura Posner Perls, built a strong psychoanalytic practice, as they had previously done in Germany. In 1936, Perls sailed his private yacht 4,000 miles from South Africa to Germany to attend an international psychoanalytic congress in Czechoslovakia. There he arranged an audience with Freud. A brief interchange with Freud left Perls feeling humiliated. Thereafter, Perls, who had been humiliated frequently by his father, dedicated himself to proving Freud and psychoanalysis wrong.

Perls immigrated to the United States in 1946. Although his ideas initially were not readily accepted, he gained prominence through the publication of *Gestalt Therapy* (1951), which he coauthored with Hefferline and Goodman. He also established the Institute for Gestalt Therapy in New York City in 1952 and offered lectures and workshops around America. In 1960 he moved to the Esalen Institute in Big Sur, California. Perls was an actor at heart and loved to parade his ideas before the public at Esalen. Laura Perls, long separated from Fritz, continued to be supportive of her husband until his death in British Columbia at the Gestalt kibbutz, a commune he had founded, in 1970 (Bankart, 1997). Perls recounted many of the more personal moments of his life in his autobiographical book, *In and Out of the Garbage Pail* (1972).

View of Human Nature

Gestaltists believe that human beings work for wholeness and completeness in life. Each person has a self-actualizing tendency that emerges through personal interaction with the environment and the beginning of self-awareness. Self-actualization is centered in the present; it "is the process of being what one is and not a process of striving to become" (Kempler, 1973, p. 262). The Gestalt view of human nature places trust on the inner wisdom of people, much as person-centered counseling does. Each person seeks to live integratively and productively, striving to coordinate the various parts of the person into a healthy, unified whole. From a Gestalt perspective, persons are more than a sum of their parts (Perls, 1969).

The Gestalt view is antideterministic: each person is able to change and become responsible (Hatcher & Himelsteint, 1997). Individuals are actors in the events around them, not just reactors to events. Overall, the Gestalt point of view takes a position that is existential, experiential, and phenomenological: the now is what really matters. One discovers different aspects of oneself through experience, not talk, and a person's own assessment and interpretation of his or her life at a given moment in time are what is most important.

According to Gestalt therapy, many troubled individuals have an overdependency on intellectual experience (Simkin, 1975). Such an emphasis diminishes the importance of emotions and the senses, limiting a person's ability to respond to various situations. Another common problem is the inability to identify and resolve unfinished business—that is, earlier thoughts, feelings, and reactions that still affect personal functioning and interfere with living life in the present. The most usual unfinished business in life is not forgiving one's parents for their mistakes. Gestaltists do not attribute either of these difficulties to any unconscious forces within persons. Rather, the focus is on awareness, "the ability of the client to be in full mental and sensory" contact of "experiencing the now" (Gilliland & James, 1998, p. 142). Every person operates on some conscious level, from being very aware to being very unaware.

Healthy individuals are those who are most aware. Such people realize that body signs, such as headaches or stomach pains, may indicate a need to change behavior. They are also aware of personal limitations. For instance, in conflicts with others, one may be able to resolve the situation or just have to dismiss it. A healthy person avoids complicating such situations by embellishing them with fantasy. Instead, the person focuses "sharply on one need (the figure) at a time while relegating other needs to the background. When the need is met, or the Gestalt is closed or completed, it is relegated to the background and a new need comes into focus (becomes the figure)" (Thompson & Rudolph, 1992, p. 66). Such functioning requires that persons recognize internal needs and learn how to manipulate those needs and the environment (Perls, 1976).

According to Gestaltists, a person may experience difficulty in several ways. First, he or she may lose contact with the environment and the resources in it. Second, the person may become overinvolved with the environment and thus out of touch with the self. Third, he or she may fail to put aside unfinished business. Fourth, he or she may become fragmented or scattered in many directions. Fifth, the person may experience conflict between the *top dog* (what one thinks one should do) and the *underdog* (what one wants to do). Finally, the person may have difficulty handling the dichotomies of life, such as love/hate, masculinity/femininity, and pleasure/pain.

Role of the Counselor

The role of the Gestalt counselor is to create an atmosphere that promotes a client's exploration of what is needed to grow. The counselor provides such an atmosphere by being intensely and personally involved with clients and being honest. Polster and Polster (1973) stress that counselors must be exciting, energetic, and fully human. Involvement occurs in the now, which is a continuing process (Perls, 1969). The now often involves having the counselor help a client focus on blocking energy and using that energy in positive and adaptive ways (Zinker, 1978). The now also entails the counselor's helping the client recognize patterns in his or her life (Fagan, 1970).

Gestalt counselors follow several rules in helping clients become more aware of the now (Levitsky & Perls, 1970):

- *The principle of now*—always using the present tense
- *I and Thou*—always addressing someone directly instead of talking about him or her to the counselor
- *The use of I*—substituting the word *I* for *it,* especially when talking about the body
- *The use of an awareness continuum*—focusing on how and what rather than why
- *The conversion of questions*—asking clients to convert questions into statements

Gestalt counselors do not use standardized assessment instruments, such as psychological tests, nor do they diagnose their clients according to DSM-IV classification standards.

Goals

The goals of Gestalt therapy are well defined. They include an emphasis on the here and now and a recognition of the immediacy of experience (Bankart, 1997). The importance of these first two goals can be seen in the fact that the term *contact* is used to refer to the sensory and motor immediacy that may be experienced when the environment is met directly (Perls et al., 1951). Further goals include a focus on both nonverbal and verbal expression, and a focus on the concept that life includes making choices (Fagan & Shepherd, 1970). The Gestalt approach concentrates on helping a client resolve the past to become integrated. This goal includes the completion of mentally growing up. It emphasizes the coalescence of the emotional, cognitive, and behavioral aspects of the person. A primary focus is the acceptance of polarities within the person (Gelso & Carter, 1985). As a group, Gestalt therapists stress action, pushing their clients to experience feelings and behaviors. They also stress the meaning of the word *now*. Perls (1970) developed a formula that expresses the word's essence: "Now = experience = awareness = reality. The past is no more and the future not yet. Only the now exists" (p. 14).

To be mature in the now, a person often must shed neurotic tendencies. Perls (1970) identifies five layers of neurosis that potentially interfere with being authentically in touch with oneself: the phony, the phobic, the impasse, the implosive, and the explosive. The *phony layer* consists of pretending to be something that one is not. At this level, there is a lot of game playing and fantasy enactment. When persons become more aware of the games they are playing, they can be more honest, open, and in touch with unpleasantness and pain.

The *phobic layer* is an attempt to avoid recognizing aspects of self that the person would prefer to deny. People who experience this layer of awareness are afraid that if they acknowledge who they are and present it to others, they will be rejected.

Below this layer is the *impasse layer,* where individuals wonder how they are going to make it in the environment. There is no sense of direction at this level, and the person is adrift in a sea of helplessness and dread.

The fourth and fifth layers, the *implosive* and *explosive,* are often grouped together. People at these layers frequently feel vulnerable to feelings. Yet as they peel back the layers of defensiveness built up over the years (implosiveness), they become alive in an explosion of joy, sorrow, or pain that leads to being authentic. When persons reach this point, the now can be experienced most fully.

Techniques

Some of the most innovative counseling techniques ever developed are found in Gestalt therapy (Harman, 1997). These techniques take two forms: exercises and experiments. *Exercises* are ready-made techniques, such as the enactment of fantasies, role playing, and psychodrama (Covin, 1977). They are employed to evoke a certain response from the client, such as anger or exploration. *Experiments*, on the other hand, are activities that grow out of the interaction between counselor and client. They are not planned, and what is learned is often a surprise to both the client and the counselor. Many of the techniques of Gestalt therapy take the form of unplanned experiments (Zinker, 1978). The concentration here, however, is on exercise-oriented counseling techniques.

One common exercise is dream work. Perls describes dreams as messages that represent a person's place at a certain time (Bernard, 1986). Unlike psychoanalysts, Gestalt counselors do not interpret. Rather, clients present dreams and are then directed to experience what it is like to be each part of the dream—a type of dramatized free association. In this way, a client can get more in touch with the multiple aspects of the self. The person with repetitive dreams is encouraged to realize that unfinished business is being brought into awareness and that there is a need to take care of the message delivered.

Another effective technique is the empty chair (see Figure 9.1). In this procedure clients talk to the various parts of their personality, such as the part that is dominant and the part that is passive. An empty chair is the focus. A client may simply talk to the chair as a representative of one part of the self, or the client may switch from chair to chair and have each chair represent a different part. In this dialogue, both rational and irrational parts of the client come into focus; the client not only sees these sides but also becomes able to deal with the dichotomies within the self. This method is not recommended for the severely emotionally disturbed (Bernard, 1986).

One of the most powerful Gestalt exercises is confrontation. Counselors point out to clients incongruent behaviors and feelings, such as a client's smiling when admitting to nervousness. Truly nervous people do not smile. Confrontation involves asking clients *what* and *how* questions. *Why* questions are avoided because they lead to intellectualization.

A counselor may purposely frustrate a client to help him or her move beyond present states of denial (Harman, 1975). The counselor hopes that the client makes valuable interpretations when confronted. Techniques that center on working in the here and now focus on helping break out of old habits and becoming more in touch with the self.

Some other powerful Gestalt exercises that are individually oriented are often used in groups (Harman, 1997).

- *Making the rounds.* This exercise is employed when the counselor feels that a particular theme or feeling expressed by a client should be faced by every person in the group.

Figure 9.1   The empty chair

The client may say, for instance, "I can't stand anyone." The client is then instructed to say this sentence to each person in the group, adding some remarks about each group member. The rounds exercise is flexible and may include nonverbal and positive feelings, too. By participating in it, clients become more aware of inner feelings.

- *I take responsibility.*   In this exercise clients make statements about perceptions and close each statement with the phrase "and I take responsibility for it." The exercise helps clients integrate and own perceptions and behaviors.
- *Exaggeration.*   Clients accentuate unwitting movement or gestures. In doing so, the inner meaning of these behaviors become more apparent.
- *May I feed you a sentence?*   The counselor, who is aware that implicit attitudes or messages are implied in what the client is saying, asks whether the client will say a certain sentence (provided by the counselor) that makes the client's thoughts explicit. If the counselor is correct about the underlying message, the client will gain insight as the sentence is repeated.

Evaluation of Uniqueness and Limitations

Gestalt therapy strengths include the following:

• The approach emphasizes helping people incorporate and accept all aspects of life. An individual cannot be understood outside the context of a whole person who is choosing to act on the environment in the present (Passons, 1975).

• The approach helps a client focus on resolving areas of unfinished business. When a client is able to make these resolutions, life can be lived productively.

• The approach places primary emphasis on doing rather than talking. Activity helps individuals experience what the process of change is about and make more rapid progress.

• The approach is flexible and not limited to a few techniques. Any activity that helps clients become more integrative can be employed in Gestalt therapy. *"The Gestalt Journal* is the literary organ that disseminates research, theory, and innovative techniques of the approach" (Gilliland & James, 1998, p. 137).

• The approach is appropriate for certain affective disorders, anxiety states, somato-form disorders, adjustment disorders, and DSM-IV diagnoses such as occupational problem and interpersonal problem (Seligman, 1997). In short, Gestalt therapy is versatile.

Gestalt therapy also has some limitations:

• The approach lacks a strong theoretical base. Some critics view Gestalt counseling as all experience and technique—that is, as too gimmicky (Corey, 1996). They maintain that it is antitheoretical. In support of this position, they cite an often-quoted line from Perls: "Lose your mind and come to your senses."

• The approach deals strictly with the now and how of experience (Perls, 1969). This two-pronged principle does not allow for passive insight and change, which some clients are more likely to use.

• The approach eschews diagnosis and testing. Some individuals need to be screened before experiencing such an intense method of counseling. Although Gestalt therapists screen their clients for appropriateness, some critics argue the process needs to be uniform and thorough.

• The approach is too concerned with individual development and is criticized for its self-centeredness. The focus is entirely on feeling and personal discovery. Although many counseling theories are centered on individual development, Gestalt therapy is considered extreme. One example of self-centeredness is the "Gestalt Prayer" (Perls, 1969, p. 4):

> I do my thing and you do your thing.
> I am not in this world to live up to your expectations
> And you are not in this world to live up to mine.
> You are you and I am I,
> And if by chance we find each other, it's beautiful.
> If not, it cannot be helped.

Summary and Conclusion

Three affective approaches have been explored in this chapter: person-centered, existential, and Gestalt. Of these three, the person-centered approach continues to be the most popular. On the surface it is one of the easiest theories to learn. Because Rogerian techniques have been discussed in depth and concretely defined, the theory has become even more attractive. Gestalt therapy also continues to generate strong interest among practitioners. Although the approach is criticized for being heavy on technique and light on theory, it produces major change in many clients. Existential counseling has just the opposite problem: it is steeped in philosophy but short on technique. Yet existential counseling also attracts adherents because of its focus on the meaning of life and other universal concerns. In recent years, existential counseling has been advocated for working with culturally diverse clients, and its popularity may increase if it is used more in multicultural counseling (Epp, 1998).

As a group, affective approaches do not make much use of psychological tests, formal diagnoses, or rigid procedures. A trademark of these approaches is that they tailor what they do to the needs of the client. Counselors assess needs by establishing strong relationship with clients. Existential counseling is the most nondirective of the theories, whereas Gestalt therapy is most directive. All the theories discussed in this chapter share the belief that clients are capable of change, integration, and positive growth. Person-centered theory has the strongest support from research data. Existential counseling is often considered more of a philosophy than a counseling approach and has the least research data to back it up.

CLASSROOM ACTIVITIES

1. Compare and contrast how a practitioner from each of the three affective approaches covered in this chapter might work with the following types of clients: an alcoholic, a school-phobic child, a spouse abuser, and an unemployed person. How are the approaches similar and different?

2. Read *A Way of Being* (1980) by Carl Rogers. In small groups discuss how Rogers's theory was influenced by his personal development and how person-centered theory might be applied to educational, political, industrial, medical, recreational, and managerial settings. Be as specific as you can in translating the theory to these settings. After you have come to some conclusions, discuss your views with the class as a whole.

3. How do you think counselors from any of the affective approaches would handle reluctant clients, such as a child sent to the counselor or a prisoner whose sentence requires counseling? Discuss your ideas in pairs and then share them with the class as a whole.

4. Rollo May believed that the best counselors are those who have been "wounded"—that is, have suffered and been healed. In small groups, discuss what experiences counselors might best use to help them understand themselves and their clients. What are the advantages of having experienced situations similar to those your clients have experienced? What are the disadvantages?

5. There are approximately 50 Gestalt institutes in the United States. With the help of your instructor or a librarian, locate as many of them as you can and find out what types of training programs they offer. If possible, interview a professional who practices Gestalt and ask how he or she compares the approach with person-centered counseling.

REFERENCES

Baldwin, C. (1989). Peaceful alternatives: Inner peace. *Journal of Humanistic Education and Development, 28,* 86–92.

Bankart, C. P. (1997). *Talking cures.* Pacific Grove, CA: Brooks/Cole.

Benjamin, P., & Looby, J. (1998). Defining the nature of spirituality in the context of Maslow's and Rogers's theories. *Counseling and Values, 42,* 92–100.

Bernard, J. M. (1986). Laura Perls: From ground to figure. *Journal of Counseling and Development, 64,* 367–373.

Boy, A. V., & Pine, G. J. (1982). *Client-centered counseling: A renewal.* Boston: Allyn & Bacon.

Braaten, L. J. (1986). Thirty years with Rogers's necessary and sufficient conditions of therapeutic personality change. *Person-centered Review, 1,* 37–49.

Brammer, L. M., Abrego, P. J. & Shostrom, E. L. (1993). *Therapeutic counseling and psychotherapy* (6th ed.). Upper Saddle River, NJ: Merrill/Prentice Hall.

Buhler, C., & Allen, M. (1972). *Introduction to humanistic psychology.* Pacific Grove, CA: Brooks/Cole.

Carkhuff, R. R. (1969a). *Helping and human relations* (Vol. 1). New York: Holt, Rinehart, & Winston.

Carkhuff, R. R. (1969b). *Helping and human relations* (Vol. 2). New York: Holt, Rinehart, & Winston.

Chandler, C. K., Holden, J. M., & Kolander, C. A. (1992). Counseling for spiritual wellness: Theory and practice. *Journal of Counseling & Development, 71,* 168–176.

Corey, G. (1996). *Theory and practice of counseling and psychotherapy* (5th ed.). Pacific Grove, CA: Brooks/Cole.

Cormier, W. H., & Cormier, L. S. (1998). *Interviewing strategies for helpers* (4th ed.). Pacific Grove, CA: Brooks/Cole.

Covin, A. B. (1977). Using Gestalt psychodrama experiments in rehabilitation counseling. *Personnel and Guidance Journal, 56,* 143–147.

Cunningham, L. M., & Peters, H. J. (1973). *Counseling theories.* Upper Saddle River, NJ: Prentice Hall.

Das, A. K. (1998). Frankl and the realm of meaning. *Journal of Humanistic Education and Development, 36,* 199–211.

Dollarhide, C. T. (1997). Counseling for meaning in work and life: An integrated approach. *Journal of Humanistic Education and Development, 35,* 178–187.

Epp, L. R. (1998). The courage to be an existential counselor: An interview with Clemmont E. Vontress. *Journal of Mental Health Counseling, 20,* 1–12.

Fagan, J. (1970). The task of the therapist. In J. Fagan & I. L. Shepherd (Eds.), *Gestalt therapy now* (pp. 88–106). Palo Alto, CA: Science and Behavior Books.

Fagan, J., & Shepherd, I. L. (1970). Theory of Gestalt therapy. In J. Fagan & I. L. Shepherd (Eds.), *Gestalt therapy now* (pp. 1–7). Palo Alto, CA: Science and Behavior Books.

Frankl, V. (1959). The spiritual dimension in existential analysis and logotherapy. *Journal of Individual Psychology, 15,* 157–165.

Frankl, V. (1962). *Man's search for meaning: An introduction to logotherapy.* New York: Washington Square Press.

Frankl, V. (1967). *Psychotherapy and existentialism: Selected papers on logotherapy.* New York: Washington Square Press.

Frankl, V. (1969a). *Psychotherapy and existentialism: Selected papers on logotherapy.* New York: Simon & Schuster.

Frankl, V. (1969b). *The will to meaning: Foundations and applications of logotherapy.* New York: New American Library.

Gazda, G. M. (1973). *Human relations development: A manual for education.* Boston: Allyn & Bacon.

Gelso, C. J., & Carter, J. A. (1985). The relationship in counseling and psychotherapy: Components, consequences, and theoretical antecedents. *Counseling Psychologist, 13,* 155–243.

Gilliland, B. E., & James, R. K. (1998). *Theories and strategies in counseling and psychotherapy* (4th ed.). Boston: Allyn & Bacon.

Goodyear, R. K. (1987). In memory of Carl Ransom Rogers. *Journal of Counseling and Development, 65,* 523–524.

Grummon, D. L. (1972). Client-centered therapy. In B. Stefflre & W. H. Grant (Eds.), *Theories of counseling* (2nd ed.). New York: McGraw-Hill.

Hackney, H., & Cormier, L. S. (1996). *The professional counselor: A process guide to helping* (3rd ed.). Boston: Allyn & Bacon.

Harman, R. L. (1975). A Gestalt point of view on facilitating growth in counseling. *Personnel and Guidance Journal, 53,* 363–366.

Harman, R. L. (1997). *Gestalt therapy techniques: Working with groups, couples, and sexually dysfunctional men.* Northvale, NJ: Aronson.

Hart, J. (1970). The development of client-centered therapy. In J. T. Hart & T. M. Tomlinson (Eds.), *New directions in client centered therapy.* Boston: Houghton Mifflin.

Hatcher, C., & Himelsteint, P. (Eds.). (1997). *The handbook of Gestalt therapy.* Northvale, NJ: Aronson.

Heppner, P. P., Rogers, M. E., & Lee, L. A. (1990). Carl Rogers: Reflections on his life. In P. P. Heppner (Ed.), *Pioneers in counseling and development* (pp. 54–59). Alexandria, VA: American Counseling Association.

Hergenhahn, B. R. (1994). *An introduction to theories of personality* (4th ed.). Upper Saddle River, NJ: Prentice Hall.

Hoffman, E. (1990). Abraham Maslow's legacy for counseling. *Journal of Humanistic Education and Development, 29,* 2–9.

Jackson, M. L. (1987). Cross-cultural counseling at the crossroads: A dialogue with Clemmont E. Vontress. *Journal of Counseling and Development, 66,* 20–23.

Kemp, C. G. (1976). Existential counseling. In G. S. Belkin (Ed.), *Counseling directions in theory and practice.* Dubuque, IA: Kendall/Hunt.

Kempler, W. (1973). Gestalt therapy. In R. Corsini (Ed.), *Current psychotherapies* (pp. 251–286). Itasca, IL: Peacock.

Levitsky, A., & Perls, F. S. (1970). The rules and games of Gestalt therapy. In J. Fagan & I. L. Shepherd (Eds.), *Gestalt therapy now* (pp. 140–149). Palo Alto, CA: Science and Behavior Books.

May, R. (1939). *The art of counseling.* New York: Abingdon-Cokesbury.

May, R. (Ed.). (1961). *Existential psychology.* New York: Random House.

May, R. (1967). Part three: Psychotherapy. In *Psychology and the human dilemma* (pp. 87–160). Princeton, NJ: Van Nostrand.

May, R. (1969). *Love and will.* New York: Norton.

May, R. (1975). *The courage to create.* New York: Bantam.

May, R. (1977). *The meaning of anxiety* (rev. ed.). New York: Norton.

May, R. (1985). *My quest for beauty.* New York: Norton.

May, R., Angel, E., & Ellenberger, H. (Eds.). (1958). *Existence.* New York: Simon & Schuster.

May, R., & Yalom, I. (1995). Existential psychotherapy. In R. J. Corsini & D. Wedding (Eds.), *Current psychotherapies* (5th ed., pp. 262–292). Itasca, IL: Peacock.

McIllroy, J. H. (1979). Career as life-style: An existential view. *Personnel and Guidance Journal, 57,* 351–354.

Miller, M. J. (1996). Client-centered reflections on career decision making. *Journal of Employment Counseling, 33,* 43–46.

Nye, R. D. (1996). *Three psychologies* (5th ed.). Pacific Grove, CA: Brooks/Cole.

Partenheimer, D. (1990). Teaching literature toward a humanistic society. *Journal of Humanistic Education and Development, 29,* 40–44.

Passons, W. R. (1975). *Gestalt approaches to counseling.* New York: Holt, Rinehart, & Winston.

Perls, F. (1969). *Gestalt therapy verbatim.* Lafayette, CA: Real People Press.

Perls, F. (1970). Four lectures. In J. Fagan & I. L. Shepherd (Eds.), *Gestalt therapy now* (pp. 14–38). Palo Alto, CA: Science and Behavior Books.

Perls, F. (1972). *In and out of the garbage pail.* New York: Bantam.

Perls, F. (1976). *The Gestalt approaches and eye witnesses to therapy.* New York: Bantam.

Perls, F., Hefferline, R. F., & Goodman, P. (1951). *Gestalt therapy.* New York: Dell.

Polster, E., & Polster, M. (1973). *Gestalt therapy integrated: Contours of theory and practice.* New York: Brunner/Mazel.

Poppen, W. A., & Thompson, C. L. (1974). *School counseling: Theories and concepts.* Lincoln, NE: Professional Educators Publications.

Rabinowitz, F. E., Good, G., & Cozad, L. (1989). Rollo May: A man of meaning and myth. *Journal of Counseling and Development, 67,* 436–441.

Raskin, N. J., & Rogers, C. R. (1995). Person-centered therapy. In R. J. Corsini & D. Wedding (Eds.), *Current psychotherapies* (5th ed., pp. 128–161). Itasca, IL: Peacock.

Reeves, C. (1977). *The psychology of Rollo May*. San Francisco: Jossey-Bass.

Rogers, C. R. (1942). *Counseling and psychotherapy*. Boston: Houghton Mifflin.

Rogers, C. R. (1951). *Client-centered therapy*. Boston: Houghton Mifflin.

Rogers, C. R. (1955). Persons or science? A philosophical question. *American Psychologist, 10,* 267–278.

Rogers, C. R. (1957). The necessary and sufficient conditions of therapeutic personality change. *Journal of Consulting Psychology, 21,* 95–103.

Rogers, C. R. (1959). A theory of therapy, personality, and interpersonal relationships, as developed in the client-centered framework. In S. Koch (Ed.), *Psychology: A study of science* (Vol. 3, pp. 184–256). New York: McGraw-Hill.

Rogers, C. R. (1961). *On becoming a person*. Boston: Houghton Mifflin.

Rogers, C. R. (1965). Client-centered therapy: Part I. In E. Shostrom (Producer), *Three approaches to psychotherapy* [film]. Santa Ana, CA: Psychological Films.

Rogers, C. R. (1967a). Autobiography. In E. G. Boring & G. Lindzey (Eds.), *A history of psychology in autobiography* (Vol. 5, pp. 341–384). New York: Appleton.

Rogers, C. R. (1967b). The conditions of change from a client-centered viewpoint. In B. Berenson & R. Carkhuff (Eds.), *Sources of gain in counseling and psychotherapy* (pp. 71–86). New York: Holt, Rinehart, & Winston.

Rogers, C. R. (1969). *Freedom to learn*. Upper Saddle River, NJ: Merrill/Prentice Hall.

Rogers, C. R. (1970). *Carl Rogers on encounter groups*. New York: Harper & Row.

Rogers, C. R. (1974). In retrospect: Forty-six years. *American Psychologist, 29,* 115–123.

Rogers, C. R. (1975). Empathic: An unappreciated way of being. *Counseling Psychologist, 5,* 2–10.

Rogers, C. R. (1977). *Carl Rogers on personal power: Inner strength and its revolutionary impact*. New York: Delacorte.

Rogers, C. R. (1980). *A way of being*. Boston: Houghton Mifflin.

Rogers, C. R. (1986). Rogers, Kohut, and Erickson: A personal perspective on some similarities and differences. *Person-centered Review, 1,* 125–140.

Rogers, C. R. (1987). The underlying theory: Drawn from experience with individuals and groups. *Counseling and Values, 32,* 38–46.

Seligman, L. (1997). *Diagnosis and treatment planning in counseling*. New York: Plenum.

Simkin, J. S. (1975). An introduction to Gestalt therapy. In F. D. Stephenson (Ed.), *Gestalt therapy primer* (pp. 3–12). Springfield, IL: Thomas.

Stevens, M. J., Pfost, K. S., & Wessels, A. B. (1987). The relationship of purpose in life to coping strategies and time since the death of a significant other. *Journal of Counseling and Development, 65,* 424–426.

Thompson, C. D., & Rudolph, L. B. (1996). *Counseling children* (4th ed.). Pacific Grove, CA: Brooks/Cole.

Wallace, W. A. (1986). *Theories of counseling and psychotherapy*. Boston: Allyn & Bacon.

Watts, R. E. (1996). Social interest and the core conditions: Could it be that Adler influenced Rogers? *Journal of Humanistic Education and Development, 34,* 165–170.

Whiteley, J. M. (1987). The person-centered approach to peace. *Counseling and Values, 32,* 5–8.

Wilbur, M. P., Roberts-Wilbur, J., & Morris, J. R. (1990). A humanistic alternative for counseling alcoholics. *Journal of Humanistic Education and Development, 28,* 146–165.

Yalom, I. D. (1980). *Existential psychotherapy*. New York: Basic Books.

Zajonc, R. (1984). On the primacy of affect. *American Psychologist, 39,* 117–123.

Zinker, J. (1978). *Creative process in Gestalt therapy*. New York: Random House.

10

RATIONAL EMOTIVE BEHAVIOR THERAPY AND TRANSACTIONAL ANALYSIS

◆

She works in a world I have never known

Full of rainbow pills and lilac candles

Woven together with simple time-stitches

A pattern of color in a gray fabric factory

Where she spends her days

spinning threads

that go to Chicago by night.

Once with a little girl smile and a giggle

She flew to Atlanta in her mind,

Opening the door to instant adventures

far from her present fatigue,

That was a journey we shared

arranging her thoughts in a patchwork pattern

until the designs and desires came together.

Cognitions are thoughts, beliefs, and internal images that people have about events in their lives (Holden, 1993b). Cognitive theories, such as social constructionism, *focus on the idea that reality is a mental construction. Cognitive counseling theories focus on mental processes and their influences on mental health. A common premise of all cognitive approaches is that how people think largely determines how they feel and behave (Beck & Weishaar, 1995). As Burns (1980) points out, "every bad feeling you have is the result of your distorted negative thinking" (p. 28). Therefore, most cognitive theorists agree in substance with Proverbs 23:7: "As people think, so shall they be." They would also agree with Shakespeare's Hamlet, who said, "There's nothing either good or bad but thinking makes it so." In short, cognitive theorists believe that if persons change their ways of thinking, their feelings and behaviors will be modified as a result.*

Among the best-known cognitive theories are Aaron Beck's cognitive therapy, David Burns's new mood therapy, Albert Ellis's rational emotive behavior therapy, and Eric Berne's transactional analysis. This chapter highlights rational emotive behavior therapy (REBT) and transactional analysis (TA) because they are two of the oldest and most widely known theories that began with a primarily cognitive emphasis. Before covering these two approaches, however, we will discuss some aspects common to all cognitive counseling theories and then highlight elements of Beck's (1976) cognitive model.

Common Aspects of Cognitive Counseling

As a rule, cognitive theories are successful with clients who have the following characteristics (Hackney & Cormier, 1996):

> They are average to above-average in intelligence.
> They have moderate to high levels of functional distress.
> They are able to identify thoughts and feelings.
> They are not psychotic or disabled by present problems.
> They are willing and able to complete systematic homework assignments.
> They possess a repertoire of behavioral skills and responses.
> They process information on a visual and auditory level.

As one might expect, cognitive approaches are frequently used with clients who have inhibited mental functioning, such as depression. But they are also employed with individuals who are not visibly impaired but suffer from dysfunctional *automatic thoughts* (involving content specific to an event) and *schemata* (general rules about themselves or the world associated with an event) (Holden, 1993b). For instance, if a person is slighted at a party, he or she may automatically think, "That person is a jerk!" The schema that follows is "I'm offended" or "I'm hurt."

To bring about change, cognitive counseling theories emphasize the modification of one's thoughts that can be generally categorized into cold, warm, and hot cognitions. A *cold cognition* is basically descriptive and nonevaluative, such as "I lost my job." A warm cognition emphasizes preferences and nonpreferences, such as "I lost my job and I really don't want to have to start looking for another one." Hot cognitions "are heavily laden emotional-demand statements" and may take a variety of forms such as "overgeneralizing, catastrophizing, magnification, . . . and all-or-none thinking," such as "I must get a job just like I lost" (Gilliland & James, 1998, p. 238). Hot cognitions usually lead to dysfunctional behaviors.

Sometimes individuals improve just by expressing their thoughts in writing, a process known as *scriptotherapy* (Pennebaker, 1990). But such a natural resolution is not usual. Therefore, a systematic plan works best. Two processes must occur for such a plan to be a success. First, a relationship must be established between client and counselor. Second, cognitive change strategies must be implemented (Burns, 1989; Schuyler, 1991). Change strategies most often involve the following:

1. Using standardized guidelines for understanding in a concrete manner the events in people's lives
2. Recording or reflecting people's thoughts about these events in a clear, precise way
3. Finding a means to identify and challenge distorted thoughts
4. Implementing new ways of thinking that are realistic and productive

Although terms and emphases differ in cognitive counseling theories, those basic four steps and the premises behind them are at the heart of change.

Beck's Cognitive Therapy

Aaron T. Beck, a Philadelphia psychiatrist, developed a cognitive approach to mental disorders at about the same time that Albert Ellis was developing his ideas about rational emotive behavior therapy (in the late 1950s and early 1960s). He emphasized the importance of cognitive thinking in his theory, especially *dysfunctional thoughts* (thoughts that are nonproductive and unrealistic) (Weinrach, 1988).

As director of the Center for Cognitive Therapy at the University of Pennsylvania's Department of Psychiatry, Beck has not only continued to refine his theory but has rigorously tested it (see, for example, Rush, Beck, Kovacs, & Hollon, 1977). He has found that cognitive therapy is effective as a short-term treatment, especially for depression and anxiety. In these cases, there are "interpretations and expectations that lead to the painful effects of sadness and anxiety, to avoidance and inhibition" (Weinrach, 1988, p. 161). The cognitive-oriented counselor trained in Beck's methodology tries to help clients become more realistic in their interpretation of events by generalizing less (in the case of depression) or projecting less (in the case of anxiety).

Overall, Beck emphasizes the following points. First, he does not try necessarily to disprove beliefs but lets his clients examine beliefs' functionality. Second, his approach employs specific profiles and treatment plans for disorders such as depression, suicide, anxiety (Dattilio & Padesky, 1990). In addition, Beck's model is exploratory and collaborative in working with clients (Holden, 1993a). Therefore, it requires empirical testing on the part of clients as researchers of their lives so they can understand that their beliefs are not functional.

In summary, Beck focuses on the importance of modifying thoughts in the treatment of mental disorders. For him, the counselor should be attuned to six cognitive distortions: arbitrary inferences, selective abstraction, overgeneralization, magnification and minimization, personalization, and dichotomous thinking (Arnkoff & Glass, 1992). (Beck is sometimes categorized as a cognitive-behavioral clinician, and his theory will be referred to again in chapter 11 in the cognitive-behavioral section).

Rational Emotive Behavior Therapy

Albert Ellis

The founder of rational emotive behavior therapy (REBT), Albert Ellis has been described by Weinrach (1980) as "abrasive, impatient, and lacking in some of the basic social graces that my mother spent hours indoctrinating me with" but also as "brilliant, sensitive, perceptive, humorous, and stimulating" (p. 152). That Ellis fits both these descriptions is partially the result of his life history.

Albert Ellis was born in 1913 into a Jewish family in Pittsburgh, Pennsylvania. His parents eventually had a daughter and another son. Early in his life, Ellis's family moved to New York City, where he has spent most of his life. Ellis describes his father in positive and neutral terms, although the elder Ellis was often absent from home. From his father, Ellis believes he acquired his intelligence, drive, and persistence (Newhorn, 1978). His mother was quite independent for her time, often idiosyncratic in her behavior as well as happy and nonsmothering. Ellis describes her way of parenting as benign neglect (Dryden, 1989).

At age 5, Ellis almost died from tonsillitis; he later suffered from acute nephritis and diabetes (Dryden, 1989; Morris & Kanitz, 1975). He thought most members of his family were pretty crazy, and by age 7 he was largely on his own (Weinrach, 1980). His parents' divorce when he was 12 years old caused him to give up plans to be a Hebrew teacher, and he became instead a self-described *probabilistic atheist*—someone who does not believe that God exists but would accept empirical evidence to the contrary.

Ellis's dream as an adolescent was to become a writer. He planned to make enough money to retire early in life and then devote his time to writing. In 1934, he graduated in business from the City College of New York and worked in the business world until the mid-1940s. When not working, he wrote fiction. His literary efforts proved unsuccessful, however, and he decided to study psychology. From Columbia University, Ellis received a master's degree in 1943 and a Ph.D. in clinical psychology in 1947.

Ellis wanted to become a psychoanalytic clinical psychologist, a wish that was at first frustrated because institutions that specialized in such training only admitted medical professionals. He finally succeeded in obtaining analysis from the Karen Horney group and practiced classic psychoanalysis in the early 1950s. Dissatisfied with that approach, Ellis began the practice of his own theory in 1955.

Rational emotive behavior therapy was primarily a cognitive theory in the beginning. Its main tenets were first published in Ellis's *Reason and Emotion in Psychotherapy*

(1962). REBT has since broadened its base considerably and now includes behavioral and emotional concepts.

Ellis has established two nonprofit institutes to promote REBT: the Institute for Rational Living, a scientific and educational foundation established in 1959, and the Institute for Rational Emotive Behavior Therapy, an institution for professional training and clinical services established in 1968. Ellis, a prolific writer, has produced over 500 articles, some 50 books, and numerous films and tapes. Each week, he sees as many as 80 clients for individual sessions and conducts up to eight group sessions. Annually, he gives about 200 workshops and talks. Yet Ellis does not consider himself a compulsive worker because he does not *have* to work or prove himself (Weinrach, 1980). He relaxes by reading, listening to music, and socializing.

Ellis has been married twice and states that he has learned something about himself and the nature of women from each marriage. Since 1964, he has had a solid love/companionship relationship with Janet Wolfe, who helped him build the Institute for Rational Emotive Behavior Therapy and does her own work there (Dryden, 1989). Besides being a devout practitioner of his own theory, Ellis is a nationally known sex therapist who has written numerous books and articles on the subject. He has been recognized in professional circles in many ways, including being named Humanist of the Year by the American Humanist Association. Although he is flamboyant in a humorous and startling manner, Ellis can be affectionate and warm (Dryden, 1989). Indeed, he is a man of contrasts who sees ways of combining ideas that on the surface might appear to clash, such as religion and REBT (Powell, 1976).

View of Human Nature

REBT assumes that people are both "inherently rational and irrational, sensible and crazy" (Weinrach, 1980, p. 154) According to Ellis (1995), this duality is biologically inherent and perpetuated unless a new way of thinking is learned (Dryden, 1994). *Irrational thinking*, or as Ellis defines it, *irrational Beliefs* (iBs), may include the invention of upsetting and disturbing thoughts. Ellis places irrational beliefs under three main headings. These fallacies, which have been used in formulating various tests, have been correlated "with various kinds of emotional disturbance" (Ellis, 1984, p. 266).

1. "I *absolutely must* perform important tasks well and be approved by significant others, or else I am an *inadequate, pretty worthless person!*" Result: Severe feelings of anxiety, depression, and demoralization, often leading to severe inhibition.
2. "Other people, especially my friends and relatives, *truly must* treat me kindly and fairly, or else they are *rotten, damnable people!*" Result: Severe feelings of anger, rage, fury, often leading to fights, child abuse, assault, rape, murder, and genocide.
3. "The condition under which I live absolutely must be comfortable, unhassled, and enjoyable, or else it's *awful*, I *can't stand* it, and my life is hardly worth living!" Result: Severe feelings of low frustration tolerance, often leading to compulsion, addiction, avoidance, inhibition, and public reaction (Ellis, 1996b, p. 77).

Although Ellis (1973) does not deal with the developmental stages of individuals, he thinks that children are more vulnerable to outside influences and irrational thinking than adults are. By nature, he believes human beings are gullible and highly suggestible and are easily disturbed. Overall, people have within themselves the means to control their thoughts, feelings, and actions, but they must first realize what they are telling themselves (*self-talk*) to gain command of their lives (Ellis, 1962). This is a matter of personal, conscious awareness. The unconscious mind is not included in Ellis's conception of human nature.

Ellis believes it is a mistake for people to evaluate or rate themselves beyond the idea that everyone is a fallible human being. He especially discourages the use of any form of the verb *to be* (*is, was, am, has been, being,* etc.) to describe a person. He reasons that human problems do not come from the id, as Freud envisioned, or from the "what if" but rather from the "is." The verb *to be* makes it difficult to separate the person from his or her actions. Therefore, Ellis advocates that individuals speak and think of their behavior as separate from their personhood—for example, "I act badly" rather than "I am bad" (Ellis & Harper, 1975). By avoiding the verb *to be*, a person fosters a more rational thought process and gains the freedom to change, to focus on altering specific behaviors instead of over-hauling the personality.

Role of the Counselor

In the REBT approach, counselors are active and direct. They are instructors who teach and correct the client's cognitions. "Countering a deeply ingrained belief requires more than logic. It requires consistent repetition" (Krumboltz, 1992). Therefore, counselors must listen carefully for illogical or faulty statements from their clients and challenge beliefs such as "I will never be any better." In the process, they show concern and care for their clients by "attending to their behavior, by frequently asking questions for clarification, by recalling personal details about the client and his or her problems, by the use of gentle humor, and by active attempts to help the client solve difficult issues" (Vernon, 1996, p. 122).

Ellis (1980) and Walen, DiGuiseppe, and Dryden (1992) have identified several characteristics desirable for REBT counselors. They need to be bright, knowledgeable, empathetic, respectful, genuine, concrete, persistent, scientific, interested in helping others, and users themselves of REBT. Counselors' main assessment instrument is evaluation of a client's thinking. Some formal tests may be employed to measure rational and irrational thinking, but the evaluation process is primarily accomplished in counselor-client sessions. As a rule, REBT practitioners do not rely heavily on the diagnostic categories in the DSM-IV.

Goals

The primary goals of REBT focus on helping people realize that they can live more rational and productive lives. "Roughly speaking, rational-emotive therapy constitutes an attempt to correct mistakes in a client's reasoning as a way of eliminating undesirable emotions" (Cohen, 1987, p. 37).

REBT is heavily influenced by stoic philosophy, and Ellis is fond of quoting a first-century stoic, Epictetus, who wrote, "Men feel disturbed not by things, but by the views which they take of them." Often individuals disturb themselves by changing wishes and desires into demands. Ellis points out that when a person uses words such as *must, should, ought, have to,* and *need,* he or she makes demands of wishes and thinks irrationally. Many individuals think that wishes must or should occur and that if a wish remains unfulfilled, the result is a catastrophe. REBT helps clients stop making such demands and becoming upset through "catastrophizing." Clients in REBT may express some negative feelings, but a major goal is to help them avoid having more of an emotional response to an event than is warranted.

Ellis frequently uses puns and other humorous devices to help his clients see how irrational thinking develops and how silly the consequences of such thinking are. He cautions clients not to "should on themselves" and advises them to avoid "musterbation." He has even composed a number of rational songs to help remind himself and others to think rationally. For example, he penned the following to the tune of the "Whiffenpoof Song":

> I cannot have all of my wishes filled—
> Whine, whine, whine!
> I cannot have every frustration stilled—
> Whine, whine, whine!
> Life really owes me the things that I miss,
> Fate has to grant me eternal bliss!
> And if I must settle for less than this—
> Whine, whine, whine!*

Besides Ellis, other REBT counselors, such as Richard Watts (1996), have penned rational emotive behavior therapy songs to such common tunes as "I've Been Working on the Railroad," "Jimmy Cracked Corn," "Twinkle, Twinkle, Little Star," and "O Suzannah." The list of common familiar tunes and the words that can be put to them is large. Through singing the songs cognitively distorted thoughts are addressed in a humorous and therapeutic way.

Another goal of REBT is to help people change self-defeating habits of thought or behavior. One way this is accomplished is through teaching clients the ABCs of REBT: *A* signifies activating experience; *B* represents how the person thinks about the experience; *C* is the emotional reaction to *B* (see Figure 10.1).

Many clients believe that an experience directly causes feelings—a concept called *cognitive bypass.* Left out of this conceptualization is the thought process that leads to the development of emotions. For example, a person may lose a job or an opportunity and assert that the experience caused depression. REBT helps such a person learn how to recognize his or her *emotional anatomy*—that is, learn how feelings are attached to thoughts.

Thoughts about experiences may be characterized in four ways: positive, negative, neutral, or mixed. A positive thought leads to positive feelings. For example, if a host at a party reminds a man that he has had too much to drink, the man may think about the host's care and concern on his behalf and have positive emotions. Or the man may have negative feelings about the same event because he thinks that the host is being critical of him, has no right to do so, and should not comment about his behavior. Neutral thoughts mean simply noting the host's actions and moving on to another thought. Mixed thoughts

---

* Source: *Rational Humorous Songs: A Garland of Rational Songs,* by A. Ellis, 1980, New York: Albert Ellis Institute. © 1980 by the Albert Ellis Institute. Reprinted by permission.

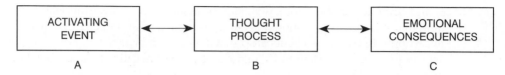

Figure 10.1   The ABCs of REBT

occur when the person has both negative and positive thoughts at once, such as "I'm glad something was said, but I dislike the way it was said." The resulting feeling is ambivalence.

REBT encourages clients to be more tolerant of themselves and others and to achieve personal goals. These goals are accomplished by having people learn to think rationally to change self-defeating behavior and by helping them learn new ways of acting.

Ellis (1996a) has devised a number of homework assignments, such as *shame attack exercises,* to help clients learn to behave differently. These exercises usually include an activity that is harmless but dreaded, such as introducing oneself to a stranger or asking for a glass of water in a restaurant without ordering anything else. By participating in such exercises, a client learns the ABCs of REBT on a personal level and comes to realize more fully that the world does not stop if a mistake is made or if a want remains unfulfilled. A client also learns that others are fallible human beings and need not be perfect. Finally, a client learns that goals may be achieved without "awfulizing" or "terriblizing" about personal situations.

Techniques

REBT encompasses a number of diverse techniques. Two primary ones are teaching and disputing. Before changes can be made, clients have to learn the basic ideas of REBT and understand how thoughts are linked with emotions and behaviors. As a process, REBT is highly didactic and very directive. In the first few sessions, counselors teach their clients the *anatomy of an emotion*: that feelings are a result of thoughts, not events, and that self-talk influences emotions. This procedure is generally known as rational-emotive education (REE) and has had a high success rate in working with children, adolescents, and adults from a wide variety of backgrounds and with an equally wide range of backgrounds (Wilde, 1996). It is critical that the client master the ability to dispute irrational thoughts.

Disputing thoughts and beliefs takes one of three forms: cognitive, imaginal, and behavioral. The process is most effective when all three forms are used (Walen et al., 1992). *Cognitive disputation* involves the use of direct questions, logical reasoning, and persuasion. Direct questions may challenge the client to prove that his or her response is logical. Sometimes these inquiries involve the use of the word *why,* which is seldom used in counseling because it puts most people on the defensive and closes off exploration. Examples of why questions in cognitive disputation include "Why must you?" and "Why must that be so?" During these inquiries, clients learn to distinguish between rational and irrational thoughts. They also learn the superiority of rational thoughts.

Another form of cognitive disputation involves the use of *syllogisms,* "a deductive form of reasoning consisting of two premises and a conclusion" (Cohen, 1987, p. 37). Syllogisms help clients and counselors more thoroughly understand inductive and deductive fallacies that underlie emotions. For example, in irrational "Can't-Stand-It-ism," the process might go as follows (Cohen, 1987, p. 39):

Major premise:	"Nobody can stand to be lied to."
Minor premise:	"I was lied to."
Conclusion:	"I can't stand it."

Imaginal disputation depends on the client's ability to imagine and employs a technique known as rational-emotive imagery (REI) (Maultsby, 1984). REI may be used in one of two ways. First, the client may be asked to imagine a situation in which he or she is likely to become upset. The client examines his or her self-talk during that imagined situation. Then the counselor asks the client to envision the same situation but this time to be more moderate in his or her self-talk. Second, the counselor asks a client to imagine a situation in which the client feels or behaves differently from some real instance. The client is then instructed to examine the self-talk used in this imagined situation. REI takes practice. It may work with clients who have vivid imaginations and, after some practice, with those who do not.

The emotional control card (ECC) is a device that helps clients reinforce and expand the practice of REI (Sklare, Taylor, & Hyland, 1985). Four emotionally debilitating categories (anger, self-criticism, anxiety, and depression) are listed on wallet-sized ECCs (Ellis, 1986). Under each category is a list of inappropriate or self-destructive feelings and a parallel list of appropriate or nondefeating feelings (see Figure 10.2). In a potentially troubling situation, a client may refer to the card and change the quality of feelings about that situation. At the next session with the counselor, the client discusses the use of the card in cognitively restructuring thoughts to make them rational.

Behavioral disputation involves behaving in a way that is the opposite of the client's usual way. Sometimes behavioral disputation may take the form of bibliotherapy, in which the client reads a self-help book. (A number of books for all ages are distributed by the Institute for Rational Emotive Behavior Therapy.) At other times, behavioral disputation includes role playing and the completion of a homework assignment in which a client actually does activities previously thought impossible to do. The client brings the completed assignment to the REBT counselor at the next counseling session and evaluates it with the counselor's help.

If disputation of irrational Beliefs (iBs) is successful, a new Effective Philosophy will emerge (Ellis, 1996a). This philosophy will include new cognitive Effect (cE) which is a restatement of original rational Beliefs (rBs). For example, "It is not awful, merely inconvenient, that I was rejected by a particular person."

Two other powerful REBT techniques are confrontation and encouragement. As previously noted, REBT counselors explicitly encourage clients to abandon thought processes that are not working and try REBT. Sometimes, the counselor will challenge a client who claims to be thinking rationally but in truth is not. At other times, the counselor encourages a client to continue working from a REBT base even when discouraged. Confrontation need not be done in the manner Ellis uses: vigorously confronting and attacking the client's beliefs (Johnson, 1980). Instead, a counselor may be empathetic and insistent at the same time.

One interesting variation on REBT is rational behavior therapy (RBT), which was formulated by Maxie Maultsby (1971, 1973, 1975, 1984). RBT emphasizes cognitive change in

Inappropriate or Self-Destructive Feelings	**Appropriate or Nondefeating Feelings**
Anger Feelings of resentment, anger, madness, fury, rage	*Irritation* Feelings of (mild or intense) irritation, displeasure, annoyance, frustration; anger at people's acts but not at their persons
Self-criticism Feelings of humiliation, shame, embarrassment, inadequacy; discounting self as a person	*Criticism of one's behavior* Feelings of (mild or intense) regret, sorrow, displeasure, doubt; criticism of one's behavior but not of one's total self
Anxiety Feelings of anxiety, nervousness, hypertension, panic, helplessness, horror	*Concern* Feelings of (mild or intense) concern, caution, vigilance; tension about one's performance but not about one's self
Depression Feelings of depression, worthlessness, undeservingness, guilt, self-downing	*Sadness* Feelings of (mild or intense) sadness, sorrow, regret, discontentment, displeasure; feeling that one is a person who has performed badly but is not a bad person

Figure 10.2   Emotional control card (revised version)

Source: From "An Emotional Control Card for Inappropriate and Appropriate Emotions in Using Rational-Emotive Imagery," by A. Ellis, 1986, *Journal of Counseling and Development, 65,* p. 206. © 1986 by ACA. Reprinted with permission. No further reproduction authorized without written permission of the American Counseling Association.

a way more behavioral than Ellis originally conceptualized. It involves checking the activating event as if one had a camera to be sure of objectivity. Disputation of a person's self-talk takes the form of a debate based on five rules for rational behavior. (See Figure 10.3 for a list of the five questions.)

In RBT, clients regularly complete homework assignments in rational self-analysis (RSA), in which they write down significant events in their lives and their thoughts and feelings associated with those events. The beliefs of the persons are then evaluated for their degree of rationality and changed in accordance with the rules of rational behavior. This method of assessing clients' thoughts is useful in maintaining a record of therapeutic progress. The standard RSA format consists of six steps, which were outlined by Maultsby (1984) and are presented in Figure 10.3.

A. ACTIVATING EVENT: What you perceived happened.

Da. CAMERA CHECK: If you perceived anything a video camera would *not show*, correct that to what a video camera *would* have shown.

B. YOUR BELIEFS: Your sincere thoughts about A, plus your attitudes about each B sentence.

Db. RATIONAL DEBATE OF B: Answer "yes" or "no" for each rational question about each B sentence or write DNA ("does not apply"). Then write *rational alternative self-talk* for each irrational B idea, and "That's rational" for each rational B idea.

B_1.

Db_1.

B_2.

Db_2.

ETC.

ETC.

C. CONSEQUENCES OF B
1. Emotional feelings
2. Actions

E. EXPECTED NEW BEHAVIORS
1. New emotional feelings
2. New actions

Five Rational Questions

1. Is my thinking here based on obvious fact?
2. Will my thinking here best help me protect my life and health?
3. Will my thinking here best help me achieve my short- and long-term goals?
4. Will my thinking here best help me avoid my most unwanted conflicts with others?
5. Will my thinking here best help me habitually feel the emotions I want to feel?

Figure 10.3 The standard RSA format
Source: From *Rational Behavior Therapy* (p. 176), by M. C. Maultsby, Jr., 1984, Upper Saddle River, NJ: Prentice Hall. © 1984 by M. C. Maultsby, Jr. Reprinted by permission of the author.

Evaluation of Uniqueness and Limitations

REBT has a number of unique dimensions and special emphases:

• The approach is clear, easily learned, and effective. Most clients have few problems in understanding the principles or terminology of REBT. Roush (1984) reports that REBT is effective with many different types of individuals, including adolescents. Seligman (1997) notes that it is appropriate for the treatment of affective disorders, anxiety disorders, and adjustment disorders. Ellis (1977) provides research data on the effectiveness of

REBT with different types of clients in specific settings across the life span, and Gilliland and James (1997) summarize its effectiveness with minority culture clients.

• The approach can easily be combined with other behavioral techniques to help clients more fully experience what they are learning. Maultsby's rational behavior therapy is a good example of this type of combination. Ellis is sometimes referred to as a forerunner of cognitive-behavioral counseling approaches. In 1993 he changed rational-emotive therapy (RET) to rational emotive behavior therapy (REBT).

• The approach is relatively short term, usually lasting 10 to 50 sessions. Clients may continue to use the approach on a self-help basis. The economical and efficiency aspects of REBT are impressive (Ellis, 1996a).

• The approach has generated a great deal of literature and research for clients and counselors. Few other theories have developed as much bibliotherapeutic material. Ellis is a prolific writer and researcher, as are many other REBT practitioners. Each year the Institute for Rational Emotive Behavior Therapy (45 E. 65th Street, New York, NY 10021-6593) produces a catalog filled with an array of books, booklets, audiotapes, and videotapes on rational emotive behavior therapy. Ellis's two nonprofit institutes are constantly engaged in empirical studies on the use of REBT with a wide variety of clients.

• The approach has continued to evolve over the years as techniques have been refined. An example of its evolution is found in the difference between inelegant and elegant REBT. *Inelegant REBT*, which developed first, focuses on the activating event and the distortions clients usually have about such events (Ellis, 1977, 1995). It does not give clients any coping strategies for dealing with situations in which the perception of an event matches reality. Instead, clients are encouraged to assure themselves that they will do better in the future or that they are good persons. *Elegant REBT*, on the other hand, concentrates on the beliefs of clients and focuses on their taking responsibility for their own feelings and not blaming others. Clients realize in the process that success in everything is not essential and that catastrophe is not the result of every unfulfilled want.

The limitations of the REBT approach are few but significant:

• The approach cannot be used effectively with individuals who have mental problems or limitations, such as schizophrenics and those with severe thought disorders. It is not productive with people who are severely mentally impaired. A person who is intellectually bright benefits most from this approach.

• The approach may be too closely associated with its founder, Albert Ellis. Many individuals have difficulty separating the theory from Ellis's eccentricities. Although Johnson (1980) urges counselors to adapt the theory and its techniques to their own personalities and styles of counseling, some counselors still eschew the approach because of its connection with Ellis.

• The approach is limited if its practitioners do not combine its early cognitive base with more behavioral and emotive techniques. Ellis says that REBT has always been a diverse approach, and he advocates its use in various settings (Weinrach, 1980). The theory is now much broader than it was originally, but many counselors still concentrate on the cognitive side of REBT, thus limiting its usefulness.

• The approach is direct, and the potential for the counselor being overzealous and not as therapeutic as would be ideal is a real possibility (Gilliland & James, 1998).

• The approach's emphasis on changing thinking may not be the simplest way of helping clients change their emotions. Instead, Gestalt theorists would challenge REBT and state that emotions should be experienced prior to efforts to make interventions.

Transactional Analysis

Eric Berne

Transactional analysis (TA), another major cognitive theory, was formulated by Eric Berne in the early 1960s. The theory rose to prominence after the publication of two best-selling books: Berne's *Games People Play* (1964) and Thomas Harris's *I'm OK; You're OK* (1967). Berne was fearful that the popularity of these books would undermine the seriousness of his work. Instead, popularity made the theory more attractive as well as familiar to the general public.

Eric Berne was born in 1910 in Montreal, Canada, where his father was a doctor and his mother was a writer and an editor. Berne was 5 years older than his only sibling, a sister. He was close to his father, who died at the age of 38 when Eric was 9 years old. Berne followed in his father's footsteps, earning a medical degree from McGill University in 1935. He then completed a psychiatric residency at Yale, set up a private practice in Connecticut and New York, became a U.S. citizen, and married. During World War II, he served as an army psychiatrist in Utah, where he started practicing group therapy.

After the war, Berne settled in Carmel, California, where he separated from his wife and completed his first book, *The Mind in Action* (1947), a critical survey of psychiatry and psychoanalysis. In California, he resumed the psychoanalytic training he had started before the war. Part of that training was his analysis, which was supervised by Erik Erikson. Erikson insisted that Berne not remarry until after the analysis was finished. Berne did as directed. He remarried in 1949 and fathered two children, as he had in his first marriage. He built a study in his house away from the noise of the children and, in 1950, began setting a demanding schedule for himself that included consultations and practice in Carmel, San Francisco, and Monterey. His only break occurred on Friday night, when he played poker at his house.

In 1956, Berne was turned down for membership in the Psychoanalytic Institute. This rejection proved to be a turning point in his life. He reacted by disassociating himself from psychoanalysis and devoting his time to the development of transactional analysis, which has a psychoanalytic flavor.

Dusay (1977) describes the formulation of TA in four phases. In the first phase (1955–1962), Berne developed the concept of ego states. His ideas were influenced by his clients' descriptions of behaving as a child, a parent, and an adult (the three ego states). In the second phase (1962–1966), he concentrated on ideas about transactions and games. During this time, the International Transactional Analysis Association was created (1964), and Berne published the popular *Games People Play*. In the third phase (1966–1970), he emphasized the reasons some individuals choose to play certain games in life. In the fourth phase (from 1970 on), he and his followers emphasized action and energy distribution.

Berne was involved in the first three phases of this development. After a second divorce in 1964, he spent a great deal of time writing. At one time, he was working on the manuscripts of six books and editing the *Transactional Analysis Bulletin*. He also gave numerous lectures and seminars. Berne's third marriage was short-lived; he died of a heart attack in 1970 at the age of 60.

View of Human Nature

Transactional analysis is an optimistic theory. Its basic assumption is that people can change despite any unfortunate events of the past. TA is also antideterministic, believing that people have choices in their lives: that what was decided can be redecided at a later date. As James and Jongeward (1971) emphasize, "transactional analysis is a rational approach to understanding behavior and is based on the assumption that all individuals can learn to trust themselves, think for themselves, make their own decisions, and express their feelings" (p. 12).

TA focuses on four major methods of understanding and predicting human behavior:

- *Structural analysis*—understanding what is happening within the individual
- *Transactional analysis*—describing what happens between two or more people
- *Game analysis*—understanding transactions between individuals that lead to bad feelings
- *Script analysis*—understanding the life plan that an individual is following

Structural Analysis.   In structural analysis, each person is considered to have three functional ego states: child, parent, and adult.

Berne (1964) defines an *ego state* as "a consistent pattern of feeling and experience directly related to a corresponding consistent pattern of behavior" (p. 364). He notes that the findings of Wilder Penfield and his associates (1952; Penfield, & Jasper, 1954) offer support for this definition. Penfield, a neurosurgeon, found that an electrode applied to different parts of the brain evokes memories and feelings long forgotten by the person. The implication of this research is that the brain functions like a tape recorder to preserve complete experiences in a sequential form recognizable as ego states.

The *child ego state* is the first to develop. It is that part of the personality characterized by childlike behaviors and feelings. Childlike behavior might be described as inquisitive, affectionate, selfish, mean, playful, whiny, and manipulative. The child ego state consists of two subdivisions: the natural (free) child and the adaptive child.

The *natural child* is the part of the person that is spontaneous, impulsive, feeling oriented, and often self-centered and pleasure loving. The natural child is also intuitive, creative, and responsive to nonverbal messages. The *adaptive child* is the compliant part of the personality that conforms to the wishes and demands of parental figures. These adaptations of natural impulses occur in response to traumas, natural life experiences, and training.

The *parent ego state* incorporates the attitudes and behaviors (the dos, shoulds, and oughts) of parental figures. Outwardly, these messages are expressed through prejudice, criticism, and nurturing behavior. Parental messages are present throughout a person's life. A response to any thoughtful question that occurs within 10 seconds usually comes from the parent ego state. This ego state consists of two subdivisions: the nurturing parent and the critical parent.

The *nurturing parent* is the part of the person that comforts, praises, and aids others. The *critical parent* is that part of the person that finds fault, displays prejudices, disapproves, and prevents others from feeling good about themselves. These two parts of the parent are recognized through nonverbal behaviors such as pointing a finger at someone and verbal statements such as "That's too bad, but don't worry."

The *adult ego state* is not subdivided or related to a person's age. It is the objective, thinking, data-gathering part of the person. The adult ego state tests reality, much as the ego does in Freud's system. The adult is rational and organized. In some ways it functions like a computer, expressing itself through phrases such as "I understand" and "I'm going to."

Sometimes the different ego states operate simultaneously. For example, a woman may observe an attractive man and go through the following self-dialogue: "He is really good looking and well spoken [adult], but he's probably stuck-up [critical parent], although I've heard he's very sensitive [nurturing parent]. I wonder how I could attract him and get him to notice me [natural child]. Oops! I had better stop looking and get back to work, or my boss will get mad at me [adaptive child]."

A major focus of transactional analysis is determining which ego state(s) a person is using. Although TA does not favor any ego state over another, the theory stresses the importance of being able to balance responses when necessary and appropriate. Those who constantly exhibit just one ego state do not function as well as those who are more flexible.

One way of assessing the ego state(s) a person most employs is through the use of an *egogram* (Dusay & Dusay, 1989). An egogram will remain "fixed" unless an individual decides to invest energy in using another ego state. The egogram of a person who responds mostly from the adult ego state is shown in Figure 10.4.

Transactional Analysis. The second way of understanding and predicting human behavior involves diagramming ego-state transactions. The diagramming of transactional analysis is interpersonal, in contrast to the intrapersonal diagramming of structural analysis. Transactions may occur on one of three levels: complementary, crossed, or ulterior.

In a *complementary transaction,* both persons are operating either from the same ego state (e.g., child to child; adult to adult) or from complementary ego states (parent to child; adult to parent). Responses are predictable and appropriate. For example, an adult-to-adult transaction might look like this:

PERSON 1: What time is it?
PERSON 2: It is 7 o'clock.

Figure 10.4   An egogram

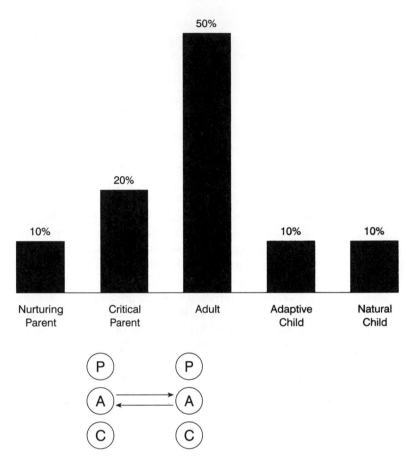

A child-to-child transaction would involve more playfulness:

PERSON 1:   Let's go play with Billy.
PERSON 2:   Yeah! We could have lots of fun with him!

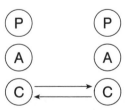

A parent-to-parent transaction, however, would be more nurturing or critical:

PERSON 1:   You never do anything right.
PERSON 2:   That's because you're always finding fault with my work.

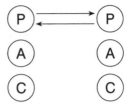

In a *crossed transaction*, an inappropriate ego state is activated, producing an unexpected response. Crossed transactions hurt. When they occur, persons tend to withdraw from each other or switch topics. An example of a crossed transaction is when a person who is operating from a child ego state and hoping for a complementary parent ego-state response receives instead a comment from the other person's adult ego state:

> PERSON 1: Can you help me carry these bags? They must weigh a ton.
> PERSON 2: Those bags weigh approximately 20 pounds, and you are capable of carrying them.

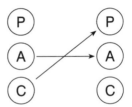

An *ulterior transaction* is one in which two ego states operate simultaneously and one message disguises the other. Ulterior transactions appear to be complementary and socially acceptable even though they are not. For example, at the end of a date one person may say to the other, "Do you want to come in and see my etchings?" On the surface this question might seem to be coming from the adult ego state. In reality it is coming from the child ego state: "Want to come in and have some fun together?"

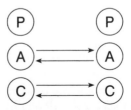

Game Analysis. *Games* are ulteriorly motivated transactions that appear complementary on the surface but end in bad feelings. People play games to structure time, achieve recognition, make others predictable, and prevent intimacy. Because intimacy involves risks, games keep people safe from exposing their thoughts and feelings. There are first-degree, second-degree, and third-degree games; all have predictable ends.

First-degree games are played in social circles with anyone who is willing to participate. They generally lead to mild upsets. An example of a first-degree game is "Seducto,"
which can initially be exciting and fun. In this game, a male and female enjoy an evening
flirting with each other until one turns the other down and both leave feeling slightly
uncomfortable.

A second-degree game occurs when the players go after bigger stakes, usually in more
intimate circles, and end up with bad feelings. An example of a second-degree game is
"Uproar," in which two persons get angrier and angrier until one or both gets very upset
about being called a name or put down.

A third-degree game usually involves tissue damage, and the players end up in jail, the
hospital, or the morgue. An example of this game is "Cops and Robbers," in which people
dare those in authority to catch them and yet leave clues about where they can be cor-
nered. At each game level, there is more danger of permanent damage. Very few games
have a positive or neutral outcome (Berne, 1964).

Individuals who play games operate from one of three positions: victim, persecutor, or
rescuer (Karpman, 1968). To keep games going there is often a switch-off where people
assume new roles. For example, in the game "Why Don't You/Yes, But," one person plays the
rescuer, responding to a complaint by the victimized other by saying, "Why don't you . . . ?"
The victim answers, "Yes, but . . . [I've tried]." After this game becomes tiresome, the rescuer
may switch to a more punishing, persecuting role. When the victim complains, he or she may
respond sarcastically, "Ain't it awful," until the game ends. The *Karpman (drama) triangle*
represents the three positions people assume during game interactions and their switch-offs.

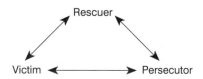

The list of possible games is almost endless, and it is easy for individuals to get
hooked into playing them. In the long run, however, game players are losers because they
avoid meaningful and healthy human interactions.

Script Analysis.   Berne believed that everyone makes a *life script,* or life plan, early in
childhood, by the age of 5. These scripts, which determine how one interacts with others,
are based on interpretations of external events. Positive messages given to a child function
as *permissions* and do not limit people in any way. Negative messages, or *injunctions,* are
more powerful and may become the basis for destructive scripts. Many parental injunctions
begin with *don't*: "don't succeed," "don't grow," "don't be that way." Unless a person makes
a conscious attempt to overcome such injunctions, the result may be a miserable life.

A life script involves the ability to get *strokes* (verbal or physical recognition) for certain behaviors. Most life scripts revolve around giving and receiving strokes. Berne points
out that negative strokes (punishments) are better than no strokes at all (being ignored).
Strokes result in the collection of either good or bad feelings, known as *stamps.* When
individuals collect enough stamps, they cash them in on behaviors. For example, a
teenager may collect enough bad feelings from failing grades to justify quitting school or

enough good feelings about studying hard to attend a party. Healthy people give and receive positive strokes most often.

The following list shows common negative script patterns:

- *Never scripts.*   A person never gets to do what he or she wants because the parent forbids it ("Marriage is bad; never get married").
- *Until scripts.*   A person must wait until a certain time to do something before he or she can have a reward ("You cannot play until you have all your work done").
- *Always scripts.*   A person tells him- or herself that it is necessary to continue doing the same thing ("You should always continue any job once you've started").
- *After scripts.*   A person expects difficulty after a certain event ("After age 40, life goes downhill").
- *Open-ended scripts.*   A person does not know what he or she is supposed to do after a given time ("Be active while you're young").

There are also miniscripts within people's lives that focus on minute-by-minute occurrences. Some of the most common miniscripts are "be perfect," "be strong," "hurry up," "try hard," "please someone." These five messages, called *drivers,* allow people to escape their life scripts, but the escape is only temporary.

The ideal life script in TA terms is informed by the position *I'm OK; you're OK* (a "get-on-with" position) (Harris, 1967). But people may operate from three other positions: *I'm OK; you're not OK* (a "get-away-from" position); *I'm not OK; you're OK* (a "get-nowhere-with" position); and *I'm not OK; you're not OK* (a "get-rid-of" position). Figure 10.5 shows these positions.

Everyone operates from each of these four positions at various times, but well-functioning individuals learn to recognize unhealthy positions and modify thoughts and behaviors accordingly. Berne held that life scripts can be rewritten if a person becomes more conscious of what he or she is thinking and makes concerted efforts to change.

Role of the Counselor

TA treatment assigns the counselor the initial role of being a teacher. He or she first must explain to the client the language and concepts of TA, a new way of thinking about self. After this is accomplished, the counselor contracts with the client for specific changes and helps the person achieve them. In essence, the counselor helps the client obtain the tools (i.e., skills) necessary for change in the present and allows the client to make constructive changes through various empowering techniques (Corey, 1996).

TA counselors do not rely heavily on formal psychological tests, although a counselor does assess client functioning. Assessment is usually done through an egogram or another less formal method. The purpose is to determine how a client is spending time and from which ego states he or she is operating. Diagnosis based on DSM-IV categories is not stressed.

Goals

Primary goals of TA focus on helping clients transform themselves from "frogs" into "princes and princesses." It is not enough that persons learn to adjust, as in psychoanaly-

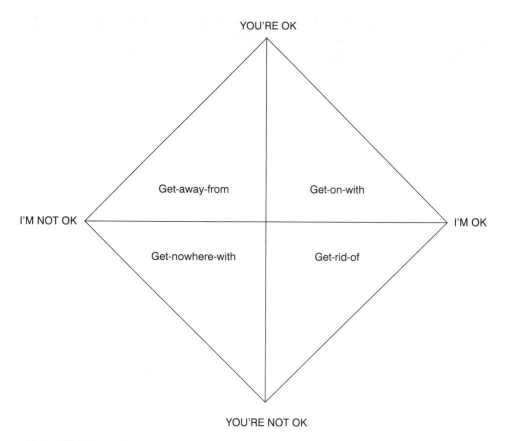

Figure 10.5   TA OK positions

sis. Instead, the emphasis is attaining health and autonomy. Counselors help their clients identify and restore distorted or damaged ego states, develop the capacity to use all ego states, use the adult ego state with its reasoning powers, alter inappropriate life scripts, and adopt a position of "I'm OK; you're OK" (Berne, 1966).

In becoming autonomous, clients exhibit more awareness, intimacy, and spontaneity; become free of games; and eliminate self-defeating scripts. They become more in touch with their past but, at the same time, are freed from previous negative influences. A major emphasis of TA is on learning about the self to decide whom one wishes to become (Goulding & Goulding, 1997).

Techniques

TA has initiated a number of techniques for helping clients reach their goals. Among the most common are structural analysis, transactional analysis, game analysis, and script analysis. Other techniques include the following:

- *Treatment contract*—a specific, concrete contract that emphasizes agreed-on responsibilities for both counselors and clients (Dusay & Dusay, 1989). The contract lets each know when counseling goals have been reached. Some behavioral approaches also use a treatment contract.
- *Interrogation*—involves speaking to a client's adult ego state until the counselor receives an adult response. The technique can be very confrontational. If not used properly, interrogation will be ineffective and supply only historical material.
- *Specification*—identification of the ego state that initiated a transaction. Specification takes place from the adult ego states of both client and counselor.
- *Confrontation*—involves the counselor's pointing out inconsistencies in the client's behavior or speech. TA's use of this technique varies little from its use in other theories.
- *Explanation*—occurs on an adult-to-adult ego state level. The counselor teaches the client about some aspect of TA.
- *Illustration*—enlightens the client or elaborates a point. An illustration is a story that is often humorous and as such speaks to both the child and the adult ego states of the client.
- *Confirmation*—used when previously modified behavior occurs again and the counselor points this out to the client. Only when the client has a firmly established adult ego state can this technique be effective.
- *Interpretation*—involves the counselor's explaining to the child ego state of the client the reasons for the client's behavior. This technique is mainly a psychodynamic procedure and is used only when the client has an effectively functioning adult ego state.
- *Crystallization*—consists of an adult-to-adult transaction in which the client comes to an awareness that individual game playing may be given up if so desired. Thus, the client is free to do as he or she chooses, and the TA process is virtually complete.

Almost all the techniques in TA involve some combination of questioning, confrontation, and dialogue. The following are among the questions most frequently asked by TA counselors:

What are the nicest and worst things your parents ever said to you?
What is your earliest memory?
What is the family story about your birth? What is your favorite fairy tale, story, or song?
How would you describe your mother and father?
How long do you expect to live?

To be most effective, a TA counselor must always be careful to assess the ego strengths of individual clients. A client is usually capable of making new decisions about life once he or she discovers different aspects of the self.

TA is presently divided into three main schools of treatment: the classical school, the cathexis school, and the redecision school (Barnes, 1977). All these schools use contracts as their primary method of intervention and have the achievement of autonomy as their final goal of treatment.

Evaluation of Uniqueness and Limitations

TA has a number of distinguishing emphases:

• The approach uses terms that are easily understood and clearly defined. Because of such clear terminology, TA can be used in a number of settings with varied populations—for example, with students who want to overcome math anxiety (Eisenberg, 1992).

• The approach is easily and effectively combined with other more action-oriented counseling theories. The use of TA and Gestalt therapy together has been especially powerful (James & Jongeward, 1971).

• The approach puts the responsibility of change on the client. Individuals can choose to change or remain the same.

• The approach is goal directed. The contractual nature of the counseling process makes it possible for both counselors and clients to know when treatment should be terminated (Gilliland & James, 1998).

• The International Transactional Analysis Association (ITAA) is active in training and certification for its members and in the publishing of a scholarly journal, the *Transactional Analysis Journal*.

Nevertheless, TA has limitations:

• The approach has been criticized for its primary cognitive orientation. To understand is only the beginning of change. TA promotes understanding, but unless the approach is used with another more action-oriented theory, TA is limited in its effectiveness.

• The approach is criticized for its simplicity, structure, and popularity. TA is so widely known that some people use the terminology but do not practice the theory. These individuals intellectualize their problems but take few actions to modify them. (In truth, the theory behind TA is sound but the practice by some is not).

• The approach does not emphasize the authenticity of the counselor (Corey, 1996). In the counseling process, the counselor and the client are seen as equals. Unlike a Rogerian approach, however, little attention is paid to the person of the counselor in the process.

• The research behind the approach is relatively weak. Methodological improvements are needed for studying populations receiving TA treatment (Miller & Capuzzi, 1984).

• The approach has not developed much since Berne's death in 1970. Although emphases within the theory have become distinct and schools of TA have emerged, few new ideas have been conceptualized. In addition, there are no prominent new theorists or disciples of TA on the national scene. Unless there is renewal within the theory and those who practice it, TA may lose prominence as a counseling modality.

Summary and Conclusion

Cognitive counseling theories vary in form and content, but all stress the importance of thinking for mental health. Two of the most prominent cognitive theories are REBT and TA. They have a number of assumptions and practices in common. For instance, both agree that if people gain insight into their thinking process, they can change. Thinking influences feeling and behavior, according to these theories. Both approaches also stress that counseling is a learning process and that counselors often operate in the role of instructors. The theories further emphasize the importance of clients' work outside formal therapeutic sessions (homework). Both theories are structured sequentially and require clients to learn new vocabularies and restructure their thoughts as well. Both REBT and TA can be used in a number of settings and with a variety of client problems.

Although these theories share some commonalities, they are also quite different. For instance, REBT incorporates more techniques into its treatment sessions than TA does. But TA counselors often combine their theory with other approaches, such as Gestalt, to make it more active and strong. REBT and its offshoots have fewer new terms for the client to learn, and REBT practitioners often have their clients working in advanced stages of counseling before TA counselors do. Yet TA has a more complex view of human nature than REBT does. Finally, TA's research database is not nearly as strong as REBT's (Solomon & Haaga, 1995).

CLASSROOM ACTIVITIES

1. Pair up with another student and discuss which of the two main theories presented in this chapter you find most attractive. Support your view with specifics from the approaches.

2. Do a rational self-analysis (RSA) on a situation that is real in your life. Have another student go over the results with you. What did you learn from this exercise that you could pass on to a client whom you ask to complete an RSA?

3. In groups of three, role-play how you think an REBT or a TA counselor would act in helping individuals with the following concerns: procrastination, interpersonal conflict, stress, adjustment to a new living situation, and grief. One student should take the role of the client, one the counselor, and the other the observer. After the role playing is over, the observer should give feedback to the counselor. The counselor and client should also explain how they experienced the process. Switch roles until everyone has had a chance to be in each role.

4. Keep a list of the number and types of "games" you find yourself playing for a week. Try to notice any patterns that emerge. Share your findings with fellow classmates in an open class discussion.

5. Which do you find most attractive: affective theories or cognitive theories? State your reasons as specifically as possible. What support does recent professional literature offer on the effectiveness of the theories you chose? Do a search of the literature for articles written in the last 3 years on your preferred theories.

REFERENCES

Arnkoff, D. B., & Glass, C. R. (1992). Cognitive therapy and psychotherapy integration. In D. K. Freedheim (Ed.), *History of psychotherapy: A century of change* (pp. 657–694). Washington, DC: American Psychological Association.

Barnes, G. (1977). Introduction. In G. Barnes (Ed.), *Transactional analysis after Eric Berne: Teach-ings and practices of three TA schools* (pp. 3–31). New York: Harper & Row.

Beck, A. T. (1976). *Cognitive therapy and emotional disorders.* New York: International Universities Press.

Beck, A. T., & Weishaar, M. E. (1995). Cognitive therapy. In R. J. Corsini & D. Wedding (Eds.), *Cur-*

rent psychotherapies (5th ed., pp. 229–261). Itasca, IL: Peacock.

Berne, E. (1947). *The mind in action.* New York: Simon & Schuster.

Berne, E. (1964). *Games people play.* New York: Grove.

Berne, E. (1966). *Principles of group treatment.* New York: Oxford University Press.

Burns, D. D. (1980). *Feeling good: The new mood therapy.* New York: Signet.

Burns, D. D. (1989). *The feeling good handbook: Using the new mood therapy in everyday life.* New York: Morrow.

Cohen, E. D. (1987). The use of syllogism in rational-emotive therapy. *Journal of Counseling and Development, 66,* 37–39.

Corey, G. (1996). *Theory and practice of counseling and psychotherapy* (5th ed.). Pacific Grove, CA: Brooks/Cole.

Dattilio, F. M., & Padesky, C. A. (1990). *Cognitive therapy with couples.* Sarasota, FL: Professional Resource Exchange.

Dryden, W. (1989). Albert Ellis: An efficient and passionate life. *Journal of Counseling and Development, 67,* 539–546.

Dryden, W. (1994). Reason and emotion in psychotherapy: Thirty years on. *Journal of Rational Emotive and Cognitive Behavior Therapy, 12,* 83–89.

Dusay, J. M. (1977). The evolution of transactional analysis. In G. Barnes (Ed.), *Transactional analysis after Eric Berne: Teachings and practices of three TA schools* (pp. 32–52). New York: Harper & Row.

Dusay, J. M., & Dusay, K. M. (1989). Transactional analysis. In R. J. Corsini & D. Wedding (Eds.), *Current psychotherapies* (4th ed., pp. 405–453). Itasca, IL: Peacock.

Eisenberg, M. (1992). Compassionate math. *Journal of Humanistic Education and Development, 30,* 157–166.

Ellis, A. (1962). *Reason and emotion in psychotherapy.* New York: Stuart.

Ellis, A. (1973). Rational-emotive therapy. In R. Corsini (Ed.), *Current psychotherapies* (pp. 167–206). Itasca, IL: Peacock.

Ellis, A. (1977). The basic clinical theory of rational-emotive therapy. In A. Ellis & R. Grieger (Eds.), *Handbook of rational-emotive therapy* (pp. 3–34). New York: Springer.

Ellis, A. (1980). Foreword. In S. R. Walen, R. DiGiuseppe, & R. L. Wessler (Eds.), *A practi-* *tioner's guide to rational-emotive therapy* (pp. vii–xii). New York: Oxford University Press.

Ellis, A. (1984). Rational-emotive therapy (RET) and pastoral counseling: A reply to Richard Wessler. *Personnel and Guidance Journal, 62,* 266–267.

Ellis, A. (1986). An emotional control card for inappropriate and appropriate emotions in using rational-emotive imagery. *Journal of Counseling and Development, 65,* 205–206.

Ellis, A. (1993). Changing rational emotive therapy (RET) to rational emotive behavior therapy (REBT). *Behavior Therapist, 16,* 257–258.

Ellis, A. (1995). Rational-emotive therapy. In R. J. Corsini & D. Wedding (Eds.), *Current psychotherapies* (5th ed., pp. 162–196). Itasca, IL: Peacock.

Ellis, A. (1996a). *Better, deeper, and more enduring brief therapy: The rational emotive behavior therapy approach.* New York: Brunner/Mazel.

Ellis, A. (1996b). The humanism of rational emotive behavior therapy and other cognitive behavior therapies. *Journal of Humanistic Education and Development, 35,* 69–88.

Ellis, A., & Harper, R. A. (1975). *A new guide to rational living.* North Hollywood, CA: Wilshire.

Gilliland, B. E., & James, R. K. (1998). *Theories and strategies in counseling and psychotherapy* (4th ed.). Boston: Allyn & Bacon.

Goulding, M., & Goulding, R. (1997). *Changing lives through redecision therapy* (rev. ed.). New York: Grove/Atlantic.

Hackney, H., & Cormier, L. S. (1996). *The professional counselor: A process guide to helping* (3rd ed.). Boston: Allyn & Bacon.

Harris, T. (1967). *I'm OK; You're OK.* New York: Harper & Row.

Holden, J. (1993a). *Cognitive counseling* [Videotape]. Greensboro, NC: ACES/Chi Sigma Iota.

Holden, J. A. (1993b). *Learning module: Cognitive counseling.* Denton, TX: Author.

James, M., & Jongeward, D. (1971). *Born to win: Transactional analysis with Gestalt experiments.* Reading, MA: Addison-Wesley.

Johnson, N. (1980). Must the RET therapist be like Albert Ellis? *Personnel and Guidance Journal, 59,* 49–51.

Karpman, S. (1968). Script drama analysis. *Transactional Analysis Bulletin, 26,* 16–22.

Krumboltz, J. D. (1992, December). Challenging troublesome career beliefs. *CAPS Digest,* EDO-CG-92-4.

Maultsby, M. C., Jr. (1971). *Handbook of rational self-counseling.* Lexington: University of Kentucky Medical Center.

Maultsby, M. C., Jr. (1973). *More personal happiness through rational self-counseling.* Lexington: University of Kentucky Medical Center.

Maultsby, M. C., Jr. (1975). *Help yourself to happiness.* New York: Institute for Rational Living.

Maultsby, M. C., Jr. (1984). *Rational behavior therapy.* Upper Saddle River, NJ: Prentice Hall.

Miller, C., & Capuzzi, D. (1984). A review of transactional analysis outcome studies. *AMHCA Journal, 6,* 30–41.

Morris, K. T., & Kanitz, M. (1975). *Rational-emotive therapy.* Boston: Houghton Mifflin.

Newhorn, P. (1978). Albert Ellis. *Human Behavior, 7,* 30–35.

Penfield, W. (1952). Memory mechanisms. *Archives of Neurology and Psychiatry, 67,* 178–198.

Penfield, W., & Jaspcr, H. (1954). *Epilepsy and the functional anatomy of the human brain.* Boston: Little, Brown.

Pennebaker, J. W. (1990). *Opening up: The healing power of confiding in others.* New York: Avon.

Powell, J. (1976). *Fully human, fully alive.* Niles, IL: Argos.

Roush, D. W. (1984). Rational-emotive therapy and youth: Some new techniques for counselors. *Personnel and Guidance Journal, 62,* 414–417.

Rush, A. J., Beck, A. T., Kovacs, M., & Hollon, S. (1977). Comparative efficacy of cognitive therapy and pharmacotherapy in the treatment of depressed outpatients. *Cognitive Therapy and Research, 1,* 17–37.

Schuyler, D. (1991). *A practical guide to cognitive therapy.* New York: Norton.

Seligman, L. (1997). *Diagnosis and treatment planning in counseling* (2nd ed.). New York: Plenum.

Sklare, G., Taylor, J., & Hyland, S. (1985). An emotional control card for rational-emotive imagery. *Journal of Counseling and Development, 64,* 145–146.

Solomon, A., & Haaga, D. (1995). Rational emotive behavior therapy research: What we know and what we need to know. *Journal of Rational-Emotive and Cognitive Behavior Therapy, 13,* 193–201.

Vernon, A. (1996). Counseling children and adolescents: Rational emotive behavior therapy and humanism. *Journal of Humanistic Education and Development, 35,* 120–127.

Walen, S. R., DiGuiseppe, R., & Dryden, W. (1992). *A practitioner's guide to rational-emotive therapy.* New York: Oxford University Press.

Watts, R. E. (1996). Some contemporary rational emotive behavior therapy songs. *Journal of Humanistic Education and Development, 35,* 117–119.

Weinrach, S. G. (1980). Unconventional therapist: Albert Ellis. *Personnel and Guidance Journal, 59,* 152–160.

Weinrach, S. G. (1988). Cognitive therapist: A dialogue with Aaron Beck. *Journal of Counseling and Development, 67,* 159–164.

Wilde, J. (1996). The efficacy of short-term rational-emotive education with fourth-grade students. *Elementary School Guidance & Counseling, 31,* 131–138.

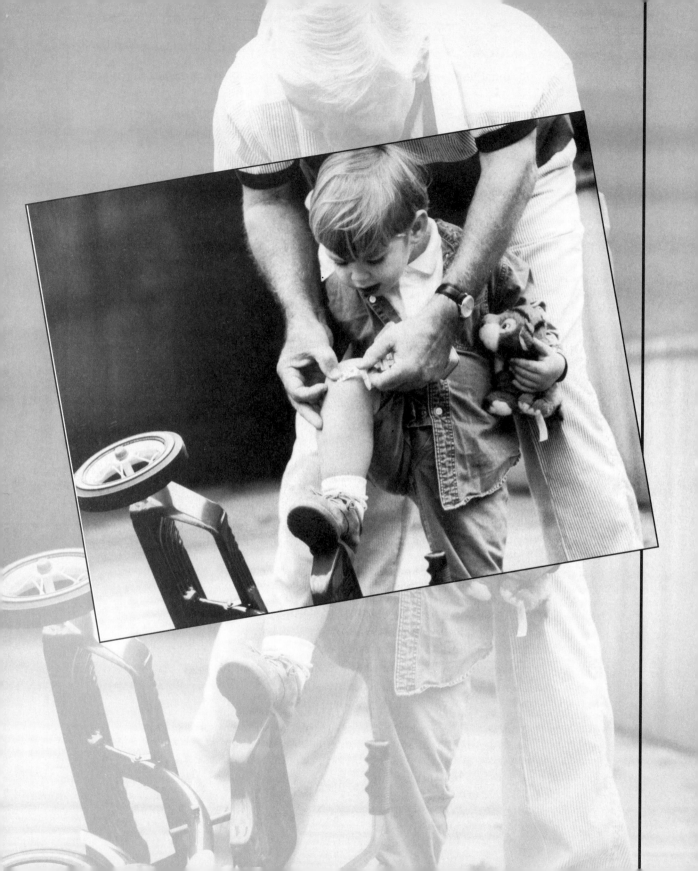

11

BEHAVIORAL, COGNITIVE-BEHAVIORAL, AND REALITY THERAPY

◆

At times I envy the band aid man

who cleaned my cuts when I was young

While painting me as "mercurochrome clown"

before he patched my pain with adhesive.

That was security to know he cared and would be around

to fix, when possible, all the hurts of childhood

that come in growing to be man.

His job, I think, was easier than mine

for in counseling I cannot always see

your past wounds, scars, and might-have-beens.

If I could, on days like today,

I might like the old man I remember

try with gentleness to cover them.

For you sit beside me with tears in your eyes

and I know how slowly it takes words to heal.

From "The Bandaid Man," by S. T. Gladding, 1975, Personnel and Guidance Journal, _53, p. 520. © 1975 by ACA._

Reprinted with permission. No further reproduction authorized without written permission of the American

Counseling Association.

Behavioral theories of counseling focus on a broad range of client behaviors. Often, a person has difficulties because of a deficit or an excess of behavior. Counselors who take a behavioral approach seek to help clients learn new, appropriate ways of acting or modify or eliminate excessive actions. In such cases, adaptive behaviors replace those that were maladaptive, and the counselor functions as a learning specialist for the client (Krumboltz, 1966). Behavioral counseling approaches are especially popular in institutional settings, such as mental hospitals or sheltered workshops. They are the approaches of choice in working with clients who have specific problems such as eating disorders, substance abuse, and psychosexual dysfunction. Behavioral approaches are also useful in addressing difficulties associated with anxiety, stress, assertiveness, parenting, and social interaction (Hackney & Cormier, 1996; Seligman, 1997).

This chapter examines the dominant forms of behavioral counseling along with cognitive-behavioral approaches. Reality therapy, a related theory that is not strictly behavioral, is also discussed. Like behaviorism, reality therapy is concerned with bringing about change in quick, overt ways. "Behaviorist, cognitive-behavioral, and reality therapies stress instrumental rationality, control over emotions, enhanced human liberty, efficiency in ways of achieving self-defined goals, and opposition to irrational authority or arbitrary privilege" (Christopher, 1996, pp. 19–20).

Overview of Behavioral Approaches

The term *behavioral* encompasses a wide range of ideas, practices, and theories. On one end of the behavioral continuum are the so-called radical behaviorists, such as B. F. Skinner (1974), who focus predominantly on learning principles and avoid examining any mentalistic concepts, such as thoughts. On the other end of the continuum are cognitive-behavioral researchers such as Donald Meichenbaum (1977, 1985), who emphasize the importance of mental processes (e.g., perceptions) in human behavior and view thoughts as a type of behavior. This latter group is collectively known as cognitive-behaviorists and form a bridge between counselors who are exclusively focused on either cognitive or behavioral changes. As we saw in the last chapter, rational emotive behavior therapy exemplifies a type of cognitive-behavioral counseling approach.

In its infancy (1900s–1930s), behaviorism was concerned almost entirely with outward observations and was promoted as a scientific approach to the study of human life. Its primary advocate, John B. Watson (1913, 1925), used his work with a child named Little Albert to demonstrate that human emotions can be conditioned and generalized (Watson & Raynor, 1920). After World War I, behaviorist ideas were explored by researchers such as Mary Cover Jones (1924), who demonstrated how a process known as counterconditioning can be employed to help overcome phobic reactions.

In the 1940s and 50s, behaviorism achieved more prominence. Clinical psychology promoted the idea that therapists could be scientific practitioners and base their work on research. Examples of the scientist-practitioner singled out at the time were B. F. Skinner (1953) and his work in operant conditioning, Joseph Wolpe (1958) and his study of respondent (i.e., classical) conditioning, Hans Eysenck (1960) and his treatment of abnormal behavior, and Albert Bandura (Bandura & Walters, 1963) and his study of the effects of vicarious learning. During the 1950s, the term *behavior therapy* was introduced as a term to describe diverse behavioral approaches to resolving client problems (Yates, 1970).

John Krumboltz (1966) is credited as one of the major personalities to popularize behaviorism in counseling. He drew upon Bandura's earlier work and in doing so revolutionized the counseling profession (Hosford, 1980). Krumboltz's ideas, as well as behaviorism in general, gained widespread acceptance in the 1970s. By the late 1980s, behavioral approaches had generally split into three main theories: the stimulus-response model, applied behavior analysis, and social-cognitive theory. *Cognitive-behavioral approaches,* in which behavioral tasks are used to modify faulty perceptions and interpretation of important life events, also emerged at this time (Bankart, 1997).

Hackney and Cormier (1996) note that the following kinds of clients have the most success with behavioral and cognitive-behavioral counseling:

- Predominantly goal oriented, with a need for achievement and results
- Action oriented, with a need to be doing something
- Interested in changing either a discrete response or a limited number of behaviors

Behavioral Theories

As already mentioned, behaviorism has had a number of prominent proponents. Each has advocated for a behavioral-based treatment strategy for counseling. The life of B. F. Skinner is briefly traced here because of his powerful and innovative ideas and his long tenure as a major researcher and advocate for behaviorism.

B. F. Skinner

B. F. (Burrhus Frederick) Skinner was born in Susquehanna, Pennsylvania, in 1904. He was the oldest of two sons, but his younger brother died at age 16. Skinner's father, a wealthy attorney, wanted his son to become an attorney; but Skinner showed skills in other areas, such as an early facility with mechanical devices: he made roller-skate scooters, blow guns, model airplanes, and a flotation system to separate green from ripe elderberries (Skinner, 1967). These inventions were precursors of later devices, such as the infant Air Crib and the Skinner Box. The young Skinner was also interested in animal behavior, and at a country fair he was highly impressed by a troupe of performing pigeons. He later used pigeons to demonstrate aspects of his theory, teaching them to do a variety of tasks.

Skinner enjoyed music and played the saxophone in a jazz band. His home environment was warm, comfortable, and stable, imbued with the virtues of small-town, middle-class America at the turn of the century (Skinner, 1976). His parents did not use corporal punishment.

Skinner wanted to be a writer. He majored in English literature at Hamilton College, where he earned Phi Beta Kappa honors and graduated in 1926. Back home, he set about the task of writing, having been encouraged in his efforts by Robert Frost. After a year, he moved to New York's Greenwich Village to live among writers and benefit from a stimulating environment. There he discovered the works of Ivan Pavlov and John B. Watson as well as those of Bertrand Russell and Francis Bacon. Soon he gave up his writing ambitions to become a psychologist, although he had never taken a psychology course in college. He was accepted for graduate study in psychology at Harvard, where he received a master's degree in 1930 and a Ph.D. in 1931. After another 5 years of postdoctoral training, he joined the faculty of the University of Minnesota in 1936, the same year he married Yvonne Blue.

Skinner's first book, *The Behavior of Organisms* (1938), was followed by other major works, and he rapidly developed a national reputation. He left Minnesota for the University of Indiana in 1945, where he chaired the department of psychology until he returned to Harvard in 1948. At Indiana, he wrote perhaps his most influential book, *Walden Two* (1948), which describes a utopian society functioning without punishment and according to the principles of learning. The writing itself was a remarkable experience for Skinner, intensively done with much emotion (Elms, 1981).

At Harvard, Skinner continued to be a prolific writer. His best book on theory, *Science and Human Behavior* (1953), describes how learning principles can be applied to all areas of society. *Beyond Freedom and Dignity* (1971), also influential, outlined the steps necessary for civilization to survive and flourish. In the early 1980s, Skinner wrote about how behavioral principles could be applied to problems of the aged (Skinner & Vaughan, 1983). Overall, Skinner can be classified as a *behavioral determinist* because of his emphasis on learning as the primary determinant of human actions. He died at the age of 86 on August 18, 1990, a much admired and respected pioneer in the helping professions (Fowler, 1990).

View of Human Nature

Despite the great diversity of thought among behaviorists, certain characteristics can be identified as basic to the overall approach. Rimm and Cunningham (1985) list these common characteristics:

- As a group, behaviorists concentrate on behavioral processes—that is, processes closely associated with overt behavior (except for cognitive-behaviorists).
- Behaviorists concentrate on the here and now as opposed to the then and there of behavior.
- Behaviorists assume that all behavior is learned, whether it be adaptive or maladaptive.
- Behaviorists believe that learning can be effective in changing maladaptive behavior.
- Behaviorists focus on setting up well-defined therapy goals with their clients.
- Behaviorists reject the idea that the human personality is composed of traits.
- Behaviorists stress the importance of obtaining empirical evidence and scientific support for any techniques they use.

As mentioned earlier, the three main approaches in contemporary behavior therapy are the stimulus-response model, applied behavior analysis, and social-cognitive theory. These ways of learning are used by all organisms, although only human learning is addressed in this chapter.

The Stimulus-Response Model

The stimulus-response model is the application of classical conditioning, sometimes called *respondent learning* or the *stimulus-response (S-R) model*. In this model, the person or organism need not be an active participant to learn. Rather, learning occurs through the association of two stimuli, also known as the *conditioning of involuntary responses*.

The best-known example of S-R learning is Pavlov's famous experiments with his laboratory dogs. Pavlov found that when a dog's food was paired with the sound of a bell (rung before the dog was fed), the dog would associate the bell with food and begin to salivate in response to the bell (before the food was served). In this case, the bell, initially a neutral stimulus, became a conditioned (learned) stimulus (CS) because of its association with an unconditioned (natural) stimulus (UCS), the food. Salivating to the sound of the bell became a conditioned (learned) response (CR), as opposed to the unconditioned response (UCR) of naturally salivating when presented with food. S-R learning in this case is represented in the following diagram (Holden, 1993b):

1. CS not → (does not initially elicit) CR
2. UCS → (elicits) UCR
3. CS + UCS (presented simultaneously or UCS immediately after CS) → UCR
4. After a few repetitions of #3 . . .
5. CS → CR

In a similar way, many human emotions, such as phobias, arise because of paired associations. For example, a person may have an accident after eating a certain food. The association of the food with the accident, even though the two are unrelated, may result in that person's eventual fear or avoidance of the food. Clients often associate feelings with certain events and vice versa. The sound of music, the smell of certain odors, the sight of certain colors, and the touch of a stranger are experiences that individuals may react to emotionally because of S-R learning. Once learned, these associations can be unlearned, with new ones taking their place, a process known as *counterconditioning*.

Applied Behavior Analysis

Applied behavior analysis is "a direct extension of Skinner's (1953) radical behaviorism" (Wilson, 1995, p. 198), which is based on operant conditioning. According to the theory of operant conditioning, for learning to occur a person must be involved as an active participant with the environment. Operant conditioning (and its successor, applied behavior analysis) focuses primarily on how individuals operate in the environment. In general, the idea is that a person is rewarded or punished for actions, thereby learning to discriminate between behaviors that bring rewards and those that do not. The person is then likely to increase behavior that is rewarded and decrease behavior that is either punished or not reinforced. Thus, "applied behavior analysis makes use of reinforcement, punishment, extinction, stimulus control, and other procedures derived from laboratory research" (Wilson, 1995, p. 198).

Skinner's (1953) basic premise, the foundation on which applied behavior analysis is built, is that when a certain behavior is followed closely by a *reinforcer* (a reward), chances increase that the behavior will recur in similar or identical circumstances. Individuals do not shape their environments as much as they are shaped by them through rewards and punishments. In other words, the consequences of a behavior determine whether that behavior will be learned or repeated.

Social-Cognitive Theory

In the social-cognitive form of learning, people acquire new knowledge and behavior by observing other people and events without engaging in the behavior themselves and without any direct consequences to themselves. Synonyms for *social-cognitive theory* include *observational learning, imitation, social modeling*, and *vicarious learning*.

"The social-cognitive approach depends on the theory that behavior is based on three separate but interacting regulatory systems (Bandura, 1986). They are (a) external stimulus events, (b) external reinforcement, and (c) cognitive mediational processes" (Wilson, 1995, p. 198). In social-cognitive learning "the behavior of an individual or a group, the model, acts as a stimulus for similar thoughts, attitudes, or behavior on the part of another individual who observes" (Perry & Furukawa, 1980, p. 131). Learning to drive a car, use the correct fork at a dinner party, give oneself positive messages, and react appropriately to a new client are often learned this way. Learning through social-cognitive processes emphasizes the self-regulation of behavior and deemphasizes the importance of external reinforcers. Learning may occur independently of reinforcement (Hergenhahn, 1994). The advantages of social-cognitive learning are many, but chief among them is saving time, energy, and effort in acquiring new skills. Social-cognitive theory is easily administered, directed toward positive behavioral change, visually appealing, and of little or no risk to clients.

Bandura (1969) finds that models closest to the observer's age, gender, race, and attitude have the greatest impact. Live models, symbolic models (those on films and videos), and multiple models (groups of people) are equally effective in producing desired behavior change. In addition, covert models (a client imagines a model performing a socially desired activity) are quite effective (Cautela, 1976).

Role of the Counselor

A counselor may take one of several roles, depending on his or her behavioral orientation and the client's goal(s). Generally, however, a behaviorally based counselor is active in counseling sessions. The client learns, unlearns, or relearns specific ways of behaving. In that process, the counselor functions as a consultant, teacher, adviser, reinforcer, and facilitator (Gilliland, James, & Bowman, 1998). He or she may even instruct or supervise support people in the client's environment who are assisting in the change process. An effective behavioral counselor operates from a broad perspective and involves the client in every phase of the counseling. Counselors who are oriented toward social-cognitive learning serve as models for emulation, whereas those who are more S-R or applied are more direct and prescriptive in offering assistance.

Counselors using a behavioral approach differ widely regarding the use of psychological tests and diagnoses. Most employ some form of client assessment device, but often these instruments measure behavior and action. Rarely do counselors use paper-and-pencil personality tests. For diagnosis, they describe clients according to the behaviors they display, many of which are listed in the DSM-IV.

Goals

The goals of behaviorists are similar to those of many other counselors. Basically, behavioral counselors want to help clients make good adjustments to life circumstances and achieve personal and professional objectives. Thus, the focus is on modifying or eliminating the maladaptive behaviors that clients display, while helping them acquire healthy, constructive ways of acting. Just to eliminate a behavior is not enough; unproductive actions must be replaced with productive ways of responding.

A major step in the behavioral approach is for counselors and clients to reach mutually agreed-on goals. Four specific steps (Blackham & Silberman, 1979) in this process are as follows:

1. *Define the problem.*   If a problem is to be solved, it must be stated concretely. Therefore, clients are asked to specify when, where, how, and with whom the problem arises. Counselors may benefit from actually observing the problem behavior, but that is not always necessary.
2. *Take a developmental history.*   It is useful for both clients and counselors to have some knowledge about how clients have handled past circumstances and whether the presenting problem might be organically based.
3. *Establish specific goals.*   Behavioral counselors help clients break down goals into small, achievable units. Counselors also set up learning experiences for clients to develop any needed skills (Krumboltz & Thoresen, 1976). For example, if a woman wishes to complete college, she must first select and then pass courses during a school's initial term. She may also need to learn new study habits and ways of interrelating with others, such as roommates.
4. *Determine the best methods for change.*   Usually several behavioral methods can help clients reach desired goals. If one method does not work, it may be modified or a new one may be tried. Continual assessment of the effectiveness of methods is critical.

In general, behavioral counselors specialize in helping clients learn how to set up and achieve specific goals and subgoals. Counselors are concrete, objective, and collaborative in their work.

Techniques

Behavioral counselors have at their disposal some of the best-researched and most effective counseling techniques available; a sample is discussed here. Because the literature is so rich, however, you are urged to consult professional behaviorally oriented publications that describe these and other techniques in more detail.

General Behavioral Techniques.   General behavioral techniques are applicable to all behavioral theories, although a given technique may be more applicable to a particular approach at a given time or in a specific circumstance.

Use of Reinforcers.   *Reinforcers* are those events that, when they follow a behavior, increase the probability of the behavior's recurring. A reinforcer may be either positive or negative. A *positive reinforcer* is valued and considered pleasurable by the person affected. There are no universal positive reinforcers, but some events and objects frequently serve in this capacity, such as social recognition, money, and food. A *negative reinforcer* is an aversive stimulus whose removal is contingent upon performance of a desired action; the removal of the aversive stimulus is reinforcing for the person involved. For example, a mother nags her daughter until the daughter washes the dishes. The nagging could be viewed as a negative reinforcer, especially if the daughter values peace. In behavioral counseling, positive reinforcers are used more frequently than negative ones. In some situations, praise from counselors when clients complete an action is a positive reinforcer.

A reinforcer may also be either primary or secondary. A *primary reinforcer* is one that is valued intrinsically, such as food. A *secondary reinforcer*, such as some kind of token (e.g., money) acquires its value by being associated with a primary reinforcer. Clients are the best experts on what activities or items are most reinforcing for them.

Schedules of Reinforcement.   When a behavior is first being learned, it should be reinforced every time it occurs—that is, by continuous reinforcement. After a behavior is established, however, it should be reinforced less frequently—that is, by intermittent reinforcement. Schedules of reinforcement operate according to either the number of responses (*ratio*) or the length of time (*interval*) between reinforcers. Both ratio and interval schedules are either fixed or variable.

A *fixed-ratio schedule* delivers reinforcement based on the number of responses made, such as being paid for the number of items produced. A *fixed-interval schedule* occurs on a regular time schedule. One example of a fixed-interval schedule of reinforcement is salary payment on a regular basis. A *variable-ratio schedule* is one in which reinforcement is obtained irregularly, such as from a slot machine, but averages out to a given figure. A *variable-interval schedule* is based on an irregular time schedule. Reinforcement takes place unpredictably, such as being congratulated by the boss twice in one day and then not again for a month. If a counselor knows what type of schedule a client most prefers, reinforcers can be set up accordingly.

Shaping.   Behavior learned gradually in steps through successive approximation is known as *shaping*. When clients are learning new skills, counselors may help break down behavior into manageable units. Shaping occurs when a person actually practices a behavior or imagines doing more of a task than he or she previously had (*focused imagery*). Before undertaking shaping, counselors and clients need to be aware of the specific response sequence they wish to establish—that is, what follows what and how, a process known as *chaining*. Implementing such a procedure, when carefully planned, will usually lead to new or improved behaviors.

Generalization. *Generalization* involves the display of behaviors in environments outside where they were originally learned (e.g., at home, at work). It indicates that transference into another setting has occurred. Generalizing behaviors and transferring them to another setting does not happen by chance. A number of procedures make it possible, including the assignment of behavioral homework, training significant others (e.g., peers or colleagues) to reinforce them for appropriate behaviors, and consulting with clients about particular problems they may have in making behavioral switches (Rose, 1983).

Maintenance. *Maintenance* is defined as being consistent in doing the actions desired without depending on anyone else for support. In maintenance, an emphasis is placed on increasing a client's self-control and self-management (Thoresen & Mahoney, 1974). One way this may be done is through self-monitoring, when clients learn to modify their own behaviors. It involves two self-monitoring related processes: self-observation and self-recording (Goldiamond, 1976). *Self-observation* requires that a person notice particular behaviors he or she does; *self-recording* focuses on recording these behaviors. Self-monitoring interferes with learned habits by having the client count the occurrences of specific behaviors that are normally done without thought. Such self-monitoring increases the client's awareness of behaviors and assures that he or she is more conscious of when and how certain actions occur. For example, in the management of weight control, individuals monitor their calorie intake and their reactions to eating certain foods.

Extinction. *Extinction* is the elimination of a behavior because of a withdrawal of its reinforcement. Few individuals will continue doing something that is not rewarding. For example, when a client is no longer reinforced for talking about the past, he or she will quit bringing it up. Talk about the subject has disappeared and is said to be extinct.

Punishment. *Punishment* involves presenting an aversive stimulus to a situation to suppress or eliminate a behavior. A counselor may punish a client with a critical statement, such as "I don't want to hear you talk like that."

One way to conceptualize the differences in behavioral consequences on behavior is illustrated in the following chart (Holden, 1993a):

THE INFLUENCE OF BEHAVIORAL CONSEQUENCES ON BEHAVIOR

	Pleasurable Stimulus	Aversive Stimulus
Increases rate or strength of response	Positive reinforcement (response is followed very quickly by pleasurable stimulus)	Negative reinforcement (response is followed very quickly by termination of aversive stimulus; response precludes occurrence of aversive stimulus)
Decreases rate or strength of response	Extinction (response is no longer followed by pleasurable stimulus)	Punishment (response is followed very quickly by aversive stimulus)

Specific Behavioral Techniques.   Specific behavioral techniques are refined behavioral methods that combine general techniques in precise ways. They are found in different behavioral approaches.

Behavioral Rehearsal.   *Behavioral rehearsal* consists of practicing a desired behavior until it is performed the way a client wishes (Lazarus, 1985). The process consists of gradually shaping a behavior and getting corrective feedback. It is frequently used after a client has viewed a model enacting the desired behavior. In such cases, especially with complex behavior, the client who wishes to acquire the behavior will practice what he or she has observed in the counselor's presence. The client will then receive feedback and suggestions on what was done and make modifications accordingly. The client receives homework designed to help him or her practice the new behavior outside the counselor's office. By practicing in real-life conditions, the client will most likely achieve success and generalization. If not, modifications can be made during the next counseling session (Kipper, 1986). Sometimes behavioral rehearsal is called *role playing* because the client is practicing a new role. Improvisational role playing of behavior inconsistent with one's previous behavior is an effective mechanism for change (Zimbardo & Leippe, 1991).

Environmental Planning.   This procedure involves a client's setting up part of the environment to promote or limit certain behaviors (Krasner & Ullmann, 1973). For example, if a client associates painful memories with a certain place, a daily schedule is planned to avoid that setting. Likewise, to control a situation and therefore promote desirable interaction, a client may arrange a room or chairs in a certain way.

Systematic Desensitization.   This technique is designed to help clients overcome anxiety in particular situations. A client is asked to describe the situation that causes anxiety and then to rank this situation and related events on a hierarchical scale (see Table 11.1), from aspects that cause no concern (0) to those that are most troublesome (100).

The higher up the scale, the more anxious the client becomes. To help the client avoid anxiety and face the situation, the counselor teaches him or her to relax physically or men-

Table 11.1   Joe's anxiety hierarchy

Amount of Anxiety (%)	Event
90	Marriage relationship
85	In-law relationship
80	Relating to my newborn child
75	Relating to my dad
70	Relating to my mother
65	General family relations and responsibilities
60	Being a project manager at work
50	Work in general
40	Coming to counseling
35	Personal finances
20	Having fun (being spontaneous)
10	Going to sleep

tally. Then the hierarchy is reviewed, starting with low-anxiety items. When the client's anxiety begins to mount, the client is helped to relax again. The idea is that a person cannot feel anxious and physically relaxed at the same time, a phenomenon called *reciprocal inhibition* (Wolpe, 1958).

Assertiveness Training.   The major tenet of assertiveness training is that a person should be free to express thoughts and feelings appropriately without feeling undue anxiety (Alberti & Emmons, 1996). The technique consists of counterconditioning anxiety and reinforcing assertiveness. A client is taught that everyone has the right (not the obligation) of self-expression. The client then learns the differences among aggressive, passive, and assertive actions.

A client tells the counselor at the beginning of the counseling relationship what his or her objectives are, such as being able to speak out at a public meeting. The counselor then gives the client feedback (both positive and negative) about present behaviors. The next steps involve modeling the desired behavior and the client's role-playing it. The counselor then reinforces the behavior and helps shape the client's actions. Finally, the client receives homework to be completed between sessions (Bellack & Hersen, 1998). Assertive behaviors should be shaped gradually to keep the client encouraged and on track. The objective of assertiveness training is for individuals to feel good about their ability to express themselves, not to encourage aggressiveness and manipulation.

Contingency Contracts.   *Contingency contracts* spell out the behaviors to be performed, changed, or discontinued; the rewards associated with the achievement of these goals; and the conditions under which rewards are to be received (Corey, 1996). Most often they are used with children rather than adults because many adults find them offensive. Usually contingency contracts are written out as quasi-formal documents.

Implosion and Flooding.   *Implosive therapy* was first introduced in the 1960s by Thomas Stampfl. It involves desensitizing a client to a situation by having him or her imagine an anxiety-producing situation that may have dire consequences. The client is not taught to relax first (as in systematic desensitization). This technique should not be used by beginning counselors or with a client who has a heart condition.

Flooding is less traumatic than implosive therapy. In flooding, the imagined anxiety-producing scene does not have dire consequences.

Aversive Techniques.   Although most behaviorists recommend that positive techniques be employed first, sometimes it is necessary to use aversive techniques, such as punishment. Such techniques are useful when one behavior must be eliminated before another can be taught. Aversive techniques vary in their severity. Some of the better known are described here.

Time-out is a technique in which a client is separated from the opportunity to receive positive reinforcement. It is a mild aversive technique that requires careful monitoring and is most effective when employed for short periods of time, such as 5 minutes. An example of time-out is separating a child from classmates when he or she misbehaves.

Overcorrection is a technique in which a client first restores the environment to its natural state and then makes it "better than normal." For example, children who throw food in the lunchroom might be required to clean up their mess and wax the floor.

Covert sensitization is a technique in which undesired behavior is eliminated by associating it with unpleasantness. It is used in treating clients who have problems with smoking, obesity, substance abuse, and sexual deviation.

In the long run, aversive stimuli are usually not effective by themselves, for three reasons: their negative emotional effects soon dissipate; they may interfere with the learning of desired behaviors; and they may encourage the client to try to escape, which, when successful, becomes a positive reinforcer. Furthermore, ethical and legal concerns are associated with all aversive techniques. Before they administer them, counselors should obtain written permission for their use, especially if minors are involved.

Cognitive-Behavioral Theory and Techniques

Some of the most exciting new techniques in counseling have been originated since the early 1980s by cognitive-behaviorists (Craighead, Craighead, Kazdin, & Mahoney, 1994; Mahoney, 1995). However, "there is no single definition of cognitive-behavioral theory." Rather "the individual theories are tied together by common assumptions, techniques, and research strategies but maintain a diversity of views about the role that cognitions play in behavior change" (Kalodner, 1995, p. 354).

Space does not allow us to examine but a few of the emphases and procedures of cognitive-behaviorists. As a group, they have much in common with both cognitive and behavioral theorists and practitioners (e.g., an emphasis on the present, the environment, and learning). "Common to cognitive-behavioral intervention is a directive style; structured, goal-directed, and time-limited treatment; use of homework assignments and skill practice; and a focus on problem-solving ability" (Kalodner, 1995, p. 364).

The overlap among cognitive, behavioral, and cognitive-behavioral theorists makes it difficult to classify what approaches and techniques are principally in one category or another. Some cognitive-behavioral interventions originate from behaviorally based theories, whereas others are derived from those that are primarily cognitively based. A case can be made for literally including dozens of interventions under the cognitive-behavioral banner. Here just three interrelated interventions to cognitive-behavioral counseling—cognitive restructuring, stress inoculation, and thought stopping—will be examined as representatives of this approach. Beck's cognitive theory, covered briefly in chapter 10, is also considered by some to be an example of a cognitive-behavioral approach because of his emphasis that affect and behavior are determined by how people cognitively structure their worlds. Likewise, Ellis's rational emotive behavioral therapy is placed in the cognitive-behavioral camp by others because of this same premise.

Cognitive Restructuring

Among the most effective cognitive-behavioral techniques is cognitive restructuring, which includes stress inoculation and thought stopping. *Cognitive restructuring* is a process in which clients are taught to identify, evaluate, and change self-defeating or irrational thoughts that negatively influence their behavior. This process is accomplished by getting them to vocalize their self-talk before others and change it, when necessary, from negative to neutral or positive. It is similar to Ellis's (1962) and Beck's (1976) proposals for modifying the way one thinks.

One of the best methods for implementing this process is through Meichenbaum's (1977) *self-instructional training*. The client is trained to become aware of his or her maladaptive thoughts (self-statements). Then the counselor models appropriate behaviors while verbalizing the reasons behind these strategies. Finally, the client performs the designated behaviors while verbally repeating the reasons behind the actions and then conducts these behaviors giving him- or herself covert messages.

Rose (1983) has identified a number of cognitive restructuring procedures, including corrective information, stress inoculation, thought stopping, reframing, disputing irrational beliefs, imagery, relaxation exercises, and systematic problem solving. Two of these, stress inoculation and thought stopping, will be covered here because of their prevalence in behavior therapy circles and the fact that they are not covered elsewhere in the text as the other techniques are.

Stress Inoculation. Stress inoculation is a preventive technique, like medical inoculation, in which individuals are taught sets of coping skills to help them handle stressful events. The process has three phases. First, the client is helped to achieve an understanding of the nature of stress and coping. Second, the client learns specific coping skills and is reinforced for using the ones he or she already possesses. The final phase emphasizes practice: the client uses coping skills in clinical settings and real situations. Overall, stress inoculation involves focusing on what lies ahead, grouping stressful events into manageable doses, thinking of ways to handle small stressful events, and practicing coping skills (Meichenbaum, 1985, 1986). The major drawback to this procedure is that its initial results sometimes do not generalize into permanent behavior changes (Arnkoff & Glass, 1992). Therefore, follow-up and booster sessions are often necessary.

Thought Stopping. Thought stopping helps clients who ruminate about the past or have irrational thoughts stop such self-defeating behavior and live more productively. A counselor initially asks the client to think in the self-defeating manner. In the midst of such thoughts, the counselor suddenly yells, "Stop." The shout interrupts the thought process and makes it impossible to continue. There are several components of the thought-stopping process (Cormier & Cormier, 1998). Basically, the technique teaches the client to progress from outside to inner control of negative thought patterns. It also helps a client replace self-defeating thoughts with assertive, positive, or neutral ones.

Evaluation of Uniqueness and Limitations

The behavioral approach has many distinguishing characteristics (including aspects that are primarily cognitive-behavioral). Among the unique and strong aspects of the behavioral approach are the following:

• The approach deals directly with symptoms. Because most clients seek help because of specific problems, counselors who work directly with symptoms are often able to assist clients immediately. Furthermore, behavioral counseling is appropriate to use with attention deficit disorders, conduct disorders, eating disorders, substance abuse disorders, psychosexual dysfunction, impulse control disorders, and phobic disorders (Seligman, 1997).

• The approach focuses on the here and now. A client does not have to examine the past to obtain help in the present. A behavioral approach saves both time and money.

• The approach offers several techniques for counselors to use. Behavioral techniques more than doubled from 1969 to 1976, and they continue to increase. Counselors may employ behavioral techniques in numerous settings. Many behaviorally oriented counseling journals are also available, such as the *Journal of Applied Behavior Analysis.*

• The approach is based on learning theory, which is a well-formulated way of documenting how new behaviors are acquired (Krumboltz & Thoresen, 1969, 1976). Learning theory continues to evolve and generate pragmatic applications for treatment in a wide variety of areas (Rescorla, 1988).

• The approach is buttressed by the Association for the Advancement of Behavior Therapy (AABT), which publishes ethical guidelines for its members (Azrin, Stuart, Risely, & Stolz, 1977). AABT promotes the practice and edification of behavioral counseling methods, while trying to protect the public from unscrupulous practitioners.

• The approach is supported by exceptionally good research on how behavioral techniques affect the process of counseling. Novice counselors may follow one of many research designs. A common denominator among all behavioral approaches is a commitment to objectivity and evaluation.

• The approach is objective in defining and dealing with problems. Thus, it demystifies the process of counseling and makes it possible for clients and outside evaluators to assess in a measurable way its level of accountability (Gilliland et al., 1998).

The behavioral approach does have several limitations, too:

• The approach does not deal with the total person, just explicit behavior. Critics contend that many behaviorists, such as Skinner, have taken the person out of personality and replaced it with an emphasis on laws that govern actions in specific environments. This emphasis may be too simple in explaining complex human interaction (Hergenhahn, 1994).

• The approach is sometimes applied mechanically. Goldstein (1973) notes that "the most common error of neophyte behavior therapists is to start employing techniques too quickly" (p. 221). Even though most behaviorists are careful to establish rapport with their clients and make counseling a collaborative effort, some do not initially stress the counselor-client relationship, a situation that has hurt the approach's image.

• The approach is best demonstrated under controlled conditions that are difficult to replicate in normal counseling situations. Implicit in this criticism is an uneasiness that much of behavioral theory has been formulated using other animal forms, such as rats and pigeons. Many counselors wonder whether a behavioral approach will work for human clients who operate in less than ideal environments.

• The approach includes techniques that may be ahead of the theory (Thoresen & Coates, 1980). A proliferation of new methods has been generated by behavioral counselors, yet the theory that should underlie these methods has not kept pace.

• The approach ignores the client's past history and unconscious forces. Although it may work quite well with someone who clearly has a behavioral concern, those who wish to resolve past issues or deal with insight from the unconscious may not be helped.

• The approach does not consider developmental stages (Sprinthall, 1971). Skinner (1974) notes that a child's world develops, but he and many other behaviorists think that developmental stages do little to explain overt behavior. Instead, they contend that learning acquisition has universal characteristics.

• The approach programs the client toward minimum or tolerable levels of behaving, reinforces conformity, stifles creativity, and ignores client needs for self-fulfillment, self-actualization, and feelings of self-worth (Gilliland et al., 1998).

Reality Therapy

Begun in the 1960s, *reality therapy* emphasizes choices that people can make to change their lives. It focuses on two general concepts: the environment necessary for conducting counseling and the procedures leading to change (Wubbolding, 1998). Usually it is necessary to establish a safe environment before change can occur. Regardless, reality therapy is a flexible, friendly, and firm approach to working with clients and is action oriented. Overall, it stresses the fulfillment of psychological needs, the resolution of personal difficulties, and the prevention of future problems. The chief architect of the theory is William Glasser.

William Glasser

William Glasser was born in Cleveland, Ohio, in 1925, the third and youngest child in a close-knit family. He has described his childhood as happy and uneventful; but like his theory, he does not emphasize the past. In school, he played in the band and developed a strong interest in sports. After graduating at age 19 from the Case Institute of Technology with a degree in chemical engineering, he began graduate work in clinical psychology. He finished work for a master's degree in 1948, but his doctoral dissertation was rejected. He then entered medical school at Western Reserve University, graduating with a medical degree in 1953.

Glasser moved with his wife, Naomi Judith Silver, to California for a psychiatric residency at UCLA, which he completed in 1957. Although he hoped to establish a private psychiatric practice, he soon found that referrals were slow in coming because of his open resistance to traditional psychoanalytic treatment. Instead, he took a position as head psychiatrist at the Ventura School for Girls, a state-operated facility for juvenile delinquents.

At Ventura in the 1960s, Glasser began to formalize his approach to counseling. As a resident, his doubts about the effectiveness of classical psychoanalysis had been supported by one of his faculty supervisors, G. L. Harrington. Harrington helped Glasser develop some of the basic tenets of reality therapy and even verify these primary concepts. Glasser's first book, *Mental Health or Mental Illness?* (1961), contains many of the ideas that were later more formally expressed in *Reality Therapy: A New Approach to Psychiatry* (1965). He developed reality therapy because he thought "conventional psychiatry wastes too much time arguing over how many diagnoses can dance at the end of a case history" (1965, p. 49). He wanted an approach that was practical and more easily understood by both clinicians and the public. He found that by using the basic principles of reality therapy, he was able to cut recidivism at the Ventura School to only 20%.

Shortly after the publication of *Reality Therapy*, Glasser founded the Institute of Reality Therapy in Canoga Park, California, where he did some of his most creative work. He applied reality therapy to school settings in *Schools without Failure* (1969) and to the areas of identity in *The Identity Society* (1972). In *Positive Addiction* (1976) he asserted that individuals can become stronger instead of weaker from so-called addictive habits. Two examples of habits that improve physical and mental health are jogging and meditation.

In 1981, Glasser linked his original ideas with control theory, which argues that all behavior is generated from inside persons. Thus, the only thing that people obtain from the outside world is information (Glasser, 1988). Two of Glasser's books, *Stations of the Mind* (1981) and *Control Theory: A New Explanation of How We Control Our Lives* (1984), reflect this theoretical stance and emphasize how the brain influences inner perceptions. However, Glasser abandoned control theory as a part of his approach in 1996, incorporating choice theory in its place. His most recent book reflects the tenets of this change.

View of Human Nature

Reality therapy does not include a comprehensive explanation of human development, as Freud's system does. Yet it offers practitioners a focused view of some important aspects of human life and human nature. A major tenet of reality therapy is its focus on consciousness: human beings operate on a conscious level; they are not driven by unconscious forces or instincts (Glasser, 1965, 1988).

A second belief about human nature is that everyone has a health/growth force (Glasser & Wubbolding, 1995), manifested on two levels: the physical and the psychological. Physically, there is the need to obtain life-sustaining necessities such as food, water, and shelter and use them. According to Glasser, human behavior was once controlled by the physical need for survival (e.g., behaviors such as breathing, digesting, and sweating). He associates these behaviors with physical, or old-brain, needs because they are automatically controlled by the body. In modern times, most important behavior is associated with psychological, or new-brain, needs. The four primary psychological needs include the following:

- *Belonging*—the need for friends, family, and love
- *Power*—the need for self-esteem, recognition, and competition
- *Freedom*—the need to make choices and decisions
- *Fun*—the need for play, laughter, learning, and recreation

Associated with meeting these psychological needs is the need for *identity*—that is, the development of a psychologically healthy sense of self. Identity needs are met by being accepted as a person by others. Especially important in this process is experiencing love and worth. When this happens, people achieve a *success identity*. Those whose needs are not met establish a *failure identity*, a maladjusted personality characterized by a lack of confidence and a tendency to give up easily. Because "almost everyone is personally engaged in a search for acceptance as a person rather than as a performer of a task," personal identity precedes performance (Glasser, 1972, p. 10).

In regard to identity in early life, Glasser thinks there are two critical periods in children's lives. First, between ages 2 and 5, children learn early socialization skills (e.g., how to relate to their parents, siblings, and friends), and they begin to deal with frustrations and disappointments. During this period, children especially need the love, acceptance, guidance, and involvement of their parents. If that is not forthcoming, a child may begin to establish a failure identity. Second, between ages 5 and 10, children are involved with school and gain knowledge and self-concept. Many children establish a failure identity during this period because of socialization difficulties or learning problems (Glasser, 1969).

Reality therapy proposes that human learning is a life-long process based on choice. If individuals do not learn something early in life, such as how to relate to others, they can choose to learn it later. In the process they may change their identity and the way they behave (Glasser & Wubbolding, 1995).

A final tenet of reality therapy comes from tenets of control theory that Glasser (1998) has written about in a new psychology of personal freedom called "choice theory." The idea is that people have mental images of their needs and behave accordingly; thus, individuals are ultimately self-determining—they choose (Glasser, 1984; Wubbolding, 1994). Individuals can choose to be miserable or mentally disturbed. They may also choose to determine the course of their lives in positive ways and give up trying to control others. People who are mentally healthy will be in noncontrolling relationships with significant others in their lives, such as a parent, child, spouse, or employee/employer. They will choose to "care, listen, support, negotiate, encourage, love, befriend, trust, accept, welcome, and esteem" rather than "coerce, force, compel, punish, reward, manipulate, boss, motivate, criticize, blame, complain, nag, badger, rank, rate, and withdraw" (Glasser, 1998, p. 21).

Role of the Counselor

The counselor serves primarily as a teacher and model, accepting the client in a warm, involved way and creating an environment in which counseling can take place. The counselor immediately seeks to build a relationship with the client by developing trust through friendliness, firmness, and fairness (Wubbolding, 1998). Counselors use "-ing" verbs, such as *angering* or *bullying,* to describe client thoughts and actions. Thus, there is an emphasis on choice, on what the client chooses to do. Counselor-client interaction focuses on behaviors that the client would like to change and ways to go about making these desires a reality. It emphasizes positive, constructive actions (Glasser, 1988). Special attention is paid to metaphors and themes clients verbalize.

There is little attempt in reality therapy to test, diagnose, interpret, or otherwise analyze client actions except to ask questions such as "What are you doing now?" "Is it working?" and "What are the consequences?" Reality therapists do not concentrate on early childhood experiences, client insights, aspects of the unconscious, mental illness, blame, or stimulus-response ways of perceiving interaction. They emphasize aspects of the client's life that he or she can control.

Goals

The primary goal of reality therapy is to help clients become psychologically strong and rational and realize they have choices in the ways they treat themselves and others. If this goal is reached, individuals become autonomous and responsible for behaviors that affect themselves and others (Wallace, 1986; Wubbolding, 1988, 1991). Responsible behavior allows individuals to take charge of actions and obtain goals as well as not interfere with others or get into trouble. It leads to the formation of a success identity that enables clients to live more productive and harmonious lives. Glasser (1981) contends that to help people "we must help them gain strength to do worthwhile things with their lives and at the same time become warmly involved with the people they need" (p. 48). In essence, reality therapy strives to prevent problems from occurring.

Related to this first goal is a second one: to help clients clarify what they want in life. It is vital for persons to be aware of life goals if they are to act responsibly. In assessing goals, reality therapists help their clients examine personal assets as well as environmental supports and hindrances. It is the client's responsibility to choose behaviors that fulfill personal needs. Glasser (1976) lists six criteria by which to judge whether a person is choosing a suitable and healthy behavior:

1. The behavior is noncompetitive.
2. The behavior is easily completed without a great deal of mental effort.
3. The behavior is done or can be done by oneself.
4. The behavior has value for the person.
5. The client believes that improvements in lifestyle will result if he or she practices the behavior.
6. The person can practice the behavior without being self-critical.

Another goal of reality therapy is to help the client formulate a realistic plan to achieve personal needs and wishes. Poor mental health is sometimes the result of a person's not knowing how to achieve what he or she has planned. Glasser advocates that plans be as specific and concrete as possible. Once a plan is formulated, alternative behaviors, decisions, and outcomes are examined, and often a contract is written. The focus is on helping individuals become more responsible and realize that no single plan is absolute.

An additional goal of reality therapy is to have the counselor become involved with the client in a meaningful relationship (Glasser, 1980, 1981). This relationship is based on understanding, acceptance, empathy, and the counselor's willingness to express faith in the client's ability to change. The counselor helps the client establish boundaries for his or her behavior but is not critical and does not give up on the client if the client is unable to complete a behavior. Often, to facilitate the development of the relationship, the counselor will risk disclosing personal information to the client.

Another goal of reality therapy is to focus on behavior and the present. Glasser (1988) believes that behavior (i.e., thought and action) is interrelated with feeling and physiology. Thus, a change in behavior also brings about other positive changes. Basically, Glasser emphasizes current activities because they are controlled by the client, who has no control over the past.

Finally, reality therapy aims to eliminate punishment and excuses from the client's life. Often, a client uses the excuse that he or she cannot carry out a plan because of punishment for failure by either the counselor or people in the outside environment. Reality therapy helps the client formulate a new plan if the old one does not work. The emphasis is on planning, revision, and eventual success rather than setbacks. The entire procedure empowers the client and enables him or her to be more productive.

Techniques

Basically, reality therapy uses action-oriented techniques that help clients realize they have choices in how they respond to events and people and that others do not control them any more than they control others (Glasser, 1998). Some of reality therapy's more effective and active techniques are teaching, employing humor, confronting, role playing, offering feedback, formulating specific plans, and composing contracts.

Reality therapy relies heavily on teaching as a primary technique. Glasser (1965) states that "the specialized learning situation . . . is made up of three separate but interwoven procedures" (p. 21). First, there is involvement between counselor and client in which the client begins to face reality and see how a behavior is unrealistic. Second, the counselor rejects the unrealistic behavior of the client without rejecting the client as a person. Finally, the counselor teaches the client better ways to fulfill needs within the confines of reality. One strategy that reality therapy counselors use is *positiveness:* the reality therapist talks about, focuses on, and reinforces positive and constructive planning and behaving (Gilliland et al., 1998).

Humor is the ability to see the absurdity within a situation and view matters from a different and amusing perspective. It is an appropriate technique in reality therapy if used sparingly. Most clients do not see difficult situations as funny; yet if a counselor times a remark just right, the client may come to see some silliness in the behavior. The ability to laugh at oneself promotes the ability to change because the situation appears in a new and often insightful way. In no case should humor in counseling be used as a sarcastic put-down. When used in that manner, it is likely to deteriorate the counseling relationship and adversely affect the process of change.

In confrontation, the counselor asks the client about a behavior as a way of helping the client accept responsibility for his or her actions. It does not differ much from confrontation in other approaches. Similarly, role playing in reality therapy is similar to that employed in other counseling approaches. But its purpose in reality therapy is to help the client bring the past or future into the present and assess how life will be different when he or she starts behaving differently. Role-plays are almost always followed by counselor feedback sessions.

From confrontation and role-plays, clients focus on formulating specific plans for improving their lives. Contracts are established to carry out these plans in a timely and systematic way.

Reality therapy uses the *WDEP system* as a way of helping counselors and clients make progress. In this system the *W* stands for *wants;* at the beginning of the counseling process counselors find out what clients want and what they have been doing (Wubbolding, 1988, 1991). Counselors in turn share their wants for and perceptions of clients' situations. The *D* in WDEP involves clients further exploring the *direction* of their lives. Effective and ineffective self-talk that they use is discussed. Basic steps strategically incorporated in these two stages include establishing a relationship and focusing on present behavior.

The *E* in the WDEP procedure stands for *evaluation* and is the cornerstone of reality therapy. Clients are helped to evaluate their behaviors and how responsible their personal behaviors are. Behaviors that do not contribute to helping clients meet their needs often alienate them from self and significant others. If clients recognize a behavior as unproductive, they may be motivated to change. If there is no recognition, the therapeutic process may break down. It is therefore crucial that clients, not the counselor, do the evaluation.

After evaluation, the final letter *P,* for *plan,* of the WDEP system comes into focus. A client concentrates on making a plan for changing behaviors. The plan stresses actions that the client will take, not behaviors that he or she will eliminate. The best plans are simple, attainable, measurable, immediate, and consistent (Wubbolding, 1998). They are also controlled by clients and committed to sometimes in the form of a written contract in which responsible alternatives are spelled out. Clients are then requested to make a commitment to the plan of action. In this procedure, the counselor is persistent and makes it clear that no excuses will be accepted for a client's not carrying out the plan of action; neither will the counselor blame or punish. In essence, responsibility is placed entirely on the client. If the client fails to accomplish the plan, Glasser thinks the client should suffer the natural or reasonable consequences of that failure (Evans, 1982).

Glasser (1965, 1980) stresses that the counselor should not give up on the client if he or she fails to accomplish a goal. Instead, the counselor stubbornly and tenaciously encourages the client to make a new plan or revise an old one. Most clients are used to being put down or abandoned when goals are not achieved. Glasser's approach gives the client an opportunity to alter that cycle of failure.

Evaluation of Uniqueness and Limitations

Reality therapy has a number of emphases:

• The approach can be applied to many different populations. It is especially appropriate in the treatment of conduct disorders, substance abuse disorders, impulse control disorders, personality disorders, and antisocial behavior. It can be employed in individual counseling with children, adolescents, adults, and the aged and in group, marriage, and family counseling. The approach has such versatility that it is helpful in almost any setting that emphasizes mental health and adjustment, such as hospitals, mental health clinics, schools, prisons, rehabilitation centers, and crisis centers (Glasser, 1986; Seligman, 1997).

• The approach is concrete. Both counselor and client are able to assess how much progress is being made and in what areas, especially if a goal-specific contract is drawn up. If a client is doing well in modifying one behavior and not another, increased attention can be given to the underdeveloped area.

• The approach emphasizes short-term treatment. Reality therapy is usually limited to relatively few sessions that focus on present behaviors. Clients work with conscious and verifiable objectives that can be achieved quickly.

• The approach has national training centers. The Institute for Reality Therapy (Los Angeles) and the Center for Reality Therapy (Cincinnati) promote a uniform educational experience among practitioners who employ this theory and publish professional literature.

• The approach promotes responsibility and freedom within individuals without blame or criticism or an attempt to restructure the entire personality. Sometimes people are not taught to take responsibility for their behavior or refuse to accept that responsibility. To act responsibly means "to fulfill one's needs, and to do so in a way that does not deprive others of the ability to fulfill their needs" (Glasser, 1965, p. 13). Many individuals need help in becoming responsible, and reality therapy addresses this aspect of human life.

• The approach has successfully challenged the medical model of client treatment. Its rationale and positive emphasis are refreshing alternatives to pathology-centered models (Gilliland et al., 1998).

• The approach addresses conflict resolution. Glasser (1984) believes that conflict occurs on two levels, true and false. On the true level, conflict develops over interpersonal disagreements about change. There is no single solution, and people are best off if they expend energy in nonconflict areas. In false conflict, change is possible if persons are willing to expend the effort, such as lose weight. Responsible behaviors in such situations can bring resolutions.

• The approach stresses the present because current behavior is most amenable to client control. Like behaviorists, Gestaltists, and rational emotive behavior therapists, reality therapists are not interested in the past.

Reality therapy also has limitations:

• The approach emphasizes the here and now of behavior so much that it sometimes ignores other concepts, such as the unconscious and personal history. Sometimes a person may be informed by the unconscious (e.g., by dreams). In other cases, a person may need to relive and resolve past traumas. Reality therapy makes little allowance for these eventualities.

• The approach holds that all forms of mental illness are attempts to deal with external events (Glasser, 1984). Mental illness does not just happen, Glasser believes; a person chooses mental illness to help control his or her world. But Glasser ignores biology as a factor in mental illness, a stance considered by some critics to be naive and irresponsible.

• The approach is too simple. Reality therapy has few theoretical constructs, although its tie to choice theory means that it is becoming more sophisticated. Still, Glasser does not deal with the full complexity of human life, preferring to ignore developmental stages. His theory lacks comprehensiveness.

• The approach is susceptible to becoming overly moralistic. Glasser (1972) disavows that reality therapy was intended to function in this way. The counselor who practices reality therapy does not judge a client's behavior; the client judges the behavior. The counselor's role is to support the client in a personal exploration of values. Still, an overzealous practitioner may impose values on a client. This criticism is aimed at a potential difficulty rather than the theory as advocated by its founder.

• The approach is dependent on establishing a good counselor-client relationship. If sufficient involvement does not ensue, counselors may settle for general client goals, force a plan, or proceed too quickly to commitment (Wubbolding, 1975).

• The approach depends on verbal interaction and two-way communication. It has limitations in helping clients who, for any reason, cannot adequately express their needs, options, and plans (Gilliland et al., 1998).

• The approach keeps changing its focus (Corey, 1996). Reality therapy has shifted its emphasis since the early 1960s, despite an initial denial by Glasser (1976). Acceptance is emphasized now more than it previously was, and the integration of control theory and then choice theory as the bedrock of the approach altered the theory's earlier focus. At present there has been no attempt to document the changes reality therapy has undergone and note which emphases are most essential to practice. Until such documentation emerges, reality therapy will not be as well understood or used as might otherwise be the case.

Development and Integration of Counseling Theories

In addition to the counseling theories covered in this text, new theories continue to develop, although at a less rapid clip than in the 1950s and 1960s. This decline has several causes:

1. A proliferation of theories (more than 400) in the preceding decades that ranged from psychoanalysis to soap opera therapy (Corsini & Wedding, 1995)
2. A refinement and broadening of already established positions
3. Stringent research requirements that must be met before any novel position will be accepted
4. Current interest in integrating already existing theories, such as cognitive theories with behavioral theories

Okun (1990) states that the present emphasis in connecting theories instead of creating them is built on the fundamental assumption that "no one theoretical viewpoint can provide all of the answers for the clients we see today" (p. xvi). Furthermore, counselors can be pragmatically flexible in adapting techniques and interventions from different approaches without actually accepting the premises of these points of view. When treating clients, counselors must consider intrapersonal, interpersonal, and external social systems. Few theories blend all these dimensions together. By necessity, many counselors must weave formerly distinct points of view into a creative, systemic, and eclectic process if they are to be effective and holistic (Gilliland et al., 1998).

Summary and Conclusion

This chapter has covered behavioral and cognitive-behavioral approaches to counseling as well as reality therapy. It is clear that these approaches to counseling have areas of overlap, yet each is unique. The basic premise of these theories is that if a person changes behavior, including mental processes, alterations in personal functioning will follow. Behaviorists, cognitive-behaviorists, and reality therapists stress that behavior or cognitive-behavioral change comes before modification of feelings. Likewise, they emphasize that change takes sustained client effort as well as counselor expertise and facilitation.

Basically, counselors who work from a behavioral, cognitive-behavioral, or reality therapy perspective focus on present actions and perceptions that clients wish to learn, unlearn, or modify. Counselors are concrete and goal directed and work in collaboration with their clients. Contracts are often established between counselor and client to identify when counseling goals have been reached.

These theories, as well as the ones examined in previous chapters, are effective in both broad and selective ways. For some clients, a specific theoretical orientation at a select time is best. For others, an eclectic approach (discussed in Chapter 8) is best. To maximize time and effort, effective counselors constantly evaluate the impact of an approach and review the professional literature on what theories work best with what type of client under what circumstances. Which theoretical orientation counselors choose depends on the counselor's personality, the client's personality, the nature of the concern, the setting, and other variables unique to a particular situation. The theories in this and previous chapters have unique emphases and limitations. As you work toward becoming a professional counselor, you need to explore each theory in depth. Such exploration continues well after a course of study has been completed.

Counseling is an ever expanding and changing process. Table 11.2 will help you gain a clearer picture of the various counseling theories covered thus far and stimulate your thinking about systematic approaches to counseling (covered in Chapter 12).

CLASSROOM ACTIVITIES

1. Which of the behavioral theories do you find most attractive? Share the reasons for your decision with other class members. Which theories do you anticipate using? Find several research articles that support the effectiveness of these theories, and share summaries of them with the class.

2. In 1956, a debate arose between Carl Rogers and B. F. Skinner: Skinner took the position that the environment is the sole determiner of behavior; Rogers proposed that human behavior is determined by self-concept. How do you think such a debate would be staged now? Stage a simulated debate in which several class members act as spokespersons for each side. Then discuss how it feels to argue as a Skinnerian or Rogerian.

3. How would you compare the main behavioral theories with Glasser's reality therapy?

Are they all really the same? If not, what makes them different? List similarities and differences among the approaches and discuss your ideas with class members.

4. What do you think of the integration of individual theories into a composite or eclectic approach? Investigate recent attempts to formulate a healthy eclecticism. In small groups discuss the strengths and limitations of working in such a way.

5. What are some activities you can do after your formal education is complete to stay abreast of developments in counseling theory and keep your counseling skills up-to-date? Survey practicing counselors to find out how they stay current. Discuss your findings with fellow classmates.

Table 11.2   Summary of counseling approaches

	Psychoanalysis	Adlerian Counseling	Person-centered Counseling	Existential Counseling
Major Theorists	Sigmund Freud Anna Freud Heinz Kohut	Alfred Adler Rudolph Dreikurs Don Dinkmeyer Thomas Sweeney	Carl Rogers Angelo Boy Gerald Pine	Rollo May Victor Frankl Abraham Maslow Irvin Yalom Sidney Jourard Clemmont Vontress
View of Human Nature	Emphasis on early childhood and psychosexual stages of development; importance of unconscious and ego defense mechanisms; focus on biological, deterministic aspects of behavior	Emphasis on social interest as a primary motivator; focus on birth order, family constellation, style of life, and teleological (future) goals as major influences on personal growth and development	Emphasis on humans as basically good, positive, forward moving and trustworthy; phenomenological view of self; person is self-directed and growth oriented if provided with the right conditions	Belief in human freedom and choice of lifestyle; focus on meaning of anxiety, meaning of life, and relevance of individual experience
Role of the Counselor	Counselor as expert; encourages transference and exploration of the unconscious; use of interpretation	Counselor in equalitarian relationship with client; models, teaches, and assesses client's situation; shares hunches; assigns homework; encourages	Stresses holism, I-Thou quality; counselor facilitates, focuses on uniqueness of client; counselor is the technique; emphasis on personal warmth, empathy, acceptance, concreteness, and genuineness	Emphasis on counselor authenticity and understanding of client as unique; stress on personal relationship, modeling, and sharing of experiences
Goals	Make the unconscious conscious; work through unresolved developmental stages; help the client learn to cope and adjust; reconstruction of personality	Cultivate social interests; correct faulty assumptions and mistaken goals; develop client insight; bring about behavioral change through acting "as if"	Self-exploration; openness to self, others; self-directed and realistic; more accepting of self, others, and environment; focus on the here and now	Helps clients realize their responsibility, awareness, freedom, and potential; shift from outward frame of reference

Table 11.2 *continued*

Gestalt Theory	Rational Emotive Behavior Therapy	Transactional Analysis	Behavioral and Cognitive-Behavioral Counseling	Reality Therapy
Fritz Perls Laura Perls Irma Lee Shepherd Joen Fagan	Albert Ellis Maxie Maultsby Janet Wolfe	Eric Berne Carl Steiner Thomas Harris Graham Barnes	John B. Watson B. F. Skinner Joseph Wolpe Albert Bandura John Krumboltz Donald Meichenbaum Aaron Beck	G. L. Harrington William Glasser Robert Wubbolding
Emphasis on importance of wholeness and completeness in human life; stress on inner wisdom of person and importance of affect; phenomenological and antideterministic; stresses change	Humans are both inherently rational and irrational; biological duality; humans can disturb themselves by what they think; children are most vulnerable; mistake for people to use form of the verb *to be* to describe themselves	Optimistic that people can change; each individual is composed of three interacting ego states of parent, adult, child; stresses importance of intrapersonal integration and analysis of transactions, games, time, and scripts for individual health and growth	All human behaviors are learned; old behaviors can be extinguished and new behaviors established; respondent learning, operant conditioning, and social modeling are the three primary ways of learning	Health or growth force in all individuals; problems occur when people don't take responsibility for behavior; learning is a life-long process; people need to love and be loved, feel worthwhile and successful, and act to control the world around them for various purposes
Counselor must be authentic, exciting, and energetic; emphasis on the now; helps client resolve unfinished business; counselor stresses verbal and nonverbal messages, congruence; use of *I* for *it*	Active, direct counselor teaches, confronts, corrects; counselor concentrates on ABCs of self-talk or on rational self-analysis	Counselor as teacher; contracts with client for change; instructs in language of TA	Counselor as teacher, director, and expert; active in sessions; assists client in clarifying goals and modifying behaviors and thoughts	Counselor as teacher and model; focuses on establishing a relationship with client; counselor is active, direct, practical, didactic
Emphasis on immediacy of experience; making choices in the now; resolving the past, becoming congruent, growing up mentally; shedding neuroses	Help clients live more relational and productive lives, stop thinking irrationally; stress elimination of oughts, shoulds, musts (i.e. making wants into demands); elimination of self-defeating habits; tolerance and acceptance of self and others	Transformation; attainment of health and autonomy; becoming more aware, game free, intimate, and OK	Helps clients make good adjustment, modify maladaptive behavior, learn productive responses; establish and achieve specific concrete goals and subgoals; change thoughts (cognitive-behavioral)	Assist individuals to become psychologically strong and rational, take responsibility, clarify goals, formulate a realistic plan, focus on behavior and the present, eliminate punishment and excuses

Table 11.2 *continued*

	Psychoanalysis	**Adlerian Counseling**	**Person-centered Counseling**	**Existential Counseling**
Techniques	Free association; dream analysis; analysis of transference; analysis of resistance; interpretation	Use of empathy, support, warmth, collaboration; stress on client strengths and responsibility through confrontation; examination of client's memories, dreams, and priorities; focus on interpretation, asking "the question," spitting in the client's soup, catching oneself, and task setting	Acceptance, clarification; reflection of feeling; use of empathy, positive regard, congruence, self-disclosure; active/passive listening; open-ended questions/statements; summarization	Counselor openness and inquiringness; acceptance of client uniqueness; emphasis on relationship; working with ambiguity; confrontation; borrowing of other active techniques that work, such as imagery or awareness exercises
Strengths	Emphasis on importance of sexuality and unconscious in human behavior; supportive of diagnostic instruments; multidimensional; continued evolution effective in select cases; focus on developmental stages of human life, especially childhood	Encouragement and support of counselor in an equalitarian relationship; versatility; useful in specific disorders; contribution of ideas to the public and professional vocabulary (e.g., inferiority complex)	Openness and evolution of theory; applicable to a wide range of human problems; effectiveness with specific disorders (e.g., adjustment disorders); short-term treatment; effectiveness with paraprofessionals; positive view of human nature	Humanistic emphasis; focus on anxiety as a motivator; use of philosophy and literature to inform/direct; stress on continuous growth; effective in cross-cultural counseling
Limitations	Time-consuming and expensive; a closed system of practice, limited mainly to psychiatry; focus on pathology; deterministic; not efficient method for less-disturbed individuals	Lack of a firm research base; vagueness of concepts/terms and the how of counseling; narrowness of approach	Lack of concreteness; works best with verbal, bright clients; ignores unconscious and innate drives; deals with surface issues	Not fully developed; lack of training approaches to learning theory; subjective, lacks uniformity; more philosophical and less functional than other theories; avoids diagnoses and testing

Table 11.2 *continued*

Gestalt Theory	Rational Emotive Behavior Therapy	Transactional Analysis	Behavioral and Cognitive-Behavioral Counseling	Reality Therapy
Use of exercises and experiments; exercises include frustration actions, fantasy, role playing, and psychodrama; experiments grow out of client-counselor interaction; use of dream work, empty chair, confrontation, making the rounds, exaggeration, and I take responsibility	Counselor uses teaching and disputing; clients learn the anatomy of an emotion; imagery, persuasion, logical reasoning, reminder devices, homework assignments, bibliotherapy, shame attacks, and rational self-analyses	Emphasis on treatment contracts, specific and concrete; use of techniques such as interrogation, specification, confrontation, illustration, and crystallization; concentration on early memories/stories; often combined with Gestalt techniques for action	Use of reinforcement—positive/negative, primary/secondary, continuous/intermittent; shaping, extinction, self-monitoring, punishment, environmental planning, systematic desensitization, implosion, flooding, time out, overcorrection, imitation, stress inoculation, thought stopping	Teaching, focusing, evaluating; helping client make a plan and commit to it; not blaming, not giving up on client, role playing, using humor, confronting, role modeling; defining limits; involvement with client; feedback
Helps individual incorporate all parts of life, resolve past; stresses doing and being active; appropriate for certain affective disorders; flexibility of techniques	Direct, clear, effective, and easily learned; combines well with other theories; treatment is short-term; centralized training centers; theory continues to evolve	Easily understood and clearly defined terminology; easy to combine with other theories; puts responsibility on client for choosing; goal directed	Focus on symptoms; focus on here and now; abundance of available procedures; based on learning theory; well-organized practitioners; effective for certain disorders; well researched; continually growing in sophistication; can be combined with other theories, especially cognitive	Applicable to many different populations; effective with certain disorders; concreteness; short-term; centralized training center; promotes responsibility and freedom without blaming; stresses here and now; integrates choice theory
Lack of a strong theoretical base; gimmicky; does not allow for passive learning; eschews testing/diagnosis; self-centeredness of approach	Not applicable to all clients, especially those who are mentally impaired; associated with unconventional theorist Albert Ellis; still viewed as primarily cognitive	Cognitive orientation limiting; simplicity and popularity dilute effectiveness; lack of emphasis on qualities of the counselor	Doesn't deal with total person, just behaviors; may be applied mechanically; sometimes difficult to replicate in actual counseling conditions; techniques getting ahead of theory; ignores past history and the unconscious; doesn't consider developmental stages	Ignores unconscious, personal history, mental illness; theoretically simplistic; may become value ladened unless supervised appropriately; ignores its own history of evolution

REFERENCES

Alberti, R. E., & Emmons, M. L. (1996). *Your perfect right: A guide to assertive behavior* (7th ed.). San Luis Obispo, CA: Impact.

Arnkoff, D. B., & Glass, C. R. (1992). Cognitive therapy and psychotherapy integration. In D. K. Freedheim (Ed.), *History of psychotherapy: A century of change* (pp. 657–694). Washington, DC: American Psychological Association.

Azrin, N. H., Stuart, R. B., Risely, T. R., & Stolz, S. (1977). Ethical issues for human services. *AABT Newsletter, 4,* 11.

Bandura, A. (1969). *Principles of behavior modification.* New York: Holt, Rinehart, & Winston.

Bandura, A. (1986). *Social foundations of thought and action: A social cognitive theory*. Upper Saddle River, NJ: Prentice Hall.

Bandura, A., & Walters, R. H. (1963). *Social learning and personality development.* New York: Rinehart & Winston.

Bankart, C. P. (1997). *Talking cures.* Pacific Grove, CA: Brooks/Cole.

Beck, A. (1976). *Cognitive therapy and the emotional disorders.* New York: International Universities Press.

Bellack, A. S., & Hersen, M. (1998). *Behavioral assessment: A practical handbook.* Boston: Allyn & Bacon.

Blackham, G. J., & Silberman, A. (1979). *Modification of child and adolescent behavior.* Belmont, CA: Wadsworth.

Cautela, J. R. (1976). The present status of covert modeling. *Journal of Behavior Therapy and Experimental Psychiatry, 6,* 323–326.

Christopher, J. C. (1996). Counseling's inescapable moral vision. *Journal of Counseling & Development, 75,* 17–25.

Corey, G. (1996). *Theory and practice of counseling and psychotherapy* (5th ed.). Pacific Grove, CA: Brooks/Cole.

Cormier, W. H., & Cormier, L. S. (1998). *Interviewing strategies for helpers: A guide to assessment, treatment, and evaluation* (4th ed.). Pacific Grove, CA: Brooks/Cole.

Corsini, R. J., & Wedding, D. (1995). *Current psychotherapies* (5th ed.). Itasca, IL: Peacock.

Craighead, L. W., Craighead, W. E., Kazdin, A. E., & Mahoney, M. J. (1994). *Cognitive and behavioral interventions: An empirical approach to mental health problems.* Boston: Allyn & Bacon.

Ellis, A. (1962). *Reason and emotion in psychotherapy.* New York: Stuart.

Elms, A. C. (1981). Skinner's dark year and Walden Two. *American Psychologist, 36,* 470–479.

Evans, D. (1982). What are you doing? An interview with William Glasser. *Personnel and Guidance Journal, 60,* 460–464.

Eysenck, H. J. (1960). *Behavior therapy and the neuroses.* New York: Pergamon.

Fowler, R. D. (1990, October). B. F. Skinner: Farewell, with admiration and affection. *APA Monitor, 21*(10), 2.

Gilliland, B. E., James, R. K., & Bowman, J. T. (1998). *Theories and strategies in counseling and psychotherapy* (4th ed.). Boston: Allyn & Bacon.

Glasser, W. (1961). *Mental health or mental illness.* New York: Harper & Row.

Glasser, W. (1965). *Reality therapy: A new approach to psychiatry.* New York: Harper & Row.

Glasser, W. (1969). *Schools without failure.* New York: Harper & Row.

Glasser, W. (1972). *The identity society.* New York: Harper & Row.

Glasser, W. (1976). *Positive addiction.* New York: Harper & Row.

Glasser, W. (1980). Reality therapy: An explanation of the steps of reality therapy. In W. Glasser (Ed.), *What are you doing? How people are helped through reality therapy.* New York: Harper & Row.

Glasser, W. (1981). *Stations of the mind.* New York: Harper & Row.

Glasser, W. (1984). *Control theory: A new explanation of how we control our lives.* New York: Harper & Row.

Glasser, W. (1986). *Control theory in the classroom.* New York: Harper & Row.

Glasser, W. (1998). *Choice theory.* New York: HarperCollins.

Glasser, W. (1988, November). *Reality therapy.* Workshop presented at the Alabama Association for Counseling and Development, Fall Conference, Birmingham.

Glasser, W., & Wubbolding, R. (1995). Reality therapy. In R. Corsini & D. Wedding (Eds.), *Current psychotherapies* (5th ed., pp. 293–321). Itasca, IL: Peacock.

Goldiamond, I. (1976). Self-reinforcement. *Journal of Applied Behavior Analysis, 9,* 509–514.

Goldstein, A. (1973). Behavior therapy. In R. Corsini (Ed.), *Current psychotherapies* (pp. 207–249). Itasca, IL: Peacock.

Hackney, H. & Cormier, L. S. (1996). *The professional counselor* (3rd ed.). Boston: Allyn & Bacon.

Hergenhahn, B. R. (1994). *An introduction to theories of personality* (4th ed.). Upper Saddle River, NJ: Prentice Hall.

Holden, J. (1993a). *Behavioral consequences on behavior.* Unpublished manuscript, University of North Texas, Denton.

Holden, J. (1993b). *Respondent learning.* Unpublished manuscript.

Hosford, R. E. (1980). The Cubberley conference and the evolution of observational learning strategies. *Personnel and Guidance Journal, 58,* 467–472.

Jones, M. C. (1924). The elimination of children's fears. *Journal of Experimental Psychology, 7,* 383–390.

Kalodner, C. R. (1995). Cognitive-behavioral theories. In D. Capuzzi & D. R. Gross (Eds.), *Counseling & psychotherapy* (pp. 353–384). Upper Saddle River, NJ: Merrill/Prentice Hall.

Kipper, D. A. (1986). *Psychotherapy through clinical role playing.* New York: Brunner/Mazel.

Krasner, L., & Ullmann, L. P. (1973). *Behavior influence and personality: The social matrix of human action.* New York: Holt, Rinehart, & Winston.

Krumboltz, J. D. (1966). Behavioral goals of counseling. *Journal of Counseling Psychology, 13,* 153–159.

Krumboltz, J. D., & Thoresen, C. E. (1969). *Behavioral counseling.* New York: Holt, Rinehart, & Winston.

Krumboltz, J. D., & Thoresen, C. E. (1976). *Counseling methods.* New York: Holt, Rinehart, & Winston.

Lazarus, A. A. (1985). Behavior rehearsal. In A. S. Bellack & M. Hersen (Eds.), *Dictionary of behavior therapy techniques* (p. 22). New York: Pergamon.

Mahoney, M. J. (1995). *Cognitive and constructive psychotherapies: Theory, research, and practice.* New York: Springer.

Meichenbaum, D. H. (1977). *Cognitive-behavior modification.* New York: Plenum.

Meichenbaum, D. H. (1985). Cognitive behavioral therapies. In S. J. Lynn & J. P. Garske (Eds.), *Contempo-rary psychotherapies: Models and methods* (pp. 261–286). Upper Saddle River, NJ: Prentice Hall.

Meichenbaum, D. (1986). Cognitive behavior modification. In F. H. Kanfer & A. P. Goldstein (Eds.), *Helping people change: A textbook of methods* (pp. 346–380). New York: Pergamon.

Okun, B. K (1990). *Seeking connections in psychotherapy.* San Francisco: Jossey-Bass.

Perry, M. A., & Furukawa, M. J. (1980). Modeling methods. In F. H. Kanfer & A. P. Goldstein (Eds.), *Helping people change* (pp. 131–171). New York: Pergamon.

Rescorla, R. A. (1988). Pavlovian conditioning: It's not what you think it is. *American Psychologist, 43,* 151–160.

Rimm, D. C., & Cunningham, H. M. (1985). Behavior therapies. In S. J. Lynn & J. P. Garske (Eds.), *Contemporary psychotherapies: Models and methods* (pp. 221–259). Upper Saddle River, NJ: Prentice Hall.

Rose, S. D. (1983). Behavior therapy in groups. In H. I. Kaplan & B. J. Sadock (Eds.), *Comprehensive group psychotherapy* (2nd ed.). Baltimore: Williams & Wilkins.

Seligman, L. (1997). *Diagnosis and treatment planning in counseling.* New York: Plenum.

Skinner, B. F. (1938). *The behavior of organisms: An experimental analysis.* Upper Saddle River, NJ: Prentice Hall.

Skinner, B. F. (1948). *Walden Two.* New York: Macmillan.

Skinner, B. F. (1953). *Science and human behavior.* New York: Macmillan.

Skinner, B. F. (1967). Autobiography. In E. G. Boring & G. Lindzey (Eds.), *A history of psychology in autobiography* (Vol. 5, pp. 387–413). New York: Appleton-Century-Crofts.

Skinner, B. F. (1971). *Beyond freedom and dignity.* New York: Knopf.

Skinner, B. F. (1974). *About behaviorism.* New York: Knopf.

Skinner, B. F. (1976). *Particulars of my life.* New York: McGraw-Hill.

Skinner, B. F., & Vaughan, M. E. (1983). *Enjoy old age.* New York: Norton.

Sprinthall, N. A. (1971). A program for psychological education: Some preliminary issues. *Journal of School Psychology, 9,* 373–382.

Thoresen, C. E., & Coates, T. J. (1980). What does it mean to be a behavior therapist? In C. E. Thoresen (Ed.), *The behavior therapist* (pp. 1–41). Pacific Grove, CA: Brooks/Cole.

Thoresen, C. E., & Mahoney, M. J. (1974). *Behavioral self-control.* New York: Holt, Rinehart, & Winston.

Wallace, W. A. (1986). *Theories of counseling and psychotherapy.* Boston: Allyn & Bacon.

Watson, J. B. (1913). Psychology as a behaviorist views it. *Psychological Review, 20,* 158–177.

Watson, J. B. (1925). *Behaviorism.* New York: Norton.

Watson, J. B., & Raynor, R. (1920). Conditioned emotional reactions. *Journal of Experimental Psychology, 3,* 1–14.

Wilson, G. T. (1995). Behavior therapy. In R. J. Corsini & D. Wedding (Eds.), *Current psychotherapies* (5th ed., pp. 197–228). Itasca, IL: Peacock.

Wolpe, J. (1958). *Psychotherapy by reciprocal inhibition building.* Stanford, CA: Stanford University Press.

Wubbolding, R. E. (1975). Practicing reality therapy. *Personnel and Guidance Journal, 53,* 164–165.

Wubbolding, R. E. (1988). *Using reality therapy.* New York: Harper/Collins.

Wubbolding, R. E. (1991). *Understanding reality therapy.* New York: Harper/Collins.

Wubbolding, R. E. (1994). The early years of control theory: Forerunners Marcus Aurelius & Norbert Wiener. *Journal of Reality Therapy, 13,* 51–54.

Wubbolding, R. E. (1996). *Basic concepts of reality therapy.* Los Angeles: Institute for Control Theory, Reality Therapy and Quality Management.

Wubbolding, R. E. (1998). *Cycle of managing, supervising, counseling, and coaching using reality therapy.* Cincinnati: Center for Reality Therapy.

Yates, A. J. (1970). *Behavior therapy.* New York: Wiley.

Zimbardo, P. G., & Leippe, M. R. (1991). *The psychology of attitude change and social influence.* Philadelphia: Temple University Press.

PART III

SKILLS AND SPECIALTIES IN THE PRACTICE OF COUNSELING

Professional counselors work in many different settings and in a variety of ways. Because of interest, background, and educational qualifications, many counselors choose to focus on specific populations, such as those people seeking marriage and family counseling or career counseling. Other counselors have more general domains. They see clients who have a wide range of problems and work with them accordingly.

Part III of this text focuses on how counselors function and what they do. It is premised on the belief that counselors, whether or not they specialize in an area, need to understand what the entire profession of counseling encompasses as well as their areas of expertise. Through such knowledge counselors will have an awareness that will make them effective in the overall process of helping and should serve them well in case they need to make a referral.

12

MARRIAGE AND FAMILY COUNSELING: SYSTEMS THEORY

◆

At thirty-five, with wife and child

a Ph.D.

and hopes as bright as a full moon

on a warm August night,

He took a role as a healing man

blending it with imagination,

necessary change and common sense

To make more than an image on an eye lens

of a small figure running quickly up steps;

Quietly he traveled

like one who holds a candle to darkness

and questions its power

So that with heavy years, long walks,

shared love, and additional births

He became as a seasoned actor,

who, forgetting his lines in the silence,

stepped upstage and without prompting

lived them.

From "Without Applause," by S. T. Gladding, 1974, Personnel and Guidance Journal, 52, *p. 586. © 1974 by ACA.*
Reprinted with permission. No further reproduction authorized without written permission of the American
Counseling Association.

Marital relations and family life are rooted in the antiquity of human society. Whether arranged by a family or the couple themselves, men and women have paired together in unions sanctioned by the religion and society for economic, societal, and procreation reasons. The terms marriage *and* family *have distinct connotations in different societies. Marriage is generally seen as a socially sanctioned union between two adults, whereas the U.S. Bureau of the Census (1991) defines a family as "a group of two or more persons related by birth, marriage, or adoption and residing together in a household" (p. 5). These definitions of* marriage *and* family *allow for maximum flexibility and can encompass a wide variety of forms.*

The strong interest in marriage and family counseling today is partly due to the rapid change in American family life since World War II. For example, in the mid-1990s, the Census Bureau reported the following statistics (Associated Press, 1994):

Family households in the United States constitute about 71% of all households (down from 81% in 1970).

The majority of American family households do not have children younger than 18 (the opposite of 1970).

There are 10.9 million single parents raising children (up from 3.8 million in 1970).

In addition, only about half of the 67 million children in the United States lived in traditional nuclear families, defined as a married couple and their shared offspring (Usdansky, 1994). The rest live in single-parent or blended (stepfamily) households.

The strains on marriages and families are further complicated by "high family mobility, the fragility of the husband-wife relationship, . . . two working parents, [and] decreased attention to parenting" (Hackney & Wrenn, 1990, p. 10). A high divorce rate, an increase in out-of-wedlock births, substantial cohabitation, and an increase in selecting a single lifestyle further attest to changes in the American family. Marriage and family life require commitment and hard work in the best of times and can be extremely difficult when unsettling changes are sanctioned by society at large (Napier, 1988).

Another major reason for the popularity of marriage and family counseling is the realization that persons are directly affected by how their families function (Goldenberg & Goldenberg, 1998). For instance, chaotic families produce offspring who have difficulty relating to others because of distance, whereas enmeshed families have children who have difficulty leaving home. Family counseling is economical in addressing family problems. Its encompassing nature makes it intrinsically appealing. Thus, the specialty attracts many counselors who wish to work on complex, multifaceted levels in the most effective way possible.

The profession of marriage and family counseling is relatively new (Framo, 1996). Its substantial beginnings are traced to the 1940s and early 1950s, but its real growth occurred in the late 1970s and the 1980s (Nichols, 1993). It differs from individual and group counseling in both emphasis and clientele (Gladding, 1999; Hines, 1988; Trotzer, 1988). For instance, most approaches to marriage and family counseling concentrate on making changes in the internal or external systems of the family, whereas individual and group counseling focus primarily on intra- and interpersonal changes. It is interesting to note that the rise of marriage and family counseling closely followed dramatic changes in the form, composition, structure, and emphasis of the American family: from a primarily nuclear unit to a complex and varied institution (Markowitz, 1994).

Some of the theories employed in marriage and family counseling are similar to those used in other settings, but many are completely different. This chapter examines the genesis and development of marriage and family counseling along with various family life forms related to the family life cycle. It also summarily delineates and compares major theoretical viewpoints.

The Beginnings of Marriage and Family Counseling

At least eight separate events have influenced the formation of marriage and family counseling since World War II. These developments and interactions have set the stage for an entirely new way of conceptualizing and working with couples and families.

Developments in Psychoanalysis

Psychoanalytic therapists began to extend their approach to include a family orientation in the late 1940s. The work of Nathan Ackerman (1958) was especially important in focusing the attention of psychoanalysis on family units. Before Ackerman, psychoanalysts had purposely excluded family members from the treatment of individual clients for fear that family involvement would be disruptive. Ackerman applied psychoanalytic practices to the treatment of families and made family therapy respected in the profession of psychiatry.

General Systems Theory

The originator of general systems theory was Ludwig von Bertalanffy (1968), a biologist. According to the theory, any living organism, including a family, is composed of interacting components—that is, people that mutually affect one another. Three basic assumptions distinguish systems theory from other counseling approaches: (a) causality is interpersonal, (b) "psychosocial systems are best understood as repeated patterns of interpersonal interaction," and (c) "symptomatic behaviors must . . . be understood from an interactional viewpoint" (Sexton, 1994, p. 250). Thus, the focus in general systems theory is on how the interaction of parts influences the operation of the system as a whole. For example, if one person in a family, such as a single parent, is not functioning up to capacity, the entire family system, including the children, will have difficulty carrying out tasks (Carnegie Task Force on Meeting the Needs of Young Children, 1994).

Circular causality is one of the main concepts introduced by this theory: the idea that events are related through a series of interacting feedback loops. By viewing family operations in this way, family dysfunctionality or health is shifted from an individual to the family unit itself. *Scapegoating* (in which one person is singled out as the cause of the family's problems) and *linear causality* (in which one action is seen as the cause of another) are eliminated.

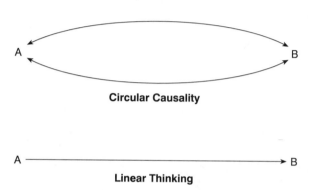

Circular Causality Versus Linear Thinking

Circular Causality

Linear Thinking

Schizophrenia and Families

Three main teams of researchers conducted pioneer studies in the area of family dynamics and the etiology of schizophrenia: the Gregory Bateson group (Bateson, Jackson, Haley, & Weakland, 1956) in Palo Alto, California; the Theodore Lidz group (Lidz, Cornelison, Fleck, & Terry, 1957) at Yale; and the Murray Bowen and Lyman Wynne groups (Bowen, 1960; Wynne, Ryckoff, Day, & Hirsch, 1958) at the National Institute of Mental Health (NIMH). All observed how couples and families functioned when a family member was diagnosed as schizophrenic. Several observations and ideas were generated, but among the most important concepts to emerge were double bind, pseudomutuality, and marital schism and skewness.

In a *double bind,* a person receives two contradictory messages at the same time and is unable to follow both. Physical and psychological symptoms (e.g., headaches, withdrawal) or even schizophrenic behavior develop as a way to lessen tension and escape. *Pseudomutuality* is a facade of family harmony that covers underlying tension between family members. *Marital schism* is overt marital conflict; *marital skewness* is a pathological marriage in which one partner dominates the other.

Emergence of Marriage Counseling

Early pioneers in marriage counseling, such as Paul Popenoe, Ernest Groves, Emily Mudd, and Abraham and Hannah Stone, were instrumental in establishing the American Association of Marriage Counselors in 1942 (Nichols, 1993). That fledgling organization grew in time to become the American Association of Marriage and Family Therapists (AAMFT). These pioneers' focus on the marriage relationship, rather than just the individuals involved, was important. The new emphasis meant that three entities were considered in a marriage relationship: two individuals and one couple. Early marriage counseling set a precedent for seeing couples together in conjoint sessions.

Growth of the Child Guidance Movement

Child guidance clinics, whose origins are based in Adlerian theory, concentrate on the treatment and prevention of emotional disorders in children through an interdisciplinary approach. Parents, as well as children, have traditionally been treated in clinics by teams of specialists from the fields of psychiatry, psychology, and social work. Although early research in this area tended to focus on parental behavior such as maternal overprotectiveness, clinicians eventually began to concentrate on the family as a whole (Levy, 1943).

Emergence of Group Counseling

The innovative ideas of the 1940s and 50s, which emerged from small group-behavior laboratories such as the National Training Laboratory (NTL) in Bethel, Maine, and the Tavistock Institute of Human Relations in London, were especially important to the development of marriage and family counseling. Experiences in group settings showed the powerful influence of groups on individuals and how a change in the membership or functioning of a group greatly affects its outcome. Techniques developed in psychodrama and Gestalt therapy, such as sculpting and choreography, further influenced work in marriage and family counseling. Some practitioners (e.g., Bell, 1975, 1976) even started treating families as a group and began the practice of couple/family group counseling (Ohlsen, 1979, 1982).

Postwar Changes

At the end of World War II, the United States experienced an unsettling readjustment from war to peace that manifested itself in three trends that had an impact on the family (Walsh, 1993). Along with the baby boom in 1946 came a sharp upturn in the number of divorces: 50% to 65% of all couples who married eventually dissolved their marriages (Martin & Bumpass, 1989; Whitehead, 1997). Further, starting in the 1960s, more women sought employment outside the home. By the mid-1980s, almost half the workforce was composed of women, many of them working mothers. A third trend, the expansion of the life span, also had an impact on family life. Couples found themselves living with the same partners longer than at any previous time in history. The need to work with families and individuals who were affected by these changes brought researchers, practitioners, and theorists together.

Multicultural Counseling

The most recent trend to influence marriage and family counseling is multiculturalism (McGoldrick, Giordano, & Pearce, 1996). Before the early 1980s, little attention was given to culture and ethnicity in family life. But the publication of *Ethnicity and Family Therapy* (McGoldrick, Pearce, & Giordano, 1982) raised the awareness of many marriage and family counselors about the importance of cultural background in treating families. Since the book's publication and its most recent update (McGoldrick et al., 1996), the concept of culture has broadened beyond the realm of ethnicity. Included in the idea of culture today are *inherited cultures* (e.g., ethnicity, nationality, religion, groupings such as baby boomers) and *acquired cultures* (learned habits, such as those of being a counselor). "The multiculturalism of the 90s has gone beyond encouraging individuals to rediscover their roots" (Markowitz, 1994, p. 23). Instead, it is aimed at exposing the link between people's culture and their behaviors within families and society.

Associations, Education, and Research

Interest in marriage and family counseling has grown rapidly since the 1970s, especially in regard to the number of individuals receiving training in this specialty. Four major professional associations attract marriage and family clinicians. The largest (over 22,000 members) and oldest (established 1942) is the American Association for Marriage and Family Therapy (AAMFT). The second association, the International Association of Marriage and Family Counselors (IAMFC), a division within the American Counseling Association (ACA), was chartered in 1986. In the late 1990s, it was the fastest-growing division within the ACA, with about 8,000 members. The third association, Division 43 (Family Psychology), a division within the American Psychological Association (APA), was formed in 1984 and has increasingly attracted psychologists to work with families. At the beginning of the 21st century it had over 3,000 members. The fourth association is the American Family Therapy Association (AFTA), formed in 1977. It is identified as an academy of about 1,000 advanced professionals interested in the exchange of ideas (Gladding, 1998).

Both the AAMFT and IAMFC have established guidelines for training professionals in working with couples and families. The AAMFT standards are drawn up and administered by the Commission on Accreditation for Marriage and Family Therapy Education (CAMFTE); those for the IAMFC are handled through the Council for Accreditation of Counseling and Related Educational Programs (CACREP). A minimum of a master's degree is required for entering this specialty, although debate persists over the exact content and sequencing of courses.

Regardless of professional affiliation and curriculum background, professionals are attracted to marriage and family counseling largely owing to a societal need for the specialty and its growing research base. Gurman and Kniskern (1981) report that approximately 50& of all problems brought to counselors are related to marriage and family issues. Unemployment, poor school performance, spouse abuse, depression, rebellion, and self-concept issues are just a few of the many situations that can be dealt with from this perspective. Okun (1984) notes that individual development dovetails with family and career issues and that each one impacts the resolution of the other in a systemic manner. Bratcher (1982) comments on the interrelatedness of career and family development, recommending the use of family systems theory for experienced counselors working with individuals seeking career counseling.

Research studies summarized by Doherty and Simmons (1996), Gurman and Kniskern (1981), Haber (1983), Pinsof and Wynne (1995), and Wohlman and Stricker (1983) report a number of interesting findings. First, family counseling interventions are at least as effective as individual interventions for most client complaints and lead to significantly greater durability of change. Second, some forms of family counseling (e.g., using structural-strategic family therapy with substance abusers) are more effective in treating problems than other counseling approaches. Third, the presence of both parents, especially noncompliant fathers, in family counseling situations greatly improves the chances for success. Similarly, the effectiveness of marriage counseling when both partners meet conjointly with the counselor is nearly twice that of counselors working with just one spouse. Fourth, when marriage and family counseling services are not offered to couples conjointly or to families systemically, the results of the intervention may be negative and problems may worsen. Finally, there is high client satisfaction from those who receive marital and family counseling services, with over 97% rating the services they received from good to excellent. Overall, the basic argument for employing marriage and family counseling is its proven efficiency. This form of treatment is logical, fast, satisfactory, and economical.

Family Life and the Family Life Cycle

Family life and the growth and developments that take place within it are at the heart of marriage and family counseling. The *family life cycle* is the name given to the stages a family goes through as it evolves over the years. These stages sometimes parallel and complement those in the individual life cycle (see Erikson, 1959; Levinson, 1978), but often they are unique because of the number of people involved and the diversity of tasks to be accomplished. Becvar and Becvar (1996) outline a nine-stage cycle that begins with the unattached adult and continues through retirement (Table 12.1).

Some families and family members are more "on time" in achieving stage-critical tasks that go with the family life cycle and their own personal cycle of growth. In such cases, a better sense of well-being is achieved (Carter & McGoldrick, 1988). Regardless of timing, all families have to deal with *family cohesion* (emotional bonding) and *family adaptability* (ability to be flexible and change). These two dimensions each have four levels, represented by Olson (1986) in the circumplex model of marital and family systems (see Figure 12.1). "The two dimensions are curvilinear in that families that apparently are very high or very low on both dimensions seem dysfunctional, whereas families that are balanced seem to function more adequately" (Maynard & Olson, 1987, p. 502).

Families that are most successful, functional, happy, and strong are not only balanced but committed, appreciate each other, spend time together, have good communication patterns, have a high degree of religious orientation, and are able to deal with crisis in a positive manner (Stinnett, 1998; Stinnett & DeFrain, 1985).

According to Wilcoxon (1985), marriage and family counselors need to be aware of the different stages within the family while staying attuned to developmental tasks of individual members. When counselors are sensitive to individual family members and the family as a whole, they are able to realize that some individual manifestations, such as depression (Lopez, 1986), career indecisiveness (Kinnier, Brigman, & Noble, 1990), and substance abuse (West, Hosie, & Zarski, 1987), are related to family structure and functioning. Consequently, they are able to be more inclusive in their treatment plans.

When evaluating family patterns and the mental health of everyone involved, it is crucial that an assessment be based on the form and developmental stage of the family constellation.

Table 12.1 Stages of the family life cycle

	Stage	Emotion	Stage-Critical Tasks
1.	Unattached adult	Accepting parent-offspring separation	a. Differentiation from family of origin b. Development of peer relations c. Initiation of career
2.	Newly married	Commitment to the marriage	a. Formation of marital system b. Making room for spouse with family and friends c. Adjusting career demands
3.	Childbearing	Accepting new members into the system	a. Adjusting marriage to make room for child b. Taking on parenting roles c. Making room for grandparents
4.	Preschool-age child	Accepting the new personality	a. Adjusting family to the needs of specific child(ren) b. Coping with energy drain and lack of privacy c. Taking time out to be a couple
5.	School-age child	Allowing child to establish relationships outside the family	a. Extending family/society interactions b. Encouraging the child's educational progress c. Dealing with increased activities and time demands
6.	Teenage child	Increasing flexibility of family boundaries to allow independence	a. Shifting the balance in the parent-child relationship b. Refocusing on mid-life career and marital issues c. Dealing with increasing concerns for older generation
7.	Launching center	Accepting exits from and entries into the family	a. Releasing adult children into work, college, marriage b. Maintaining supportive home base c. Accepting occasional returns of adult children
8.	Middle-aged adult	Letting go of children and facing each other	a. Rebuilding the marriage b. Welcoming children's spouses, grandchildren into family c. Dealing with aging of one's own parents
9.	Retirement	Accepting retirement and old age	a. Maintaining individual and couple functioning b. Supporting middle generation c. Coping with death of parents, spouse d. Closing or adapting family home

Source: From *Family Therapy: A Systematic Integration* (pp. 128–129), by Dorothy Stroh Becvar and Raphael J. Becvar. © 1993 by Allyn & Bacon. All rights reserved. Reprinted with permission.

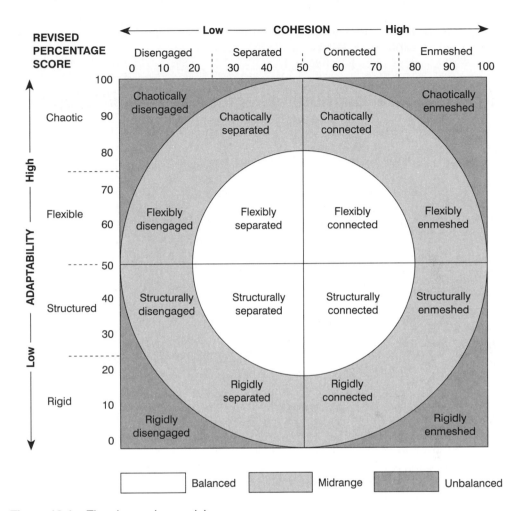

Figure 12.1 The circumplex model
Source: From Prepare/Enrich, Inc., David H. Olson, president, Minneapolis, MN. © 1979 (rev. 1986). Reprinted with permission.

To facilitate this process, Carter and McGoldrick (1988) propose sets of developmental tasks for traditional and nontraditional families, such as those headed by single parents or blended families. It is important to note that nontraditional families are not pathological because of their differences; they are merely on a different schedule of growth and development.

Bowen (1978) suggests terms such as *enmeshment* and *triangulation* to describe family dysfunctionality regardless of the family form. (*Enmeshment* refers to family environments in which members are overly dependent on each other or are undifferentiated. *Triangulation* describes family fusion situations in which one person is pulled in two different directions by the other members of the triangle.) Counselors who effectively work with couples and families have guidelines for determining how, where, when, or whether to intervene in the family process. They do not fail to act (e.g., neglect to engage everyone in the therapeutic process), nor do they overreact (perhaps place too much emphasis on verbal expression) (Gladding, 1998).

Marriage/Family Counseling versus Individual/Group Counseling

There are similarities and differences in the approaches to marriage or family counseling and individual or group counseling. A major similarity centers on theories. Some theories used in individual or group counseling (e.g., the person-centered approach, Gestalt therapy, Adlerian counseling, reality therapy, transactional analysis) are used with couples and families (Horne & Passmore, 1991). Other approaches (e.g., structural, strategic, solution-focused family therapy) are unique to marriage and family counseling. Counselors must learn about additional theorists, terms, and theories as well as new applications of previous theories to become skilled at working with couples or families.

Marriage or family counseling and individual counseling share a number of assumptions. For instance, both recognize the importance the family plays in the individual's life, both focus on problem behaviors and conflicts between the individual and the environment, and both are developmental. A difference is that individual counseling usually treats the person outside his or her family, whereas marriage or family counseling generally includes the involvement of other family members. Further, marriage and family counseling works at resolving issues within the family as a way of helping individual members better cope with the environment (Nichols & Schwartz, 1998).

Marriage and family counseling sessions are similar to those in group counseling in organization, basic dynamics, and stage development. Furthermore, both types of counseling have an interpersonal emphasis. But the family is not like a typical group, although a knowledge of group process may be useful. For example, family members are not equal in status and power. In addition, families may perpetuate myths, whereas groups are initially more objective in dealing with events. More emotional baggage is also carried among family members than members of another type of group because the arrangement in a family is not limited in time and is related to sex roles and affective bonds that have a long history (Becvar, 1982). While the family may be a group, it is not well suited to work that takes place only through group theory.

Finally, the emphasis of marriage and family counseling is generally on dynamics as opposed to linear causality as in much individual and some group counseling. In other words, the dynamics behind marriage and family counseling generally differ from the other two types of counseling. In making the transition from an individual perspective to a family orientation, Resnikoff (1981) stresses specific questions that counselors should ask themselves to understand family functioning and dynamics. By asking the right questions, the counselor becomes more attuned to the family as a client and how best to work with it.

- What is the outward appearance of the family?
- What repetitive, nonproductive sequences are noticeable?
- What is the basic feeling state in the family, and who carries it?
- What individual roles reinforce family resistance, and what are the most prevalent family defenses?

- How are family members differentiated from one another, and what are the subgroup boundaries?
- What part of the life cycle is the family experiencing, and what are its problem-solving methods?

Counselors working with couples also ask many of these questions.

Marriage and Couples Counseling

Persons seek marriage and couples counseling for a wide variety of reasons, including finances, children, fidelity, communication, and compatibility. Almost any situation can serve as the impetus to seek help.

Regardless of who initiates the request, it is crucial that the counselor see both members of the couple from the beginning. Whitaker (1977) notes that if a counselor is not able to structure the situation in this way, he or she will probably not help the couple and may do harm. Trying to treat one spouse alone for even one or two sessions increases the other spouse's resistance to counseling and his or her anxiety. Moreover, if one member of a couple tries to change without the other's knowledge or support, conflict is bound to ensue. Wilcoxon and Fenell (1983) have developed a therapist-initiated letter explaining the process of marriage therapy to an absent partner. It outlines the perils of treating just one partner and is sent by counselors to the nonattending partner to help him or her see the possibilities that can accrue when working with both members of the couple (see Figure 12.2).

After both partners have decided to enter marriage and couples counseling, the counselor may take a variety of approaches. Five of the main approaches are psychoanalytic, social-cognitive, Bowen family systems, structural-strategic, and rational emotive behavior (Ellis, Sichel, Yeager, DiMattia, & DiGuiseppe, 1989; Jacobson & Gurman, 1996). Although a number of other treatment methods exist, they will not be covered here because of their lack of proven effectiveness.

Psychoanalytic Theory

Psychoanalytically based marriage counseling is premised on the *theory of object relations,* which addresses how relationships are developed across the generations (Slipp, 1988). *Objects* are significant others in one's environment, such as a mother with whom children form an interactive emotional bond. Preferences for certain objects as opposed to others are developed in early childhood in parent-child interactions. Individuals bring these unconscious forces into a marriage relationship.

To help the marriage, the counselor focuses with each partner on obtaining emotional insight into early parent-child relationships. The treatment may be both individual and conjoint. In the process, the counselor uses *transference* in which each partner restructures internally based perceptions of, expectations of, and reactions to self and others and projects them onto the counselor. Other techniques include taking individual histories of each partner and a history of the marriage relationship. Interpretation, dream work, and an analysis of resistance are often incorporated into the treatment (Baruth & Huber, 1984).

(Date)

Mr. John Jones
111 Smith Street
Anytown, USA 00000

Dear Mr. Jones,

As you may know, your wife, Jill, has requested therapy services for difficulties related to your marriage. However, she has stated that you do not wish to participate in marital therapy sessions.

As a professional marriage therapist, I have an obligation to inform each of you of the possible outcome of marital therapy services to only one spouse. The available research indicates that one-spouse marital therapy has resulted in reported increases in marital stress and dissatisfaction for both spouses in the marriage. On the other hand, many couples have reported that marital therapy which includes both spouses has been helpful in reducing marital stress and enhancing marital satisfaction.

These findings reflect general tendencies in marital research and are not absolute in nature. However, it is important for you and Jill to be informed of potential consequences which might occur through marital therapy in which only your spouse attends. Knowing this information, you may choose a course of action which best suits your intentions.

After careful consideration of this information, I ask that you and Jill discuss your options regarding future therapy services. In this way, all parties will have a clear understanding of another's intentions regarding your relationship.

As a homework assignment for Jill, I have asked that each of you read this letter and sign in the spaces provided below to verify your understanding of the potential consequences to your relationship by continuing one-spouse marital therapy. If you are interested in joining Jill for marital therapy, in addition to your signature below, please contact my office to indicate your intentions. If not, simply sign below and have Jill return the letter at our next therapy session. I appreciate your cooperation in this matter.

Sincerely,

Therapist X
_____

We verify by our signatures below that we have discussed and understand the potential implications of continued marital therapy with only one spouse in attendance.

_____   _____
Attending Spouse   Date

_____   _____
Non-Attending Spouse   Date

Figure 12.2   Letter to engage a nonattending spouse

Source: From "Engaging the Non-Attending Spouse in Marital Therapy through the Use of a Therapist-Initiated Written Communication," by A. Wilcoxon and D. Fennel, pp. 199–203. Reprinted from Vol. 9, No. 2 of the *Journal of Marital and Family Therapy.* © 1983 by American Association for Marriage and Family Therapy. Reprinted with permission.

Catharsis, the expression of pent-up emotion, is a must. The goal of this approach is for individuals and couples to gain new insights into their lives and change their behaviors.

Social-Cognitive Theory

Social-cognitive theory is a form of behaviorism that stresses learning through modeling and imitation (Bandura, 1977). Sometimes it is referred to as *social-learning*. It suggests that behaviors are learned through observing others and that marriage partners either have a deficit or excess of needed behaviors. A deficit may be the result of one or both partners' never having witnessed a particular skill, such as how to fight fairly. An excess may come as a result of one or both partners' thinking that just a little more of a certain behavior will solve problems. For example, one partner tells the other everything he or she likes and does not like in the marriage in the hope that honest communication will be beneficial. While such honesty may be admired, research shows that marriages grow more through positive reciprocity than negative feedback (Gottman, 1994). Select communication and interaction with one's spouse seem to work best.

The focus in social-cognitive marriage counseling is on skill building in the present. Events in the past that have disrupted the marriage may be recognized but receive little focus. Within the treatment process, counselors may use a wide variety of behavioral strategies to help couples change, such as self-reports, observations, communication enhancement training exercises, contracting, and homework assignments (Stuart, 1980). Much of social-cognitive theory is based on linear thinking.

Bowen Family Systems Theory

The focus of Bowen family systems marital theory is on *differentiation,* or distinguishing one's thoughts from one's emotions and oneself from others (Kerr & Bowen, 1988). Couples marry at the same level of emotional maturity, with those who are less mature being prone to have a more difficult time in their marriage relationships than those who are more mature. When a great deal of friction exists in a marriage, the less mature partners tend to display a high degree of *fusion* (undifferentiated emotional togetherness) or *cutoff* (physical or psychological avoidance). They have not separated themselves from their families of origin in a healthy way, nor have they formed a stable self-concept. When they are stressed as persons within the marriage, they tend to *triangulate* (focus on a third party) (Papero, 1996). The third party can be the marriage itself, a child, or even a somatic complaint. Regardless, it leads to unproductive couple interactions.

Techniques in this approach focus on ways to differentiate oneself from one's extended family-of-origin system. In the process, there is an attempt to create an individuated person with a healthy self-concept who can couple and not experience undue anxiety every time the relationship becomes stressful. Ways of achieving this goal include assessment of self and family through a *genogram* (a three-generational family tree) and a focus on cognitive processes, such as asking content-based questions of one's family (Bowen, 1976). The sequencing and pacing of this process differ from spouse to spouse, but the therapeutic interaction takes place with both spouses together.

Structural-Strategic Theory

Structural-strategic theory is based on the belief that when dysfunctional symptoms occur in a marriage, they are an attempt to help couples adapt. This approach sees problems as occurring within a developmental framework of the family life cycle. Marital difficulties are generated by the system the couple is in, and these symptoms consequently help maintain the marital system in which they operate (Todd, 1986). Therefore, the job of a structural-strategic marriage counselor is to get couples to try new behaviors because their old behaviors are not working. Usually, a specific behavior is targeted for change. If this behavior can be modified, it will tend to have a spillover effect, helping couples make other behavior changes as well.

To bring about change, counselors are active, direct, and goal oriented as well as problem focused, pragmatic, and brief (Todd, 1986). *Relabeling* (giving a new perspective to a behavior) is frequently used, as are *paradoxing* (insisting on just the opposite of what one wants) and *prescribing the symptom* (having the couple display voluntarily what they had previously manifested involuntarily, such as fighting). The counselor often asks clients to pretend to make changes or carry out homework assignments (Madanes, 1984; Minuchin, 1974). The idea behind this approach is to bring about new functional behaviors that will help couples achieve a specific goal.

Rational Emotive Behavior Theory (REBT)

The premise behind REBT is that couples, like individuals, often become disturbed because of what they think rather than because of specific actions that occur in the relationship. *Irrational thinking* that is "highly exaggerated, inappropriately rigid, illogical, and especially absolutist" is what leads to neurosis and relationship disturbance (Ellis et al., 1989, p. 17). To combat disturbances, couples need to challenge and change their belief systems about activating events; otherwise, they continue to "awfulize" and "catastrophize" about themselves and their marriage. The essence of this theory is what Ellis (1988) calls "double systems therapy," in which emphasis is placed on personal and family systems change.

As with individual counseling, the REBT counselor concentrates on thinking, but within a couples context. The focus is on helping individuals first and marriages second (Ellis et al., 1989). After assessing what is occurring with the couple, the REBT counselor works with them separately and together in the ABC method of REBT (see Chapter 5). A special emphasis is placed, however, on some particular marital problems, such as jealousy and sexuality.

Evaluation of Marriage and Couples Counseling

The theoretical basis for most marriage and couples counseling is not as strong as it is for family counseling, for several reasons. For example, many marriage and couples counselors are primarily practitioners, not researchers or writers. Moreover, until recently, marriage and couples counseling has been viewed as a subspecialty within family counseling; most research and theory have focused on families. However, marriage and couples counseling is now becoming a stronger discipline (Jacobson & Gurman, 1996).

Family Counseling

Families enter counseling for a number of reasons. Usually, there is an *identified patient* (IP) (an individual who is seen as the cause of trouble within the family structure) whom family members use as their ticket of entry. Most family counseling practitioners do not view one member of a family as the problem but instead work with the whole family system. Occasionally, family therapy is done from an individual perspective (Nichols, 1988).

Family counseling has expanded rapidly since the mid-1970s and encompasses many aspects of couples counseling. Seven of its main theoretical orientations will be covered here. Although a few family counselors are linearly based and work on cause-and-effect or constructivist perspective, most are not. Rather, the majority operate from a general systems framework and conceptualize the family as an open system that evolves over the family life cycle in a sociocultural context. Functional families follow rules and are flexible in meeting the demands of family members and outside agencies. Family systems counselors stress the idea of circular causality. They also emphasize the following concepts:

- *Nonsummativity.* The family is greater than the sum of its parts. It is necessary to examine the patterns within a family rather than the actions of any specific member alone.
- *Equifinality.* The same origin may lead to different outcomes, and the same outcome may result from different origins. Thus, the family that experiences a natural disaster may become stronger or weaker as a result. Likewise, healthy families may have quite dissimilar backgrounds. Therefore, treatment focuses on interactional family patterns rather than particular conditions or events.
- *Communication.* All behavior is seen as communicative. It is important to attend to the two functions of interpersonal messages: *content* (factual information) and *relationship* (how the message is to be understood). The *what* of a message is conveyed by how it is delivered.
- *Family rules.* A family's functioning is based on explicit and implicit rules. Family rules provide expectations about roles and actions that govern family life. Most families operate on a small set of predictable rules, a pattern known as the *redundancy principle.* To help families change dysfunctional ways of working, family counselors have to help them define or expand the rules under which they operate.
- *Morphogenesis.* The ability of the family to modify its functioning to meet the changing demands of internal and external factors is known as morphogenesis. Morphogenesis usually requires a *second-order change* (the ability to make an entirely new response) rather than a *first-order change* (continuing to do more of the same things that have worked previously) (Watzlawick, Weakland, & Fisch, 1974). Instead of just talking, family members may need to try new ways of behaving.
- *Homeostasis.* Like biological organisms, families have a tendency to remain in a steady, stable state of equilibrium unless otherwise forced to change. When a family member unbalances the family through his or her actions, other members quickly try to rectify the situation through negative feedback. The model of functioning can be compared to a furnace, which comes on when a house falls below a set temperature and cuts off once the temperature is reached. Sometimes homeostasis can be advanta-

geous in helping a family achieve life-cycle goals, but often it prevents the family from moving on to another stage in its development.

Counselors who operate from a family systems approach work according to the concepts just listed. For instance, if family rules are covert and cause confusion, the counselor helps the family make these regulations overt and clear. All members of the family are engaged in the process so that communication channels are opened. Often, a genogram is constructed to help family members and the counselor detect intergenerational patterns of family functioning that have an impact on the present (McGoldrick & Gerson, 1985) (see Figure 12.3).

For a genogram, three generations of the family should be drawn. Names, dates of birth, marriage, separation, and divorce should be indicated, along with basic information such as current age and occupation. A genogram can also be used in a multicultural context to assess the worldview and cultural factors that often influence family members' behaviors (Thomas, 1998). Overall, "the genogram appears to provide an effective and personally meaningful strategy to facilitate systems thinking," especially by new client fami-

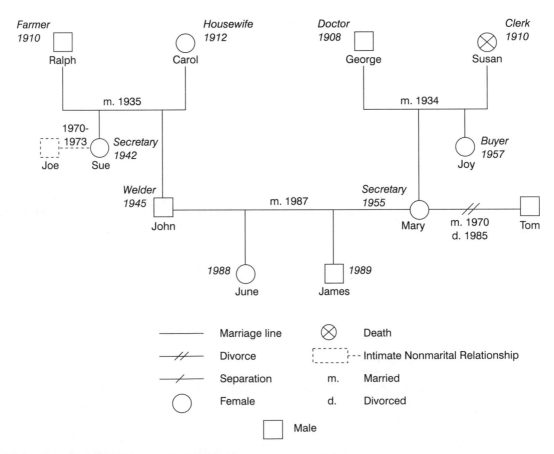

Figure 12.3   Family genogram (basic structure)

lies and counselors who are just beginning to work with families (Pistole, 1997, p. 339). For a more thorough explanation of genograms, McGoldrick and Gerson's (1985) book is an excellent place to begin.

Psychodynamic Family Counseling

As traditionally practiced, psychodynamic counseling concentrates on individuals rather than social systems such as the family. Ackerman (1966), however, broke with tradition by working with intact families. He believed that family difficulties resulted from *interlocking pathologies* (unconscious and dysfunctional ways of acting) present in the couple and family system. An initial goal of psychodynamic family counseling is to change the personalities of family members so they can work with one another in a healthy and productive way. Nichols and Schwartz (1998) point out that psychodynamic counselors who follow Ackerman most often employ an eclectic mix of psychoanalytic and systems concepts.

A unique contribution that psychodynamic practitioners have made to family counseling is the use of object relations as a primary emphasis in treatment. Object relations, as mentioned previously, are internalized residues of early parent-child interactions. In dysfunctional families, object relations continue to exert a negative influence in present interpersonal relationships. Dysfunctional families are those with a greater degree of unconscious, unresolved conflict, or loss (Paul & Paul, 1975). Three main ways of working with these families are developing a stronger parent coalition, defining and maintaining generation boundaries, and modeling sex-linked roles (Walsh, 1993).

Overall, psychodynamic family counselors concentrate on (a) helping family members obtain insight and resolve family-of-origin conflicts or losses, (b) eliminating distorted projections, (c) reconstructing relationships, and (d) promoting individual and family growth. Prominent practitioners associated with this approach include Nathan Ackerman, James Framo, Theodore Lidz, and Norman Paul.

Experiential Family Counseling

Experientialist family counselors are concerned as much with individuals as with family systems and consider intrapsychic problems when explaining psychopathology. Unlike most other family counselors, experientialists describe patterns of family dysfunction using the individual or a dyad as the unit of analysis. They believe that dysfunctional families are made up of people who are incapable of autonomy or real intimacy—that is, people who are alienated from themselves and others. These individuals are emotionally dead. Therefore, the goal of counseling is growth and opening family members to new experiences.

Two prominent practitioners in the experiential school are Virginia Satir and Carl Whitaker. Satir (1967, 1972) stresses the importance of clear communications, while Whitaker (1976, 1977) is an existential maverick whose interactions with families have sometimes been unconventional but always very creative. Satir believes that when family members are under stress they may handle their communications in one of four nonproductive roles:

- *Placater:* agrees and tries to please
- *Blamer:* dominates and finds fault

- *Responsible analyzer:* remains emotionally detached and intellectual
- *Distractor:* interrupts and constantly chatters about irrelevant topics

Satir helps families by teaching members to own personal feelings and express them clearly, a process she calls *leveling*. To promote intimacy, individuals are instructed to listen to one another. Satir stresses the importance of obtaining and providing feedback and negotiating differences when they arise. Her primary focus is on communication skills. She uses experiential exercises and props to help families and their members become more aware.

Whitaker, who takes a less structured approach to working with families, represents the extreme side of the experiential school. He advocates nonrational, creative experiences and lets the form of his methods develop as he works. He is unconventional, sometimes using *absurdity* (a statement that is half true and even silly if followed out to its conclusion) in working with families. To be effective, Whitaker uses a cotherapist. He has been known to go to sleep, have a dream, and share it with a family. Messages that come from such events are hard for family members to dismiss or resist. Families begin to change their patterns of behaving and become more honest, open, and spontaneous with each other as a result. Overall, Whitaker (1989) emphasizes uncovering and using the unconscious life of the family.

Behavioral Family Counseling

Behavioral family counselors use theory techniques originally devised for treating individuals in their approach to working with families. With the exception of functional family therapists (e.g., Alexander & Parsons, 1982), they are nonsystemic in conceptualizing and clinically working with families. Instead, most behavioral family counselors stress the importance of learning. They emphasize the importance of family rules and skills training (Walsh, 1993) and believe that behaviors are determined by consequences rather than antecedents.

The goals of behavioral family counseling are specific and usually limited. Behaviorists try to modify troublesome behavior patterns to alleviate undesirable interactions. Much of their work focuses on changing dyadic interaction through teaching, modeling, and reinforcing new behaviors. Stuart (1998) has described a variation of behavior therapy with couples as "principled pragmatism." Behaviorists believe that change is best achieved through accelerating positive behavior than decelerating negative behavior. Most of their work is concentrated in three main areas: behavioral parent training (Patterson, 1971), behavioral marriage counseling (Stuart, 1980, 1998), and treatment of sexual dysfunctions (LoPiccolo, 1978; Masters & Johnson, 1970). A protocol for a routine first session in behaviorally oriented couples' therapy is presented in Figure 12.4.

Structural Family Counseling

Salvador Minuchin (1974), the founder of structural family counseling, defines *structure* as the informal way in which a family organizes itself and interacts. Structural family counseling practitioners advocate structural changes in the organization of the family unit, with particular attention on changing interactional patterns in subsystems of the family such as in the marital dyad and establishing clear boundaries among family members (Minuchin, Montalvo, Guerney, Rosman, & Schumer, 1967). The approach is based on general systems theory.

Prior to the first in-person contact, make first appointment through phone contact with both partners if possible, using this call to

1. Determine whether you have the skills needed to help the clients, whether they are suitable for your practice, and whether your approach is likely to be acceptable to them.
2. Explain the terms of your therapeutic contract (e.g., fees, hours, etc.).
3. Establish initial rapport with each by asking about and expressing interest in their concerns.

First Session

1. A. Ask the seemingly most relaxed partner for a brief (i.e., 5-minute) description of her or his personal history (including past major relationships).
   B. Ask other partner to do the same.
2. Devote approximately 5 minutes to asking both partners to describe how they met and how their relationship developed.
   A. Ask seemingly more committed partner to describe what first attracted him and/or her to the other.
   B. Ask other to do the same.
3. A. Devote approximately 5 minutes to asking the less committed partner to describe aspects of the current relationship that are pleasing and aspects he and/or she would like changed.
   B. Ask other to do the same.
4. Ask both partners about their commitment to stay together.
   A. If both are committed, explain the logic of treatment.
      1. Your use of the smart-client model in which you explain the principles guiding your work and then help them apply these principles to meet their goals.
      2. Your use of a series of mini-experiments in which they are coinvestigators and participants in an effort to learn which intervention techniques help.
      3. Your search for negotiated two-winner solutions to problems.
      4. The three stages of the therapy you offer.
         a. You begin by suggesting specific changes.
         b. Once they learn the principles, you then coach the partners to identify goals and plan actions.
         c. At the end of therapy, you serve as consultant on the changes that the partners have negotiated.
   B. If either partner is inclined to end the relationship, offer treatment as a means of reducing uncertainty, which can allow both to participate in the process of deciding their fate so that both are more likely to accept the outcome. Stress the importance of acting as if change were possible, interpreting these efforts as experiments rather than as signs of renewed commitment.
5. Solicit a commitment from both partners to begin the process of exploring interaction change, revising the agreement until it is acceptable to both.
6. Initiate caring days by framing it as helping the partners to draw closer and demonstrate that they can both begin to feel better if each will make small, positive behavior changes.
7. After the first session, identify areas of stress and develop a general plan for developing the necessary insights, understanding, and skills in each partner.

Figure 12.4 Protocol for routine first sessions in behaviorally oriented couples' therapy

Source: From "Updating Behavior Therapy with Couples," by R. B. Stuart, 1998, *Family Journal, 6,* p. 11, copyright © 1998 by American Association for Marriage and Family Therapy. Reprinted by permission of Sage Publications, Inc.

In working with families, structural family counselors join with the family in a position of leadership. They map within their minds the structure of the family and determine how it is stuck in a dysfunctional pattern. They then employ a number of techniques aimed at getting the family to change the way it operates (Minuchin & Fishman, 1981). One primary technique is to work with the family's interaction. When family members repeat nonproductive sequences of behavior or demonstrate a disengaged or enmeshed position in the family structure, the counselor will rearrange the physical environment so they have to act in a different way. The technique may be as simple as having people face each other when they talk.

Structural family counselors also use *reframing*, a technique that involves helping the family see its problem from a different and more positive perspective. For example, if a child is misbehaving, the behavior may be labeled "naughty" instead of "crazy." As a consequence, the child and his or her actions will be viewed as less pathological. By helping families change their structure, reframe their problems, establish a hierarchy with the parents in charge, and create clear (as opposed to diffuse or rigid) boundaries and appropriate ways of interacting, structuralists help families use resources within themselves to function in a productive and healthy way.

Strategic (Brief) Family Counseling

Jay Haley (1973), Cloe Madanes (1991), and the Milan Group (Selvini-Palazzoli, Boscolo, Cecchin, & Prata, 1978) are prominent leaders in the strategic school of family counseling. Strategic counselors take a systemic view of problem behaviors and focus on the process rather than the content of dysfunctional interactions. They strive to resolve presenting problems and pay little attention to instilling insight. They are brief therapists and limit the number of times families can see them.

One powerful technique is to *prescribe the symptom*. This approach places targeted behaviors, such as family fights, under the control of the counselor by making a behavior voluntary if family members comply and eliminating a behavior if the family group resists the counselor's instructions. Strategic family counselors *accept the presenting problems* of families and view symptoms as serving the positive purpose of communication.

The Milan Group often has families go through *ordeals*, such as traveling or suffering, during the treatment process. The idea is that if families have to make sacrifices to get better, then the long-term improvements of treatment are enhanced. A major aspect of strategic family counseling is the assignment of original *homework* tasks (often given in the form of prescriptions or directives) that are to be completed between sessions. Many strategic counselors work in teams. Overall, this treatment is quite pragmatic.

Solution-Focused Family Counseling

Solution-focused family counseling is both an extension of strategic family counseling and a distinct entity. It traces its roots to the work of Milton Erickson (1954), particularly his *utilization principle:* using whatever clients present in counseling "as a basis and means for client solutions and change" (Lawson, 1994, p. 244). Erickson felt that people have within themselves the resources and abilities to solve their own problems. "Additionally, Erickson . . . believed that a small change in one's behavior is often all that is necessary to lead to more profound changes in a problem context" (Lawson, 1994, p. 244). This viewpoint was adapted by Jay Haley and has been formulated into solution-focused family counseling by Steve deShazer and Bill O'Hanlon (deShazer, 1985, 1988; O'Hanlon & Weiner-Davis, 1989).

The essence of solution-focused family counseling is that clients create problems because of their perceptions, such as "I am always depressed." Counselors try to help clients get a different perspective on their situations by having them notice *exceptions* to the times when they are distressed. Client families are then directed toward solutions to situations that already exist in these exceptions (West, Bubenzer, Smith, & Hamm, 1997). Thus, the focus of sessions and homework is on positives and possibilities either now or in the future (Walter & Peller, 1992). One way of helping individuals change perspective (from concentrating on the negative to emphasizing the positive) is called the *miracle question,* which basically goes as follows: "Let's suppose tonight while you were sleeping a miracle happened that solved all the problems that brought you here. How would you know it? What would be different?" (deShazer, 1991).

Advantages of solution-focused family counseling include its brevity and its empowerment of client families (Fleming & Rickord, 1997). This approach also has great flexibility and excellent research in support of its effectiveness.

Narrative Family Counseling

Narrative family counseling, the newest family counseling approach to gain prominence, was originated by Michael White and David Epston (1990). It is a postmodern and social constructionist approach to change that sees counselors as collaborators and masters of asking questions (Walsh & Keenan, 1997). The approach is based on *narrative reasoning*, which is characterized by stories, meaningfulness, and liveliness. According to the narrative family viewpoint, "people live their lives by stories" (Kurtz & Tandy, 1995, p. 177). Therefore the emphasis in this approach is shifted to a narrative way of conceptualizing and interpreting the world.

The narrative approach emphasizes developing unique and alternative stories in the hope that families will come up with novel options and strategies for living. *Reauthoring* lives is a focus of treatment that makes change more possible (White, 1995). In changing their stories, families are encouraged to *externalize problems* to solve them. Externalization separates people from problems and objectifies difficulties so that the resources of a family can be focused on how a situation negatively impacting the family unit, such as depression or chaos, can be constructively addressed. Counselors send letters to families about their progress and formally celebrate the termination of their treatment. In the narrative approach blame is alleviated and dialogue is generated as everyone works to solve a common problem (Walsh & Keenan, 1997).

Summary and Conclusion

The professions of marriage and family counseling have grown rapidly since the 1940s for a number of reasons, including theory development, needs within the population, and proven research effectiveness. The field of marriage counseling is sometimes incorporated into family counseling models; but since the 1970s, it has become stronger as a separate entity. There are five main approaches to marriage counseling: psychoanalytic, social-cognitive, Bowen family systems, structural-strategic, and rational emotive behavior therapy (REBT). Family counseling has a wider range of approaches, but the dominant ones are psychodynamic, experiential, behavioral, structural, strategic (brief), solution focused, and narrative.

In working as either a marriage or a family counselor, the helping professional must be aware of the theoretical basis of his or her approach and keep in mind where marriage or family members are in their individual and family life cycles. Counselors must also realize how individual or group theories may complement or detract from work with families.

SUMMARY TABLE
Select Marriage and Family Counseling Approaches

Psychodyamic Family Theory

Theorists
Sigmund Freud, Nathan Ackerman, Ivan Boszormenyi-Nagy, James Framo, Theodore Lidz, Norman Paul, Lyman Wynne

Underlying Premises
Unconscious processes link family members together and influence individuals in the decisions about whom they marry. Objects (i.e., significant others in one's life) are identified with or rejected. Unconscious forces must be worked through.

Role of the Counselor
The counselor is a teacher and interpreter of experience.

Unit of Treatment
Individuals, sometimes the individuals within a family

Goals of Treatment
To break dysfunctional interactions within the family based on unconscious processes; to resolve individual dysfunctionality as well

Techniques
Transference, dream analysis, confrontation, focusing on strengths, life history

Unique Aspects
Concentrates on potency of unconscious in human behavior; examines basic defense mechanisms in family relations; offers in-depth treatment of dysfunctionality

Bowen Family Theory

Theorists
Murray Bowen, Michael Kerr

Underlying Premises
Theory and therapy are the same. Family patterns are likely to repeat. It is important to differentiate oneself from one's family of origin. Uncontrolled anxiety results in family dysfunctionality.

Role of the Counselor
The counselor acts as a coach and teacher and concentrates on boundary and differentiation issues.

Unit of Treatment
Individual or couple

Goals of Treatment
To prevent triangulation and help couples and individuals relate on a cognitive level; to stop dysfunctional repetitive intergenerational patterns of family relations

Techniques
Genograms, going home again, detriangulation, person-to-person relationships, differentiation of self

Unique Aspects
Emphasis on intergenerational relationships and repeating patterns; systemic, in-depth theory

Experiential Family Counseling

Theorists
Virginia Satir, Carl Whitaker, Fred Duhl, Bunny Duhl, Walter Kempler, Augustus Napier, David Keith, Susan Johnson, Peggy Papp

Underlying Premises
Family problems are rooted in suppression of feelings, rigidity, denial of impulses, lack of awareness, emotional deadness.

Role of the Counselor
Counselors use their own personalities. They must be open, spontaneous, empathic, and sensitive and must demonstrate caring and acceptance. They must deal with regression therapeutically and teach family members new skills that clearly communicate their feelings.

Unit of Treatment
Focuses on individuals and couple dyads, except for Whitaker, who concentrates on three-generational families

Goals of Treatment
To emphasize growth, change, creativity, flexibility, spontaneity, and playfulness; to make the covert overt; to increase emotional closeness and disrupt rigidity; to unlock defenses; to enhance self-esteem

Techniques
Family sculpting and choreography, clear communication skills, humor, family art therapy, role playing, family reconstruction; disregards theory and emphasizes intuitive spontaneity; shares feelings and creates an emotionally intense atmosphere; makes suggestions and gives directives

Unique Aspects
Promotes creativity and spontaneity in families; encourages family members to change roles and increase understanding of themselves and others; is humanistic and treats all members of the family as being equal in status; increases awareness of feelings within and among family members; encourages growth

Behavioral Family Counseling

Theorists
B. F. Skinner, John Watson, Richard Stuart, Norman Epstein, Neil Jacobson, Gerald Patterson, Robert Weiss, Gayola Margolin, Albert Bandura, Walter Mischel, William Masters, Virginia Johnson, Joseph Wolpe, Aaron Beck, Donald Meichenbaum, Ed Katkin

Underlying Premises
Behavior is maintained or eliminated by consequences. Maladaptive behaviors can be unlearned or modified. Adaptive behaviors can be learned. Likewise, cognitions are either rational or irrational. They can be modified and as a result bring about a change.

Role of the Counselor
Direct, careful assessment and intervention; the counselor is seen as a teacher, expert, and reinforcer, with a focus on presenting problems.

Unit of Treatment
Parent training, marriage relationship and couple communication, and the treatment of sexual dysfunctions; emphasis on dyadic interactions, except in functional family therapy

Goals of Treatment
To bring about behavioral changes by modifying the antecedents or consequences of an action; to pay special attention to modifying the consequences; to emphasize eliminating undesirable behavior and accelerating positive behavior; to teach social skills and prevent problems from reoccurring; to promote competence in individuals and couples and foster an understanding of the dynamics of behavior

Techniques
Operant conditioning, classical conditioning, social learning theory, and cognitive-behavioral strategies; techniques include systematic desensitization, positive reinforcement, intermittent reinforcement, generalization, fading, extinction, modeling, reciprocity, punishment, token economies, quid pro quo exchanges, charting, psychoeducational methods

Unique Aspects
Approaches are straightforward with attention paid to observations, measurements, and use of scientific

theory. They emphasize the treatment of presenting problems. A considerable amount of time is spent teaching new social skills and eliminating dysfunctional ones. The relationship is built on positive controls and enlightened education procedures rather than punishment. Behaviorism is a simple and pragmatic intervention with a variety of workable techniques (such as use of contracts). Excellent research data accompany these approaches and measure their effectiveness. Treatment is generally short-term.

Structural Family Theory

Theorists
Salvador Minuchin, Braulio Montalvo, Charles Fishman, Bernie Rosman, Harry Aponte, Duncan Stanton, Thomas Todd

Underlying Premises
Family functioning involves family structure, subsystems, and boundaries. Overt and covert rules and hierarchies must be understood and changed to help family adjust to new situations.

Role of the Counselor
Counselors map families mentally and work actively in counseling sessions. Like theater directors, they instruct families to interact through enactments and spontaneous sequences.

Unit of Treatment
The family is treated as a system or subsystem, yet individual needs are not ignored.

Goals of Treatment
To bring problematic behaviors out in the open so that counselors can observe and help change them; to bring about structural changes within families, such as organizational patterns and action sequences

Techniques
Joining, accommodating, restructuring, working with interaction (enactment, spontaneous behaviors), intensifying, unbalancing, reframing, shaping competence, making boundaries

Unique Aspects
First developed for families with low socioeconomic standing; very pragmatic; influential in getting the pro-

fession of psychiatry to respect family counseling as an approach to treatment; tenets and techniques stated clearly by Minuchin and others; effective in working with families of addicts, those with eating disorders, and suicidals; well researched, systemic, problem focused in the present, brief (generally less than 6 months); counselors and families active during the sessions

Strategic (Brief) and Solution-Focused Theories

Theorists
Strategic: Jay Haley, Cloe Madanes, Milton Erickson, Paul Watzlawick, John Weakland, Richard Fisch, Mara Selvini Palazzoli, Luigi Boscolo, Gianfranco Cecchin, Guiliana Pata, Karl Tomm, Lynn Hoffman, Peggy Papp, Olga Siverstein, Peggy Penn, Richard Rabkin, Joel Bergman, Carlos Sluzki

Solution-focused: Steve deShazer, Insoo Berg, Bill O'Hannon, Michele Weiner-Davis

Underlying Premises
People and families can change quickly. Treatment should be simple and pragmatic and concentrate on changing symptomatic behaviors and rigid rules. Change is brought about through enactment, ordeals, paradox, pretense, and rituals (strategic and systemic therapies); focuses on exceptions to dysfunctionality, hypothetical solutions, and small changes (solution-focused therapies).

Role of the Counselor
The counselor is responsible for overcoming resistance in the family and designing novel strategies for solving problems. He or she overcomes resistance by positively accepting whatever problem the family brings. The counselor is much like a physician in taking responsibility for the success of treatment and must plan ahead and develop strategies.

Unit of Treatment
The family as a system, although these approaches can be selectively used with dyads and individuals

Goals of Treatment
To resolve present problems, find solutions, bring about change; to target definable behavioral goals; to minimize insight; to ignore what is not a problem

Techniques

Reframing (including positive connotation), directives, compliance- and defiance-based paradox (including prescribing the symptoms), promoting second-order change, discouraging interpretation, pretending, cooperative hierarchies, ordeals, rituals, teams, circular questioning, hypothetical solutions (i.e., asking the "miracle question")

Unique Aspects

There is an emphasis on seeing symptoms in a positive way. Treatment is short-term (usually 10 sessions or fewer). Focus is on changing present problematic behavior. Techniques are tailor-made for each family. Innovative treatments are highlighted. Approaches are flexible, evolving, and creative. Many are easily combined with other theories.

Narrative Family Theory

Theorists

Michael White, David Epston

Underlying Premises

People live their lives according to stories and their meaningfulness. Families that reauthor their lives and make their stories more meaningful live healthier.

Role of the Counselor

The counselor questions and examines the meaningfulness of situations for families and helps them create new stories for their lives.

Unit of Treatment

The entire family when possible

Goals of Treatment

To get families to look for exceptions to their dilemmas and to focus on solutions to their problems

Techniques

Externalization of problems, examining how problems and people influence one another, raising dilemmas, predicting setbacks, using questions to challenge family perceptions, writing letters to families, holding celebrations at the closure of treatment

Unique Aspects

This approach is based on narrative reasoning (i.e., the meaning of stories) rather than systems theory. It emphasizes externalizing problems, reauthoring lives, using questions to challenge family perceptions, and writing letters to families as a way of providing them feedback and doing clinical notes.

CLASSROOM ACTIVITIES

1. Do you think the family life cycle has as much influence on a person as the individual life cycle? What conflicts might occur between these two cycles? Discuss the cycles with a group of three other classmates.

2. Determine where you are in your own individual and family life cycles. Talk with a classmate about what changes you anticipate making in the next few years because of life-cycle demands.

3. What are the advantages and disadvantages of working with individuals with family concerns on a one-to-one basis rather than a family counseling basis? Do you think it is

possible to work effectively with only one member of a couple or family? Divide the class into two teams and debate the issue.

4. Which approach to marriage or family counseling do you prefer? What are the reasons behind your decision? Form groups with classmates who share your view and present your rationale to other class members.

5. Research how some of the family counseling approaches not described in this chapter (e.g., person-centered, Gestalt, transactional analysis) work with families to bring about change. What data support the use of these theories?

REFERENCES

Ackerman, N. W. (1958). *The psychodynamics of family life*. New York: Basic Books.

Ackerman, N. W. (1966). *Treating the troubled family*. New York: Basic Books.

Alexander, J., & Parsons, B. V. (1982). *Functional family therapy*. Pacific Grove, CA: Brooks/Cole.

Bandura, A. (1977). *Social learning theory*. Upper Saddle River, NJ: Prentice Hall.

Baruth, L. G., & Huber, C. H. (1984). *An introduction to marital theory and therapy*. Pacific Grove, CA: Brooks/Cole.

Bateson, G., Jackson, D. D., Haley, J., & Weakland, J. (1956). Toward a theory of schizophrenia. *Behavioral Science, 1*, 251–264.

Becvar, D. S. (1982). The family is not a group: Or is it? *Journal for Specialists in Group Work, 7*, 88–95.

Becvar, D. S., & Becvar, R. J. (1996). *Family therapy: A systematic integration* (3rd ed.). Boston: Allyn & Bacon.

Bell, J. E. (1975). *Family therapy*. New York: Aronson.

Bell, J. E. (1976). A theoretical framework for family group therapy. In P. J. Guerin (Ed.), *Family therapy: Theory and practice* (pp. 129–143). New York: Gardner.

Bertalanffy, L. von. (1968). *General systems theory: Foundations, development, application*. New York: Brazillier.

Bowen, M. (1960). A family concept of schizophrenia. In D. D. Jackson (Ed.), *The etiology of schizophrenia* (pp. 346–372). New York: Basic Books.

Bowen, M. (1976). Theory in the practice of psychotherapy. In P. J. Guerin, Jr. (Ed.), *Family therapy: Theory and practice* (pp. 42–90). New York: Gardner.

Bowen, M. (1978). *Family therapy in clinical practice*. New York: Aronson.

Bratcher, W. E. (1982). The influence of the family on career selection: A family systems perspective. *Personnel and Guidance Journal, 61*, 87–91.

Carnegie Task Force on Meeting the Needs of Young Children. (1994). *Starting points: Meeting the needs of our youngest children*. New York: Carnegie Corporation.

Carter, B., & McGoldrick, M. (1988). *The changing family life cycle* (2nd ed.). New York: Gardner.

deShazer, S. (1985). *Keys to solution in brief family therapy*. New York: Norton.

deShazer, S. (1988). *Clues: Investigating solutions in brief therapy*. New York: Norton.

deShazer, S. (1991). *Putting differences to work*. New York: Norton.

Doherty, W. J., & Simmons, D. S. (1996). Clinical practice patterns of marriage and family therapists: A national survey of therapists and their clients. *Journal of Marital and Family Therapy, 22*, 9–25.

Ellis, A. (1988). *How to stubbornly refuse to make yourself miserable about anything: Yes, anything!* Secaucus, NJ: Stuart.

Ellis, A., Sichel, J. L., Yeager, R. J., DiMattia, D. J., & DiGuiseppe, R. (1989). *Rational-emotive couples therapy*. New York: Pergamon.

Erickson, M. (1954). Special techniques of brief hypnotherapy. *Journal of Clinical and Experimental Hypnosis, 2*, 109–129.

Erikson, E. H. (1959). *Identity and the life cycle: Psychological issues*. New York: International Universities Press.

Fleming, J. S., & Rickord, B. (1997). Solution-focused brief therapy: One answer to managed mental health care. *Family Journal, 5*, 286–294.

Framo, J. L. (1996). A personal retrospective of the family therapy field: Then and now. *Journal of Marital and Family Therapy, 22*, 289–316.

Gladding, S. T. (1998). *Family therapy: History, theory, and practice* (2nd ed.). Upper Saddle River, NJ: Merrill/Prentice Hall.

Gladding, S. T. (1999). *Group work: A counseling specialty* (3rd ed.). Upper Saddle River, NJ: Merrill/Prentice Hall.

Goldenberg, H. & Goldenberg, I. (1998). *Counseling today's family* (3rd ed.). Pacific Grove, CA: Brooks/Cole.

Gottman, J. (1994). *What predicts divorce? The relationship between marital processes and marital outcomes*. Hillsdale, NJ: Erlbaum.

Gurman, A., & Kniskern, D. (1981). Family therapy outcome research: Knowns and unknowns. In A. Gurman & D. Kniskern (Eds.), *Handbook of family therapy* (pp. 742–775). New York: Brunner/Mazel.

Haber, R. A. (1983). The family dance around drug abuse. *Personnel and Guidance Journal, 61*, 428–430.

Hackney, H., & Wrenn, C. G. (1990). The contemporary counselor in a changed world. In H. Hackney

(Ed.), *Changing contexts for counselor preparation in the 1990s* (pp. 1–20). Alexandria, VA: Association for Counselor Education and Supervision.

Haley, J. (1973). *Uncommon therapy.* New York: Norton.

Hines, M. (1988). Similarities and differences in group and family therapy. *Journal for Specialists in Group Work, 13,* 173–179.

Horne, A. M., & Passmore, J. L. (1991). *Family counseling and therapy* (2nd ed.). Itasca, IL: Peacock.

Jacobson, N. S., & Gurman, A. S. (Eds.) (1996). *Clinical handbook of couple therapy.* New York: Guilford.

Kerr, M. E., & Bowen, M. (1988). *Family evaluation: An approach based on Bowen theory.* New York: Norton.

Kinnier, R. T., Brigman, S. L., & Noble, F. C. (1990). Career indecision and family enmeshment. *Journal of Counseling and Development, 68,* 309–312.

Kurtz, P. D., & Tandy, C. C. (1995). Narrative family interventions. In A. C. Kilpatrick & T. P. Holland (Eds.), *Working with families* (pp. 177–197). Boston: Allyn & Bacon.

Lawson, D. (1994). Identifying pretreatment change. *Journal of Counseling and Development, 72,* 244–248.

Levinson, D. (1978). *The seasons of a man's life.* New York: Knopf.

Levy, D. (1943). *Marital overprotection.* New York: Columbia University Press.

Lidz, T., Cornelison, A., Fleck, S., & Terry, D. (1957). Intrafamilial environment of schizophrenic patients II: Marital schism and marital skew. *American Journal of Psychiatry, 20,* 241–248.

Lopez, F. G. (1986). Family structure and depression: Implications for the counseling of depressed college students. *Journal of Counseling and Development, 64,* 508–511.

LoPiccolo, J. (1978). Direct treatment of sexual dysfunction. In J. LoPiccolo & L. LoPiccolo (Eds.), *Handbook of sex therapy* (pp. 1–18). New York: Plenum.

Madanes, C. (1984). *Behind the one-way mirror: Advances in the practice of strategic therapy.* San Francisco: Jossey-Bass.

Madanes, C. (1991). Strategic family therapy. In A. S. Gurman & D. P. Kniskern (Eds.), *Handbook of family therapy* (Vol. 2, pp. 396–416). New York: Brunner/Mazel.

Markowitz, L. M. (1994, July/August). The cross-culture of multiculturalism. *Family Therapy Networker, 18,* 18–27, 69.

Martin, T., & Bumpass, L. (1989). Recent trends in marital disruption. *Demography, 26,* 37–51.

Masters, W. H., & Johnson, V. E. (1970). *Human sexual inadequacy.* Boston: Little, Brown.

Maynard, P. E., & Olson, D. H. (1987). Circumplex model of family systems: A treatment tool in family counseling. *Journal of Counseling and Development, 65,* 502–504.

McGoldrick, M., & Gerson, R. (1985). *Genograms in family assessment.* New York: Norton.

McGoldrick, M., Giordano, J., & Pearce, J. K. (Eds.). (1996). *Ethnicity and family therapy* (2nd ed.). New York: Guilford.

McGoldrick, M., Pearce, J. K., & Giordano, J. (Eds.). (1982). *Ethnicity and family therapy.* New York: Guilford.

Minuchin, S. (1974). *Families and family therapy.* Cambridge, MA: Harvard University Press.

Minuchin, S., & Fishman, H. C. (1981). *Family therapy techniques.* Cambridge, MA: Harvard University Press.

Minuchin, S., Montalvo, B., Guerney, B., Rosman, B., & Schumer, F. (1967). *Families of the slums.* New York: Basic Books.

Napier, A. Y. (1988). *The fragile bond.* New York: Harper & Row.

Nichols, M. (1988). *The self in the system: Expanding the limits of family therapy.* New York: Brunner/Mazel.

Nichols, M., & Schwartz, R. C. (1998). *Family therapy: Concepts and methods* (4th ed.). Boston: Allyn & Bacon.

Nichols, W. C. (1993). *The AAMFGC: 50 years of marital and family therapy.* Washington, DC: American Association of Marriage and Family Therapists.

O'Hanlon, W. H., & Weiner-Davis, M. (1989). *In search of solutions: A new direction in psychotherapy.* New York: Norton.

Ohlsen, M. M. (1979). *Marriage counseling in groups.* Champaign, IL: Research Press.

Ohlsen, M. M. (1982). Family therapy with the triad model. In A. M. Horne & M. M. Ohlsen (Eds.), *Family counseling and therapy* (pp. 412–434). Itasca, IL: Peacock.

Okun, B. R. (1984). *Working with adults: Individual, family and career development.* Pacific Grove, CA: Brooks/Cole.

Olson, D. H. (1986). Circumplex model VII: Validation studies and FACES III. *Family Process, 25,* 337–351.

Papero, D. V. (1996). Bowen family systems and marriage. In N. S. Jacobson & A. S. Gurman (Eds.), *Clinical handbook of marital therapy*. New York: Guilford.

Patterson, G. R. (1971). *Families: Applications of social learning to family life*. Champaign, IL: Research Press.

Paul, N. L., & Paul, B. B. (1975). *A marital puzzle: Transgenerational analysis in marriage*. New York: Norton.

Pinsof, W. M., & Wynne, L. C. (1995). The efficacy of marital and family therapy: An empirical overview, conclusions and recommendations. *Journal of Marital and Family Therapy, 21*, 585–614.

Pistole, M. C. (1997). Using the genogram to teach systems thinking. *Family Journal, 5*, 337–341.

Resnikoff, R. D. (1981). Teaching family therapy: Ten key questions for understanding the family as patient. *Journal of Marital and Family Therapy, 7*, 135–142.

Satir, V. M. (1967). *Conjoint family therapy*. Palo Alto, CA: Science and Behavior Books.

Satir, V. M. (1972). *Peoplemaking*. Palo Alto, CA: Science and Behavior Books.

Selvini-Palazzoli, M., Boscolo, L., Cecchin, G., & Prata, G. (1978). *Paradox and counterparadox*. New York: Monson.

Sexton, T. L. (1994). Systemic thinking in a linear world: Issues in the application of interactional counseling. *Journal of Counseling and Development, 72*, 249–258.

Slipp, S. (1988). *The technique and practice of object relations family therapy*. New York: Aronson.

Stinnett, N. (1998). *Good families*. New York: Doubleday.

Stinnett, N., & DeFrain, J. (1985). *Secrets of strong families*. Boston: Little, Brown.

Stuart, R. B. (1980). *Helping couples change: A social learning approach to marital therapy*. New York: Guilford.

Stuart, R. B. (1998). Updating behavior therapy with couples. *Family Journal, 6*, 6–12.

Thomas, A. J. (1998). Understanding culture and worldview in family systems: Use of the multicultural genogram. *Family Journal, 6*, 24–32.

Todd, T. C. (1986). Structural-strategic marital therapy. In N. S. Jacobson & A. S. Gurman (Eds.), *Clinical handbook of marital therapy* (pp. 71–105). New York: Guilford.

Trotzer, J. P. (1988). Family theory as a group resource. *Journal for Specialists in Group Work, 13*, 180–185.

U.S. Bureau of the Census (1991). *Statistical abstracts of the United States 1991* (11th ed.). Washington, DC: U.S. Government Printing Office.

Usdansky, M. L. (1994, August 30). More kids live in changing families. *USA Today*, p. 1A.

Walsh, F. (1993). Conceptualizations of normal family functioning. In F. Walsh (Ed.), *Normal family processes* (2nd ed., pp. 3–42). New York: Guilford.

Walsh, W. M., & Keenan, R. (1997). Narrative family therapy. *Family Journal, 5*, 332–336.

Walter, J., & Peller, J. (1992). *Becoming solution-focused in brief therapy*. New York: Brunner/Mazel.

Watzlawick, P., Weakland, J., & Fisch, R. (1974). *Change: Principles of problem formation and problem resolution*. New York: Norton.

West, J. D., Bubenzer, D. L., Smith, J. M., & Hamm, T. L. (1997). Insoo Kim Berg and solution-focused therapy. *Family Journal, 5*, 286–294.

West, J. D., Hosie, T. W., & Zarski, J. J. (1987). Family dynamics and substance abuse: A preliminary study. *Journal of Counseling and Development, 65*, 487–490.

Whitaker, C. (1976). The hindrance of theory in clinical work. In P. J. Guerin (Ed.), *Family therapy: Theory and practice* (pp. 154–164). New York: Gardner.

Whitaker, C. (1977). Process techniques of family therapy. *Interaction, 1*, 4–19.

Whitaker, C. (1989). *Midnight musings of a family therapist*. New York: Norton.

White, M. (1995). *Re-authoring lives*. Adelaide, Australia: Dulwich Centre Publications.

White, M., & Epston, D. (1990). *Narrative means to therapeutic ends*. New York: Norton.

Whitehead, B. D. (1997). *The divorce culture*. New York: Knopf.

Wilcoxon, S. A. (1985). Healthy family functioning: The other side of family pathology. *Journal of Counseling and Development, 63*, 495–499.

Wilcoxon, S. A., & Fenell, D. (1983). Engaging the non-attending spouse in marital therapy through the use of therapist-initiated written communication. *Journal of Marital and Family Therapy, 9*, 199–203.

Wohlman, B., & Stricker, G. (1983). *Handbook of family and marital therapy.* New York: Plenum.

Wynne, L. C., Ryckoff, I., Day, J., & Hirsch, S. I. (1958). Pseudo-mutuality in the family relationships of schizophrenics. *Psychiatry, 21,* 205–220.

13

GROUPS IN COUNSELING

Who am I in this pilgrim group

whose members differ so in perception?

Am I timid like a Miles Standish,

letting others speak for me

because the experience of failure is softened

if a risk is never personally taken?

Or am I more like a John Alden

speaking boldly for others in the courting of beauty

but not seeking such for myself?

Perhaps I am more than either man

or maybe I'm both at different times!

In the silence and before others, I ponder the question anew.

Working in groups is a counseling specialty that is often effective in helping individuals resolve personal and interpersonal concerns. Organized groups make use of people's natural tendency to gather and share thoughts and feelings as well as work and play cooperatively. "Groups are valuable because they allow members to experience a sense of belonging, to share common problems, to observe behaviors and consequences of behaviors in others, and to find support during self-exploration and change" (Nims, 1998, p. 134). By participating in a group, people develop social relationships, emotional bonds, and often become enlightened (Posthuma, 1996).

Yet before such possibilities become a reality, certain misperceptions about groups need to be clarified (Gladding, 1999). Most misperceptions involve counseling and psychotherapy groups (as opposed to psychoeducational and task/work groups). Some prevalent myths about groups are as follows (Childers & Couch, 1989):

- *They are artificial and unreal.*
- *They are second-rate structures for dealing with problems.*
- *They force people to lose their identity by tearing down psychological defenses.*
- *They require people to become emotional and spill their guts.*
- *They are touchy-feely, confrontational, and hostile; they brainwash participants.*

Contrary to these myths is reality. Groups have a long and distinguished history in the service of counseling. Joseph Hersey Pratt, a Boston physician, is generally credited with starting the first psychotherapy/counseling group in 1905. Pratt's group members were tubercular outpatients at Massachusetts General Hospital who found the time they regularly spent together informative, supportive, and therapeutic. The following people were also pioneers in the group movement:

- *Jacob L. Moreno, who introduced the term* group psychotherapy *into the counseling literature in the 1920s*
- *Alexander Wolf and Emanuel Schwartz, who started the first certification program in group therapy at New York Medical College in the late 1940s*
- *Kurt Lewin, whose field theory concepts in the 1930s and 1940s became the basis for the Tavistock small study groups in Britain and the T-group movement in the United States*
- *Fritz Perls, whose Gestalt approach to groups attracted new interest in the field*
- *W. Edwards Deming, who conceptualized and implemented the idea of quality work groups to improve the processes and products people produced and build morale among workers in businesses*
- *William Schutz and Jack Gibb, who emphasized a humanistic aspect to T-groups that focused on personal growth as a legitimate goal*
- *Carl Rogers, who devised the basic encounter group in the 1960s that became the model for growth-oriented group approaches*

This chapter examines the following aspects of groups: their place in counseling, including the types of groups most often used; their theoretical basis; issues and stages in groups; and qualities of effective group leaders. Both national and local organizations have been established for professionals engaged primarily in leading groups. One of the most comprehensive (and the one to which most professional counselors belong) is the Association for Specialists in Group Work (ASGW), a national division of American Counseling Association (ACA). This organization, which has a diverse membership, was chartered by the ACA in 1974 (Carroll & Levo, 1985). It has been a leader in establishing educational and ethical guidelines for group leaders and publishes a quarterly periodical, the Journal for Specialists in Group Work. *Other prominent group organizations are the American Group Psychotherapy Association (AGPA), the American Society of Group Psychotherapy and Psychodrama (ASGPP), and the Group Psychology and Group Psychotherapy division of the American Psychological Association (APA) (Division 49).*

The Place of Groups in Counseling

A *group* is defined as two or more people interacting together to achieve a goal for their mutual benefit. Groups have a unique place in counseling. Everyone typically spends some time in group activities each day—for example, with schoolmates or business associates. Gregariousness is part of human nature, and many personal and professional skills are learned through group interactions. It is only natural, then, for counselors to make use of this primary way of human interaction. Groups are an economical and effective means of helping individuals who share similar problems and concerns. Counselors who limit their competencies to individual counseling skills limit their options for helping.

Most counselors have to make major decisions about when, where, and with whom to use groups. In some situations groups are not appropriate ways of helping. For instance, a counselor employed by a company would be unwise to use groups to counsel employees with personal problems who are unequal in rank and seniority in the corporate network. Likewise, a school counselor would be foolish to use a group setting as a way of working with children who are all behaviorally disruptive. But a group may be ideal for helping people who are not too disruptive or unequal in status and who have common concerns. In such cases, counselors generally schedule a regular time for people to meet in a quiet, uninterrupted setting and interact together.

Groups differ in purpose, composition, and length. Basically, however, they all involve *work,* which Gazda (1989) describes as "the dynamic interaction between collections of individuals for prevention or remediation of difficulties or for the enhancement of personal growth/enrichment" (p. 297). Hence, the term *group work* is often used to describe what goes on within groups. The ASGW (1992) defines *group work* as "a broad professional practice that refers to the giving of help or the accomplishment of tasks in a group setting. It involves the application of group theory and process by a capable professional practitioner to assist an interdependent collection of people to reach their mutual goals, which may be personal, interpersonal, or task-related in nature" (p. 14).

Groups have a number of general advantages. For example, group members can come to realize that they are not alone, unique, or abnormal in their problems and concerns. Through their interaction with one another, they learn more about themselves in social situations. In groups, people can try out new behaviors and ways of interacting because the group atmosphere provides a safe environment to experiment with change and receive feedback. Members also observe how others attack and resolve problems, thereby picking up skills vicariously. Finally, the group may serve as a catalyst to help persons realize a want or a need for individual counseling or the accomplishment of a personal goal.

If set up properly, groups have specific advantages that can be beneficial in helping individuals with a variety of problems and concerns. Literally hundreds of studies describe group approaches and statistically support the effectiveness of various forms of groups. Documentation of group experiences is occurring at such a fast rate, however, that it is difficult to stay abreast of the latest developments. Some researchers in the field, such as Zimpfer (1990), regularly write comprehensive reviews on select group activities that help practitioners become better informed.

Some recent findings about groups reveal the following:

- Group counseling can be used to help 9th- and 10th-grade students learn social problem-solving behaviors that help them in career decision preparation (Hutchinson, Freeman, & Quick, 1996).
- Learning groups geared toward cooperative sharing can help participants achieve their goals more easily (Avasthi, 1990).
- Support groups can help older women cope with divorce and its aftermaths (Blatter & Jacobsen, 1993).
- Group counseling and psychoeducational programs can help persons who have sustained heart attacks deal better with stressors in their lives (Livneh & Sherwood-Hawes, 1993).

Yet groups are not a panacea for all people and problems. They have definite limitations and disadvantages. For example, many client concerns and personalities are not well suited for groups. The problems of individuals may not be dealt with in enough depth within groups. In addition, group pressure may force a client to take action, such as self-disclosure, before being ready. Groups may also lapse into a *groupthink* mentality, in which stereotypical, defensive, and stale thought processes become the norm and creativity and problem solving are squelched. Another drawback to groups is that individuals may try to use them for escape or selfish purposes and disrupt the group process. Furthermore, it may be difficult for leaders to find a suitable time to conduct groups so that all who wish to can participate. Another concern is whether groups will reflect the social milieu in which individual members normally operate. Otherwise, what is learned from the group experience may not be relevant. Finally, if groups do not work through their developmental stages successfully, they may become regressive and engage in nonproductive and even destructive behaviors such as scapegoating, group narcissism, and projection (McClure, 1994).

Types of Groups

Groups come in many forms: "there seems to be a group experience tailored to suit the interests and needs of virtually anyone who seeks psychotherapy, personal growth, or simply support and companionship from others" (Lynn & Frauman, 1985, p. 423). There are a number of group models appropriate for a wide variety of situations. Although lively debate persists about how groups should be categorized, especially in regard to goals and process (Waldo & Bauman, 1998), the following types of groups have training standards developed by the ASGW (1992).

Guidance/Psychoeducational Groups

Guidance/psychoeducational groups are preventive and instructional (Brown, 1998; Pence, Paymar, Ritmeester, & Shepard, 1998). Their purpose is to teach group participants how to deal with a potential threat (such as AIDS), a developmental life event (such as growing older), or an immediate life crisis (such as the death of a loved one). These types of groups are often found in educational settings. One of the most important parts of the process in such groups revolves around group discussions of how members will personalize the information presented in the group context (Ohlsen, 1977). In school settings, instructional materials such as unfinished stories, puppet plays, films, audio interviews, and guest speakers are employed in psychoeducational groups. In adult settings, other age-appropriate means, usually written materials, are used.

An example of a psychoeducational group is the promotion of student development on college and university campuses. During the traditional college-age years, "students grow and change in complexity along a variety of dimensions" (Taub, 1998, p. 197). Their development can be enhanced through psychoeducational groups that address issues important to them such as control of anger, dating relationships, and study skills. These groups are relatively brief in duration and meet for only a limited time. Yet, they prepare those who attend more adequately for the issues that are covered.

Counseling/Interpersonal Problem-Solving Groups

Counseling groups "seek to help group participants to resolve the usual, yet often difficult, problems of living through interpersonal support and problem solving. An additional goal is to help participants to develop their existing interpersonal problem-solving competencies so they may be better able to handle future problems. Non-severe career, educational, personal, social, and developmental concerns are frequently addressed" (ASGW, 1992, p. 14).

Gazda (1989) distinguishes group counseling from group guidance in the following ways:

- Group counseling is recommended for individuals who are having temporary or continuing problems, whereas group guidance is recommended on a regular basis as a personal educational measure.
- Group counseling is more direct than group guidance in attempting to modify attitudes and behaviors. For instance, group counseling stresses the affective involvement

of participants, whereas group guidance concentrates more on the cognitive understanding of its members.
- Group counseling is conducted in a small, intimate setting, whereas group guidance is more applicable to classroom-size environments.

In fact, at times group counseling and group guidance may overlap (Taub, 1998; Waldo & Bauman, 1998). An example of a brief but effective group counseling approach that overlaps some with group guidance is a structured group for high school seniors making the transition to college and to military service (Goodnough & Ripley, 1997). These groups are held for soon-to-be high school graduates. They give the students an opportunity to deal with the complex set of emotions they are experiencing while providing them with information that will assist them in gaining a helpful cognitive perspective on what they are about to do. In group counseling such as this, participants get "airtime," an opportunity to speak about their own concerns. The interaction of group members and the personalizing of the information is greater than in a pure psychoeducational group.

Psychotherapy/Personality Reconstruction Groups

Psychotherapy groups are set up to help individual group members remediate in-depth psychological problems. "Because the depth and extent of the psychological disturbance is significant, the goal is to aid each individual to reconstruct major personality dimensions" (ASGW, 1992, pp. 14–15).

Sometimes there is overlap in group counseling and group psychotherapy, but the emphasis on major reconstruction of personality dimensions usually distinguishes the two. Group psychotherapy often takes place in inpatient facilities, such as psychiatric hospitals or other mental health facilities, because greater control may be necessary for the people involved. Certain types of individuals are poor candidates for outpatient, intensive group psychotherapy. Among them are depressives, incessant talkers, paranoids, schizoid and sociopathic personalities, suicidals, and extreme narcissists (Yalom, 1995). It may be easier to identify group psychotherapy candidates who should be excluded than choose those who should be included. Regardless, group psychotherapy is an American form of treatment and has provided much of the rationale for group counseling.

Task/Work Groups

Task groups help members apply the principles and processes of group dynamics to improve practices and accomplish identified work goals. "The task/work group specialist is able to assist groups such as task forces, committees, planning groups, community organizations, discussion groups, study circles, learning groups, and other similar groups to correct or develop their functions" (ASGW, 1992, p. 14).

The classic example of a task group is a team. In athletics, art, and employment settings, teams are often formed to accomplish objectives that would be impossible for an individual to achieve alone. The *quality circle*, an employee-run group of workers who meet weekly to examine the processes they are using in their jobs and devise ways to improve them, is a business example of a task group (Johnson & Johnson, 1997). However, counselors often work in teams to resolve internal and external situations as well as to plan and implement ideas, so these groups have broad applicability.

Traditional and Historical Groups

Several traditional and historical groups belong in one of the four categories of specialty groups just described. Some of these groups, however, do not fit into any category well. Furthermore, all these types of groups developed before groups were classified as they are today. T-groups and encounter groups are seldom conducted in their original forms anymore but are important because of their contributions to the evolution of group work. Psychodrama, group marathons, and support/self-help groups continue to be used in their traditional ways and are important therapeutically.

T-Groups

The first T-group (the *T* stands for training) was conducted at the National Training Laboratories (NTL) in Bethel, Maine, in 1947. These groups appeared at a time when neither group counseling nor group psychotherapy was popular. Kurt Lewin's ideas about group dynamics formed the basis for the original groups. Since that time, T-groups have evolved from a focus on task accomplishment to a primary emphasis on interpersonal relationships. Although it is difficult to classify T-groups in just one way, members of such groups are likely to learn from the experience how one's behavior in a group influences others' behavior and vice versa. In this respect, T-groups are similar to forms of family counseling in which the emphasis is on both how the system operates and how an individual within the system functions.

Encounter Groups

According to Lynn and Frauman (1985), encounter groups emerged from T-groups in an attempt to focus on the growth of individual group members rather than the group itself. Encounter groups are intended for "normally functioning" people who want to grow, change, and develop (Lieberman, 1991). These groups took many forms in their heyday (the 1970s), from the minimally structured groups of Carl Rogers (1970) to the highly structured, open-ended groups of William Schutz (1971). Regardless of the structure, the primary emphasis of such groups was and is on individual expression and recognition of affect.

Group Marathon

A group marathon is an extended, one-session group experience that breaks down defensive barriers that individuals may otherwise use. It usually lasts for a minimum of 24 hours. The concept was pioneered by Frederick Stoller and George Bach in the 1960s. Group marathons have been used successfully in working with substance abusers in rehabilitation programs and normally functioning individuals in group counseling settings. Often labor and peace negotiations are held in a group marathon setting to achieve breakthroughs.

Psychodrama

J. L. Moreno, a Viennese psychiatrist, is credited as the originator of psychodrama. This type of group experience, employed for decades with mental patients at Saint Elizabeth's Hospital in Washington, DC, was initially used with ordinary citizens in Vienna, Austria (Moreno's home). In group psychodrama, members enact unrehearsed role plays, with the group leader serving as the director. Other group members are actors in the protagonist's play, give feedback to the protagonist as members of the audience, or do both. This type of group is popular with behaviorists, Gestaltists, and affective-oriented group leaders who have adapted it as a way of helping clients experience the emotional qualities of an event.

Self-Help/Support Groups

Since the 1970s, self-help and support groups have grown in prominence. A *self-help group* usually develops spontaneously, centers on a single topic, and is led by a layperson with little formal group training but with experience in the stressful event that brought the group together (Riordan & Beggs, 1987). For example, residents in a neighborhood may meet to help each other make repairs and clean up after a natural disaster, or they may assemble to focus government attention on an issue, such as toxic waste, that directly affects the quality of their lives. Self-help groups can be either short- or long-term, but they basically work to help their members gain greater control of their lives. Over 10 million people are involved in approximately 500,000 such groups in the United States and the number continues to increase.

A *support group* is similar to a self-help group in its focus on a particular concern or problem, but it is organized by an established professional helping organization or individual (such as Alcoholics Anonymous, Lamplighters, or Weight Watchers) (Gladding, 1999). Some support groups charge fees; others do not. The involvement of laypeople as group leaders varies. Like self-help groups, support groups center around topics that are physical, emotional, or social (L'Abate & Thaxton, 1981).

Self-help and support groups partly fill the needs of populations who can best be served in group formats and that might otherwise not receive services. They meet in churches, recreation centers, schools, and other community buildings as well as in mental health facilities. Lieberman (1994) sees self-help and support groups as healthy for the general public, and Corey (1995) thinks such groups are complementary to other mental health services. Like other group experiences, however, "cohesion is always a vital characteristic for success," and proper guidelines must be set up to ensure the group will be a positive, not a destructive, event (Riordan & Beggs, 1987, p. 428).

Theoretical Approaches in Conducting Groups

Theoretical approaches to counseling in groups vary as much as individual counseling approaches. In many cases, the theories are the same. For instance, within group work there are approaches based on psychoanalytic, Gestalt, person-centered, rational emotive behavior, transactional analysis, cognitive, and behavioral theories. Because the basic positions of these theories are examined elsewhere in this text, they will not be reviewed here. Yet the implementation of any theoretical approach differs when employed with a group because of *group dynamics* (the interaction of members within the group).

In an evaluation of seven major theoretical approaches to groups, Ward (1982) analyzes the degree to which each approach pays attention to the individual, interpersonal, and group levels of the process (see Table 13.1). For instance, the psychoanalytic, Gestalt, and behavioral approaches are strong in focusing on the individual but weak on the other two components of the group process. On the other hand, the Rogerian approach is strong on the individual level and medium on the interpersonal and group level. Ward points out the limiting aspects of each approach and the importance of considering other factors, such as the group task and membership maturity, in conducting comprehensive group assignments.

Similarly, Frey (1972) outlines how eight approaches to group work can be conceptualized on a continuum from insight to action and rational to affective (Figure 13.1); whereas Hansen, Warner, and Smith (1980) conceptualize group approaches on a continuum from process to outcome and leader centered to member centered (Figure 13.2). Group leaders and potential group members must know how theories differ to make wise choices. Overall, multiple theoretical models provide richness and diversity for conducting groups.

Three factors, in addition to the ones already mentioned, are useful for group leaders to consider when deciding on what theoretical approach to take:

1. Do I need a theoretical base for conducting the group?
2. What uses will the theory best serve?
3. What criteria will be employed in the selection process?

A theory is a lot like a map. In a group, it provides direction and guidance in examining basic assumptions about human beings. It is also useful in determining goals for the group, clarifying one's role and functions as a leader, and explaining the group interactions. Finally, a theory can help in evaluating the outcomes of the group. Trying to lead a

Table 13.1   Rating of theory strength at three group levels

	Levels			
Theory	**Individual**	**Interpersonal**	**Group**	**Limiting Factors**
Freud	Strong	Weak	Weak	Task, members, leader
Perls	Strong	Weak	Weak	Task, members, leader
Behavioral	Strong	Weak	Weak	Task, leader
Ellis	Strong	Medium	Weak	Task, leader
Berne	Strong	Strong	Weak	Task
Rogers	Strong	Medium	Medium	Style

Source: From "A Model for the More Effective Use of Theory in Group Work," by D. E. Ward, 1982, *Journal for Specialists in Group Work, 7,* p. 227. © 1982 by ACA. Reprinted with permission. No further reproduction authorized without written permission of the American Counseling Association.

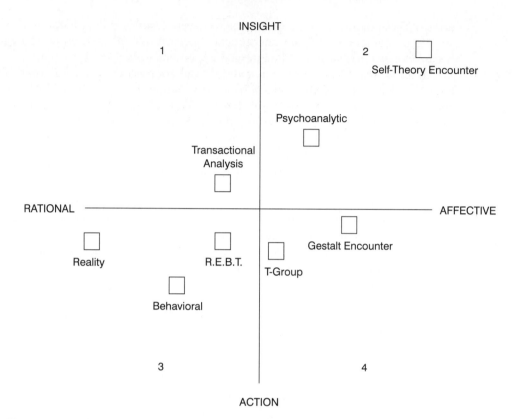

Figure 13.1   Group approaches conceptualized
Source: From "Conceptualizing Counseling Theories," by D. H. Frey, 1972, *Counselor Education and Supervision, 11,* p. 245. © 1972 by ACA. Reprinted with permission. No further reproduction authorized without written permission from the American Counseling Association.

group without an explicit theoretical rationale is similar to attempting to fly an airplane without a map and knowledge of instruments. Either procedure is foolish, dangerous, and likely to lead to injury.

A good theory also serves practical functions (Gladding, 1999). For example, it gives meaning to and a framework for experiences and facts that occur within a setting. Good theory helps make logical sense out of what is happening and leads to productive research. With so many theories from which to choose, the potential group leader is wise to be careful in selecting an approach.

Ford and Urban (1998) believe counselors should consider four main factors when selecting a theory: personal experience, consensus of experts, prestige, and a verified body of knowledge. All these criteria contain liabilities and advantages. Therefore, it is crucial for beginning counselors to listen to others and read the professional literature critically to evaluate the theories that are most verifiable and that fit in with their personality styles (Gladding, 1999).

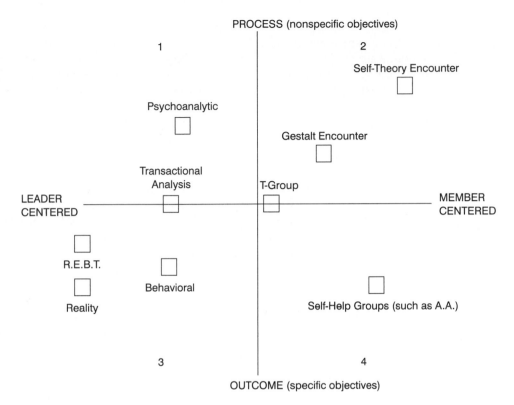

Figure 13.2   Group approaches conceptualized
Source: From *Group Counseling: Theory and Process* (2nd ed., p. 322), by J. C. Hansen, R. W. Warner, and E. J. Smith, 1980, Boston: Houghton Mifflin. © 1980, 1976 by Houghton Mifflin Company. Reprinted by permission.

Stages in Groups

Groups, like other living systems, go through stages. If an individual or group leader is not aware of these stages, the changes that occur within the group may appear confusing rather than meaningful and the benefits may be few. Leaders can maximize learning by either setting up conditions that facilitate the development of the group or "using developmentally based interventions, at both individual and group levels" (Saidla, 1990, p. 15). In either case, group members and leaders benefit.

There is debate in the professional literature about what and when groups go through stages. Developmental stages have been identified in various types of groups, such as learning groups and training groups, yet much of the debate about stages centers around group counseling. Group counseling is most often broken into four or five stages, but some models depict as few as three stages and others as many as six. Tuckman's stage model is considered mainstream.

Tuckman (1965) was one of the first theorists to design a stage process for group counseling. He believed there were four stages of group development: forming, storming, norming, and performing. This concept was later expanded to include a fifth stage: adjourning (Tuckman & Jensen, 1977) or mourning/morning (Waldo, 1985). In each stage certain tasks are performed. For example, in the *forming stage,* the foundation is usually laid down for what is to come and who will be considered in or out of group deliberations. In this stage (the group's infancy), members express anxiety and dependency and talk about nonproblematic issues. One way to ease the transition into the group at this stage is to structure it so that members are relaxed and sure of what is expected of them. For example, before the first meeting, members may be told they will be expected to spend 3 minutes telling others who they are (McCoy, 1994).

In the second stage, *storming,* considerable turmoil and conflict usually occur, as they do in adolescence. Conflict within the group at this and other times "forces group members to make some basic decisions about the degree of independence and interdependence in their relationship with one another" (Rybak & Brown, 1997, p. 31). Group members seek to establish themselves in the hierarchy of the group and deal successfully with issues concerning anxiety, power, and future expectations. Sometimes the group leader is attacked at this stage.

The third stage, *norming,* is similar to young adulthood, in which "having survived the storm the group often generates enthusiasm and cohesion. Goals and ways of working together are decided on" (Saidla, 1990, p. 16). This stage is sometimes combined with the storming stage, but whether it is combined or not, it is followed by *performing,* which parallels adulthood in a developmental sense. In the performing stage, group members become involved with each other and their individual and collective goals. This is the time when the group, if it works well, is productive. Finally, in the *adjourning* or *mourning/morning* stage, the group comes to an end, and members say good-bye to one another and the group experience. In termination, members feel either fulfilled or bitter. Sometimes there is a celebration experience at this point of the group; almost always at least a closure ceremony takes place.

Table 13.2 offers a brief breakdown of the characteristics of each of the five stages discussed here with the characteristics most prevalent in the storming/norming combined.

Overall, the developmental stages of a group are not always easily differentiated at any one point in time. "A group does not necessarily move step by step through life stages, but may move backward and forward as a part of its general development" (Hansen et al., 1980, p. 476). The question of what stage a group is in and where it is heading can best be answered through retrospection or insightful perception.

Issues in Groups

Conducting successful groups entails a number of issues. Some deal with procedures for running groups; others deal with training and ethics. Before a group is set up, the leader of the group needs to have a clear idea of why the group is being established and what its intermediate as well as ultimate goals are. It is only from such a process that a successful group will emerge.

Table 13.2 Four stages of groups

	Forming	Storming/Norming	Working	Terminating
Emphasis	Help members feel they are part of the group. Develop trust and inclusiveness.	Leader and members work through overt and covert tension, frustration, and conflict as they find their place in the group and develop a sense of cohesiveness (i.e., "we-ness.").	Productivity, purposefulness, constructiveness, achievement, and action are highlighted.	Completeness, closure, and accomplishment of tasks/goals are highlighted along with celebration and ultimately the dismissal of the group.
Dynamics/ Characteristics	Members initiate conversations/ actions that are safe; interactions are superficial.	Energy, anxiety, and anticipation increase temporarily. Focus on functioning of group as an entity heightens. Cooperation and security increase toward end of this stage.	Members are more trusting of self and others. Increased risk taking, hopefulness, problem solving, and inclusiveness of others in achieving goals/ objectives. Leader less involved in directing or structuring group. Members become increasingly responsible for running group.	About 15% of the group's time is spent concentrating and reflecting on events signifying the end of the group, such as completion of a task. Members deal with the issue of loss, as well as celebration, individually or collectively.
Role of Leader	Leader sets up a structured environment where members feel safe; clarifies purpose of group; establishes rules; makes introductions. Leader models appropriate behaviors; initiates ice-breaker activities; engages in limited self-disclosure; outlines vision of the group.	Leader manages conflict between members; emphasizes rules and regulations regularly; helps group become a more unified entity.	Leader concentrates on helping members and group as a whole achieve goals by encouraging interpersonal interactions. Prevention of problems through use of helping skills and renewed focus on reaching goal(s). Modeling of appropriate behavior(s) by leader.	The leader helps members assess what they have learned from the group and encourages them to be specific. Leader provides a structure for dealing with loss and celebration of group as well as its ending; arranges for follow-up and evaluation.

Table 13.2 *continued*

	Forming	Storming/Norming	Working	Terminating
Role of Members	Members need to dedicate themselves to "owning" the group and becoming involved. They need to voice what they expect to get out of the group as well as what they plan to give to it.	Members seek and receive feedback from others, which changes from more negative to neutral/positive as group works through power issues and becomes more unified. "I statements" become more necessary and prevalent.	Members concentrate on individual and group accomplishments; give and receive input in the form of feedback about their ideas and behaviors.	Group members focus on the work they have accomplished and what they still need to achieve. Members celebrate their accomplishments, resolve unfinished business with others, and incorporate their group experiences in both unique and universal ways.
Problem Areas	Inactive, unfocused, or uninvolved group members will inhibit the group from progressing. Too much openness is also detrimental. Anxiety that is denied or unaddressed will surface again.	Group may deteriorate and become chaotic and conflictual with less involved members. Corrective feedback may be misunderstood and underused. A sense of cohesiveness may fail to develop, and group may regress and become more artificial.	Unresolved conflicts or issues may resurface. Inappropriate behaviors may be displayed and inhibit the growth of the group. Rules may be broken.	Members may deny the group is ending and be unprepared for its final session(s). Members may also be reluctant to end the group and may ask for an extension. Leaders may not prepare members for the ending and may in fact foster dependency.

Selection and Preparation of Group Members

Screening and preparation are essential for conducting a successful group (Couch, 1995). Some individuals who wish to be members of groups are not appropriate candidates for them. If such persons are allowed to join a group, they may end up being difficult group members (e.g., by monopolizing or manipulating) and cause the group leader considerable trouble (Kottler, 1994b). Or they may join with others who are at an equally low level of functioning and contribute to the regression of the group. When this happens, members become psychologically damaged, and the group is unable to accomplish its goals (McClure, 1990).

Screening and preparation are usually accomplished through pregroup interviews and training, which take place between the group leader and prospective members. The ASGW's *Ethical Guidelines for Group Counselors* (1992) states that during a *pregroup*

Table 13.2 *continued*

	Forming	Storming/Norming	Working	Terminating
Intervention Techniques	Set up the group room where it is conducive to interpersonal interaction, such as arranging chairs in a circle. Help group members feel relaxed, welcomed, and valued. Invest energy in giving group members a say or air time so they are energized and invested in the group.	Leader may introduce structured experiences, rely more on spontaneity, and use increased self-discloure. Leader may employ helping skills, such as active listening and linking, to build trust and sense of togetherness and purposefulness. Leader and members may take limited risks. Acknowledgment of differences as strengths.	More time may be allotted for discussion and interaction of goals and processes. Group may try acknowledgment of what is occurring and using the ideas of the group in reaching a resolution. A reminder to the group of agreed on goal(s) and the finiteness of the group's time may be helpful.	Both the group leader and members may actively remind each other of the conclusion of the process. Groups may be helped through good-bye events, such as celebrations, written or verbal feedback assignments on what they have learned from the group experience, and the joint planning of last sessions and the date of a follow-up.
Ideal Outcome	Leader and members are clear on purpose of group, dedicated to that purpose, and feel a sense of trust in the group and their ability to contribute to it. Anxiety within the group lessens as members get to know each other and the purposes of the group better. Enthusiasm and commitment are heightened.	Differences and similarities within group members are recognized and used. Group becomes cooperative and leader/members invest in it with shared goals/objectives. Conflicts between members are resolved. Group becomes poised to begin the working stage.	Group stays focused and productive; works as a team. Risk taking, creativity, and pride in group and its accomplishments occur. Group makes a transition toward termination.	Group members will have pride in having accomplished planned projects/goals and be able to point to tangible results. Everyone in the group will have dealt successfully with the loss in ending the group. Everyone will leave the group stronger and better connected with other group participants. Everyone will make a successful transition back from the life of the group to everyday life.

interview group members will be selected "whose needs and goals are compatible with the established goals of the group; who will not impede the group process; and whose well-being will not be jeopardized by the group experience" (p. 3). Research indicates that *pregroup training*, in which members learn more about a group and what is expected of them, provides important information for participants and gives them a chance to lower their anxiety (Sklare, Petrosko, & Howell, 1993).

In following ASGW ethical guidelines for group counselors, certain individuals may need to be screened out or may elect to screen themselves out of the group. Screening is a two-way process. Potential group members may not be appropriate for a certain group at a particular time with a designated leader. They should be advised of their options if they are not selected for a group, such as joining another group or waiting for a group to form that is better able to address their situation. In selecting group members, a group leader should heed Gazda's (1989) advice that individuals in the group be able to identify with other group members at least on some issues. In essence, the screening interview "lays the foundation upon which the group process will rest" (McCoy, 1994, p. 18).

Before the group begins, group members and leaders need to be informed as much as possible about *group process* (how group member interactions influence the development of the group). For instance, in *homogeneous groups* (in which members are more alike than unalike), there is usually less conflict and risk taking, more cohesion and support, and better attendance. In contrast, in *heterogeneous groups* (in which members are more unalike than alike), there is more conflict initially, greater risk taking, but support and cohesion may lag and members may drop out (Merta, 1995). It is the process of the group, not the content, focus, or purpose, that will eventually determine whether a group succeeds. In successful groups, process is balanced with content (Donigian & Malnati, 1997; Kraus & Hulse-Killacky, 1996) (see Figure 13.3). "When either the content or the process of . . . groups becomes disproportionate, the group may experience difficulty accomplishing work" (Nelligan, 1994, p. 8). Veterans of group experiences usually need minimal information about how a group will be conducted, whereas novice participants may require extensive preparation. Members who are informed about the procedures and focus of a group before they begin will do better in the group once it starts.

In joining a group, it is important to check first with the group organizer and become clear about what possibilities and outcomes are expected in a group experience. Corey (1995) lists issues that potential participants should clarify before they enroll in a group. The following are among the most important:

- A clear statement of the group's purpose
- A description of the group format, ground rules, and basic procedures
- A statement about the educational and training qualifications of the group leader(s)
- A pregroup interview to determine whether the potential group leader and members are suited for one's needs at the time
- A disclosure about the risks involved in being in a group and the members' rights and responsibilities
- A discussion about the limitations of confidentiality and the roles group leaders and participants are expected to play within the group setting

Regardless of the perceived need for information, research supports the idea that "providing a set of expectations for participants prior to their initiation into a group improves the

Figure 13.3 Balanced process and content

Source: From "Leadership in Groups: Balancing Process and Content," presentation at the annual convention of the American Counseling Association, April 1994, Minneapolis, MN. Reprinted with permission of Diane Hulse-Killacky, University of New Orleans.

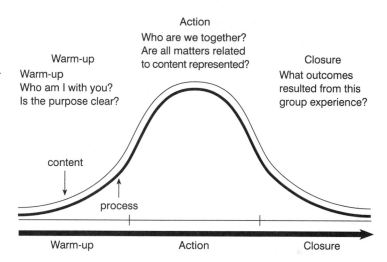

Focus Questions:

Action
Who are we together?
Are all matters related to content represented?

Warm-up
Warm-up
Who am I with you?
Is the purpose clear?

Closure
What outcomes resulted from this group experience?

content

process

Warm-up   Action   Closure

possibility of members having a successful group . . . experience" (Sklare, Keener, & Mas, 1990, p. 145). Specifically, group leaders can facilitate "here and now group counseling . . . by discouraging 'you' and 'we' language, questioning, speaking in the third person, seeking approval, rescuing, and analyzing. Group leaders must model the behaviors they wish others to emulate, such as using 'I messages,'" as the following cartoon shows (Sklare et al., p. 145):

Source: © 1994 by Kurt Kraus. Used with permission.

Finally, group leaders must know how to handle challenges to their leadership and resistance from individual group members or the group as a whole.

Group Size and Duration

A group's size is determined by its purpose and preference. Large groups are less likely to spotlight the needs of individual members. Therefore, outside of group guidance there is an optimal number of people that should be involved. A generally agreed-on number is six to eight group members, although Gazda (1989) notes that if groups run as long as 6 months, up to 10 people may productively be included. Group size and duration affect each other. Corey (1995) states, "For ongoing groups of adults, about eight members with one leader seems to be a good size. Groups with children may be as small as three or four. In general, the group should have enough people to afford ample interaction so it doesn't drag and yet be small enough to give everyone a chance to participate frequently without . . . losing the sense of 'group'" (p. 90).

Open versus Closed Groups

Open-ended groups admit new members after they have started; *closed-ended groups* do not. Lynn and Frauman (1985) point out that open-ended groups are able to replace lost members rather quickly and maintain an optimal size. Many long-term outpatient groups are open ended. Closed-ended groups, although not as flexible in size, promote more cohesiveness among group members and may be productive in helping members achieve stated goals.

Confidentiality

Groups function best when members feel a sense of *confidentiality*—that is, what has been said within the group setting will not be revealed outside. To promote a sense of confidentiality and build trust, a group leader must be active. In the prescreening interview the subject of confidentiality should be raised. The importance of confidentiality needs to be stressed during the first meeting of the group and on a regular basis thereafter (Corey, Corey, & Callanan, 1998).

The ASGW has published guidelines on confidentiality that emphasize group leaders' role in protecting their members by clearly defining what confidentiality is and the importance and difficulty of enforcing it. Whenever any question arises about the betrayal of confidentiality within a group, it should be dealt with immediately. Otherwise, the problem grows and the cohesiveness of the group breaks down. Olsen (1971) points out that counselors must realize they can only guarantee their own adherence to the principles of confidentiality. Still, they must strive to ensure the rights of all group members.

Physical Structure

Where a group is conducted is either an asset or a liability. Terres and Larrabee (1985) emphasize the need for a physical structure (a room or a setting) that ensures the safety and growth of group members. Groups within schools and community agencies need to be conducted in places that promote the well-being of the group. The furnishings of the space (attractive) and the way the group is assembled (preferably in a circle) can facilitate the functioning of the group.

Co-leaders

It is not necessary for groups to have *co-leaders* (two leaders), but such an arrangement can be beneficial to the group and the leaders, especially if the group is large (over 10 members). With co-leaders, one leader can work with the group while the other monitors the group process. A co-leader arrangement may also be beneficial when an inexperienced leader and experienced leader are working together. In such a setup, the inexperienced leader can learn from the experienced one. Many group specialists advocate that an inexperienced leader co-lead a group first before attempting the process alone (Ritter, 1982).

Dinkmeyer and Muro (1979) suggest that successful, experienced co-leaders (a) possess a similar philosophical and operational style, (b) have similar experience and competence, (c) establish a model relationship for effective human interaction, (d) are aware of splitting and member loyalty ties to one leader or the other and help the group deal with this, and (e) agree on counseling goals and the processes to achieve them so that power struggles are avoided.

Pietrofesa, Hoffman, and Splete (1984) recommend that co-leaders sit opposite each other in a group so that leader responsibility and observation are maximized. They point out that it is not necessary for group co-leaders to be of the opposite sex; skills, not gender, matter most.

Self-disclosure

Shertzer and Stone (1981) define *self-disclosure* as "here and now feelings, attitudes, and beliefs" (p. 206). The process of self-disclosure is dependent on the trust that group members have for one another (Bunch, Lund, & Wiggins, 1983). If there is high trust, greater self-disclosure will ensue. An interesting aspect of this phenomenon is that self-disclosure builds on itself. During the first stages of the group, it may have to be encouraged. Morran (1982) suggests that leaders, in the beginning sessions of a group, use self-disclosure often to serve as a model for others and promote the process. As Stockton, Barr, and Klein (1981) document, group members who make few verbal self-disclosures are more likely than others to drop out of a group.

Feedback

Feedback is a multidimensional process that consists of group members' responding to the verbal messages and nonverbal behaviors of one another. It is one of the most important and abused parts of any group experience. When feedback is given honestly and with care, group members can gauge the impact of their actions on others and attempt new behaviors.

Corey (1995) distinguishes between group feedback given at the end of a session and that given at the termination of a group. During the latter process, Corey encourages group members to be clear, concise, and concrete with one another. Group members should give themselves feedback about how they have changed during the group experience. After processing feedback information, group members should record some of the things said during final feedback sessions so they will not forget and can make use of the experience in evaluating progress toward their goals.

To promote helpful feedback, Pietrofesa, Hoffman, and Splete (1984) list criteria for feedback evaluation. Here are some important recommendations:

- Feedback should be beneficial to the receiver and not serve the needs of the giver.
- Feedback is more effective when it is based on describable behavior.
- In the early stages of group development, positive feedback is more beneficial and more readily accepted than negative feedback.
- Feedback is most effective when it immediately follows a stimulus behavior and is validated by others.
- Feedback is of greater benefit when the receiver is open and trusts the giver. (p. 376)

Follow-up

Follow-up is used in a group to keep in touch with members after the group has terminated to determine how well they are progressing on personal or group goals. Often group leaders fail to conduct proper follow-up. This failure is especially prevalent in short-term counseling groups or groups led by an outside leader (Gazda, 1989). ASGW's *Ethical Guidelines for Group Counselors* (1992) states that leaders shall provide for follow-up after the termination of a group "as needed or requested." Follow-up helps group members and leaders assess what they gained in the group experience and allows the leader to refer a group member for help, if appropriate (Gladding, 1999). Follow-up sessions maximize the effects of a group experience and encourage members to keep pursuing original goals (Jacobs, Harvill, & Masson, 1998).

Corey (1995) suggests that a follow-up session for a short-term group be conducted about 3 months after termination. He points out that the process of mutual feedback and support from other group members at this time can be very valuable. If group members are aware during the termination stage of their group that they will meet again for a follow-up, they are more likely than not to continue pursuing their goals. In addition to a whole group follow-up, individual follow-up between leaders and group members is important, even if these sessions are conducted by phone.

Qualities of Effective Group Leaders

There are distinguishing qualities of effective and ineffective group leaders. For instance, group leaders who are authoritarian, aggressive, confrontational, or emotionally removed from the group are ineffective and produce *group casualties* (members who drop out or are worse after the group experience) (Yalom & Lieberman, 1971). On the other hand, four leadership qualities have a positive effect on the outcome of groups, if they are not used excessively (Yalom, 1995):

- *Caring*—the more, the better
- *Meaning attribution*—includes clarifying, explaining, and providing a cognitive framework for change
- *Emotional stimulation*—involves activity, challenging, risk taking, self-disclosure
- *Executive function*—entails developing norms, structuring, and suggesting procedures

It is vital that group leaders find a position between the two extremes of emotional stimulation and executive function for the group's well-being. Leaders should not allow members to experience so much emotion that they are unable to process the material being discovered in the group or structure the situation so rigidly that no emotion is expressed.

Kottler (1994a) states that effective leaders understand the forces operating within a group, recognize whether these forces are therapeutic, and, if they are not, take steps to better manage the group with the assistance of its members. His assessment of leadership complements that of Yalom's (1995) and Osborne's (1982), who believe that good group leaders behave with intentionality because they are able to anticipate where the group process is moving and recognize group needs. An example of this phenomenon is the ability of group leaders to treat the group homogeneously when there is a need to manage group tensions and protect members and to emphasize heterogeneous qualities when the group has become too comfortable and is not working.

In addition, Corey (1995) maintains that effective group leaders are committed "to the never-ending struggle" to become effective as human beings. He lists a number of personal qualities that are "vitally related to effective group leadership" (p. 54). Among them are presence, personal power, courage, willingness to confront oneself, sincerity, authenticity, enthusiasm, sense of identity, and inventiveness/creativity.

A final quality of effective group leaders is that they are well educated in group theory, practice, and techniques. For instance, in group counseling and psychotherapy, "the group leader's task is to translate symptoms into interpersonal issues" (Pistole, 1997, p. 7). By so doing, the leader helps participants in groups learn how to develop distortion-free and gratifying relationships. Regardless of the type of group, leaders employ a number of techniques such as those listed in Table 13.3.

The Future of Group Work

The future of group work is filled with possibilities. It is headed in many directions. One focus of group work is the development of new ways of working in groups that are theory driven. For example, solution-focused counseling and brief therapy groups appear to be gaining popularity and have been found through research to be effective (LaFountain, Garner, & Eliason, 1996; Shapiro, Peltz, & Bernadett-Shapiro, 1998). These groups differ from problem-solving groups in their "focus on beliefs about change, beliefs about complaints, and creating solutions" (LaFountain et al., 1996, p. 256).

Groups are also becoming more preventive. Life-skill training in groups is one example of the prevention emphasis (Gazda, 1989). Four areas of this approach are (a) interpersonal communication and human relations, (b) problem solving and decision making, (c) physical fitness and health maintenance, and (d) development of identity and purpose of life. But the

Table 13.3 Overview of group leadership skills

Skills	Description	Aims and Desired Outcomes
Active Listening	Attending to verbal and nonverbal aspects of communication without judging or evaluating.	To encourage trust and client self-disclosure and exploration.
Restating	Saying in slightly different words what a participant has said to clarify its meaning.	To determine whether the leader has understood correctly the client's statement; to provide support and clarification.
Clarifying	Grasping the essence of a message at both the feeling and the thinking levels; simplifying client statements by focusing on the core of the message.	To help clients sort out conflicting and confused feelings and thoughts; to arrive at a meaningful understanding of what is being communicated.
Summarizing	Pulling together the important elements of an interaction or session.	To avoid fragmentation and give direction to a session; to provide for continuity and meaning.
Questioning	Asking open-ended questions that lead to self-exploration of the "what" and "how" of behavior.	To elicit further discussion; to get information; to stimulate thinking; to increase clarity and focus; to provide for further self-exploration.
Interpreting	Offering possible explanations for certain behaviors, feelings, and thoughts.	To encourage deeper self-exploration; to provide a new perspective for considering and understanding one's behavior.
Confronting	Challenging participants to look at discrepancies between their words and actions or body messages and verbal communication; pointing to conflicting information or messages.	To encourage honest self-investigation; to promote full use of potentials; to bring about awareness of self-contradictions.
Reflecting Feelings	Communicating understanding of the content of feelings.	To let members know that they are heard and understood beyond the level of words.
Supporting	Providing encouragement and reinforcement.	To create an atmosphere that encourages members to continue desired behaviors; to provide help when clients are facing difficult struggles; to create trust.
Empathizing	Identifying with clients by assuming their frames of references.	To foster trust in the therapeutic relationship; to communicate understanding; to encourage deeper levels of self-exploration.

Table 13.3 *continued*

Skills	Description	Aims and Desired Outcomes
Facilitating	Opening up clear and direct communication within the group; helping members assume increasing responsibility for the group's direction.	To promote effective communication among members; to help members reach their own goals in the group.
Initiating	Taking action to bring about group participation and to introduce new directions in the group.	To prevent needless group floundering; to increase the pace of group process.
Goal Setting	Planning specific goals for the group process and helping participants define concrete and meaningful goals.	To give direction to the group's activities; to help members select and clarify their goals.
Evaluating	Appraising the ongoing group process and the individual and group dynamics.	To promote deeper self-awareness and better understanding of group movement and direction.
Giving Feedback	Expressing concrete and honest reactions based on observation of members' behaviors.	To offer an external view of how the person appears to others; to increase the client's self-awareness.
Suggesting	Offering advice and information, direction, and ideas for new behavior.	To help members develop alternative courses of thinking and action.
Protecting	Safeguarding members from unnecessary psychological risks in the group.	To warn members of possible risks in group participation; to reduce these risks.
Disclosing Oneself	Revealing one's reactions to here-and-now events in the group.	To facilitate deeper levels of interaction in the group; to create trust; to model ways of making oneself known to others.
Modeling	Demonstrating desired behavior through actions.	To provide examples of desirable behavior; to inspire members to fully develop their potential.
Dealing with Silence	Refraining from verbal and nonverbal communication.	To allow for reflection and assimilation; to sharpen focus; to integrate emotionally intense material; to help the group use its own resources.
Blocking	Intervening to stop counterproductive behavior in the group.	To protect members; to enhance the flow of group process.
Terminating	Preparing the group to end a session or finalize its history.	To prepare members to assimilate, integrate, and apply in-group learning to everyday life.

Note: The format of this chart is based on Edwin J. Nolan's article "Leadership Interventions for Promoting Personal Mastery," *Journal for Specialists in Group Work,* 1978, *3*(3), 132–138.

Source: From *Theory and Practice of Group Counseling* (4th ed., pp. 72–73) by Gerald Corey. Copyright © 1995 Brooks/Cole Publishing Company. Reprinted by permission of Wadsworth Publishing Company.

biggest manifestation of prevention in groups is in managed health care, where financial premiums are attached to helping individuals stay well or prevent future difficulties.

Overall, the future of group work seems robust and headed toward more diversity in both its theory and practice (DeLucia-Waack, 1996). Multicultural issues, especially in regard to awareness of others, self, training, and research, are receiving more attention (Merta, 1995). For example, Conyne (1998) has developed a set of "multicultural sensitizers" that can be used along with Hanson's (1972) original group process observation guidelines to help students and other trainees become more aware of multicultural issues in group work. Likewise, guidelines for groups that focus on working with specific cultural minorities have been devised. For instance, ways of working with African-American women in groups have been formulated and published (Pack-Brown, Whittington-Clark, & Parker, 1998). More such developments should occur in the 21st century.

Summary and Conclusion

Groups are an exciting, necessary, and effective way to help people. They can take an educational, preventive, or remedial form. The ASGW has formulated standards for psychoeducational groups, counseling groups, psychotherapy groups, and task groups. The theories and some of the techniques used in groups are often the same as those employed in working with individuals. There are differences in application, however.

To be maximally effective, group leaders must be competent in dealing with individual as well as group issues. Learning how to do this is a developmental process. Effective group leaders know what type of groups they are leading and share this information with potential members. Leaders follow ethical, legal, and procedural guidelines of professional organizations. They are concerned with the general well-being of their groups and the people in them. They anticipate problems before they occur and take proactive steps to correct them. They systematically follow up with group members after the group has terminated. They keep up with the professional literature about groups and are constantly striving to improve their personal and professional levels of functioning.

Overall, groups are a stage-based and expanding way of working with people to achieve individual and collective goals. Professional counselors must acquire group skills if they are to be well rounded and versatile.

CLASSROOM ACTIVITIES

1. Reflect on the types of groups mentioned in this chapter. Discuss those groups you are most knowledgeable and comfortable with now. Anticipate the types of groups you might lead in the future.

2. Divide into pairs and discuss the problems and potentials you see in leading a group.

Pretend you have been asked to lead a group of your own choosing. What feelings do you have about this upcoming event? How do you see yourself behaving and thinking during each stage of the process?

3. Examine copies of professional counseling journals from the past 5 years. Report to

the class on articles about groups that you are particularly interested in. Compare your findings with those of other class members.

4. Imagine you are a counselor without any group skills. How do you see yourself functioning in the following settings: a school, an employee assistance program, a private practice? Discuss with the class your thoughts about counselor engagement in various types of groups.

5. Select a topic that is interesting to a wide variety of individuals (e.g., proper diet or dealing with anger), and present a group guidance lesson to your classmates based on information you have researched. Process this experience directly with the class as soon as you complete it. How difficult or easy was the project?

REFERENCES

Association for Specialists in Group Work (ASGW). (1992). *Ethical guidelines for group counselors (1989) and professional standards for training group workers (1990)*. Alexandria, VA: Author.

Avasthi, S. (1990). Native American students targeted for math and sciences. *Guidepost, 33*(6), 1, 6, 8.

Blatter, C. W., & Jacobsen, J. J. (1993). Older women coping with divorce: Peer support groups. *Women and Therapy, 14,* 141–154.

Brown, N. W. (1998). *Psychoeducational groups*. Muncie, IN: Accelerated Development.

Bunch, B. J., Lund, N. L., & Wiggins, F. K. (1983). Self-disclosure and perceived closeness in the development of group process. *Journal for Specialists in Group Work, 8,* 59–66.

Carroll, M. R., & Levo, L. (1985). The association for specialists in group work. *Journal for Counseling and Development, 63,* 453–454.

Childers, J. H., Jr., & Couch, R. D. (1989). Myths about group counseling: Identifying and challenging misconceptions. *Journal for Specialists in Group Work, 14,* 105–111.

Conyne, R. K. (1998). What to look for in groups: Helping trainees become more sensitive to multicultural issues. *Journal for Specialists in Group Work, 23,* 22–32.

Corey, G. (1995). *Theory and practice of group counseling* (4th ed.). Pacific Grove, CA: Brooks/Cole.

Corey, G., Corey, M. S., & Callanan, P. (1998). *Issues and ethics in the helping profession* (5th ed.). Pacific Grove, CA: Brooks/Cole.

Couch, R. D. (1995). Four steps for conducting a pre-group screening interview. *Journal for Specialists in Group Work, 20,* 18–25.

DeLucia-Waack, J. L. (1996). Multiculturalism is inherent in all group work. *Journal for Specialists in Group Work, 21,* 218–223.

Dinkmeyer, D. C., & Muro, J. J. (1979). *Group counseling: Theory and practice* (2nd ed.). Itasca, IL: Peacock.

Donigian, J., & Malnati, R. (1997). *Systemic group therapy: A triadic model*. Pacific Grove, CA: Brooks/Cole.

Ford, D., & Urban, H. (1998). *Systems of psychotherapy: A comparative study* (2nd ed.). New York: Wiley.

Frey, D. H. (1972). Conceptualizing counseling theories. *Counselor Education and Supervision, 11,* 243–250.

Gazda, G. M. (1989). *Group counseling: A developmental approach* (4th ed.). Boston: Allyn & Bacon.

Gladding, S. T. (1999). *Group work: A counseling specialty* (3rd ed.). Upper Saddle River, NJ: Merrill/Prentice Hall.

Goodnough, G. E., & Ripley, V. (1997). Structured groups for high school seniors making the transition to college and to military service. *School Counselor, 44,* 230–234.

Hansen, J. C., Warner, R. W., & Smith, E. J. (1980). *Group counseling* (2nd ed.). Chicago: Rand McNally.

Hanson, P. (1972). What to look for in groups: An observation guide. In J. Pfeiffer & J. Jones (Eds.), *The 1972 annual handbook for group facilitators* (pp. 21–24). San Diego: Pfeiffer.

Hutchinson, N. L., Freeman, J. G., & Quick, V. E. (1996). Group counseling intervention for solving problems on the job. *Journal of Employment Counseling, 33,* 2–19.

Jacobs, E. E., Harvill, R. L., & Masson, R. L. (1998). *Group counseling* (3rd ed.). Pacific Grove, CA: Brooks/Cole.

Johnson, D. W., & Johnson, F. P. (1997). *Joining together* (6th ed.). Boston: Allyn & Bacon.

Kottler, J. A. (1994a). *Advanced group leadership*. Pacific Grove, CA: Brooks/Cole.

Kottler, J. A. (1994b). Working with difficult group members. *Journal for Specialists in Group Work*, *19*, 3–10.

Kraus, K., & Hulse-Killacky, D. (1996). Balancing process and content in groups: A metaphor. *Journal for Specialists in Group Work, 21*, 90–93.

L'Abate, L., & Thaxton, M. L. (1981). Differentiation of resources in mental health delivery: Implications of training. *Professional Psychology, 12*, 761–767.

LaFountain, R. M., Garner, N. E., & Eliason, G. T. (1996). Solution-focused counseling groups: A key for school counselors. *School Counselor, 43*, 256–267.

Lieberman, M. A. (1991). Group methods. In F. H. Kanfer & A. P. Goldstein (Eds.), *Helping people change: A textbook of methods* (4th ed.). Boston: Allyn & Bacon.

Lieberman, M. A. (1994). Self-help groups. In H. I. Kaplan & B. J. Sadock (Eds.), *Comprehensive group psychotherapy* (3rd ed.). Baltimore: Williams & Wilkins.

Livneh, H., & Sherwood-Hawes, A. (1993). Group counseling approaches with persons who have sustained myocardial infarction. *Journal of Counseling and Development, 72*, 57–61.

Lynn, S. J., & Frauman, D. (1985). Group psychotherapy. In S. J. Lynn & J. P. Garske (Eds.), *Contemporary psychotherapies: Models and methods* (pp. 419–458). Upper Saddle River, NJ: Merrill/Prentice Hall.

McClure, B. A. (1990). The group mind: Generative and regressive groups. *Journal for Specialists in Group Work*, *15*, 159–170.

McClure, B. A. (1994). The shadow side of regressive groups. *Counseling and Values, 38*, 77–89.

McCoy, G. A. (1994, April). A plan for the first group session. *ASCA Counselor, 31*, 18.

Merta, R. J. (1995). Group work: Multicultural perspectives. In J. G. Ponterotto, J. M. Casas, L. A. Suzuki, & C. M. Alexander (Eds.), *Handbook of multicultural counseling* (pp. 567–585). Thousand Oaks, CA: Sage.

Morran, D. K. (1982). Leader and member self-disclosing behavior in counseling groups. *Journal for Specialists in Group Work, 7,* 218–223.

Nelligan, A. (1994, Fall). Balancing process and content: A collaborative experience. *Together, 23*, 8–9.

Nims, D. R. (1998). Searching for self: A theoretical model for applying family systems to adolescent group work. *Journal for Specialists in Group Work, 23*, 133–144.

Ohlsen, M. M. (1977). *Group counseling* (2nd ed.). New York: Holt, Rinehart, & Winston.

Olsen, L. D. (1971). Ethical standards for group leaders. *Personnel and Guidance Journal, 50,* 288.

Osborne, W. L. (1982). Group counseling: Direction and intention. *Journal for Specialists in Group Work, 7,* 275–280.

Pack-Brown, S. P., Whittington-Clark, L. E., & Parker, W. M. (1998). *Images of me: A guide to group work with African-American women*. Boston: Allyn & Bacon.

Pence, E., Paymar, M. Ritmeester, T., & Shepard, M. (1998). *Education groups for men who batter: The Duluth model* New York: Springer.

Pietrofesa, J. J., Hoffman, A., & Splete, H. H. (1984). *Counseling: An introduction* (2nd ed.). Boston: Houghton Mifflin.

Pistole, M. C. (1997). Attachment theory: Contributions to group work. *Journal for Specialists in Group Work, 22*, 7–21.

Posthuma, B. W. (1996). *Small groups in counseling and therapy: Process and leadership* (2nd ed.). Boston: Allyn & Bacon.

Riordan, R. J., & Beggs, M. S. (1987). Counselors and self-help groups. *Journal of Counseling and Development, 65,* 427–429.

Ritter, K. Y. (1982). Training group counselors: A total curriculum perspective. *Journal for Specialists in Group Work, 7,* 266–274.

Rogers, C. R. (1970). *Carl Rogers on encounter groups*. New York: Harper & Row.

Rybak, C. J., & Brown, B. M. (1997). Group conflict: Communication patterns and group development, *Journal for Specialists in Group Work, 22,* 31–42.

Saidla, D. D. (1990). Cognitive development and group stages. *Journal for Specialists in Group Work, 15,* 15–20.

Schutz, W. (1971). *Here comes everybody: Bodymind and encounter culture.* New York: Harper & Row.

Shapiro, J. L., Peltz, L. S., Bernadett-Shapiro, S. (1998). *Brief group treatment: Practical training for therapists and counselors.* Pacific Grove, CA: Brooks/Cole.

Shertzer, B., & Stone, S. C. (1981). *Fundamentals of guidance* (4th ed.). Boston: Houghton Mifflin.

Sklare, G., Keener, R., & Mas, C. (1990). Preparing members for "here-and-now" group counseling. *Journal for Specialists in Group Work, 15,* 141–148.

Sklare, G., Petrosko, J., & Howell, S. (1993). The effect of pre-group training on members' level of anxiety. *Journal for Specialists in Group Work, 18,* 109–114.

Stockton, R., Barr, J. E., & Klein, R. (1981). Identifying the group dropout: A review of the literature. *Journal for Specialists in Group Work, 6,* 75–82.

Taub, D. J. (1998). Promoting student development through psychoeducational groups: A perspective on the goals and process matrix. *Journal for Specialists in Group Work, 23,* 196–201.

Terres, C. K., & Larrabee, M. J. (1985). Ethical issues and group work with children. *Elementary School Guidance and Counseling, 19,* 190–197.

Tuckman, B. (1965). Developmental sequence in small groups. *Psychological Bulletin, 63,* 384–399.

Tuckman, B. W., & Jensen, M. A. (1977). Stages of small group development revisited. *Group and Organizational Studies, 2,* 419–427.

Waldo, M. (1985). Curative factor framework for conceptualizing group counseling. *Journal for Counseling and Development, 64,* 52–58.

Waldo, M., & Bauman, S. (1998). Regrouping the categorization of group work: A goal and process (GAP) matrix for groups. *Journal for Specialists in Group Work, 23,* 164–176.

Ward, D. E. (1982). A model for the more effective use of theory in group work. *Journal for Specialists in Group Work, 7,* 224–230.

Yalom, I. D. (1995). *The theory and practice of group psychotherapy* (4th ed.). New York: Basic Books.

Yalom, I. D., & Lieberman, M. (1971). A study of encounter group casualties. *Archives of General Psychiatry, 25,* 16–30.

Zimpfer, D. G. (1990). Publications in group work, 1989. *Journal for Specialists in Group Work, 15,* 179–189.

14

CAREER COUNSELING
OVER THE LIFE SPAN

◆
_____

Far in the back of his mind he harbors thoughts

like small boats in a quiet cove

ready to set sail at a moment's notice.

I, seated on his starboard side,

listen for the winds of change

ready to lift anchor with him

and explore the choppy waves of life ahead.

Counseling requires a special patience

best known to seamen and navigators—

courses are only charted for times

when the tide is high and breezes steady.

From "Harbor Thoughts," by S. T. Gladding, 1985, Journal of Humanistic Education and Development, 23, *p. 68.*
© 1985 by ACA. Reprinted with permission. No further reproduction authorized without written permission of
the American Counseling Association.

The counseling profession began charting its course when Frank Parsons (1909) outlined a process for choosing a career and initiated the vocational guidance movement. According to Parsons, it is better to choose a vocation than merely to hunt a job. Since his ideas first came into prominence, a voluminous amount of research and theory has been generated in the field of career development and counseling.

Choosing a career is more than simply deciding what one will do to earn a living. Occupations influence a person's whole way of life, including physical and mental health. "There are interconnections between work roles and other life roles" (Imbimbo, 1994, p. 50). Thus, income, stress, social identity, meaning, education, clothes, hobbies, interests, friends, life-style, place of residence, and even personality characteristics are tied to one's work life (Herr & Cramer, 1996; NCDA, 1990). Work groups are also cultures in which social needs are met and values developed (Tart, 1986). The nature and purpose of a person's work is related to his or her sense of well-being as well (Burlew, 1992; Campbell, 1981). Therefore, it is important for individuals to choose their careers wisely.

Nevertheless, systematically exploring and choosing careers often does not happen. Nearly one in five American workers reports getting his or her current job by chance, and more than 60% of workers in the United States would investigate job choices more thoroughly if they could plan their work lives again (Hoyt, 1989). Therefore, it is important that individuals obtain career information early and enter the job market with carefully made plans.

The process of selecting a career is unique to each individual. It is influenced by a variety of factors. For instance, personality styles, developmental stages, and life roles come into play (Drummond & Ryan, 1995). Happenstance (Miller, 1983), family background (Bratcher, 1982; Helwig & Myrin, 1997), gender (Hotchkiss & Borow, 1996), and age (Canaff, 1997) may also influence the selection of a career. In addition, the global economy at the time one decides on a career is a factor (Borgen, 1997). In the industrial age, skills needed to be successful were punctuality, obedience, and rote work performance; in the present technoservice economy emphasis is on "competitive teamwork, customer satisfaction, continual learning, and innovation" (Staley & Carey, 1997, p. 379).

Because an enormous amount of literature on careers is available, this chapter can provide only an overview of the area. It will concentrate on career development and counseling from a holistic, life-span perspective (as first proposed by Gysbers [1975]). In the process theories and tasks appropriate for working with a variety of clients will be examined. Specific career assessment instruments will not be covered here but will be reviewed in Chapter 20.

Chapter 14 • Career Counseling Over the Life Span **351**

The Importance of Career Counseling

Despite its long history and the formulation of many models, career counseling has not enjoyed the same degree of prestige that other forms of counseling or psychotherapy have (Burlew, 1992). This is unfortunate for both the counseling profession and the many people who need these services. Surveys of high school juniors and seniors and college undergraduates show that one of the counseling services they most prefer is career counseling. Brown (1985) also posits that career counseling may be a viable intervention for some clients who have emotional problems related to nonsupportive, stress-producing environments. The contribution of career counseling to personal growth and development is well documented (Imbimbo, 1994; Krumboltz, 1994).

Crites (1981, pp. 14–15) lists important aspects of career counseling, which include the following:

1. "The need for career counseling is greater than the need for psychotherapy." Career counseling deals with the inner and outer world of individuals, whereas most other counseling approaches deal only with internal events.
2. "Career counseling can be therapeutic." A positive correlation exists between career and personal adjustment (Crites, 1969; Krumboltz, 1994; Super, 1957; Williams, 1962; Williams & Hills, 1962). Clients who successfully cope with career decisions may gain skill and confidence in the ability to tackle other problem areas. They may invest more energy into resolving noncareer problems because they have clarified career objectives. While Brown (1985) provides a set of assessment strategies that are useful in determining whether a client needs personal or career counseling first, Krumboltz (1994) asserts that career and personal counseling are inextricably intertwined and often must be treated together. Indeed, research data refute the perspective "that career help seekers are different from non-career help seekers" (Dollarhide, 1997, p. 180). For example, people who lose jobs and fear they will never find other positions have both a career problem and a personal anxiety problem. It is imperative to treat such people in a holistic manner by offering information on the intellectual aspects of finding a career and working with them to face and overcome their emotional concerns about seeking a new job or direction in life.
3. "Career counseling is more difficult than psychotherapy." Crites states that to be an effective career counselor a person must deal with both personal and work variables and know how the two interact. "Being knowledgeable and proficient in career counseling requires that counselors draw from a variety of both personality and career development theories and techniques and that they continuously be able to gather and provide current information about the world of work" (Imbimbo, 1994, p. 51). The same is not true to the same degree for counseling that often focuses on the inner world of the client.

Career Counseling Associations and Credentials

The National Career Development Association (NCDA) (formerly the National Vocational Guidance Association [NVGA]) and the National Employment Counselors Association

(NECA) are the two divisions within the American Counseling Association (ACA) primarily devoted to career development and counseling. The NCDA, the oldest division within the ACA, traces its roots back to 1913 (Sheeley, 1978, 1988; Stephens, 1988). The association comprises professionals in business and industry, rehabilitation agencies, government, private practice, and educational settings who affiliate with the NCDA's special-interest groups, such as Work and Mental Health, Substance Abuse in the Workplace, and Employee Assistance Programs (Parker, 1994; Smith, Engels, & Bonk, 1985). The NECA's membership is also diverse but more focused. Until 1966, it was an interest group of the NCDA (Meyer, Helwig, Gjernes, & Chickering, 1985). Both divisions publish quarterly journals: the *Career Development Quarterly* (formerly the *Vocational Guidance Quarterly*) and the *Journal of Employment Counseling*, respectively.

There is also a national credentialing body for career counselors: the National Council for Credentialing Career Counselors (NCCCC). The NCDA started this organization in 1981; since 1985, it has been affiliated with the National Board of Certified Counselors (NBCC). Potential candidates must first achieve the entry-level certification of national certified counselors (NCCs). Then they must pass the Career Counseling Specialty Examination and meet minimal educational course work and experience requirements to advance to the level of a national certified career counselor (NCCC). Minimum competencies for this credential include demonstrated knowledge in six areas: general counseling, information, individual-group assessment, consultation, management-administration, and implementation (Smith & Karpati, 1985). Career counselors should be masters of applied technology, too, especially the use of computers and electronic career searches (Bratina & Bratina, 1998).

Among the many functions that NCCCs perform are administering and interpreting tests and inventories; conducting personal counseling sessions; developing individualized career plans; helping clients integrate vocational and avocational life roles; facilitating decision-making skills; and providing support for persons experiencing job stress, job loss, or career transitions.

The Scope of Career Counseling and Careers

Career counseling is a hybrid discipline, often misunderstood and not always fully appreciated by many professionals or the public (Burlew, 1992; Imbimbo, 1994). The NCDA conceptualizes *career counseling* as a "one-to-one or small group relationship between a client and a counselor with the goal of helping the client(s) integrate and apply an understanding of self and the environment to make the most appropriate career decisions and adjustments" (Sears, 1982, p. 139). More elaborately, Brown and Brooks (1991) define career counseling and related terms as follows:

> Career counseling is an interpersonal process designed to assist individuals with career development problems. Career development is that process of choosing, entering, adjusting to and advancing in an occupation. It is a lifelong process that interacts dynamically with other life roles. Career problems include, but are not limited to, career indecisions and undecidedness, work performance, stress and adjustment, incongruence of the person and work environment, and inadequate or unsatisfactory integration of life roles with other life roles (e.g., parent, friend, citizen). (p. 5)

Throughout its history, career counseling has been known by a number of different names, including *vocational guidance, occupational counseling*, and *vocational counseling*. Crites (1981) emphasizes that the word *career* is more modern and inclusive than the word *vocation*. *Career* is also broader than the word *occupation*, which Herr and Cramer (1996) define as a group of similar jobs found in different industries or organizations. A *job* is merely an activity undertaken for economic returns (Fox, 1994). Regardless of which term they use, career counselors clearly must consider many factors when helping persons make career decisions.

To understand these factors, it is important first to define a career specifically. Super (1976) provides an excellent definition that incorporates a number of experiences. He views a *career* as

> the course of events that constitutes a life; the sequence of occupations and other life roles which combine to express one's commitment to work in his or her total pattern of self-development; the series of remunerated and nonremunerated positions occupied by a person from adolescence through retirement, of which occupation is only one. A career includes work-related roles such as those of student, employee, and pensioner together with complementary avocational, familial, and civic roles. Careers exist only as people pursue them; they are person-centered. (p. 4)

Although not disagreeing with Super, McDaniels (1984) broadens the definition to emphasize the idea of leisure even more. He contends that leisure will occupy an increasingly important role in the lives of all individuals in the future. The integration and interaction of work and leisure in "one's career over the life span is fundamental," according to McDaniels, and expressed in the formula "C = W + L" (where *C* equals career; *W,* work; and *L,* leisure) (Gale, 1998, p. 206).

All theories of counseling are potentially applicable and useful in working with individuals on career choices, but people gain understanding and insight about themselves and how they fit into the world of work through educational means as well as counseling relationships. Well-informed persons may need fewer counseling services than others and respond more positively to this form of helping.

Career Information

The NCDA (then the NVGA) has defined *career information* as "information related to the world of work that can be useful in the process of career development, including educational, occupational, and psychosocial information related to working, e.g., availability of training, the nature of work, and status of workers in different occupations" (Sears, 1982, p. 139). As has been discussed in previous chapters, the word *guidance* is usually reserved for activities that are primarily educational. *Career guidance* involves all activities that seek to disseminate information about present or future vocations in such a way that individuals become more knowledgeable and aware about who they are in relationship to the world of work (NOICC, 1994). Guidance activities can take the form of

- *career fairs* (inviting practitioners in a number of fields to explain their jobs),
- library assignments,
- outside interviews,
- computer-assisted information experiences,
- *career shadowing* (following someone around on his or her daily work routine),
- didactic lectures, and
- experiential exercises such as role-playing.

Career guidance and the dissemination of career information is traditionally pictured as a school activity. But this process is often conducted outside a classroom environment—for example, at governmental agencies, industries, libraries, and homes or with a private practitioner (Burlew, 1992; Harris-Bowlsbey, 1992). According to C. H. Patterson, career guidance is "for people who are pretty normal and have no emotional problems that would interfere with developing a rational approach to making a vocational or career choice" (Freeman, 1990, p. 292). Many government and educational agencies (such as the National Career Information System [NCIS] in Eugene, Oregon) computerize information about occupations and disseminate it through libraries. Overall, the ways of becoming informed about careers are extensive.

Not all ways of learning are as effective as others are, however, and those who fail to personalize career information to specific situations often have difficulty making vocational decisions. The result may be *unrealistic aspirations*, goals beyond a person's capabilities (Salomone & McKenna, 1982). Therefore, it is vital to provide qualitative and quantitative information to individuals who are deciding about careers including the nature of the career decision process, such as mentioning that "career decidedness develops over time" and "the decision-making process is complex, not simple" (Krieshok, 1998). Knowledge of career information and processes associated with it does not guarantee self-exploration in career development, but good career decisions cannot be made without these data. A lack of enough information or up-to-date information is one reason that individuals fail to make decisions or make unwise choices.

Several publications are considered classic references for finding in-depth and current information on careers and trends. They include the government-published *Dictionary of Occupational Titles* and the *Occupational Outlook Handbook*. Some self-help books, such as Bolles's (1998) *What Color Is Your Parachute?* and Leape and Vacca's (1991) *Harvard Guide to Careers*, outline practical steps most individuals, from late adolescence on, can follow to define personal values and successfully complete career-seeking tasks, such as writing a résumé. These books also provide a wealth of information on how to locate positions of specific interest.

A number of *computer-assisted career guidance systems* (CAGSs) offer career information and help individuals sort through their values and interests or just find job information. One of the beauties of computer-based career planning systems is their accessibility: they are available in many settings and with diverse people across cultures and the life span (Harris-Bowlsbey, 1992). Some of the top programs include SIGI-Plus (System of Interactive Guidance and Information, with "Plus" indicating a refinement of the system), DISCOVER, and NOICC (National Occupational Information Coordinating Committee; includes state branches).

DISCOVER and SIGI-Plus are the two programs most widely used in the United States for career planning, whereas NOICC and its state branches are used for specific job listings. "DISCOVER consists of four components: (a) self-assessment (Self-Information), (b) identification of occupational alternatives (Strategies for Identifying Occupations), (c) reviewing occupational information (Occupational Information), and (d) identification of educational alternatives (Searches for Educational Institutions)" (Sampson, Shahnasarian, & Reardon, 1987, p. 416). SIGI-Plus contains five components with a focal point on (a) self-assessment (Values), (b) identification of occupational alternatives (Locate), (c) reviewing occupational information (Compare), (d) reviewing information on preparation programs (Planning), and (e) make tentative occupational choices (Strategy). Ways of enhancing computer-assisted career guidance systems are constantly being implemented, including interactive programs (Sampson & Reardon, 1990; Zunker, 1998).

Career Development Theories and Counseling

Career development theories try to explain why individuals choose careers. They also deal with the career adjustments people make over time because, as Jesser (1983) notes, the average person changes jobs five times in a working life. Modern theories, which are broad and comprehensive in regard to individual and occupational development, began appearing in the literature in the 1950s (Gysbers, Heppner, & Johnston, 1998). "The theories of Donald Super and John Holland are the primary career development and choice approaches currently in use" (Weinrach, 1996, p.6), although a number of other career theories have been generated and some are currently evolving (Zunker, 1998). The theories described here (i.e., trait-and-factor, psychodynamic, developmental, social-cognitive) and the counseling procedures that go with them are among the most prominent. There are presently attempts at developing a comprehensive theory of career counseling, too.

Trait-and-Factor Theory

The origin of trait-and-factor theory can be traced back to Frank Parsons. It stresses that the traits of clients should first be assessed and then systematically matched with factors inherent in various occupations. Its most widespread influence occurred during the Great Depression when E. G. Williamson (1939) championed its use. It was out of favor during the 1950s and 1960s but has resurfaced in a more modern form, which is best characterized as "structural" and is reflected in the work of researchers such as John Holland (1997). The trait-and-factor approach has always stressed the uniqueness of persons. Original advocates of the theory assumed that a person's abilities and traits could be measured objectively and quantified. Personal motivation was considered relatively stable. Thus, satisfaction in a particular occupation depended on a proper fit between one's abilities and the job requirements.

In its modern form, trait-and-factor theory stresses the interpersonal nature of careers and associated lifestyles as well as the performance requirements of a work position. Holland (1997) identifies six categories in which personality types and job environments can be classified: realistic, investigative, artistic, social, enterprising, and conventional (RIASEC) (see Figure 14.1).

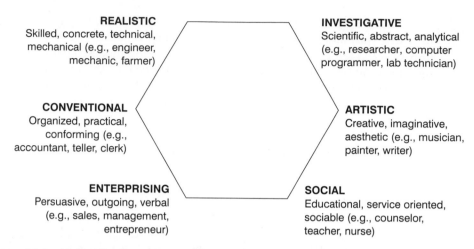

Figure 14.1   Holland's six categories of personality and occupation

Personal satisfaction in a work setting depends on the degree of congruence between the personality type and the work environment (Gade, Fuqua, & Hurlburt, 1988; Holland & Gottfredson, 1976; Savickas, 1989). For example, an artistic person will probably not fit well into a conventional job environment, such as that of office manager. There are exceptions, of course; and as Salomone and Sheehan (1985) and Brown and Brooks (1991) point out, it is likely that some nonpsychological factors, such as economic, social, or cultural influences, account for why many professional and nonprofessional workers accept and keep their jobs.

Nevertheless, as Holland emphasizes, it is vital for persons to have adequate knowledge of themselves and occupational requirements to make informed career decisions. According to Holland, a three-letter code represents a client's overall personality. Thus, a profile of SAE would suggest a person is most similar to a social type, then an artistic type, and finally an enterprising type. However, it is the interaction of letter codes that influences the makeup of the person and his or her fit in an occupational environment. Miller (1998) suggests that instead of using the three highest scores on Holland's hexagon for such a purpose that the top two, middle two, and lowest two scores be paired and presented to give the client a fuller picture of his or her personality profile and similarity to others in a given career. Given the first criteria, Donald Super's profile would be S/I/R, whereas John Holland's would be A/E/IRS. The second criteria would yield a profile for Super of SI/RA/EC, with Holland's profile being AE/IR/SC (Weinrach, 1996).

Trait-and-factor career counseling is sometimes inappropriately caricatured as "three interviews and a cloud of dust." The first interview session is spent getting to know a client's background and assigning tests. The client then takes a battery of tests and returns for the second interview to have the counselor interpret the results of the tests. In the third session, the client reviews career choices in light of the data presented and is sent out by the counselor to find further information on specific careers. Williamson (1972) originally implemented this theory to help clients learn self-management skills. But as Crites (1969, 1981) notes, trait-and-factor career counselors may ignore the psychological realities of decision making and fail to promote self-help skills in their clients. Such counselors may overemphasize test information, which clients either forget or distort.

Psychodynamic Theory

Psychodynamic theory is best exemplified by the writings of Anne Roe (Roe & Lunneborg, 1991; Wrenn, 1985), although Robert Hoppock (1976) outlines some similar ideas by stressing the importance of unconscious motivation and meeting emotional needs. Roe theorized that vocational interests develop as a result of the interaction between parents and their children. Career choices reflect the desire to satisfy needs not met by parents in childhood. From the psychodynamic point of view, the first few years of childhood are primarily responsible for shaping the pattern of life. Roe believes there is an unconscious motivation from this period that influences people to choose a career in which these needs can be expressed and satisfied.

Roe (1956) describes three different parent-child relationship climates (see Figure 14.2). The first is characterized by an emotional concentration on the child that may take one of two forms. The first is overprotection, in which the parents do too much for the child and encourage dependency. The other is overdemanding, in which the parents emphasize achievement. Children who grow up in these types of environments usually develop a need for constant feedback and rewards. They frequently choose careers that provide recognition from others, such as the performing arts.

The second child-rearing pattern is avoidance of the child. There are two extremes within this pattern. One is neglectful parenting, in which little effort is made to satisfy the child's needs. The other is rejecting parenting, in which no effort is made to satisfy the child's needs. Roe speculates that children reared in such environments will concentrate on careers that involve scientific and mechanical interests as a way of finding gratification in life. They are more prone to deal with things and ideas.

The final pattern of child-parent relationships is acceptance of the child. Acceptance may be casual or more actively loving; in either case, independence is encouraged. Children from these families usually seek careers that balance the personal and nonpersonal aspects of life, such as teaching or counseling.

Although not extensively used today in its original form, Roe's psychodynamic theory has generated considerable research. Unfortunately, research on the whole has failed to verify Roe's basic propositions (Beale, 1998). However, some career instruments are based on Roe's ideas, such as the Remak Interest Inventory and the Courses Interest Inventory, and are currently being tested (Meir, 1994; Meir, Rubin, Temple, & Osipow, 1997).

The model underlying psychodynamic career counseling was constructed primarily by Bordin (1968, 1991). His view, which is based on psychodynamic theories such as Roe's, holds that career choices involve a client's needs and are developmental in nature. A major limitation of the approach is its strong emphasis on internal factors, such as motivation, and its lack of attention to external variables (Ginzberg, Ginsburg, Axelrad, & Herma, 1951). The process of career counseling from this perspective is considered overly complex.

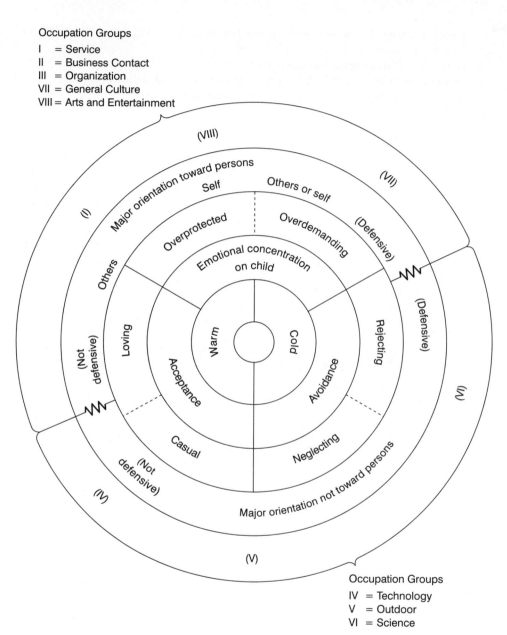

Occupation Groups

I   = Service
II = Business Contact
III = Organization
VII = General Culture
VIII = Arts and Entertainment

Occupation Groups

IV = Technology
V = Outdoor
VI = Science

Figure 14.2   Roe's conceptualization of occupational categories

Source: From *The Origin of Interests* (p. 6), by A. Roe and M. Seligman, 1964, Washington, DC: American Personnel and Guidance Association. © 1964 by ACA. Reprinted with permission. No further reproduction authorized without written permission of the American Counseling Association.

One offshoot of psychodynamic career counseling, which is more concrete but still complex, is based on the work of Murray Bowen (1980) and has been amplified by McGoldrick and Gerson (1985). According to this approach, the uniqueness of people is interconnected with their family of origin. One way of mapping family-of-origin patterns is to draw either a family or career genogram. (Family genograms were discussed in Chapter 12 on family counseling; see Figure 12.3.)

> The career genogram is particularly useful because it provides a direct and relevant frame-work for use with clients to shed light on many topics, including their world views, possible environmental barriers, personal-work-family role conflicts, racial identity status and issues, and levels of acculturation. It has substantial face validity for clients because it provides them with an opportunity to tell their story within the career counseling context. (Gysbers et. al., 1998, p. 157)

Okiishi (1987) has used genograms and a psychodynamically based theory to provide career counseling for undergraduate students. Okiishi's results were successful, illustrating that complex psychodynamic career counseling can still be pragmatic.

Developmental Theories

As stated earlier, the two most widely known career theories are those associated with Donald Super and Eli Ginzberg. They are both based on personal development. The original developmental theory proposed by Ginzberg and his associates has had great influence and has been revised (Ginzberg, 1972). But Super's theory is examined in detail here because more extensive work has been done with it.

Compared with other approaches, developmental theories are generally more inclusive, more concerned with longitudinal expression of career behavior, and more inclined to highlight the importance of self-concept. Super (1957, 1990) believes that career development is the process of implementing a self-concept. People's views of who they are is reflected in what they do. He suggests that vocational development unfolds in five stages, each of which contains a developmental task to be completed (see Table 14.1). The first stage is growth (from birth to age 14). During this stage, with its substages of fantasy (ages 4–10), interest (ages 11–12), and capacity (ages 13–14), children form a mental picture of themselves in relation to others. During the process of growth, children become oriented to the world of work.

The second stage, exploration (ages 15–24), has three substages: tentative (ages 15–17), transition (ages 18–21), and trial (ages 22–24). The major task of this stage is a general exploration of the world of work and the specification of a career preference.

The third stage is known as establishment (ages 25–44). Its two substages, trial (ages 25–30) and advancement (ages 31–44), constitute the major task of becoming established in a preferred and appropriate field of work. Once established, persons can concentrate on advancement until they tire of their job or reach the top of the profession.

The fourth stage, maintenance (ages 45–64), has the major task of preserving what one has already achieved. The final stage, decline (age 65 to death), is a time for disengagement from work and alignment with other sources of satisfaction. It has two substages: deceleration (ages 65–70) and retirement (age 71 to death).

Table 14.1 Super's stages

Growth	Exploration	Establishment	Maintenance	Decline
Birth to Age 14 Self-concept develops through identification with key figures in family and school; needs and fantasy are dominant early in this stage; interest and capacity become more important with increasing social participation and reality testing; learn behaviors associated with self-help, social interaction, self-direction, industrialness, goal setting, persistence.	**Ages 14 to 24** Self-examination, role try-outs and occupational exploration take place in school, leisure activities, and part-time work.	**Ages 24 to 44** Having found an appropriate field, an effort is made to establish a permanent place in it. Thereafter changes which occur are changes of position, job, or employer, not of occupation.	**Ages 44 to 64** Having made a place in the world of work, the concern is how to hold on to it. Little new ground is broken, continuation of established pattern. Concerned about maintaining present status while being forced by competition from younger workers in the advancement stage.	**Ages 64 and Beyond** As physical and mental powers decline, work activity changes and in due course ceases. New roles must be developed: first, selective participant and then observer. Individual must find other sources of satisfaction to replace those lost through retirement.
Substages *Fantasy* (4–10) Needs are dominant; role playing in fantasy is important. *Interest* (11–12) Likes are the major determinant of aspirations and activities. *Capacity* (13–14) Abilities are given more weight and job requirements (including training) are considered.	**Substages** *Tentative* (15–17) Needs, interests, capacities, values and opportunities are all considered; tentative choices are made and tried out in fantasy, discussion, courses, work, etc. Possible appropriate fields and levels of work are identified.	**Substages** *Trial-Commitment and Stabilization* (25–30) Settling down. Securing a permanent place in the chosen occupation. May prove unsatisfactory resulting in one or two changes before the life work is found or before it becomes clear that the life work will be a succession of unrelated jobs. *Advancement* (31–44) Effort is put forth to stabilize, to make a secure place in the world of work. For most persons these are the creative years. Seniority is acquired; clientele are developed; superior performance is demonstrated; qualifications are improved.		**Substages** *Deceleration* (65–70) The pace of work slackens, duties are shifted, or the nature of work is changed to suit declining capacities. Many find part-time jobs to replace their full-time occupations. *Retirement* (71 on) Variation on complete cessation of work or shift to part-time, volunteer, or leisure activities.

Tasks

Developing a picture of the kind of person one is.

Developing an orientation to the world of work and an understanding of the meaning of work.

Task—Crystallizing a Vocational Preference

Transition (18–21) Reality considerations are given more weight as the person enters the labor market or professional training and attempts to implement a self-concept. Generalized choice is converted to specific choice.

Task—Specifying a Vocational Preference

Trial-Little Commitment (22–24) A seemingly appropriate occupation having been found, a first job is located and is tried out as a potential life work. Commitment is still provisional, and if the job is not appropriate, the person may reinstitute the process of crystallizing, specifying, and implementing a preference. Implementing a vocational preference. Developing a realistic self-concept. Learning more about more opportunities.

Tasks

Finding opportunity to do desired work.
Learning to relate to others.
Consolidation and advancement.
Making occupational position secure.
Settling down in a permanent position.

Tasks

Accepting one's limitations.
Identifying new problems to work on.
Developing new skills.
Focusing on essential activities.
Preservation of achieved status and gains.

Tasks

Developing nonoccupational roles.
Finding a good retirement spot.
Doing things one has always wanted to do.
Reducing working hours.

Source: From *Career Guidance and Counseling through the Life Span: Systematic Approaches* (5th ed., p. 321), by Edwin L. Herr and Stanley H. Cramer, New York: HarperCollins. © 1988 by Edwin L. Herr and Stanley H. Cramer. Reprinted by permission of HarperCollins Publishers, Inc.

The major contributions of developmental career counseling are its emphases on the importance of the life span in career decision making and on career decisions that are influenced by other processes and events in a person's life. This "life pattern paradigm for career counseling encourages counselors to consider a client's aptitudes and interests in a matrix of life experiences, not just in comparison to some normative group" (Savickas, 1989, p. 127).

The developmental approach can be conceptualized as career-pattern counseling (Super, 1954). Although this method has been criticized for its historical and descriptive emphases, these features, along with the conceptual depth of the theory, have also been considered strengths (Herr, 1997). Overall, developmental career counseling is strong and continues to grow beyond the comprehensive *rainbow theory* that Super conceptualized toward the end of his life (Super, 1990; Super, Thompson, & Lindeman, 1988) (see Figure 14.3).

Social-Cognitive Theories

Social-cognitive theories of career development have evolved from cognitive-behavioral and social learning theories first formulated in the 1960s. Two of the most prominent models, those of Tiedeman and Knefelkamp, have a developmental base. Tiedeman (1961) and his associates rely on Erikson's (1963) developmental crisis model; Knefelkamp and

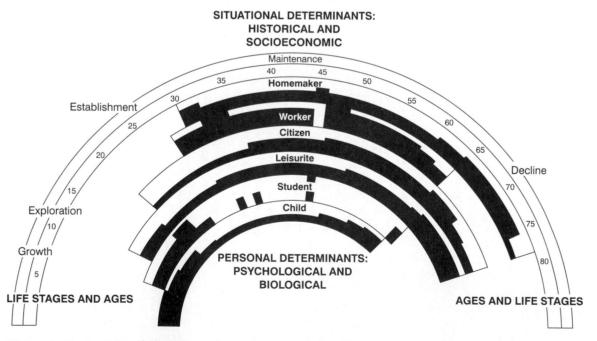

Figure 14.3   Super's rainbow theory: Six life roles in schematic life space
Source: From "A Life-Span, Life-Space Approach to Career Development," by D. E. Super, 1980, *Journal of Vocational Behavior, 16,* pp. 282–298. Copyright 1980 by Academic Press. Reprinted by permission.

Slepitza (1976) build on the work of Perry (1968), which focuses on the intellectual and ethical development of college students.

Tiedeman and O'Hara's (1963) social-cognitive approach outline a seven-stage model of career decision: exploration (ages 14–18), crystallization (ages 18–21), choice (ages 18–25), clarification (ages 18–25), induction (ages 21–30), reformation (ages 21–30), and integration (ages 30–40). There is some overlap among the stages, but each requires the individual to make a decision. This emphasis on the cognitive restructuring of the person from "within to without" is Tiedeman's unique contribution to career development theory. He and his associates view people as more active in the formation of careers than Super does. Careers satisfy needs (Beale, 1998).

Knefelkamp and Slepitza (1976) also focus on a hierarchical structure of cognitive development and the behaviors that accompany such development in describing the career decision making in college students. Their model of career planning takes into account nine variables, such as locus of control, analysis, synthesis, and openness to alternative perspectives. A major weakness of the theory is its lack of measurement of the processes on which it focuses. Moreover, it has not been studied in a noncollege population.

Krumboltz (1979) has formulated an equally comprehensive but less developmental social-cognitive approach. He takes the position that four factors influence a person's career choice: genetic endowment, conditions and events in the environment, learning experiences, and task-approach skills (e.g., values, work habits). According to Krumboltz, career decisions are controlled by both internal and external processes; that is, one has some control over the events one finds reinforcing.

Comprehensive Career Counseling

In contrast to these theories, comprehensive systems of career counseling have been developed. One is the *career-development assessment and counseling model (C-DAC) model* (Hartung et al., 1998). Another is Crites's (1981) model based on the general systems of counseling and psychotherapy, such as those described by Corsini and Wedding (1995), and his own wide experience as a career counselor.

The C-DAC model views a client as an individual in a constantly changing environment (Osborne & Niles, 1994; Super, Osborne, Walsh, Brown, & Niles, 1992). It assesses career maturity and identifies values placed on work and occupational career using a battery of tests and interest inventories, such as the Career Development Inventory, the Adult Career Concerns Inventory, the Strong Interest Inventory, the Value Scales, and the Salience Inventory (Osborne, Brown, Niles, & Miner, 1997). Clients high in career salience and ready for career decision-making activities work with a counselor to objectify their interests, abilities and values. They then take a final step of subjectively assessing life themes and patterns they can identify (Hartung et al., 1998).

The C-DAC model is employed over the life span and holds great promise for multicultural career theory and practice because it already incorporates "important culturally based variables such as work role importance and values" (Hartung et al., 1998, p. 277).

Crites's model advocates that counselors make three diagnoses of a client's career problems: *differential* (what the problems are), *dynamic* (why problems have occurred), and *decisional* (how the problems are being dealt with). Such diagnoses result from a close working relationship between the client and counselor and are facilitated by open communication. Once made, diagnoses form the basis for problem resolution strategies that can be expected to produce more fully functioning individuals, intellectually, personally, socially, and vocationally.

Crites employs eclectic methods in his career counseling. He uses client-centered and developmental counseling at the beginning to identify problems. The middle stage of his process is dominated by psychodynamic techniques, such as interpretation, to clarify how problems have occurred. The final stage of the process uses trait-and-factor and behavioral approaches to help the client resolve problem areas. Crites's version of comprehensive career counseling also advocates the use of tests in working with clients. The focus in test use, however, is on *interpreting the tests without the tests*—that is, letting the client and counselor share responsibility for interpreting what the test results mean independently of standardized norms. Finally, this model of career counseling stresses the use of career information and recommends that counselors orient clients to such information and reinforce them when they make use of it. Crites (1978) developed the Career Maturity Inventory to help counselors determine how knowledgeable clients are about career information and themselves.

Career Counseling with Diverse Populations

Career counseling and education are conducted with a wide variety of individuals in diverse settings. Brown (1985) observes that career counseling typically is offered in college counseling centers, rehabilitation facilities, employment offices, and public schools. He thinks it could be applied with great advantage in many other places as well, including mental health centers and private practice offices. Jesser (1983) agrees, asserting that there is a need to provide career information and counseling to potential users, such as the unemployed, the learning disabled, prisoners, and those released from mental hospitals who seek to reenter the job market. Reimbursement is a drawback to offering career counseling outside its traditional populations and settings. Career concerns are not covered in the DSM-IV, and most health care coverage excludes this service from reimbursement (Burlew, 1992).

Because the concept of careers encompasses the life span, counselors who specialize in this area find themselves working with a full age range of clients, from young children to octogenarians. Consequently, many different approaches and techniques have been developed for working effectively with select groups.

Career Counseling with Children

The process of career development begins in the preschool years and becomes more direct in elementary schools. Herr and Cramer (1996) cite numerous studies to show that during the first 6 years of school, many children develop a relatively stable self-perception and make a tentative commitment to a vocation. These processes are observed whether career counseling and guidance activities are offered or not. Nevertheless, it is beneficial for children, especially those who live in areas with limited employment opportunities, to have a broad, systematic program of career counseling and guidance in the schools. Such a program should focus on awareness rather than firm decision making. They should provide as many experiential activities as possible and should help children realize that they have career choices. As children progress in the elementary school grades, they should receive more detailed information about careers and become acquainted with career opportunities that might transcend socioeconomic levels and gender (Bobo, Hildreth, & Durodoye, 1998).

Jesser (1983) suggests that levels of career awareness in elementary school children may be raised through activities such as field trips to local industries, bakeries, manufacturing plants, or banks. For example, "because pizza is an immediate attention getter with elementary school children, a field trip to a pizza restaurant can provide an entertaining learning experience" (Beale & Nugent, 1996, p. 294) (see Figure 14.4). When such trips are carefully preplanned, implemented, and followed up with appropriate classroom learning exercises (e.g., class discussions), children become aware of a wider spectrum of related occupations, the value of work, and the importance of teams in carrying out tasks.

Other ways of expanding children's awareness of careers are through parent career days or class visitors. "This is an opportune time to introduce the concept of school as work and students as workers" (NOICC, 1994, p. 9).

Splete (1982) outlines a comprehensive program for working with children that includes parent education and classroom discussions jointly planned by teacher and counselor. He emphasizes that there are three key career development areas at the elementary school level: self-awareness (i.e., one's uniqueness), career awareness and exploration, and decision making. Well-designed career guidance and counseling programs that are implemented at an early age and coordinated with programs across all levels of the educational system can go a long way toward dispelling irrational and decision-hindering career development myths, such as "a career decision is an event that should occur at a specific point in time" (Lewis & Gilhousen, 1981, p. 297).

Career Counseling with Adolescents

To meet the career needs of adolescents, the American School Counselor Association (ASCA) has developed role statements on the expectations and responsibilities of school counselors engaged in career guidance (ASCA, 1985; Campbell & Dahir, 1997). These statements emphasize that school counselors should involve others, both inside and outside the school, in the delivery of career education to students.

Cole (1982) stresses that in middle and junior high school, career guidance activities should include the exploration of work opportunities and students' evaluation of their own strengths and weaknesses in regard to possible future careers. Assets that students should become aware of and begin to evaluate include talents and skills, general intelligence, motivation level, friends, family, life experience, appearance, and health (Campbell, 1974). "Applied arts curriculum such as industrial arts (applied technology), home economics (family life education) and computer literacy classes . . . offer ideal opportunities for integrated career education. Libraries and/or career centers may have special middle level computerized career information delivery systems (CIDS) for student use" (NOICC, 1994, p. 9). The four components common to most CIDS are "assessment, occupational search, occupational information, and educational information" (Gysbers et al., 1998, p. 135).

Name _____   Date _____

Activity Sheet #5
Pizza Connection Word Scramble

See how many of these words you can unscramble. The words are from your field trip to a pizza restaurant.

1. risdhawshe   _____

2. eanmarg   _____

3. norew   _____

4. tinjoar   _____

5. oshetss   _____

6. tisasrwe   _____

7. fhec   _____

8. tawire   _____

9. ihcsrea   _____

10. uertntraas   _____

11. azpazari   _____

12. psbuoerns   _____

Answers: (1)dishwasher; (2)manager; (3)owner; (4)janitor; (5)hostess; (6)waitress; (7)chef; (8)waiter; (9)cashier; (10)restaurant; (11)pizzeria; and (12)busperson.

Figure 14.4   Pizza connection word scramble

Source: From "The Pizza Connection: Enhancing Career Awareness," by A. V. Beale and D. G. Nugent, 1996, *Elementary School Guidance and Counseling, 30*, p. 301. © 1996 by ACA. Reprinted with permission. No further reproduction authorized without written permission of the American Counseling Association.

At the senior high school, career guidance and counseling activities are related to students' maturity. The greatest challenge and need for career development programs occur on this level, especially in the area of acquiring basic skills (Bynner, 1997). In general, career counseling at the high school level has three emphases: stimulating career development, providing treatment, and aiding placement. More specifically, counselors provide students with reassurance, information, emotional support, reality testing, planning strategies, attitude clarification, and work experiences, depending on a student's needs and level of functioning (Herr & Cramer, 1996).

Several techniques have proven quite effective in helping adolescents crystallize ideas about careers. Some involve the providing of fundamental information about career entry and development. Others use guided fantasies, such as imagining a typical day in the future, an awards ceremony, a midcareer change, or retirement (Morgan & Skovholt, 1977). More concrete exercises might include completing an occupational family tree (see Figure 14.5) to find out how present interests compare with the careers of family members (Dickson & Parmerlee, 1980).

Another career focus in high schools is youth apprenticeships, a popular approach that provides work-based learning for adolescents. Apprenticeships help students who are not college-bound make a smooth transition from high school to the primary work environment. Although apprenticeships hold much promise, they pose several challenges for career counselors such as (Hoyt, 1994):

> (a) helping clients learn adaptive skills that will enable them to change with change, (b) helping clients find ways to acquire the kinds of work [identified in government reports], and (c) helping clients to develop a personally meaningful set of work values that will enable them to humanize the workplace for themselves and thus receive the personal satisfaction that comes from true work. (p. 222)

In addition to helping youth in school, career counselors must make special efforts to help the estimated 15% to 29% of high school students who leave school before graduation (Rumberger, 1987). These young people are at risk of unemployment or underemployment for the rest of their lives. Educational programs, such as Mann's (1986) *four Cs* (cash, care, computers, and coalitions), can help students at risk become involved in career exploration

Figure 14.5 Occupational family tree

Source: From "The Occupational Family Tree: A Career Counseling Technique," by G. L. Dickson and J. R. Parmerlee, 1980, *School Counselor, 28*, p. 101. © 1980 by ACA. Reprinted with permission. No further reproduction without written permission of the American Counseling Association.

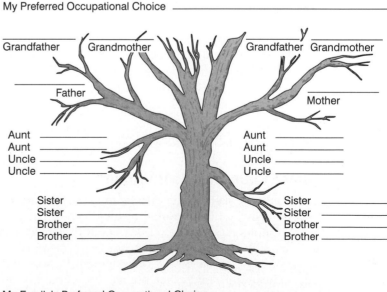

My Preferred Occupational Choice _____

My Family's Preferred Occupational Choice _____

and development. According to Bloch (1988, 1989), successful educational counseling programs for students at risk of dropping out should follow six guidelines:

1. They make a connection between a student's present and future status (i.e., cash, students are paid for attending).
2. They individualize programs and communicate caring.
3. They form successful coalitions with community institutions and businesses.
4. They integrate sequencing of career development activities.
5. They offer age- and stage-appropriate career development activities.
6. They use a wide variety of media and career development resources, including computers.

Career Counseling with College Students

Approximately half of all college students experience career-related problems (Herr & Cramer, 1996). Therefore, college students value career counseling services. Even students who have already decided on their college majors and careers seek such services.

In responding to student needs, comprehensive career guidance and counseling programs in institutions of higher education attempt to provide a number of services. Among these services are

- helping with the selection of a major field of study;
- offering self-assessment and self-analysis through psychological testing;
- helping students understand the world of work;
- facilitating access to employment opportunities through career fairs, internships, and campus interviews;
- teaching decision-making skills; and
- meeting the needs of special populations (Herr & Cramer, 1996).

Another important service is exploring with students the role of leisure in proposed career and lifestyle plans (Weiner & Hunt, 1983). Anticipating problems related to work and intimate relationships, such as preparing to live in a dual-career family, are also important career-counseling services for college students (Hester & Dickerson, 1982). In a review of the published literature on career interventions with college students, Pickering and Vacc (1984) found that most counseling approaches are effective to some degree and short-term behavioral interventions prevalent.

Career Counseling with Adults

Career interest patterns tend to be more stable after college than during college. Nevertheless, many adults continue to need career counseling (Swanson & Hansen, 1988). Indeed, adults experience cyclical periods of stability and transition throughout their lives, and career change is a developmental as well as situational expectation at this stage of life (Borgen, 1997; Kerka, 1991). Developmentally, some adults have a midlife career change that occurs as they enter their 40s and what Erik Erikson described as a stage of generativity versus stagnation. At this time, adults may change careers as they become more introspective and seek to put more meaning in their lives. Situationally, adults may seek career changes after a trauma such as a death, layoff, or divorce (Marino, 1996).

Adults may have particularly difficult times with their careers and career decisions when they find "themselves unhappy in their work yet feel appropriately ambivalent about switching directions" (Lowman, 1993, p. 549). In such situations they may create illogical or troublesome career beliefs that become self-fulfilling and self-defeating (Krumboltz, 1992). An example of such a belief is "I'll never find a job I really like." It is crucial in such cases to help people change their ways of thinking and become more realistic.

There are two dominant ways of working with adults in career counseling: the differential approach and the developmental approach. The *differential approach* stresses that "the typology of persons and environments is more useful than any life stage strategies for coping with career problems" (Holland & Gottfredson, 1976, p. 23). It avoids age-related stereotypes, gender and minority group issues, and the scientific and practical difficulties of dealing with life span problems. "At any age, the level and quality of a person's vocational coping is a function of the interaction of personality type and type of environment plus the consistency and differentiation of each" (Holland & Gottfredson, 1976, p. 23).

According to this view, a career counselor who is aware of typological formulations such as Holland's can predict the characteristic ways a given person may cope with career problems. For example, a person with a well-defined social/artistic personality (typical of many individuals employed as counselors) would be expected to have high educational and vocational aspirations, to have good decision-making ability, to have a strong and life-long interest in learning, to have moderate personal competency, and to have a marked interest in creative and high-level performance rather than in leadership (Holland, 1997). A person with such a profile would also have a tendency to remold or leave an environment in the face of adversity. A major advantage of working from this approach is the ease with which it explains career shifts at any age. People who shift careers, at any point in life, seek to find more consistency between personality and environment.

The *developmental approach* examines a greater number of individual and environmental variables. "The experiences people have with events, situations and other people play a large part in determining their identities (i.e., what they believe and value, how they respond to others, and what their own self images are)" (Gladstein & Apfel, 1987, p. 181). Developmental life-span career theory proposes that adults are always in the process of evaluating themselves in regard to how they are affected by outside influences (e.g., spouse, family, friends) and how they impact these variables. Okun (1984) and Gladstein and Apfel (1987) believe the interplay of other people and events strongly influences career decisions in adulthood.

Gladstein and Apfel's approach to adult career counseling focuses on a combination of six elements: developmental, comprehensive, self-in-group, longitudinal, mutual commitment, and multimethodological. These elements work together in the process of change at this stage of life. This model, which has been implemented on a practical level at the University of Rochester Adult Counseling Center, considers the person's total identity over time. In a related model, Chusmir (1990) stresses the interaction of multiple factors in the process that men undergo when choosing *nontraditional careers* (careers in which people of one gender are not usually employed) (see Figure 14.6). Whether or not careers are nontraditional, the fact is that many forces enter into career decisions.

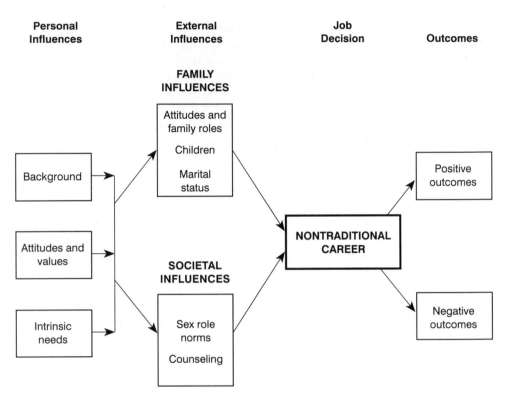

Figure 14.6   Factors contributing to men's adoption of nontraditional careers
Source: From "Men Who Make Nontraditional Career Choices," by L. H. Chusmir, 1990, *Journal of Counseling and Development, 69*, p. 21. © 1990 by ACA. Reprinted with permission. No further reproduction authorized without written permission of the American Counseling Association.

Career Counseling with Women and Cultural Minorities

From the late 1980s to 2000, people of color, women, and immigrants made up more than five-sixths of net additions to the U.S. workforce (Markowitz, 1994). Yet, in the United States women and cultural minorities have historically received less adequate career counseling than European American males have. The reason has often involved stereotypical beliefs and practices connected with these two groups (Herr & Niles, 1994). For example, society has generally assumed that women will have discontinuous career patterns to accommodate their families' needs. Likewise, cultural minorities have often been viewed as interested in only a limited number of occupations. The growing social activism among women and cultural minority groups are helping to challenge constraining negative forces.

Women.   Gender-based career patterns for women have changed for several reasons. For one thing, "children are being exposed to greater and more varied career choices. Additionally, women have moved into careers previously reserved for men, thereby creating a broader range in the role models they provide girls" (Bobo et al., 1998, pp. 40–41).

Since 1970, there has been a dramatic rise in research on and interest in the career development of women (Scott & Hatalla, 1990; Walsh & Osipow, 1994). The trend parallels the increase in women's participation in the civilian work force, from roughly 20% in 1900 to 50% in the 1970s to approximately 75% in the 1990s. Unfortunately, most theories of career development cannot be appropriately applied to women because they were formulated for men or are incomplete (Cook, 1993; Holland, 1966).

In working with women, counselors need to watch out for occupational sex-role stereotyping, even at the elementary school level (McMahon & Patton, 1997). Common stereotypes include viewing women as primarily mothers (nurturing), children (dependent), iron maidens (hard driving), and sex objects (Gysbers et al., 1998). In addition, there is the *"glass ceiling" phenomenon* in which women can rise only so far in a corporation because they are not seen as being able to perform top-level executive duties. In addition, many people often assume that as a group females prefer social, artistic, and conventional occupations (as opposed to realistic, investigative, and enterprising occupations for men) (Tomlinson & Evans-Hughes, 1991). Therefore, girls and women are sometimes not challenged to explore their abilities and possibilities. As a result, some women fail to develop their abilities to the fullest. Consequently, they never work; develop a low or moderate commitment to work; or focus on "safe," traditional, female-dominated occupations such as teaching, nursing, or social work (Betz & Fitzgerald, 1987; Walsh & Osipow, 1994).

To understand why many women choose career paths as they do, Scott and Hatalla (1990) surveyed an extensive number of women from a large, urban, mid-Atlantic university 30 years after their graduations in 1959 and 1960. They found that three factors were common to the sample group, regardless of work history: "the contingency factors of Perception of Interests and Awareness of Skills, and the chance factor of Unexpected Personal Events" (p. 24). These researchers believe the last factor, Unexpected Personal Events, needs further investigation and exploration.

Another area that warrants counselors' attention is demographics and trends. The labor market has shifted from goods-producing to service-producing industries (Van Buren, Kelly, & Hall, 1993). Service jobs are those such as sales clerk and computer operator. If young women take these jobs rather than pursue higher-paying, nontraditional careers in skilled trades, they will be more subjected to economic forces such as poverty, social welfare, and dependence on men that are not in their or society's best interest. Therefore, there is "an urgent need for career counseling interventions" offered through live or video modeling "that will persuade young women to consider the economic benefits of nontraditional career choices" (Van Buren et al., 1993, p. 101).

In addition to girls and young women, two other groups of women workers, displaced homemakers and late entrants, have received and should continue to receive considerable attention. *Displaced homemakers*, who enter the job market out of necessity, and *late-entry or delayed-entry women*, who decide to enter the job market after considerable time at home, pose considerable challenges for career counselors (Isaacson & Brown, 1997). The displaced homemaker often finds herself in a financial strain, uninformed about current job market trends, without a support system, and with a shaky self-concept. Career counselors must first help such women sort out or resolve some of these problems before dealing with major career decisions. In the process, they may assist these women in finding temporary employment, but long-term solutions to career satisfaction take time.

Late-entry women, because of their own motivation and status, do not face the same problems to the same degree. Nevertheless, they usually need more information on careers and, like displaced homemakers, have to identify skills and deal with self-concept and family responsibilities.

Cultural Minorities.

Cultural minorities are so diverse that it is impossible to focus on all the factors that career counselors must deal with in working with them individually or collectively. Many cultural minorities have difficulty obtaining meaningful employment because of employers' discrimination practices, lack of marketable skills, and limited access to informal networks that lead to good jobs (Leong, 1995). In addition, the interest patterns of cultural minorities (as a group) have tended not to fall within Holland's (1997) circular RIASEC ordering in the same way European Americans have, thus presenting challenges for many career counselors in regard to helping them (Osipow & Fitzgerald, 1996). Whereas about 27% of adults in the United States express a need for assistance in finding information about work, the rate is much higher among specific minority populations: African Americans (44%), Asian/Pacific Islanders (36%), and Hispanics/Latinos (35%) (NCDA, 1990).

Counselors must remember that cultural minorities have special needs in regard to establishing themselves in careers. Counselors must be sensitive to such issues and at the same time help individuals overcome artificial and real barriers that prohibit them from maximizing their potential. For instance, some African-American youths who have lived in poverty all their lives are characterized as vocationally handicapped because "they have few positive work-related experiences, limited educational opportunities, and frequently lack positive work role models" (Dunn & Veltman, 1989, pp. 156–157). Structured programs for these individuals use positive role models and experiences to affirm cultural or ethnic heritage and abilities, thus working to address and overcome traditional restrictions (Drummond & Ryan, 1995; Locke & Faubert, 1993).

Career awareness programs for Chinese- and Korean-American parents have also proven beneficial (Evanoski & Tse, 1989). In these Asian cultures, parents traditionally make career decisions for their children, regardless of the children's interests. By staging neighborhood workshops to introduce parents to American career opportunities, a greater variety of choices is opened to all concerned. The success of such workshops is due to bilingual role models and career guidance materials written in the participants' language. Chapter 4 addresses issues of multicultural counseling more thoroughly.

Gays/Lesbians/Bisexuals.

A special minority group not often considered in career counseling are those individuals with gay, lesbian, or bisexual lifestyles. These individuals face unique concerns as well as many that are common to other groups. Of special concern to many gays, lesbians, and bisexuals is whether to be overt or covert in disclosing their sexual orientation at work (Chojnacki & Gelberg, 1994). Persons with minority sexual orientations face personal and professional developmental concerns, including discrimination, if they openly acknowledge their beliefs and practices.

Although traditional career-counseling methods are usually appropriate with individuals of all sexual orientations, special attention should be given to helping gays, lesbians, and bisexuals assess the fit between their lifestyle preferences and specific work environments. Sexual orientation cannot be ignored as an important variable in career counseling if the process is to be constructive (Croteau & Thiel, 1993).

Summary and Conclusion

This chapter has covered information on various aspects of career counseling including its importance and the associations within counseling, such as the NCDA and NECA, that are particularly concerned with its development. Major theories of career counseling—trait-and-factor, psychodynamic, developmental, and social-cognitive—were reviewed along with two recent attempts to develop a comprehensive theory of career counseling. Career counseling with particular populations, especially individuals at different ages, women, and cultural minorities, was examined, too.

Multiple factors, including inner needs and drives and external circumstances such as the economy, gender, educational attainment, ethnicity, and the social milieu, combine to influence career decisions. Developments around the world, especially in technology, are impacting the field of careers as well. "The information age continues to alter the number of job openings as well as the way in which a wide variety of jobs are done" (Walls & Fullmer, 1996, p. 154). As advancing technology creates new or modifies old kinds of jobs, previously valued skills and entire occupations may diminish or vanish. Therefore, career counseling is becoming ever more important, and counselors who are going to be relevant to their clients must be knowledgeable about procedures and practices in this field across the life span.

CLASSROOM ACTIVITIES

1. Think back to your childhood and the careers you were aware of at that time. How do your early career dreams (before age 12) relate to your present professional aspirations? With the class discuss your memories and how they have or continue to influence you.

2. With another classmate discuss your opinions about the importance of including the concept of leisure in the definition of career. Do you agree with McDaniels's emphasis, or do you think leisure is really a separate entity? Share your ideas with the class as a whole.

3. Read about and evaluate a technique that could be used in career information guid-

ance with an age group that you are interested in. Share your information with the class in an oral report.

4. Evaluate Roe's theory of career choice in relation to an individual you know who is established in a career. Interview the person, if possible. Discuss with your classmates how Roe's theory was or was not verified by the information you obtained.

5. Which particular group covered in this chapter appeals to you most in regard to career counseling? Divide the class into groups according to preferences. Focus on areas you consider crucial for your group to master in regard to career decision making. Report your results back to the class as a whole.

REFERENCES

American School Counselor Association (ASCA). (1985). The role of the school counselor in career guidance: Expectations and responsibilities. *School Counselor, 32,* 164–168.

Beale, A. V. (1998). Facilitating the learning of career development theories. *Career Development Quarterly, 46,* 294–300.

Beale, A. V., & Nugent, D. G. (1996). The pizza connection: Enhancing career awareness. *Elementary School Guidance & Counseling, 30,* 294–303.

Betz, N., & Fitzgerald, L. (1987). *The career psychology of women.* New York: Academic Press.

Bloch, D. P. (1988). *Reducing the risk: Using career information with at-risk youth.* Eugene, OR: Career Information Systems.

Bloch, D. P. (1989). Using career information with dropouts and at-risk youth. *Career Development Quarterly, 38,* 160–171.

Bobo, M., Hildreth, B. L., & Durodoye, B. (1998). Changing patterns in career choices among African-American, Hispanic, and Anglo children. *Professional School Counseling, 1*(4), 37–42.

Bolles, R. N. (1998). *What color is your parachute?* Berkeley, CA: Ten Speed Press.

Bordin, E. S. (1968). *Psychological counseling* (2nd ed.). New York: Appleton-Century-Crofts.

Bordin, E. S. (1991). Psychodynamic model of career choice and satisfaction. In D. Brown, L. Brooks, & Associates (Eds.), *Career choice and development: Applying contemporary theories to practice* (2nd ed., pp. 102–144). San Francisco: Jossey-Bass.

Borgen, W. A. (1997). People caught in changing career opportunities: A counseling perspective. *Journal of Employment Counseling, 34,* 133–143.

Bowen, M. (1980). *Key to the genogram.* Washington, DC: Georgetown University Hospital.

Bratcher, W. E. (1982). The influence of the family on career selection: A family systems perspective. *Personnel and Guidance Journal, 61,* 87–91.

Bratina, T. G., & Bratina, T. A. (1998). Electronic career search. *Journal of Employment Counseling, 35,* 1725.

Brown, D. (1985). Career counseling: Before, after or instead of personal counseling. *Vocational Guidance Quarterly, 33,* 197–201.

Brown, D., & Brooks, L. (1991). *Career counseling techniques.* Boston: Allyn & Bacon.

Burlew, L. (1992, Winter). My job, my mind. *American Counselor, 1,* 24–27.

Bynner, J. M. (1997). Basic skills in adolescents' occupational preparation. *Career Development Quarterly, 45,* 300–321.

Campbell, A. (1981). *The sense of well-being in America: Recent patterns and trends.* New York: McGraw-Hill.

Campbell, C. A., & Dahir, C. A. (1997). *The national standards for school counseling programs.* Alexandria, VA: American School Counseling Programs.

Campbell, D. (1974). *If you don't know where you're going you'll probably end up somewhere else.* Niles, IL: Argus.

Canaff, A. L. (1997). Later life career planning: A new challenge for career counselors. *Journal of Employment Counseling, 34,* 85–93.

Chojnacki, J. T., & Gelberg, S. (1994). Toward a conceptualization of career counseling with gay/lesbian/bisexual persons. *Journal of Career Development, 21,* 3–9.

Chusmir, L. H. (1990). Men who make nontraditional career choices. *Journal of Counseling and Development, 69,* 11–16.

Cole, C. G. (1982). Career guidance for middle junior high school students. *Vocational Guidance Quarterly, 30,* 308–314.

Cook, E. P. (1993). The gender context of life: Implications for women's and men's career-life plans. *Career Development Quarterly, 41,* 227–237.

Corsini, R., & Wedding, D. (1995). *Current psychotherapies* (5th ed.). Itasca, IL: Peacock.

Crites, J. O. (1969). *Vocational psychology.* New York: McGraw-Hill.

Crites, J. O. (1978). *Theory and research handbook for the Career Maturity Inventory.* Monterey, CA: CTB/McGraw-Hill.

Crites, J. O. (1981). *Career counseling: Models, methods, and materials.* New York: McGraw-Hill.

Croteau, J. M., & Thiel, M. J. (1993). Integrating sexual orientation in career counseling: Acting to end a form of the personal-career dichotomy. *Career Development Quarterly, 42,* 174–179.

Dickson, G. L., & Parmerlee, J. R. (1980). The occupation family tree: A career counseling technique. *School Counselor, 28,* 99–104.

Dollarhide, C. T. (1997). Counseling for meaning in work and life: An integrated approach. *Journal of Humanistic Education and Development, 35,* 178–187.

Drummond, R. J., & Ryan, C. W. (1995). *Career counseling: A development approach.* Upper Saddle River, NJ: Merrill/Prentice Hall.

Dunn, C. W., & Veltman, G. C. (1989). Addressing the restrictive career maturity patterns of minority youth: A program evaluation. *Journal of Multicultural Counseling and Development, 17,* 156–164.

Erikson, E. H. (1963). *Childhood and society* (2nd ed.). New York: Norton.

Evanoski, P. O., & Tse, F. W. (1989). Career awareness programs for Chinese and Korean American parents. *Journal of Counseling and Development, 67,* 472–474.

Fox, M. (1994). *The reinvention of work: A new vision of livelihood for our time.* San Francisco: Harper.

Freeman, S. C. (1990). C. H. Patterson on client-centered career counseling: An interview. *Career Development Quarterly, 38,* 291–301.

Gade, E., Fuqua, D., & Hurlburt, G. (1988). The relationship of Holland's personality types to educational satisfaction with a Native-American high school population. *Journal of Counseling Psychology, 35,* 183–186.

Gale, A. U. (1998). Carl McDaniels: A life of transitions. *Journal of Counseling and Development, 76,* 202–207.

Ginzberg, E. (1972). Toward a theory of occupational choice: A restatement. *Vocational Guidance Quarterly, 20,* 169–176.

Ginzberg, E., Ginsburg, S. W., Axelrad, S., & Herma, J. L. (1951). *Occupational choice.* New York: Columbia University Press.

Gladstein, G. A., & Apfel, F. S. (1987). A theoretically based adult career counseling center. *Career Development Quarterly, 36,* 178–185.

Gysbers, N. C. (1975). Beyond career development: Life career development. *Personnel and Guidance Journal, 53,* 647–652.

Gysbers, N. C., Heppner, J. A., & Johnson, J. A. (1998). *Career counseling: Process, issues, & techniques.* Boston: Allyn & Bacon.

Harris-Bowlsbey, J. (1992, December). Building blocks of computer-based career planning systems. *CAPS Digest,* EDO-CG-92-7.

Hartung, P. J., Vandiver, B. J., Leong, F. T. L., Pope, M., Niles, S. G., & Farrow, B. (1998). Appraising cultural identity in career-development assessment and counseling. *Career Development Quarterly, 46,* 276–293.

Helwig, A. A., & Myrin, M. D. (1997). Ten-year stability of Holland codes within one family. *Career Development Quarterly, 46,* 62–71.

Herr, E. L. (1997). Super's life-span, life-space and its outlook for refinement. *Career Development Quarterly, 45,* 238–246.

Herr, E. L., & Cramer, S. H. (1996). *Career guidance and counseling through the lifespan* (5th ed.). New York: HarperCollins.

Herr, E. L., & Niles, S. G. (1994). Multicultural career guidance in the schools. In P. Pedersen & J. C. Carey (Eds.), *Multicultural counseling in schools* (pp. 177–194). Boston: Allyn & Bacon.

Hester, S. B., & Dickerson, K. G. (1982). The emerging dual-career life-style: Are your students prepared for it? *Journal of College Student Personnel, 23,* 514–519.

Holland, J. L. (1966). *The psychology of vocational choice.* Waltham, MA: Blaisdell.

Holland, J. L. (1997). *Making vocational choices: A theory of vocational preferences and work environments* (3rd ed.). Odessa, FL: Psychological Assessment Resources.

Holland, J. L., & Gottfredson, G. D. (1976). Using a typology of persons and environments to explain careers: Some extensions and clarifications. *Counseling Psychologist, 6,* 20–29.

Hoppock, R. (1976). *Occupational information* (4th ed.). New York: Harper & Row.

Hotchkiss, L., & Borow, H. (1996). Sociological perspective on work and career development. In D. Brown, L. Brooks, & Associates (Eds.), *Career choice and development* (3rd ed.). San Francisco: Jossey-Bass.

Hoyt, K. B. (1989). Policy implications of selected data from adult employed workers in the 1987 Gallup Career Development Survey. In D. Brown & C. W. Minor (Eds.), *Working in America: A status report on planning and problems* (pp. 6–24). Alexandria, VA: National Career Development Association.

Hoyt, K. B. (1994). Youth apprenticeship "American style" and career development. *Career Development Quarterly, 42,* 216–223.

Imbimbo, P. V. (1994). Integrating personal and career counseling: A challenge for counselors. *Journal of Employment Counseling, 31,* 50–59.

Isaacson, L. E., & Brown, D. (1997). *Career information, career counseling, and career development* (6th ed.). Boston: Allyn & Bacon.

Jesser, D. L. (1983). Career education: Challenges and issues. *Journal of Career Education, 10,* 70–79.

Kerka, S. (1991). Adults in career transition. *ERIC Digest,* ED338896.

Knefelkamp, L. L., & Slepitza, R. (1976). A cognitive developmental model of career development: An adaptation of Perry's scheme. *Counseling Psychologist, 6,* 53–58.

Krieshok, T. S. (1998). An anti-introspectivist view of career decision making. *Career Development Quarterly, 46,* 210–229.

Krumboltz, J. D. (1979). *Social learning and career decision making.* New York: Carroll.

Krumboltz, J. D. (1992, December). Challenging troublesome career beliefs. *CAPS Digest,* EDO-CG-92-4.

Krumboltz, J. D. (1994). Integrating career and personal counseling. *Career Development Quarterly, 42,* 143–148.

Leape, M. P., & Vacca, S. M. (1991). *The Harvard guide to careers.* Cambridge, MA: Harvard University Press.

Leong, F. T. L. (Ed.). (1995). *Career development and vocational behavior of racial and ethnic minorities.* Hillsdale, NJ: Erlbaum.

Lewis, R. A., & Gilhousen, M. R. (1981). Myths of career development: A cognitive approach to vocational counseling. *Personnel and Guidance Journal, 59,* 296–299.

Locke, D. C., & Faubert, M. (1993). Getting on the right track: A program for African American high school students. *School Counselor, 41,* 129–133.

Lowman, R. L. (1993). The inter-domain model of career assessment and counseling. *Journal of Counseling and Development, 71,* 549–554.

Mann, D. (1986). Dropout prevention: Getting serious about programs that work. *NASSP Bulletin, 70,* 66–73.

Marino, T. W. (1996, July). Looking for greener pastures. *Counseling Today,* 16.

Markowitz, L. M. (1994, July/August). The cross-currents of multiculturalism. *Family Therapy Networker, 18,* 18–27, 69.

McDaniels, C. (1984). The work/leisure connection. *Vocational Guidance Quarterly, 33,* 35–44.

McGoldrick, M., & Gerson, R. (1985). *Genograms in family assessment.* New York: Norton.

McMahon, M., & Patton, W. (1997). Gender differences in children and adolescents' perceptions of influences on their career development. *School Counselor, 44,* 368–376.

Meir, E. I. (1994). Comprehensive interests measurement in counseling for congruence. *Career Development Quarterly, 42,* 314–324.

Meir, E. I., Rubin, A., Temple, R., & Osipow, S. H. (1997). Examination of interest inventories based on Roe's classification. *Career Development Quarterly, 46,* 48–61.

Meyer, D., Helwig, A., Gjernes, O., & Chickering, J. (1985). The National Employment Counselors Association. *Journal of Counseling and Development, 63,* 440–443.

Miller, M. J. (1983). The role of happenstance in career choice. *Vocational Guidance Quarterly, 32,* 16–20.

Miller, M. J. (1998). Broadening the use of Holland's hexagon with specific implications for career counselors. *Journal of Employment Counseling, 35,* 2–6.

Morgan, J. I., & Skovholt, T. M. (1977). Using inner experience: Fantasy and daydreams in career counseling. *Journal of Counseling Psychology, 24,* 391–397.

National Career Development Association (NCDA). (1990). *National survey of working America, 1990: Selected findings.* Alexandria, VA: Author.

National Occupational Information Coordinating Committee (NOICC). (1994). *Program guide: Planning to meet career development needs in school-to-work transition programs.* Washington, DC: U.S. Government Printing Office.

Okiishi, R. W. (1987). The genogram as a tool in career counseling. *Journal of Counseling and Development, 66,* 139–143.

Okun, B. F. (1984). *Working with adults: Individual, family, and career development.* Pacific Grove, CA: Brooks/Cole.

Osborne, W. L., Brown, S., Niles, S., & Miner, C. U. (1997). *Career development, assessment &*

counseling. Alexandria, VA: American Counseling Association.

Osborne, W. L., & Niles, S. G. (1994, November). *A tribute to Donald Super.* Paper presented at the Southern Association for Counselor Education and Supervision Conference, Charlotte, NC.

Osipow, S. H., & Fitzgerald, L. F. (1996). *Theories of career development* (4th ed.). Boston: Allyn & Bacon.

Parker, M. (1994, March). SIG updates. *Career Developments, 9,* 14–15.

Parsons, F. (1909). *Choosing a vocation.* Boston: Houghton Mifflin.

Perry, W. G. (1968). *Forms of intellectual and ethical development in the college years: A scheme.* New York: Holt, Rinehart, & Winston.

Pickering, J. W., & Vacc, N. A. (1984). Effectiveness of career development interventions for college students: A review of published research. *Vocational Guidance Quarterly, 20,* 149–159.

Roe, A. (1956). *The psychology of occupations.* New York: Wiley.

Roe, A., & Lunneborg, P. W. (1991). Personality development and career choice. In D. Brown, L. Brooks, & Associates (Eds.), *Career choice and development: Applying contemporary theories to practice* (2nd ed., pp. 68–101). San Francisco: Jossey-Bass.

Rumberger, R. W. (1987). High school dropouts. *Review of Educational Research, 57,* 101–122.

Salomone, P. R., & McKenna, P. (1982). Difficult career counseling cases. I: Unrealistic vocational aspirations. *Personnel and Guidance Journal, 60,* 283–286.

Salomone, P. R., & Sheehan, M. C. (1985). Vocational stability and congruence: An examination of Holland's proposition. *Vocational Guidance Quarterly, 34,* 91–98.

Sampson, J. P., Jr., & Reardon, R. C. (1990). *Enhancing the design and use of computer-assisted career guidance systems.* Alexandria, VA: American Counseling Association.

Sampson, J. P., Jr., Shahnasarian, M., & Reardon, R. C. (1987). Computer-assisted career guidance: A national perspective on the use of DISCOVER and SIGI. *Journal of Counseling and Development, 65,* 416–419.

Savickas, M. L. (1989). Annual review: Practice and research in career counseling and development, 1988. *Career Development Quarterly, 38,* 100–134.

Scott, J., & Hatalla, J. (1990). The influence of chance and contingency factors on career patterns of college-educated women. *Career Development Quarterly, 39,* 18–30.

Sears, S. (1982). A definition of career guidance terms: A National Vocational Guidance Association perspective. *Vocational Guidance Quarterly, 31,* 137–143.

Sheeley, V. L. (1978). *Career guidance leadership in America: Pioneering professionals.* Falls Church, VA: National Vocational Guidance Association.

Sheeley, V. L. (1988). Historical perspectives on NVGA/NCDA: What our leaders think. *Career Development Quarterly, 36,* 307–320.

Smith, R. L., Engels, D. W., & Bonk, E. C. (1985). The past and future: The National Vocational Guidance Association. *Journal of Counseling and Development, 63,* 420–423.

Smith, R. L., & Karpati, F. S. (1985). Credentialing career counselors. *Journal of Counseling and Development, 63,* 611.

Splete, H. H. (1982). Planning for a comprehensive career guidance program in the elementary schools. *Vocational Guidance Quarterly, 30,* 300–307.

Staley, W. L., & Carey, A. L. (1997). The role of school counselors in facilitating a quality twenty-first century workforce. *School Counselor, 44,* 377–383.

Stephens, W. R. (1988). Birth of the National Vocational Guidance Association. *Career Development Quarterly, 36,* 293–306.

Super, D. E. (1954). Career patterns as a basis for vocational counseling. *Journal of Counseling Psychology, 1,* 12–19.

Super, D. E. (1957). *The psychology of careers.* New York: Harper.

Super, D. E. (1976). *Career education and the meaning of work* [Monograph]. Washington, DC: Office of Career Education, U.S. Office of Education.

Super, D. E. (1990). A life-span, life-space approach to career development. In D. Brown, L. Brooks, & Associates (Eds.), *Career choice and development: Applying contemporary theories to practice* (2nd ed., pp. 197–261). San Francisco: Jossey-Bass.

Super, D. E., Osborne, L., Walsh, D., Brown, S., & Niles, S. (1992). Developmental career assessment and counseling: The C-DAC model. *Journal of Counseling and Development*, *71*, 74–80.

Super, D. E., Thompson, A. S., & Lindeman, R. H. (1988). *Adult career concerns inventory.* Palo Alto, CA: Consulting Psychologists Press.

Swanson, J. L., & Hansen, J. C. (1988). Stability of vocational interests over 4-year, 8-year, and 12-year intervals. *Journal of Vocational Behavior, 33,* 185–202.

Tart, C. T. (1986). *Waking up: Overcoming the obstacles to human potential.* Boston: New Science library.

Tiedeman, D. V. (1961). Decision and vocational development: A paradigm and its implications. *Personnel and Guidance Journal, 40,* 15–20.

Tiedeman, D. V., & O'Hara, R. P. (1963). *Career development: Choice and adjustment.* New York: College Entrance Examination Board.

Tomlinson, S. M., & Evans-Hughes, G. (1991). Gender, ethnicity, and college students' responses to the Strong-Campbell Interest Inventory. *Journal of Counseling and Development*, *70*, 151–155.

Van Buren, J. B., Kelly, K. R., & Hall, A. S. (1993). Modeling nontraditional career choices: Effects of gender and school location on response to a brief videotape. *Journal of Counseling and Development*, *72*, 101–104.

Walls, R. T., & Fullmer, S. L. (1996). Comparing rehabilitated workers with the United States workforce. *Rehabilitation Counseling Bulletin, 40*(2), 153–164.

Walsh, W. B., & Osipow, S. H. (1994). *Career counseling for women.* Hillsdale, NJ: Erlbaum.

Weiner, A. I., & Hunt, S. L. (1983). Work and leisure orientations among university students: Implications for college and university counselors. *Personnel and Guidance Journal, 61,* 537–542.

Weinrach, S. G. (1996). The psychological and vocational interest patterns of Donald Super and John Holland. *Journal of Counseling & Development, 75,* 5–16.

Williams, J. E. (1962). Changes in self and other perceptions following brief educational-vocational counseling. *Journal of Counseling Psychology, 9,* 18–30.

Williams, J. E., & Hills, D. A. (1962). More on brief educational-vocational counseling. *Journal of Counseling Psychology, 9,* 366–368.

Williamson, E. G. (1939). *How to counsel students.* New York: McGraw-Hill.

Williamson, E. G. (1972). Trait-and-factor theory and individual differences. In B. Stefflre & W. H. Grant (Eds.), *Theories of counseling* (2nd ed., pp. 136–176). New York: McGraw-Hill.

Wrenn, R. L. (1985). The evolution of Anne Roe. *Journal of Counseling and Development, 63,* 267–275.

Zunker, V. G. (1998). *Career counseling* (5th ed.). Pacific Grove, CA: Brooks/Cole.

15

ELEMENTARY, MIDDLE, AND SECONDARY SCHOOL COUNSELING

◆

I skip down the hall like a boy of seven

before the last bell of school

and the first day of summer

My ivy-league tie flying through the stagnant air

that I break into small breezes as I bobbingly pass.

At my side, within fingertip touch,

a first grade child with a large cowlick

roughly traces my every step

filling in spaces with moves of his own

on the janitor's just waxed floor.

"Draw me a man"

I stop and request

And with no thought of crayons and paper

he shyly comes with open arms

to quietly embrace me.

Each year over three and a half million children begin their formal education in the United States. These children are diverse in both their backgrounds and abilities. Some are developmentally ready and eager to begin their education. Others are disadvantaged because of physical, mental, cultural, and socioeconomic factors. Yet a third group enters school carrying the burden of traumas, such as various forms of abuse, through no fault of their own (Richardson & Norman, 1997). Like children in other lands, American school children face a barrage of complex events and processes that have temporary and permanent impacts on them as they progress in their formal educational experience. Alcohol and other drug abuse, changing family patterns, poor self-esteem, hopelessness, AIDS, racial and ethnic tensions, crime and violence, teenage pregnancy, sexism, and the explosion of knowledge have a direct and often times negative influence on these children (Keys & Bemak, 1997; McGowan, 1995).

Schools are like families, in that they attempt to foster children's development in the midst of an environment that is often less than ideal. Furthermore, schools are like families in that they may face persistent problems that arise in them owing to patterns of interaction rather than isolated events. Schools are like other systems, too, in being "homeostatic"; that is, interaction patterns remain constant. Problems can result in such systems from power struggles, poor communication, and unproductive coalitions (Carns & Carns, 1997).

More than 30 years of research have concluded that in school environments "counseling interventions have a substantial impact on students' educational and personal development" (Borders & Drury, 1992, p. 495). School counselors and the services they provide help children and adolescents become better adjusted academically and mentally. However, "school counselors often struggle to prove their worth to superintendents, principals, teachers, students, and parents who sometimes misunderstand what they do" (Guerra, 1998, p. 20). Part of the problem for this misunderstanding is due to its complexity of the school counselor's job, the history of school counseling, and the organization of schools.

The field of school counseling involves a wide range of ages, developmental stages, background experiences, and types of problems (Paisley & Hubbard, 1994). Within the field, the professional literature focuses on three distinct school-age populations: elementary school children (grades K–5), middle school children (grades 6–8), and secondary school children (grades 9–12). Counselors who work in schools on the precollege level most often affiliate professionally with the American School Counselor Association (ASCA) (801 N. Fairfax Street, Suite 310, Alexandria, VA 22314), which publishes a periodical, Professional School Counseling, *that encompasses all levels of working with young people in educational settings.*

This chapter examines the unique and overlapping roles of school counselors at the elementary, middle, and secondary levels. It addresses the special situational and devel-

opmental aspects of dealing with each school-age population. Furthermore, it empha-sizes that school counselors at all levels must be sensitive to children's cultural back-grounds and differing worldviews as well as their own personal assumptions, values, and biases (Baker, 1994; Hobson & Kanitz, 1996; Whitledge, 1994). Particular attention is given to prevention and treatment issues associated with children in schools. "Managing stress and learning healthy life-style behaviors are lifelong skills, which need to be taught early, practiced, and reinforced throughout the school years" (Romano, Miller, & Nord-ness, 1996, p. 269). Wherever possible, prevention and treatment for children need to be linked so that schools, families, and communities are working together in an interactive and informed way (Keys & Bemak, 1997).

In addition, this chapter explores in an integrated manner the three major areas of student development associated with school counseling: academic development, career development, and personal/social development (Campbell & Dahir, 1997).

Elementary School Counseling and Guidance

Elementary school counseling and guidance is a relatively recent development. The first book on this subject was not published until the 1950s, and the discipline was virtually nonexistent before 1965 (Dinkmeyer, 1973, 1989). In fact, fewer than 10 universities offered course work in elementary school counseling in 1964 (Muro, 1981).

The development of elementary school counseling was slow for three reasons (Peters, 1980; Schmidt, 1999). First, many people believed that elementary school teachers should serve as counselors for their students because they worked with them all day and were in an ideal position to identify specific problems. Second, counseling at the time was primarily concerned with vocational development, which is not a major focus of elementary school-children. Finally, many people did not recognize a need for counseling on the elementary school level. Psychologists and social workers were employed by some secondary schools to diagnose emotional and learning problems in older children and offer advice in difficult family situations, but full-time counseling on the elementary level was not considered.

The first elementary school counselors were employed in the late 1950s, but elementary school counseling did not gain momentum until the 1960s (Faust, 1968). In 1964, Congress passed the National Defense Education Act (NDEA) Title V-A, and counseling services were extended to include elementary schoolchildren (Minkoff & Terres, 1985). Two years later, the Joint Committee on the Elementary School Counselor (a cooperative effort between the Association for Counselor Education and Supervision [ACES] and ASCA) issued a report defining the roles and functions of the elementary school counselor, which emphasized counseling, consultation, and coordination (ACES-ASCA, 1966). Government grants to establish training institutes for elementary school counselors were authorized in 1968; by 1972, more than 10,000 elementary school counselors were employed (Dinkmeyer, 1973).

During the 1970s, the number of counselors entering the elementary school counseling specialty leveled off and then fell temporarily owing to declining school enrollments and economic problems (Baker, 1995). In the late 1980s, however, accrediting agencies and state departments of public instruction began mandating that schools provide counseling services on the elementary level, and a surge in demand for elementary school counselors ensued. This renewed interest in the specialty was a result of publications such as *A Nation at Risk*, which was released by the National Commission of Excellence in Education (Schmidt, 1999). Although it does not refer to elementary school counseling, the report emphasizes accountability and effectiveness within schools at all levels.

Emphases and Roles

Elementary school counselors are a vanguard in the mental health movement (Gysbers & Henderson, 1994). No other profession has ever been organized to work with individuals from a purely preventive and developmental perspective. Among the tasks that elementary school counselors regularly perform are the following:

* implement effective classroom guidance,
* provide individual and small group counseling,
* assist students in identifying their skills and abilities,
* work with special populations,
* develop students' career awareness,
* coordinate school, community, and business resources,
* consult with teachers and other professionals,
* communicate and exchange information with parents/guardians, and
* participate in school improvement and interdisciplinary teams (Campbell & Dahir, 1997).

As Wilson and Rotter (1980) point out, "the elementary school counselor is charged with facilitating optimal development of the whole child" (p. 179).

A study in California of the perceived, actual, and ideal roles of elementary school counselors found that the majority of counselors who were surveyed spent a large portion of their time in counseling, consultation, and parental-help activities (Furlong, Atkinson, & Janoff, 1979). Their actual and ideal roles were nearly identical. Schmidt and Osborne (1982) found similar results in a study of North Carolina elementary school counselors, whose top activities were counseling with individuals and groups and consulting with teachers. Morse and Russell (1988) also found preferences involving consultation, counseling, and group work when they analyzed roles of Pacific Northwest elementary school counselors in K–5 settings. Three of the five highest-ranked actual roles of these counselors involved consultation activities, while two of the five included individual counseling with students. These counselors ranked four of their top five ideal activities as those that involved working with groups of students. Indeed, it appears that elementary school counselors desire to spend more time in group activities with children (Partin, 1993).

The lowest-ranked and most inappropriate tasks that other school personnel try to assign elementary school counselors include substitute teaching, monitoring lunchrooms or playgrounds, and acting as school disciplinarian or student records clerk. The emphases that elementary school counselors place on such noncounseling services have important consequences for them and the children and schools they serve. If counselors are used in such ways, they lose their effectiveness and everyone suffers.

In an important article on the effectiveness of elementary school counseling, Gerler (1985) reviewed research reports published in *Elementary School Guidance and Counseling* from 1974 to 1984. He focused on studies designed to help children from behavioral, affective, social, and mental image/sensory awareness perspectives. Gerler found strong evidence that elementary school counseling programs "can positively influence the affective, behavioral, and inter-personal domains of children's lives and, as a result, can affect children's achievement positively" (1985, p. 45). In another article, Keat (1990) detailed how elementary school counselors can use a multimodal approach called HELPING (an acronym for health; emotions; learning; personal relationships; imagery; need to know; and guidance of actions, behaviors, and consequences) to help children grow and develop.

The fact that elementary school counselors can and do make a difference in the lives of the children they serve is a strong rationale for keeping and increasing their services. It is easier to handle difficulties during the younger years than at later times (Bailey, Deery, Gehrke, Perry, & Whitledge, 1989; Campbell & Dahir, 1997).

Activities

Elementary school counselors engage in a number of activities. Some of these are prescribed by law, such as the reporting of child abuse. "In the United States, all 50 states and the District of Columbia have laws that require schools and their agents to report suspicions or allegations of child abuse and neglect to a local agency mandated to protect children" (Barrett-Kruse, Martinez, & Carll, 1998, p. 57). Most activities of elementary school counselors are not so legally mandated, however, and include a plethora of preventive and remedial activities. Prevention is preferred because of its psychological payoff in time invested and results.

Prevention.   Elementary school counseling programs strive to create a positive school environment for students. They emphasize the four *C*s: counseling services, coordination of activities, consultation with others, and curriculum development. The last activity, curriculum development, is both developmental and educational. It focuses on formulating "guidance classes [on] life skills and in preventing . . . difficulties" that might otherwise occur (Bailey et al., 1989, p. 9). As an example of proactive classroom guidance, Magnuson (1996) developed a lesson for fourth graders that compared the web the spider, Charlotte, spins for physical nutrition in the book *Charlotte's Web* (White, 1952) with the webs human beings spin for person nurturing. Just as Charlotte needed a variety of insects to stay healthy, the lesson stressed people need to attract a variety of friends and support to live life to the fullest. The lesson ended with children not only discussing the parallels between Charlotte and themselves but also drawing a "personal web" filled with significant and important persons in their lives (see Figure 15.1).

A first priority for elementary school counselors is making themselves known and establishing links with others. "School personnel are not usually viewed by young children as the first source of help" (Bachman, 1975, p. 108). Therefore, elementary school coun-

Figure 15.1 Source: From "Charlotte's Web: Expanding a Classroom Activity for a Guidance Lesson," by S. Magnuson, 1996, *Elementary School Guidance and Counseling, 31*, p. 76. © 1996 by ACA. Reprinted with permission. No further reproduction authorized without written permission of the American Counseling Association.

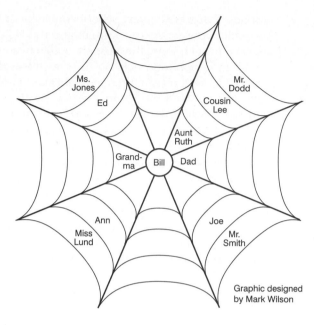

selors need to publicize who they are, what they do, and how and when they can help. This process is usually handled best through orientation programs, classroom visits, or both. The important point is to let children, parents, teachers, and administrators know that counseling and guidance services are a vital part of the total school environment.

For instance, in situations in which very young children (3- to 5-year-olds) are part of the school environment, elementary school counselors can make themselves known by offering special assistance to these children and their families such as monitoring developmental aspects of the children's lives (Hohenshil & Hohenshil, 1989). Many children in this age range face a multitude of detrimental conditions including poverty, family/community violence, and neglect (Carnegie Task Force on Meeting the Needs of Young Children, 1994). The efforts of elementary school counselors with these children may include offering prosocial classroom guidance lessons centered around socialization skills (Morganett, 1994; Paisley & Hubbard, 1994). Furthermore, elementary school counselors can consult with teachers and other mental health professionals to be sure that efforts at helping these young children are maximized.

It is especially important to work with parents and the community when children, regardless of age, are at risk for developing either low self-concepts or antisocial attitudes. Family counseling interventions by school counselors are increasingly used approaches that focus on three primary subsystems: the family, the school, and the subsystem formed by the family and school interactions (Lewis, 1996). Elementary school counselors (and for that matter middle and secondary school counselors, too) avoid assuming that most student problems are a result of dysfunctional families and instead focus on constructively addressing all three subsystems as needed. Another way of combating potential destructiveness is known as *multiple concurrent actions*. In this approach, counselors access more than one set of services within the community at a time—for example, social services and learning disabilities specialists. This type of coordinated action between school and community agencies is collaborative and integrative, and it requires energy and commitment on the part of the counselor (Keys, Bemak, Carpenter, & King-Sears, 1998).

Simultaneous with publicizing their services and establishing relationships with others, elementary school counselors must be active in their schools in a variety of ways, especially in guidance activities. Myrick (1993) recommends a proactive, developmental, comprehensive approach to guidance programs: two to three large classroom meetings each week and twice as many small-group sessions. These activities focus on structured learning, such as understanding oneself, decision making, problem solving, establishing healthy girl-boy relations, and how to get along with teachers and make friends (Coppock, 1993; Snyder & Daly, 1993). Classroom guidance should also address conflict resolution and peer mediation in which students learn peaceful and constructive ways of settling differences and preventing violence (Carruthers, Sweeney, Kmitta, & Harris, 1996).

Other preventive services offered by elementary school counselors include setting up peer counselor programs and consultation/education activities. *Peer counselors* are specially selected and trained students who serve the school and the counselor in positive and unique ways. They may help students get to know one another, create an atmosphere of sharing and acceptance, or provide opportunities for other students to resolve personal difficulties by acting as counselor assistants (Garner, Martin, & Martin, 1989). In these ways, peer counselors help elementary school counselors reach a number of individuals they might otherwise miss. They also enhance the overall cooperative atmosphere and problem-solving skills of the students (Joynt, 1993).

By implementing consultation/education sessions for teachers, administrators, and parents, counselors address common concerns and teach new ways of handling old problems by getting many people committed to working in a cooperative manner (Dougherty, 1986). For example, helping establish culturally compatible classrooms in which student diversity is recognized, appreciated, and used is a service counselors can provide constituents (Herring & White, 1995). Promoting communication skills between teachers and students is another crucial cooperative service school counselors can set up (Hawes, 1989). Yet a third cooperative service school counselors can provide is a class on parenting skills that emphasize effective communication procedures and behavior management (Ritchie & Partin, 1994).

Skilled elementary school counselors can even use their counseling role in a preventive way, too. For instance, by meeting regularly in individual sessions with at-risk children (those most likely to develop problems because of their backgrounds or present behaviors) counselors can assess how well these children are functioning and what interventions, if any, might be helpful to them or significant others (Webb, 1992). Preventive counseling services are also needed for gifted and talented students. Although this subgroup of students may appear to function well, in reality these individuals may have some concerns, such as underachieving, overextending, and handling stress (Kaplan & Geoffroy, 1993).

In working with children and the topic of divorce, elementary school counselors can do much good on the preventive level (Crosbie-Burnett & Newcomer, 1989). Preventively, they can address divorce as a topic in classroom guidance classes. Such classes should be informationally humane in intent and aimed at alleviating much of the negative stereotyping and myths that surround divorce. Elementary school counselors can use small groups to concentrate on specific children's needs regarding divorce too, thus preventing further problems. Groups for children experiencing divorce have been found effective in reducing dysfunctional behaviors, especially if both the custodial and noncustodial parents are involved (Frieman, 1994).

Remediation.   *Remediation* is the act of trying to make a situation right. The word implies that something is wrong and that it will take work to implement correction. In elementary school counseling, a number of activities come under the remediation heading. One example is children's self-esteem.

Children's self-esteem is related to their *self-concept,* how they "perceive themselves in a variety of areas, academically, physically, socially, and so forth" (McWhirter, McWhirter, McWhirter, & McWhirter, 1994, p. 190). *Self-esteem* results from the comparison of oneself to others in a peer group. Although it may be situational or characterological, self-esteem is basically how well individuals like what they see—how people evaluate themselves (Street & Isaacs, 1998). To enhance self-esteem is an arduous process. For such a task, counselors need to focus on helping low self-esteem children, who are at risk for failure, improve in the following areas: critical school academic competencies, self-concept, communication skills, coping ability, and control. McWhirter et al. calls these the "Five Cs of Competency" (1994, p. 188). Counselors can enhance self-esteem in these areas by focusing on skill building, such as improving social skills, problem-solving skills, and coping skills (Street & Isaacs, 1998). In working in remediation, elementary school counselors must rely on their individual and group counseling skills, as well as their social action abilities in making environmental changes and modifications.

One way of determining what needs to be remediated and at what level is to use a needs assessment. *Needs assessments* are structured surveys that focus on the systematic appraisal of the types, depths, and scope of problems in particular populations (Cook, 1989; Rossi & Freeman, 1993). Needs assessments may be purchased commercially, borrowed and modified from others, or originated by an institution's staff. In school settings, counselors can gain a great deal of useful information if they regularly take the time to survey students, teachers, parents, and support personnel. This knowledge helps them address specific problems (Stiltner, 1978). Typically, concerns uncovered through needs assessments fall into four main areas: school, family relations, relationships with others, and the self (Dinkmeyer & Caldwell, 1970). The Survey of Student Concerns (Berube & Berube, 1997) is an excellent example of a needs assessment (see Figure 15.2).

In remediation sessions, young children often respond best to counseling strategies built around techniques that require active participation. Play therapy, bibliotherapy, and the use of games are three strategic interventions that help counselors establish rapport with young children and facilitate their self-understanding.

Play therapy is a specialized way of working with children that requires skill and training. It, along with art therapy, is "less limited by cultural differences" between counselors and clients "than are other forms of interventions" (Cochran, 1996, p. 287). Therefore, this form of counseling is covered more and more frequently in counselor education programs (Landreth, 1991). Basically, children express emotions by manipulating play media such as toys. When counselors participate with children in the play process—that is, communicate by acknowledging children's thoughts and feelings—they establish rapport and a helping relationship (Campbell, 1993b). By expressing their feelings in a natural way, children are more able to recognize and constructively deal with volatile affect (Thompson & Rudolph, 1996). A number of approaches can be used in play therapy, but Jungian (Allan & Brown, 1993) and person centered (Landreth, 1993) are two of the most popular.

When conducting play sessions with children, it is ideal to have a well-equipped playroom. But most schools do not, so counselors usually need a tote bag in which to store their materials (Landreth, 1987). Play materials fall into one of three broad categories: real-life toys, acting-out or aggressive toys, and toys for creative expression or release (Landreth, 1987). Items frequently include puppets, masks, drawing materials, and clay. Sand play has been effective in working with children who have low self-esteem, poor academic progress, high anxiety, and mild depression (Allan & Brown, 1993; Carmichael, 1994). In some situations, counselors may work with parents to continue play therapy sessions at home (Guerney, 1983); in other cases, counselors may hold counseling sessions for students who are involved in play therapy (Landreth, 1983).

Bibliotherapy can be used, too, in counseling and guidance activities with elementary schoolchildren (Borders & Paisley, 1992; Gladding & Gladding, 1991). Bibliotherapy is "the use of books [or media] as aids to help children gain insight into their problems and find appropriate solutions" (Hollander, 1989, pp. 184–185). For example, books and videos that emphasize diversity, such as *Babe, Pocahontas, The Lion King*, or *The Little Mermaid*, may be used to promote acceptance and tolerance (Richardson & Norman, 1997). These counseling tools are especially helpful if counselors summarize stories for children, openly discuss characters' feelings, explore consequences of a character's action, and sometimes draw conclusions (Schrank, 1982).

School counselors who work directly with children who have been abused may also choose to use bibliotherapy because of the way media promote nonthreatening relationships. A number of books can be used therapeutically with children who have been sexually abused. Two of the best are *I Can't Talk about It*, a book about how a young girl deals with her father touching her private parts, and *My Body Is Private*, a book about a young girl's awareness of her body and her discussion with her mother about keeping one's body private.

Games are yet a third way to work with elementary schoolchildren in counseling. Games "offer a safe, relatively non-threatening connection to children's problems" (Friedberg, 1996, p. 17). They are also familiar to children and valued by them. What's more, games are considered fun and enhance the counseling relationship. For example, playing with a Nerf ball may relax a nervous child and lead to the revealing by the child of troublesome behaviors.

A number of games have been professionally developed to deal with such common elementary schoolchild problems as assertiveness, anger, self-control, anxiety, and depression (Berg, 1986, 1989, 1990a, 1990b, 1990c). In addition, counselors can make up games, the best of which are simple, flexible, and connected with the difficulties the child is experiencing (Friedberg, 1996).

Middle School Counseling and Guidance

Emphasis on middle school counseling and guidance is an even more recent phenomenon than elementary school counseling. It came into prominence in the 1970s as a hybrid

<table>
<tr><td colspan="3" align="center">**Survey of Student Concerns**</td></tr>
</table>

I am in Grade_____   Please check one: Boy____   Girl____

Please check the space which best describes your answer to the following statements. Use the scale below.

Concerned a lot: Means that you spend a lot of time thinking or worrying about it.
Concerned a little: Means that you spend some time thinking or worrying about it.
Not concerned: Means that you seldom think or worry about it, or it may be a problem you have already solved.

After each category, there is a place marked "Other." If you have a concern that was not listed in that category, write it down and mark the proper space.

Remember: There are no right or wrong answers! Your answers will be confidential since no name is to be put on the survey.

	Concerned a lot	Concerned a little
Health and growth		
1. My weight	_____	_____
2. My size	_____	_____
3. My physical development	_____	_____
4. Sickness/not feeling well	_____	_____
5. A physical handicap	_____	_____
6. How I look	_____	_____
7. Other	_____	_____
My personality		
1. Not being smart enough	_____	_____
2. My temper	_____	_____
3. Daydreaming	_____	_____
4. Being easily hurt	_____	_____
5. Being shy or bashful	_____	_____
6. Being teased or made fun of	_____	_____
7. Lacking self-confidence	_____	_____
8. Feeling guilty	_____	_____
9. Feeling jealous	_____	_____
10. Mistakes I have made	_____	_____
11. Being popular	_____	_____
12. Other	_____	_____

Figure 15.2   Survey of Student Concerns

School and school work
1. Getting poor grades/not passing   _____   _____
2. Getting into trouble   _____   _____
3. Too much school work to do at home   _____   _____
4. Can't concentrate   _____   _____
5. School is too strict   _____   _____
6. Don't like school   _____   _____
7. Being called on in class   _____   _____
8. Don't understand the work   _____   _____
9. Other   _____   _____

Home and family
1. Money problems at home   _____   _____
2. Family relationships   _____   _____
3. Parents not understanding me   _____   _____
4. Parents telling me what to do   _____   _____
5. Parents expect too much from me   _____   _____
6. Quarreling or arguing with family members   _____   _____
7. Seldom discuss things   _____   _____
8. Being treated like a baby   _____   _____
9. Other   _____   _____

Friends and other people
1. Making friends   _____   _____
2. My clothes   _____   _____
3. People gossiping   _____   _____
4. Being bored   _____   _____
5. Not being a member of a certain group   _____   _____
6. Having a girlfriend/boyfriend   _____   _____
7. Problems with other kids   _____   _____
8. Other   _____   _____

My future
1. How will violence in the world affect me   _____   _____
2. How to earn money   _____   _____
3. Deciding what to do after high school   _____   _____
4. What am I going to be   _____   _____
5. Death/dying   _____   _____
6. Pollution and environment   _____   _____
7. Other   _____   _____

Current issues
1. Making choices about alcohol use   _____   _____
2. Making choices about smoking and other drugs   _____   _____
3. Making choices about dating   _____   _____

Figure 15.2 *continued*

Source: From "Creating Small Groups Using School and Community Resources to Meet Student Needs," by E. Berube and L. Berube, 1997, *School Counselor, 44*, pp. 300–302. © 1997 by ACA. Reprinted with permission. No further reproduction authorized without written permission of the American Counseling Association.

way to offer services for students who did not fit the emphases given by either elementary school or high school counselors (Cole, 1988; Stamm & Nissman, 1979). The idea of a special curriculum and environment for preadolescents and early adolescents was first implemented as a junior high concept—an attempt to group younger adolescents (ages 12–14 and grades 7–9) from older adolescents.

Middle schools typically enroll children between the ages of 10 and 14 and encompass grades 6 through 9. Children at this age and grade level are often referred to as *transescents* (Cole, 1988; Eichhorn, 1968) or *bubblegummers* (Thornburg, 1978). "In addition to experiencing the normal problems that exist in the family, school, and community, middle school boys and girls adjust to changes in the body, pressure from peers, demands by the school for excellence, conflicting attitudes of parents, and other problems with establishing self-identity" (Matthews & Burnett, 1989, p. 122). There is little homogeneity about them, and their most common characteristic is unlikeness.

According to Dougherty (1986), we know less about this age group than any other. Part of the reason is that few middle school counselors conduct research or publish their findings about this population (St. Clair, 1989). Yet the Gesell Institute of Child Development and other child study centers offer a description of cognitive, physical, and emotional factors that can be expected during this time (Johnson & Kottman, 1992). Too few counselors avail themselves of this data. On a general level, however, most middle school counselors are aware of the major physical, intellectual, and social developmental tasks that middle school children must accomplish. Thornburg (1986) outlines them:

- Becoming aware of increased physical changes
- Organizing knowledge and concepts into problem-solving strategies
- Making the transition from concrete to abstract symbols
- Learning new social and sex roles
- Identifying with stereotypical role models
- Developing friendships
- Gaining a sense of independence
- Developing a sense of responsibility (pp. 170–171)

Elkind (1986) notes that in addition to developmental tasks, middle graders also must deal successfully with three basic stress situations. A *Type A* stress situation is one that is foreseeable and avoidable, such as not walking in a dangerous area at night. A *Type B* situation is neither foreseeable nor avoidable, such as an unexpected death. A *Type C* situation is foreseeable but not avoidable, such as going to the dentist.

Overall, middle school children tend to experience more anxiety than either elementary or high school students. Therefore, they are at risk for not achieving or successfully resolving developmental tasks (Matthews & Burnett, 1989). Thus, middle school counselors can be most helpful during times of stress because they can provide opportunities for children to experience themselves and their worlds in different and creative ways (Schmidt, 1991). They can also help middle schoolers foster a sense of uniqueness as well as identify with universal common concerns. In such a process counselors help middle schoolers overcome their restlessness and moodiness and counter influences by peers and the popular culture that suggest violence or other destructive behaviors are an acceptable solution to complex, perplexing problems (Peterson & O'Neal, 1998).

Emphases and Roles

Often schools neglect the physical and social development of the child while stimulating intellectual growth (Thornburg, 1986). Middle school counseling and guidance, like elementary school counseling and guidance, seeks to correct this imbalance by focusing on the child's total development. The emphasis is holistic: counselors stress not only growth and development but also the process of transition involved in leaving childhood and entering adolescence (Schmidt, 1999). Their activities include

- working with students individually and in groups,
- working with teachers and administrators,
- working in the community with education agencies, social services, and businesses, and
- partnering with parents to address unique needs of specific children (Campbell & Dahir, 1997).

These roles may be fulfilled more easily if counselors develop capacities and programs in certain ways. The necessary capacities, according to Thornburg (1986), include general information about developmental characteristics of middle schoolers and specific tasks students are expected to achieve. In addition, counselors must understand the specific child with whom they are interacting and his or her perspective on a problem. Finally, counselors need to know how to help students make decisions so that students can help themselves in the future.

The ideal role of middle school counselors also includes providing individual counseling, group experiences, peer support systems, teacher consultation, student assessment, parent consultation, and evaluation of guidance services (Bonebrake & Borgers, 1984; Schmidt, 1999). In a survey of Kansas principals and counselors, Bonebrake and Borgers found that participants not only agreed on the ideal role of the middle school counselor but also agreed on a counselor's lowest priorities: serving as principal, supervising lunchroom discipline, and teaching nonguidance classes. This survey is encouraging because it shows the close agreement between principals and counselors concerning ideal roles. After all, principals usually "determine the role and function of counselors within the school" (Ribak-Rosenthal, 1994, p. 158). Yet outside the school, various groups have different perceptions and priorities about the purpose of middle school counselors. To ease the tension that may arise from such evaluations, Bonebrake and Borgers recommend that counselors document their functions and run "a visible, well-defined, and carefully evaluated program" (p. 198). Middle school counselors also need to be in constant communication with their various publics about what they do and when. Publicity as well as delivery of services is as crucial at this level as it is in elementary schools (Ribak-Rosenthal, 1994).

Activities

Working with middle school children requires both a preventive and a remedial approach. It is similar to dealing with elementary schoolchildren except that counselors must penetrate more barriers if they are to be truly helpful in a holistic way.

Prevention.   One of the most promising prevention programs for middle schoolers is the Succeeding in School approach (Gerler & Anderson, 1986). Composed of 50-minute classroom guidance units, this program is geared toward helping children become comfortable with themselves, their teachers, and their schools (Gerler, 1987). The approach is multimodal and asks children to participate actively in the learning process. Each lesson plan focuses in on a prosocial aspect of personal and institutional living, such as identifying with successful people, being comfortable in school, cooperating with peers and teachers, and recognizing the bright side of life events (Gerler, Drew, & Mohr, 1990).

A complement to the Succeeding in School program is Morganett's (1990) group counseling activities for young adolescents. These activities develop skills for living. Because her exercises for small groups can be used in various ways, middle school counselors have flexibility in helping students deal with sensitive areas such as anger, grief, stress, divorce, assertiveness, and friendship.

In addition to classroom guidance and group work, middle school counselors (like elementary school counselors) can use individual counseling, peer counseling, and consultation activities to foster problem prevention (Thompson & Rudolph, 1996). Another preventive type of program is *peer mentoring*. In this arrangement, an older student, such as an eighth grader is paired up with a younger student, such as a sixth grader. The older student both accepts and teaches the younger student through a cooperative learning arrangement. Noll (1997) reports that in a cross-age mentoring program she set up to help younger students with learning disabilities acquire social skills, the arrangement worked well. The younger students made significant gains in their social development, and the older students achieved an increase in their "ability to relate better to parents, an increase in self-esteem, better conflict resolution skills, and enhanced organization skills" (p. 241).

Remediation.   One of the best ways to work remedially with middle school students is to combine it with a preventive approach. According to Stamm and Nissman (1979), the activities of middle school counselors are best viewed as services that revolve around "a Human Development Center (HDC) that deals with sensitive human beings (students, teachers, parents, and the community as a whole)" (p. 52). They recommend developing a rapport with these persons and coordinating middle school counseling and guidance services with others to provide the most productive program possible. Stamm and Nissman outline eight service areas that they believe are vital to a comprehensive middle school counseling and guidance program (see Figure 15.3).

Each service cluster is linked with the others. But middle school counselors cannot perform all the recommended functions alone, so they must delegate responsibility and solicit the help of other school personnel, parents, and community volunteers. A counselor's job, then, entails coordinating service activities as well as delivering direct services when able.

The *communication service cluster* is primarily concerned with public relations. It is the counselor's outreach arm and is critical for informing the general public about what the school counseling program is doing. *Curriculum service,* on the other hand, concentrates on facilitating course placements and academic adjustment. Middle school counselors need to help teachers "psychologize" the curriculum so that students can deal with significant issues in their lives, such as peer relationships and values (Beane, 1986). If the curriculum is not relevant to children at this age, they often divert their energy to nonpro-

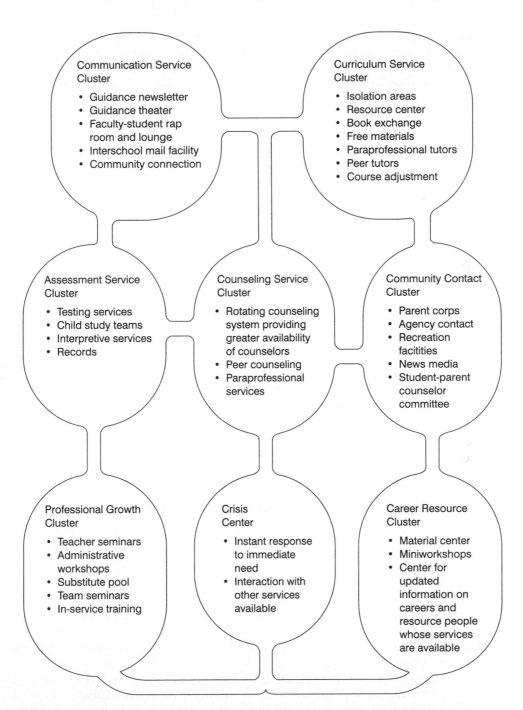

Figure 15.3 Areas vital to a middle school counseling and guidance program

Source: From *Improving Middle School Guidance* (p. 54), by M. L. Stamm and B. S. Nissman, 1979, Boston: Allyn & Bacon. © 1979 by Allyn & Bacon. All rights reserved. Reprinted with permission.

ductive activities. The *assessment service cluster* provides testing and evaluation services and is often linked to the *career resource cluster,* which focuses on the student's future goals and vocation.

The *counseling service cluster* and the *crisis center cluster* are also closely connected. Counseling services are provided on an individual, peer, and group level and are offered during off-school and in-school hours. Sometimes counseling activities are aimed at *self-counseling,* which is "when people (including middle graders) think the ideas that they believe, then react to those ideas with logical emotional reactions and logical physical behaviors" (Maultsby, 1986, p. 207). Rational self-counseling is one research-based way to help students help themselves deal effectively with their emotions. At other times, peer facilitators help middle schoolers make friends and learn about their environments and schoolwork (Bowman, 1986; Sprinthall, Hall, & Gerler, 1992).

There is also someone designated in the Stamm and Nissman model as a *crisis person* during the school day. This individual deals with emergencies and, with the help of the counselor, finds an appropriate way to assist the child who is experiencing sudden distress. On an individual level, a crisis and distress may be connected with loss or internal or external pressures that result in a child acting out or withdrawing. On a group level, a crisis and the resulting distress may involve "cases of trauma that affect large numbers of students such as homicide, suicide, accidental death, or severe accident" (Lockhart & Keys, 1998, p. 4). (It is vital that elementary and secondary school counselors have both a crisis plan as well as a crisis person in their school counseling programs.)

The *community contact cluster* focuses on working with parents and other interested people to open the lines of communication between the school and other agencies. The *professional growth cluster* provides programs for school staff and paraprofessionals. This last task is critical to the counselor's success. If the total school environment is to be positively affected, middle school counselors must help "teachers develop skills related to enhancing the students' self-concept and self-esteem" (Beane, 1986, p. 192).

Secondary School Counseling and Guidance

"There are few situations in life more difficult to cope with than an adolescent son or daughter during their attempt to liberate themselves" (Freud, 1958, p. 278). Although most adolescents make it through this period of their lives in a healthy way, some experience great difficulty. Secondary school counselors must deal with this difficult population and the problems unique to it. They may take some comfort in the fact that some problems in adolescence are more cyclical than others. For example, "delinquent behaviors are rare in early adolescence, almost universal by midadolescence (ages 15 to 17), and decrease thereafter" (McCarthy, Brack, Lambert, Brack, & Orr, 1996, p. 277). However, many other concerns are connected with this population that are situational and unpredictable.

Secondary school counseling and guidance began in the early 1900s when its primary emphasis was on guidance activities that would help build better citizens (Gysbers & Guidance Program Field Writers, 1990) (see Chapter 1). Frank Parsons influenced the early growth of the profession, although John Brewer really pushed for the establishment of secondary school guidance in the 1930s (Aubrey, 1979). Brewer believed that both guidance and education meant assisting young people in living. His ideas did not gain wide acceptance at the time, but under the name *life skills training* they have become increasingly popular (Gazda, 1989).

The growth of secondary school counseling was particularly dramatic during the 1960s. Counselor employment in this specialty more than tripled from about 12,000 in 1958–1959 to more than 40,000 in 1969–1970 (Shertzer & Stone, 1981). According to the *Occupational Outlook Handbook*, an estimated 63,000 people worked as public school counselors during 1986, with a ratio of 3 to 1 in favor of secondary school counselors over elementary school counselors. Several thousand more counselors worked in private schools. Furthermore, the number of employment opportunities for school counselors began increasing in the late 1980s as many counselors who had trained in the NDEA institutes began to retire and more states mandated better counseling services in the schools at all levels (Baker, 1995). Today, there are an estimated 100,000 counselors in schools, many of them working on the secondary level.

Emphases and Roles

Counselors in high school environments concentrate on the following tasks:

- providing direct counseling services individually and in groups,
- providing educational and support services to parent,
- offering consultation and in-service programs to teachers and staff,
- facilitating referrals to outside agencies,
- networking to postsecondary schools and businesses, and
- advising academically (Campbell & Dahir, 1997).

Aubrey (1979) argues that a real conflict exists for secondary school counselors, who are faced with two needs: (a) engaging in student counseling and (b) doing academic and administrative tasks, such as scheduling, which school administrative personnel often require. He contends that school counselors, especially on the high school level, frequently get bogged down in nonprofessional activities. Brown (1989) states that dysfunctional counselors are frequently misunderstood or misdirected by their principals, are poorly educated, lack a plan of action, are not engaged in public relations, and violate ethical standards. To combat attempts to cast them into inappropriate roles, secondary school counselors need to develop and publicize what they do and how they do it, not only to students but to teachers, principals, and administrators as well (Guerra, 1998). They can do this by "writing monthly newsletters, posting the counselor's schedule, distributing the American School Counselor Association (ASCA) role statement, developing a guidance service handbook, making presentations at faculty meetings," and pointing out to others the cost efficiency of allowing counselors to do their jobs correctly (Ribak-Rosenthal, 1994, p. 163).

Peer (1985) elicited the opinions of state directors of guidance and counseling and others in regard to views about the role of secondary school counselors. He found mixed opinions. Those who held secondary school programs in highest regard were principals, superintendents, students, college and university personnel, other secondary school counselors, and counselor educators. Teachers, parents, community leaders, and business leaders were less positive. State directors overwhelmingly reported that secondary school counselors are "probably" or "definitely" heavily involved in nonprofessional activities. If this is true, it is understandable why secondary school counselors have come under heavy criticism from people outside the school environment.

The Peer survey also discovered that secondary school counselors are not seen as being actively involved in group counseling or group guidance, not serving as consultants, and not making an impact on the majority of students. Overall, programs at this level are not viewed as favorably as those in elementary schools in the same district. On a positive note, however, respondents perceived secondary counselors as avoiding disciplinarian roles, well qualified, and helpful to individual students, especially those bound for college. Significantly, respondents thought counselors could effect changes in counseling programs.

Ways of improving the perception and behavior of the secondary school counselor include an emphasis on roles that meet real needs. Jones (1977), for instance, stresses that school counselors must be facilitators of healthy learning environments. He thinks the primary functions of secondary school counselors should include facilitating problem solving within the regular classroom, developing professional growth groups, and improving staff communications. All these roles give counselors maximum exposure among groups who have traditionally held them in low esteem. By functioning as facilitators in student-adult interactions and adult-adult transactions, counselors provide the means for a productive exchange between divergent and often isolated groups of people.

An important function for any school counselor is the constant remodeling of the counseling program (Gysbers & Henderson, 1994). A systematic plan is crucial to this process. It includes not only implementation of services but also evaluation of these activities. Some stress can be expected in setting up and restructuring guidance and counseling activities within the school, but a great deal of satisfaction also results. Secondary school counselors must be in constant touch with their constituents if they are to keep their services and roles appropriate and current.

Activities

The activities of secondary school counselors can be divided into several areas. In addition to evaluating their own activities, they are involved in prevention, remediation and intervention, and cooperation and facilitation. These categories are not mutually exclusive, and there are a multitude of concerns under each heading.

Prevention.   Secondary school counselors, like elementary and middle school counselors, stress preventive services. These efforts "need to be comprehensive, multifaceted, and integrated" (Keys & Bemak, 1997, p. 257). The reason is that adolescent problems outside the classroom and school problems are interrelated (McCarthy et al., 1996). Therefore, to address one situation and neglect the other usually will not work.

Sprinthall (1984) notes that primary prevention in the secondary school creates "classroom educative experiences that affect students' intellectual and personal development simultaneously" (p. 494). Through primary preventive, students become more self-reliant and less dominated by their peer group. They also become less egocentric, more attuned to principles as guidelines in making decisions, and more empathic. Relationships between teacher and counselor and student and counselor are enhanced in this process, too.

There are a multitude of ways to build primary prevention programs. One way for counselors to practice prevention is for them to become familiar with current popular songs (Ostlund & Kinnier, 1997). By listening attentively to the lyrics of these songs, secondary school counselors become "more knowledgeable about adolescent subcultures and may be better able to help many teenagers cope with typical adolescent problems" (pp. 87–88).

Another way for counselors to be proactive in secondary school environments is occasionally to teach prevention-based curriculum offerings in classes (Martin, 1983). Anxieties about school and tests, study skills, interpersonal relationships, self-control, and career planning may be dealt with in this way. Such an approach has two major advantages: less time needs to be devoted to remediation and intervention activities, and the counselor maintains a positive high profile with teachers and students. As an adjunct or an integrated part of curriculum offerings, counselors can have class members participate in an interactive bibliotherapy process in which they read either fiction or nonfiction books on specific subjects and discuss their reactions with the counselor. (This process may be individualized in personal counseling, too). Books dealing with illness and death, family relations, self-destructive behaviors, identity, abuse, race and prejudice, and sex and sexuality are readily available; Christenbury, Beale, and Patch (1996) suggest several of them. Other works are easily attainable through *Books for You* (Christenbury, 1995).

Four examples of problem areas in which prevention can make a major difference are substance abuse, adolescent suicide/homicide, prevention of HIV infection/AIDS, and abusive relationships. Programs for preventing substance abuse work best when they are started early in students' lives, based on social influence models, tailored to the age and stage of different student groups, and "involve students, parents, teachers, and community members in the planning process" (Mohai, 1991). A specific effective model is "Here's Looking at You Two" in which counselors work with potentially susceptible at-risk students in a multidimensional curriculum approach that is systematically evaluated (Robinson, 1989). In general, multidimensional approaches increase self-esteem, reduce negative peer influence, and provide drug information. Student assistance programs (SAPs) set up by counselors in schools are effective also (Moore & Forster, 1993). SAP teams are composed of school personnel from a variety of backgrounds and function in ways similar to multidisciplinary special education teams in schools.

Suicide and homicide prevention programs follow broad-based approaches that stress the seriousness of such violence and alternatives. Suicide is "the fastest-growing cause of death among adolescents in American society" (Malley & Kush, 1994, p. 191), and the number of youth homicides, especially those involving multiple deaths in schools, has increased dramatically in recent years. There is a suicide attempt by an adolescent almost every minute, making approximately 500,000 attempts annually (Hicks, 1990). Although girls attempt more suicides than boys, boys are more successful in carrying them out. Boys also tend to be almost the exclusive perpetrators of adolescent homicides.

Because antisocial behaviors like suicide and homicide are multidetermined phenomena, a variety of interventions are needed to prevent them (Dykeman, Daehlin, Doyle, & Flameer, 1996). Some ways to prevent suicides and homicides are to help students, parents, and school personnel become aware of their danger signs and alert counselors and other mental health helpers to the professional and legal standards that deal with breaking confidentiality (Peach & Reddick, 1991; Remley & Sparkman, 1993; Sheeley & Herlihy, 1989). Involving school peers, families, and significant others in the community is also vital (Cashwell & Vacc, 1996; Ritchie, 1989). It is important that suicide and homicide prevention programs in schools be proactive rather than reactive as well as systematically designed. One approach to such aggression is a concept known as *wrap-around programs* (Cautilli & Skinner, 1996). These programs have multiple services provided by a team of many mental health professionals, including counselors, who work together to provide direct assistance to the youth at risk of violence as well as his or her family and community/school personnel who come in contact with the youth.

A common factor among suicidal and homicidal youth is feelings of depression and anger. Therefore, preventive programs, such as support or psychoeducational groups, that deal with improving self-esteem and coping with loss and rejection are important. Likewise, programs aimed at preventing copy-cat and cluster suicides and to provide community awareness are vital (Popenhagen & Qualley, 1998). Individual identification of youth at risk for either suicide or homicide is crucial, too. Youth intervention programs tailored to the needs and circumstances of potential suicide victims and homicide perpetrators are essential. A plan of action for dealing with suicide and homicide potential should be as broad-based as possible (Capuzzi, 1994).

When working to prevent HIV/AIDS, counselors may or may not persuade students to change their sexual activity. But they can help them avoid contracting AIDS and other sexually transmitted diseases by employing both an informational and skills-based intervention system (Stevens-Smith & Remley, 1994). For instance, the school counselor can make sure students know how HIV is spread and what behaviors, such as sharing intravenous needles and unprotected casual sex, put them into greatest danger (Keeling, 1993). In addition, counselors can offer students opportunities for interpersonal skill building by simulating situations that are potentially hazardous. They can also support teenagers who decide to try new and positive behaviors such as changing their habits or environments. Support groups, workshops for parents and administrators, and peer education programs can also be used. Peer education is one of the strongest means of dissuading adolescents from engaging in destructive behaviors and helping them focus on productive action (Campbell, 1993a).

Finally, interpersonal violence (i.e., abusive relationships) can be prevented through school counselor interventions (Becky & Farren, 1996). In such programs, counselors work with students in groups to emphasize to them that slapping, pushing, and emotionally threatening language are not a normal or necessary part of interpersonal relationships. Furthermore, they focus on teaching students anger control, assertiveness, and responsible communication. Dating Safely is one model available in a programmed format that is easy to follow.

Overall, as these examples show, school counselors are in a strong position because of their skills, training, and knowledge "to be leaders in the development of . . . school- and community-based intervention" programs (Stevens-Smith & Remley, 1994, p. 182).

Remediation and Intervention.

Secondary school counselors initiate remediation and intervention programs to help students with specific problems that are not amenable to prevention techniques. Some common mental disorders of childhood and adolescents manifest themselves clearly at this time, such as problems centering around adjustment, behavior, anxiety, substance abuse, and eating (Geroski, Rodgers, & Breen, 1997). The identification, assessment, referral, and in some cases treatment of these disorders found in the *Diagnostic and Statistical Manual of Mental Disorders,* fourth edition (DSM-IV), is one of the most valuable services a secondary school counselor, or any school counselor, can render (often in consultation with other mental health providers). Because of time and resources, secondary school counselors usually do not deal directly in treating severe mental disorders but rather focus on other specific problematic behaviors that occur in their settings. Three of the most prevalent of these problems are depression, parental divorce, and teenage parenting.

Depression is related in adolescence to negative life stress (Benson & Deeter, 1992). Forrest (1983) states that about 15% of all schoolchildren may be depressed because of external stressors and inadequate individual response abilities. He lists common emotional, physical, intellectual, and behavioral indicators of depression (see Table 15.1). Furthermore, he emphasizes the need for school counselors to use a variety of approaches in dealing with the problem. Among the most prominent include using Lazarus's multimodal model; teaching the student how to develop self-esteem; helping the student become aware of depression and the stress factors that influence it; and teaching relaxation procedures, new coping skills, and ways of modifying negative self-messages. All these approaches require a significant investment of time and energy.

Approximately one million children experience parental divorces each year, and it is estimated 45% of all American children can expect their families to break up before they reach the age of 18 (Whitehead, 1997). Secondary school counselors can help children, parents, and teachers adjust to divorce through both direct and indirect services (Cook & McBride, 1982). Interventions that directly address the problems of divorce are individual and group counseling services within the school for the children. Structured, short-term group work can make a positive impact in helping secondary school students sort out and resolve their feelings about the divorce experience (Morganett, 1995). More indirect services can also be implemented, such as consulting with teachers and parents about the children's feelings. Teachers and parents need information about what to expect from children of divorce and what useful interventions they might employ in the process of helping.

Teenage parenting is filled with emotional issues for both society and teens. When parenting results from an out-of-wedlock pregnancy, feelings run high. The challenge for school counselors is to develop outreach strategies for working with members of this population. In addition, counselors must address personal and career concerns of young parents and make necessary referrals. Usually the process is accomplished best through collaborative efforts between school counselors and community mental health workers (Kiselica & Pfaller, 1993). One essential task is to prevent teenage parents from having a second child. Another crucial aspect is keeping unwed mothers (and fathers) in school and increasing their success in academic, personal, and interpersonal arenas (DeRidder, 1993).

Cooperation and Facilitation.   Cooperation and facilitation involve the counselor in a variety of community and school activities beyond that of caregiver. Counselors who are not aware of or involved in community and school groups are not as effective as they could otherwise be (Bradley, 1978). Part of a counselor's responsibility is becoming

Table 15.1   Common indicators of depression

Emotional (Affective)	Physical (Somatic)	Intellectual (Cognitive)	Behavior (Doing)
Sadness	Fatigue	Negative self-concept	Soft spoken, slow speech
Anxiety	Sleep disorders	Negative view of world	Withdrawals from normal social contact
Guilt	Eating disorders	Negative expectations for future	Engages in fewer pleasurable activities
Anger	Dyspepsia	Self-blame	Seldom smiles or laughs
Fear	Constipation	Self-criticism	Eats alone Studies alone
Unhappiness	Poorly defined plan	Loss of interest	Does not speak up in class or social encounters
Pessimism	Menstrual irregularity	Inability to concentrate	Avoids expressing hostile tendencies
Mood variation	High pulse rate with appearance apathy	Poverty of thought	Avoids groups Reduces involvement in sports and games
Helplessness	Headaches	Ambivalence	Drab dress Grades take sudden drop
Worthlessness	Stomach aches	Indecisiveness	Sighs often and cries easily Procrastinates

Source: From "Depression: Information and Interventions for School Counselors," by D. V. Forrest, 1983, *School Counselor, 30*, p. 270. © 1983 by ACA. Reprinted with permission. No further reproduction authorized without written permission of the American Counseling Association.

involved with others in ways outside of direct counseling services (Lee & Walz, 1998). Thus, secondary school counselors often have to take the initiative in working with teachers and other school personnel. By becoming more involved with teachers, administrators, and sponsors of extracurricular activities, counselors integrate their views into the total life of schools and "help create the kind of school environments that stimulate growth and learning" (Glosoff & Koprowicz, 1990, p. 10).

In a very practical article on the role of the school counselor as service coordinator, DeVoe and McClam (1982) stress the importance of counselors' being accountable for performing three roles. The first role is *information retriever.* Here, the counselor either collects information or works with other professionals to collect information about particularly complex situations, such as the abused and drug-dependent pregnant teenager. The second role is related to *service coordination.* The counselor determines whether he or she has the expertise to meet particular students' needs. If the counselor does not have the expertise, an appropriate referral is made. The third role is *information administrator.* The counselor coordinates a plan in which individuals or agencies in nonschool counseling settings deliver student services. This activity involves planning and implementing continuous communication among service providers.

A less involved but important way in which counselors can cooperate with others in the school and community is through participation in *individualized education programs* (IEPs)—that is, educational programs tailored to the specialized needs of certain children (Humes, 1980). Counselors engage in either direct interventions or support services with students for whom IEPs are drawn up. Regardless of special considerations, counselors can work closely with other school and community personnel to ensure that atypical students receive appropriate educational and support services. Thus, fewer students drop out of school or are lost to the communities in which they live (Kushman & Kinney, 1989).

Summary and Conclusion

This chapter has covered various aspects of counseling in elementary, middle, and secondary schools, offering a brief history of how practices in these areas have evolved. The tasks of school counselors at each level are uniquely developmental, yet all focus on intrapersonal and interpersonal relationships. Counselors who work in schools must be flexible and skilled in knowing how to work with children, parents, and other school personnel who come from many different environments and have various worldviews. They must know what situations are best handled in what manner (through counseling, consultation, curriculum development, etc.).

Elementary school counselors focus on offering preventive services and increasing student awareness of individual needs and ways of meeting them in a healthy, prosocial manner. Much work on this level is the result of emphasizing curriculum issues (i.e., classroom guidance), conducting small groups, and providing consultation to others. Middle school counselors, on the other hand, are more focused on helping students make the smoothest possible transition from childhood to adolescence. They offer many activities that parallel those on the elementary school level, and they especially focus on situations of major concern to children in this age range, such as how to handle anxiety, develop good girl-boy relationships, and so on.

Secondary school counseling has traditionally emphasized counseling services. Since the 1980s, however, it has become more multidimensional. Secondary school counselors are more involved in making an impact on the whole school environment and implementing both prevention and remediation programs. They assist students in making a transition from a school environment into the world of work or further study. Resolving developmental and situational factors associated with this transition are equally important to them.

Overall, school counselors have multiple tasks and responsibilities. There is a new awareness that passive or poorly educated school counselors have not and will not work for the good of children and society (Cecil & Cobia, 1990; Guerra, 1998). To rectify problems associated with the education of school counselors, the Dewitt-Wallace Reader's Digest Fund in 1998 chose 10 colleges and universities around the United States to make suggestions about revamping the school counselor education curriculum at institutions of higher education. The guidelines that result from this effort will influence school counseling in the future.

CLASSROOM ACTIVITIES

1. In groups of three, talk about your perceptions of and experiences with counselors in your elementary, middle, and high schools. How did they exemplify the roles outlined in this chapter? What were the best things they did for you or your school? What could they have done differently to improve their services?

2. Read several articles focusing on counseling elementary school children, and compare them with articles focused on working with adolescents. What similarities and differences do you notice? What does this information tell you about the concerns of counselors in select settings? Share your thoughts with the class.

3. Reflect on your life as a middle school student. What were your greatest concerns then, and how did you handle them? With another classmate, share your reflections (to the point you feel comfortable doing so). What counselor-related activities do you think might have been helpful to you then?

4. What do you think are the greatest concerns of high school students today? Write down your top five ideas. Share them with other classmates in groups of three, and then compare your rank-ordered group list with the class as a whole. How much agreement exists among the class? As a class, discuss ways of addressing one of these problems.

5. Pretend that you are an elementary school counselor. Design a guidance lesson on the topic of your choice. Then either tell or show the class how you would carry out your plan. What is your rationale for choosing your topic? How might children in your class eventually benefit from the experience?

REFERENCES

ACES-ASCA Joint Committee on the Elementary School Counselor. (1966). The elementary school counselor: Preliminary statement. *Personnel and Guidance Journal, 44,* 658–661.

Allan, J., & Brown, K. (1993). Jungian play therapy in elementary schools. *Elementary School Guidance and Counseling, 28,* 30–41.

Aubrey, R. F. (1979). Relationship of guidance and counseling to the established and emerging school curriculum. *School Counselor, 26,* 150–162.

Bachman, R. W. (1975). Elementary school children's perceptions of helpers and their characteristics. *Elementary School Guidance and Counseling, 10,* 103–109.

Bailey, W. R., Deery, N. K., Gehrke, M., Perry, N., & Whitledge, J. (1989). Issues in elementary school counseling: Discussion with American School Counselor Association leaders. *Elementary School Guidance and Counseling, 24,* 4–13.

Baker, S. B. (1994). Serving students with differing worldviews. *School Counselor, 41,* 313.

Baker, S. B. (1995). *School counseling for the twenty-first century* (2nd ed.). Upper Saddle River, NJ: Merrill/Prentice Hall.

Barrett-Kruse, C., Martinez, E., & Carll, N. (1998). Beyond reporting suspected abuse: Positively influencing the development of the student within the classroom. *Professional School Counseling, 1,* 57–60.

Beane, J. A. (1986). The self-enhancing middle-grade school. *School Counselor, 33,* 189–195.

Becky, D., & Farren, P. M. (1997). Teaching students how to understand and avoid abusive relationships. *School Counselor, 44,* 303–308.

Benson, L. T., & Deeter, T. E. (1992). Moderators of the relation between stress and depression in adolescence. *School Counselor, 39,* 189–194.

Berg, B. (1986). *The assertiveness game.* Dayton, OH: Cognitive Counseling Resources.

Berg, B. (1989). *The anger control game.* Dayton, OH: Cognitive Counseling Resources.

Berg, B. (1990a). *The anxiety management game.* Dayton, OH: Cognitive Counseling Resources.

Berg, B. (1990b). *The depression management game.* Dayton, OH: Cognitive Counseling Resources.

Berg, B. (1990c). *The self-control game.* Dayton, OH: Cognitive Counseling Resources.

Berube, E., & Berube, L. (1997). Creating small groups using school and community resources to meet student needs. *School Counselor, 44,* 294–302.

Bonebrake, C. R., & Borgers, S. B. (1984). Counselor role as perceived by counselors and principals. *Elementary School Guidance and Counseling, 18,* 194–199.

Borders, L. D., & Drury, S. M. (1992). Comprehensive school counseling programs: A review for policymakers and practitioners. *Journal of Counseling and Development, 70,* 487–498.

Borders, S., & Paisley, P. O. (1992). Children's literature as a resource for classroom guidance. *Elementary School Guidance and Counseling, 27,* 131–139.

Bowman, R. P. (1986). Peer facilitator programs for middle graders: Students helping each other grow up. *School Counselor, 33,* 221–229.

Bradley, M. K. (1978). Counseling past and present: Is there a future? *Personnel and Guidance Journal, 57,* 42–45.

Brown, D. (1989). The perils, pitfalls, and promises of school counseling program reform. *School Counselor, 37,* 47–53.

Campbell, C. A. (1993a). *Managing your school counseling program.* Minneapolis: Educational Media Corporation.

Campbell, C. A. (1993b). Play, the fabric of elementary school counseling programs. *Elementary School Guidance and Counseling, 28,* 10–16.

Campbell, C. A., & Dahir, C. A. (1997). *The national standards for school counseling programs.* Alexandria, VA: American School Counseling Programs.

Capuzzi, D. (1994). *Suicide prevention in the schools.* Alexandria, VA: American Counseling Association.

Carmichael, K. D. (1994). Sand play as an elementary school strategy. *Elementary School Guidance and Counseling, 28,* 302–307.

Carnegie Task Force on Meeting the Needs of Young Children. (1994). *Starting points: Meeting the needs of our youngest children.* New York: Author.

Carns, A. W., & Carns, M. R. (1997). A systems approach to school counseling. *School Counselor, 44,* 218–223.

Carruthers, W. L., Sweeney, B., Kmitta, D., & Harris, G. (1996). Conflict resolution: An examination of the research literature and a model for program evaluation. *School Counselor, 44,* 5–18.

Cashwell, C. S., & Vacc, N. A. (1996). Family functioning and risk behaviors: Influences on adolescent delinquency. *School Counselor, 44,* 105–114.

Cautilli, J., & Skinner, L. (1996, September). Combating youth violence through wrap-around service. *Counseling Today,* 12.

Cecil, J. H., & Cobia, D. C. (1990). Educational challenge and change. In H. Hackney (Ed.), *Changing contexts for counselor preparation in the 1990s* (pp. 21–36). Alexandria, VA: Association for Counselor Education and Supervision.

Christenbury, L. (Ed.). (1995). *Books for you.* Chicago: National Council of Teachers of English.

Christenbury, L., Beale, A. V., & Patch, S. S. (1996). Interactive bibliocounseling: Recent fiction and nonfiction for adolescents and their counselors. *School Counselor, 44,* 133–145.

Cochran, J. L. (1996). Using play and art therapy to help culturally diverse students overcome barriers to school success. *School Counselor, 43,* 287–298.

Cole, C. G. (1988). *Guidance in middle level schools: Everyone's responsibility*. Columbus, OH: National Middle School Association.

Cook, A. S., & McBride, J. S. (1982). Divorce: Helping children cope. *School Counselor, 30,* 89–94.

Cook, D. W. (1989). Systematic need assessment: A primer. *Journal of Counseling and Development, 67,* 462–464.

Coppock, M. W. (1993). Small group plan for improving friendships and self-esteem. *Elementary School Guidance and Counseling, 28,* 152–154.

Crosbie-Burnett, M., & Newcomer, L. L. (1989). A multimodal intervention for group counseling with children of divorce. *Elementary School Guidance and Counseling, 23,* 155–166.

DeRidder, L. M. (1993). Teenage pregnancy: Etiology and educational interventions. *Educational Psychology Review, 5,* 87–103.

DeVoe, M. W., & McClam, T. (1982). Service coordination: The school counselor. *School Counselor, 30,* 95–100.

Dinkmeyer, D. (1973). Elementary school counseling: Prospects and potentials. *School Counselor, 52,* 171–174.

Dinkmeyer, D. (1989). Beginnings of "Elementary School Guidance and Counseling." *Elementary School Guidance and Counseling, 24,* 99–101.

Dinkmeyer, D. C., & Caldwell, C. E. (1970). *Developmental counseling and guidance: A comprehensive school approach*. New York: McGraw-Hill.

Dougherty, A. M. (1986). The blossoming of youth: Middle graders "on the grow." *School Counselor, 33,* 167–169.

Dykeman, C., Daehlin, W., Doyle, S., & Flamer, H. S. (1996). Psychological predictors of school-based violence: Implications for school counselors. *School Counselor, 44,* 35–47.

Eichhorn, D. H. (1968). Middle school organization: A new dimension. *Theory into Practice, 7,* 111–113.

Elkind, D. (1986). Stress and the middle grader. *School Counselor, 33,* 196–206.

Faust, V. (1968). *History of elementary school counseling: Overview and critique*. Boston: Houghton Mifflin.

Forrest, D. V. (1983). Depression: Information and interventions for school counselors. *School Counselor, 30,* 269–279.

Freud, A. (1958). Adolescence. *Psychoanalytic Study of the Child, 13,* 255–278.

Friedberg, R. D. (1996). Cognitive-behavioral games and workbooks: Tips for school counselors. *Elementary School Guidance & Counseling, 31,* 11–19.

Frieman, B. B. (1994). Children of divorced parents: Action steps for the counselor to involve fathers. *School Counselor, 28,* 197–205.

Furlong, M. J., Atkinson, D. R., & Janoff, D. S. (1979). Elementary school counselors' perceptions of their actual and ideal roles. *Elementary School Guidance and Counseling, 14,* 4–11.

Garner, R., Martin, D., & Martin, M. (1989). The PALS program: A peer counseling training program for junior high school. *Elementary School Guidance and Counseling, 24,* 68–76.

Gazda, G. M. (1989). *Group counseling: A developmental approach* (4th ed.). Boston: Allyn & Bacon.

Gerler, E. R. (1987). Classroom guidance for success in overseas schools. *International Quarterly, 5,* 18–22.

Gerler, E. R., Jr. (1985). Elementary school counseling research and the classroom learning environment. *Elementary School Guidance and Counseling, 20,* 39–48.

Gerler, E. R., & Anderson, R. F. (1986). The effects of classroom guidance on children's success in school. *Journal of Counseling and Development, 65,* 78–81.

Gerler, E. R., Drew, N. S., & Mohr, P. (1990). Succeeding in middle school: A multimodal approach. *Elementary School Guidance and Counseling, 24,* 263–271.

Geroski, A. M., Rodgers, K. A., & Breen, D. T. (1997). Using the DSM-IV to enhance collaboration among school counselors, clinical counselors, and primary care physicians. *Journal of Counseling & Development, 75,* 231–239.

Gladding, S. T., & Gladding, C. (1991). The ABCs of bibliotherapy for school counselors. *School Counselor, 39,* 7–13.

Glosoff, H. L., & Koprowicz, C. L. (1990). *Children achieving potential*. Alexandria, VA: American Counseling Association.

Guerney, L. (1983). Client-centered (nondirective) play therapy. In C. E. Schaeffer & K. J. O'Connor

(Eds.), *Handbook of play therapy* (pp. 21–64). New York: Wiley.

Guerra, P. (1998, January). Advocating for school counseling. *Counseling Today*, 20.

Gysbers, N. C., & Guidance Program Field Writers. (1990). *Comprehensive guidance programs that work*. Ann Arbor, MI: ERIC/CAPS.

Gysbers, N. C., & Henderson, P. (1994). *Developing and managing your school guidance program* (2nd ed.). Alexandria, VA: American Counseling Association.

Hawes, D. J. (1989). Communication between teachers and children: A counselor consultant/trainer model. *Elementary School Guidance and Counseling, 24,* 58–67.

Herring, R. D., & White, L. M. (1995). School counselors, teachers, and the culturally compatible classroom: Partnerships in multicultural education. *Journal of Humanistic Education and Development, 34,* 52–64.

Hicks, B. B. (1990). *Youth suicide*. Bloomington, IN: National Educational Services.

Hobson, S. M., & Kanitz, H. M. (1996). Multicultural counseling: An ethical issue for school counselors. *School Counselor, 43,* 245–255.

Hohenshil, T. H., & Hohenshil, S. B. (1989). Preschool counseling. *Journal of Counseling and Development, 67,* 430–431.

Hollander, S. K. (1989). Coping with child sexual abuse through children's books. *Elementary School Guidance and Counseling, 23,* 183–193.

Humes, C. W., (1980). Counseling IEPs. *School Counselor, 28,* 87–91.

Johnson, W., & Kottman, T. (1992). Developmental needs of middle school students: Implications for counselors. *Elementary School Guidance and Counseling, 27,* 3–14.

Jones, V. F. (1977). School counselors as facilitators of healthy learning environments. *School Counselor, 24,* 157–164.

Joynt, D. F. (1993). *A peer counseling primer*. Danbury, CT: Author.

Kaplan, L. S., & Geoffroy, K. E. (1993). Copout or burnout? Counseling strategies to reduce stress in gifted students. *School Counselor, 40,* 247–252.

Keat, D. B., II. (1990). Change in child multimodal counseling. *Elementary School Guidance and Counseling, 24,* 248–262.

Keeling, R. P. (1993). HIV disease: Current concepts. *Journal of Counseling and Development, 71,* 261–274.

Keys, S. G., & Bemak, F. (1997). School-family-community linked services: A school counseling role for changing times. *School Counselor, 44,* 255–263.

Keys, S. G., Bemak, F., Carpenter, S. L., & King-Sears, M. E. (1998). Collaborative consultant: A new role for counselors serving at-risk youth. *Journal of Counseling & Development, 76,* 123–133.

Kiselica, M. S., & Pfaller, J. (1993). Helping teenage parents: The independent and collaborative roles of counselor educators and school counselors. *Journal of Counseling and Development, 72,* 42–48.

Kushman, J. W., & Kinney, P. (1989). Understanding and preventing school dropout. In D. Capuzzi & D. R. Gross (Eds.), *Youth at risk* (pp. 345–366). Alexandria, VA: American Counseling Association.

Landreth, G. (1983). Play therapy in elementary school settings. In C. E. Schaeffer & K. J. O'Connor (Eds.), *Handbook of play therapy* (pp. 200–212). New York: Wiley.

Landreth, G. (1987). Play therapy: Facilitative use of child's play in elementary school counseling. *Elementary School Guidance and Counseling, 21,* 253–261.

Landreth, G. (1991). *Play therapy: The art of the relationship*. Muncie, IN: Accelerated Development.

Landreth, G. (1993). Child-centered play therapy. *Elementary School Guidance and Counseling, 28,* 17–29.

Lee, C. C., & Walz, G. R. (Eds.). (1998). *Social action: A mandate for counselors*. Alexandria, VA: American Counseling Association.

Lewis, W. (1996). A proposal for initiating family counseling interventions by school counselors. *School Counselor, 44,* 93–99.

Lockhart, E. J., & Keys, S. G. (1998). The mental health counseling role of school counselors. *Professional School Counseling, 1(4),* 3–6.

Magnuson, S. (1996). Charlotte's web: Expanding a classroom activity for a guidance lesson. *Elementary School Guidance & Counseling, 31,* 75–76.

Malley, P. B., & Kush, F. (1994). Comprehensive and systematic school-based suicide prevention programs: A checklist for counselors. *School Counselor, 41,* 191–194.

Martin, J. (1983). Curriculum development in school counseling. *Personnel and Guidance Journal, 61,* 406–409.

Matthews, D. B., & Burnett, D. D. (1989). Anxiety: An achievement component. *Journal of Humanistic Education and Development, 27,* 122–131.

Maultsby, M. C., Jr. (1986). Teaching rational self-counseling to middle graders. *School Counselor, 33,* 207–219.

McCarthy, C. J., Brack, C. J., Lambert, R. G., Brack, G., & Orr, D. P. (1996). Predicting emotional and behavioral risk factors In adolescents. *School Counselor, 43,* 277–286.

McGowan, A. S. (1995). "Suffer the little children": A developmental perspective. *Journal of Humanistic Education and Development, 34,* 50–51.

McWhirter, J. J., McWhirter, B. T., McWhirter, A. M., & McWhirter, E. H. (1994). High- and low-risk characteristics of youth: The five Cs of competency. *School Counselor, 28,* 188–196.

Minkoff, H. B., & Terres, C. K. (1985). ASCA perspective: Past, present, and future. *Journal of Counseling and Development, 63,* 424–427.

Mohai, C. E. (1991). *Are school-based drug prevention programs working?* Ann Arbor, MI: CAPS Digest (EDO-CG-91-1).

Moore, D. D., & Forster, J. R. (1993). Student assistance programs: New approaches for reducing adolescent substance abuse. *Journal of Counseling and Development, 71,* 326–329.

Morganett, R. S. (1990). *Skills for living: Group counseling for young adolescents.* Champaign, IL: Research Press.

Morganett, R. S. (1994). *Skills for living: Group counseling activities for elementary students.* Champaign, IL: Research Press.

Morganett, R. S. (1995). *Skills and techniques for group work with youth.* Champaign, IL: Research Press.

Morse, C. L., & Russell, T. (1988). How elementary counselors see their role: An empirical study. *Elementary School Guidance and Counseling, 23,* 54–62.

Muro, J. J. (1981). On target: On top. *Elementary School Guidance and Counseling, 15,* 307–314.

Myrick, R. D. (1993). *Developmental guidance and counseling: A practical approach* (2nd ed.). Minneapolis: Educational Media Corporation.

Ostlund, D. R., & Kinnier, R. T. (1997). Values of youth: Messages from the most popular songs of four decades. *Journal of Humanistic Education and Development, 36,* 83–91.

Paisley, P. O., & Hubbard, G. T. (1994). *Developmental school counseling programs: From theory to practice.* Alexandria, VA: American Counseling Association.

Partin, R. (1993). School counselors' time: Where does it go? *School Counselor, 40,* 274–281.

Peach, L., & Reddick, T. L. (1991). Counselors can make a difference in preventing adolescent suicide. *School Counselor, 39,* 107–110.

Peer, G. G. (1985). The status of secondary school guidance: A national survey. *School Counselor, 32,* 181–189.

Peters, H. J. (1980). *Guidance in the elementary schools.* New York: Macmillan.

Peterson, K. S., & O'Neal, G. (1998, March 25). Society more violent; so are its children. *USA Today,* 3A.

Popenhagen, M. P., & Qualley, R. M. (1998). Adolescent suicide: Detection, intervention, and prevention. *Professional School Counseling, 1,* 30–35.

Remley, T. P., Jr., & Sparkman, L. B. (1993). Student suicides: The counselor's limited legal liability. *School Counselor, 40,* 164–169.

Ribak-Rosenthal, N. (1994). Reasons individuals become school administrators, school counselors, and teachers. *School Counselor, 41,* 158–164.

Richardson, R. C., & Norman, K. I. (1997). "Rita dearest, it's OK to be different": Teaching children acceptance and tolerance. *Journal of Humanistic Education and Development, 35,* 188–197.

Ritchie, M. H. (1989). Enhancing the public image of school counseling: A marketing approach. *School Counselor, 37,* 54–61.

Ritchie, M. H., & Partin, R. L. (1994). Parent education and consultation activities of school counselors. *School Counselor, 41,* 165–170.

Robinson, S. E. (1989). "Why say no?": Substance abuse among teenagers. In D. Capuzzi & D. R. Gross (Eds.), *Youth at risk* (pp. 325–341). Alexandria, VA: American Counseling Association.

Romano, J. L., Miller, J. P., & Nordness, A. (1996). Stress and well-being in the elementary school: A classroom curriculum. *School Counselor, 43,* 268–276.

Rossi, P. H., & Freeman, H. E. (1993). *Evaluation: A systematic approach* (5th ed.). Beverly Hills, CA: Sage.

St. Clair, K. L. (1989). Middle school counseling research: A resource for school counselors. *Ele-*

mentary School Guidance and Counseling, 23, 219–226.

Schmidt, J. J. (1991). *A survival guide for the elementary/middle school counselor.* West Nyack, NY: Center for Applied Research in Education.

Schmidt, J. J. (1999). *Counseling in schools* (3rd ed.). Boston: Allyn & Bacon.

Schmidt, J. J., & Osborne, W. L. (1982). The way we were (and are): A profile of elementary counselors in North Carolina. *Elementary School Guidance and Counseling, 16,* 163–171.

Schrank, F. A. (1982). Bibliotherapy as an elementary school counseling tool. *Elementary School Guidance and Counseling, 16,* 218–227.

Sheeley, V. L., & Herlihy, B. (1989). Counseling suicidal teens: A duty to warn and protect. *School Counselor, 37,* 89–97.

Shertzer, B., & Stone, S. C. (1981). *Fundamentals of guidance* (4th ed.). Boston: Houghton Mifflin.

Snyder, B. A., & Daly, T. P. (1993). Restructuring guidance and counseling programs. *School Counselor, 41,* 36–42.

Sprinthall, N. A. (1984). Primary prevention: A road paved with a plethora of promises and procrastinations. *Personnel and Guidance Journal, 62,* 491–495.

Sprinthall, N. A., Hall, J. S., & Gerler, E. R., Jr. (1992). Peer counseling for middle school students experiencing family divorce: A deliberate psychological education model. *Elementary School Guidance and Counseling, 26,* 279–294.

Stamm, M. L., & Nissman, B. S. (1979). *Improving middle school guidance.* Boston: Allyn & Bacon.

Stevens-Smith, P., & Remley, T. P., Jr. (1994). Drugs, AIDS, and teens: Intervention and the school counselor. *School Counselor, 41,* 180–184.

Stiltner, B. (1978). Needs assessment: A first step. *Elementary School Guidance and Counseling, 12,* 239–246.

Street, S., & Isaacs, M. (1998). Self-esteem: Justifying its existence. *Professional School Counseling, 1,* 46–50.

Thompson, C. L., & Rudolph, L. B. (1996). *Counseling children* (4th ed.). Pacific Grove, CA: Brooks/Cole.

Thornburg, H. D. (1978). *The bubblegum years: Sticking with kids from 9 to 13.* Tucson: HELP Books.

Thornburg, H. D. (1986). The counselor's impact on middle-grade students. *School Counselor, 33,* 170–177.

Webb, W. (1992). Empowering at-risk children. *Elementary School Guidance and Counseling, 27,* 96–103.

White, E. B. (1952). *Charlotte's web.* New York: Trophy.

Whitehead, B. D. (1997). *The divorce culture.* New York: Knopf.

Whitledge, J. (1994). Cross-cultural counseling: Implications for school counselors in enhancing student learning. *School Counselor, 41,* 314–318.

Wilson, N. H., & Rotter, J. C. (1980). Elementary school counselor enrichment and renewal. *Elementary School Guidance and Counseling, 14,* 178–187.

16

COLLEGE COUNSELING AND STUDENT LIFE SERVICES

♦
_____

Just like fall foliage

we watch what you bring forth each September.

Your changes are not as dramatic as the red of Maples,

or as warm as the orange of twilight fires;

But your presence, both individually and collectively,

like leaves adds color to a campus

that would otherwise be bland

in the shades of administration gray.

We celebrate your coming

much as we look forward to the crisp cool air

at the end of summer.

We welcome your spirit

for it enlivens us to the metaphors and ideals

that live unchanging lives . . .

From "Through the Seasons to New Life," by S. T. Gladding, 1982, Humanist Educator, 20, *122. © 1982 by ACA.*
Reprinted with permission. No further reproduction authorized without written permission of the American
Counseling Association.

Higher education is one of the most valued experiences in the United States, enrolling between 12 and 13 million people annually. At the start of the 21st century, over 25% of U.S. adults ages 25–34 had completed 4 years or more of higher education. That rate compared with a similar percentage in Japan, 18% in Canada, and 12% in the United Kingdom, France, and Germany (Horton, 1994). In higher education, student life services are offered in addition to courses. These services are primarily in the form of cocurricular activities, support programs, and counseling (Komives, Woodard, & Delworth, 1996).

Student life services and counseling on U.S. college and university campuses first emerged at the beginning of the 20th century. E. G. Williamson, dean of students at the University of Minnesota in the 1930s and 1940s, articulated what would later be called the student personnel point of view *(Williamson, 1939). His model of student personnel services set the standard for the time. It was largely a direct and counselor-centered approach. The emphasis was "It is not enough to help counselees become what they want to become; rather it is more important to help them become what they ought to want to become" (Ewing, 1990, p. 104). The student personnel point of view, sometimes called the Minnesota point of view, remained in place until after World War II. At that time the federal government began pouring money into higher education for diverse services, and competing points of view emerged.*

Ideas about the importance of student life services, student development, and counseling have increasingly been accepted since the 1940s. They have been a part of what is known as the field of student affairs since the 1970s (Canon, 1988; Winston & Creamer, 1997). Sometimes student life services and college counseling are connected in specific ways (Evans, Carr, & Stone, 1982); sometimes they are not. Regardless, they share much common ground (e.g., emphasis on the health and development of the whole person) and are included together in this chapter because of the way they dovetail and influence the total campus life of students, faculty, staff, and administrators.

Professionals who work with college students outside the classroom vary in background and training (Bloland, 1992; Komives et al., 1996). They include those employed in financial aid, admissions, career planning and placement, health education, campus unions, registration, residence life, advising, and international activities. The services they offer include the following (Kuh, 1996; Kuh, Bean, Bradley, & Coomes, 1986):

- *Services connected with student behaviors (e.g., achievement, attrition, campus activities)*
- *Services associated with describing student characteristics (e.g., aptitudes, aspirations)*
- *Services concerned with student growth (e.g., cognitive, moral, social/emotional)*
- *Services connected with academic performance (e.g., study skills)*

Counselors and student services personnel emphasize a common concern about the total development of the persons they serve (Brown & Helms, 1986; Johnson, 1985; Komives et al., 1996). Many hold multiple memberships in professional organizations.

One of the most diverse professional groups is the American College Personnel Association (ACPA), an affiliate of the ACA until 1992. This association, which was officially organized in 1924, has undergone three name changes. Its members are employed in a number of areas related to student services. Another important professional group is the American College Counseling Association (ACCA), a division of the ACA since 1992. The ACCA's members are professionals who primarily work in colleges and universities and identify themselves as counselors (Davis, 1998; Dean, 1994). Other organizations in the student life services field include the National Association of Student Personnel Administrators (NASPA), Division 17 (Counseling Psychology) of the APA, and the postsecondary division of the American School Counselor Association (ASCA).

Several attempts have been made through the years to form a united organization of professionals who work in various college student life services, but none has completely succeeded (Sheeley, 1983). This failure is partly attributable to different backgrounds and training (Bloland, 1992). Because college professionals who work with students are employed in different areas, they tend to concentrate their services on specific issues and people. Institutional focus also makes a difference. Some universities emphasize research and scholarship (known as the German university tradition), some the education of the whole person (the English residential liberal arts tradition), and some vocational or professional preparation (the U.S. paradigm) (Rodgers, 1989; Rubin, 1990). Quite often, student life specialists have their perceptions, opinions, and values about programs shaped or directed by the institutions that employ them (Canon, 1985).

Moreover, publications in student life services tend to be diverse. The leading periodicals are the Journal of College Student Development, *the* National Association of Student Personnel Administrators Journal, *and the* Journal of College Counseling. *The theme-oriented quarterly series,* New Directions for Student Services *(published by Jossey-Bass), is also influential and popular.*

The Beginning of Student Life Services and College Counseling

Student life services in higher education, including counseling, began largely by default. "Historically, the participation of faculty in what are now called student services functions gradually changed from total involvement to detachment" (Fenske, 1989b, p. 16). This change was the result of significant developmental factors in the growth of American higher education over its nearly 300-year history, including the following:

- The passage of the Morrill Land Grant Act in 1862, which influenced the establishment and eventual dominance of state universities in American higher education
- The growth of pluralistic opinions and populations among U.S. college students

- A change in faculty role: professors and teachers no longer fostered students' moral character, took charge of character development, or adhered to a policy of in loco parentis (in place of parents)
- An increase in faculty interest in research and intellectual development (e.g., Hutchins, 1936)
- Lack of faculty interest in the daily implementation of institutional governance
- The emergence of counseling and other helping professions
- The documentation by Sanford (1962, 1979) that student development during the college years can be promoted by challenge and support and that curriculum and co-curriculum activities can "initiate, accelerate, or inhibit developmental change" (Canon, 1988, p. 451)

Student life services as a profession grew rapidly in higher education between the end of World War I and the depression of the 1930s (Fenske, 1989a). During this period, many hoped that student life professionals would be integrated into the mainstream of academic programs. But they were not, and a strong theoretical rationale for implementing student life programs was not formulated. In addition, many student life professionals were terminated during the Great Depression because of a lack of money and the failure of employed practitioners to define themselves adequately. Thus, student life services, then as now, occupies the paradoxical position "of being both indispensable and peripheral" (Fenske, 1989b, p. 6).

College counseling as a profession did not begin until the late 1940s. Before that time faculty and college presidents served as students' counselors (Pace, Stamler, Yarris, & June, 1996). The delay of college counseling was due to the prevailing cultural view that most students who entered college were well adjusted and that the only professionals helpful to mentally distressed college students were psychiatrists. It was not until after World War II that counseling psychologists and counselors were allowed to work with students in newly formed campus counseling centers. Such structures were set up because large numbers of veterans returned to colleges and needed more help than could otherwise be provided. Furthermore, during and immediately after World War II, counseling psychologists won the right to work clinically with clients just as psychiatrists did (Ewing, 1990).

The Theoretical Bases and Professional Preparation for Working with College Students

College counseling and student life services involve understanding how college students of all ages learn, grow, and develop. Yet as Bloland (1986) points out, some "entry-level and not a few seasoned professionals know little of student development theory or practice" (p. 1). This fact is unfortunate because working with students effectively requires this specialized knowledge. It is important that college counselors in particular distinguish between problems students have tied to normal developmental struggles, such as autonomy, identity, and intimacy, and more serious or chronic forms of psychological disturbance (Sharkin, 1997). Even among professionals with the best of intentions, ethically or legally questionable behavior may cause harm if one is not closely attuned to both the developmental and disordered aspect of the college population (Canon, 1989; Kitchener, 1985).

Theoretical Bases

Professionals in college counseling and student life services can use a number of theoretical models as guides in working with students experiencing predictable developmental situations. From an ideological viewpoint, three traditions dominate: in loco parentis, student services, and student development (Rodgers, 1989). *In loco parentis* gives faculty and staff the parental role of teaching moral values. *Student services* emphasizes the student as consumer and mandates services that facilitate development. This approach stresses a cafeteria-style manner of program offerings that students select according to what they think they need. *Student development* focuses on creating research-based environments that "help college students learn and develop" (Rodgers, 1989, p. 120). Student development is proactive because it makes opportunities available for special groups of students.

Within student development, at least four kinds of developmental theories guide professionals' activities: psychosocial, cognitive-structural, person-environment interaction, and typological. *Psychosocial theories* are embodied most thoroughly in the writings of Arthur Chickering (e.g., Chickering & Reisser, 1994). He contends that there are seven specific developmental tasks of college students: competence, autonomy, managing emotions, identity, purpose, integrity, and relationships (Garfield & David, 1986). These tasks are in line with Erik Erikson's (1968) ideas about the developmental processes of youth. A major strength of Chickering is that he elaborates and specifies Erikson's concepts in such a way that college counselors and student life professionals can plan and evaluate their practices and programs around three key issues: career development, intimacy, and formulation of an adult philosophy of life. For example, first-year students and seniors differ in their specific levels of development, with first-year students being more preoccupied than seniors with establishing competence, managing emotions, and developing autonomy. Seniors, on the other hand, concentrate more on issues such as establishing identity, freeing interpersonal relationships, developing purpose, and establishing integrity (Rodgers, 1989).

Cognitive-structural theories focus on how individuals develop a sense of meaning in the world. They deal with perception and evaluation and are best described in the moral and intellectual models of Perry (1970) and Kohlberg (1984). These models are process oriented, hierarchical, and sequential. For example, Perry's model assumes growth from "simple dualism (positions 1 and 2) through multiplicity (positions 3 and 4) and relativism (positions 5 and 6) to commitment within a relativistic framework (positions 7 through 9)." Kohlberg's model "outlines three levels of moral development: the preconventional, the conventional, and the postconventional" (Delve, Mintz, & Stewart, 1990b, p. 8). According to these theories, each new stage contains the previous one and is a building block for the next one. Cognitive discomfort is the impetus for change. Explicit in this approach is the idea that "people need the opportunity to learn how to think and act responsibly in order to control their own behavior in a democratic society" (Herman, 1997, p. 147).

The *person-environment interaction model* "refers to various conceptualizations of the college student and the college environment and the degree of congruence that occurs when they interact" (Rodgers, 1989, p. 121). Congruence is believed to lead to "satisfaction, stability, and perhaps, development" (Rodgers, 1980, p. 77). The theories in this model stress that development is a holistic process that involves all parts of the person with the environment in an interacting way. It is similar to the psychosocial approach in assuming that development in one area of life can facilitate growth in another. For example, when students participate and take leadership positions in student organizations, their life management skills develop more positively than those of students who are more passive (Cooper, Healy, & Simpson, 1984). Likewise, students who volunteer in community service initiatives (also known as "service learning") become more informed about environmental needs, less egocentric, and more empathetic (Delve, Mintz, & Stewart, 1990a). Unlike psychosocial theories, person-environment theories "are not developmental per se" (Rodgers, 1980, p. 77). In many ways, they are rooted in Kurt Lewin's (1936) formula: $B = f(P, E)$, where behavior (B) is a function (f) of person (P) and environment (E).

Typological theories focus on individual differences, such as temperament, personality type, and patterns of socialization. These differences are assumed to persist over time, and most often individuals are combinations of types. Patterns of personality influence individuals to vary in their developmental growth patterns and are related to their motivation, effort, and achievement. This approach is exemplified in the writings of John Holland (1997), which study how personalities fit with work environments.

Professional Preparation

Proper preparation is one of the difficulties in the field of college counseling and student life services. Because there is such diversity in the functions of student life professionals, no single professional preparation program can meet the needs of all graduate students. Those who enter this specialty "do not need the same kind of graduate work" (Sandeen, 1988, p. 21). Therefore, the CACREP provides different specialty standards for the field. CACREP accreditation in the student affairs area includes programs in student affairs with college counseling and student affairs with professional practice (Hollis, 1997). Specific course work and experiences needed for graduation have also been outlined by the Council for the Advancement of Standards for Student Services/Development Programs (1994). It is vital that specialization decisions be made as soon as possible in one's graduate career because the outcomes of each course of study vary considerably.

College Counseling

Emphases and Roles

The emphases and roles of college counselors vary and are influenced by the models under which they operate. Traditionally, there have been four main models of counseling services that college/university counseling centers have followed (Westbrook et al., 1993):

1. *Counseling as psychotherapy.* This model emphasizes long-term counseling with a small percentage of students. The counselor deals with personality change and refers other vocational and educational concerns to student academic advisers.

2. *Counseling as vocational guidance.* This model emphasizes helping students productively relate academic and career matters. The counselor deals with academic or vocationally undecided students and refers those with personal or emotional problems to other agencies.
3. *Counseling as traditionally defined.* This model emphasizes a broad range of counseling services, including short- or long-term relationships and those that deal with personal, academic, and career concerns. The counselor's role is diverse.
4. *Counseling as consultation.* This model emphasizes working with the various organizations and personnel who have a direct impact on student mental health. The counselor offers indirect services to students through strategic interventions.

A fifth model, *counseling as global* (i.e., an interactive, interdependent, community system), has recently been advocated (Pace et al., 1996). This model is dynamic and fluid. It proposes that counseling center staff work interactively with other members of a college/university community to create a mentally healthy environment and use personnel and other resources within a campus. The idea is an evolution of the cube concept (Morrill, Oetting, & Hurst, 1974, p. 355) that specifies target (individual, primary group, associational group, and institution or community), purposes (remedial, preventive, or developmental), and methods (direct, consultation and training, or media) as places for counselors to intervene. The global model changes the role of the counselor and the focus of the college counseling center by having center staff be more flexible and interactive (see Figure 16.1).

In reality, most college counseling centers offer a variety of services to help their diverse client populations and meet local campus needs.

Activities

The activities of college counselors are similar to those of student life professionals in being comprehensive and varied. Some services of these two groups even overlap. Lewing and Cowger (1982) identify nine counseling functions that generally dictate the agendas of college counselors:

- Academic and educational counseling
- Vocational counseling
- Personal counseling
- Testing
- Supervision and training
- Research
- Teaching
- Professional development
- Administration

In truth, three of these activities—personal, vocational, and educational counseling—account for more than 50% of college counselors' time. Most of the counseling theories covered in this book are implemented in college counseling centers. For instance, Thur-

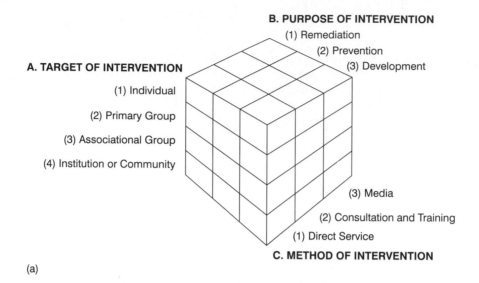

A. TARGET OF INTERVENTION

    (1) Individual

    (2) Primary Group

    (3) Associational Group

    (4) Institution or Community

B. PURPOSE OF INTERVENTION

    (1) Remediation

    (2) Prevention

    (3) Development

    (3) Media

    (2) Consultation and Training

    (1) Direct Service

C. METHOD OF INTERVENTION

(a)

Evolution of the Cube

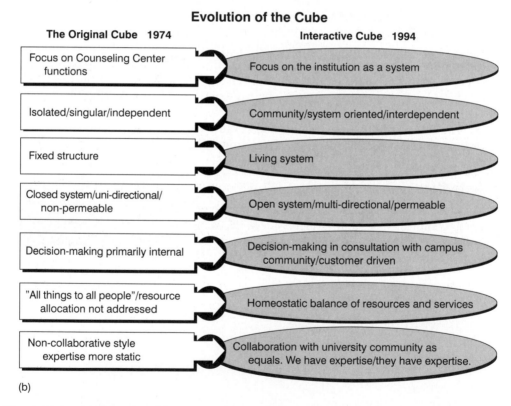

The Original Cube 1974   **Interactive Cube 1994**

The Original Cube 1974	Interactive Cube 1994
Focus on Counseling Center functions	Focus on the institution as a system
Isolated/singular/independent	Community/system oriented/interdependent
Fixed structure	Living system
Closed system/uni-directional/non-permeable	Open system/multi-directional/permeable
Decision-making primarily internal	Decision-making in consultation with campus community/customer driven
"All things to all people"/resource allocation not addressed	Homeostatic balance of resources and services
Non-collaborative style expertise more static	Collaboration with university community as equals. We have expertise/they have expertise.

(b)

Figure 16.1 (a) The cube; (b) evolution of the cube

Sources: (a) "Dimensions of Counselor Functioning," by W. H. Morrill, E. R. Oetting, and J. C. Hurst, 1974, *Personnel and Guidance Journal, 42*, p. 355. © 1972 by Morrill, Oetting, and Hurst. Reprinted with permission. (b) From "Rounding Out the Cube: Evolution to a Global Model for Counseling Centers," by D. Pace, V. L. Stamler, E. Yarris, and L. June, 1996, *Journal of Counseling and Development, 74*, p. 325. Reprinted with permission.

man (1983) found that rational emotive behavior therapy, including the use of rational emotive imagery, can be effective in reducing Type A behavior (time-urgent, competitive, and hostile) among college students and help them become healthier achievers. Watkins (1983), on the other hand, found a person-centered approach to be most effective in helping students evaluate present and future plans and decide whether to stay in college. Even systems theory, most often used in marriage and family counseling, has proven effective in helping students understand family dynamics and patterns of interaction and how family patterns continue to influence important decisions about education (Openlander & Searight, 1983). Brief therapy, a form of systems theory, has been employed in college counseling centers to help expand the "therapeutic framework to include nonfamilial members [who] can affect therapeutic progress" for better or worse (Terry, 1989, p. 352). In this treatment, conflictual nonfamily members within a campus community are brought together to form meaningful relationships and make changes in problematic situations. The idea behind the treatment is that students within a campus can help each other problem-solve and make their environments healthier through the resolution of problem behaviors. In the process, blaming and scapegoating cease.

One challenge that college counselors face is a constantly changing student culture (Bishop, 1992). Behaviors among college students change with each generation. The culture of "Generation X" (the current student population) is not the same as its predecessors. Indeed, college counseling center practitioners in recent years "have been expressing a sense of urgency about increasing numbers of students who present with serious psychological problems as well as an overall increase in the severity of presenting problems" (Sharkin, 1997, p. 275). College counseling centers are "seeing as many as 20 per cent of the students in counseling sessions each year, and they expect the proportion to continue to rise" (Geraghty, 1997, A32). Therefore, both educational and preventive programs must regularly be modified to help students handle current issues.

When services are varied and numerous at the professional level, everyone benefits. The College Adjustment Scales is a means of screening college students for common developmental and psychological problems (Anton & Reed, 1991). These nine scales measure psychological distress in the following areas: anxiety, depression, suicidal ideation, substance abuse, self-esteem problems, interpersonal problems, family problems, academic problems, and career problems. It is an important assessment instrument for college counseling centers to use in deciding what services and programs they will emphasize.

Peer counselors are also an effective way of reaching students beyond the traditional college counseling center. As a rule, students turn first to friends for help, then to close relatives, before finally turning to faculty and counseling services. Ragle and Krone (1985) found that 1st-year students who had previously undergone a summer orientation program at the University of Texas at Austin were, as a result, overwhelmingly at ease in talking with peer advisers over the telephone about various concerns. Furthermore, they felt that contact with peer counselors was helpful and indicated that it made the university seem less impersonal.

Sometimes peer counselors take the role of resident assistants (RAs) (Nickerson & Harrington, 1968). In this arrangement, RAs are assigned to live in selected residence halls. Their services, which include dealing with remedial, preventive, and developmental issues, are given high exposure (Schuh, Shipton, & Edman, 1986). RAs provide crisis intervention, short-term counseling, conflict mediation, and referral services (Blimling & Miltenberger, 1981). They help students keep favorable attitudes toward counseling and counseling-related services and, at the same time, become more aware of opportunities offered by college counseling centers (Johnson, Nelson, & Wooden, 1985). In addition, RAs sponsor programs for residents on mental and physical health topics, bringing in faculty and staff from across the campus to give presentations. RAs usually receive ongoing professional training and supervision from the campus counseling center. This arrangement benefits the RAs, students in the residence halls, and the campus as a whole because of its integrative and preventive focus.

College counselors can also offer services and programs in conjunction with other student life professionals. Three of the most needed services relate to alcohol, sexual abuse and violence, and eating disorders. Nearly 90% of students drink alcohol sometime during an academic year, and approximately 20% qualify as heavy drinkers, averaging one ounce of alcohol per day per month (Steenbarger, 1998). Thus, it is not surprising that alcohol-related problems, including the abuse of alcohol and its concomitant disorders, are prevalent on college campuses. *Binge drinking* (having five or more drinks at a time for men and four or more drinks for women) appears to be increasing, and one in three college students drinks primarily to get drunk (Commission on Substance Abuse at College and Universities, 1994). In addition, irresponsible drinking may lead to violence in the form of date rape, unsafe sex, academic difficulties, and suicide. Even riots on or near college campuses occur when college administrators ban alcohol at certain campus events or areas (Lively, 1998).

Thus, alcohol abuse is likely to bring students in contact with counselors and other student life professionals (Gill-Wigal, Heaton, Burke, & Gleason, 1988). Systematic steps are usually implemented to help students get through denial they may have connected with alcohol abuse because before effective treatment can take place, students need to realize their need for help in correcting out-of-control behavior. Intervention is sometimes done individually, but often it involves a group and usually a wide variety of treatments, including insight and behavioral change.

Many students who abuse alcohol have grown up in dysfunctional families. They frequently experience problems related to growing up in such environments (e.g., workaholism, depression, dependency, antisocial tendencies, food addictions). Specific interventions counselors use with these students include helping them define more clearly the roles they played in their family-life dramas and then helping them break nonproductive patterns of interaction (Crawford & Phyfer, 1988). One way counselors can break nonproductive patterns is to respond to these students in functionally healthy ways that contrast with the behaviors they have experienced before (see Table 16.1). Peer counseling may also be helpful to an extent in this process.

Sexual assault and violence, including incest and rape, are matters that many students, primarily women, must deal with during their college experience. The dynamics surrounding sexual crimes have similarities and differences. A common denominator in many cases is alcohol abuse: 90% of campus rapes occur when alcohol has been consumed by the assailant, the victim, or both (Commission on Substance Abuse at Colleges and Universities, 1994). There are at least two stages in the recovery process: (a) the acute, which is characterized by disorganization, and (b) long-term reorganization, which includes dealing

Table 16.1 Intervention strategies for survival roles

Survival Role	Manifestations	Counseling Techniques
Hero	Overachievement Anxiety Stress Overcontrol	Self-esteem enhancement; exercises to establish sources of internal reinforcement including self-statements Exploration of leisure activities for personal renewal and growth Examination of irrational beliefs regarding perfectionism and the need for approval
Scapegoat	Delinquency Role infraction Impulsiveness Substance abuse	Impulse control through self-talk Behavioral contracting for delay of gratification Treatment for abuse disorder, if present
Lost Child	Social isolation Shyness Obesity Depression	Interpersonal skills training Behavioral contracting for not reinforcing social isolation Self-esteem enhancement exercises Cognitive restructuring for interpreting experience positively
Mascot	Fear Clowning Hypochondriasis Hyperactivity	Self-esteem enhancement exercises Exercises in responsibility-taking Assertiveness training

Source: From "Adult Children of Alcoholics: A Counseling Model," by R. L. Crawford and A. Phyfer, 1988, *Journal of College Student Development, 29*, p. 110. © 1988 by ACA. Reprinted with permission. No further reproduction authorized without written permission of the American Counseling Association.

with the pain of trauma and rebuilding one's life through support (Burgess & Holstrom, 1974; Scrignar, 1984).

Eating disorders, especially bulimia and anorexia nervosa, are the third area in which college counselors can team up with other student life professionals in offering services. There is a great need to address eating disorders in universities, where it is estimated that up to 65% of women in their first year of college display "some behavioral and psychological characteristics of disturbed eating" (Meyer & Russell, 1998, p. 166). To address these needs, eating disorders must "be considered within a developmental framework" (Sharkin, 1997, p. 275). Programs that emphasize the characteristics of eating disorders as well as highlight ways of combating such tendencies before they become full blown can do much to educate those most likely to experience them. Furthermore, such programming can give participants sources to which they can turn if either they or someone they know becomes caught up in a bulimic cycle.

In addressing issues pertinent to college students, counselors in cooperation with student life professionals can take preventive action on tertiary, secondary, and primary levels. "*Tertiary prevention* is akin to remediation and includes direct services to victims" (Roark, 1987, p. 369; my emphasis). It includes encouraging the reporting of aggression and helping the victim use available resources. *Secondary prevention* is geared toward problems, such as date rape, already in existence on campus and is aimed at raising consciousness among potential victims and perpetrators and setting policies to stop known abuses. *Primary prevention* focuses on stopping problems from ever developing. It involves modifying the physical environment as well as addressing causes and providing training to create awareness and change values. For example, to help students manage stress, a program referred to by the acronym BRIMS (breathing, relaxing, imagery, message, and signs) might be offered (Carrese, 1998). This program is a type of cognitive self-hypnosis that helps students relax both physically and mentally while giving themselves positive messages and physical signs that help them recall constructive ways of feeling and viewing a situation. In the process, students "transform negative thoughts into constructive energy, allowing control over situations that produce unnecessary anxiety" (p. 140).

Student Life Professionals

Emphases and Roles

Initially, college/university student life services concentrated on helping new students adjust to campus life (Williamson, 1961). This focus still exists but now includes an emphasis on older returning students and an increased concern for all aspects of the college/university community, such as working with minority culture students and students with learning disabilities (Boesch & Cimbolic, 1994; Lynch & Gussel, 1996; Tate & Schwartz, 1993). There is a humanistic quality among individuals who choose student life services as a profession: they try to maximize, personalize, and individualize the higher education of students, helping them fully use the environment to promote their development. An important by-product of this process is that students are greatly assisted in making successful transitions from their communities to institutional life and back again (Berdie, 1966; Brown, 1986; Kuh, 1996). Thus, student life professionals are institutional integrators who facilitate the accomplishment of student and college/university goals.

At times during the college year (orientation, midterm examinations, and the end of the term) the work of student life professionals increases dramatically (Houston, 1971). Although certain problems are universal regardless of one's developmental age or stage (including health, anxiety, and depression), other concerns are related directly to specific college student populations. For example, first-year college students may especially need help during their initial months in college. Graduation from high school involves a loss of identity and a need for reevaluation and goal commitment that is often unavailable to entering students before they matriculate (Hayes, 1981). In addition, first-year college students face the challenges of managing time effectively, making choices about what courses to take, taking academic tests, and coping with fellow students while simultaneously handling finances, family, and personal problems (Carrese, 1998). "Some of the most commonly reported crises in the first year involve difficulties in social adjustment manifested as feelings of homesickness and loneliness" (Gerdes & Mallinckrodt, 1994, p. 281). There is often the experience of psychological pain because of the disruption in established friendship networks and new stress (Ponzetti & Cate, 1988).

Another unique problem is Greek life and rush. The rush system of fraternities and sororities, though exciting and fulfilling for many students, may also produce feelings of depression among students who are not offered bids. In helping students during these times, student life professionals must be sensitive to individual needs, offer support, and try to help rejected students find a fulfilling peer group (Atlas & Morier, 1994).

In line with transitional problems, Grites (1979) found that 12 of the 43 items on the Social Readjustment Rating Scale (Holmes & Rahe, 1967) almost exclusively apply to first-year college students in their adjustment to a new environment. When translated into life-change units, these factors yield a combined score of 250, which the authors of this instrument consider to be in the "moderate life crisis" category. As a group, individuals in this category have a 51% greater risk of a deteriorating health change than those who score 150 or below.

Grites further observes that new students who face other changes outside the college/university environment (e.g., the death of a family member or friend) are likely to move into the "major life crisis" category, becoming an even greater risk for a detrimental health change. Therefore, many colleges and universities now employ special student life staff to work with each incoming class to enhance the first-year experience and initially promote positive individual development as well as a sense of community (Loxley & Whiteley, 1986; Whiteley, 1982).

Regardless of such attempts at prevention, approximately 10% of all students encounter an emotional difficulty during their years that is serious enough to impair academic performance (Mathiasen, 1984). In addition, stress on college students to pass examinations or get into a professional school increase the incidents of major depression in this population (Clay, Anderson, & Dixon, 1993). If appropriate intervention is not offered (e.g., training in appropriate anger expression or stress management), students experience emotional, social, or academic problems to such a degree that they drop out of school. Unfortunately, between 40% and 60% of students who begin 4-year institutions do not graduate (Brown, 1986; Gerdes & Mallinckrodt, 1994). Even more tragically, students may take their own lives. Annually approximately 6 of every 100,000 college students in the United States commit suicide (Chisolm, 1998).

Some of the strongest predictors of staying in school and maintaining good mental health are amenable to student life services (Polansky, Horan, & Hanish, 1993). To help students have a successful and productive college experience, student life professionals offer campus-wide programs and individual assistance. The goal of comprehensive programs is to make a positive impact on students and help them identify problems or concerns at strategic points where intervention strategies may be most beneficial. The emphases and roles of student life professionals are aimed at helping sensitize students to the multiple issues that face them and constructively deal with these unfolding issues and themselves (Creamer & Associates, 1990; Deegan & O'Banion, 1989). For example, college students face the challenge of maintaining some form of separation from their parents and families while establishing their own identity through individuation. There is a correlation between student adjustment to college and attachment to parents (Rice & Whaley, 1994). "Research suggests that college students benefit from (a) secure attachment to parents in which there is mutual trust, communication, and little conflict or alienation, and (b) relationships with parents in which their separateness and individuality are mirrored, acknowledged, and supported" (Quintana & Kerr, 1993, p. 349). By helping students separate positively and yet stay connected with their families, student life professionals assist students in their overall adjustment and achievement at college and beyond.

Activities

The activities of student life professionals are related to the specialty area in which they work: administration, development, or counseling. "The *administrative model* . . . is based on the premise that the student services profession is an administrative, service-oriented unit in higher education that provides many facilitating and development activities and programs for students" (Ambler, 1989, p. 247; my emphasis). Examples of these services include admissions, records, food, health, and financial aid. The *developmental model* is one that stresses education, such as helping students learn decision-making skills by offering leadership seminars or facilitating increased autonomy in residence-life activities. Finally, the *counseling model* is one that emphasizes social and emotional growth in interpersonal and vocational decisions and includes conducting highly personalized seminars around a topic of interest, such as dating, careers, or stress (Forrest, 1989).

Not all student life specialists follow these models, and not all student life activities are conducted by professionals. Indeed, a national survey found that 72% of college/university student affairs divisions use student paraprofessionals to supplement and implement their offerings (Winston & Ender, 1988). These paraprofessionals are "undergraduate students who have been selected and trained to offer services or programs to their peers. These services are intentionally designed to assist in the adjustment, satisfaction, and/or persistence of students" (p. 466). Student paraprofessionals are frequently employed in residence halls and orientation programs; they also work with crisis lines, student judiciaries, academic advising, financial aid, international student programs, and student activities.

By involving student paraprofessionals in structured programs, student life specialists directly and indirectly offer them leadership opportunities, improve the quality of life on campus, and accomplish critical tasks. More than 600 U.S. colleges and universities offer students some type of formal leadership training, and the number is growing (Freeman, Knott, & Schwartz, 1996; Gregory & Britt, 1987). Yet, certain core beliefs, underlying principles, and necessary curriculum topics must be dealt with before any such activity can be effective (Roberts & Ullom, 1989). Student life professionals have become increasingly interested in improving their leadership abilities at the same time that they have devoted additional time and effort to helping students in this area (McDade, 1989). This dual focus may help colleges take more initiative overall and promote a greater sense of community.

Counseling and Student Life Services with Nontraditional Students

In addition to working with mainstream groups, college counselors and student life professionals address the needs of nontraditional students. These may be older students, first-generation college students, or even student athletes. In all likelihood, those who are today called nontraditional students will become the norm in the early part of the 21st century (Benshoff & Lewis, 1992).

Many nontraditional students are adults who are older than the traditional college age. One-third to one-half of undergraduate students and more than 50% of all graduate students are over age 30 (Brazziel, 1989). As a group, they are highly motivated, prefer interactive learning, have family and financial concerns, view education as an investment, and have multiple commitments and responsibilities that are not related to school (Richter-Antion, 1986). Within this large group there are two basic subgroups: students ages 25–50 and those ages 50–80.

The first subgroup is usually motivated to return to college because of changing job or career requirements or opportunities that include family life transitions (e.g., marriage, divorce) (Aslanian & Brickell, 1980). Building up self-esteem and providing academic and social support are particularly important for these younger nontraditional students. The latter subgroup, often called *senior students,* come to campus for many purposes, which include obtaining degrees and finding personal enrichment. When working with senior students, college counselors and student life professionals must take several factors into consideration, such as modifications to the environment (perhaps brighter lighting or warmer room temperatures), the clients' developmental stage (e.g., dealing with issues of generativity or integration), the pace of the counseling sessions (slower may be better), potentially difficult areas (such as transference), and the use of counseling techniques (e.g., bibliotherapy, journal writing) (Huskey, 1994). With an increase in the number of older people, the numbers of senior students will most likely continue to grow.

Regardless of how fast the number of senior students grows, the overall number of nontraditional students will increase because of business down-sizing, the rapid advance of technology, and increased opportunities for professional development. Community and technical colleges and public universities are most likely to enroll the majority of these nontraditional students. As is the case with traditional students, more females than males will enroll, there will be an increase in the number of part-time students, and more cultural and racial minorities will seek a college education (Hodgkinson, Outtz, & Obarakpor, 1992). All these events will test the limits of counseling and other student life services.

A second group of nontraditional students *is first-generation college students*—that is, students who are the first in their family to enter college. The individuals in this category come from a wide variety of backgrounds, including second-generation immigrants and upwardly mobile poor (Hodgkinson et al., 1992). "Family support for education is the key difference between first generation and second generation students. Family support is also a fundamental variable in the decision to attend college and in the successful completion of college" (Fallon, 1997, p. 385).

Thus, first-generation college students have numerous needs. They must master knowledge of the college environment, including its specific vocabulary—for example, *credit hours, GPA,* and *dean* (Fallon, 1997). They must also become committed to the role of being a student, decipher the value systems of second-generation college students, as well as learn to understand student life services and study skills. Language barriers and social or cultural customs must also be addressed.

A third group of nontraditional students is student athletes. Many of these students have "problems in relating to the university system and the larger society" (Engstrom & Sedlacek, 1991, p. 189). They are often seen by others as problem students who have trouble relating either socially or academically (Burke, 1993). In addition, many are from minority cultural groups and are the first within their families to attend college (Kirk & Kirk, 1993). A sports-oriented environment may foster dependence on a coach or a team. Therefore, these students may become isolated and alienated from the mainstream of college life. Teaching time management and social skills are areas where counselors and student life specialists can help.

In addition, when student athletes lose their athletic identity through loss of eligibility or because of injury, they need assistance in making an integrative transition back to college life (Wooten, 1994). Counselors and student life professionals need to work with student athletes on both an emotional and cognitive basis by helping them identify and express their feelings and confront and correct irrational thoughts. Student athletes also need help in learning to see themselves beyond the college years, most likely as nonprofessional athletes. Therefore, career counseling and life-planning skills are important services to provide.

Summary and Conclusion

The professions of college counseling and student life services have much in common. Both emphasize the total growth and maturation of students in college/university environments, and each has an optimistic outlook, focusing on the benefits of certain environments and events as catalysts to make students more self-aware and use their abilities fully. These specialties also share a common historical parallel: their influence at colleges and universities has ebbed and flowed over time. In the 21st century, however, both specialties are well established and contributing positively to the overall functioning of institutions of higher education.

This chapter has covered the historical, philosophical, and pragmatic qualities of college student development and growth as they relate to counseling and student life services. The quality and variety of activities associated with these specialties are strong. In college counseling centers, emphasis is increasingly placed on global outreach and interaction and a proactive stance in the delivery of services (Bishop, 1990; Pace et al., 1996). These services include consultation, career counseling, crisis management, retention, personalization and humanization of the campus environment, establishment of self-help programs, and cooperation with other campus units (Stone & Archer, 1990). Student life services are also becoming more fluid and dynamic. As the dialogue between professionals in each aspect of student life becomes more open, the ability to serve students and the systems in which they operate will continue to increase.

CLASSROOM ACTIVITIES

1. Check your college library to see which of the journals mentioned in this chapter they subscribe to. Examine recent issues of the journals and find an article that you think is interesting. Summarize the contents of this article for your classmates in an oral report.

2. Invite a resident assistant at your college/university to discuss his or her job with the class. How does the actual job compare with your idea of what it could be? What parts of the position do you find appealing or not appealing?

3. Ask a professional in the student life services division at your college/university to describe the universal and unique aspects of his or her job with your class. Discuss how student life services activities relate to academic activities. How might the two be linked even more closely?

4. College/university students are bright and articulate. What theories do you imagine might be effective with this population that would not be as useful with a less educated group?

5. What concerns or problems on your college campus do you think college counselors and student life professionals should address? Pretend that you have been asked to set up programs to take care of these situations. What are some steps you might take to be effective?

REFERENCES

Ambler, D. A. (1989). Designing and managing programs: The administrator role. In U. Delworth, G. R. Hanson, & Associates (Eds.), *Student services: A handbook for the profession* (2nd ed., pp. 247–264). San Francisco: Jossey-Bass.

Anton, W. D., & Reed, J. R. (1991). *College adjustment scales professional manual*. Odessa, FL: Psychological Assessment Resources.

Aslanian, C. B., & Brickell, H. M. (1980). *Americans in transition: Life changes as reasons for adult learning*. New York: College Entrance Examination Board.

Atlas, G., & Morier, D. (1994). The sorority rush process: Self- selection, acceptance criteria, and the effect of rejection. *Journal of College Student Development, 35,* 346-353.

Benshoff, J. M., & Lewis, H. A. (1992, December). Nontraditional college students. *CAPS Digest* (EDO-CG-92-21).

Berdie, R. F. (1966). Student personnel work: Definition and redefinition. *Journal of College Student Personnel, 7,* 131-136.

Bishop, J. B. (1990). The university counseling center: An agenda for the 1990s. *Journal of Counseling and Development, 68,* 408-413.

Bishop, J. B. (1992). The changing student culture: Implications for counselors and administrators. *Journal of College Student Psychotherapy, 6,* 37-57.

Blimling, G. S., & Miltenberger, L. J. (1981). *The resident assistant*. Dubuque, IA: Kendall/Hunt.

Bloland, P. A. (1986). Student development: The new orthodoxy? Part 1. *ACPA Developments, 13,* 1, 13.

Bloland, P. A. (1992). The professionalization of student affairs staff. *CAPS Digest* (EDO-CG-92-25).

Boesch, R., & Cimbolic, P. (1994). Black students' use of college and university counseling centers. *Journal of College Student Development, 35,* 212-216.

Brazziel, W. F. (1989). Older students. In A. Levine & Associates (Eds.), *Shaping higher education's future: Demographic realities and opportunities, 1990-2000* (pp. 116-132). San Francisco: Jossey-Bass.

Brown, R. D. (1986). Editorial. *Journal of College Student Personnel, 27,* 99.

Brown, T., & Helms, J. (1986). The relationship between psychological development issues and anticipated self- disclosure. *Journal of College Student Personnel, 27,* 136–141.

Burgess, A. W., & Holstrom, L. L. (1974). Rape trauma syndrome. *American Journal of Psychiatry, 131,* 981–986.

Burke, K. L. (1993). The negative stereotyping of student athletes. In W. D. Kirk & S. V. Kirk (Eds.), *Student athletes: Shattering the myths and sharing the realities* (pp. 93–98). Alexandria, VA: American Counseling Association.

Canon, H. J. (1985). Ethical problems in daily practice. In H. J. Cannon & R. D. Brown (Eds.), *Applied ethics in student services* (pp. 5–15). San Francisco: Jossey-Bass.

Canon, H. J. (1988). Nevitt Sanford: Gentle prophet, Jeffersonian rebel. *Journal of Counseling and Development, 66,* 451–457.

Canon, H. J. (1989). Guiding standards and principles. In U. Delworth, G. R. Hanson, & Associates (Eds.), *Student services: A handbook for the professional* (2nd ed., pp. 57-79). San Francisco: Jossey-Bass.

Carrese, M. A. (1998). Managing stress for college success through self-hypnosis. *Journal of Humanistic Education and Development, 36,* 134–142.

Chickering, A. W., & Reisser, L. (1994). *Education and identity* (2nd ed.). San Francisco: Jossey-Bass.

Chisolm, M. S. (1998, May 15). Colleges need to provide early treatment of students' mental illnesses. *Chronicle of Higher Education, 44,* B6–B7.

Clay, D. L., Anderson, W. P., & Dixon, W. A. (1993). Relationship between anger expression and stress in predicting depression. *Journal of Counseling and Development, 72,* 91–94.

Commission on Substance Abuse at Colleges and Universities. (1994). *Rethinking rites of passage: Substance abuse on America's campuses.* New York: Center on Addiction and Substance Abuse at Columbia University.

Cooper, D. L., Healy, M. & Simpson, J. (1994). Student development through involvement: Specific changes over time. *Journal of College Student Development, 35,* 98–101.

Council for the Advancement of Standards for Student Services/Development Programs. (1994). *CAS standards and guidelines for student services/development programs.* College Park: University of Maryland.

Crawford, R. L., & Phyfer, A. Q. (1988). Adult children of alcoholics: A counseling model. *Journal of College Student Development, 29,* 105–111.

Creamer, D. G., & Associates (1990). *College student development: Theory and practices for the 1990s.* Alexandria, VA: American College Personnel Association.

Davis, D. C. (1998). The American College Counseling Association: A historical view. *Journal of College Counseling, 1,* 7–9.

Dean, L. A. (1994, June). Chimney building. *Visions, 2,* 3–4.

Deegan, W. L., & O'Banion, T. (Eds.). (1989). *Perspectives on student development.* San Francisco: Jossey-Bass.

Delve, C. I., Mintz, S. D., & Stewart, G. M. (1990a). Editors' notes. In C. I. Delve, S. D. Mintz, & G. M. Stewart (Eds.), *Community service as values education* (pp. 1–5). San Francisco: Jossey-Bass.

Delve, C. I., Mintz, S. D., & Stewart, G. M. (1990b). Promoting values development. In C. I. Delve, S. D. Mintz, & G. M. Stewart (Eds.), *Community service as values education* (pp. 7–28). San Francisco: Jossey-Bass.

Engstrom, C. M., & Sedlacek, W. E. (1991). A study of prejudice toward university student-athletes. *Journal of Counseling and Development, 70,* 189–193.

Erikson, E. H. (1968). *Identity: Youth and crisis.* New York: Norton.

Evans, N. J., Carr, J., & Stone, J. E. (1982). Developmental programming: A collaborative effort of residence life and counseling center staff. *Journal of College Student Personnel, 23,* 48–53.

Ewing, D. B. (1990). Direct from Minnesota: E. G. Williamson. In P. P. Heppner (Ed.), *Pioneers in counseling and development: Personal and professional perspectives* (pp. 104–111). Alexandria, VA: American Counseling Association.

Fallon, M. V. (1997). The school counselor's role in first generation students' college plans. *School Counselor, 44,* 384–393.

Fenske, R. H. (1989a). Evolution of the student services professional. In U. Delworth, G. R. Hanson, & Associates (Eds.), *Student services: A handbook for the profession* (2nd ed., pp. 25–56). San Francisco: Jossey-Bass.

Fenske, R. H. (1989b). Historical foundations of student services. In U. Delworth, G. R. Hanson, & Associates (Eds.), *Student services: A handbook for the profession* (2nd ed., pp. 5–24). San Francisco: Jossey-Bass.

Forrest, L. (1989). Guiding, supporting, and advising students: The counselor role. In U. Delworth, G. R. Hanson, & Associates (Eds.), *Student services: A handbook for the profession* (2nd ed., pp. 265–283). San Francisco: Jossey-Bass.

Freeman, F. H., Knott, K. B., & Schwartz, M. K. (1996). *Leadership education: A source book*. Greensboro, NC: Center for Creative Leadership.

Garfield, N. J., & David, L. B. (1986). Arthur Chickering: Bridging theory and practice in student development. *Journal of Counseling and Development, 64,* 483–491.

Geraghty, M. (1997, August 1). Campuses see steep increase in students seeking counseling. *Chronicle of Higher Education,* A32.

Gerdes, H., & Mallinckrodt, B. (1994). Emotional, social, and academic adjustment of college students: A longitudinal study of retention. *Journal of Counseling and Development, 72,* 281–288.

Gill-Wigal, J., Heaton, J., Burke, J., & Gleason, J. (1988). When too much is too much. *Journal of College Student Development, 29,* 274–275.

Gregory, R. A., & Britt, S. (1987). What the good ones do: Characteristics of promising leadership development programs. *Campus Activities Programming, 20,* 33–35.

Grites, T. J. (1979). Between high school counselor and college advisor: A void. *Personnel and Guidance Journal, 58,* 200–204.

Hayes, R. L. (1981). High school graduation: The case for identity loss. *Personnel and Guidance Journal, 59,* 369–371.

Herman, W. E. (1997). Values acquisition: Some critical distinctions and implications. *Journal of Humanistic Education and Development, 35,* 146–155.

Hodgkinson, H. L., Outtz, J. H., & Obarakpor, A. M. (1992). *The nation and the states: A profile and data book of America's diversity*. Washington, DC: Institute for Educational Leadership.

Holland, J. L. (1997). *Making vocational choices: A theory of vocational personalities and work environments* (3rd ed.). Odessa, FL: Psychological Assessment Resources.

Hollis, J. W. (1997). *Counselor preparation, 1996–1998* (9th ed.). Muncie, IN: Accelerated Development.

Holmes, T. H., & Rahe, R. H. (1967). The social readjustment rating scale. *Journal of Psychosomatic Research, 11,* 213–218.

Horton, N. (1994, October 10). United States has most educated population. *Higher Education and National Affairs, 43,* 3.

Houston, B. K. (1971). Sources, effects and individual vulnerability of psychological problems for college students. *Journal of Counseling Psychology, 18,* 157–161.

Huskey, H. H. (1994, April). Counseling the senior student. *Visions, 2,* 10–11.

Hutchins, R. M. (1936). *The higher learning in America.* New Haven, CT: Yale University Press.

Johnson, C. S. (1985). The American College Personnel Association. *Journal of Counseling and Development, 63,* 405–410.

Johnson, D. H., Nelson, S. E., & Wooden, D. J. (1985). Faculty and student knowledge of university counseling center services. *Journal of College Student Personnel, 26,* 27–32.

Kirk, W. D., & Kirk, S. V. (1993). The African American student athlete. In W. D. Kirk & S. V. Kirk (Eds.), *Student athletes: Shattering the myths and sharing the realities* (pp. 99–112). Alexandria, VA: American Counseling Association.

Kitchener, K. S. (1985). Ethical principles and ethical decisions in student affairs. In H. J. Canon & R. D. Brown (Eds.), *Applied ethics in student services* (pp. 17–29). San Francisco: Jossey-Bass.

Kohlberg, L. (1984). *Essays on moral development* (Vol. 2), *The psychology of moral development: The nature and validity of moral stages.* New York: Harper & Row.

Komives, S. R., Woodard, D. B., Jr., & Delworth, U. (1996). *Student services: A handbook for the profession* (3rd ed.). San Francisco: Jossey-Bass.

Kuh, G. D. (1996). *Student learning outside the classroom: Transcending artificial boundaries.* Washington, DC: George Washington University.

Kuh, G. D., Bean, J. R., Bradley, R. K., & Coomes, M. D. (1986). Contributions of student affairs journals to the literature on college students. *Journal of College Student Personnel, 27,* 292–304.

Lewin, K. (1936). *Principles of topological psychology.* New York: McGraw-Hill.

Lewing, R. J., Jr., & Cowger, E. L., Jr., (1982). Time spent on college counselor functions. *Journal of College Student Personnel, 23,* 41–48.

Lively, K. (1998, May 15). At Michigan State, a protest escalated into a night of fires, tear gas, and arrests. *Chronicle of Higher Education, 44,* A46.

Loxley, J. C., & Whiteley, J. M. (1986). *Character development in college students.* Alexandria, VA: American Counseling Association.

Lynch, R. T., & Gussel, L. (1996). Disclosure and self-advocacy regarding disability-related needs: Strategies to maximize integration in postsecondary education. *Journal of Counseling & Development, 74,* 352–357.

Mathiasen, R. E. (1984). Attitudes and needs of the college student-client. *Journal of College Student Personnel, 25,* 274–275.

McDade, S. A. (1989). Leadership development: A key to the new leadership role of student affairs professionals. *NASPA Journal, 27,* 33–41.

Meyer, D. F., & Russell, R. K. (1998). Caretaking, separation from parents, and the development of eating disorders. *Journal of Counseling & Development, 76,* 166–173.

Morrill, W. H., Oetting, E. R., & Hurst, J. C. (1974). Dimensions of counselor functioning. *Personnel and Guidance Journal, 53,* 354–359.

Nickerson, D. L., & Harrington, J. T. (1968). *The college student as counselor.* Moravia, NY: Chronicle Guidance Publications.

Openlander, P., & Searight, R. (1983). Family counseling perspectives in the college counseling center. *Journal of College Student Personnel, 24,* 423–427.

Pace, D., Stamler, V. L., Yarris, E., & June, L. (1996). Rounding out the Cube: Evolution to a global model for counseling centers. *Journal of Counseling & Development, 74,* 321–325.

Perry, W. G., Jr. (1970). *Forms of intellectual and ethical development in the college years.* New York: Holt, Rinehart, & Winston.

Polansky, J., Horan, J. J., & Hanish, C. (1993). Experimental construct validity of the outcomes of study skills training and career counseling as treatments for the retention of at-risk students. *Journal of Counseling and Development, 71,* 488–492.

Ponzetti, J. J., Jr., & Cate, R. M. (1988). The relationship of personal attributes and friendship variables in predicting loneliness. *Journal of College Student Development, 29,* 292–298.

Quintana, S. M., & Kerr, J. (1993). Relational needs in late adolescent separation-individuation. *Journal of Counseling and Development, 71,* 349–354.

Ragle, J., & Krone, K. (1985). Extending orientation: Telephone contacts by peer advisors. *Journal of College Student Personnel, 26,* 80–81.

Rice, K. G., & Whaley, T. J. (1994). A short term longitudinal study of within-semester stability and change in attachment and college student adjustment. *Journal of College Student Development, 35,* 324–330.

Richter-Antion, D. (1986). Qualitative differences between adult and younger students. *NASPA Journal, 23,* 58–62.

Roark, M. L. (1987). Preventing violence on college campuses. *Journal of Counseling and Development, 65,* 367–371.

Roberts, D., & Ullom, C. (1989). Student leadership program model. *NASPA Journal, 27,* 67–74.

Rodgers, R. F. (1980). Theories underlying student development. In D. G. Creamer (Ed.), *Student development in higher education* (pp. 10–96). Cincinnati, OH: American College Personnel Association.

Rodgers, R. F. (1989). Student development. In U. Delworth, G. R. Hanson, & Associates (Eds.), *Student services: A handbook for the profession* (2nd ed., pp. 117–164). San Francisco: Jossey-Bass.

Rubin, S. G. (1990). Transforming the university through service learning. In C. I. Delve, S. D. Mintz, & G. M. Stewart (Eds.), *Community services as values education* (pp. 111–124). San Francisco: Jossey-Bass.

Sandeen, A. (1988). *Student affairs: Issues, problems and trends.* Ann Arbor, MI: ERIC/CAPS.

Sanford, N. (1962). *The American college.* New York: Wiley.

Sanford, N. (1979). Freshman personality: A stage in human development. In N. Sanford & J. Axelrod

(Eds.), *College and character.* Berkeley, CA: Montaigne.

Schuh, J. J., Shipton, W. C., & Edman, N. (1986). Counseling problems encountered by resident assistants: An update. *Journal of College Student Personnel, 27,* 26–33.

Scrignar, C. B. (1984). *Post-traumatic stress disorder, diagnosis, treatment and legal issues.* New York: Praeger.

Sharkin, B. S. (1997). Increasing severity of presenting problems in college counseling centers: A closer look. *Journal of Counseling & Development, 75,* 275–281.

Sheeley, V. L. (1983). NADW and NAAS: 60 years of organizational relationships. In B. A. Belson & L. E. Fitzgerald (Eds.), *Thus, we spoke: ACPA-NAWDAC, 1958–1975.* Alexandria, VA: American College Personnel Association.

Steenbarger, B. N. (1998). Alcohol abuse and college counseling: An overview of research and practice. *Journal of College Counseling, 1,* 81–92.

Stone, G. L., & Archer, J., Jr., (1990). College and university counseling centers in the 1990s: Challenges and limits. *Counseling Psychologist, 18,* 539–607.

Tate, D. S., & Schwartz, C. L. (1993). Increasing the retention of American Indian students in professional programs in higher education. *Journal of American Indian Education, 32,* 21–31.

Terry, L. L. (1989). Assessing and constructing a meaningful system: Systemic perspective in a college counseling center. *Journal of Counseling and Development, 67,* 352–355.

Thurman, C. (1983). Effects of a rational-emotive treatment program on Type A behavior among college students. *Journal of College Student Personnel, 24,* 417-423.

Watkins, E. (1983). Project retain: A client centered approach to student retention. *Journal of College Student Personnel, 24,* 81.

Westbrook, F. D., Kandell, J. J., Kirkland, S. E., Phillips, P. E., Regan, A. M., Medvene, A., & Oslin, Y. D. (1993). University campus consultation: Opportunities and limitations. *Journal of Counseling and Development, 71,* 684–688.

Whiteley, J. M. (1982). *Character development in college students.* Alexandria, VA: American Counseling Association.

Williamson, E. G. (1939). *How to counsel students: A manual of techniques for clinical counselors.* New York: McGraw-Hill.

Williamson, E. G. (1961). *Student personnel services in colleges and universities.* New York: McGraw-Hill.

Winston, R. B., Jr., & Creamer, D. G. (1997). *Improving staffing practices in student affairs.* San Francisco: Jossey-Bass.

Winston, R. B., Jr., & Ender, S. C. (1988). Use of student paraprofessionals in divisions of college student affairs. *Journal of Counseling and Development, 66,* 466–473.

Wooten, H. R. (1994). Cutting losses for student-athletes in transition: An integrative transition model. *Journal of Employment Counseling, 31,* 2–9.

17

MENTAL HEALTH, SUBSTANCE ABUSE, AND REHABILITATION COUNSELING

◆

As our sessions go on you speak of your scars

and show me the places where you have been burned.

Sadly, I hear your fiery stories

reliving with you, through your memories and words,

all of the tension-filled blows and events

that have beaten and shaped your life.

"I wish I were molten steel" you say,

"And you were a blacksmith's hammer.

Maybe then, on time's anvil, we could structure together

a whole new person, with soft smooth sounds,

inner strength and glowing warmth."

From "Scars," by S. T. Gladding, 1977, Personnel and Guidance Journal, 56, _p. 246. © 1977 by ACA. Reprinted with permission. No further reproduction authorized without written permission of the American Counseling Association._

This chapter examines mental health, substance abuse, and rehabilitation counseling from a theoretical, structural, and functional viewpoint. Counselors who work in the mental health, substance abuse, and rehabilitation fields are often members of the American Mental Health Counselor Association (AMHCA), the International Association of Addictions and Offender Counseling (IAAOC), or the American Rehabilitation Counselor Association (ARCA). However, counselors from varied backgrounds deal with clients who have mental health, substance abuse, or rehabilitation concerns. Counselors in such circumstances focus on prevention in the form of wellness and the promotion of good overall health, as well as treatment. The essence of such counseling is promoting healthy lifestyles, identifying and eliminating stressors, modifying toxic environments where possible, and preserving or restoring mental health. Specific ways in which clients are served depends on counselors' skills and the needs of client populations.

Federal legislation has been an impetus through the years in establishing services for mental health, substance abuse, and rehabilitation. Two such acts were the Community Mental Health Centers Act of 1963 and the Americans with Disabilities Act of 1990. The Community Mental Health Centers Act provided funding for the establishment of more than 2,000 community mental health centers nationwide. It also made it possible for local communities to employ counselors as well as mental health professionals and focus on health and outreach programs. The Americans with Disabilities Act heightened awareness of the needs of the over 40 million people in the United States with disabilities and increased national efforts in providing multiple services for people with mental, behavioral, and physical disabilities.

Throughout the years, counselors who work in mental health, substance abuse, and rehabilitation have been strongly influenced by other legislative acts that have set standards for the delivery of their services. Counselors in these specific areas have been active in supporting federal and state legislation that has recognized them professionally as well.

Mental Health Counseling

Mental health counseling has been defined in many ways during its relatively brief history. Initially, it was described as a specialized form of counseling performed in noneducational, community-based, or mental health settings (Seiler & Messina, 1979). Over the years, however, different views of mental health counseling have evolved, including those that are developmental (Ivey, 1989); relationship focused (Ginter, 1989); and slanted toward treatment, advocacy, or personal and environmental coping (Hershenson, Power, & Seligman, 1989). The Council for Accreditation of Counseling and Related Educational Programs (CACREP; 1994) has developed a detailed description of this specialty, along with requirements for course work, basic knowledge, and skills.

It is clear that "mental health counseling is interdisciplinary in its history, practice settings, skills/knowledge, and roles performed" (Spruill & Fong, 1990, p. 19). This interdisciplinary nature is an asset in generating new ideas and energy. At the same time, it is a drawback in helping those who identify themselves as mental health counselors distinguish themselves from some closely related mental health practitioners (Wilcoxon & Puleo, 1992).

Regardless, many practitioners within the counseling profession use the term *mental health* counselor to describe themselves, and some states designate licensed counselors under this title. As a group, mental health counselors work in a variety of settings, including mental health centers, community agencies, psychiatric hospitals, health maintenance organizations (HMOs), employee assistance programs (EAPs), health and wellness promotion programs (HWPs), geriatric centers, crisis control agencies, and child guidance clinics. Some are private practitioners, too. They counsel a diverse group of clients, including rape victims, depressives, families, potential suicide victims, and those with diagnosable disorders. In addition, they consult, educate, and at times perform administrative duties (Hosie, West, & Mackey, 1988; West, Hosie, & Mackey, 1987). They often work closely with other helping professionals, such as psychiatrists, psychologists, clinical social workers, and psychiatric nurses, and become part of a team effort (Hansen, 1998). Thus, it is crucial that mental health counselors know the *Diagnostic and Statistical Manual* (DSM-IV) classifications so they can converse intelligently with other health professionals and skillfully treat dysfunctional clients (Hinkle, 1994; Vacc, Loesch, & Guilbert, 1997).

Mental health counselors have basic counseling skills as well as specialty skills related to the needs and interests of particular populations or problems. Major duties of counselors in mental health are assessing and analyzing background and current information on clients, diagnosing mental and emotional conditions, exploring possible solutions, and developing treatment plans. Preventive mental health activities and recognition of the relationship between physical and mental health have also become prominent. As a group, mental health counselors are interested in professional development related to applied areas of counseling such as marriage and family counseling, substance abuse/chemical dependency, third-party reimbursement, and small-group counseling (Wilcoxon & Puleo, 1992). Such interest is understandable in light of the fact that most mental health counselors are practitioners and earn a living by offering services for remuneration.

The American Mental Health Counselor Association (AMHCA; 801 N. Fairfax Street, Suite 304, Alexandria, VA 22314) has initiated a number of task forces to help its members broaden their horizons and develop practical skills and knowledge. These task forces cover such areas as business and industry, aging and adult development, treatment of various disorders, and prevention. Such concentrations are important because they allow professional mental health counselors to obtain in-depth knowledge and skills in particular domains.

The AMHCA also emphasizes total health and health counseling. This aspect of mental health counseling is vital because changes made within a community can be upsetting or cause regressive behaviors if people are unprepared. By providing people with health information and support, counselors can prevent more serious problems (e.g., alcoholism) from occurring (Sperry, Carlson, & Lewis, 1993). Such an emphasis is unique in the helping professions, which as a whole tend to be treatment based.

In addition, the AMHCA has set up certification standards for counselors to become Certified Clinical Mental Health Counselors (CCMHC). This procedure initially involved the establishment of the National Academy of Certified Clinical Mental Health Counselors (NAC-CMHC) as an independently incorporated certification group in 1978. However, in 1993, the NACCMHC merged with the National Board for Certified Counselors (NBCC). Professionals who wish to obtain the CCMHC credential first become national certified counselors (NCCs).

Theories and Functions

Mental health counselors are diverse in the ways they use theories and techniques in their practices, in part because they work in such varied settings and have wide range functions. One theoretical position, existential theory, has been advocated as "congruent with the essential principles of mental health counseling" (Bauman & Waldo, 1998, p. 27), but a large number of theories have been used in the field. The selection of theories by mental health counselors depends on their clients' needs. Generally, the literature about mental health counseling focuses on two major issues that have theoretical implications: (a) prevention and promotion of mental health and (b) treatment of disorders and dysfunctions. Both topics are likely to continue attracting attention because they are considered primary roles of mental health counselors.

Primary Prevention and the Promotion of Mental Health.   A primary philosophical emphasis throughout the history of mental health counseling has been on prevention and promotion of mental health services. "Many mental health counselors are actively involved in primary prevention types of programs through the schools, colleges, churches, community health centers, and public and private agencies" where they are employed (Weikel & Palmo, 1989, p. 15). *Primary prevention* is characterized by its "before the fact quality"; it is intentional and "group- or mass-, rather than individually, oriented" (Baker & Shaw, 1987, p. 2). It may be directly or indirectly implemented, but it ultimately results in healthier and better-adjusted individuals.

One place where primary prevention is emphasized is in the area of suicide. In the United States suicide is "the ninth ranking cause of death for adults and third for young people ages 17 and under" (Carney & Hazler, 1998, p. 28). When assessing clients for suicide, mental health counselors may use the SAD PERSONS scale (Patterson, Dohn, Bird, & Patterson, 1983) for adults or the Adapted-SAD PERSONS scale (A-SPS) for children (Juhnke, 1996) to surmise which individuals are most likely to be at high risk. The letters in this scale stand for the following:

*S*ex (male)
*A*ge (older clients)
*D*epression
*P*revious attempt
*E*thanol (alcohol) abuse
*R*ational thinking loss
*S*ocial support system lacking (lonely, isolated)
*O*rganized plan
*N*o spouse
*S*ickness (particularly chronic or terminal illness)

It is the combination of these factors in an interactive process that is likely to yield information pertinent for the mental health counselor to use in prevention.

Another form of prevention is emphasizing healthy development—that is, positive coping and growth (Hershenson, 1982, 1992b). "Insofar as counseling derives from a model based on healthy development, it can reasonably hope to achieve its purpose of promoting healthy development in its clients" (Hershenson, 1982, p. 409). Erik Erikson (1963) and Abraham Maslow (1962) offer bases from which mental health counselors can work. The writings of these researchers were based on observations about human development and emphasized the promotion of healthy lifestyles. The integration of these two systems of thought yields six personal development trends: survival, growth, communication, recognition, mastery, and understanding. The first two trends focus on the self, the middle two on interpersonal functions, and the final two on the accomplishment of tasks. Mental health counseling is geared toward the improvement of the self in interpersonal relationships and task performances.

In an important and related article on healthy personal development, Heath (1980) outlines a comprehensive model of healthy maturation. He points out that research demonstrates that an adolescent's psychological maturity is a major predictor of adult mental health and vocational adaptation and that the degree of adult maturity is related to marital sexual adjustment and vocational adaptation. Heath proposes practical general principles that counselors can apply in promoting client development. Four are listed here (Heath, 1980, p. 395):

1. "Encourage the anticipatory rehearsal of new adaptations," such as those that deal with jobs and intimate relationships.
2. "Require constant externalization of what is learned and its correction by action." In essence, Heath believes practice makes perfect the accomplishment of all human tasks. Learning is accomplished through feedback.
3. "Allow a person to experience the consequences of his or her decisions and acts." Heath agrees with Alfred Adler on this idea. He notes that inappropriate or excessive rewards may have an unhealthy effect on a person's development.
4. "Appreciate and affirm strengths." Reinforcement, according to behaviorist principles, is crucial to new learning. Heath agrees and says that the acknowledgment and acceptance of people's strengths can bolster self-confidence and help them take risks necessary for new learning.

Focusing on persons' environments is another preventive emphasis of mental health counselors. Huber (1983) sums up the research in this growing area of interest, noting that environments have personalities just as people do. Some environments are controlling and rigid, whereas others are more flexible and supportive. To make effective use of *this social-ecological perspective,* mental health counselors should do the following:

• Identify the problem as one essentially connected with a particular setting. Some environments elicit or encourage specific behaviors that may not be healthy.
• Gain the agreement of clients and significant others that the environment is the client. It is much easier for most people to see a difficulty as simply a matter related to the individual.

- Assess the dynamic variables within an environment. Moos (1973) developed a number of ways to evaluate environments. Counselors can work with clients to determine how environments function in favor of or counter to the clients' needs.
- Institute social change. The counselor helps the client with specific methods for improving the present environment.
- Evaluate the outcome. There is no one way to do this, but the more clearly the client states his or her criteria for the ideal environment, the better the evaluation possibility.

Related to the social-ecological perspective is *ecosystemic thinking:* "thinking that recognizes the indivisible interconnectedness of individual, family, and sociocultural context" (Sherrard & Amatea, 1994, p. 5). In this view, mental health counseling is enlarged to consider the cultural contexts in which people relate and communicate.

Marriage is a situation that illustrates the importance of both personal and environmental factors in individuals' well-being. Wiggins, Moody, and Lederer (1983) conducted a study on marital satisfaction and found that the most significant predictor was the compatibility of couples' tested personality typologies. They concluded, as has Holland (1997), that individuals express "satisfaction with and seek interaction in environments that meet their psychological needs" (Wiggins et al., 1983, p. 177). In interracial marriages, which are increasing, mental health counselors can be therapeutic in helping couples identify and address predictable stressors in their lives, such as prejudice or identity issues regarding biracial children, and helping them find support or marriage enrichment groups (Solsberry, 1994).

An overall emphasis in mental health prevention is on *positive wellness* (health-related activities that are both preventive and remedial and have a therapeutic value to individuals who practice them consistently). Such activities include eating natural foods, taking vitamins, going to health spas, meditating, participating in regular exercise, and exploring a variety of humanistic and transpersonal approaches to helping (O'Donnell, 1988). "For the person to be a whole, healthy, functioning organism, one must evaluate the physical, psychological, intellectual, social, emotional, and environmental processes" (Carlson & Ardell, 1988, p. 383). Signs of the holistic movement toward health and well-being are apparent everywhere as Americans of all ages have become more aware of positive and negative habits.

Research backs up the basis for this movement and in some ways leads it. In an extensive review of the literature on the effectiveness of physical fitness on measures of personality, Doan and Scherman (1987) found strong support for the idea that regular exercise can have a beneficial effect on people's physical and psychological health. Their review supports counselors who prescribe health habits to accompany regular counseling practices. Other strategies for working from a wellness perspective include having counselors dwell on positive, life-enhancing things the individual can do; alter traditional screening to include more emphasis on overall health; conduct more research; and highlight the physical feature dimension as one aspect of what Lazarus (1989) calls *multimodal therapy* (BASIC I.D.: behavior, affect, sensation, imagery, cognition, interpersonal relationships, and drugs/biology).

Treatment of Disorders and Dysfunctions.   The number of people who need and seek mental health services cannot adequately be dealt with by the nation's mental health providers, even if the treatment of clients were the only activity in which these professionals were engaged (Lichtenberg, 1986; Meehl, 1973). For example, an estimated 7.5

million children, or 12% of the residents of the United States, "under 18 years of age have a diagnosable mental disorder, and nearly half of these are severely handicapped by their disabilities. The population of children with serious emotional and behavioral problems has been growing dramatically, concomitant with the growth of such social problems as poverty, homelessness, and substance abuse" (Collins & Collins, 1994, p. 239).

To address societal needs, mental health counselors concentrate on *secondary prevention* (controlling mental health problems that have already surfaced but are not severe) and *tertiary prevention* (controlling serious mental health problems to keep them from becoming chronic or life threatening). In such cases (in contrast to primary prevention), mental health counselors use theories and techniques developed by major theorists such as Rogers, Ellis, Skinner, and Glasser to treat symptoms and core conditions (Weikel & Palmo, 1989). In this respect, mental health counseling is more like other helping disciplines, such as psychology, social work, and psychiatric nursing (Hansen, 1998; Waldo, Horswill, & Brotherton, 1993). As already noted, mental health counselors also assess disorders using the DSM-IV. (See Appendix C for a list of major disorders covered in the DSM-IV.)

A survey of articles in the *Journal of Mental Health Counseling* reveals that mental health counselors have a stronger tendency to deal with treatment in their discussions of the essence of mental health counseling than they do prevention (Kiselica & Look, 1993). This emphasis on treatment links mental health counseling more to allied health professions rather than to the traditional developmental emphasis of counseling. In addition, an emphasis on treatment presents a problem in regard to politics and inclusion within health systems. Some of the areas mental health counselors focus on in treatment are general and specific life-span disorders, such as mild depression (Kolenc, Hartley, & Murdock, 1990), smoking cessation (Pinto & Morrell, 1988), obsessive-compulsive behavior (Dattilio, 1993), and bulimia (Gerstein & Hotelling, 1987). The reason treatment is highlighted in mental health counseling and will continue to be is related to a trend in mental health to shorten the length of inpatient hospital stays for severely disturbed clients. These shortened stays mean more disturbed individuals are being seen in outpatient facilities where many mental health counselors work (Hansen, 1998).

Substance Abuse Counseling

The area of abuse involves the misuse or exploitation of people and things. Although abuse is multidimensional, it can be broken down into two broad categories: substance abuse and physical abuse. Counselors work in both areas, but substance abuse will be the focus of this section. Abuse of substances damages people mentally, physically, emotionally, socially, and spiritually. It is "one of the major public health issues in today's society" and cuts across "gender, socioeconomic levels, ethnicity, age, religion, profession, geography, and most dimensions of human existence and background" (Stevens-Smith & Smith, 1998, p. iii).

The Nature of Substance Abuse

Substance abuse is broadly defined as the habitual and often addictive use of alcohol, drugs, and tobacco. Drugs are any substance other than food that can affect the way a person's mind and body works, including stimulants, depressants, and hallucinogens. Abuse of substances is one of the most frequently occurring mental health problems in the United States. For instance, "1 in 10 American adults in the general population has significant problems related to his or her own use of alcohol" (Miller & Brown, 1997, p. 1269). In addition, it is estimated that there are up to four times as many other people adversely affected by alcohol abuse such as family members, friends, or associates (Vick, Smith, & Herrera, 1998). Between "12% to 30% of all hospitalized patients abuse alcohol," too, and "health care costs among alcoholic families are twice as great as those of nonalcoholic families" (Steenbarger, 1998, p. 81). In summary, the estimated financial cost of alcohol abuse to Americans per year is over $150 billion (Lam et al., 1996).

Besides alcoholism, approximately half a million Americans are heroin addicts, and 4 million are regular users of marijuana. Over 25% of American adults (48 million individuals) smoke cigarettes as well (Wetter et al., 1998), 3 million of whom are adolescents. Furthermore, "approximately 80% of alcoholics smoke" in addition to drinking, increasing their risk for a premature death or injury (Barker, 1997, p. 53).

Americans in general, and adolescents in particular, overwhelmingly see the use of drugs as the greatest problem they face. For adolescents, in fact, drugs far outrank crime, social pressure, grades, or sex as a hazard to their development and well-being (Center on Addiction and Substance Abuse, 1995). The U.S. Department of Education estimates that up to 3 million teenagers are alcoholics, half are users of marijuana, and 1 out of 10 has tried cocaine (Gibson & Mitchell, 1995).

On the surface, substance abuse appears to be an individual problem and one that is related to a particular substance. In reality, however, substance abuse is much more complex. Often people who abuse one substance abuse other substances as well. *Polysubstance abuse* (the abuse of two or more substances simultaneously) is a growing phenomenon. In addition, abuse of substances often becomes a way of life related to social conditions. For example, many people begin smoking as adolescents in response to an unsatisfactory life rooted in poverty and hopelessness. Peer pressure, poor school performance, parental smoking, minority ethnic status, and an external locus of control make smoking more likely until addiction occurs (Hilts, 1996).

Likewise, one of the factors related to substance abuse is an attempt by young adults to protect and stabilize dysfunctional families by keeping their attention off overall dynamics and on predictable problematic behaviors (Stanton & Todd, 1982). Substance abuse may serve as a substitute for sex as well and promote *pseudo-individuation* (a false sense of self). These complex and interrelated factors make it difficult to help people caught up in substance abuse patterns to change behaviors without an intensive social action approach designed to change dysfunctional systems (Lee & Walz, 1998).

Often the abuse of substances involves *addiction,* which is defined "as a persistent and intense involvement with and stress upon a single behavior pattern, with a minimization or even exclusion of other behaviors, both personal and interpersonal" (L'Abate, 1992, p. 2). A primary characteristic of addicts is that they become preoccupied with one object that controls their behaviors, thus limiting their other actions over time. Addictive behaviors, even socially acceptable ones such as workaholism and gambling, continue to be major problems in the United States (L'Abate, Farrar, & Serritella, 1992).

The International Association of Addictions and Offender Counseling (IAAOC) is one of the leading groups that focuses on the prevention, treatment, and description of abusive and addictive behaviors. Its members publish material, such as the *Journal of Addictions & Offender Counseling*, that informs professional counselors about the latest developments in the field. Increasingly the number of academic programs that educate counselors with an emphasis on substance abuse counseling is growing (Hollis, 1997), and since 1994 NBCC has had a certification process for becoming a substance abuse counselor.

Preventing Substance Abuse

As previously stated, substance abuse appears to be problem of individuals. In some cases, preventive strategies are aimed at individuals and are appropriate. For example, a bibliotherapeutic approach may work with some individuals (Hipple, Comer, & Boren, 1997). In this approach abusers and addicts read books or view/listen to media and discuss ideas related to what they have experienced. For example in working with adolescents, substance abusers might be asked to read *Go Ask Alice* by Anonymous, a nonfiction novel about teen drug abuse, or *Imitate the Tiger* by Jan Cheripko, a novel on teenage alcohol abuse. They would then discuss their reactions with a counselor including how they are like or not like the main characters of the book and what insights they gleaned from the reading.

However, usually substance abuse and addiction prevention programs are tied into a community and seek to prevent abuse community wide. One such preventive measure is the "Just Say No" campaign found in schools and public agencies sponsored by local governments. Children learn through this program how to be assertive and how to refuse offers of harmful drugs. For example, they learn that they can simply ignore or walk away from drug related situations as well as say "No thanks" or make an excuse for refusing an offer of drugs. Another program, often found in late elementary and early middle school grades, that has a uniform prevention curriculum is D.A.R.E. (Drug Abuse Resistance Education). D.A.R.E. uses police as instructors and provides case scenarios fifth and sixth graders are challenged to think about and answer (Ben Gladding, personal correspondence, May 22, 1998).

On the high school level, there are national chapters of S.A.D.D. (Students against Drunk Driving) and M.A.D.D. (Mothers against Drunk Driving). Both of these associations, plus those found on college and university campuses, help educate and orient young people about the hazards of drug abuse and the dangers of addiction.

Another form of an effective educational programming involves teens who use tobacco and potential and real cocaine addicts (Mudore, 1997; Sunich & Doster, 1995). The emphasis in these programs is focused on both external and internal factors important to these individuals. External factors include the impact of smoking on one's breath, teeth, and clothes as well as monetary costs. Internal factors include such variables as lifestyle choices, time management, and nutrition. For younger individuals, external factors may be more effective in influencing their decisions to stop smoking or doing drugs, whereas for older adolescents internal factors are more powerful.

A common element in approaches to substance abuse and addiction prevention involves group pressure and dynamics. In setting up preventive programs, counselors are wise to use their knowledge of groups. The reason is that most people, especially adolescents, who get involved in the use of drugs do so because their friends use drugs (Center on Addiction and Substance Abuse at Columbia University, 1995). Therefore, when a group perceives drugs as hazardous to their health or dangerous, members of such a group are less likely to engage in experimenting with these substances. The group norm becomes one of discouraging members from trying drugs (Serritella, 1992). Thus, educational and support groups are a valuable tool for counselors to employ in warding off abuse and addictive behaviors in preventive programs (Gladding, 1999).

Treating Substance Abuse

Approximately 25% of counseling cases relate to substance abuse and addiction problems either directly or indirectly. As indicated earlier, abuse and addictions of any type are difficult to work with because of the dysfunctional dynamics that surround them. For example, families often organize themselves around alcoholism in a systemic way and thus enable family members to drink excessively (Bateson, 1971; Steinglass, 1979). In the alcoholic family system, there is an overresponsible/underresponsible phenomenon, with the overresponsible person(s) being a so-called "codependent" (Berenson, 1992). "An essential characteristic of someone who is codependent is that they continually invest their self-esteem in the ability to control and influence behavior and feelings in others as well as in themselves, even when faced with adverse consequences such as feelings of inadequacy after failure" (Springer, Britt, & Schlenker, 1998, p. 141). In such a situation, it is easier and more productive to work with the overfunctioning person(s) and modify that phenomenon than to try to get the underfunctioning person(s) to change.

Among the most prevalent factors affecting treatment for substance abuse are "motivation, denial, dual diagnosis, matching, control, and relapse" (L'Abate, 1992, p. 11). *Motivation* has to do with a desire to change that most substance abusers do not wish to do because of their self-centeredness and comfort. *Denial* is basically minimizing the effects of substance abuse on either oneself or others. It minimizes the harm that is being done. A *dual diagnosis* is one in which an abuser has more than one aspect of personality that is open to labeling. For instance, a substance abuser may be impulsive or depressed in addition to be addicted. *Matching* concerns the right treatment for a disorder. Some substance abuses, such as overdosing with cocaine, require specialized treatment (Washton, 1989). *Control* has to do with the regulation of behavior which substance abusers tend to disregard. Finally, *relapse* is the recidive or reoccurrence of dysfunctional behaviors once they have been treated. It is discouraging to have substance abusers go through structured programs and end up acting the way they did before.

Treating Alcohol Abuse

Alcoholics Anonymous (AA) is the oldest successful treatment program in the world for working with alcoholics, having been founded in the 1930s (AA World Services, 1976). It is "both a fellowship and a rehabilitation program" (Warfield & Goldstein, 1996, p. 196). Alcoholics suffer from what AA describes as "character defects" (AA World Services, 1976). "These are feelings, beliefs, and behaviors that dispose them to seek a sense of well-being by abusing alcohol" (Warfield & Goldstein, 1996, p. 197). AA meetings are conducted in small group settings where literature—for example, "The Big Book" (AA World Services, 1976)—is used along with group discussion.

AA also uses a 12-step program with a spiritual foundation. This program "has been adapted to treat many other problems such as narcotic addiction, cocaine abuse, overeating, compulsive gambling, compulsive sexual behavior, and the pain of children of alcoholics" (James & Hazler, 1998, p. 124). Group discussions in AA meetings center on helping members realize they need and have the support of others and a dependence on a higher power. The spiritual dimension in AA results in an emphasis on members admitting their powerlessness over alcohol (or other substances). Members who abstain from the use and abuse of alcohol are never "cured"; rather, they are "in recovery." There is also an emphasis within AA on responsibility, forgiveness, restitution (when possible), affirmation, ritual, and fellowship.

Some counselors are uncomfortable with the spiritual qualities of AA (Bristow-Braitman, 1995) and prefer to discuss needed recovery qualities in cognitive-behavioral or humanistic language. Rational emotive behavior therapy (REBT) has led the way in setting up recovery groups that are nonspiritual in nature.

Along with treating the person who is abusing alcohol, the counselor also needs to working with his or her family and community. The support or scapegoating that abusers of alcohol receive from family and community systems in which they live makes a tremendous difference in their ability to abstain from the use of alcohol. AA and other recovery programs have special groups for family members of persons who are substance abusers.

Treating Other Drug Addictions

Individuals who are addicted to other drugs besides alcohol, such as cocaine, often receive treatment based on the AA model. However, because of society's greater disapproval of these drugs and their illegality, the context in which treatment is offered is often not the same. For example, one context in which treating illegal drug abuse is provided is jail. A prototype of this type of program is "Stay 'n Out" in Staten Island, New York. "Its secret is a captive audience; participants don't have any choice about showing up for therapy. It's be there—or you're off to a meaner cellblock" (Alter, 1995, pp. 20–21). Although the ethical dimensions of this program are debatable, the results are a recidivism rate of only 25%, much lower than average. Also, a substance abuse program such as Stay 'n Out saves money for communities to use in other ways because recovering addicts require less health care and criminal justice costs.

Families and Substance Abuse Treatment

Families also play a large part in promoting or enabling substance abuse behaviors, and it is difficult to help substance abusers without including everyone in the family (Doweiko, 1990). "Students from homes in which parents are chemically dependent or abuse alcohol or other drugs (CDs) are at risk for a wide range of developmental problems" (Buelow, 1995, p. 327). Many alcoholic families especially tend to be isolated and children within them consequently suffer from a lack of positive role models. As children get older, they seem to be particularly affected for the worse from growing up in these families.

Treatment services can take the form of providing information, but often counselors must be confrontational with the family as a whole over the effects of substance abuse on the family as a unit as well as its individual members. Such an intervention cannot be made without an intensive systems approach that involves a number of people and agencies since substance abuse is often a way of organizing and stabilizing dysfunctional families by keeping their attention off overall dynamics and on predictable problematic behaviors (Kaufman & Kaufman, 1992; Morgan, 1998). Substance abuse is also used as a way to relieve stress, reduce anxiety, and structure time (Robinson, 1995).

Counselors who realize the dysfunctional impact of substance abuse, especially in regard to alcohol and drug misuse in families, can work to help clients deal with feelings, such as anger, and defense mechanisms, such as denial, within a family context. They can also help the family take responsibility for their behaviors (Krestan & Bepko, 1988). In essence, they can help the family get back on track as a functional system by getting "involved in the treatment process" and "helping the abusing member overcome . . . addiction rather than serving as a force that maintains it" (Van Deusen, Stanton, Scott, Todd, & Mowatt, 1982, p. 39). In the process, families and their individual members are assisted in regard to resolving developmental issues as well.

Working with Addiction

Counselors work with addicts as well as substance abusers in a number of ways. It is important to remember that either an addict or a substance abuser must be "dry" or not currently taking an addictive substance before any effective treatment can be started. Being "dried out" for a period of 30 or more days gives the addict or substance abuser a "clean" body and mind to use in doing something different and positive. Some guidelines for working with addicts are specific to situations, while others are more general in nature. Robinson (1995, p. 33) recommends the following steps for working with clients who are addicted, especially those recovering from work addiction:

- "Help them slow down their pace." Give them examples of how they can make a conscious effort to slow down their daily lives through deliberate means.
- "Teach them to learn to relax." Learning meditation or yoga, reading an inspirational book, or even soaking in a hot tub is healthy and helpful in moderation.
- "Assist them in evaluating their family climate." Interactions with family members, especially of a positive nature, can be meaningful and relaxing. Therefore, it behooves recovering addicts to explore ways they "can strengthen family ties."
- "Stress the importance of celebrations and rituals." Activities such as celebrations and rituals are the glue that hold families together and make life personally rich and rewarding.
- "Help them [clients] get back into the social swing." This strategy involves devising a plan for developing social lives and friendship. If successful, it "explores ways of building social networks outside of work."
- "Address living in the now." By appreciating the present, recovering addicts can enjoy experiences more and not become anxious about or preoccupied with the future.

- "Encourage clients to nurture themselves." Often individuals who have become addicts find it hard, if not impossible, to indulge themselves. However, the practice of self-nurturing can be beneficial.
- "Stress the importance of proper diet, rest, and exercise." It is hard to function if a person is running on a deficit either physically or emotionally. Therefore, getting clients to balance their lives in regard to diet, rest, and exercise can go a long way to helping them recover from their addiction.
- "Help clients grieve the loss of their childhoods" and "address self-esteem." Many addicts feel ashamed, saddened, angry, or even determined by their past. Helping them realize they can recover from past times and experiences can go a long way in assisting clients to become functional.
- "Inform clients [that] 12-step programs [are] available as a complement to the individual work you do with them." Almost all addicts in recovery can benefit from a 12-step program that emphasizes human relationships in concert with a higher power.

Women and Cultural Groups in Substance Abuse Treatment

In working with the chemically dependent, there is some question about whether men and women should be treated differently. Although women alcoholics constitute about one-third of the membership in Alcoholics Anonymous, "there is little empirical evidence on the benefits of AA and NA to the female alcoholic or addict" (Manhal-Baugus, 1998, p. 82). Therefore, new theories and alternative treatment strategies are developing for women that reflect the broader context of women's lives and draw on community resources. One of these approaches is "Women for Sobriety," a mutual help group based on a cognitive behavior modification approach that helps teach women to change their thinking so they may overcome feelings of helplessness, powerlessness, guilt, and dependence. It has 13 Affirmations that promote positive thinking in a supportive relationship environment run by women for women (Manhal-Baugus, 1998).

In addition to gender difference, cultural differences may play a part, too, in the recovery process. Native Americans, for instance, may find spiritual elements different from non–Native American traditions important in helping them. Therefore, counselors who work with this population may want to consult a medicine man or medicine woman before trying to work with persons or groups seeking recovery (Vick et al., 1998). The same principle of seeking culturally appropriate support systems rings true in treating other culturally specific groups as well.

Rehabilitation Counseling

Rehabilitation counseling focuses on serving individuals with disabilities. Because of this distinct emphasis, rehabilitation practice is seen as differing from the practice of other counseling specialties (Emener & Cottone, 1989). In some ways this perception is correct. *Rehabilitation* is defined as the reeducation of disabled individuals who have previously lived independent lives. A related area, *habilitation,* focuses on educating clients who have been disabled from early life and have never been self-sufficient (Bitter, 1979).

Rehabilitation counselors also distinguish between having a disability and being handicapped. A person with a *disability* has either a physical or a mental condition that limits that person's activities or functioning (U.S. Department of Health, Education, and Welfare, 1974). The Americans with Disabilities Act (1990) projects that there are over 40 million people with disabilities in the United States. These people "continually encounter misconceptions, biases, and harassment about their disabilities that affect their everyday social interactions" (Leierer, Strohmer, Leclere, Corwell, & Whitten, 1996, p. 89). As a result, a large percentage of persons with disabilities are unemployed and unable to achieve an independent-living status (Blackorby & Wagner, 1996).

A *handicap,* which is linked to but distinct from a disability, is "an observable or discernible limitation that is made so by the presence of various barriers" (Schumacher, 1983, p. 320). It is the cumulative result of obstacles that disabilities interpose between persons and their maximum level of functioning (Olkin, 1994; Wright, 1983). An example of a disabled person with a handicap is a quadriplegic assigned to a third-floor apartment in a building without an elevator or a partially deaf person receiving instructions orally. Rehabilitation counselors help clients in these types of situations overcome handicaps and effectively cope with their disabilities.

Another aspect of rehabilitation counseling that distinguishes it from other forms of counseling is its historical link with the *medical model* of delivering services (Ehrle, 1979). The prominence of the medical model is easy to understand when one recalls how closely rehabilitation professionals are involved with the physically challenged. "Rehabilitation counseling practice requires knowledge in areas of medical terminology, diagnosis, prognosis, vocational evaluation of disability-related limitations, and job placement in the context of a socioeconomic system" (Emener & Cottone, 1989, p. 577).

Although the medical model originally dominated rehabilitation counseling, more pragmatic models of helping have emerged (Anthony, 1980; Livneh, 1984). Two such models are the *minority model,* which assumes that persons with disabilities are a minority group rather than people with pathologies, and the *peer counselor model,* which assumes that people with direct experience with disabilities are best able to help those who have recently acquired disabilities (Olkin, 1994).

The Education, Certification, and Affiliation of Rehabilitation Counselors

Like other counseling specialties, counselors who concentrate on working in rehabilitation receive their education and certification from organizations that deal with this area. The Council of Rehabilitation Education (CORE) accredits institutions that offer rehabilitation counseling. Over 100 CORE accredited programs operate in the United States. The Commission of Rehabilitation Counselor Certification (CRCC) certifies rehabilitation counselors who complete CORE-accredited programs. It requires applicants to complete specific courses and experience requirements. There are presently over 13,000 certified rehabilitation counselors in the United States.

Rehabilitation counselors also belong to specialty groups. One of these organizations is the American Rehabilitation Counselor Association (ARCA). The formation and development of the ARCA resulted from three events coming together. First, an interest was present. Before the founding of the ARCA, there was a void for a professional counseling organization within rehabilitation. Soon after World War II, ARCA was organized as an interest group of the National Vocational Guidance Association (NVGA). ARCA became a part of ACA (then APGA) as the Division of Rehabilitation Counseling (DRC) in 1958 and as ARCA in 1961.

A second event that led to ARCA's founding was federal legislation. Rehabilitation has a long history of involvement with the federal government, beginning in 1920 when Congress passed the Vocational Rehabilitation Act. Initially, rehabilitation activities were focused on the physically disabled. However, over the years these services have broadened.

A final event in the development of rehabilitation counseling was opportunity. Traditionally, most rehabilitation counselors have been hired by federal, state, and local agencies. Since the late 1960s, however, more have moved into for-profit agencies and private practice (Lewin, Ramseur, & Sink, 1979). The movement from the public sector into private employment is the result of several developments, such as economic changes, new emphases by businesses and insurance companies, national professional certification requirements, and state licensure laws that have affected all counselors.

Theories and Techniques

Clients of rehabilitation counselors include those with physical, emotional, mental, and behavioral disabilities. Ways these disabilities are manifested include alcoholism, arthritis, blindness, cardiovascular disease, deafness, developmental disabilities, cerebral palsy, epilepsy, mental retardation, drug abuse, neurological disorders, orthopedic disabilities, psychiatric disabilities, renal failure, speech impairments, and spinal cord conditions. "The literature suggests that people with disabilities may encounter a variety of challenges and barriers to career development," including low self-esteem, limited early life experiences, lack of confidence in decision making, social stigma, a restricted range of available occupations, and few successful role models (Enright, 1997, p. 285).

> In working with a client to develop or to restore work adjustment, the role of the rehabilitation counselor is to assess the client's current level of work adjustment and environmental situation and to bring the rehabilitation services system to bear on:
> (a) reintegrating the work personality,
> (b) restoring or replacing competencies that were lost or failed to develop,
> (c) reformulating work goals, and
> (d) restructuring the working environment to maximize supports and to minimize barriers. (Hershenson, 1996, p. 7)

To accomplish all of these goals, rehabilitation counselors use a wide variety of counseling theories and techniques. Virtually all of the affective, behavioral, cognitive, and systemic theories of counseling are employed. Systems theories in rehabilitation practice have become especially popular in recent years (Cottone, Grelle, & Wilson, 1988; Hershenson, 1996).

The actual theories and techniques used in rehabilitation counseling are dictated by the skills of counselors as well as the needs of clients (Bitter, 1979). For example, a disabled client with sexual feelings may need a psychoeducational approach on how to handle these emotions, while another disabled client who is depressed may need a more cognitive or behavioral intervention (Boyle, 1994). Ideally, theories and techniques are chosen with regard to specific situations and are aimed at enhancing the overall functioning of clients.

Livneh and Evans (1984) point out that rehabilitation clients who have physical disabilities (e.g., blindness or spinal cord injuries) go through 12 phases of adjustment that may distinguish them from others: shock, anxiety, bargaining, denial, mourning, depression, withdrawal, internalized anger, externalized aggression, acknowledgment, acceptance, and adjustment/adaptation. There are behavioral correlates that accompany each phase and intervention strategies appropriate for each as well. For example, the client who is in a state of shock may be immobilized and cognitively disorganized. Intervention strategies most helpful during this time include comforting the person (both physically and verbally), listening and attending, offering support and reassurance, allowing the person to ventilate feelings, and referring the person to institutional care if appropriate.

Livneh and Evans believe that, as a general rule, affective and insight strategies are appropriate for the early phases of the adjustment process and that action and rational orientations work best in later phases. They also contend that disabled clients with low intelligence or low energy levels may best be served by more direct, action-oriented counseling theories and techniques, such as Bandura's modeling, Skinner's operant conditioning, Krumboltz's behavioral counseling, and Glasser's reality therapy. On the other hand, rehabilitation clients with relatively high levels of energy and intelligence may respond better to more indirect counseling strategies: Rogers's person-centered approach, May's or Frankl's existential therapy, Adler's individual counseling, and Perls's Gestalt therapy.

Coven (1977) notes that little in the research literature supports the effectiveness of indirect counseling methods in rehabilitation counseling. Therefore, he advocates that rehabilitation counselors use more action-oriented approaches, such as those generated by behavioral and Gestalt theories. Coven believes that Gestalt psychodrama can be especially powerful in helping rehabilitation clients become more involved in the counseling process and accept responsibility for their lives. Techniques such as role playing, fantasy enactment, and psychodrama can be learned and used by clients to help in adjustment.

A few other examples dealing with spinal cord injuries, mental limitations, persons with HIV/AIDS, and persons who are minorities will illustrate some specific ways in which rehabilitation counselors provide services. Physical injuries such as spinal cord damage produce a major loss for an individual and consequently have a tremendous physical and emotional impact (Krause & Anson, 1997). Rehabilitation in such cases requires concentration on both the client's and the family's adjustment to the situation. Everyone involved needs help working through the mourning process, and all need to be included in developing detailed medical, social, and psychological evaluations. A long-term counselor commitment involves carefully timed supportive counseling, crisis intervention, confrontation, life-planning activities, sex counseling, and group counseling. In short, the rehabilitation counselor must help the person with an injured spinal cord develop an internal locus of control for accepting responsibility for his or her life (Povolny, Kaplan, Marme, & Roldan, 1993). In addition to serving as a counselor, a professional who works with the physically disabled must be an advocate, a consultant, and an educator. The task is comprehensive and involves a complex relationship among job functions.

Mentally limited clients include those who have mild to severely limited cognitive as well as physical abilities. Children are one example. In these cases, the counselor's tasks and techniques may be similar to those employed with a physically disabled adult or adolescent (supportive counseling and life-planning activities), but young clients with mental deficiencies require more and different activities. Parents must be helped as well in working through their feelings about their disabled child or children and finding ways of promoting positive interactions that promote maximum development (Huber, 1979). When working with adolescents who have mental difficulties due to head injuries, a counselor must address social issues as well as therapeutic activities (Bergland & Thomas, 1991). As a general rule, increased time and effort in attending to psychosocial issues are required for working with anyone who has been mentally impaired, regardless of the client's age or the cause of the impairment (Kaplan, 1993).

Rehabilitation counselors (as well as other types of counselors) also provide services for persons with HIV/AIDS (All & Fried, 1994; Glenn, Garcia, Li, & Moore, 1998). HIV is now considered a chronic illness, and people with AIDS are classified as disabled under the Americans with Disabilities Act. A large percentage of people who are HIV-positive or who have AIDS are already socially stigmatized, so rehabilitation counselors must first examine their own attitudes and feelings before attempting to deal with this special population. Then their job is to assist clients in dealing with psychosocial tasks, such as maintaining a meaningful quality of life, coping with loss of function, and confronting existential or spiritual issues. Common client emotions include shock, anger, anxiety, fear, resentment, and depression. Therefore, counselors must help clients face these emotions as well. In addition, practical considerations such as preparing for treatment or death must be handled in a sensitive and caring way (Dworkin & Pincu, 1993).

In dealing with minority groups, such as women workers with disabilities, counselors must be aware of the developmental processes typical in such populations and be prepared with appropriate counseling techniques for the problems peculiar to each group. Counseling disabled women, for example, involves four interrelated elements: "(a) job or skill training or education; (b) family support services; (c) trait-and-factor job matching and placement services; and (d) soft counseling support services" (Hollingsworth & Mastroberti, 1983, p. 590).

Clearly, the rehabilitation counselor must be versatile. He or she must not only provide services directly but also coordinate services with other professionals and monitor clients' progress in gaining independence and self-control. Thus, a counselor needs skills from an array of theories and techniques and adaptability in shifting professional roles.

Roles and Functions

A rehabilitation counselor must also be a professional with a clear sense of purpose (Wright, 1980, 1987). There are several competing, but not necessarily mutually exclusive, ideas about what roles and functions rehabilitation counselors should assume. In the late 1960s, Muthard and Salomone conducted the first systematic investigation of rehabilitation counselors' work activities (Bolton & Jaques, 1978). They found eight major activities that characterize the counselor's role and noted a high degree of importance attached to affective counseling, vocational counseling, and placement duties (Muthard & Salomone, 1978). In this survey, rehabilitation counselors reported spending about 33% of their time in counseling activities, 25% in clerical duties, and 7% in client placement.

In 1970 the U.S. Labor Department listed 12 major functions of rehabilitation counselors, which are still relevant (Schumacher, 1983):

1. *Personal counseling.*   This function entails working with clients individually from one or more theoretical models. It plays a vital part in helping clients make complete social and emotional adjustments to their circumstances.
2. *Case finding.*   Rehabilitation counselors attempt to make their services known to agencies and potential clients through promotional and educational materials.
3. *Eligibility determination.*   Rehabilitation counselors determine, through a standard set of guidelines, whether a potential client meets the criteria for funding.
4. *Training.*   Primary aspects of training involve identifying client skills and purchasing educational or training resources to help clients enhance them. In some cases, it is necessary to provide training for clients to make them eligible for employment in a specific area.
5. *Provision of restoration.*   The counselor arranges for needed devices (e.g., artificial limbs or wheelchairs) and medical services that will make the client eligible for employment and increase his or her general independence.
6. *Support services.*   These services range from providing medication to offering individual and group counseling. They help the client develop in personal and interpersonal areas while receiving training or other services.
7. *Job placement.*   This function involves directly helping the client find employment. Activities range from supporting clients who initiate a search for work to helping less motivated clients prepare to exert more initiative.
8. *Planning.*   The planning process requires the counselor to include the client as an equal. The plan they work out together should change the client from a recipient of services to an initiator of services.
9. *Evaluation.*   This function is continuous and self-correcting. The counselor combines information from all aspects of the client's life to determine needs and priorities.
10. *Agency consultation.*   The counselor works with agencies and individuals to set up or coordinate client services, such as job placement or evaluation. Much of the counselor's work is done jointly with other professionals.
11. *Public relations.*   The counselor is an advocate for clients and executes this role by informing community leaders about the nature and scope of rehabilitation services.
12. *Follow-along.*   This function involves the counselor's constant interaction with agencies and individuals who are serving the client. It also includes maintaining contact with the clients themselves to assure steady progress toward rehabilitation.

Rehabilitation counseling is a multidimensional task whose success is dependent on many things. "The rehabilitation counselor is expected to be a competent case manager as well as a skilled therapeutic counselor" (Cook, Bolton, Bellini, & Neath, 1997, p. 193). Because some rehabilitation counselors are better at case management and some better at counseling, counselor competency in rehabilitation is helped when counselors are provided with schema to help them in assisting their clients to the fullest. Hershenson (1992a) has proposed one way of helping counselors perform their tasks even better. He has devised a practical way to conceptualize a disability and provide appropriate services. He contends that disabilities result from one of four forces: supernatural, medical, natural, or societal. Therefore, treatment can be based on explanations and techniques emphasizing faith (for the supernatural), logic (for the medical and natural), and power (for the societal). If the rehabilitation counselor and client agree on the nature of cause and treatment, services can be provided in a more accepting and therapeutic way.

Summary and Conclusion

The specialty areas of mental health, substance abuse, and rehabilitation counseling are distinct and yet interrelated. They emphasize the dynamics behind psychological adjustments, prevention programs, and treatment strategies.

Although mental health counseling is among the youngest counseling specialties, it has made a major impact on the general public and the counseling profession. Since the mid-1970s, mental health counseling has stressed the promotion of mental health services through prevention, treatment, and influencing federal and state legislation. Mental health counseling is an important part of the counseling profession on all levels. The field continues to develop at a rapid pace.

The treatment of substance abusers is an important focus in counseling as well. The consumption of substances, such as alcohol, tobacco, and drugs, has a deleterious impact on individuals, families, and society in general. To work with members of this population, counselors must focus on prevention and treatment. Prevention can come through educational programs, especially for children and youth. Treatment programs are usually more focused on adults and include systemic, spiritually focused groups, such as Alcoholics Anonymous, as well as programs run by professionals for those who are incarcerated or in treatment facilities.

Rehabilitation counseling is like mental health and substance abuse counseling in that it focuses on both prevention and the providing of services. Rehabilitation counselors see themselves as distinct since they focus mainly on helping individuals with disabilities and have traditionally been tied in with the medical model. Their programs and certification are accredited by CORE and the Commission of Rehabilitation Counselor Certification (CRCC) instead of the CACREP and NBCC. Nevertheless, rehabilitation counseling is similar to other types of counseling in that it has programs and guidelines that practitioners follow, and many of the approaches used by rehabilitation counselors are also employed by mental health and substance abuse counselors.

CLASSROOM ACTIVITIES

1. In small groups, examine how legislation has influenced the development of mental health, substance abuse, and rehabilitation services in the United States and your state. Report your findings to the class.

2. Attend an open meeting of Alcoholics Anonymous, or interview a substance abuse counselor about the services he or she presently provides. Inform the class about what you experienced at the AA meeting or what you found out from your interview with the substance abuse counselor.

3. As a class, generate ideas about what you consider to be the most pressing societal needs in the next decade. Describe how the professions of mental health, substance abuse, and rehabilitation counseling can

help alleviate problems associated with these needs. Apply your ideas to a specific setting in which you hope to be employed.

4. Khan and Cross (1984) found similarities and differences in the value systems held by three professional mental health groups: psychiatrists, psychologists, and social workers. Discuss with class members how values affect the delivery of counseling services in mental health, substance abuse, and rehabilitation counseling.

5. Investigate the educational training of rehabilitation counselors and the certification they obtain compared to mental health and substance abuse counselors. How do these groups differ? How are they alike?

REFERENCES

AA World Services, Inc. (1976). *Alcoholics Anonymous: The story of how many thousands of men and women have recovered from alcoholism* (3rd ed.). New York: Author.

All, A. C., & Fried, J. H. (1994). Psychosocial issues surrounding HIV infection that affect rehabilitation. *Journal of Rehabilitation, 60,* 8–11.

Alter, G. (1995, May 29). *What works.* Newsweek, 18–24.

Americans with Disabilities Act. (1990, July 26). Public Law 101-336. Washington, DC: Government Printing Office.

Anthony, W. A. (1980). A rehabilitation model for rehabilitating the psychiatrically disabled. *Rehabilitation Counseling Bulletin, 24,* 6–21.

Baker, S. B., & Shaw, M. C. (1987). *Improving counseling through primary prevention.* Upper Saddle River, NJ: Prentice Hall.

Barker, S. B. (1997). Nicotine addiction: An interview with Lori Karan. *Journal of Addiction and Offender Counseling, 17,* 50–55.

Bateson, G. H. (1971). The cybernetics of "self": A theory of alcoholism. *Psychiatry, 34,* 1–18.

Bauman, S., & Waldo, M. (1998). Existential theory and mental health counseling: If it were a snake it would have bitten! *Journal of Mental Health Counseling, 20,* 13–27.

Berenson, D. (1992). The therapist's relationship with couples with an alcoholic member. In E. Kaufman & P. Kaufman (Eds.), *Family therapy of drug and alcohol abuse* (pp. 224–235). Boston: Allyn & Bacon.

Bergland, M. M., & Thomas, K. R. (1991). Psychosocial issues following severe head injury of adolescence: Individual and family perceptions. *Rehabilitation Counseling Bulletin, 35,* 5–22.

Bitter, J. A. (1979). *Introduction to rehabilitation.* St. Louis: Mosby.

Blackorby, J., & Wagner, M. (1996). Longitudinal postschool outcomes of youth with disabilities: Findings from the national longitudinal transition study. *Exceptional Children, 62,* 399–413.

Bolton, B., & Jaques, M. E. (1978). Rehabilitation counseling research: Editorial introduction. In B. Bolton & M. E. Jaques (Eds.), *Rehabilitation counseling: Theory and practice* (pp. 163–165). Baltimore: University Park Press.

Boyle, P. S. (1994). Rehabilitation counselors as providers: The issue of sexuality. *Journal of Applied Rehabilitation Counseling, 25,* 6–10.

Bristow-Braitman, A. (1995). Addiction recovery: 12-step program and cognitive-behavioral psychology. *Journal of Counseling and Development, 73,* 414–418.

Buelow, G. (1995). Comparing students from substance abusing and dysfunctional families: Implications for counseling. *Journal of Counseling and Development, 73,* 327–330.

Carlson, J., & Ardell, D. E. (1988). Physical fitness as a pathway to wellness and effective counseling. In R. Hayes & R. Aubrey (Eds.), *New directions for counseling and human development* (pp. 383–396). Denver: Love.

Carney, J. V., & Hazler, R. J. (1998). Suicide and cognitive-behavioral counseling: Implications for mental health counselors. *Journal of Mental Health Counseling, 20,* 28–41.

Center on Addiction and Substance Abuse. (1995). *American adolescence.* New York: Columbia University Press.

Collins, B. G., & Collins, T. M. (1994). Child and adolescent mental health: Building a system of care. *Journal of Counseling and Development, 72,* 239–243.

Cook, D., Bolton, B., Bellini, J., & Neath, J. (1997). A statewide investigation of the rehabilitation counselor generalist hypothesis. *Rehabilitation Counseling Bulletin, 40,* 192–201.

Cottone, R. R., Grelle, M., & Wilson, W. C. (1988). The accuracy of systemic versus psychological evidence in judging vocational evaluator recommendations: A preliminary test of a systemic theory of vocational rehabilitation. *Journal of Rehabilitation, 54,* 45–52.

Council for Accreditation of Counseling and Related Educational Programs (CACREP). (1994). *Accreditation procedures manual and application.* Alexandria, VA: Author.

Coven, A. B. (1977). Using Gestalt psycho-drama experiments in rehabilitation counseling. *Personnel and Guidance Journal, 56,* 143–147.

Dattilio, F. M. (1993). A practical update on the treatment of obsessive-compulsive disorders. *Journal of Mental Health Counseling, 15,* 244–259.

Doan, R. E., & Scherman, A. (1987). The therapeutic effect of physical fitness on measures of personality: A literature review. *Journal of Counseling and Development, 66,* 28–36.

Dworkin, S., & Pincu, L. (1993). Counseling in the era of AIDS. *Journal of Counseling and Development, 71,* 275–281.

Ehrle, R. A. (1979). Rehabilitation counselors on the threshold of the 1980s. *Counselor Education and Supervision, 18,* 174–180.

Emener, W. G., & Cottone, R. R. (1989). Professionalization, deprofessionalization, and reprofessionalization of rehabilitation counseling according to criteria of professions. *Journal of Counseling and Development, 67,* 576–581.

Enright, M. S, (1997). The impact of short-term career development programs on people with disabilities. *Rehabilitation Counseling Bulletin, 40,* 285–300.

Erikson, E. H. (1963). *Childhood and society* (2nd ed.). New York: Norton.

Gerstein, L. H., & Hotelling, K. (1987). Length of group treatment and changes in women with bulimia. *Journal of Mental Health Counseling, 9,* 162–173.

Ginter, E. J. (1989). Slayers of monster watermelons found in the mental health patch. *Journal of Mental Health Counseling, 11,* 77–85.

Gladding, S. T. (1999). *Group work: A counseling specialty* (3rd ed.). Upper Saddle River, NJ: Merrill/Prentice Hall.

Glenn, M., Garcia, J., Li, L., & Moore, D. (1998). Preparation of rehabilitation counselors to serve people living with HIV/AIDS. *Rehabilitation Counseling Bulletin, 41,* 190–200.

Hansen, J. T. (1998). Do mental health counselors require training in the treatment of mentally disordered clients? A challenge to the conclusions of Vacc, Loesch, and Guilbert. *Journal of Mental Health Counseling, 20,* 183–188.

Heath, D. H. (1980). Wanted: A comprehensive model of healthy development. *Personnel and Guidance Journal, 58,* 391–399.

Hershenson, D. B. (1982). A formulation of counseling based on the healthy personality. *Personnel and Guidance Journal, 60,* 406–409.

Hershenson, D. B. (1992a). Conceptions of disability: Implications for rehabilitation. *Rehabilitation Counseling Bulletin, 35,* 154–159.

Hershenson, D. B. (1992b). A genuine copy of a fake Dior: Mental health counseling's pursuit of pathology. *Journal of Mental Health Counseling, 14,* 419–421.

Hershenson, D. B. (1996). A systems reformulation of a developmental model of work adjustment. *Rehabilitation Counseling Bulletin, 40,* 2–10.

Hershenson, D. B., Power, P. W., & Seligman, L. (1989). Mental health counseling theory: Present status and future prospects. *Journal of Mental Health Counseling, 11,* 44–69.

Hilts, P. J. (1996). *Smokescreen: The truth behind the tobacco industry cover-up.* Reading, MA: Addison-Wesley.

Hinkle, J. S. (1994). DSM-IV: Prognosis and implications for mental health counselors. *Journal of Mental Health Counseling, 16,* 174–183.

Hipple, T., Comer, M., & Boren, D. (1997). Twenty recent novels (and more) about adolescents for bibliotherapy. *Professional School Counseling, 1,* 65–67.

Holland, J. L. (1997). *Making vocational choices: A theory of vocational personalities and work environments* (3rd ed.). Odessa, FL: Psychological Assessment Resources.

Hollingsworth, D. K., & Mastroberti, C. J. (1983). Women, work, and disability. *Personnel and Guidance Journal, 61,* 587–591.

Hollis, J. W. (1997). *Counselor preparation, 1996–1998* (9th ed.). Muncie, IN: Accelerated Development.

Hosie, T. W., West, J. D., & Mackey, J. A. (1988). Employment and roles of mental health counselors in substance-abuse centers. *Journal of Mental Health Counseling, 10,* 188–198.

Huber, C. H. (1979). Parents of the handicapped child: Facilitating acceptance through group counseling. *Personnel and Guidance Journal, 57,* 267–269.

Huber, C. H. (1983). A social-ecological approach to the counseling process. *AMHCA Journal, 5,* 4–11.

Ivey, A. E. (1989). Mental health counseling: A developmental process and profession. *Journal of Mental Health Counseling, 11,* 26–35.

James, M. D., & Hazler, R. J. (1998). Using metaphors to soften resistance in chemically dependent clients. *Journal of Humanistic Education and Development, 38,* 122–133.

Juhnke, G. A. (1996). The adapted-SAD PERSONS: A suicide assessment scale designed for use with children. *Elementary School Guidance and Counseling, 30,* 252–258.

Kaplan, S. P. (1993). Five year tracking of psychosocial changes in people with severe traumatic brain injury. *Rehabilitation Counseling Bulletin, 36,* 151–159.

Kaufman, E., & Kaufman, P. (Eds.). (1992). *Family therapy of drug and alcohol abuse.* Boston: Allyn & Bacon.

Khan, J. A., & Cross, D. G. (1984). Mental health professionals: How different are their values? *AMHCA Journal, 6,* 42–51.

Kiselica, M. S., & Look, C. T. (1993). Mental health counseling and prevention: Disparity between philosophy and practice? *Journal of Mental Health Counseling, 15,* 3–14.

Kolenc, K. M., Hartley, D. L., & Murdock, N. L. (1990). The relationship of mild depression to stress and coping. *Journal of Mental Health Counseling, 12,* 76–92.

Krause, J. S., & Anson, C. A. (1997). Adjustment after spinal cord injury: Relationship to participation in employment or educational activities. *Rehabilitation Counseling Bulletin, 40,* 202–214.

Krestan, J., & Bepko, C. (1988). Alcohol problems and the family life cycle. In B. Carter & M. McGoldrick (Eds.), The changing family life cycle (2nd ed., pp. 483–511). New York: Gardner.

L'Abate, L. (1992). Introduction. In L. L'Abate, G. E. Farrar, & D. A. Serritella (Eds.), *Handbook of differential treatments for addiction* (pp. 1–4). Boston: Allyn & Bacon.

L'Abate, L., Farrar, G. E., & Serritella, D. A. (Eds.). (1992). *Handbook of differential treatments for addiction.* Boston: Allyn & Bacon.

Lam, C. S., Hilburger, J., Kornbleuth, M., Jenkins, J., Brown, D., & Racenstein, J. M. (1996). A treatment matching model for substance abuse rehabilitation clients. *Rehabilitation Counseling Bulletin, 39,* 202–216.

Lee, C. C., & Walz, G. R. (Eds.). (1998). *Social action: A mandate for counselors.* Alexandria, VA: American Counseling Association.

Leierer, S. J., Stohmer, D. C., Leclere, W. A., Cornwell, B.J., & Whitten, S. L. (1996). The effect of counselor disability, attending behavior, and client problem on counseling. *Rehabilitation Counseling Bulletin, 40,* 92–96.

Lewin, S. S., Ramseur, J. H., & Sink, J. M. (1979). The role of private rehabilitation: Founder, catalyst, competitor. *Journal of Rehabilitation, 45,* 16–19.

Lichtenberg, J. W. (1986). Counseling research: Irrelevant or ignored? *Journal of Counseling and Development, 64,* 365–366.

Livneh, H. (1984). Psychiatric rehabilitation: A dialogue with Bill Anthony. *Journal of Counseling and Development, 63,* 86–90.

Livneh, H., & Evans, J. (1984). Adjusting to disability: Behavioral correlates and intervention strategies. *Personnel and Guidance Journal, 62,* 363–368.

Manhal-Baugus, M. (1998). The self-in-relation theory and Women for Sobriety: Female-specific theory and mutual help group for chemically dependent women. *Journal of Addiction and Offender Counseling, 18,* 78–87.

Maslow, A. H. (1962). *Toward a psychology of being.* Princeton, NJ: Van Nostrand.

Meehl, P. (1973). *Psychodiagnosis: Selected papers.* New York: Norton.

Miller, W. R., & Brown, S. A. (1997). Why psychologists should treat alcohol and drug problems. *American Psychologist, 52,* 1269–1279.

Moos, R. (1973). Conceptualization of human environments. *American Psychologist, 28,* 652–665.

Morgan, O. J. (1998). Addiction, family treatment, and healing Resources: An interview with David Berenson. *Journal of Addiction and Offender Counseling, 18,* 54–62.

Mudore, C. F. (1997). Assisting young people in quitting tobacco. *Professional School Counseling, 1,* 61–62.

Muthard, J. E., & Salomone, P. R. (1978). The role and function of the rehabilitation counselor. In B. Bolton & M. E. Jaques (Eds.), *Rehabilitation counseling: Theory and practice* (pp. 166–175). Baltimore: University Park Press.

O'Donnell, J. M. (1988). The holistic health movement: Implications for counseling theory and practice. In R. Hayes & R. Aubrey (Eds.), *New directions for counseling and human development* (pp. 365–382). Denver: Love.

Olkin, R. (1994, Fall). Introduction to the special issue on physical and sensory disabilities. *Family Psychologist, 10,* 6–7.

Patterson, W., Dohn, H., Bird, J., & Patterson, G. (1983). Evaluation of suicide patients: The SAD PERSONS scale. *Psychosomatics, 24,* 343–349.

Pinto, R. P., & Morrell, E. M. (1988). Current approaches and future trends in smoking cessation programs. *Journal of Mental Health Counseling, 10,* 95–110.

Povolny, M. A., Kaplan, S., Marme, M., & Roldan, G. (1993). Perceptions of adjustment issues following a spinal cord injury: A case study. *Journal of Applied Rehabilitation Counseling, 24,* 31–34.

Robinson, B. E. (1995, July). Helping clients with work addiction: Don't overdo it. *Counseling Today, 38,* 31–32.

Schumacher, B. (1983). Rehabilitation counseling. In M. M. Ohlsen (Ed.), *Introduction to counseling* (pp. 313–324). Itasca, IL: Peacock.

Seiler, G., & Messina, J. J. (1979). Toward professional identity: The dimensions of mental health counseling in perspective. *AMHCA Journal, 1,* 3–8.

Sherrard, P. A. D., & Amatea, E. S. (1994). Through the looking glass: A preview. *Journal of Mental Health Counseling, 16,* 3–5.

Solsberry, P. W. (1994). Interracial couples in the United States of America: Implications for mental health counseling. *Journal of Mental Health Counseling, 16,* 304–316.

Sperry, L., Carlson, J., & Lewis, J. (1993). Health counseling strategies and interventions. *Journal of Mental Health Counseling, 15,* 15–25.

Springer, C. A., Britt, T. W., & Schlenker, B. R. (1998). Codependency: Clarifying the construct. *Journal of Mental Health Counseling, 20,* 141–158.

Spruill, D. A., & Fong, M. L. (1990). Defining the domain of mental health counseling: From identity confusion to consensus. *Journal of Mental Health Counseling, 12,* 12–23.

Stanton, M., & Todd, T. (1982). *The family therapy of drug abuse and addiction.* New York: Guilford.

Steenbarger, B. N. (1998). Alcohol abuse and college counseling: An overview of research and practice. *Journal of College Counseling, 1,* 81–92.

Steinglass, P. (1979). Family therapy with alcoholics: A review. In E. Kaufman & P. N. Kaufman (Eds.), *Family therapy of drug and alcohol abuse* (pp. 147–186). New York: Gardner.

Stevens-Smith, P., & Smith, R. L. (1998). *Substance abuse counseling: Theory and practice.* Upper Saddle River, NJ: Merrill/Prentice Hall.

Sunich, M. F., & Doster, J. (1995, June). Cocaine—Part II. *Amethyst Journal, 1,* 1–2.

U.S. Department of Health, Education, and Welfare. (1974). Vocational rehabilitation program: Implementation provisions, rules and regulations. *Federal Register, 39,* 42470–42507.

Vacc, N., Loesch, L., & Guilbert, D. (1997). The clientele of certified clinical mental health counselors. *Journal of Mental Health Counseling, 19,* 165–170.

Van Deusen, J. M., Stanton, M. D., Scott, S. M., Todd, S. C., & Mowatt, D. T. (1982). Getting the addict to agree to involve the family of origin: The initial contact. In M. D. Stanton, T. C. Todd, & Associates (Eds.), *The family therapy of drug abuse and addiction* (pp. 39–59). New York: Guilford.

Vick, R. D., Smith, L. M., & Herrera, C. I. R. (1998). The healing circle: An alternative path to alcoholism recovery. *Counseling and Values, 42,* 133–141.

Waldo, M., Horswill, R. K., & Brotherton, W. D. (1993). Collaborating with state departments to achieve recognition of mental health counselors. *Journal of Mental Health Counseling, 15,* 342–346.

Warfield, R. D., & Goldstein, M. B. (1996). Spirituality: The key to recovery from alcoholism. *Counseling and Values, 40,* 196–205.

Washton, A. (1989). *Cocaine addiction.* New York: Norton.

Weikel, W. J., & Palmo, A. J. (1989). The evolution and practice of mental health counseling. *Journal of Mental Health Counseling, 11,* 17–25.

West, J. D., Hosie, T. W., & Mackey, J. A. (1987). Employment and roles of counselors in mental health agencies. *Journal of Counseling and Development, 66,* 135–138.

Wetter, D. W., Fiore, M. C., Gritz, E. R., Lando, H. A., Stitzer, M. L., Hasselblad, V., & Baker, T. B. (1998). The agency for health care policy and research smoking cessation clinical practice guideline. *American Psychologist, 53,* 657–669.

Wiggins, J. D., Moody, A. D., & Lederer, D. A. (1983). Personality typologies related to marital satisfaction. *AMHCA Journal, 5,* 169–178.

Wilcoxon, S. A., & Puleo, S. G. (1992). Professional-development needs of mental health counselors: Results of a national survey. *Journal of Mental Health Counseling, 14,* 187–195.

Wright, B. (1983). *Physical disability: A psychosocial approach* (2nd ed.). New York: Harper & Row.

Wright, G. N. (1980). *Total rehabilitation.* Boston: Little, Brown.

Wright, G. N. (1987). Rehabilitation counselors' qualifications and client responsibilities structure their professional relationships. *Journal of Applied Rehabilitation Counseling, 18,* 18–20.

18

CONSULTATION

◆

She went about kissing frogs

for in her once-upon-time mind

that's what she had learned to do.

With each kiss came expectations

of slimy green changing to Ajax white.

With each day came realizations

that quick-tongued, fly-eating, croaking creatures

Don't magically turn to instant princes

from the after effects of a fast-smooching,

smooth-talking helping beauty.

So with regret she came back from a lively lily-pond

to the sobering stacks of the village library

To page through the well-worn stories again

and find in print what she knew in fact

that even loved frogs sometimes stay frogs

no matter how pretty the damsel or how high the hope.

Although counselors in a variety of work settings provide "some consulting services as part of their professional responsibilities, the formal literature on consultation as a function of counselors did not emerge until the late 1960s and early 1970s" (Randolph & Graun, 1988, p. 182). Initially, consultant *was defined as an expert with special knowledge to share with the consultee. Therefore, certain theoretical approaches to counseling (such as Adlerian, cognitive, and behavioral) were considered to be best suited for this activity because of their emphases on teaching and pragmatic application. Affective theories were considered to be less desirable because of their focus on close personal relationships and their generally less precise structure. However, as time has shown, consultation can be premised on a variety of theoretical concepts depending on the need of the client or the group.*

Regardless of the orientation, consultation is a function expected of all counselors and one that is receiving increased attention (Hollis, 1997). Sometimes counselors who function in this capacity are referred to as counselor-consultants *(Randolph & Graun, 1988); at other times, only the word* consultant *is used. "First and foremost, [consultation is] a human relationship" process (Dougherty, 1995, p. v). It requires a personal touch as well as professional input if it is to be effective. It also requires an acute sensitivity to cultural nuances and multicultural issues (Jackson & Hayes, 1993).*

Consultation: Defining a Multifaceted Activity

Many attempts have been made through the years to define *consultation*, although there is still no universal agreement on the definition. As early as 1970, Caplan defined it as "a process between two professional persons, the consultant, who is a specialist, and the consultee, who invokes the consultant's help in regard to current work problems" (p. 19). In the late 1970s, two special issues of the *Personnel and Guidance Journal* (February and March 1978) were published on consultation, which were followed 7 years later by a special issue of *The Counseling Psychologist* (July 1985) devoted exclusively to the same topic. Eight years later, two issues of the *Journal for Counseling and Development* (July/August and November/December 1993) addressed the subject of consultation again in multiple ways. All five publications, and others like them, brought consultation to the forefront of counseling and helped professionals delineate common aspects of the consultation process: its problem-solving focus, its tripartite nature, and its emphasis on improvement (Dougherty, 1995).

In spite of all the attention it has received, consultation is not well conceptualized by many counselors, who often do not understand its exact nature (Drapela, 1983). Consequently, some counselors misinterpret the concept, feel uncomfortable about engaging in consultative activities, or both (Goodyear, 1976). Brown (1983) relates the story of a man whose image of a consultant was "someone who blows in, blows off, and blows out" (p. 124). As inaccurate as this idea is, it may well reflect the impreciseness implied by the term.

Although consultation has "proliferated wildly" since the early 1970s, "theory and research lag far behind" actual practice (Gallessich, 1985, p. 336). The reasons for this lag include the following:

- There is an atheoretical attitude toward consultation that inhibits its development. Consultation originated in many different settings with various groups and has multiple forms, thereby making it hard to organize (Gallessich, 1982). In addition, many counseling consultants do not conceptualize or practice consultation as a specialized professional process.
- Consultation is not the primary activity of all professionals or of any professional group. It lacks "the organizational support, leadership, and resources necessary for theory-building and research" (Gallessich, 1985, p. 342).
- Consultation practices have changed rapidly. Unlike most other forms of helping, consultation reacts quickly to social, political, or technical changes. For example, the humanistic consultation practices of the late 1960s were not widely employed in the more conservative 1980s.

Other factors inhibiting the growth and development of consultation involve difficulties in (a) defining variables and obtaining permission to do specialized research in organizational settings and (b) understanding the changing nature of goals in the consultation process. In other words, initial goals may change.

Some debate still persists about the exact definition of *consultation* (Kurpius & Fuqua, 1993). One of the best definitions, was adapted in pre-1995 editions of the ACA code of ethics. It was originated by Kurpius (1978), who defined *consultation* as "a voluntary relationship between a professional helper and help-needing individual, group, or social unit in which the consultant is providing help to the client(s) in defining and solving a work-related problem or potential problem with a client or client system."

In general, consulting approaches have the following characteristics in common (Gallessich, 1985; Kurpius & Fuqua, 1993; Newman, 1993):

- Consultation is content based (supported by a recognized body of knowledge).
- Consultation is goal oriented; it has an objective, often a work-related one.
- Consultation is governed by variable roles and relationship rules.
- Consultation is process oriented; it involves gathering data, recommending solutions, and offering support.
- Consultation is triadic.
- Consultation is based on ideologies, value systems, and ethics.

Kurpius (1986, 1988) also stresses that consultation is systems oriented. It aims to help change aspects of the system, such as its structure or people, to change the system itself. Forces within systems either facilitate or inhibit their receptivity to the consultation process (Kurpius, Fuqua, & Rozecki, 1993). (See Figure 18.1.)

Because of its importance to the overall role of counselors, "a generic consultation course is required in many counselor training programs, and consultation experiences have

Figure 18.1   System openness and balance of forces

Source: From "The Consulting Process: A Multidimensional Approach," by D. J. Kurpius, D. R. Fuqua, and T. Rozecki, 1993, *Journal of Counseling and Development, 71,* p. 602. © 1993 by ACA. Reprinted with permission. No further reproduction authorized without written permission of the American Counseling Association.

	System is Closed to Change	System is Open to Change
Equilibrium	1. Do Not Accept Contract—Little Chance for Helping	2. Accept Contract But Inform Members That Change May Be Slower
Disequilibrium	3. Accept Contract But Expect High Conflict and Slow Change	4. Best Chance for Successful Helping

been included in the Council for Accreditation of Counseling and Related Programs (CACREP) . . . standards for accreditation of such programs" (Randolph & Graun, 1988, p. 182).

Consultation versus Counseling

Schmidt and Osborne (1981) found that in actual practice most counselors they surveyed did not distinguish between consultation and counseling activities. These researchers concluded "the ultimate goals of both are so similar that it is difficult to differentiate between the two when studying them as general processes" (p. 170). Indeed, many of the principles and processes are similar. For example, consultation and counseling may be offered on a primary (preventive) level, and both are interpersonal processes. Yet there are distinctions.

One of the differences between consultation and counseling is that "the content of the consulting interview, unlike counseling, is a unit external to the counselee" (Stum, 1982, p. 297). Most consultation takes place in a natural setting (often the consultee's work environment), whereas most counseling occurs at the designated center where a counselor is employed (Kurpius, 1986).

A further distinction between counseling and consultation is that consultation services are usually sought when a "system is in decline or crisis" (Nelson & Shifron, 1985, p. 301). Some people do not seek counseling until they are under stress or in distress; others seek counseling for primary prevention reasons or in anticipation of situational or developmental concerns.

Skill in communication is another area in which there are contrasts between these two activities. Communication skills employed in consultation do not differ much from those used in counseling (Kurpius, 1988; Schmidt, 1999). Both counselors and consultants listen, attend, question, clarify, confront, and summarize. But consultants initially focus more on content than feeling because the process concentrates primarily on problems and issues.

Another difference between consultation and counseling is in the role of practitioners. Professionals who operate from either position try to initiate change in the people with whom they work. Yet consultants play more of a catalyst role because they do not have "direct control over the consultee or the consultee's client" (Kurpius, 1986, p. 58).

Finally, even though the goals of counseling and consulting are similar ("to help individuals become more efficient, effective, independent, and resourceful in their abilities to solve the problems that they face"), consultation activities work indirectly rather than directly (Nelson & Shifron, 1985, p. 298). Often consultants teach consultees a skill that can be applied to a third party, whereas counseling skills are usually focused on and directly applicable to a specific individual, group, or system with which counselors work.

Four Conceptual Models

Many different models of consultation exist, but only a few of them are comprehensive and useful in counseling. Four of the most comprehensive models of consultation elaborated on by a number of experts (Keys, Bemak, Carpenter, & King-Sears, 1998; Kurpius, 1978; Kurpius & Brubaker, 1976; Schein, 1978) follow:

1. *Expert or provision model.* In the expert model, consultants provide a direct service to consultees who do not have the time, inclination, or perceived skills to deal with a particular problem area. This model of consultation was the first to develop (Kurpius & Robinson, 1978). It was used extensively in the 1940s and early 1950s. The advantage of the model is that experts can handle difficult problems and leave consultees free to manage their other duties without work conflicts. The major disadvantage is that consultants are blamed if a particular problem does not get better.

2. *Doctor-patient or prescription model.* In the prescription model, consultants advise consultees about what is wrong with the targeted third party and what should be done about it. A good way to conceptualize this method is to compare it with the traditional medical model in which patients' problems are diagnosed and a prescription to rectify their situations is given. This model is usually implemented when consultees lack confidence in their own intervention strategies. It does not require consultants to bring about a change or a cure, as the provision model does.

3. *Mediation model.* Consultants act as coordinators in the mediation model. Their main function is to unify the services of a variety of people who are trying to solve a problem. They accomplish this goal by (a) coordinating the services already being provided or (b) creating an alternative plan of services that represents a mutually acceptable synthesis of several solutions. A consultant might work this way in a school system in which a disabled child is receiving a variety of different services that are disruptive to both the child and school. Through mediation, services are offered in a systematic way, and less disruption results.

4. *Process consultation or collaboration model.* Consultants are facilitators of the problem-solving process in the collaboration model. Their main task is to get consultees actively involved in finding solutions to the present difficulties they have with clients. Thus, in a school situation consultees (i.e., parents, educators, youth, counselors, and community agency professionals) would define their problems clearly, analyze them thoroughly, design workable solutions, and then implement and evaluate

their own plans of action. This approach does not assume that any one person has sufficient knowledge to develop and implement solutions and that the group assembled must work as an interdependent team (Keys et al., 1998).

Setting up an atmosphere in which this process can happen is a major task for collaboration consultants. It requires the use of a number of interpersonal counseling skills, such as empathy, active listening, and structuring. In addition, counselors who work as consultants in these situations must be highly intelligent and analytical thinkers who are able to generate enthusiasm, optimism, and self-confidence in others. They must also be able to integrate and use affective, behavioral, and cognitive dimensions of problem solving.

Levels of Consultation

Consultation services may be delivered on several levels. Three of the most common ways to implement the process involve working at the individual, group, and organizational/community level (Kurpius, 1985).

Individual Consultation

Kisch (1977) has discussed aspects of one-to-one consultation. He employs a *role-reversal process,* in which a client role-plays either an active or passive consultant while the counselor role-plays the client. The client sits in different chairs when playing the separate roles. When passive, the client gives only familiar, safe, nonthreatening advice in response to the presented problem, and there is no confrontation. When active, the client reflects "thoughts, feelings, and strategies that are assertive, confrontive, and may be novel and frightening" (p. 494). In each case, counselors ask clients about the payoffs and risks of the client-consultant ideas for change.

Another form of individual consultation involves teaching self-management skills. Kahn (1976) points out that externally maintained treatment modalities are not very effective. To replace them, he proposes a four-part interdependent component model with the following requirements:

- *Self-monitoring:* persons observe their own behavior.
- *Self-measurement:* persons validate the degree to which the problem exists.
- *Self-mediation:* persons develop and implement strategies of change.
- *Self-maintenance:* persons continually monitor and measure the desired effects of the self-management process.

Kahn gives examples of excessive and deficit behaviors that can be managed through this model, including cigarette smoking, obesity, assertiveness, and depression. He points out that when individuals learn the steps of self-management, they can take preventive and remedial actions on their own.

Kurpius (1986) emphasizes that "mutual trust and respect are essential" on an individual consultation level (p. 61). For example, Fogle (1979) suggests that teaching individuals a constructive negative-thinking process can sometimes alleviate anxiety, restore motivation, promote risk-taking behaviors, and shift attention to the present. In this process, clients are instructed to think negatively about future-oriented events and make contingency plans if the worst possible situation occurs. They are instructed only to follow the instructions of the consultant if they believe what is being suggested will work.

Overall, at the individual consultation level, a consultant is often required to model a skill or prescribe a solution. Working on an individual level is appropriate if the consultee clearly has an individual problem, a systems intervention is inappropriate or impossible, or individual change would be more beneficial and efficient (Fuqua & Newman, 1985).

Group Consultation

Group consultation is employed when several individuals share a similar problem (e.g., in a work setting). Kurpius (1986) states that in work situations in which group consultation is employed, the group may be focused on either problem solving or persons. In problem-solving groups, the consultant acts as catalyst and facilitator. In person-focused groups, the consultant may help group members build teams to understand and resolve person problems.

The *C group* was one of the first effective collaborative consultation models (Dinkmeyer, 1971, 1973; Dinkmeyer & Carlson, 1973). All aspects of the approach begin with a *C:* collaboration, consultation, clarification, confrontation, concern, confidentiality, and commitment. Its primary purpose is to present new knowledge about human behavior to members of the group. It encourages group members to work together as equals (collaboration); give and receive input from each other (consultation); understand the relationship among beliefs, feelings, and actions (clarification); share openly with each other (confrontation); empathize with one another (concern); keep information within the group (confidentiality); and make plans for specific changes (commitment). Although the C group has the potential to influence parent-child interactions dramatically, the group is always composed of adults because its Adlerian orientation assumes that adults control parent-child interactions for better or worse. Furthermore, it is never used for counseling purposes, only for sharing information and mutual support.

Voight, Lawler, and Fulkerson (1980) have developed a program that assists women who are making midlife decisions. It has some parallels to C groups because it is directed toward promoting self-help and providing information in a group setting. The program makes use of women's existing social networks to help them become psychologically stronger and more informed about community resources and opportunities. A lasting advantage is that participants not only become better educated and self-directed but continue to live in an environment where they can receive support and input from others who have gone through the same experience. Similarly, a self-help center for adolescents has been designed to function as a form of group consultation (O'Brien & Lewis, 1975). At the center, which was originally set up for substance abusers, clients are empowered with information and methods of helping themselves and each other.

Organization/Community Consultation

Because organization and community consultations are much larger in scope than individual or group consultations, consultants must possess sophisticated knowledge of systems to operate effectively on this level. Unlike individual or group consultants, organization or community consultants are external to the project, although most of their activities involve individuals or groups. For example, counselors may function as political consultants because they are "in a pivotal position to effectively communicate the concerns of people they serve to policy makers at local, state, and national levels of government" (Solomon, 1982, p. 580). Such activities involve lobbying with individual representatives as well as testifying before and making recommendations to special committees.

Conyne (1975) mentions other ways of consulting on a community or organizational level. He emphasizes the individual within the environment, stressing *environmental mapping*. In other words, he believes that when counselors find individuals who exist in less-than-optimal mental health settings, they can work as change agents to improve the situation of the target population. Focusing on social action improves clients' conditions and their mental health while lessening their need sometimes for counseling (Lee & Walz, 1998).

Barrow and Prosen (1981) also address the importance of working as consultants on environmental factors, but they advocate a global-change process. In addition to helping clients find coping techniques to deal with stress, counselors must help clients change stress-producing environments. This process is best achieved by working to change the structure of the system rather than the person within it. Aplin (1985) formulated a model that depicts the content and process areas that a consultant should be aware of when working on an organizational or community basis (see Figure 18.2).

Stages and Attitudes in Consultation

Developmental stages are an important part of many consultation activities (Wallace & Hall, 1996). Two well-known theories propose distinct consultation stages. The first is Splete's (1982) nine-stage process based on the premise that clients collaborate with consultants to work on predetermined concerns. The order of the stages in this approach are as follows:

1. *Precontract.*   The consultant clarifies personal skill and areas of expertise that can be used in the consultation process.
2. *Contract and exploration of relationship.*   The consultant discusses a more formal arrangement between him- or herself and the consultee. The consultee's readiness and the consultant's ability to respond must be determined.
3. *Contracting.*   A mutual agreement is set up that defines what services are to be offered and how.
4. *Problem identification.*   Both the consultant and consultee determine and define the precise problem to be worked on and the desired outcome.
5. *Problem analysis.*   The focus is on reviewing pertinent information and generating possible solutions.
6. *Feedback and planning.*   Here the alternative solutions generated in stage 5 are evaluated and the probabilities of success determined. One or more solution plans are then systematically implemented.
7. *Implementation of the plan.*   The consultee carries out the proposed plan with the consultant's support.

Figure 18.2 Aplin's model

Source: From "Business Realities and Organizational Consultation," by J. C. Aplin, 1978, *Counseling Psychologist, 13*, p. 400, copyright © 1978 by Sage Publications, Inc. Reprinted by permission of Sage Publications, Inc.

8. *Evaluation of the plan.* Both the consultant and consultee determine how well the plan worked in relationship to the desired outcome.
9. *Conclusion and termination of relationship.* Both parties in the process review what has happened and plan for any follow-up, either independently or with the consultant.

Although Splete's plan is detailed and useful, it does not elaborate on counselor skills contained within the process. A second model that does has been proposed by Dustin and Ehly (1984). It outlines a five-stage process of consultation along with counselor techniques and behaviors that accompany each stage. The model assumes that the consultant is working in a school setting with either a parent or teacher, but it has potential usefulness outside the school environment—for example, in business, government, corrections, and rehabilitation. Its stages are as follows:

1. *Phasing in.*   The focus is on relationship building and can be compared with Splete's (1982) precontract stage. The consultant uses skills such as active listening, self-disclosure, and empathy and promotes a sense of trust.
2. *Problem identification.*   Comparable to stages 2 through 4 in the Splete model, this step focuses on determining whether a suspected third-party problem really exists. Consultants employ focusing skills as well as other counseling techniques, such as paraphrasing, restatement, genuineness, and goal setting.
3. *Implementation.*   Similar to stages 5 through 7 of Splete's scheme, this stage defines strategies and sets up a time frame. Feedback is an important part of this process. Flexibility, dealing with resistance and negative feelings, and patience are other counselor skills involved.
4. *Follow-up and evaluation.*   This stage merges with stage 3 at times, but its focus is distinct. It concentrates on the results gained from the consultation process, especially if the consultee is satisfied with the outcome of changes. Counselor skills include risk taking, openness, and persistence. These skills are especially important if the consultee is dissatisfied or frustrated.
5. *Termination.*   The consultant helps bring closure to previous activities. Relationship skills such as empathy and genuineness are again employed. Giving and asking for feedback time are important. It is vital that the consultant and consultee evaluate what was most profitable for each and what aspects of the procedure were less effective.

Splete (1982) also lists four attitude areas that are important for consultants. First, they must display an attitude of professionalism. They must take responsibility for helping their clients deal with immediate and long-term problems. Second, consultants must show maturity. They have to be willing to stand up for their own views, take risks, and deal with hostility or rejection. Third, consultants need to demonstrate open-mindedness and not close off ideas and input into the problem-solving process too soon. Finally, they need to believe in the importance of individuals and place people above technology.

Specific Areas of Consultation

Consultation often takes place in schools and community agencies, but the process may take place in almost any environment. In this section, some of the work conducted in schools and agencies will be examined as examples of the kinds of consultation programs that can be set up.

School Consultation

Kahnweiler (1979) has traced the concept of school counselors as consultants from its beginnings in the late 1950s. As he points out, the accompanying literature has evolved in theory and practice. The development of school consultation has been summarized by Bundy and Poppen (1986), who surveyed articles from *Elementary School Guidance and Counseling* and *The School Counselor* over 28 years and found that consultation was effective in prevention and intervention in schools. Consultation by school counselors also enhances overall school achievement, improves student self-concept, reduces stress in certain populations, leads to better classroom management skills, and facilitates the moral growth of students (Cecil & Cobia, 1990; Conoley & Conoley, 1992). As a process, "consultation is an efficient method of impacting the well-being and personal development of many more students than can be seen directly by a counselor" (Otwell & Mullis, 1997, p. 25).

Generally, school counselors are in the perfect position to act as consultants and change agents (Podemski & Childers, 1980). On most school organizational charts, the counselor is positioned as a staff authority rather than a line authority. Persons in staff authority positions are expected to have specialized knowledge, such as familiarity with local, state, and federal laws (McCarthy & Sorenson, 1993). Therefore, they can act in an advisory and supportive way for others. By functioning in this manner, school counselors help bring about environmental and systemic changes (Schmidt, 1999). They advise persons in positions of power about what conditions need modifying and then support efforts to make improvements.

Umansky and Holloway (1984) view the many aspects of consultation as a way of serving students and the larger population of the school community without increasing expenditures. They advocate four approaches to consultation in the schools: Adlerian, behavioral, mental health, and organizational development.

The *Adlerian-based approach* is a psychological education model and assumes that individuals, groups, and communities lack information. The consultant teaches within the organizational structure of the school and emphasizes ways to promote positive behavior in children.

The behavioral approach, also geared to teaching, concentrates on instructing consultees how to use behavioral principles in working with students and collect empirical data to validate each intervention strategy.

The *mental health approach* is based on the broader community mental health approach developed by Caplan (1970). Psychodynamic theory underlies mental health consultation. The goal of this approach is to help teachers and other powerful personnel in the school gain new insight into themselves and their students.

Finally, the *organizational development approach* emphasizes the context in which problems arise. Thus, if students and teachers have problems, the climate of the school becomes the focus of concern. To be most helpful, the consultant has to work on changing the school's atmosphere and structure. Sometimes the task requires the support of administrators who may not favor such an objective. In other cases, it involves asking school counselors to set up an environment in which other school personnel, mainly teachers, feel "that it is natural to consult and work with counselors" (Edgemon, Remley, & Snoddy, 1985, p. 298).

Group consultation sessions with teachers are an effective way to provide services for them and the schools in general. Offering consultation services for exceptional children, students, parents, curriculum developers, and community organizations takes time and effort but is worth it. Theoretical bases in the group consultation process include those that are person centered, Adlerian, and behavioral.

School counselors can also work from a parent-counselor consulting model, which aims to solve student problems (behavioral, attitudinal, or social) and educate parents on how to help their children with particular situations (Campbell, 1993; Ritchie & Partin, 1994). In offering consultation services to parents, counselors may face resistance, such as

- excuses ("I can't come during the day"),
- negative mind-sets ("My child is doing well; why bother me?"), and
- denial ("There is nothing wrong with my child's relationship to the school").

To overcome resistance, school counselors can be empathetic, arrange for parental observations of a child, help the parent refocus or reframe situations, and share parables (i.e., stories of similar situations).

One aspect of school consultation (which can be used in agency consultation too) is the use of peers. In the Structured Peer Consultation Model for School Counselors (SPCM-SC), a total of nine 90-minute sessions are held every other week in which counselors "use their basic helping skills" to help one another progress in their growth as professionals (Benshoff & Paisley, 1996, p. 314). Such a model makes use of talent within a group of similarly employed counselors and can be as useful and productive as more formalized supervision sessions.

Agency Consultation

According to Werner (1978), agency consultation resulted from the passage of the Community Mental Health Centers Act of 1963. Implicit within the act is the philosophy that mental health should be viewed from a local community perspective with an emphasis on prevention.

Caplan (1964) sets forth a three-level definition of *prevention.* The first level consists of *primary prevention,* a reduction in the incidents of mental disorders. This goal is achieved within the general population "by actively changing environments and settings and by teaching life skills" (Goodyear, 1976, p. 513). One of the primary activities at this level of intervention is consultation. *Secondary prevention,* a reduction in the duration of mental disorders, is the next focus. This goal is achieved by working with individuals to forestall or alleviate problem areas and attempting early detection and reversal of acute psychological crises. Finally, *tertiary prevention* is a reduction in the impairment that may result from psychological disorders. One way to conceptualize this level of prevention is as treatment. The more successful primary and secondary prevention are, the less need there is for tertiary prevention.

Examples abound of primary prevention in agency settings. Werner (1978) and Caplan and Caplan (1993) propose six levels of community mental health consultation:

1. *Client-centered case consultation.*   The goal is to enable the consultee to deal more effectively with the current situation and similar situations in the future.
2. *Consultee-centered case consultation.*   The goal is collaboratively to identify consultee difficulties in working with certain types of clients and help the consultee develop skills to deal effectively with this and similar situations in the future.
3. *Program-centered administrative consultation.*   The goal is to help the consultee deal more effectively with specific parts of a mental health program and improve his or her abilities to function with similar program problems in the future.
4. *Consultee-centered administrative consultation.*   The goal is to identify consultee problems generated by implementing a mental health program and develop collaboratively the consultee's skills in dealing with similar problems.

5. *Community-centered ad hoc consultation.* The goal is to enable an ad hoc consultee to deal more effectively with community problems encountered while developing a temporary program of mental health services.

6. *Consultee-centered ad hoc consultation.* The goal is to identify collaboratively the ad hoc consultee's problems generated in providing temporary mental health services and take steps to help the consultee develop skills in dealing with these problems.

Aplin (1985) points out that consultants who work with agencies such as public corporations, governments, or universities must be aware of trends that affect the process of consultation itself. He lists five trends that have continued to influence agency consultation:

- Downsizing of organizations
- Creation of semiautonomous work units brought about by mergers
- Rebirth of commitment leadership by managers
- Process-based technologies (such as robotics and computers) in manufacturing
- Egalitarian social and organizational values

Because of the rapid changes in agencies, consultation skills are in great demand, but "the key to successfully implementing systems change programs is to increase the basic skills the consultant brings to the change process." Aplin (1985) stresses that the demands on consultants "will grow in direct proportion to growth in organizational complexity and turbulence associated with underlying social and economic change" (p. 401).

Training in Consultation

Since the late 1970s, a number of models for training individuals in consultation skills have been proposed and developed (Brown, 1993; Brown, Pryzwansky, & Schulte, 1998; Conoley, 1981; Kratochwill & Bergan, 1978; Randolph, 1980). Most models are competency based and emphasize various modes of training consultants, such as didactic, laboratory, field placement, and supervision (Gallessich, 1974).

Stum's (1982) Directed Individual Response Educational Consulting Technique (DIRECT) is an excellent example of a model that has attempted to synthesize previous knowledge and help students learn what they are supposed to do in a consulting interview and how they are supposed to do it. Stum views consulting as a systematic process with sequential steps. The model is structured so that beginning students can conceptualize the consultation process developmentally. It includes the following steps: (a) establish consulting relationship, (b) identify and clarify the problem situation, (c) determine desired outcome, (d) develop ideas and strategies, (e) develop a plan, (f) specify the plan, and (g) confirm consulting relationship. The DIRECT model also specifies four sequential leads for each of the seven developmental steps. Based on systematic human relations training, these leads provide guidelines for the consultant and consultee to enter, initiate, educate, and evaluate each step in the consulting process. Cue words are provided for the consultant trainee at each step and level of the process. An evaluation chart, the Technique and Relationship Evaluation Chart (TREC), is available to assess the degree of competency that the consultant trainee achieves (see Figure 18.3).

Step A—Establish Consulting Format

Behavior	Lead
Level 1 The consultant listens, observes, repeats, and paraphrases. Attending and responding promotes understanding.	"You're saying that _____" "The problem seems to be _____" "So, the situation is _____"
Level 2 The consultant uses the term *consult* or *collaborate* in regards to working together. Explaining the use of a systematic process sets the tone for the interview.	"We can consult together about _____" "In our work, we'll use a problem-solving process."
Level 3 The consultant briefly explains the initial steps in the problem-resolution process. This is the first "teaching" of the model and further establishes the direction for the consulting interview.	"We'll go through several steps working together." "First, in clarifying the problem, we'll be _____" "Later on, we'll be trying to set some goals in regards to _____"
Level 4 The consultant "checks-in" regarding this step and then suggests moving ahead to the next step.	"Can we work together along these lines?" "Let's go ahead and clarify the problem further."

Step B—Identify-Clarify the Problem

Behavior	Lead
Level 1 The consultant clarifies the history, environment, causes and effects of the problem-situation.	"Tell me more about the background of _____" "What do you see as the effects of _____" "So, your position in this is that of _____"
Level 2 The consultant summarizes the major factors presented in the problem-situation. A dominant "theme" is stated.	The major factor seems to be _____" "Then to summarize, _____"

Figure 18.3 DIRECT chart

Source: From "DIRECT—A Consultation Skills Training Model," by D. Stum, 1982, *Personnel and Guidance Journal, 60*, p. 300. © 1982 by ACA. Reprinted with permission. No further reproduction authorized without written permission of the American Counseling Association.

Brown (1985, 1993) also proposes developmental stages for training human services consultants. He stresses didactic, laboratory, and field placement competencies that must be mastered. In addition, he elaborates on problems (e.g., resistance) and strategies to overcome these problems (e.g., ways to select proper interventions). His model requires instructors to help trainees master consultation skills by analyzing case histories, modeling cognitive strategies by talking through cases, and employing a Socratic method of inquiry. Brown emphasizes that the well-trained consultant should master conceptual and relationship skills at five discernable stages of consultation: (a) relationship or entry, (b) assessment or problem identification, (c) goal setting, (d) choosing and implementing change strategies, and (e) evaluation and termination.

Gallessich (1985) advocates that future consultation models and training be based on one of three models, which are not mutually exclusive:

- *Scientific/technological consultation.*   In this model, which focuses on knowledge deficits, the consultant's primary role is that of an expert on information and technique.
- *Human-development consultation.*   The consultant's primary role, according to this model, is to be an educator and facilitator in affective and cognitive processes that influence professional and personal relationships in an organization.
- *Social/political consultation.*   In this model, the consultant takes a partisan role to help change organizations so that they conform with particular values, such as democracy. Methods of training consultants in this model are still being developed.

In addition to training consultants, Zins (1993) emphasizes the need to educate consultees in skills such as problem solving, communication, and intervention techniques before the actual consultation process. If consultees have these skills, they can make better use of consultation services within specific environments.

Summary and Conclusion

Consultation is a systematic concept with a set of skills (Parsons, 1996). Although it is growing in importance, it is still in the process of being defined. Several definitions of *consultation* emphasize that it is primarily an indirect service; usually triadic; voluntary; and based on roles, rules, values, and goals. Consultation and counseling have distinct differences, such as the directness of the activity, the setting in which it is conducted, and the way communications are focused. Counselors are in an ideal position to function as human service consultants, but they must receive specialized training to do so (Brown, 1993).

The four models of comprehensive consultation found in the literature (i.e., expert [provision], doctor-patient [prescription], mediation, and process/collaboration) emphasize the multidimensional aspects of consultation. There are distinct consultation levels (individual, group, and organizational) and definite stages that the process goes through (e.g., phasing in, identifying problems, implementing, following up, terminating). Important skills and attitudes make up the complete process. Consultation is implemented in schools and agencies, and training models are being used to teach consultation skills. The concept and implementation of counselor as consultant are ideas that are still developing.

CLASSROOM ACTIVITIES

1. How do you distinguish consultation from counseling? Discuss your ideas with a fellow classmate and then with the class as a whole.
2. Which of the four comprehensive models of consultation do you think is most appropriate for clients you plan to work with in the future? Why? Which of these models do you consider least appropriate for your future work? Discuss your opinions with another classmate and then with the class as a whole.
3. Which stage in the consultation process do you think is most important? Which one do you think is most difficult? Are they the same? With three other classmates discuss what skills you possess that will enable you to be an effective consultant. Identify skills

you must refine or develop within yourself to work in this capacity.
4. What theoretical approach do you find most attractive as a basis for consultation services? Divide the class into groups based on similar orientations. After each group has had an opportunity to discuss its ideas, share them with fellow classmates.
5. Do you think there are other proactive activities counselors can engage in that cannot be classified as a part of counseling or consultation? What specific behaviors would you place in this category? Discuss your ideas in groups of four and then with the class as a whole.

REFERENCES

Aplin, J. C. (1985). Business realities and organizational consultation. *Counseling Psychologist, 13,* 396–402.

Barrow, J. C., & Prosen, S. S. (1981). A model of stress and counseling interventions. *Personnel and Guidance Journal, 60,* 5–10.

Benshoff, J. M., & Paisley, P. O. (1996). The structured peer consultation model for school counselors. *Journal of Counseling & Development, 74,* 314–318.

Brown, D. (1985). The preservice training and supervision of consultants. *Counseling Psychologist, 13,* 410–425.

Brown, D. (1993). Training consultants: A call to action. *Journal of Counseling and Development, 72,* 139–143.

Brown, D., Pryzwansky, W. B., & Schulte, A. C. (1998). *Psychological consultation* (4th ed.). Boston: Allyn & Bacon.

Brown, J. A. (1983). Consultation. In J. A. Brown & R. H. Pate, Jr. (Eds.), *Being a counselor: Directions and challenges* (pp. 124–146). Pacific Grove, CA: Brooks/Cole.

Bundy, M. L., & Poppen, W. A. (1986). School counselors' effectiveness as consultants: A research

review. *Elementary School Guidance and Counseling, 20,* 215–222.

Campbell, C. (1993). Strategies for reducing parent resistance to consultation in the schools. *Elementary School Guidance and Counseling, 28,* 83–90.

Caplan, G. (1964). *Principles of preventive psychiatry.* New York: Basic Books.

Caplan, G. (1970). *The theory and practice of mental health consultation.* New York: Basic Books.

Caplan, G., & Caplan, R. (1993). *Mental health consultation and collaboration.* San Francisco: Jossey-Bass.

Cecil, J. H., & Cobia, D. C. (1990). Educational challenge and change. In H. Hackney (Ed.), *Changing contexts for counselor preparation in the 1990s* (pp. 21–36). Alexandria, VA: Association for Counselor Education and Supervision.

Conoley, J. C. (1981). Emergent training issues in consultation. In J. C. Conoley (Ed.), *Consultation in schools: Theory, research procedures* (pp. 223–263). New York: Academic Press.

Conoley, J. C., & Conoley, C. W. (1992). *School consultation: Practice and training* (2nd ed.). Boston: Allyn & Bacon.

Conyne, R. K. (1975). Environmental assessment: Mapping for counselor action. *Personnel and Guidance Journal, 54,* 150–154.

Dinkmeyer, D. C. (1971). The "C" group: integrating knowledge and experience to change behavior. *Counseling Psychologist, 3,* 63–72.

Dinkmeyer, D. C. (1973). The parent C group. *Personnel and Guidance Journal, 52,* 4.

Dinkmeyer, D. C., & Carlson, J. (1973). *Consulting: Facilitating human potential and processes.* Upper Saddle River, NJ: Prentice Hall.

Dougherty, A. M. (1995). *Consultation: Practice and perspectives* (2nd ed.). Pacific Grove, CA: Brooks/Cole.

Drapela, V. J. (1983). Counseling, consultation, and supervision: A visual clarification of their relationship. *Personnel and Guidance Journal, 62,* 158–162.

Dustin, D., & Ehly, S. (1984). Skills for effective consultation. *School Counselor, 31,* 23–29.

Edgemon, A. W., Remley, T. P., Jr., & Snoddy, H. N. (1985). Integrating the counselor's point of view. *School Counselor, 32,* 296–301.

Fogle, D. O. (1979). Preparing students for the worst: The power of negative thinking. *Personnel and Guidance Journal, 57,* 364–367.

Fuqua, D. R., & Newman, J. L. (1985). Individual consultation. *Counseling Psychologist, 13,* 390–395.

Gallessich, J. (1974). Training the school psychologist for consultation. *Journal of School Psychology, 12,* 138–149.

Gallessich, J. (1982). *The profession and practice of consultation.* San Francisco: Jossey-Bass.

Gallessich, J. (1985). Toward a meta-theory of consultation. *Counseling Psychologist, 13,* 336–354.

Goodyear, R. K. (1976). Counselors as community psychologists. *Personnel and Guidance Journal, 54,* 512–516.

Hollis, J. W. (1997). *Counselor preparation, 1996–1998: Programs, personnel, trends* (9th ed.). Muncie, IN: Accelerated Development.

Jackson, D. N., & Hayes, D. H. (1993). Multicultural issues in consultation. *Journal of Counseling and Development, 72,* 144–147.

Kahn, W. J. (1976). Self-management: Learning to be our own counselor. *Personnel and Guidance Journal, 55,* 176–180.

Kahnweiler, W. M. (1979). The school counselor as consultant: A historical review. *Personnel and Guidance Journal, 57,* 374–380.

Keys, S. G., Bemak, F., Carpenter, S. L., & King-Sears, M. E. (1998). Collaborative consultant: A new role for counselors serving at-risk youths. *Journal of Counseling and Development, 76,* 123–133.

Kisch, R. M. (1977). Client as "consultant-observer" in the role-play model. *Personnel and Guidance Journal, 55,* 494–495.

Kratochwill, T. R., & Bergan, J. R. (1978). Training school psychologists: Some perspectives on competency-based behavioral consultation models. *Professional Psychology, 9,* 71–82.

Kurpius, D. J. (1978). Consultation theory and process: An integrated model. *Personnel and Guidance Journal, 56,* 335–338.

Kurpius, D. J. (1985). Consultation interventions: Successes, failures, and proposals. *Counseling Psychologist, 13,* 368–389.

Kurpius, D. J. (1986). Consultation: An important human and organizational intervention. *Journal of Counseling and Human Service Professions, 1,* 58–66.

Kurpius, D. J. (1988). *Handbook of consultation: An intervention for advocacy and outreach.* Alexandria, VA: American Counseling Association.

Kurpius, D. J., & Brubaker, J. C. (1976). *Psycho-educational consultation: Definitions-functions-preparation.* Bloomington: Indiana University Press.

Kurpius, D. J., & Fuqua, D. R. (1993). Fundamental issues in defining consultation. *Journal of Counseling and Development, 71,* 598–600.

Kurpius, D. J., Fuqua, D. R., & Rozecki, T. (1993). The consulting process: A multidimensional approach. *Journal of Counseling and Development, 71,* 601–606.

Kurpius, D. J., & Robinson, S. E. (1978). An overview of consultation. *Personnel and Guidance Journal, 56,* 321–323.

Lee, C. C., & Walz, G. R. (1998). *Social action: A mandate for counselors.* Alexandria, VA: American Counseling Association.

McCarthy, M., & Sorenson, G. (1993). School counselors and consultants: Legal duties and liabilities. *Journal of Counseling and Development, 72,* 159–167.

Nelson, R. C., & Shifron, R. (1985). Choice awareness in consultation. *Counselor Education and Supervision, 24,* 298–306.

Newman, J. L. (1993). Ethical issues in consultation. *Journal of Counseling and Development, 72,* 148–156.

O'Brien, B. A., & Lewis, M. (1975). A community adolescent self-help center. *Personnel and Guidance Journal, 54,* 212–216.

Otwell, P. S., & Mullis, F. (1997). Counselor-led staff development: An efficient approach to teacher consultation. *Professional School Counseling, 1,* 25–30.

Parsons, R. D. (1996). *The skilled consultant: A systematic approach to the theory and practice of consultation.* Boston: Allyn & Bacon.

Podemski, R. S., & Childers, J. H., Jr. (1980). The counselor as change agent: An organizational analysis. *School Counselor, 27,* 168–174.

Randolph, D. (1980). Teaching consultation for mental health and educational settings. *Counselor Education and Supervision, 33,* 117–123.

Randolph, D. L., & Graun, K. (1988). Resistance to consultation: A synthesis for counselor-consultants. *Journal of Counseling and Development, 67,* 182–184.

Ritchie, M. H., & Partin, R. L. (1994). Parent education and consultation activities of school counselors. *School Counselor, 41,* 165–170.

Schein, E. H. (1978). The role of the consultant: Content expert or process facilitator? *Personnel and Guidance Journal, 56,* 339–343.

Schmidt, J. J. (1999). *Counseling in schools* (3rd ed.). Boston: Allyn & Bacon.

Schmidt, J. J., & Osborne, W. L. (1981). Counseling and consultation: Separate processes or the same? *Personnel and Guidance Journal, 60,* 168–170.

Solomon, C. (1982). Special issue on political action: Introduction. *Personnel and Guidance Journal, 60,* 580.

Splete, H. H. (1982). Consultation by the counselor. *Counseling and Human Development, 15,* 1–7.

Stum, D. (1982). DIRECT: A consultation skills training model. *Personnel and Guidance Journal, 60,* 296–302.

Umansky, D. L., & Holloway, E. L. (1984). The counselor as consultant: From model to practice. *School Counselor, 31,* 329–338.

Voight, N. L., Lawler, A., & Fulkerson, K. F. (1980). Community- based guidance: A "Tupperware party" approach to mid-life decision making. *Personnel and Guidance Journal, 59,* 106–107.

Wallace, W. A., & Hall, D. L. (1996). *Psychological consultation: Perspectives and applications.* Pacific Grove, CA: Brooks/Cole.

Werner, J. L. (1978). Community mental health consultation with agencies. *Personnel and Guidance Journal, 56,* 364–368.

Zins, J. E. (1993). Enhancing consultee problem-solving skills in consultative interactions. *Journal of Counseling and Development, 72,* 185–188.

19

EVALUATION AND RESEARCH

◆

There you sit Alice Average

midway back in the long-windowed classroom

in the middle of Wednesday's noontime blahs,

Adjusting yourself to the sound of a lecture

and the cold of the blue plastic desk that supports you.

In a world full of light words, hard rock,

Madonnas, long hair, confusion and change

Dreams fade like blue jeans

and "knowing" goes beyond the books

that are bound in semester days

and studied until the start of summer. . . .

Evaluation and research are essential parts of counseling. It is not enough for counselors to be warm, caring, and empathetic persons trained in the theories, methods, and techniques of counseling. Rather, counselors must be evaluators and researchers, too, for it is through evaluation and research that they come to understand and improve their practices (Hadley & Mitchell, 1995; May, 1996). Counselors who lack research and evaluation abilities place themselves and the counseling profession in jeopardy with the general public, third-party payers, and specific clients who rightfully demand accountability. A failure to evaluate and research counseling methods also puts counselors in danger of being unethical because they cannot prove that the counseling services they offer have a reasonable promise of success as the ethical codes of the professional counseling associations require (Sexton & Whiston, 1996).

Thus, evaluation and research are ways counselors can ensure quality client care and positive outcomes (Herman, 1993). These counseling procedures also help counselors pause and examine their practices. At such times, counselors may "think differently about, and even behave differently in counseling," thereby improving themselves and the profession (Watkins & Schneider, 1991, p. 288).

Being an evaluator, a researcher, and a consumer of evaluations and research demands time and a thorough understanding of the commonly used methods in these domains (Sexton, 1996). This chapter explores the processes of evaluation and research in counseling, with the assumption that counselors can cultivate skills in these areas.

The Nature of Evaluation and Research

Evaluation and research are different, yet they have much in common. Wheeler and Loesch (1981) note that the two terms have often been paired conceptually and are frequently used interchangeably. Krauskopf (1982) asserts that there is "essentially no difference between the two. The same empirical attitude is there, and the same tools are needed" (p. 71). However, Burck and Peterson (1975) make a distinction between the concepts. According to these authors, *evaluation* "is more mission-oriented, may be less subject to control, is more concerned with providing information for decision makers, tends to be less rigorous or sophisticated, and is concerned primarily with explaining events and their relationship to established goals and objectives" (p. 564). For example, in counselor preparation programs, students may prepare a portfolio as an end of the term project on which they will be evaluated (i.e., receive a grade). Based on their grade, faculty and students decide how much progress has been made and whether to continue their course of study. Whether academic or clinical, "quality services, careful evaluation, and good communication of evaluation" are the three main components of a solid counseling program (Ohlsen, 1983, p. 357). If evaluation is not conducted or positive results are not disseminated, a counseling program will most likely suffer.

Research, on the other hand, is "more theory-oriented and discipline-bound, exerts greater control over the activity, produces more results that may not be immediately applicable, is more sophisticated in terms of complexity and exactness of design, involves the use of judgment on the part of the researcher, and is more concerned with explaining and predicting phenomena" (Burck, & Peterson, 1975, p. 564). For example, counselors may conduct research to assess which of several theoretical techniques has the most positive results when applied to a client population all suffering from the same disorder, such as anxiety. In such a setting, variables, such as age, gender, and cultural background, are controlled as tightly as possible so that the researcher can be accurate in gaining a clear picture of what works and on whom so that the results can be reported and the findings translated appropriately. In counseling research, most counselors are *applied researchers:* they use knowledge from research studies in their own work settings.

In the following sections, we will explore how evaluation and research are commonly employed in the practical world of professional counseling.

Evaluation

Evaluation usually involves gathering meaningful information on various aspects of a counseling program to guide decisions about the allocation of resources and assure maximum program effectiveness (Gay, 1996; Wheeler & Loesch, 1981). Evaluation has a quality of immediate utility. In clinical settings, it gives counselors direct feedback on the services they provide and insight into what new services they need to offer. It also enables clients to have systematic, positive input into a counseling program. Some type of evaluation should be provided for every counseling program regardless of the setting (Hosie, 1994; Oetting, 1976).

Incorrect Evaluation Methods

Although many solid models of evaluation are available, there are a number of incorrect evaluation procedures used by the uninformed (Daniels, Mines, & Gressard, 1981). These ill-conceived methods, which produce invalid and unreliable results, have some or all of the following defects (Burck & Peterson, 1975):

- They restrict opinion sampling.
- They make comparisons between nonequivalent groups.
- They promote services rather than evaluate.
- They try to assess a program without any clear goals.

Steps in Evaluation

Program evaluation should be systematic and follow a sequential step-by-step process. The steps may vary in different evaluations, but a procedure that Burck and Peterson (1975) have laid out for implementing an evaluation program is a solid one to follow.

According to Burck and Peterson, the first step in formulating an evaluation program involves a *needs assessment*. If counselors are to be accountable, they must first identify problems or concerns within their programs. A *need* is "a condition among members of a specific group . . . that reflects an actual lack of something or an awareness (perception) that something is lacking" (Collison, 1982, p. 115). Needs are assumed to exist based on a number of factors, such as institutional or personal philosophy, government mandate, available resources, history or tradition, and expert opinion. "Need assessment techniques include clearly identifying the target of the survey, specifying a method of contact, and resolving measurement-related issues" (Cook, 1989, p. 463).

The second step in evaluation is "stating goals and performance objectives." Here, both *terminal program outcomes* (those that are most immediately recognizable) and *ultimate program outcomes* (those that are most enduring) are described in terms of measurable performance objectives. There are normally "several performance objectives for each goal statement" (Burck & Peterson, 1975, p. 567).

The third step in evaluation is designing a program. When a program is developed to meet stated objectives, activities that focus on the stated goals can be precisely designed. The fourth step is revising and improving a program. Specific activities and the adequacy of communication patterns are both evaluated at this point.

The fifth and final step is "noting and reporting program outcome" (Burck & Peterson, 1975, p. 567). This task is performed primarily by disseminating the findings of the program evaluation to the general public. Such consumer information is vital for potential clients if they are to make informed decisions, and counselors within a clinical program need this kind of feedback to improve their skills and services.

Evaluators must get others involved in the evaluation process for the results of the study to have any direct impact on a program. Individuals who have an investment in conducting a needs assessment are more likely to help counselors meet identified needs and establish program goals than those people who are not involved.

Selecting an Evaluation Model

Because evaluation is a continual part of their profession, counselors must prepare accordingly (Wheeler & Loesch, 1981). Part of this preparation includes setting aside time to conduct evaluations. Equally important is educating oneself and others about the different models of evaluation available. House (1978) offers a list of evaluation models and the critical dimensions of each (see Table 19.1). The models are systems analysis, behavioral objectives, decision making, goal free, art criticism, accreditation, adversary, and transaction.

Daniels et al. (1981) studied the dimensions along which these major evaluation models are judged and have offered some practical ways of comparing them to determine the most appropriate model for a specific situation. They note that both internal and external restrictions "define the limits to which each model may be effectively applied" (p. 580). They provide a framework to help counselors judge which model to employ in given situations (see Figure 19.1).

Questions raised before an evaluation (i.e., a priori questions) are more likely to be answered satisfactorily than those brought up after an evaluation is complete (ex post facto questions). Therefore, evaluators must ask themselves at the outset what they wish

Table 19.1 Comparison of major evaluation models

Type of Model	Major Audiences	Outcome	Consensual Assumptions	Methodology	Typical Questions
Systems analysis	Economists managers	Program efficiency	Goals, known cause and effects, quantified variables	PPBS, cost-benefit analysis	Are the expected effects achieved? What are the most efficient programs?
Behavioral objectives	Managers, psychologists	Productivity, accountability	Prespecified objectives, quantified variables	Behavioral objectives, achievement tests	Are the students achieving the objectives? Is the teacher producing?
Decision making	Administrators	Effectiveness, quality control	General goals, evaluation criteria	Surveys, questionnaires, interviews, natural variation	Is the program effective? What parts are effective?
Goal free	Consumers	Consumer choices, social utility	Consequences, evaluation criteria	Bias control, logical analysis	What are all of the effects of the program?
Art criticism	Connoisseurs, consumers	Improved standards	Critics, standards of criticism	Critical review	Would a critic approve this program?
Accreditation	Professional peers, public	Professional acceptance	Panel of peers, procedures and criteria for evaluation	Review by panel, self-study	How would professionals rate this program?
Adversary	Jury, public	Resolution	Procedures, judges	Quasi-legal procedures	What are the arguments for and against the program?
Transaction	Client practitioners	Understanding	Negotiations, activities	Case studies, interviews, observations	What does the program look like to different people?

Source: From "A Meta-model for Evaluating Counseling Programs," by M. H. Daniels, R. Mines, and C. Gressard, 1981 (adapted from House, 1978), *Personnel and Guidance Journal, 59*, p. 579. © 1981 by ACA. Reprinted with permission. No further reproduction authorized without written permission of the American Counseling Association.

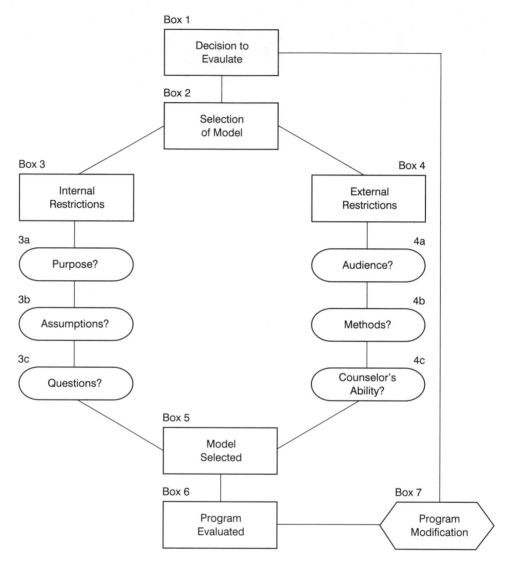

Figure 19.1   An evaluation framework

Source: From "A Meta-model for Evaluating Counseling Programs," by M. H. Daniels, R. Mines, and C. Gressard, 1981, *Personnel and Guidance Journal, 59*, p. 581. © 1981 by ACA. Reprinted with permission. No further reproduction authorized without written permission of the American Counseling Association.

to evaluate and how they are going to do it (Davidson, 1986). Two models incorporate these concerns: the planning, programming, budgeting systems (PPBS) and the context-input-process-product (CIPP) model (Humes, 1972; Stufflebeam et al., 1971).

The *PPBS model* emphasizes planning programs with specifically stated goals, objectives, and evaluation criteria. The situation, population, and treatment involved are all major concerns of this model. Humes (1972) points out that information derived from a

PPBS model is *criterion referenced* (related directly to the dimension being measured) rather than *normative referenced* (related to other members of a group, as is the case when standardized tests are used). Therefore, if proper planning and programming are carried out, the evaluator is able to demonstrate that effective counseling is an important variable in a client's progress. Moreover, when budgeting decisions are being made, the impact of counseling and its cost-effectiveness can be clearly shown and program strengths and weaknesses can be documented. Counseling services administrators are in a better position at such times to justify requests for funds for developing and delivering services not currently being provided. This aspect of program analysis is vital.

The *CIPP model* presents four types of evaluation. In the first, *context evaluation*, a comparison is made between what the program set out to do and what it actually accomplished. In the second, *input evaluation*, information is gathered about what resources are needed and which are available to meet program objectives. This part of the evaluation demonstrates cost-effectiveness and points out the need for additional resources as well. The third type of evaluation, *process evaluation*, focuses on the strengths and weaknesses of the program's design. If there are weaknesses, such as the design of communication flow, corrective measures may be taken. The fourth type of evaluation, *product evaluation*, focuses on the final results of the entire program. At this stage evaluators ask how effective the program really was. Plans can be made to continue, reuse, expand, or eliminate the program. Regardless of the type of evaluation used, most evaluation processes employ research in reaching their conclusions.

Counselors and Research

The profession of counseling has had "a long and ambivalent relationship" with research (Sprinthall, 1981, p. 465). "The word research has a certain mystique about it" (Leedy, 1997, p. 5). It suggests an activity that is exclusive, elusive, and removed from everyday life. Some counselors are drawn to research because of its mystique and their own general interests in investigation. However, "research typically evokes emotional reactions of fear, anxiety, and even disdain" among other counselors (Fall & VanZandt, 1997, p. 2). These counselors feel that the majority of research studies are poorly related to their practical needs. Furthermore, they perceive research as cold and impersonal (Krauskopf, 1982).

Some practitioners find that the demands of daily work with clients leaves them little time to be investigative let alone keep up with the latest findings and outcome studies (Sexton, 1993). Therefore, most counselors do not engage in research activities, and there appears to be a serious gap in the integration of research into the practice of counseling (Sexton & Whiston, 1996). Indeed, a number of counselor practitioners have even "shown evidence of hostility and resentment toward researchers" and research (Robinson, 1994, p. 339).

Counselors' negative feelings about research and their reluctance to spend time and energy on it is related to a number of factors, chief among which are:

- a lack of knowledge about research methods,
- an absence of clear goals and objectives for the programs in which they work,

- a lack of awareness of the importance of research in planning effective treatment procedures,
- a fear of finding negative results,
- a discouragement from peers or supervisors,
- a lack of financial support, and
- low aptitudes and limited abilities for conducting investigative studies (Heppner & Anderson, 1985; Sexton, 1993).

In addition, some counseling theories deemphasize the importance of empirical investigations.

Yet, despite the strain between some counselors and research, there are similarities between the activities of counseling practice and outcome research. Both involve a six-stage process (Whiston, 1996) (see Table 19.2).

For instance, the first stage in both processes involves identification. In counseling the identification is of a client's problem or difficulty while in research the focus is on identifying a question or questions to investigate. Similarly, in step 2, there is an analogy in formulating treatment goals and formulating a research design. Then a determining stage follows in which in counseling interventions are selected, whereas in research methods for ensuring treatment integrity are chosen. In the fourth stage action occurs in the form of either implementing counseling or collecting data, followed by an appraisal and evaluation of progress in counseling or data analysis in research. Finally, both processes end with either the completion of counseling or the interpretation and conclusions from research.

Research

There are many definitions of research, but Barkley (1982) gives one of the best: "*Research is the systematic collection, organization, and interpretation of observations in order to answer questions as unambiguously as possible*" (p. 329; my emphasis). The challenge of

Table 19.2 Analogous stages of counseling practice and the research process

Stages in Counseling	Stages in Outcome Research
1. Identification of problems or difficulties	1. Identification of research question(s)
2. Formulation of goals	2. Formulation of research design
3. Determine interventions	3. Determine methods for ensuring treatment integrity and measures of outcome
4. Implementation of counseling	4. Data collection
5. Appraisal and evaluation of progress	5. Data analysis
6. Termination	6. Interpretation and conclusions

Source: From "Accountability through Action Research: Research Methods for Practitioners," by S. C. Whiston, 1996, *Journal of Counseling and Development, 74,* p. 617. © 1996 by ACA. Reprinted with permission. No further reproduction authorized without written permission of the American Counseling Association.

research is to answer questions that do not yield truths easily. The quality of research depends on the degree to which resistance can be overcome and ways can be devised to answer questions with maximum confidence by minimizing contaminating influences.

Steps in the Research Process

Good research is scientific in the broadest definition of the word. It begins with systematic observations that concentrate on a particular population, variable, or question (Gay, 1996; Heppner, Kivlighan, & Wampold, 1992). Such complete and systematic observation attempts to explain relations among variables and why certain events happen. Explanation leads to understanding and eventually to some degree of prediction and control.

Some guidelines for conducting research investigations are available. Campbell and Katona (1953), for instance, developed a flowchart to indicate the sequence of steps involved in carrying out surveys. More recently, Ary (1996) devised the following eight-step process for conducting research. It is ideally suited for clinical work but is also applicable to other areas of counseling research.

1. *Statement of the problem.* This statement must be clear and concise. If there is confusion at this step, the investigative endeavor will probably produce little of value. An example of a clear problem statement is "The purpose of this research is to test the hypothesis that eye contact between counselor and client is related to the effectiveness of the counseling process."

2. *Identification of information needed to solve the problem.* This step may include a variety of information derived from sources such as psychological or educational tests or systematic observations, including experiments. Some data that investigators need may be impossible to collect. They must then decide whether to modify the problem statement or end the research.

3. *Selection or development of measures for gathering data.* Common measures for gathering data are surveys, tests, and observational report sheets. If researchers cannot find an existing appropriate measure, they must develop one and test its reliability and validity.

4. *Identification of the target population and sampling procedures.* If a group is small enough, an entire population may be studied. Otherwise, a sample is selected by careful standard sampling procedures.

5. *Design of the procedure for data collection.* This step involves determining how, when, where, and by whom information will be collected.

6. *Collection of data.* A systematic procedure is implemented to obtain the desired information. Usually this process involves careful monitoring and a substantial investment of time.

7. *Analysis of data.* Select procedures are employed at this step to organize the data in a meaningful fashion and determine whether they provide an answer to the problem being investigated.

8. *Preparation of a report.* Research results should be made available to others in some meaningful form, such as a journal article or a professional presentation.

The Relevance of Research

One primary question raised by readers of counseling research focuses on the relevance of a study's results for practitioners. Much research does not produce results relevant to practical issues and is not useful (Goldman, 1976, 1977, 1978, 1979, 1986, 1992). Many research efforts lack vision, concentrating instead on small details. Researchers who conduct their work in such a way have too readily accepted the experimental research designs of the physical and biological sciences and, in the process, have failed to develop research methods appropriate for counseling. What they pass on as research is often sterile and trivial.

The argument for research relevancy centers on the fact that not all knowledge is equally useful for counselors (Krumboltz & Mitchell, 1979). Therefore, limited funds and energy should be directed toward studies that are likely to make a difference in the way in which counselors function. One way to define relevance in research is to emphasize studies that focus on the reasons individuals seek counseling, such as their goals, intentions, and purposes (Howard, 1985). Another important way to assess relevance is to determine "how closely the research approximates what is done in the counseling office" (Gelso, 1985, p. 552). Such research is called *experience-near research.* Because it is applicable to counselors, it is likely to be read and used. *Action research* is a form of experience-near research. It focuses on resolving practical problems that counselors routinely encounter, such as how to help manage a child with learning disabilities or evaluate the effects of a self-esteem program on a group of children (Gillies, 1993). Action research includes studies aimed at diagnostic action, participant action, empirical action, and experimental action. Some of this research is likely to be less controlled and not as easily generalized as more rigorous research. To help solve the problem of relevancy in research, Gelso (1985) suggests reading all research studies with certain questions in mind—for example, "How was this research conducted?" and "How will it influence the way I practice counseling?"

Choosing a Research Method

Despite problems inherent in counseling research, counselors regularly employ a number of investigative methodologies. Kaplan (1964) defines a *method* as a procedure that is applicable to many disciplines. In contrast, a *technique* is a discipline-specific procedure. Most counseling research uses procedures, such as controlled observations, that are common to other disciplines. Therefore, the term *method* rather than *technique* is appropriate when referring to ways of doing counseling research. None of these methods is considered "best to test the counseling process" (Hill, 1982, p. 16). Rather, different research methods address different research questions (Watkins & Schneider, 1991). Ultimately, research methods provide answers to research questions by controlling select variables that have an impact on the counseling process (Kerlinger, 1986).

All research methods have what Gelso (1979) describes as *bubbles,* or flaws. Gelso says that selecting research methods is like putting a sticker on a car windshield. Bubbles always appear; and even though one may try to eliminate as many bubbles as possible, some remain. The only way to eliminate the bubbles totally is to remove the sticker. In research, the only way to avoid all flaws is not to do research. Yet as imperfect as research methods are, they are necessary for professional edification and development. The alternative is to remain uninformed about the effects of counseling and forgo the development of newer methods and techniques.

Emphases of Research

Counseling research has several different emphases. Four of the most prominent can be represented as contrasts (Bloland, 1992; Gelso, 1979; Hill, 1982; Neimeyer & Resnikoff, 1982):

- Laboratory versus field research
- Basic versus applied research
- Process versus outcome research
- Quantitative (group) versus qualitative (individual) research

Each of these emphases is concerned with the contrast between two investigative dimensions. The various dimensions are not mutually exclusive; many research studies, such as those that quantitatively report the outcome of counseling techniques in a laboratory setting, include more than one of them.

The first emphasis is on laboratory research versus field research. *Laboratory research* concentrates on conducting the investigation within a confined environment, such as a counseling lab, where as many extraneous variables as possible may be controlled (Dobson & Campbell, 1986). Under such conditions, some researchers think they can obtain the most reliable information. Practitioners of *field research,* on the other hand, see laboratory investigations as artificial and believe that counseling theories and techniques are best observed and recorded in actual counseling situations, such as counseling centers and clinics. They argue that these settings are realistic and that the results are likely to be applicable to other practitioners.

The second emphasis is basic research versus applied research. *Basic research* is oriented to theory, and those who practice it are "interested in investigating some puzzle or problem that is suggested by theory" (Forsyth & Strong, 1986, p. 113). An example is the work of Wilder Penfield in probing select parts of the brain to verify Eric Berne's theory of distinct ego states within the person. In contrast, *applied research* focuses on examining practical problems and applying their findings to existing problems. An example of applied research is the work of Jesness (1975), who compared the effectiveness of transactional analysis and behavior modification in counseling delinquents. Tracey (1991) offers one way of distinguishing basic and applied research (see Figure 19.2).

Figure 19.2 Relation of basic research, applied research, and practice

Source: From "Counseling Research as an Applied Science," by T. J. Tracey, 1991, in C. E. Watkins, Jr., and L. J. Schneider (Eds.), *Research in Counseling* (p. 27), Hillsdale, NJ: Erlbaum. © 1991 by Lawrence Erlbaum Associates, Inc. Used with permission.

The third emphasis is process research versus outcome research. According to Hill (1991), *process research* focuses on what "happens in counseling and therapy sessions" (p. 85). She states that identifying the changes in counseling "can be quite overwhelming and frustrating" (1982, p. 7). It demands a concentrated amount of time and energy focused on a few variables, such as the reactions of the counselor to the client. The burnout rate among process-oriented researchers is high. Yet such research is indispensable in enlightening counselors about the dynamics of the counseling relationship itself. An example of process research is the work of Allen Ivey (1980) in assessing the importance of counselor skills in select stages of counseling. *Outcome research,* on the other hand, is "the experimental investigation of the impact of counseling on clients" (Lambert, Masters, & Ogles, 1991, p. 51). It is "typified by measurement before and after treatment on specified dependent variables" (Hill, 1982, p. 7). An example of outcome research would be the effect of person-centered counseling with depressed persons. Outcome research emphasizes results rather than the factors producing them.

The fourth emphasis is quantitative research versus qualitative research (i.e., naturalistic inquiry). Neimeyer and Resnikoff (1982) describe *quantitative research* as deductive and objective, usually subordinating subjective understanding to clarity, precision, and reproducibility of objective phenomena. A quantitative approach is based on a positive-reductive conceptual system that "values objectivity, linearity, cause and effect, repeatability, and reproductivity, predictability, and the quantification of data" (Merchant & Dupuy, 1996, p. 538).

In contrast, *qualitative research* is "inductive and phenomenological, placing primary emphasis on understanding the unique frameworks within which persons make sense of their feelings, thoughts, and behaviors" (Neimeyer & Resnikoff, 1982, p. 84). It focuses on understanding a complex social situation without previously defined parameters (Jencius & Rotter, 1998). Furthermore, "qualitative research examines what people are doing and how they interpret what is occurring rather than pursuing patterns of cause and effect in a controlled setting" (Merchant & Dupuy, 1996, p. 537).

Thus, the emphasis of these two approaches differs because of the different assumptions each makes about the goals of research (Bloland, 1992; May, 1996; Merchant & Dupuy, 1996). Neither quantitative nor qualitative research is superior to the other per se. Rather, the use of each depends on what question is being asked and for what reason. The major strength of quantitative research is its emphasis on analyzing large amounts of data in a clear, mathematical fashion. The major strength of qualitative research is the way it picks up subtle, individually focused, developmental, and experientially reported aspects of counseling (Denzin & Lincoln, 1994; Mertens, 1998).

Counseling is moving toward espousing research that is more qualitative (versus quantitative) and more field oriented (versus laboratory) (Goldman, 1992; Watkins & Schneider, 1991). Clients are seen as active rather than passive in the counseling process (Gelso, 1985; Howard, 1985). Overall, a more holistic emphasis within counseling research is being proposed (Froehle, 1985).

Major Research Methods

The research methods that counselors choose are determined by the questions they are trying to answer, their special interests, and the amount of time and resources they have available for the study (Heppner et al., 1992). Methods should be the slaves of research, not the masters (Smith, 1981). No method is suitable for all research attempts. Indeed, as Ohlsen (1983) states, "developing and clarifying a research question is a slow, painstaking process" (p. 361). A *research question* provides the context in which one begins to consider a method. There are so many quantitative and qualitative methods and designs available that deciding on one can take considerable time.

Methods and ways of obtaining data may differ for research conducted in personal, group, or couple/family counseling. A research strategy, which is "the guiding or underlying force that directs" a research project, is intended to place the investigator "in the most advantageous position" possible (Husband & Foster, 1987, p. 53). The primary research method can be chosen from among those that present data from historical, descriptive, or experimental points of view (Galfo & Miller, 1976; Vacc & Loesch, 1994). The procedures used in these methods are not mutually exclusive. For example, Tracey (1983) reports that *N of 1 research,* which focuses on the study of a single qualitative entity (such as a person), may be employed in historical studies, case studies, and intensive design studies. Such research may be either associational or experimental. The fact that this and other research methods are so flexible gives investigators more latitude in planning their strategies and carrying out their studies.

Historical Methods. Historical research has been largely neglected in counseling (Goldman, 1977). The reasons are numerous, but among the most salient is the association of historical research with psychohistory (Frey, 1978). Psychohistory has been closely linked to the theory of psychoanalysis, and its usefulness as a way of understanding persons and events has been questioned (Thoresen, 1978). Yet as Frey (1978) reports, psychohistory as practiced by Erik Erikson (1958) and the Wellfleet group (whose members included Kenneth Keniston and Robert Coles) involves two aspects:

- experiencing and reporting events and procedures from earlier times that have influenced the development of the profession, and
- embellishing current theories and generating new research hypotheses.

For the most part, counseling journals limit their dealings with historical research to printing obituaries of prominent counselors and featuring interviews with pioneers in the profession (Heppner, 1990). Although the methods used in historical research are usually less rigorous and more qualitative than those employed in other research, they produce both interesting and enlightening results. They have an important place in the understanding of persons, as exemplified in Gordon Allport's idiographic studies of traits and personality. This approach to research is clearly open to further development.

Descriptive Methods. Descriptive research concentrates on depicting present factors in a profession. It has three subcategories: surveys, case studies, and comparative studies.

Surveys. Surveys are one of the most popular and widely used methods for gathering information about the occurrence of behaviors and describing the characteristics of those that are not well understood (Fong, 1992; Heppner et al., 1992). Surveys are similar to other methods of research: they begin with the formation of a research question, then generate hypotheses, select a research design, and collect and analyze data (Kerlinger, 1986). Survey data can be collected in four ways: personal interviews, mailed question-naires, telephone interviews, and nonreactive measures such as existing records or archives (Hackett, 1981; Marken, 1981; Moser & Kalton, 1972). Data are gathered in either a structured or nonstructured way with either a *cross-section* of people (many people at one point in time) or *longitudinally* (the same people at two or more points in time).

If conducted properly, survey research can provide counselors with a great deal of information about how clients perceive them and their programs. Surveys can also offer information about clients' needs (Heppner et al., 1992; Hosie, 1994). Nevertheless, four major problems often plague survey research. First, survey instruments may be poorly constructed. Second, they may not generate a very high rate of return. Third, the sample surveyed is sometimes nonrandom and unrepresentative of the population (Hackett, 1981; Marken, 1981). In any of these three cases, the results are essentially useless because the design and methodology of the survey research lack rigor (Fong, 1992). A final prob-lem of survey research (or almost any research, for that matter) is that it can be expensive (Robinson, 1994).

The social impact of well-conceived and well-conducted survey research is apparent in the work of Kinsey on the sexual practices of men and women. The Hollis (1997) survey is an example of the usefulness of the method for counseling. Every few years Hollis has gathered information for a published directory of counselor education programs. This survey is quanti-tative in emphasis and yields relevant data about national program trends in counseling.

Case Studies.   A *case study* is an attempt to understand one unit, such as a person, group, or program, through an intense and systematic investigation of that unit longitudinally. "Almost any phenomenon can be examined by means of the case study method" (Leedy, 1997, p. 157). Some case studies rely on self-report methods that are not very reliable; oth-ers involve naturalistic inquiry in which the study extends over a period of time (Smith, 1981). The difficulties involved in naturalistic research are many and include issues such as what constitutes good research, the high cost of labor, the problems of establishing causal-ity, and restrictions on generalizing results. In addition, they often demonstrate problems of observed bias and the *halo effect* (a favorable observation generalized to a person or sit-uation as a whole) (Goldman, 1977). To help minimize such problems, Anton (1978) and Huber (1980) describe several intensive experimental designs suitable for case studies. Counselors with limited time and resources may find them useful in tracing changes over time. These designs will be discussed in a later section on experimental methods.

Comparative Studies.   *Comparative research studies* (also called *correlational studies*) form a link between historical/case study methods and experimental and quasi-experimen-tal designs. They make directional and quantitative comparisons between sets of data. Such studies are nonmanipulative (Cozby, 1997). They simply note similarities in variations among factors with no effort to discern cause-and-effect relationships. An example of such a study is the relationship of scores on a test of religiosity with scores on instruments mea-suring various aspects of mental health (Gladding, Lewis, & Adkins, 1981). A major finding of this study was that people who scored high on the religiosity test also scored high on the mental health instruments. The results do not suggest that religiosity causes a person to have better mental health; rather, it simply compares the direction of the scores. Any study that compares measures in this manner is an example of comparative research.

Experimental Methods. *Experimental research* methods are employed to describe, compare, and analyze data under controlled conditions (Galfo & Miller, 1976; Heppner et al., 1992; McLeod, 1995;). Experimental methods used in counseling research have their origin in the natural sciences. The purpose of using these methods is to determine the effect of one variable on another by controlling for other factors that might explain the effect. In other words, researchers who use this method are seeking to determine causation. To do this, they define independent and dependent variables. The *independent variable* is the one manipulated by the researcher, such as treatment. The *dependent variable* is the one in which the potential effect is recorded, such as the client's behavior. The researcher assumes that if the effect of other factors is eliminated, then any change in the dependent variable will be a result of the independent variable. Examples of independent variables in counseling might be the age, gender, personal attractiveness, or physical appearance of the counselor. Examples of dependent variables are client's reactions to these counselor traits, such as degree of relaxation, cooperation, and overall responsiveness in the counseling setting. The reactions could be measured by a variety of procedures, including an analysis of an audio- or videotape or a postcounseling interview or questionnaire.

Cohen (1990) recommends two general principles for those who are conducting research with independent and dependent variables: less is more, and simple is better. The fewer variables there are to keep track of and the more clearly they can be reported (e.g., through graphs), the easier it is for researchers and consumers to understand the significance of counseling research studies.

It is imperative in conducting experimental research that the counselor be sure to control for *contaminating variables* (variables that invalidate a study, such as one group of clients that is healthier than another). One of the most common ways of controlling for potentially contaminating variables is by establishing equivalent experimental and control groups. When the independent variable is manipulated for the experimental group while being held constant for the control group, the effect of the independent variable can be determined by comparing the postexperimental data for the two groups. Campbell and Stanley (1963) describe in detail the problems involved in experimental and quasi-experimental research; their work is recommended to readers who wish to pursue the issue further.

Traditional experimental research has involved group comparison studies. Since the 1970s, however, *single-subject research*, commonly known as *N of 1* research, has become increasingly popular. Miller (1985, p. 491) summarizes six major advantages that single-subject research has over traditional group studies. (His study is derived from Hill, Carter, & O'Farrell [1983] and Sue [1978]).

1. It allows a more adequate description of what happens between a counselor and client.
2. Positive and negative outcomes can be understood in terms of process data.
3. Outcome measures can be tailored to the client's specific problems.
4. It allows for the study of a rare or unusual phenomenon.

5. It is flexible enough to allow for novel procedures in diagnosis and treatment.
6. It can be used in evaluating the effectiveness of an intervention strategy on a single client.

A potential problem in single-subject studies is "when they are used following a period of standard treatment that has not worked. Some general improvement may occur that has nothing to do with the treatment being used but is a *regression toward the mean* (i.e., "the tendency of an extreme value when it is remeasured to be closer to the mean"; Aldridge, 1994, p. 337). To overcome this problem, especially if medication is involved, the researcher may allow for a *washout period*: a time when no treatment occurs and there is an opportunity for previous effects (such as medication) to leave the body by natural means.

Anton (1978) and Huber (1980) describe three intense experimental designs that focus on individuals: simple time series, reversal design, and multiple baseline design.

Simple Time Series.   A simple time series, the most common intense experimental design method, is referred to as an *AB design*. First, a baseline (A) is established by having the client observe and record the occurrence of the targeted behavior every day. Then an intervention strategy (B) is introduced. The client continues to record the targeted behavior in the same way as before. The manifestation of the targeted behavior is compared during these two periods and trends are noted. By graphing results, counselors can determine what, if any, effect the intervention strategy had.

Reversal Design.   A reversal design is more complex than a simple time series. It involves a reversal—an *ABAB design*. The first part is executed as it is in the simple time series, but the intervention strategy (B) is discontinued after a time, and a second baseline and intervention follow. "If the second intervention period produces proportionately the same results as the first intervention period, then it can be safely assumed that it is the strategy itself that is causing the changes in the level of interactions made" (Huber, 1980, p. 212).

Multiple Baseline Design.   The most complex of these experimental designs, the multiple baseline design permits greater generalization of the results. There are three types of multiple baseline research designs: across individuals, across situations, and across behaviors (Schmidt, 1974). Each emphasizes a different focus. The common trait of all three is that intervention is initially employed with a select individual, situation, or behavior while the researcher continues to gather baseline data on other persons, situations, or behaviors. When intervention strategies are extended to the baseline populations, counselors are able to see more clearly the power of the intervention. As with other designs, it is important to graph the results.

Overall, there are five steps in intensive experimental designs on individuals:

1. identify an observable problem that can be monitored for change,
2. gather baseline data,
3. decide on the intervention to be studied,
4. carry out the intervention strategy within one of the three research designs, and
5. evaluate the changes, if any, in the targeted behavior.

Guidelines for Using Research

Counselors who use research as a base for their practices can follow certain guidelines. They include recognizing the flaws and strengths of research methods, taking care to define terms carefully, and not overgeneralizing beyond the scope of particular findings. Such procedures help consumers evaluate studies as objectively as possible so that they can employ the results more skillfully and ethically.

Recently, several writers have been concerned about the fair assessment of gender differences (McHugh, Koeske, & Frieze, 1986; Wakefield, 1992). Altmaier, Greiner, and Griffin-Pierson (1988, p. 346) offer some of the most salient advice on this issue:

- Readers should note the values on which particular research studies are based.
- Counselors should look for findings that are in accord with their experiences and findings that converge across settings and studies.
- Consumers of research should not overlook topics of importance to women, such as childbearing.
- The assumption should not be made that differences between men and women fall along one continuum in a bipolar fashion.
- The magnitude of effects should be considered in reading research about gender differences. In other words, the reader should note how much variance in the observed behavior is accounted for by the significance of gender difference.

In the final analysis, counselors who use research should do so in relation to the skills they acquired in their graduate and continuing education programs. Clinicians must study research methodology well so that their practices reflect only the best professional knowledge available.

Statistics

All counselors should be aware of several research tools, such as libraries and their resources, computers and their software, techniques of measurement, and statistics. Statistics are not a fixed part of evaluation and research, and "using statistics, or not, is not what 'makes' or 'breaks' a good study" (Leedy, 1997, p. 18). Rather, statistics are simply a means for researchers to use in analyzing and interpreting findings and communicating those findings to others (Wilson & Yager, 1981). As Barkley (1982) emphasizes, "it is possible to be a good researcher and know nothing about sophisticated statistical techniques. It is also possible to know a great deal about statistics and be a mediocre or poor researcher" (p. 327). The distinction between research and statistics is important.

Statistical Concepts.   There are some statistical concepts that every counselor must know to read and evaluate research reports intelligently. One is *measures of the central tendency*—that is, the median, the mean, and the mode. All these measures encompass different meanings of the term *average* (Galfo & Miller, 1976). The *median* is the midpoint of a distribution of scores ranked highest to lowest. The *mean* is the arithmetic average of scores. The *mode* is the score or measure that occurs most often in a distribution.

In a true normally distributed population (which can be graphed as a *bell-shaped or normal curve*), the median, mean, and mode are the same. But in actuality this situation rarely occurs.

Two other important statistical concepts are standard deviation and sampling procedure. A *standard deviation* is "a measure of the dispersion of scores about their mean" (Marken, 1981, p. 42). It indicates how much response variability is reflected in a set of scores; that is, it is a measure of how homogeneous a group is. "The larger the standard deviation, the greater the variability among the individuals" (Thorndike, 1997, p. 41). *Sampling* is important because it determines how applicable research findings are. If a sample does not adequately represent the population on which it is based, the results cannot be considered applicable to the population. When samples are chosen in a representative, random way, results can be generalized to the population with confidence.

Statistical Methods.   Descriptive, correlational, and inferential statistics are the three most widely used statistical methods in research (Mertens, 1998). *Descriptive statistics* literally describe characteristics of a sample. They are devices used to organize and summarize data as well. They are used in analyzing single-subject research and simply describing populations (Miller, 1985). Mean and standard deviation are examples of descriptive statistics. *Correlational statistics* describe the strength and connection of relationships—for example, the strength of a relationship between one's attitude toward drugs and actually using drugs. Finally, *inferential statistics* allow for group comparisons or make predictions about an entire population from a given sample. They determine whether research results are due to chance or the treatment of variables in a study (Cozby, 1997).

A number of statistical tests have been devised to measure the probability of change occurring by chance in an experimental research design. Two broad categories of tests are used for this purpose: parametric and nonparametric. Parametric tests are usually more powerful. They assume "that most populations have at least one parameter" that is "a characteristic or quality of a population that, in concept, is a constant but whose value is variable" like the radius of circles (Leedy, 1997, p. 150). Parametric tests are used when it is thought that the population being described has evenly distributed characteristics that could be represented by a bell-shaped curve. Examples of parametric tests are the Pearson product moment correlation and *t* tests. Nonparametric tests are used when no normal curve distribution can be assumed but sharp dichotomies can. Nonparametric tests require larger sample sizes to yield a level of significance similar to parametric tests. Examples of nonparametric tests are the Spearman rank-order correlation and chi-square.

In addition, statistics can be used to compare research findings across studies. One prominent approach is through an empirically based method known as *meta-analysis* (Glass, 1976; Willson, 1981). Before the conceptualization of meta-analysis, researchers were forced to compare studies through narrative methods that were often filled with errors. With meta-analysis, large amounts of data can be compared and contrasted (Baker, Swisher, Nadenichek, & Popowicz, 1984). Statistics are invaluable to the counselor who wants to understand, organize, communicate, and evaluate data (Remer, 1981).

Summary and Conclusion

This chapter focused on the relationship between evaluation and research. Although the terms are sometimes defined identically, each has an individual purpose. Evaluation aims at helping counselors decide how programs are meeting the goals and objectives of staff and clients. A major first step in conducting an evaluation is to do a needs assessment. Several excellent models are available for counselors to use in completing this task.

Research scares many counselors. Yet this fear may diminish as counselors become more aware that there are many ways to conduct investigative studies. Three main research methods are historical, descriptive, and experimental. For years, experimental research has been valued most highly, but this emphasis is changing. Case studies and intensive experimental designs are gaining popularity. In addition, the difference between understanding research methods and statistical concepts is growing; that is, people are realizing that the two approaches are not the same. Both are important, but it is possible for researchers to be stronger in one area than the other.

Counselors must constantly strive to update their research and evaluation skills and stay current. The life span of knowledge is brief, and counselors who do not exercise their minds and find areas of needed change will become statistics instead of an influence.

CLASSROOM ACTIVITIES

1. In small groups, visit a mental health agency or school and find out what procedures are used to evaluate services and personnel. Read the institution's annual reports, and assess how uniformly an evaluative method is employed in describing the institution's activities. Report your field study findings to the class. Discuss what recommendations you would make to the agency or school.

2. As a class, gather examples of needs assessments from schools and agencies. Evaluate the instruments according to the step-by-step procedure outlined in this chapter. What are the strengths and weaknesses of these assessments? What improvements would you make if you were put in charge of the procedure? Have select members of the class role-play the steps they would take when conducting a needs assessment at a particular site.

3. As a class, choose two three-person teams to debate the pros and cons of this statement:

Counseling research must be relevant. What definition of *relevant* does each side advocate? How does an interpretation of the term influence the type of research recommended? After the debate, discuss the merits of doing basic and applied research.

4. Which of the three major types of research (historical, descriptive, or experimental) would you be most comfortable conducting? Divide the class according to research interests, and, in individual groups, discuss the reasons behind your choice. After your group agrees on a combined rationale for choosing a particular research approach, report your ideas to the class as a whole.

5. What are your feelings about statistics? In triads, discuss how feelings can either promote or interfere with learning statistical procedures. Practice taking a thinking approach to learning statistics. Does thinking rather than feeling affect your attitude and approach to learning these proce-

dures? Discuss your impressions with the class. Does your class believe there are any counseling approaches that would be use-

ful in helping a person overcome anxiety related to learning statistics? Which ones?

REFERENCES

Aldridge, D. (1994). Single-case research designs for the creative art therapist. *Arts in Psychotherapy, 21,* 333–342.

Altmaier, E. M., Greiner, M., & Griffin-Pierson, S. (1988). The new scholarship on women. *Journal of Counseling and Development, 66,* 345–346.

Anton, J. L. (1978). Intensive experimental designs: A model for the counselor/researcher. *Personnel and Guidance Journal, 56,* 273–278.

Ary, D., (1996). *Introduction to research in education* (5th ed.). New York: Harcourt Brace.

Baker, S. B., Swisher, J. D., Nadenichek, P. E., & Popowicz, C. L. (1984). Measured effects of primary prevention strategies. *Personnel and Guidance Journal, 62,* 459–464.

Barkley, W. M. (1982). Introducing research to graduate students in the helping professions. *Counselor Education and Supervision, 21,* 327–331.

Bloland, P. A. (1992, December). Qualitative research in student affairs. *CAPS Digest,* EDO-CG-92-26.

Burck, H. D., & Peterson, G. W. (1975). Needed: More evaluation, not research. *Personnel and Guidance Journal, 53,* 563–569.

Campbell, A., & Katona, G. (1953). The sample survey: A technique for social science research. In L. Festinger & D. Katz (Eds.), *Research methods in the behavioral sciences* (pp. 15–55). New York: Dryden.

Campbell, D. T., & Stanley, J. C. (1963). *Experimental and quasi-experimental designs for research.* Chicago: Rand McNally.

Cohen, J. (1990). Things I have learned (so far). *American Psychologist, 45,* 1304–1312.

Collison, B. B. (1982). Needs assessment for guidance program planning: A procedure. *School Counselor, 30,* 115–121.

Cook, D. W. (1989). Systematic need assessment: A primer. *Journal of Counseling and Development, 67,* 462–464.

Cozby, P. C. (1997). *Methods in behavioral research* (6th ed.). Palo Alto, CA: Mayfield.

Daniels, M. H., Mines, R., & Gressard, C. (1981). A meta-model for evaluating counseling programs. *Personnel and Guidance Journal, 5*(9), 578–582.

Davidson, J. P., III. (1986, March). *Developing an effective evaluation plan.* Paper presented at the Jefferson County (Alabama) Model School Program, Birmingham, AL.

Denzin, N. K., & Lincoln, Y. S. E. (1994). *Handbook of qualitative research.* Thousand Oaks, CA: Sage.

Dobson, J. E., & Campbell, N. J. (1986). Laboratory outcomes of personal growth groups. *Journal for Specialists in Group Work, 11,* 9–15.

Erikson, E. H. (1958). *Young man Luther.* New York: Norton.

Fall, M., & VanZandt, C. E. Z. (1997). Partners in research: School counselors and counselor educators working together. *Professional School Counseling, 1,* 2–3.

Fong, M. L. (1992). When a survey isn't research. *Counselor Education and Supervision, 31,* 194–195.

Forsyth, D. R., & Strong, S. R. (1986). The scientific study of counseling and psychotherapy. *American Psychologist, 41,* 113–119.

Frey, D. H. (1978). Science and the single case in counseling research. *Personnel and Guidance Journal, 56,* 263–268.

Froehle, T. C. (1985). Guest editorial. *Counselor Education and Supervision, 24,* 323–324.

Galfo, A. J., & Miller, E. (1976). *Interpreting educational research* (3rd ed.). Dubuque, IA: Brown.

Gay, L. R. (1996). *Educational research* (5th ed.). Upper Saddle River, NJ: Merrill/Prentice Hall.

Gelso, C. J. (1979). Research in counseling: Methodological and professional issues. *Counseling Psychologist, 8,* 7–36.

Gelso, C. J. (1985). Rigor, relevance, and counseling research: On the need to maintain our course between Scylla and Charybdis. *Journal of Counseling and Development, 63,* 551–553.

Gillies, R. M. (1993). Action research in school counseling. *School Counselor, 41,* 69–72.

Gladding, S. T., Lewis, E. L., & Adkins, L. (1981). Religious beliefs and positive mental health: The GLA scale and counseling. *Counseling and Values, 25,* 206–215.

Glass, G. V. (1976). Primary, secondary, and meta-analyses of research. *Educational Researcher, 5,* 3–8.

Goldman, L. G. (1976). A revolution in counseling research. *Journal of Counseling Psychology, 23,* 543–552.

Goldman, L. G. (1977). Toward more meaningful research. *Personnel and Guidance Journal, 55,* 363–368.

Goldman, L. G. (1978). Science, research, and practice: Confusing the issues. *Personnel and Guidance Journal, 56,* 641–642.

Goldman, L. G. (1979). Research is more than technology. *Counseling Psychologist, 8,* 41–44.

Goldman, L. G. (1986). Research and evaluation. In M. D. Lewis, R. L. Hayes, & J. A. Lewis (Eds.), *The counseling profession* (pp. 278–300). Itasca, IL: Peacock.

Goldman, L. G. (1992). Qualitative assessment: An approach for counselors. *Journal of Counseling and Development, 70,* 616–621.

Hackett, G. (1981). Survey research methods. *Personnel and Guidance Journal, 59,* 599–604.

Hadley, R. G., & Mitchell, L. K. (1995). *Counseling research and program evaluation.* Pacific Grove, CA: Brooks/Cole.

Heppner, P. P. (1990). *Pioneers in counseling and development: Personal and professional perspectives.* Alexandria, VA: American Counseling Association.

Heppner, P. P., & Anderson, W. P. (1985). On the perceived non-utility of research in counseling. *Journal of Counseling and Development, 63,* 545–547.

Heppner, P. P., Kivlighan, Jr., D. M., & Wampold, B. E. (1992). *Research design in counseling.* Pacific Grove, CA: Brooks/Cole.

Herman, K. C. (1993). Reassessing predictors of therapist competence. *Journal of Counseling and Development, 72,* 29–32.

Hill, C. E. (1982). Counseling process research: Philosophical and methodological dilemmas. *Counseling Psychologist, 10,* 7–19.

Hill, C. E. (1991). Almost everything you ever wanted to know about how to do process research on counseling and psychotherapy but didn't know who to ask. In C. E. Watkins, Jr., & L. J. Schneider (Eds.), *Research in counseling* (pp. 85–118). Hillsdale, NJ: Erlbaum.

Hill, C. E., Carter, J. A., & O'Farrell, M. K. (1983). A case study of the process and outcomes of time-limited counseling. *Journal of Counseling Psychology, 30,* 3–18.

Hollis, J. W. (1997). *Counselor preparation, 1996–1998* (9th ed.). Muncie, IN: Accelerated Development.

Hosie, T. W. (1994). Program evaluation: A potential area of expertise for counselors. *Counselor Education and Supervision, 33,* 349–355.

House, E. R. (1978). Assumptions underlying evaluation models. *Educational Researcher, 7,* 4–12.

Howard, G. S. (1985). Can research in the human sciences become more relevant to practice? *Journal of Counseling and Development, 63,* 539–544.

Huber, C. H. (1980). Research and the school counselor. *School Counselor, 27,* 210–216.

Humes, C. W., II. (1972). Accountability: A boon to guidance. *Personnel and Guidance Journal, 51,* 21–26.

Husband, R., & Foster, W. (1987). Understanding qualitative research: A strategic approach to qualitative methodology. *Journal of Humanistic Education and Development, 26,* 50–63.

Ivey, A. E. (1980). *Counseling and psychotherapy: Skills, theories, and practice.* Upper Saddle River, NJ: Prentice Hall.

Jencius, M., & Rotter, J. C. (1998, March). *Applying natural studies to counseling.* Paper presented at the World Conference of the American Counseling Association, Indianapolis, IN.

Jesness, C. (1975). Comparative effectiveness of behavior modification and transactional analysis programs for delinquents. *Journal of Consulting and Clinical Psychology, 43,* 759–779.

Kaplan, A. (1964). *The conduct of inquiry.* San Francisco: Chandler.

Kerlinger, F. N. (1986). *Foundations of behavioral research* (3rd ed.). New York: Holt, Rinehart, & Winston.

Krauskopf, C. J. (1982). Science and evaluation research. *Counseling Psychologist, 10,* 71–72.

Krumboltz, J. D., & Mitchell, L. K. (1979). Relevant rigorous research. *Counseling Psychologist, 8,* 50–52.

Lambert, M. J., Masters, K. S., & Ogles, B. M. (1991). Outcome research in counseling. In C. E. Watkins, Jr., & L. J. Schneider (Eds.), *Research in counseling* (pp. 51–83). Hillsdale, NJ: Erlbaum.

Lee, C. C., & Walz, G. R. (Eds.). (1998). *Social action: A mandate for counselors.* Alexandria, VA: American Counseling Association.

Leedy, P. D. (1997). *Practical research* (6th ed.). Upper Saddle River, NJ: Merrill/Prentice Hall.

Lewis, W. A., & Hutson, S. P. (1983). The gap between research and practice on the question of counseling effectiveness. *Personnel and Guidance Journal, 61,* 532–535.

Martin, D., & Martin, M. (1989). Bridging the gap between research and practice. *Journal of Counseling and Development, 67,* 491–492.

May, K. M. (1996). Naturalistic inquiry and counseling: Contemplating commonalities. *Counseling and Values, 40,* 219–229.

McHugh, M. C., Koeske, R. D., & Frieze, I. H. (1986). Issues to consider in conducting nonsexist psychological research. *American Psychologist, 41,* 879–890.

McLeod, J. (1995). *Doing counselling research.* Thousand Oaks, CA: Sage.

Marken, R. (1981). *Methods in experimental psychology.* Pacific Grove, CA: Brooks/Cole.

Merchant, N., & Dupuy, P. (1996). Multicultural counseling and qualitative research: Shared worldview and skills. *Journal of Counseling and Development, 74,* 537–541.

Mertens, D. M. (1998). *Research methods in education and psychology.* Thousand Oaks, CA: Sage.

Miller, M. J. (1985). Analyzing client change graphically. *Journal of Counseling and Development, 63,* 491–494.

Moser, C. A., & Kalton, G. (Eds.). (1972). *Survey methods in social investigation* (2nd ed.). New York: Basic Books.

Neimeyer, G., & Resnikoff, A. (1982). Qualitative strategies in counseling research. *Counseling Psychologist, 10,* 75–85.

Oetting, E. R. (1976). Planning and reporting evaluative research: Part 2. *Personnel and Guidance Journal, 55,* 60–64.

Ohlsen, M. M. (1983). Evaluation of the counselor's services. In M. M. Ohlsen (Ed.), *Introduction to counseling* (pp. 357–372). Itasca, IL: Peacock.

Remer, R. (1981). The counselor and research: An introduction. *Personnel and Guidance Journal, 59,* 567–571.

Robinson, E. H., III. (1994). Critical issues in counselor education: Mentors, models, and money. *Counselor Education and Supervision, 33,* 339–343.

Schmidt, J. A. (1974). Research techniques for counselors: The multiple baseline. *Personnel and Guidance Journal, 53,* 200–206.

Sexton, T. L. (1993). A review of the counseling outcome research. In G. R. Walz & J. C. Bleuer (Eds.), *Counselor efficacy* (pp. 79–119). Ann Arbor, MI: ERIC/CAPS.

Sexton, T. L. (1996). The relevance of counseling outcome research: Current trends and practical implications. *Journal of Counseling and Development, 74,* 590–600.

Sexton, T. L., & Whiston, S. C. (1996). Integrating counseling research and practice. *Journal of Counseling & Development, 74,* 588–589.

Smith, M. L. (1981). Naturalistic research. *Personnel and Guidance Journal, 59,* 585–589.

Sprinthall, N. A. (1981). A new model for research in service of guidance and counseling. *Personnel and Guidance Journal, 59,* 487–496.

Stufflebeam, D. L., Foley, W. J., Gephart, W. J., Guba, E. G., Hammond, R. L., Merriman, H. D., & Provus, M. M. (1971). *Educational evaluation and decision-making.* Bloomington, IN: Phi Delta Kappa.

Sue, D. W. (1978). Editorial. *Personnel and Guidance Journal, 56,* 260.

Thoresen, C. E. (1978). Making better science, intensively. *Personnel and Guidance Journal, 56,* 279–282.

Thorndike, R. M. (1997). *Measurement and evaluation in psychology and education* (6th ed.). Upper Saddle River, NJ: Merrill/Prentice Hall.

Tracey, T. J. (1983). Single case research: An added tool for counselors and supervisors. *Counselor Education and Supervision, 22,* 185–196.

Tracey, T. J. (1991). Counseling research as an applied science. In C. E. Watkins, Jr., & L. J. Schneider (Eds.), *Research in counseling* (pp. 3–32). Hillsdale, NJ: Erlbaum.

Vacc, N. A., & Loesch, L. C. (1994). *A professional orientation to counseling* (2nd ed.). Muncie, IN: Accelerated Development.

Walz, G., & Bleuer, J. C. (Eds.). (1993). *Counselor efficacy*. Greensboro, NC: ERIC/CAPS.

Wakefield, J. C. (1992). The concept of mental disorder: On the boundary between biological facts and social values. *American Psychologist, 47*, 373–388.

Watkins, C. E., Jr., & Schneider, L. J. (1991). Research in counseling: Some concluding thoughts and ideas. In C. E. Watkins, Jr., & L. J. Schneider (Eds.), *Research in counseling* (pp. 287–299). Hillsdale, NJ: Erlbaum.

Wheeler, P. T., & Loesch, L. (1981). Program evaluation and counseling: Yesterday, today, and tomorrow. *Personnel and Guidance Journal, 59*, 573–578.

Whiston, S. C. (1996). Accountability through action research: Research methods for practitioners. *Journal of Counseling & Development, 74*, 616–623.

Willson, V. L. (1981). An introduction to the theory and conduct of meta-analysis. *Personnel and Guidance Journal, 59*, 582–584.

Wilson, F. R., & Yager, G. G. (1981). A process model for prevention program research. *Personnel and Guidance Journal, 59*, 590–595.

20

TESTING, ASSESSMENT, AND DIAGNOSIS IN COUNSELING

◆

I read the test data like a ticker tape

from the New York Stock Exchange.

Your "neurotic" scales are slightly up

with a large discrepancy in your Wechsler scores.

Myers-Briggs extroversion is in the moderate range

with an artistic interest expressed in your Strong profile.

At first, like a Wall Street wizard,

I try to assess and predict your future,

But in talking about expected yields

I find the unexpected. . . .

Alone, you long for the warmth of relationships

as well as for the factual information at hand.

In the process of discussion,

a fellow human being emerges.

Behind what has been revealed on paper

is the uniqueness of a person.

From "Thoughts of a Wall Street Counselor," by S. T. Gladding, 1986/1995, Journal of Humanistic Education and Development, 24, *p. 176.* © 1986 by ACA. Reprinted with permission. No further reproduction authorized without written permission of the American Counseling Association.

Testing, assessment, and diagnosis "are integral components of the counseling process" that are used in all stages of counseling from referral to follow-up (Hohenshil, 1996, p. 65). Today, virtually all counselors are involved in testing, assessment, and diagnosis. The amount they do of each is dependent on their theoretical backgrounds, education, values, and settings. Therefore, it is essential for counselors to understand procedures connected with each process.

Counselors interested in activities that require the use of measurement and associated procedures usually belong to the Association for Assessment in Counseling (AAC), if they are members of the American Counseling Association. This division, originally named the Association for Measurement and Evaluation in Guidance (AMEG), was chartered as the seventh division of the ACA in 1965 (Sheeley & Eberly, 1985). It publishes a quarterly journal, Measurement and Evaluation in Counseling and Development. *Several American Psychological Association (APA) divisions are involved with tests, assessment, and diagnosis, too. Clinical Psychology (Division 12), School Psychology (Division 16), and Counseling Psychology (Division 17) are among the most prominent. Both the ACA and APA have clearly established standards for psychological and educational tests (ACA, 1989; APA, 1985). In addition, the Joint Committee on Testing Practices (1988) has drawn up guidelines for fair testing practices in education.*

This chapter examines the nature of tests, assessment, and diagnosis and how each fits into the counseling profession. It covers basic concepts associated with testing, such as validity, reliability, and standardization. In addition, it reviews some of the major tests that counselors use and are expected to understand. Finally, it examines the nature of assessment and diagnosis and their usefulness.

Tests and Test Scores

Anastasi (1982) defines a *psychological test* (or *test*, for short) as "essentially an objective and standardized measure of behavior" (p. 22). Most often test results are reported as *test scores*, statistics that have meaning only in relation to a person. A *score* is a reflection of a particular behavior at a moment in time. Test scores are important in counseling despite their limitations, for they provide information that might not be obtained in any other way and do so with comparatively small investments of time and effort. Although tests and test scores have been criticized for a number of reasons, testing is an indispensable part of an evaluation process. How tests and test scores are used depends on the user (Anastasi, 1992). As Loesch (1977) observes, "we usually don't have a choice about whether we will be involved with testing" (p. 74). There is a choice, however, about whether counselors will be informed and responsible.

To understand a test, counselors must know

- the characteristics of its standardization sample,
- the types and degree of its reliability and validity,
- the reliability and validity of comparable tests,
- the scoring procedures,
- the method of administration,
- the limitations, and
- the strengths (Kaplan & Saccuzzo, 1997).

Much of this information is contained in test manuals that accompany standardized tests, but acquiring a thorough knowledge of a particular test takes years of study and practice. Because it is important that counselors use tests to the fullest extent possible, they are wise to "prepare local experience tables" so they can give test takers more specific information about what their scores mean in relation to a particular community or situation (Goldman, 1994a, p. 216).

Today, in the United States approximately 10 million "counselees each year complete 'tests,' 'inventories,' and other 'assessments' and that estimate does not include school achievement tests or college entrance exams" (Prediger, 1994, p. 228). Some counseling professionals specialize in the administration and interpretation of tests. Those employed as testing and appraisal specialists are known as *psychometrists* (Harper, 1981). Most professionals who deal with tests, however, are not full-time psychometrists. Usually they are counselors and other helping professionals who are sometimes surprisingly uncomfortable with testing instruments and the negative connotation of the word *test*. A test is often linked to "a heavy emphasis on objectivity" (Loesch, 1977, p. 74), and the process of testing can be mechanical, creating psychological distance between examiner and client. To overcome such barriers, counselors who test need to be trained in the use of the most frequently given tests and become familiar with other standardized instruments.

Many periodicals review standardized tests, including *Measurement and Evaluation in Counseling and Development*, the *Journal of Counseling Psychology*, the *Journal of Counseling and Development*, and the *Review of Educational Research*. A number of authoritative reference books on tests are also available. O. K. Buros originated a series of reference books on personality tests, vocational tests, and other similar instruments. His most well known reference was entitled *Tests in Print*. It continues to be updated periodically by the institute he established (i.e., Buros Institute of Mental Measurements (www.unl.edu/buros/catalog.html#mmy). Buros also edited eight editions of *Mental Measurements Yearbook*, which is considered his best work in this area and is now in its 13th edition (Impara & Plake, 1998).

A History of Tests in Counseling

The employment of tests by counselors has a long, paradoxical, and controversial history. The origin of present-day tests developed and "grew out of the late 19th century study of individual differences" (Bradley, 1994, p. 224). Since the early years of the 20th century, when Frank Parsons (1909) asserted that vocational guidance should be based on formal assessment, counselors have been part of the testing movement.

During World War I, the field of psychometrics developed. At that time, the army hired a group of psychologists to construct paper-and-pencil intelligence tests to screen inductees (Aiken, 1997). These test pioneers, led by Arthur Otis and Robert Yerkes, built on the work of Alfred Binet (an originator of an early intelligence test), Charles Spearman (an important early contributor to test theory), Sir Francis Galton (an inventor of early techniques for measuring abilities), and James M. Cattell (an early researcher into the relationship of scores to achievement) (Anastasi, 1988). The testing movement, which gained impetus in the 1920s, gave counselors a new identity and respectability. It linked them closely to the psychometric dimension of psychology and gave them an expanded theoretical rationale on which to base their job descriptions, especially in schools.

As a group, counselors have varied in their degree of involvement with tests. The 1930s and 1960s are two distinct periods of high counselor involvement with assessment and testing. Vocational testing was emphasized in the 1930s because of the Great Depression. The University of Minnesota's Employment Stabilization Research Institute led the vocational testing movement during those years. Its personnel assembled and administered batteries of tests in an effort to help the unemployed find suitable work. Paterson and Darley (1936) estimated that up to 30% of unemployed workers in the 1930s were mismatched with their stated job preferences and training. In 1957 the Soviet Union's launch of *Sputnik* raised U.S. interest in testing because many Americans believed that the United States had fallen behind in science. Congress subsequently passed the National Defense Education Act (NDEA), which contained a provision, Title V, for funding testing in the secondary schools to identify students with outstanding talents and encourage them to continue their education, especially in the sciences.

In 1959, the *Journal of Counseling and Development*, then known as the *Personnel and Guidance Journal*, began to publish test reviews to supplement the *Mental Measurements Yearbook* (MMY) (Watkins, 1990). These reviews were discontinued in 1966, but they were revived in 1984 and continue to be published on occasions today. The *Journal of Counseling and Development* reviews both new and revised tests, focusing on theoretical and timely topics related to what tests do and do not measure (Tyler, 1984). *Measurement and Evaluation in Counseling* does the same.

The 1970s and 1980s brought greater criticism of testing. Goldman (1972) set this tone in an article that declared that the marriage between counseling and testing had failed. In the same year, the National Education Association (NEA) passed Resolution 72-44, which called for a moratorium on the use of standardized intelligence, aptitude, and achievement tests (Engen, Lamb, & Prediger, 1982; Zytowski, 1982). Since that time, many court suits have been filed to challenge the use of tests, and several bills have been introduced in state legislatures to prohibit the administration of certain tests. Jepsen (1982) has observed that the trends of the 1970s make it more challenging than ever to select tests and interpret scores carefully. His observations on testing can be generalized to other areas of counseling. As Tyler (1984) notes, "the antitesting movement has become a force to be reckoned with" (p. 48). Ironically, the use of tests in schools is more popular now than ever; a majority of school counselors on all levels spend 1 to 5 hours a week on this activity, considering it either important or very important to their work (Elmore, Ekstrom, Diamond, & Whittaker, 1993). They use such assessment devices as intelligence and achievement tests, substance abuse screening instruments, and career inventories (Giordano, Schwiebert, & Brotherton, 1997).

Many of the problems with testing in the schools and other settings are being addressed through the revision of problematic instruments (Cronbach, 1990). Indeed, Anastasi (1982) observes that "psychological testing today does not stand still long enough to have its picture taken" (p. v). For instance, in comparing the fourth (1976) and fifth (1982) editions of Anastasi's classic, *Psychological Testing*, one sees that more than a third of the tests included in the revised text are either new or substantially revised. That trend continues, as does an emphasis on revising test standards (DeAngelis, 1994; Zytowski, 1994). Renewed attention is also being paid to the education of counseling students and the continuing education of counselors in the use and abuse of psychoeducational tests (Chew 1984). But more needs to be done. According to Goldman (1994b), we need a "large decrease in the number of standardized tests bought for use by counselors, a great increase in the use of qualitative assessment, and . . . [more dedication to the AAC] being a consumer organization" (p. 218). In other words, the AAC should inform counselors about the strengths and limitations of standardized tests.

Problems and Potential of Using Tests

There are similarities between the tests administered by counselors and those used by psychologists (Bubenzer, Zimpfer, & Mahrle, 1990). However, the ways in which tests are given is more crucial for their success in serving the welfare of clients and the general public than the professional identity of who administers them (Harris, 1994).

Tests may be used alone or as part of a group (a *test battery*). Cronbach (1979) asserts that test batteries have little value unless competent, well-educated counselors are available to interpret them. The same is true for individual tests. Many of the problems associated with testing are usually the result of the way in which instruments are employed and interpreted rather than problems with the tests themselves. Nevertheless, both test administration and interpretation have received serious criticism (Talbutt, 1983).

Shertzer and Stone (1980) maintain that opponents of testing generally object to them for the following reasons:

1. Testing encourages client dependency on both the counselor and an external source of information for problem resolution.
2. Test data prejudice the counselor's picture of an individual.
3. Test data are invalid and unreliable enough so that their value is severely limited. (p. 311)

Other critics conclude that tests are biased and discriminatory, measure irrelevant skills, obscure talent, are used mechanically, invade privacy, can be faked, and foster undesirable competition (Prescott, Cavatta, & Rollins, 1977; Shertzer & Linden, 1979; Talbutt, 1983). "Over-reliance on test results, especially in isolation from other information about an individual, is one of the most serious test misuse problems" (Elmore et al., 1993, p. 76). Another criticism is that tests are regressive and used for predictability rather than screening or self-exploration (Goldman, 1994b).

The use of tests with minorities has been an especially controversial area and one in which abuse has occurred (Suzuki & Kugler, 1995; Suzuki, Meller, & Ponterotto, 1996). Assessment instruments must take into consideration the influences and experiences of persons from diverse cultural, ethnic, and racial backgrounds if they are going to have any meaning. Oakland (1982) points out that testing can be a dehumanizing experience, and minority culture students may spend years in ineffective or inappropriate programs as a result of test scores. To avoid cultural bias, the AAC has developed multicultural assessment standards (Prediger, 1993). Ethical guidelines for test use are also contained in the *Ethical Standards of the American Counseling Association.* These standards, as well as those drawn up by other professional associations, should be consulted when trying to prevent test abuse with minority populations (Hansen, 1994). In assessing bias it should be recognized that prejudicial acts may result from omission as well as acts of commission (Chernin, Holden, & Chandler, 1997).

Success or failure with tests is related to the sensitivity, ability, and knowledge of the counselors who select, administer, and interpret them. "Counselors have a general obligation to take an empirical approach to their instruments, especially those for which there are not complete norms and substantial validation" (Carlson, 1989, p. 489). If they do not consider multiple criteria in the selection process, counselors are likely to make mistakes that are costly to clients and themselves. To avoid these situations, some counselors include clients in the process of test selection.

Learner (1981) and Oakland (1982) report that the general public's attitude toward testing is positive, even among minorities, perhaps because people believe that tests serve many useful purposes. From the public's perspective, the primary function of tests is to help clients make better decisions about their futures. Tests may also help in the following ways (Shertzer & Stone, 1980):

- Help clients gain self-understanding
- Help counselors decide if clients' needs are within their range of expertise
- Help counselors better understand clients
- Help counselors determine which counseling methods might be most appropriately employed
- Help counselors predict the future performance of clients in select areas, such as mechanics, art, or graduate school
- Help counselors stimulate new interests within their clients
- Help counselors evaluate the outcome of their counseling efforts

Qualities of Good Tests

All tests are not created equal, but those that do the job best have certain qualities in common. Among the most important qualities are validity, reliability, and standardization and norms, which facilitate the interpretation of scores (Aiken, 1997; Cronbach, 1990).

Validity.   *Validity* is unquestionably the most important test quality. It is "the degree to which a test actually measures what it purports to measure" (Anastasi, 1982, p. 27). If a test does not fulfill this function, it is basically useless. The validity of a test is determined by comparing its results with measures of a separate and independent criterion. Thus, if a test purports to measure an individual's probability of succeeding in a professional field such as medicine, law, or counseling, the test scores are correlated with measures of success, such as grades and ratings of instructors, once the tested individual completes his or her education. If scores on the testing instrument correlate highly and positively with these independent measures of success, then the instrument is said to possess a high degree of validity.

There are three types of validity: content, construct, and criterion-based (Anastasi, 1988, 1992; Kaplan & Saccuzzo, 1997). *Content validity,* sometimes referred to as *face validity,* is an indication of the degree to which a test appears to measure what it is supposed to measure (Aiken, 1997). More important, content validity is concerned with whether the test includes a fair sample of the universe of factors it is supposed to assess. As a general rule, content validity is associated with achievement, aptitude, and ability tests.

Construct validity, the most general type of validity, is "the extent to which the test may be said to measure the theoretical construct or trait" it purports to measure, such as empathy or intelligence (Anastasi, 1982, p. 144). Much depends on the test maker's definition of the construct, but generally construct validity is applied to personality and interest inventories.

Criterion-based validity refers to the comparison of test scores with a person's actual performance of a certain skill across time and situations. For example, a test that measures a person's fine-motor skills may be validated against that person's ability to type. When the criterion is available at the time of testing, then the concurrent validity of the test is being measured. When the criterion is not available until after the test is administered, then the predictive validity of the test is being measured (Aiken, 1997). Two well-known criterion-based instruments are frequently used in counseling: the Minnesota Multiphasic Personality Inventory-2 (MMPI-2), a test with concurrent validity (Butcher & Williams, 1992), and the revised Strong Interest Inventory (SII), a test with predictive validity (Osborne, Brown, Niles, & Miner, 1997).

Reliability.   *Reliability* is usually defined as a measure of the degree to which a test produces consistency of test scores when people are retested with the same or an equivalent instrument (Anastasi, 1988; Cronbach, 1990). Although reliability is related to validity, a test score may be reliable but not valid. There are three traditional ways of determining reliability:

- *Test-retest,* in which the same test is given again after a period of time
- *Parallel forms,* in which two equivalent forms of the same test are administered
- *Internal consistency analysis,* in which the scores of two arbitrarily selected halves of a test are compared

Tests are neither reliable nor unreliable. Rather, "reliability refers to the results obtained with an evaluation instrument and not the instrument itself. . . . Thus, it is . . . appropriate to speak of the reliability of 'test scores' or of the 'measurement' rather than of the 'test' or the 'instrument'" (Gronlund & Linn, 1990, p. 78).

Standardization and Norms.   *Standardization* refers to the uniform conditions under which a test is administered and scored (Aiken, 1997). Standardization makes possible the comparison of an individual's successive scores over time as well as the comparison of scores of different individuals. *Norms,* or average performance scores for specified groups, make possible meaningful comparisons among people in regard to what can be expected (Kaplan & Saccuzzo, 1997). Test norms have their limitations and may be misused. For example, a major criticism of some tests is that their norms were established on members of the majority population; therefore, they may discriminate against cultural minorities and the disadvantaged (Talbutt, 1983). Counselors must carefully examine the norming procedures of tests, and they should also establish their own local norms. In this way prejudice and the inappropriate use of tests can be minimized.

Classification of Tests

There are many classifications of tests. Shertzer and Stone (1981) list seven:

1. *Standardized versus nonstandardized*—tests that are administered and scored according to specific directions (e.g., the Self-Directed Search) as opposed to those that are not (e.g., an experimental projective test)
2. *Individual versus group*—tests that are designed to be given to one person at a time (e.g., the Kaufman Assessment Battery for Children [Kamphaus, Beres, Kaufman & Kaufman, 1996]) as opposed to those that are given to groups (e.g., Minnesota School Attitude Survey [Callis, 1985])
3. *Speed versus power*—tests that must be completed within a specified period of time (e.g., most achievement tests) as opposed to those that allow for the demonstration of knowledge within generous time boundaries (e.g., many individually administered intelligence tests)
4. *Performance versus paper and pencil*—tests that require the manipulation of objects (e.g., the Object Assembly subtest of the Wechsler Intelligence Scale for Children-III [WISC-III]) as opposed to those in which subjects mark answers or give written responses (e.g., the Adjective Check List)
5. *Objective versus subjective*—tests that require the scorer not to make a judgment (e.g., short answer, true-false, matching, multiple-choice [Aiken, 1997]) as opposed to those that require the scorer to exercise a judgment (e.g., the Vocabulary subtest of the Wechsler Adult Intelligence Scale-Revised [WAIS-R] [Wechsler, 1981])
6. *Maximum versus typical performance*—tests that require the examinees to do their best (e.g., tests of intelligence and special abilities) as opposed to those that measure what a person most likes to do or usually does (e.g., tests that indicate interests or attitudes)
7. *Norm versus criterion based*—tests that compare an individual's score with scores within a group (e.g., intelligence or achievement test) as opposed to those that measure a person's score compared to a desirable level or standard (e.g., a reading test) (Aiken, 1997; Cronbach, 1990)

Another way in which tests may be classified, and one that is even more important for counselors, is "by the purpose for which they are designed or by the aspects of behavior they sample" (Shertzer & Stone, 1981, p. 242). In this classification Shertzer and Stone list six categories of tests: mental ability, aptitude, achievement, interests, career development, and personality. Yet another system of classification includes the following categories: educational, vocational, or personal aspects of counseling (Elmore & Roberge, 1982). A third classification scheme, originated by Sylvania (1956), groups tests according to frequency of use: intelligence/scholastic aptitude, vocational (and other aptitude), and achievement/diagnostic. All these classification systems have their merits and limitations. Counselors are usually involved in dealing with four distinct but sometimes overlapping categories of tests: intelligence/aptitude, interest/career, personality, and achievement.

Intelligence/Aptitude.

Among the most controversial but popular types of tests are those that attempt to measure general intelligence and special aptitude. *Intelligence* is defined in many different ways, and there is no absolute meaning associated with the word (Gardner, 1993). Indeed, Anastasi (1982) reports that most intelligence tests "are usually overloaded with certain functions, such as verbal ability, and completely omit others" (p. 228). She notes that many intelligence tests are "validated against measures of academic achievement" and "are often designated as tests of scholastic aptitude" (Anastasi, 1982, p. 228). In line with her observation is Aiken's (1997) definition of an *intelligence test* as an instrument designed to measure an individual's aptitude for scholastic work or other kinds of occupations requiring reasoning and verbal ability. Many intelligence tests are used primarily as screening devices in counseling and are followed by more specialized aptitude tests that assess aptitude in particular areas, such as music or mechanics.

Most modern intelligence tests are descendants of the original scales developed in France by Alfred Binet in the early 1900s. The Stanford-Binet Intelligence Scale, a revision of the Binet-Simon scales, was prepared by L. M. Terman and published in 1916; it is the grandfather of American intelligence tests. The test is individually administered and has traditionally been used with children rather than adults. In 1986, it underwent a fourth revision to include more material appropriate for adults.

Another popular series of individually administered intelligence tests are those originated by David Wechsler. They are the Wechsler Preschool and Primary Scale of Intelligence-Revised (WPPSI-R), designed for ages 4 years, 0 months to 6 years, 6 months; the Wechsler Intelligence Scale for Children-III (WISC-III), designed for ages 6 years, 0 months to 16 years, 11 months; and the Wechsler Adult Intelligence Scale-Revised (WAIS-R), designed for ages 16 years and older. The Wechsler intelligence tests provide a verbal IQ, performance IQ, and full-scale IQ score. Extensive research has been done on all the Wechsler scales, and they are often the instruments of choice in the evaluation of intelligence (Piotrowski & Keller, 1989; Thorndike, 1997).

There are a number of other widely respected individually administered intelligence tests. Among them are the Bayley Scales of Infant Development, the Vineland Social Maturity Scale, the Kaufman Assessment Battery for Children (K-ABC), the McCarthy Scales of Children's Abilities, the Peabody Picture Vocabulary Test (revised), and the Kaufman Adolescent and Adult Intelligence Test (KAIT).

Also available are numerous intelligence scales intended to be administered to groups. These instruments were first developed during World War I when the United States Army created its Alpha and Beta intelligence tests, the best-known forerunners of today's group intelligence instruments. These tests were initially employed to screen army inductees and classify them for training according to ability level. Among the most widely used and respected group intelligence tests are the Otis-Lennon School Ability Test, the College

Board Scholastic Aptitude Test (SAT), the American College Testing (ACT) Assessment, and the Miller Analogies Test (MAT).

Aptitude tests are similar in many ways to intelligence tests, but they are designed to tap a narrower range of ability. Aiken (1997) defines an *aptitude* as a capability for a task or type of skill and an *aptitude test* as one that measures a person's ability to profit from further training or experience in an occupation or skill. Aptitude tests are usually divided into two categories: (a) multiaptitude batteries, which test a number of skills by administering a variety of tests, and (b) component ability tests, which assess a single ability or skill, such as music or mechanical ability (Bradley, 1984). Some of the best-known multiaptitude batteries are the General Aptitude Test Battery (GATB), the Differential Aptitude Test (DAT), and the Armed Services Vocational Aptitude Battery (ASVAB) (Anastasi, 1988; Bradley, 1984; Rogers, 1996).

Interest/Career.   Although there is an expected relationship between ability and an interest in exercising that ability, tests that best measure interests are those designed specifically for the purpose. Aiken (1997) defines an *interest inventory* as a test or checklist that assesses a person's preferences for activities and topics. Responses derived from such tests are compared with the scores of others at either a similar developmental level (e.g., in an educational setting) or with people already working in a particular area (e.g., in a vocational setting). Anastasi (1982) notes that "the study of interests has probably received its strongest impetus from educational and career counseling" because a person's achievement in a learning situation or a career is greatly influenced by his or her interests (p. 534). Indeed, "interest inventory interpretation is one of the most frequently used interventions in career counseling" (Savickas, 1998, p. 307).

Instruments that measure career interests began in a systematic and standardized way with the 1927 publication of the Strong Vocational Interest Blank (SVIB). The test has been revised and expanded half a dozen times since its inception, with the latest edition of this instrument in 1994, the Strong Interest Inventory (SII), encompassing 207 occupations. The test's founder, E. K. Strong, Jr., devised only 10 Occupational Scales for the original test (Donnay, 1997). SII test results are explained in three forms: General Occupational Themes, Basic Interest Scales, and Occupational Scales. Thus, they help clients examine themselves in both a general and specific way. Another attractive feature of the instrument is its link to John Holland's theory of career development, which proposes six major types of people and environments: realistic (R), investigative (I), artistic (A), social (S), enterprising (E), and conventional (C) (RIASEC) (Holland, 1997). The closer the correlation between people and environment types, the more satisfying the relationship. Overall, the SII offers a breadth and depth in the measurement of occupational interests that are unmatched by any other single instrument. The accompanying user's guide suggests ways of employing the test with adults, cross-cultural groups, and special populations (Drummond, 1996). In addition, strong theoretical underpinnings, empirical construction, and a long history are major benefits of this inventory.

Another popular career inventory, also based on Holland's six personality/environmental types, is the Self-Directed Search (SDS), an instrument also revised in 1994 (Holland, 1994). This instrument is self-administered, self-scored, and sometimes self-interpreted. It comprises 228 items divided into three sets: activities, competencies, and occupations (Krieshok, 1987). After scoring, clients examine a three-letter Occupational Code, comparing it with career codes found in the *Dictionary of Occupational Titles* (DOT). The inventory includes Form E, which is designed for poor readers, and test takers from ages 15 to 70 report that the SDS is enjoyable and useful.

A third popular interest/career inventory is the Kuder Occupational Interest Survey (KOIS), which was first published in 1939 and continues to evolve (Kuder, 1939, 1977). The latest revision of the KOIS was in 1991 (Betsworth & Fouad, 1997). There are six forms of this activity preference, item-type, untimed instrument, but each form has a forced-choice, triad-response format (Zytowski, 1992). Some forms of the test are computer scored; others are self-scored. Clients respond to each triad by selecting the most and least preferred activity. Scores on the Kuder correlate highly with commonly expressed interests of select career groups and college majors (Zytowski & Holmberg, 1988). The test's 10 broad career areas include the following (Zytowski, 1992, pp. 245–246):

- *Social services*—"preference of helping people"
- *Persuasive*—"preference for meeting and dealing with people and promoting projects or selling things and ideas"
- *Clerical*—"preference for tasks that require precision and accuracy"
- *Computational*—"preference for working with numbers"
- *Musical*—"preference for going to concerts, playing musical instruments, singing, and reading about music and musicians"
- *Artistic*—"preference for creative work involving attractive design, color, form, and materials"
- *Literary*—"preference for reading and writing"
- *Mechanical*—"preference for working with machines and tools"
- *Outdoor*—"preference for activities that keep you outside most of the time, and usually deal with animals and plants"
- *Scientific*—"preference for discovering new facts and solving problems"

A fourth instrument, primarily career focused, is the Career Beliefs Inventory (CBI) (Krumboltz, 1991). "The CBI is an instrument which, when used sensitively by a qualified professional, can help people identify the beliefs that might be blocking them" (Krumboltz, 1992, p. 1). It is most usefully employed at the beginning of a career-counseling session. It makes possible the exploration of deep-seated attitudes and assumptions.

Other well-known interest/career tests include the California Occupational Preference System, the Jackson Vocational Interest Survey, the Ohio Vocational Interest Survey, the Unisex Edition of the ACT Interest Inventory, and the Vocational Preference Inventory.

For non-college-bound students, Bradley (1984) reports three interest inventories designed to "measure interests in occupations that do not require college training" (p. 7). These include the Minnesota Vocational Interest Inventory, the Career Assessment Inventory, and the Career Guidance Inventory in Trades, Services, and Technologies. Interest tests designed for more specialized use are the Bem Sex-Role Inventory, the Jenkins Activity Survey, the Personal Orientation Inventory, the Survey of Values, and the Survey of School Attitudes.

In selecting appropriate interest/career instruments, "you [must] know what you are looking for and . . . what you are getting" (Westbrook, 1988, p. 186). Two excellent resource books describe career decision-making and assessment measures: *Handbook of Vocational Psychology* (Walsh & Osipow, 1996) and *A Counselor's Guide to Career Assessment Instruments* (Kapes, Mastie, & Whitfield, 1995). This latter text reviews 52 major career assessment instruments and annotates 250 others as well as describes their intended populations.

Personality.   *Personality* can be defined many ways; what is considered normal in one culture may be perceived as abnormal in another. Nevertheless, there are a number of personality theories that examine the biological, social, and environmental aspects of human beings. The most popular 20th-century theorist of personality assessment was Henry A. Murray. He was especially cognizant of needs (or environmental forces/presses) and how they determined behavior (Drummond, 1996).

A *personality test* may be defined as any of several methods of analyzing personality, such as checklists, personality inventories, and projective techniques (Aiken, 1997). Such tests may be divided into two main categories: objective and projective. Some of the best-known objective tests are the Minnesota Multiphasic Personality Inventory-2 (MMPI-2), the Myers-Briggs Type Indicator (MBTI), and the Edwards Personal Preference Schedule (EPPS). These tests yield scores that are independent of any opinion or judgment of the scorer, as are all objective tests. Projective tests include the Rorschach, the Thematic Apperception Test (TAT), and the House-Tree-Person (HTP) Test. These types of tests yield measures that, in varying degrees, depend on the judgments and interpretations of administrators/scorers.

The prototype of the personality test was a self-report inventory developed during World War I by R. S. Woodworth, known as the Personal Data Sheet (Kaplan & Saccuzzo, 1997). The first significant projective test was the Rorschach Inkblot Test, published in 1921 (Erdberg, 1996). Because objectively scored personality tests are more widely used in counseling, we will begin our discussion with a review of them.

The Minnesota Multiphasic Personality Inventory-2 (MMPI-2) is the most widely used psychological test in the world (Butcher, 1994). It is a revision of the original MMPI. Instead of being normed on a limited population, however, this version uses a geographically and ethnically diverse reference group representative of the population of the United States. The restandardized MMPI-2 is also on tape for blind, illiterate, semiliterate, or disabled individuals (Drummond, 1996). It has several forms, including one for adolescents (the MMPI-A), but the most popular form consists of 567 affirmative statements that clients respond to in one of three ways: true, false, or cannot say. There are 10 clinical scales on the MMPI-2 (see Table 20.1) and three major validity scales: Lie (L), Infrequency (F), and Correction (K). In addition, there is a "?" scale, which is a compilation of unanswered questions throughout the test. In addition to distinguishing individuals who are experiencing psychiatric problems, the MMPI-2 is able to discern important characteristics such as anger, alienation, Type A behavior, and even marital distress. Extensive training and experience are necessary for counselors to use this instrument accurately and appropriately. Overall, uses of the MMPI-2 are still being refined (Austin, 1994).

The Myers-Briggs Type Indicator (MBTI) is a test that reflects Carl Jung's theory of personality type (Myers, 1962, 1980). The inventory contains 166 two-choice items concerning preferences or inclinations in feelings and behaviors (Aiken, 1997). It yields four indexes: extroversion versus introversion (EI), sensing versus intuition (SN), thinking ver-

Table 20.1 Clinical scales on the Minnesota Multiphasic Personality Inventory—2

Scale	Item Total	Item Content
Hypochondriasis (Hs)	(32)	Undue concern with physical health
Depression (D)	(57)	Depression, denial of happiness and personal worth, lack of interest, withdrawal
Hysteria (Hy)	(60)	Specific somatic complaints, denial of psychological or emotional problems, discomfort in social situations
Psychopathic deviate (Pd)	(50)	Antisocial acting-out impulses, constricted social conformity
Masculinity-femininity (Mf)	(56)	Identification with culturally conventional masculine and feminine choices, aesthetic interests, activity-passivity
Paranoia (Pa)	(40)	Delusions of persecution and ideas of reference, interpersonal sensitivity, suspiciousness, moral self-righteousness
Psychasthenia (Pt)	(48)	General dissatisfaction with life, difficulty with concentration, indecisiveness, self-doubt, obsessional aspects
Schizophrenia (Sc)	(78)	Feeling of being different, feelings of isolation, bizarre thought processes, poor family relationships, sexual identity concerns, tendency to withdraw
Hypomania (Ma)	(46)	Elevated energy level, flight of ideas, elevated mood, increased motor activity, expansiveness, grandiosity
Social introversion-extroversion	(69)	Introversion-extroversion, social insecurity

Source: From *Appraisal Procedures for Counselors and Other Helping Professionals* (2nd ed., p. 181), by R. J. Drummond, Upper Saddle River, NJ: Prentice Hall. © 1992. Reprinted by permission of Prentice Hall, Inc., Upper Saddle River, NJ.

sus feeling (TF), and judgment versus perception (JP). The MBTI consists of four bipolar scales (Goodyear, 1989):

- *Extroversion or introversion* (EI)—whether perception and judgment are directed to the outer (E) or inner (I) world

- *Sensing or intuitive* (SN)—which kind of perception is preferred when one needs to perceive
- *Thinking or feeling* (TF)—which kind of judgment is trusted when a decision needs to be made
- *Judgment or perception* (JP)—whether to deal with the world in the judgment attitude (using thinking or feeling) or in the perceptual attitude (using sensing or intuitive)

Combinations of these four indexes result in 16 possible personality types. A clear understanding of personality type provides counselors with constructive information on how clients perceive and interact with their environments (Lynch, 1985). Research indicates that different MBTI types appear to be attracted to certain occupations and lifestyles (Healy & Woodward, 1998). For example, 76% of tested counseling students score high on the intuitive/feeling scales of the MBTI and are described as insightful, enthusiastic, and able to handle challenging situations with personal warmth (Myers, 1980).

The Edwards Personal Preference Schedule (EPPS) is based on the need-press theory of personality developed by Henry Murray (1938). It consists of 225 forced-choice questions that examine the strength of 15 individual needs in relation to a person's other needs (Anastasi, 1988). The scores are plotted on a percentile chart based on group norms for college students or adults in general. Other objectively scored, self-report personality tests are the California Psychological Inventory (CPI), the Guilford-Zimmerman Temperament Survey, the Mooney Problem Check List, the Sixteen Personality Factor Questionnaire (16 PF), and the State-Trait Anxiety Inventory (STAI).

Projective personality tests are much less structured and far more difficult to score, but they are harder for the client to fake. Advocates claim that these tests measure deeper aspects of a client's personality than do other instruments. In recent years, some researchers and clinicians, such as Exner (1991, 1993, 1995), have tried to standardize the methods by which projectives are administered and scored. Although there has been success for some instruments, the scoring of many other projectives, such as the Thematic Apperception Test, is questionable. In addition to the tests already mentioned in this section, projective tests include the Holtzman Inkblot Technique, the Bender Gestalt, the Draw-a-Person Test, the Children's Apperception Test, and the Rotter Incomplete Sentences Blank.

Achievement.   An *achievement test* is a measure of an individual's degree of accomplishment or learning in a subject or task (Aiken, 1997). Achievement tests are much more direct as measurement instruments than any other type of test. Their results give clients a good idea of what they have learned in a certain area as compared with what others have learned. The tests give clients the type of information they need to make sound educational and career decisions (Bradley, 1984). If a client has aptitudes, interests, or personality dispositions suitable for select career areas but has little knowledge or skill, he or she can take positive steps to correct these deficiencies.

Achievement tests may be either teacher made or standardized. The advantages of teacher-made tests are that they measure specific units of study emphasized in an educational setting, are easy to keep up-to-date, and reflect current emphases and information. Standardized tests, on the other hand, measure more general educational objectives, are usually more carefully constructed, and give the test taker a good idea about how he or she compares with a wider sample of others in a particular subject. Teacher-made and standardized tests complement each other, and both may be used profitably in the helping process.

Various achievement tests are employed for distinct purposes. In a school setting, a combination of teacher-made and standardized tests is linked to age and grade levels. General achievement batteries used in elementary and secondary schools measure basic skills. They include the California Achievement Tests, the Iowa Tests of Basic Skills, the SRA Achievement Series, the Metropolitan Achievement Tests, the Wide Range Achievement Test, and the Stanford Achievement Test (Anastasi, 1988; Bradley, 1984). School counselors must become especially knowledgeable about these instruments to converse intelligently and efficiently with teachers, parents, administrators, students, and educational specialists.

Instruments are also available that measure adult achievement. Professionally oriented achievement tests include the National Teacher Examination, Law School Admissions Test, and the National Board of Certified Counselors Examination. They help to protect the public and the professions they represent by ensuring that individuals who pass them have achieved a minimum level of informational competence.

Administration and Interpretation of Tests

A major criticism of test use in counseling focuses on administration and interpretation. The process of administering a test is described in the manual that accompanies each one, and most tests specify uniform procedures to be followed at each step, from preparing the room to giving instructions. Some tests have specialized instructions, and counselors must follow these procedures if they expect to obtain valid test results.

One question usually not addressed in manuals is whether a test taker should be involved in selecting the test and, if so, how much should he or she be involved. In some cases, such as the administration of achievement tests in elementary schools, it is inappropriate for test takers to be involved in test selection. But on other occasions participation is beneficial. Goldman (1971) lists several advantages of involving test takers in test selection. Among the reasons for involving test takers in test selection are:

- the willingness of the tested population to accept test results,
- the promotion of independence,
- the value of the decision-making experience that might generalize to other decision-making opportunities,
- the opportunity for diagnosis based on the test taker's reactions to various tests, and
- the selection of tests that best fit the needs of the tested population.

After tests are selected, administered, and scored, counselors need to interpret the results for the tested population in an understandable way. Four basic interpretations can be helpful to test takers, depending on the test (Goldman, 1971; Hanna, 1988):

1. *Descriptive interpretation*, which provides information on the current status of the test taker
2. *Genetic interpretation*, which focuses on how the tested person got to be the way he or she is now

3. *Predictive interpretation*, which concentrates on forecasting the future
4. *Evaluative interpretation*, which includes recommendations by the test interpreter

Unfortunately, some counselors fail to learn how to administer or interpret tests (Tinsley & Bradley, 1986). "Misuse occurs in all three basic testing areas, employment, educational, and clinical" (Azar, 1994, p. 16). Misuse can result from administering and interpreting a good test in the wrong way or giving it to the wrong person for the wrong reason. In any case, when tests are misused, clients may not understand the meaning of "the numbers, charts, graphs or diagrams presented to them" (Miller, 1982, p. 87) and may leave counseling as uninformed and unenlightened as when they began.

> By maintaining conditions of standardization when tests are administered, by knowing the strengths and limitations of the norms, reliability and validity of particular instruments, and by translating raw test data into meaningful descriptions of current or predicted behavior, counselors assure that tests are used to promote the welfare of their clients. (Harris, 1994, p. 10)

Several ways have been suggested to correct deficiencies associated with test interpretation. For example, besides making sure that those who give tests are well educated and sensitive, Hanna (1988, p. 477) recommends using a person's *percentile rank* ("the percentage of persons in a reference group who scored lower than the person") as one way to provide descriptive interpretation clearly and concisely (see Figure 20.1).

Another way of rectifying deficiencies in interpretive skills depends on counselor-client preparation for the process of interpretation. First, counselors should be educated in test theory and construction. Counselors cannot explain test results unless they are well informed about the instruments with which they are dealing.

Second, Tyler (1984) points out that scores are only clues and should be seen as such. Scores must be considered in light of what else is known about a client. The total combination of information can form the basis for a more meaningful and productive dialogue between counselor and client. Goldman (1971) points out that if a test is given on an individual basis, counselors notice many things about clients that otherwise would be missed. This extra information, when combined with the test scores, often allows for a more complete assessment of the client (Loesch, 1977; Pate, 1983).

Third, Tinsley and Bradley (1986), Miller (1982), and Strahan and Kelly (1994) advocate concrete ways of dealing with test results. Tinsley and Bradley believe that before meeting with a client, the counselor must be prepared to make a clear and accurate interpretation of test results. They advise against interpreting off the cuff. A reasonable plan is to begin the interpretation with concrete information, such as interest or achievement

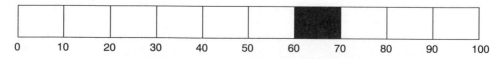

Figure 20.1   Percentile rank band for a percentile range of 60 to 70 on a standardized test of 0 to 100

scores, and then move to abstract information, such as personality or ability results. If the interpretation of information is to be meaningful, the emotional needs of the client must be considered and the information must be fresh in the counselor's mind. One way to achieve both goals is to *interpret test results on an as-needed basis*—that is, only interpret the scores the client needs to know at a point in time (Goldman, 1971). There is less information to deal with when this approach is followed, and both counselor and client are likely to remember results better. The major disadvantage of this approach is that it may become fragmented.

Tinsley and Bradley (1986) propose that when interpretation occurs, a client should be prepared through the establishment of rapport between counselor and client. Test information can then be delivered in a way that focuses on what the client wants to know. Client feedback is promoted and dialogue encouraged.

Miller (1982) makes similar remarks in his five-point plan for interpreting test results to clients. First, he has his client remember feelings on the test day and give impressions of the test or tests. He then reviews with the client the purpose of testing and how test scores are presented (e.g., by percentiles). Next, he and the client actually examine the test results together and discuss what the scores mean. Meaning is elicited by asking the client open-ended questions. Then the client can integrate scores with other aspects of self-knowledge. The final stage involves incorporating all knowledge into a client-originated plan for continuing self-study. Counselors can help clients formulate a plan, but the plan itself should come from the client.

A final way of making test results concrete is to present them in simple graph displays (Strahan & Kelly, 1994). Graphical data help clients see test results in a simple, clear, and interesting way. For example, if the data from the RIASEC code of the Strong Interest Inventory are graphed from most to least degree of liking, the results of a particular profile might look like the graph depicted in Figure 20.2.

Overall, test interpretation may be the most sensitive part of any assessment process. Clients benefit greatly when it is done properly (Miller, 1977).

Assessment

In addition to and supplementing testing is *assessment*, the procedures and processes of collecting information and measures of human behavior outside of test data. According to Cormier and Cormier (1998, p. 151) assessment has six purposes:

- "To obtain information on a client's presenting problem and on other, related problems."
- "To identify the controlling or contributing variables associated with the problem."
- "To determine the client's goals/expectations for counseling outcomes."
- "To gather baseline data that will be compared to subsequent data to assess and evaluate client progress and the effects of treatment strategies."
- "To educate and motivate the client" by sharing the counselor's view of the situation, increasing client receptivity to treatment, and contributing to therapeutic change.
- "To use the information obtained from the client to plan effective treatment inventions and strategies. The information obtained during the assessment process should

Figure 20.2 A simple graph display

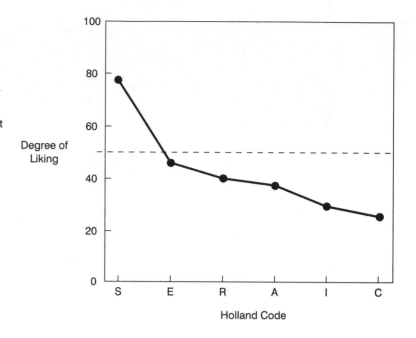

help to answer this well-thought-out question: '*What* treatment, by *whom*, is most effective for *this* individual with *that* specific problem and under *which* set of circumstances?'(Paul, 1967, p. 111)."

Assessment can be obtained "through a variety of formal and informal techniques including standardized tests, diagnostic interviews, projective personality measures, questionnaires, mental status examinations, checklists, behavioral observation, and reports by significant others (medical, educational, social, legal, etc.)" (Hohenshil, 1996, p. 65). Usually it involves a combination of procedures and not just one method (Hood & Johnson, 1997). The word *assessment* emphasizes the humanness of counseling. Included in "humanness" is a total picture of the person being evaluated. According to Anastasi (1992), "the term assessment is being used increasingly to refer to the intensive study of an individual, leading to recommendations for action in solving a particular problem" (p. 611).

As stated previously, the goal of the assessment process is a comprehensive evaluation of individuals usually in the present. Often it includes a formulation of a treatment plan that will result in positive and predictable outcomes (Groth-Marnat, 1997; Kaplan & Saccuzzo, 1997). To help counselors formulate such treatment plans, commercial as well as local treatment planners are available. For instance, Jongsma and Peterson (1995) have produced a manual that includes definitions of problematic behaviors along with long- and short-term goals. In addition, therapeutic interventions as well as bibliotherapy suggestions are given.

One way of conducting assessment is through the use of biographical and behavioral measures. Numerous *structured clinical interviews* are available for collecting this type of information. "In general, a structured clinical interview consists of a list of relevant behaviors, symptoms, and events to be addressed during an interview, guidelines for conducting the interview, and procedures for recording and analyzing the data" (Vacc & Juhnke, 1997, p. 471). The questions are asked in an ordered sequence; from the results of the interview, an assessment is made that is either diagnostic (specifically related to the *Diagnostic and Statistical Manual*) or descriptive (indicating the degree of psychopathology that is present or giving a non-DSM dysfunctional descriptor).

Overall, assessment is crucial because it allows counselors not only to determine what a client's problem is but to learn the client's orientation to problem solving (Hood & Johnson, 1997). Such a procedure helps counselors and clients to avoid blaming and to work collaboratively in finding solutions that bring about positive change rather than repeating past patterns. Assessment then makes sense to the degree that it contributes to learning and to formulating interventions in counseling that work (Egan, 1998). In clinical settings, assessment is a continuous process since once initial difficulties are resolved new ones sometimes arise or come more into focus.

Diagnosis

"*Diagnosis* . . . is the meaning or interpretation that is derived from assessment information and is usually translated in the form of some type of classification system" (Hohenshil, 1993, p. 7). A diagnosis is a description of a person's condition and not a judgment of a person's worth (Rueth, Demmitt, & Burger, 1998). For instance, the DSM-IV (American Psychiatric Association, 1994), recommends referring to clients as

> people with particular types of mental disorders, such as "a person with schizophrenia" or "a person with mental retardation," rather than using terms like the "mentally retarded" or the "schizophrenics." . . . Using labeling in this way emphasizes that the mental disorder is only one characteristic of the individual, not a descriptor of the whole person. (Hohenshil, 1996, p. 65)

Like test interpretation, some diagnostic categories are appropriately shared with clients. However, most diagnoses are withheld from clients and instead used to guide the counselor in formulating a treatment plan for helping. Usually a diagnosis does the following:

- Describes a person's current functioning
- Provides a common language for clinicians to use in discussing the client
- Leads to a consistent and continual type of care
- Helps direct and focus treatment planning
- Helps counselors fit clients within their scope of treatment (Rueth et al., 1998)

Diagnoses are important for three reasons. First, some insurance companies will only reimburse counselors and other mental health workers for their services if clients are diagnosed. Second, a diagnosis is often helpful, if not essential, in developing a proper treatment plan for a client. Finally, to work with psychiatrists, psychologists, and some medical specialists, counselors must be able to speak and understand their language, which is often conceptualized in the form of diagnosis (Hamann, 1994).

To make proper diagnoses, counselors must receive extensive training and supervision. They should know diagnostic categories, particularly those in the DSM-IV. They should also realize that diagnostic decisions are an evolving process and not a static event (Hohenshil, 1996). "Diagnosis and treatment planning are now such standard components of counseling practice" that a failure to diagnose on some level or a lack of professional diagnostic training may be construed as unethical (Sommers-Flanagan & Sommers-Flanagan, 1998, p. 189).

In making a diagnosis a counselor must observe a client for signs of symptoms. In doing so, a counselor must take into account cultural, developmental, socioeconomic, and spiritual aspects of a client's life as well as coping mechanisms, stressors, and learned behavior (Rueth et al., 1998). Sometimes a behavior in a client's life is merely a symptom of a situational problem in living, while at other times it is due to the manifestation of a severe disorder. It is crucial for counselors to neither overdiagnose nor underdiagnose. "When a formal diagnosis is made, certain symptoms must exist; [and] they must be severe enough to interfere significantly with the client's life" (Hohenshil, 1996, p. 65).

Summary and Conclusion

This chapter has covered the intricacies of testing, assessment, and diagnosis in counseling, with a particular emphasis on the qualities of useful test instruments and the types of tests counselors use. Testing is almost as old as the profession of counseling itself, but the popularity of test use in counseling has varied over the years. Nevertheless, testing will most likely remain an essential part of counseling. Therefore, counselors must be well versed in the types of tests available and their appropriate use in counseling. With this knowledge they can attain greater professional competence and help clients live healthier, more productive lives. Being well informed involves an awareness of the validity, reliability, standardization, and norms of the instruments used. A test that is reliable but not valid is inappropriate. Similarly, an instrument that discriminates against cultural minorities because it has been normed only on the majority population has no value; in fact, it can be quite harmful.

Counselors usually encounter four main types of tests: intelligence/aptitude tests, interest/career tests, personality tests, and achievement tests. A wide variety of instruments is available in each category. Counselors who work with tests must constantly examine current research results to ensure that various instruments are appropriate. They also need to consult with clients to be certain that the tests give clients the type of information they want.

Finally, counselors must be sensitively involved with the interpretation of test data. From the interpretation of tests and other analysis of data, such as behaviors, counselors make assessments and diagnoses. It is on their assessments and diagnoses that counselors base treatment plans and help their clients change their behaviors, thoughts, or feelings. Therefore, to be accountable and competent, counselors must master all three processes so that their clients benefit and they provide the best services possible.

CLASSROOM ACTIVITIES

1. Send away for educational and psychological test catalogs from major test publishers. Examine the variety of tests available and the information the publisher gives you about each. Try to group these tests under the four categories outlined in this chapter. What tests are easy to classify? Which ones are most difficult? Report your results to the class.

2. In pairs, do an in-depth report on one of the tests mentioned in this chapter or one recommended by your instructor. Be sure to notice the validity, reliability, standardization, and norms of the instrument. When you report your results to the class, explain when you think the instrument could be appropriately used in counseling.

3. Some counselors do not think that tests should be used in counseling. Divide the class into two debate teams. One side should take the position that counseling and testing are not compatible (see Goldman, 1972, 1994). The other side should advocate the use of tests in counseling (see Tinsley & Bradley, 1986). Discuss your conclusions.

4. In triads, discuss times when you have had a test interpreted for you. What did you think when the test interpreter explained your results? How do you remember feeling at the time and how did you behave? How does this experience still affect your reaction to tests, test interpretations, and the assessment process?

5. In groups of four, discuss the ethical and legal considerations of diagnosis. What issues does your group think are most sensitive? Consult the ethical codes and guidelines of professional associations on diagnosis. Share your group's findings and opinions with the class as a whole.

REFERENCES

Aiken, L. R., Jr. (1997). *Psychological testing and assessment* (9th ed.). Boston: Allyn & Bacon.

American Counseling Association (ACA). (1989, May 11). Responsibilities of users of standardized tests (rev.). *Guidepost*, pp. 12, 16, 18, 27, 28.

American Psychiatric Association. (1994). *Diagnostic and statistical manual of mental disorders* (4th ed.). Washington, DC: Author.

American Psychological Association (APA). (1985). *Standards for educational and psychological tests*. Washington, DC: Author.

Anastasi, A. (1976). *Psychological testing* (4th ed.). New York: Macmillan.

Anastasi, A. (1982). *Psychological testing* (5th ed.). New York: Macmillan.

Anastasi, A. (1988). *Psychological testing* (6th ed.). New York: Macmillan.

Anastasi, A. (1992). What counselors should know about the use and interpretation of psychological tests. *Journal of Counseling and Development, 70*, 610–615.

Austin, J. T. (1994). Minnesota Multiphasic Personality Inventory (MMPI-2). *Measurement and Evaluation in Counseling and Development, 27*, 178–185.

Azar, B. (1994, June). Could "policing" test use improve assessment? *APA Monitor, 25*, 16.

Betsworth, D. G., & Fouad, N. A. (1997). Vocational interests: A look at the past 70 years and a glance at the future. *Career Development Quarterly, 46*, 23–47.

Bradley, L. J. (1984). Lifespan career assessment for counselors and educators. *Counseling and Human Development, 16*, 1–16.

Bradley, R. W. (1994). Tests and counseling: How did we ever become partners? *Measurement and Evaluation in Counseling and Development, 26*, 224–226.

Bubenzer, D., Zimpfer, D., & Mahrle, C. (1990). Standardized individual appraisal in agency and private practice: A survey. *Journal of Mental Health Counseling, 12*, 51–66.

Butcher, J. N. (1994). The MMPI-2: A new standard for personality assessment and research in counseling settings. *Measurement and Evaluation in Counseling and Development, 27*, 131–150.

Butcher, J. N., & Williams, C. L. (1992). *Essentials of MMPI-2 and MMPI-A interpretation*. Minneapolis: University of Minnesota Press.

Callis, R. (1985). Minnesota School Attitude Survey, Lower and Upper Forms. *Journal of Counseling and Development, 63*, 382.

Campbell, V. L. (1987). Strong-Campbell Interest Inventory, fourth edition. *Journal of Counseling and Development, 66*, 53–56.

Carlson, J. G. (1989). Rebuttal. The MBTI: Not ready for routine use in counseling. A reply. *Journal of Counseling and Development, 67*, 489.

Chernin, J., Holden, J. M., & Chandler, C. (1997). Bias in psychological assessment: Heterosexism. *Measurement and Evaluation in Counseling and Development, 30*, 68–76.

Chew, A. L. (1984). Training counselors to interpret psychoeducational evaluations: A course model. *Counselor Education and Supervision, 24*, 114–119.

Cormier, S., & Cormier, B. (1998). *Interviewing strategies for helpers* (4th ed.). Pacific Grove, CA: Brooks/Cole.

Cronbach, L. J. (1979). The Armed Services Vocational Aptitude Battery: A test battery in transition. *Personnel and Guidance Journal, 57*, 232–237.

Cronbach, L. J. (1990). *Essentials of psychological testing* (5th ed.). New York: Harper & Row.

DeAngelis, T. (1994, June). APA and other groups revise testing standards. *APA Monitor, 25*, 17.

Donnay, D. A. C. (1997). E. K. Strong's legacy and beyond: 70 years of the Strong Interest Inventory. *Career Development Quarterly, 46*, 2–22.

Drummond, R. J. (1996). *Appraisal procedures for counselors and helping professionals* (3rd ed.). Upper Saddle River, NJ: Merrill/Prentice Hall.

Egan, G. (1998). *The skilled helper* (6th ed.). Pacific Grove, CA: Brooks/Cole.

Elmore, P. B., Ekstrom, R. B., Diamond, E. E., & Whittaker, S. (1993). School counselors' test use patterns and practices. *School Counselor, 41*, 73–80.

Elmore, T. M., & Roberge, L. P. (1982). Assessment and experiencing: On measuring the marigolds. *Measurement and Evaluation in Guidance, 15*, 95–102.

Engen, H. B., Lamb, R. R., & Prediger, D. J. (1982). Are secondary schools still using standardized tests? *Personnel and Guidance Journal 60*, 287–290.

Erdberg, P. (1996). The Rorschach. In C. S. Newmark (Ed.), *Major psychological assessment instruments* (2nd ed.). Boston: Allyn & Bacon.

Exner, J. E. (1991). *The Rorschach: A comprehensive system: Interpretation, Vol. 2* (2nd ed.). New York: Wiley.

Exner, J. E. (1993). *The Rorschach: A comprehensive system: Basic foundations, Vol. 1* (3rd ed.). New York: Wiley.

Exner, J. E. (1995). *The Rorschach: A comprehensive system: Assessment of children and adolescents, Vol. 3* (2nd ed.). New York: Wiley.

Gardner, H. (1993). *Frames of mind: The theory of multiple intelligences*. New York: Basic Books.

Giordano, F. G., Schwiebert, V. L., & Brotherton, W. D. (1997). School counselors' perceptions of the usefulness of standardized test, frequency of their use, and assessment training needs. *School Counselor, 44*, 198–205.

Goldman, L. (1971). *Using tests in counseling* (2nd ed.). New York: Appleton-Century-Crofts.

Goldman, L. (1972). Tests and counseling: The marriage that failed. *Measurement and Evaluation in Guidance, 4*, 213–220.

Goldman, L. (1994a). The marriage between tests and counseling redux: Summary of the 1972 article. *Measurement and Evaluation in Counseling and Development, 26*, 214–216.

Goldman, L. (1994b). The marriage is over . . . for most of us. *Measurement and Evaluation in Counseling and Development, 26*, 217–218.

Goodyear, R. K. (1989). A debate: Resolved, that the Myers-Briggs Type Indicator is a useful tool in counseling. *Journal of Counseling and Development, 67*, 435.

Gronlund, N. E., & Linn, R. L. (1990). *Measurement and evaluation in teaching* (6th ed.). New York: Macmillan.

Groth-Marnat, G. (1997). *Handbook of psychological assessment* (3rd ed.). New York: Wiley.

Hamann, E. E. (1994). Clinicians and diagnosis: Ethical concerns and clinical competence. *Journal of Counseling and Development, 72,* 259–260.

Hanna, G. S. (1988). Using percentile bands for meaningful descriptive test score interpretations. *Journal of Counseling and Development, 66,* 477–483.

Hansen, J-I. C. (1994). Multiculturalism in assessment. *Measurement and Evaluation in Counseling and Development, 27,* 67.

Harper, F. D. (1981). *Dictionary of counseling techniques and terms.* Alexandria, VA: Douglass.

Harris, F. (1994, April). Everyday ethics. *ACCA Visions, 2,* 7–8, 10.

Healy, C. C., & Woodward, G. A. (1998). The Myers-Briggs Type Indicator and career obstacles. *Measurement and Evaluation in Counseling and Development, 31,* 74–85.

Hohenshil, T. H. (1993). Assessment and diagnosis in the *Journal of Counseling and Development. Journal of Counseling and Development, 72,* 7.

Hohenshil, T. H. (1996). Role of assessment and diagnosis in counseling. *Journal of Counseling & Development, 75,* 64–67.

Holland, J. L. (1997). *Making vocational choices: A theory of careers* (3rd ed.). Odessa, FL: Psychological Assessment Resources.

Hood, A. B., & Johnson, R. W. (1997). *Assessment in counseling* (2nd ed.). Alexandria, VA: American Counseling Association.

Impara, J. C., & Plake, B. S. (Eds.). (1998). *The thirteenth mental measurements yearbook.* Lincoln: University of Nebraska, Buros Institute of Mental Measurement.

Jepsen, D. A. (1982). Test usage in the 1970s: A summary and interpretation. *Measurement and Evaluation in Guidance, 15,* 164–168.

Joint Committee on Testing Practices. (1988). *Code of fair testing practices in education.* Washington, DC: Author.

Jongsma, A. E., Jr., & Peterson, L. M. (1995). *The complete psychotherapy treatment planner.* New York: Wiley.

Kamphaus, R. W., Beres, K. A., Kaufman, A. S., & Kaufman, N. L. (1996). The Kaufman Assessment Battery for Children (K-ABC). In C. S. Newmark (Ed.), *Major psychological assessment instruments* (2nd ed.). Boston: Allyn & Bacon.

Kapes, J. T., Mastie, M. M., & Whitfield, E. A. (1995). *A counselor's guide to career assessment instruments* (3rd ed.). Alexandria, VA: National Career Development Association and Association for Assessment in Counseling.

Kaplan, R. M., & Saccuzzo, D. P. (1997). *Psychological testing: Principles, applications, and issues* (4th ed.). Pacific Grove, CA: Brooks/Cole.

Krieshok, T. S. (1987). Review of the Self-Directed Search. *Journal of Counseling and Development, 65,* 512–514.

Krumboltz, J. D. (1991). *Manual for the Career Beliefs Inventory.* Palo Alto, CA: Consulting Psychologists Press.

Krumboltz, J. D. (1992, December). Challenging troublesome career beliefs. *CAPS Digest,* EDO-CG-92-4.

Kuder, F. (1939). *Manual for the Preference Record.* Chicago: Science Research Associates.

Kuder, F. (1977). *Activity interest and occupational choice.* Chicago: Science Research Associates.

Learner, B. (1981). Representative democracy, "men of zeal," and testing legislation. *American Psychologist, 36,* 270–275.

Loesch, L. (1977). Guest editorial. *Elementary School Guidance and Counseling, 12,* 74–75.

Lynch, A. Q. (1985). The Myers-Briggs Type Indicator: A tool for appreciating employee and client diversity. *Journal of Employment Counseling, 22,* 104–109.

Miller, G. M. (1977). After the testing is over. *Elementary School Guidance and Counseling, 12,* 139–143.

Miller, G. M. (1982). Deriving meaning from standardized tests: Interpreting test results to clients. *Measurement and Evaluation in Guidance, 15,* 87–94.

Murray, H. A. (1938). *Explorations in personality.* New York: Oxford University Press.

Myers, I. B. (1962). *Manual for the Myers-Briggs Type Indicator.* Palo Alto, CA: Consulting Psychologists Press.

Myers, I. B. (1980). *Gifts differing.* Palo Alto, CA: Consulting Psychologists Press.

Oakland, T. (1982). Nonbiased assessment in counseling: Issues and guidelines. *Measurement and Evaluation in Guidance, 15,* 107–116.

Osborne, W. L., Brown, S., Niles, S., & Miner, C. U. (1997). *Career development, assessment & counseling.* Alexandria, VA: American Counseling Association.

Parsons, F. (1909). *Choosing a vocation.* Boston: Houghton Mifflin.

Pate, R. H., Jr. (1983). Assessment and information giving. In J. A. Brown & R. H. Pate, Jr. (Eds.), *Being a counselor* (pp. 147–172) Pacific Grove, CA: Brooks/Cole.

Paterson, D. J., & Darley, J. (1936). *Men, women, and jobs.* Minneapolis: University of Minnesota Press.

Paul, G. L. (1967). Strategy of outcome research in psychotherapy. *Journal of Consulting Psychology, 31,* 109–118.

Piotrowski, C., & Keller, J. (1989). Psychological testing in outpatient mental health facilities: A national study. *Professional Psychology: Research and Practice, 20,* 423–425.

Prediger, D. J. (Ed.). (1993). *Multicultural assessment standards: A compilation for counselors.* Alexandria, VA: Association for Assessment in Counseling.

Prediger, D. J. (1994). Tests and counseling: The marriage that prevailed. *Measurement and Evaluation in Counseling and Development, 26,* 227–234.

Prescott, M. R., Cavatta, J. C., & Rollins, K. D. (1977). The fakability of the Personality Orientation Inventory. *Counselor Education and Supervision, 17,* 116–120.

Rogers, J. E. (1996). Review of the Armed Services Vocational Aptitude Battery (ASVAB) career exploration program. *Measurement and Evaluation in Counseling and Development, 29,* 176–182.

Rueth, T., Demmitt, A., & Burger, S. (1998, March). *Counselors and the DSM-IV: Intentional and unintentional consequences of diagnosis.* Paper presented at the American Counseling Association World Conference, Indianapolis, IN.

Savickas, M. L. (1998). Interpreting interest inventories: A case example. *Career Development Quarterly, 46,* 307–319.

Sheeley, V. L., & Eberly, C. G. (1985). Two decades of leadership in measurement and evaluation. *Journal of Counseling and Development, 63,* 436–439.

Shertzer, B., & Linden, J. D. (1979). *Fundamentals of individual appraisal, assessment techniques for counselors.* Boston: Houghton Mifflin.

Shertzer, B., & Linden, J. D. (1982). Persistent issues in counselor assessment and appraisal. *Measurement and Evaluation in Guidance, 15,* 9–14.

Shertzer, B., & Stone, S. C. (1980). *Fundamentals of counseling* (3rd ed.). Boston: Houghton Mifflin.

Shertzer, B., & Stone, S. C. (1981). *Fundamentals of guidance* (4th ed.). Boston: Houghton Mifflin.

Sommers-Flanagan, J., & Sommers-Flanagan, R. (1998). Assessment and diagnosis of conduct disorder. *Journal of Counseling & Development, 76,* 189–197.

Strahan, R. F., & Kelly, A. E. (1994). Showing clients what their profiles mean. *Journal of Counseling and Development, 72,* 329–331.

Suzuki, L. A., & Kugler, J. F. (1995). Intelligence and personality assessment. In J. G. Ponterotto, J. M. Casas, L. A. Suzuki, & C. M. Alexander (Eds.), *Handbook of multicultural counseling* (pp. 493–515). Thousand Oaks, CA: Sage.

Suzuki, L. A., Meller, P. J., & Ponterotto, J. G. (Eds.). (1996). *Handbook of multicultural assessment: Clinical, psychological, and educational applications.* San Francisco: Jossey-Bass.

Sylvania, K. C. (1956). Test usage in counseling centers. *Personnel and Guidance Journal, 34,* 559–564.

Talbutt, L. C. (1983). The counselor and testing: Some legal concerns. *School Counselor, 30,* 245–250.

Thorndike, R. M. (1997). *Measurement and evaluation in psychology and education* (6th ed.). Upper Saddle River, NJ: Merrill/Prentice Hall.

Tinsley, H. E. A., & Bradley, R. W. (1986). Test interpretation. *Journal of Counseling and Development, 65,* 462–466.

Tyler, L. E. (1984). What tests don't measure. *Journal of Counseling and Development, 63,* 48–50.

Vacc, N. A., & Juhnke, G. A. (1997). The use of structured clinical interviews for assessment in counseling. *Journal of Counseling & Development, 75,* 470–480.

Walsh, W. B., & Osipow, S. H. (Eds.) (1996). *Handbook of vocational psychology* (2nd ed.). Hillsdale, NJ: Erlbaum.

Watkins, C. E., Jr. (1990). The testing of the test section of the *Journal of Counseling and Development:* Historical, contemporary, and future perspectives. *Journal of Counseling and Development, 69,* 70–74.

Wechsler, D. (1981). *Wechsler Adult Intelligence Scale-Revised: Manual.* San Antonio, TX: Psychological Corporation.

Westbrook, B. W. (1988). Suggestions for selecting appropriate career assessment instruments. *Measurement and Evaluation in Counseling and Development, 20,* 181–186.

Zytowski, D. G. (1982). Assessment in the counseling process for the 1980s. *Measurement and Evaluation in Guidance, 15,* 15–21.

Zytowski, D. G. (1992). Three generations: The continuing evolution of Frederic Kuder's interest inventories. *Journal of Counseling and Development, 71,* 245–248.

Zytowski, D. G. (1994). Test and counseling: We are still married and living in discriminate analysis. *Measurement and Evaluation in Counseling and Development, 26,* 219–223.

Zytowski, D. G., & Holmberg, K. S. (1988). Preferences: Frederic Kuder's contributions to the counseling profession. *Journal of Counseling and Development, 67,* 150–156.

ETHICAL STANDARDS OF THE AMERICAN COUNSELING ASSOCIATION

PREAMBLE

The American Counseling Association is an educational, scientific and professional organization whose members are dedicated to the enhancement of human development throughout the life span. Association members recognize diversity in our society and embrace a cross-cultural approach in support of the worth, dignity, potential, and uniqueness of each individual.

The specification of a code of ethics enables the Association to clarify to current and future members, and to those served by members, the nature of the ethical responsibilities held in common by its members. As the code of ethics of the Association, this document establishes principles that define the ethical behavior of Association members. All members of the American Counseling Association are required to adhere to the *Code of Ethics* and the *Standards of Practice*. The Code of Ethics will serve as the basis for processing ethical complaints initiated against members of the Association.

CODE OF ETHICS
Section A: The Counseling Relationship
A.1. Client Welfare

a. *Primary Responsibility.* The primary responsibility of counselors is to respect the dignity and to promote the welfare of clients.

b. *Positive Growth and Development.* Counselors encourage client growth and development in ways which foster the clients' interest and welfare; counselors avoid fostering dependent counseling relationships.

c. *Counseling Plans.* Counselors and their clients work jointly in devising integrated, individual counseling plans that offer reasonable promise of success and are consistent with abilities and circumstances of clients. Counselors and clients regularly review counseling plans to ensure their continued viability and effectiveness, respecting clients' freedom of choice. (See A.3.b.)

d. *Family Involvement.* Counselors recognize that families are usually important in clients' lives and strive to enlist family understanding and involvement as a positive resource, when appropriate.

e. *Career and Employment Needs.* Counselors work with their clients in considering employment in jobs and circumstances that are consistent with the clients' overall abilities, vocational limitations, physical restrictions, general temperament, interest and aptitude patterns, social skills, education, general qualifications, and other relevant characteristics and needs. Counselors neither place nor participate in placing clients in positions that will result in damaging the interest and welfare of clients, employers, or the public.

A.2. Respecting Diversity

a. *Nondiscrimination.* Counselors do not condone or engage in discrimination based on age, color, culture, disability, ethnic group, gender, race, religion, sexual orientation, marital status, or socioeconomic status. (See C.5.a., C.5.b., and D.1.i.)

b. *Respecting Differences.* Counselors will actively attempt to understand the diverse cultural backgrounds of the clients with whom they work. This includes, but is not limited to, learning how the counselor's own cultural/ethnic/racial identity impacts her/his values and beliefs about the counseling process. (See E.8. and F.2.i.)

A.3. Client Rights

a. *Disclosure to Clients.* When counseling is initiated, and throughout the counseling process as necessary, counselors inform clients of the purposes, goals, techniques, procedures, limitations, potential risks and benefits of services to be performed and other pertinent information. Counselors take steps to ensure that clients understand the implications of diagnosis, the intended use of tests and reports, fees, and billing arrangements. Clients have the right to expect confidentiality and to be provided with an explanation of its limitations, including supervision and/or treatment team professionals; to obtain clear information about their case records; to participate in the ongoing counseling plans; and to refuse any recommended services and be advised of the consequences of such refusal. (See E.5.a. and G.2.)

b. *Freedom of Choice.* Counselors offer clients the freedom to choose whether to enter into a counseling relationship and to determine which professional(s) will provide counseling. Restrictions that limit choices of clients are fully explained. (See A.1.c.)

c. *Inability to Give Consent.* When counseling minors or persons unable to give voluntary informed consent, counselors act in these clients' best interests. (See B.3.)

A.4. Clients Served by Others

If a client is receiving services from another mental health professional, counselors, with client consent, inform the professional persons already involved and develop clear agreements in order to avoid confusion and conflict for the client. (See C.6.c.)

A.5. Personal Needs and Values

a. *Personal Needs.* In the counseling relationship, counselors are aware of the intimacy and responsibilities inherent in the counseling relationship, maintain respect for clients, and avoid actions that seek to meet their personal needs at the expense of clients.

b. *Personal Values.* Counselors are aware of their own values, attitudes, beliefs, and behaviors and how these apply in a diverse society, and avoid imposing their values on clients. (See C.5.a.)

A.6. Dual Relationships

a. *Avoid When Possible.* Counselors are aware of their influential positions with respect to clients, and they avoid exploiting the trust and dependency of clients. Counselors make every effort to avoid dual relationships with clients that could impair professional judgment or increase the risk of harm to clients. (Examples of such relationships include, but are not limited to, familial, social, financial, business, or close personal relationships with clients.) When a dual relationship cannot be avoided, counselors take appropriate professional precautions such as informed consent, consultation, supervision, and documentation to ensure that judgment is not impaired and no exploitation occurs. (See F.1.b.)

b. *Superior/Subordinate Relationships.* Counselors do not accept as clients superiors or subordinates with whom they have administrative, supervisory, or evaluative relationships.

A.7. Sexual Intimacies with Clients

a. *Current Clients.* Counselors do not have any type of sexual intimacies with clients and do not counsel persons with whom they have had a sexual relationship.

b. *Former Clients.* Counselors do not engage in sexual intimacies with former clients within a minimum of two years after terminating the counseling relationship. Counselors who engage in such relationship after two years following termination have the responsibility to thoroughly exam and document that such relations did not have an exploitative nature, based on factors such as duration of counseling, amount of time since counseling, termination circumstances, client's personal history and mental status, adverse impact on the client, and actions by the counselor suggesting a plan to initiate a sexual relationship with the client after termination.

A.8. Multiple Clients

When counselors agree to provide counseling services to two or more persons who have a relationship (such as husband and wife, or parents and children), counselors clarify at the outset which person or persons are clients and the nature of the relationships they will have with each involved person. If it becomes apparent that counselors may be called upon to perform potential conflicting roles, they clarify, adjust, or withdraw from roles appropriately. (See B.2. and B.4.d.)

A.9. Group Work

a. *Screening.* Counselors screen prospective group counseling/therapy participants. To the extent possible, counselors select members whose needs and goals are compatible with goals of the group, who will not impede the group process, and whose well-being will not be jeopardized by the group experience.

b. *Protecting Clients.* In a group setting, counselors take reasonable precautions to protect clients from physical or psychological trauma.

A.10. Fees and Bartering (See D.3.a. and D.3.b.)

a. *Advance Understanding.* Counselors clearly explain to clients, prior to entering the counseling relationship, all financial arrangements related to professional services including the use of collection agencies or legal measures for non-payment (A.11.c).

b. *Establishing Fees.* In establishing fees for professional counseling services, counselors consider the financial status of clients and locality. In the event that the established fee structure is inappropriate for a client, assistance is provided in attempting to find comparable services of acceptable cost. (See A.10.d., D.3.a., and D.3.b.)

c. *Bartering Discouraged.* Counselors ordinarily refrain from accepting goods or services from clients in return for counseling services because

such arrangements create inherent potential for conflicts, exploitation, and distortion of the professional relationship. Counselors may participate in bartering only if the relationship is not exploitive, if the client requests it, if a clear written contract is established, and if such arrangements are an accepted practice among professionals in the community. (See A.6.a.)

d. *Pro Bono Service.* Counselors contribute to society by devoting a portion of their professional activity to services for which there is little or no financial return (pro bono).

A.11. Termination and Referral

a. *Abandonment Prohibited.* Counselors do not abandon or neglect clients in counseling. Counselors assist in making appropriate arrangements for the continuation of treatment, when necessary, during interruptions such as vacations, and following termination.

b. *Inability to Assist Clients.* If counselors determine an inability to be of professional assistance to clients, they avoid entering or immediately terminate a counseling relationship. Counselors are knowledgeable about referral resources and suggest appropriate alternatives. If clients decline the suggested referral, counselors should discontinue the relationship.

c. *Appropriate Termination.* Counselors terminate a counseling relationship, securing client agreement when possible, when it is reasonably clear that the client is no longer benefiting, when services are no longer required, when counseling no longer serves the client's needs or interests, when clients do not pay fees charged, or when agency or institution limits do not allow provision of further counseling services. (See A.10.b. and C.2.g.)

A.12. Computer Technology

a. *Use of Computers.* When computer applications are used in counseling services, counselors ensure that: (1) the client is intellectually, emotionally, and physically capable of using the computer application; (2) the computer application is appropriate for the needs of the client; (3) the client understands the purpose and operation of the computer applications; and (4) a follow-up of client use of a computer application is provided to correct possible misconceptions, discover inappropriate use, and assess subsequent needs.

b. *Explanation of Limitations.* Counselors ensure that clients are provided information as a part of the counseling relationship that adequately explains the limitations of computer technology.

c. *Access to Computer Applications.* Counselors provide for equal access to computer applications in counseling services. (See A.2.a.)

Section B: Confidentiality

B.1. Right to Privacy

a. *Respect for Privacy.* Counselors respect their clients' right to privacy and avoid illegal and unwarranted disclosures of confidential information. (See A.3.a. and B.6.a.)

b. *Client Waiver.* The right to privacy may be waived by the client or their legally recognized representative.

c. *Exceptions.* The general requirement that counselors keep information confidential does not apply when disclosure is required to prevent clear and imminent danger to the client or others or when legal requirements demand that confidential information be revealed. Counselors consult with other professionals when in doubt as to the validity of an exception.

d. *Contagious, Fatal Diseases.* A counselor who receives information confirming that a client has a disease commonly known to be both communicable and fatal is justified in disclosing information to an identifiable third party, who by his or her relationship with the client is at a high risk of contracting the disease. Prior to making a disclosure the counselor should ascertain that the client has not already informed the third party about his or her disease and that the client is not intending to inform the third party in the immediate future. (See B.1.c. and B.1.f.)

e. *Court Ordered Disclosure.* When court ordered to release confidential information without a client's permission, counselors request to the court that the disclosure not be required due to potential harm to the client or counseling relationship. (See B.1.c.)

f. *Minimal Disclosure.* When circumstances require the disclosure of confidential information, only essential information is revealed. To the extent possible, clients are informed before confidential information is disclosed.

g. *Explanation of Limitations.* When counseling is initiated and throughout the counseling process as necessary, counselors inform clients of the limitations of confidentiality and identify foreseeable situations in which confidentiality must be breached. (See G.2.a.)

h. *Subordinates.* Counselors make every effort to ensure that privacy and confidentiality of clients are maintained by subordinates including employees, supervisees, clerical assistants, and volunteers. (See B.1.a.)

i. *Treatment Teams.* If client treatment will involve a continued review by a treatment team, the client will be informed of the team's existence and composition.

B.2. Groups and Families

a. *Group Work.* In group work, counselors clearly define confidentiality and the parameters for the specific group being entered, explain its importance, and discuss the difficulties related to confidentiality involved in group work. The fact that confidentiality cannot be guaranteed is clearly communicated to group members.

b. *Family Counseling.* In family counseling, information about one family member cannot be disclosed to another member without permission. Counselors protect the privacy rights of each family member. (See A.8., B.3., and B.4.d.)

B.3. Minor or Incompetent Clients

When counseling clients who are minors or individuals who are unable to give voluntary, informed consent, parents or guardians may be included in the counseling process as appropriate. Counselors act in the best interests of clients and take measures to safeguard confidentiality. (See A.3.c.)

B.4. Records

a. *Requirement of Records.* Counselors maintain records necessary for rendering professional services to their clients and as required by laws, regulations, or agency or institution procedures.

b. *Confidentiality of Records.* Counselors are responsible for securing the safety and confidentiality of any counseling records they create, maintain, transfer, or destroy whether the records are written, taped, computerized, or stored in any other medium. (See B.1.a.)

c. *Permission to Record or Observe.* Counselors obtain permission from clients prior to electronically recording or observing sessions. (See A.3.a.)

d. *Client Access.* Counselors recognize that counseling records are kept for the benefit of clients and therefore provide access to records and copies of records when requested by competent clients unless the records contain information that may be misleading and detrimental to the client. In situations involving multiple clients, access to records is limited to those parts of records that do not include confidential information related to another client. (See A.8., B.1.a., and B.2.b.)

e. *Disclosure or Transfer.* Counselors obtain written permission from clients to disclose or transfer records to legitimate third parties unless exceptions to confidentiality exist as listed in Section B1. Steps are taken to ensure that receivers of counseling records are sensitive to their confidential nature.

B.5. Research and Training

a. *Data Disguise Required.* Use of data derived from counseling relationships for purposes of training, research, or publication is confined to content that is disguised to ensure the anonymity of the individuals involved. (See B.1.g. and G.3.d.)

b. *Agreement for Identification.* Identification of a client in a presentation or publication is permissible only when the client has reviewed the material and has agreed to its presentation or publication. (See G.3.d.)

B.6. Consultation

a. *Respect for Privacy.* Information obtained in a consulting relationship is discussed for professional purposes only with persons clearly concerned with the case. Written and oral reports present data germane to the purposes of the consultation, and every effort is made to protect client identity and avoid undue invasion of privacy.

b. *Cooperating Agencies.* Before sharing information, counselors make efforts to ensure that there are defined policies in other agencies serv-

ing the counselor's clients that effectively protect the confidentiality of information.

Section C: Professional Responsibility

C.1. Standards Knowledge

Counselors have a responsibility to read, understand, and follow the *Code of Ethics* and the *Standards of Practice*.

C.2. Professional Competence

a. *Boundaries of Competence.* Counselors practice only within the boundaries of their competence, based on their education, training, supervised experience, state and national professional credentials, and appropriate professional experience. Counselors will demonstrate a commitment to gain knowledge, personal awareness, sensitivity, and skills pertinent to working with a diverse client population.

b. *New Specialty Areas of Practice.* Counselors practice in specialty areas new to them only after appropriate education, training, and supervised experience. While developing skills in new specialty areas, counselors take steps to ensure the competence of their work and to protect others from possible harm.

c. *Qualified for Employment.* Counselors accept employment only for positions for which they are qualified by education, training, supervised experience, state and national professional credentials, and appropriate professional experience. Counselors hire for professional counseling positions only individuals who are qualified and competent.

d. *Monitor Effectiveness.* Counselors continually monitor their effectiveness as professionals and take steps to improve when necessary. Counselors in private practice take reasonable steps to seek out peer supervision to evaluate their efficacy as counselors.

e. *Ethical Issues Consultation.* Counselors take reasonable steps to consult with other counselors or related professionals when they have questions regarding their ethical obligations or professional practice (See H.1.).

f. *Continuing Education.* Counselors recognize the need for continuing education to maintain a reasonable level of awareness of current scientific and professional information in their fields of activity. They take steps to maintain competence in the skills they use, are open to new procedures, and keep current with the diverse and/or special populations with whom they work.

g. *Impairment.* Counselors refrain from offering or accepting professional services when their physical, mental or emotional problems are likely to lead to harm to a client or others. They are alert to the signs of impairment, seek assistance for problems, and, if necessary, limit, suspend, or terminate their professional responsibilities. (See A.11.c.)

C.3. Advertising and Soliciting Clients

a. *Accurate Advertising.* There are no restrictions on advertising by counselors except those that can be specifically justified to protect the public from deceptive practices. Counselors advertise or represent their services to the public by identifying their credentials in an accurate manner that is not false, misleading, deceptive, or fraudulent. Counselors may only advertise the highest degree earned which is in counseling or a closely related field from a college or university that was accredited when the degree was awarded by one of the regional accrediting bodies recognized by the Council on Post-secondary Accreditation.

b. *Testimonials.* Counselors who use testimonials do not solicit them from clients or other persons who, because of their particular circumstances, may be vulnerable to undue influence.

c. *Statements by Others.* Counselors make reasonable efforts to ensure that statements made by others about them or the profession of counseling are accurate.

d. *Recruiting Through Employment.* Counselors do not use their places of employment or institutional affiliation to recruit or gain clients, supervisees, or consultees for their private practices. (See C.5.e.)

e. *Products and Training Advertisements.* Counselors who develop products related to their profession or conduct workshops or training events ensure that the advertisements concerning these products or events are accurate and disclose adequate information for consumers to make informed choices.

f. *Promoting to Those Served.* Counselors do not use counseling, teaching, training, or supervisory relationships to promote their products or training events in a manner that is deceptive or would exert undue influence on individuals who may be vulnerable. Counselors may adopt textbooks they have authored for instruction purposes.

g. *Professional Association Involvement.* Counselors actively participate in local, state, and national associations that foster the development and improvement of counseling.

C.4. Credentials

a. *Credentials Claimed.* Counselors claim or imply only professional credentials possessed and are responsible for correcting any known misrepresentations of their credentials by others. Professional credentials include graduate degrees in counseling or closely related mental health fields, accreditation of graduate programs, national voluntary certifications, government-issued certifications or licenses, ACA professional membership, or any other credential that might indicate to the public specialized knowledge or expertise in counseling.

b. *ACA Professional Membership.* ACA professional members may announce to the public their membership status. Regular members may not announce their ACA membership in a manner that might imply they are credentialed counselors.

c. *Credential Guidelines.* Counselors follow the guidelines for use of credentials that have been established by the entities that issue the credentials.

d. *Misrepresentation of Credentials.* Counselors do not attribute more to their credentials than the credentials represent, and do not imply that other counselors are not qualified because they do not possess certain credentials.

e. *Doctoral Degrees from Other Fields.* Counselors who hold a master's degree in counseling or a closely related mental health field, but hold a doctoral degree from other than counseling or a closely related field do not use the title, "Dr." in their practices and do not announce to the public in relation to their practice or status as a counselor that they hold a doctorate.

C.5. Public Responsibility

a. *Nondiscrimination.* Counselors do not discriminate against clients, students, or supervisees in a manner that has a negative impact based on their age, color, culture, disability, ethnic group, gender, race, religion, sexual orientation, or socioeconomic status, or for any other reason. (See A.2.a.)

b. *Sexual Harassment.* Counselors do not engage in sexual harassment. Sexual harassment is defined as sexual solicitation, physical advances, or verbal or nonverbal conduct that is sexual in nature, that occurs in connection with professional activities or roles, and that either: (1) is unwelcome, is offensive, or creates a hostile workplace environment, and counselors know or are told this; or (2) is sufficiently severe or intense to be harassing to a reasonable person in the context. Sexual harassment can consist of a single intense or severe act or multiple persistent or pervasive acts.

c. *Reports to Third Parties.* Counselors are accurate, honest, and unbiased in reporting their professional activities and judgments to appropriate third parties including courts, health insurance companies, those who are the recipients of evaluation reports, and others. (See B.1.g.)

d. *Media Presentations.* When counselors provide advice or comment by means of public lectures, demonstrations, radio or television programs, prerecorded tapes, printed articles, mailed material, or other media, they take reasonable precautions to ensure that (1) the statements are based on appropriate professional counseling literature and practice; (2) the statements are otherwise consistent with the *Code of Ethics* and the *Standards of Practice*; and (3) the recipients of the information are not encouraged to infer that a professional counseling relationship has been established. (See C.6.b.)

e. *Unjustified Gains.* Counselors do not use their professional positions to seek or receive unjustified personal gains, sexual favors, unfair advantage, or unearned goods or services. (See C.3.d.)

C.6. Responsibility to Other Professionals

a. *Different Approaches.* Counselors are respectful of approaches to professional counseling that differ from their own. Counselors know and take into account the traditions and practices of other professional groups with which they work.

b. *Personal Public Statements.* When making personal statements in a public context, counselors clarify that they are speaking from their personal perspectives and that they are not speaking on behalf of all counselors or the profession. (See C.5.d.)

c. *Clients Served by Others.* When counselors learn that their clients are in a professional relationship with another mental health professional, they request release from clients to inform the other professionals and strive to establish positive and collaborative professional relationships. (See A.4.)

Section D: Relationships with Other Professionals

D.1. Relationships with Employers and Employees

a. *Role Definition.* Counselors define and describe for their employers and employees the parameters and levels of their professional roles.

b. *Agreements.* Counselors establish working agreements with supervisors, colleagues, and subordinates regarding counseling or clinical relationships, confidentiality, adherence to professional standards, distinction between public and private material, maintenance and dissemination of recorded information, workload, and accountability. Working agreements in each instance are specified and made known to those concerned.

c. *Negative Conditions.* Counselors alert their employers to conditions that may be potentially disruptive or damaging to the counselor's professional responsibilities or that may limit their effectiveness.

d. *Evaluation.* Counselors submit regularly to professional review and evaluation by their supervisor or the appropriate representative of the employer.

e. *In-Service.* Counselors are responsible for in-service development of self and staff.

f. *Goals.* Counselors inform their staff of goals and programs.

g. *Practices.* Counselors provide personnel and agency practices that respect and enhance the rights and welfare of each employee and recipient of agency services. Counselors strive to maintain the highest levels of professional services.

h. *Personnel Selection and Assignment.* Counselors select competent staff and assign responsibilities compatible with their skills and experiences.

i. *Discrimination.* Counselors, as either employers or employees, do not engage in or condone practices that are inhumane, illegal, or unjustifiable (such as considerations based on age, color, culture, disability, ethnic group, gender, race, religion, sexual orientation, or socioeconomic status) in hiring, promotion, or training. (See A.2.a. and C.5.b.)

j. *Professional Conduct.* Counselors have a responsibility both to clients and to the agency or institution within which services are performed to maintain high standards of professional conduct.

k. *Exploitive Relationships.* Counselors do not engage in exploitive relationships with individuals over whom they have supervisory, evaluative, or instructional control or authority.

l. *Employer Policies.* The acceptance of employment in an agency or institution implies that counselors are in agreement with its general policies and principles. Counselors strive to reach agreement with employers as to acceptable standards of conduct that allow for changes in institutional policy conducive to the growth and development of clients.

D.2. Consultation (See B.6.)

a. *Consultation as an Option.* Counselors may choose to consult with any other professionally competent persons about their clients. In choosing consultants, counselors avoid placing the consultant in a conflict of interest situation that would preclude the consultant, being a proper party to the counselor's efforts to help the client. Should counselors be engaged in a work setting that compromises this consultation standard, they consult with other professionals whenever possible to consider justifiable alternatives.

b. *Consultant Competency.* Counselors are reasonably certain that they have or the organization represented has the necessary competencies and resources for giving the kind of consulting services needed and that appropriate referral resources are available.

c. *Understanding with Clients.* When providing consultation, counselors attempt to develop with their clients a clear understanding of problem definition, goals for change, and predicted consequences of interventions selected.

d. *Consultant Goals.* The consulting relationship is one in which client adaptability and growth toward self-direction are consistently encouraged and cultivated. (See A.1.b.)

D.3. Fees for Referral

a. *Accepting Fees from Agency Clients.* Counselors refuse a private fee or other remuneration for rendering services to persons who are entitled to such services through the counselor's employing agency or institution. The policies of a particular agency may make explicit provisions for agency clients to receive counseling services from members of its staff in private practice. In such instances, the clients must be informed of other options open to them should they seek private counseling services. (See A.10.a., A.11.b., and C.3.d.)

b. *Referral Fees.* Counselors do not accept a referral fee from other professionals.

D.4. Subcontractor Arrangements

When counselors work as subcontractors for counseling services for a third party, they have a duty to inform clients of the limitations of confidentiality that the organization may place on counselors in providing counseling services to clients. The limits of such confidentiality ordinarily are discussed as part of the intake session. (See B.1.e. and B.1.f.)

Section E: Evaluation, Assessment, and Interpretation

E.1. General

a. *Appraisal Techniques.* The primary purpose of educational and psychological assessment is to provide measures that are objective and interpretable in either comparative or absolute terms. Counselors recognize the need to interpret the statements in this section as applying to the whole range of appraisal techniques, including test and nontest data.

b. *Client Welfare.* Counselors promote the welfare and best interests of the client in the development, publication, and utilization of educational and psychological assessment techniques. They do not misuse assessment results and interpretations and take reasonable steps to prevent others from misusing the information these techniques provide. They respect the client's right to know the results, the interpretations made, and the bases for their conclusions and recommendations.

E.2. Competence to Use and Interpret Tests

a. *Limits of Competence.* Counselors recognize the limits of their competence and perform only those testing and assessment services for which they have been trained. They are familiar with reliability, validity, related standardization, error of measurement, and proper application of any technique utilized. Counselors using computer-based test interpretations are trained in the construct being measured and the specific instrument being used prior to using this type of computer application. Counselors take reasonable measures to ensure the proper use of psychological assessment techniques by persons under their supervision.

b. *Appropriate Use.* Counselors are responsible for the appropriate application, scoring, interpretation, and use of assessment instruments, whether they score and interpret such tests themselves or use computerized or other services.

c. *Decisions Based on Results.* Counselors responsible for decisions involving individuals or policies that are based on assessment results have a thorough understanding of educational and psychological measurement, including validation criteria, test research, and guidelines for test development and use.

d. *Accurate Information.* Counselors provide accurate information and avoid false claims or misconceptions when making statements about assessment instruments or techniques. Special efforts are made to avoid unwarranted connotations of such terms as IQ and grade equivalent scores. (See C.5.c.)

E.3. Informed Consent

a. *Explanation to Clients.* Prior to assessment, counselors explain the nature and purposes of assessment and the specific use of results in language the client (or other legally authorized per-

son on behalf of the client) can understand, unless an explicit exception to this right has been agreed upon in advance. Regardless of whether scoring and interpretation are completed by counselors, by assistants, or by computer or other outside services, counselors take reasonable steps to ensure that appropriate explanations are given to the client.

b. *Recipients of Results.* The examinee's welfare, explicit understanding, and prior agreement determine the recipients of test results. Counselors include accurate and appropriate interpretations with any release of individual or group test results. (See B.1.a. and C.5.c.)

E.4. Release of Information to Competent Professionals

a. *Misuse of Results.* Counselors do not misuse assessment results, including test results, and interpretations, and take reasonable steps to prevent the misuse of such by others. (See C.5.c.)

b. *Release of Raw Data.* Counselors ordinarily release data (e.g. protocols, counseling or interview notes, or questionnaires) in which the client is identified only with the consent of the client or the client's legal representative. Such data are usually released only to persons recognized by counselors as competent to interpret the data. (See B.1.a.)

E.5. Proper Diagnosis of Mental Disorders

a. *Proper Diagnosis.* Counselors take special care to provide proper diagnosis of mental disorders. Assessment techniques (including personal interview) used to determine client care (e.g., locus of treatment, type of treatment, or recommended follow-up) are carefully selected and appropriately used. (See A.3.a. and C.5.c.)

b. *Cultural Sensitivity.* Counselors recognize that culture affects the manner in which clients' problems are defined. Clients' socioeconomic and cultural experience is considered when diagnosing mental disorders.

E.6. Test Selection

a. *Appropriateness of Instruments.* Counselors carefully consider the validity, reliability, psychometric limitations, and appropriateness of instruments when selecting tests for use in a given situation or with a particular client.

b. *Culturally Diverse Populations.* Counselors are cautious when selecting tests for culturally diverse populations to avoid inappropriateness of testing that may be outside of socialized behavioral or cognitive patterns.

E.7. Conditions of Test Administration

a. *Administration Conditions.* Counselors administer tests under the same conditions that were established in their standardization. When tests are not administered under standard conditions or when unusual behavior or irregularities occur during the testing session, those conditions are noted in interpretation and the results may be designated as invalid or of questionable validity.

b. *Computer Administration.* Counselors are responsible for ensuring that administration programs function properly to provide clients with accurate results when a computer or other electronic methods are used for test administration. (See A.12.b.)

c. *Unsupervised Test-Taking.* Counselors do not permit unsupervised or inadequately supervised use of tests or assessments unless the tests or assessments are designed, intended, and validated for self-administration and/or scoring.

d. *Disclosure of Favorable Conditions.* Prior to test administration, conditions that produce most favorable test results are made known to the examinee.

E.8. Diversity in Testing

Counselors are cautious in using assessment techniques, making evaluations, and interpreting the performance of populations not represented in the norm group on which an instrument was standardized. They recognize the effects of age, color, culture, disability, ethnic group, gender, race, religion, sexual orientation, and socioeconomic status on test administration and interpretation and place test results in proper perspective with other relevant factors. (See A.2.a.)

E.9. Test and Scoring Interpretation

a. *Reporting Reservations.* In reporting assessment results, counselors indicate any reservations that

exist regarding validity or reliability because of the circumstances of the assessment or the inappropriateness of the norms for the person tested.

b. *Research Instruments.* Counselors exercise caution when interpreting the results of research instruments possessing insufficient technical data to support respondent results. The specific purposes for the use of such instruments are stated explicitly to the examinee.

c. *Testing Services.* Counselors who provide test scoring and test interpretation services to support the assessment process confirm the validity of such interpretations. They accurately describe the purpose, norms, validity, reliability, and applications of the procedures and any special qualifications applicable to their use. The public offering of an automated test interpretations service is considered a professional-to-professional consultation. The formal responsibility of the consultant is to the consultee, but the ultimate and overriding responsibility is to the client.

E.10. Test Security

Counselors maintain the integrity and security of tests and other assessment techniques consistent with legal and contractual obligations. Counselors do not appropriate, reproduce, or modify published tests or parts thereof without acknowledgment and permission from the publisher.

E.11. Obsolete Tests and Outdated Test Results

Counselors do not use data or test results that are obsolete or outdated for the current purpose. Counselors make every effort to prevent the misuse of obsolete measures and test data by others.

E.12. Test Construction

Counselors use established scientific procedures, relevant standards, and current professional knowledge for test design in the development, publication, and utilization of educational and psychological assessment techniques.

Section F: Teaching, Training, and Supervision

F.1. Counselor Educators and Trainers

a. *Educators as Teachers and Practitioners.* Counselors who are responsible for developing, implementing, and supervising educational programs are skilled as teachers and practitioners. They are knowledgeable regarding the ethical, legal, and regulatory aspects of the profession, are skilled in applying that knowledge, and make students and supervisees aware of their responsibilities. Counselors conduct counselor education and training programs in an ethical manner and serve as role models for professional behavior. Counselor educators should make an effort to infuse material related to human diversity into all courses and/or workshops that are designed to promote the development of professional counselors.

b. *Relationship Boundaries with Students and Supervisees.* Counselors clearly define and maintain ethical, professional, and social relationship boundaries with their students and supervisees. They are aware of the differential in power that exists and the student's or supervisee's possible incomprehension of that power differential. Counselors explain to students and supervisees the potential for the relationship to become exploitive.

c. *Sexual Relationships.* Counselors do not engage in sexual relationships with students or supervisees and do not subject them to sexual harassment. (See A.6. and C.5.b.)

d. *Contributions to Research.* Counselors give credit to students or supervisees for their contributions to research and scholarly projects. Credit is given through coauthorship, acknowledgment, footnote statement, or other appropriate means, in accordance with such contributions.(See G.4.b. and G.4.c.)

e. *Close Relatives.* Counselors do not accept close relatives as students or supervisees.

f. *Supervision Preparation.* Counselors who offer clinical supervision services are adequately prepared in supervision methods and techniques. Counselors who are doctoral students serving as practicum or internship supervisors to master's level students are adequately prepared and supervised by the training program.

g. *Responsibility for Services to Clients.* Counselors who supervise the counseling services of others take reasonable measures to ensure that counseling services provided to clients are professional.

h. *Endorsement.* Counselors do not endorse students or supervisees for certification, licensure, employment, or completion of an academic or training program if they believe students or supervisees are not qualified for the endorsement. Counselors take reasonable steps to assist students or supervisees who are not qualified for endorsement to become qualified.

F.2. Counselor Education and Training Programs

a. *Orientation.* Prior to admission, counselors orient prospective students to the counselor education or training program's expectations, including but not limited to the following: (1) the type and level of skill acquisition required for successful completion of the training; (2) subject matter to be covered; (3) basis for evaluation; (4) training components that encourage self-growth or self-disclosure as part of the training process; (5) the type of supervision settings and requirements of the sites for required clinical field experiences; (6) student and supervisee evaluation and dismissal policies and procedures; and (7) up-to-date employment prospects for graduates.

b. *Integration of Study and Practice.* Counselors establish counselor education and training programs that integrate academic study and supervised practice.

c. *Evaluation.* Counselors clearly state to students and supervisees, in advance of training, the levels of competency expected, appraisal methods, and timing of evaluations for both didactic and experiential components. Counselors provide students and supervisees with periodic performance appraisal and evaluation feedback throughout the training program.

d. *Teaching Ethics.* Counselors make students and supervisees aware of the ethical responsibilities and standards of the profession and the students' and supervisees' ethical responsibilities to the profession. (See C.1. and F.3.e.)

e. *Peer Relationships.* When students or supervisees are assigned to lead counseling groups or provide clinical supervision for their peers, counselors take steps to ensure that students and supervisees placed in these roles do not have personal or adverse relationships with peers and that they understand they have the same ethical obligations as counselor educators, trainers, and supervisors. Counselors make every effort to ensure that the rights of peers are not compromised when students or supervisees are assigned to lead counseling groups or provide clinical supervision.

f. *Varied Theoretical Positions.* Counselors present varied theoretical positions so that students and supervisees may make comparisons and have opportunities to develop their own positions. Counselors provide information concerning the scientific bases of professional practice. (See C.6.a.)

g. *Field Placements.* Counselors develop clear policies within their training program regarding field placement and other clinical experiences. Counselors provide clearly stated roles and responsibilities for the student or supervisee, the site supervisor, and the program supervisor. They confirm that site supervisors are qualified to provide supervision and are informed of their professional and ethical responsibilities in this role.

h. *Dual Relationships as Supervisors.* Counselors avoid dual relationships such as performing the role of site supervisor and training program supervisor in the student's or supervisee's training program. Counselors do not accept any form of professional services, fees, commissions, reimbursement, or remuneration from a site for student or supervisee placement.

i. *Diversity in Programs.* Counselors are responsive to their institution's and program's recruitment and retention needs for training program administrators, faculty, and students with diverse backgrounds and special needs. (See A.2.a.)

F.3. Students and Supervisees

a. *Limitations.* Counselors, through on-going evaluation and appraisal, are aware of the academic and personal limitations of students and supervisees that might impede performance. Counselors assist students and supervisees in securing remedial assistance when needed, and dismiss from the training program supervisees who are unable to provide competent service due to academic or personal limitations. Counselors seek professional consultation and document their decision to dismiss or refer students or supervisees for assistance. Counselors assure that students and supervisees have recourse to address decisions made to require them to seek assistance or to dismiss them.

b. *Self-Growth Experiences.* Counselors use professional judgment when designing training experiences conducted by the counselors themselves that require student and supervisee self-growth or self-disclosure. Safeguards are provided so that students and supervisees are aware of the ramifications their self-disclosure may have upon counselors whose primary role as teacher, trainer, or supervisor requires acting upon ethical obligations to the profession. Evaluative components of experiential training experiences explicitly delineate predetermined academic standards that are separate and not dependent upon the student's level of self-disclosure. (See A.6.)

c. *Counseling for Students and Supervisees.* If students or supervisees request counseling, supervisors or counselor educators provide them with acceptable referrals. Supervisors or counselor educators do not serve as counselor to students or supervisees over whom they hold administrative, teaching, or evaluative roles unless this is a brief role associated with a training experience. (See A.6.b.)

d. *Clients of Students and Supervisees.* Counselors make every effort to ensure that the clients at field placements are aware of the services rendered and the qualifications of the students and supervisees rendering those services. Clients receive professional disclosure information and are informed of the limits of confidentiality. Client permission is obtained in order for the students and supervisees to use any information concerning the counseling relationship in the training process. (See B.1.e.)

e. *Standards for Students and Supervisees.* Students and supervisees preparing to become counselors adhere to the *Code of Ethics* and the *Standards of Practice.* Students and supervisees have the same obligations to clients as those required of counselors. (See H.1.)

Section G: Research and Publication

G.1. Research Responsibilities

a. *Use of Human Subjects.* Counselors plan, design, conduct, and report research in a manner consistent with pertinent ethical principles, federal and state laws, host institutional regulations, and scientific standards governing research with human subjects. Counselors design and conduct research that reflects cultural sensitivity appropriateness.

b. *Deviation from Standard Practices.* Counselors seek consultation and observe stringent safeguards to protect the rights of research participants when a research problem suggests a deviation from standard acceptable practices. (See B.6.)

c. *Precautions to Avoid Injury.* Counselors who conduct research with human subjects are responsible for the subjects' welfare throughout the experiment and take reasonable precautions to avoid causing injurious psychological, physical, or social effects to their subjects.

d. *Principal Researcher Responsibility.* The ultimate responsibility for ethical research practice lies with the principal researcher. All others involved in the research activities share ethical obligations and full responsibility for their own actions.

e. *Minimal Interference.* Counselors take reasonable precautions to avoid causing disruptions in subjects' lives due to participation in research.

f. *Diversity.* Counselors are sensitive to diversity and research issues with special populations. They seek consultation when appropriate. (See A.2.a. and B.6.)

G.2. Informed Consent

a. *Topics Disclosed.* In obtaining informed consent for research, counselors use language that is understandable to research participants and that: (1) accurately explains the purpose and procedures to be followed; (2) identifies any procedures that are experimental or relatively untried; (3) describes the attendant discomforts and risks; (4) describes the benefits or changes in individuals or organizations that might be reasonably expected; (5) discloses appropriate alternative procedures that would be advantageous for subjects; (6) offers to answer any inquiries concerning the procedures; (7) describes any limitations on confidentiality; and (8) instructs that subjects are free to withdraw their consent and to discontinue participation in the project at any time. (See B.1.f.)

b. *Deception.* Counselors do not conduct research involving deception unless alternative procedures are not feasible and the prospective value of the research justifies the deception. When the methodological requirements of a study necessitate concealment or deception, the investigator is required to explain clearly the reasons for this action as soon as possible.

c. *Voluntary Participation.* Participation in research is typically voluntary and without any penalty for refusal to participate. Involuntary participation is appropriate only when it can be demonstrated that participation will have no harmful effects on subjects and is essential to the investigation.

d. *Confidentiality of Information.* Information obtained about research participants during the course of an investigation is confidential. When the possibility exists that others may obtain access to such information, ethical research practice requires that the possibility, together with the plans for protecting confidentiality, be explained to participants as a part of the procedure for obtaining informed consent. (See B.1.e.)

e. *Persons Incapable of Giving Informed Consent.* When a person is incapable of giving informed consent, counselors provide an appropriate explanation, obtain agreement for participation and obtain appropriate consent from a legally authorized person.

f. *Commitments to Participants.* Counselors take reasonable measures to honor all commitments to research participants.

g. *Explanations After Data Collection.* After data are collected, counselors provide participants with full clarification of the nature of the study to remove any misconceptions. Where scientific or human values justify delaying or withholding information, counselors take reasonable measures to avoid causing harm.

h. *Agreements to Cooperate.* Counselors who agree to cooperate with another individual in research or publication incur an obligation to cooperate as promised in terms of punctuality of performance and with regard to the completeness and accuracy of the information required.

i. *Informed Consent for Sponsors.* In the pursuit of research, counselors give sponsors, institutions, and publication channels the same respect and opportunity for giving informed consent that they accord to individual research participants. Counselors are aware of their obligation to future research workers and ensure that host institutions are given feedback information and proper acknowledgment.

G.3. Reporting Results

a. *Information Affecting Outcome.* When reporting research results, counselors explicitly mention all variables and conditions known to the investigator that may have affected the outcome of a study or the interpretation of data.

b. *Accurate Results.* Counselors plan, conduct, and report research accurately and in a manner that minimizes the possibility that results will be misleading. They provide thorough discussions of the limitations of their data and alternative hypotheses. Counselors do not engage in fraudulent research, distort data, misrepresent data, or deliberately bias their results.

c. *Obligation to Report Unfavorable Results.* Counselors communicate to other counselors the results of any research judged to be of professional value. Results that reflect unfavorably on institutions, programs, services, prevailing opinions, or vested interests are not withheld.

d. *Identity of Subjects.* Counselors who supply data, aid in the research of another person, report research results, or make original data available take due care to disguise the identity of respective subjects in the absence of specific authorization from the subjects to do otherwise. (See B.1.g. and B.5.a.)

e. *Replication Studies.* Counselors are obligated to make available sufficient original research data to qualified professionals who may wish to replicate the study.

G.4. Publication

a. *Recognition of Others.* When conducting and reporting research, counselors are familiar with and give recognition to previous work on the topic, observe copyright laws, and give full credit to those to whom credit is due. (See F.1.d. and G.4.c.)

b. *Contributors.* Counselors give credit through joint authorship, acknowledgment, footnote statements, or other appropriate means to those who have contributed significantly to research or concept development in accordance with such contributions. The principal contributor is listed first and minor technical or professional contributions are acknowledged in notes or introductory statements.

c. *Student Research.* For an article that is substantially based on a student's dissertation or thesis, the student is listed as the principal author. (See F.1.d. and G.4.a.)

d. *Duplicate Submission.* Counselors submit manuscripts for consideration to only one journal at a time. Manuscripts that are published in whole or in substantial part in another journal or published work are not submitted for publication without acknowledgment and permission from the previous publication.

e. *Professional Review.* Counselors who review material submitted for publication, research, or other scholarly purposes respect the confidentiality and proprietary rights of those who submitted it.

Section H: Resolving Ethical Issues
H.1. Knowledge of Standards

Counselors are familiar with the *Code of Ethics* and the *Standards of Practice* and other applicable ethics codes from other professional organizations of which they are members, or from certification and licensure bodies. Lack of knowledge or misunderstanding of an ethical responsibility is not a defense against a charge of unethical conduct. (See F.3.e.)

H.2. Suspected Violations

a. *Ethical Behavior Expected.* Counselors expect professional associates to adhere to Code of Ethics. When counselors possess reasonable cause that raises doubts as to whether a counselor is acting in an ethical manner, they take appropriate action. (See H.2.d. and H.2.e.)

b. *Consultation.* When uncertain as to whether a particular situation or course of action may be in violation of Code of Ethics, counselors consult with other counselors who are knowledgeable about ethics, with colleagues, or with appropriate authorities.

c.   *Organization Conflicts.* If the demands of an organization with which counselors are affiliated pose a conflict with Code of Ethics, counselors specify the nature of such conflicts and express to their supervisors or other responsible officials their commitment to Code of Ethics. When possible, counselors work toward change within the organization to allow full adherence to Code of Ethics.

d.   *Informal Resolution.* When counselors have reasonable cause to believe that another counselor is violating an ethical standard, they attempt to first resolve the issue informally with the other counselor if feasible, providing that such action does not violate confidentiality rights that may be involved.

e.   *Reporting Suspected Violations.* When an informal resolution is not appropriate or feasible, counselors, upon reasonable cause, take action such as reporting the suspected ethical violation to state or national ethics committees, unless this action conflicts with confidentiality rights that cannot be resolved.

f.   *Unwarranted Complaints.* Counselors do not initiate, participate in, or encourage the filing of ethics complaints that are unwarranted or intend to harm a counselor rather than to protect clients or the public.

H.3. Cooperation with Ethics Committees

Counselors assist in the process of enforcing Code of Ethics. Counselors cooperate with investigations, proceedings, and requirements of the ACA Ethics Committee or ethics committees of other duly constituted associations or boards having jurisdiction over those charged with a violation. Counselors are familiar with the ACA Policies and Procedures and use it as a reference in assisting the enforcement of the Code of Ethics.

STANDARDS OF PRACTICE

All members of the American Counseling Association (ACA) are required to adhere to the *Standards of Practice* and the *Code of Ethics*. The *Standards of Practice* represent minimal behavioral statements of the *Code of Ethics*. Members should refer to the applicable section of the Code of Ethics for further

interpretation and amplification of the applicable Standard of Practice (SP).

Section A: The Counseling Relationship

SP-1: Nondiscrimination. Counselors respect diversity and must not discriminate against clients because of age, color, culture, disability, ethnic group, gender, race, religion, sexual orientation, marital status, or socioeconomic status. (See A.2.a.)

SP-2: Disclosure to Clients. Counselors must adequately inform clients, preferably in writing, regarding the counseling process and counseling relationship at or before the time it begins and throughout the relationship. (See A.3.a.)

SP-3: Dual Relationships. Counselors must make every effort to avoid dual relationships with clients that could impair their professional judgment or increase the risk of harm to clients. When a dual relationship cannot be avoided, counselors must take appropriate steps to ensure that judgment is not impaired and that no exploitation occurs. (See A.6.a. and A.6.b.)

SP-4: Sexual Intimacies with Clients. Counselors must not engage in any type of sexual intimacies with current clients and must not engage in sexual intimacies with former clients within a minimum of two years after terminating the counseling relationship. Counselors who engage in such relationship after two years following termination have the responsibility to thoroughly exam and document that such relations did not have an exploitative nature.

SP-5: Protecting Clients during Group Work. Counselors must take steps to protect clients from physical or psychological trauma resulting from interactions during group work. (See A.9.b.)

SP-6: Advance Understanding of Fees. Counselors must explain to clients, prior to their entering the counseling relationship, financial arrangements related to professional services. (See A.10.a.-d.) and A.11.c.)

SP-7: Termination. Counselors must assist in making appropriate arrangements for the continuation of treatment of clients, when necessary, following termination of counseling relationships. (See A.11.a.)

SP-8: Inability to Assist Clients. Counselors must avoid entering or immediately terminate a counseling relationship if it is determined that they are unable to be of professional assistance to a client. The counselor may assist in making an appropriate referral for the client. (See A.11.b.)

Section B: Confidentiality

SP-9: Confidentiality Requirement. Counselors must keep information related to counseling services confidential unless disclosure is in the best interest of clients, is required for the welfare of others, or is required by law. When disclosure is required, only information that is essential is revealed and the client is informed of such disclosure. (See B.1.a.-f.)

SP-10: Confidentiality Requirements for Subordinates. Counselors must take measures to ensure that privacy and confidentiality of clients are maintained by subordinates. (See B.1.h.)

SP-11: Confidentiality in Group Work. Counselors must clearly communicate to group members that confidentiality cannot be guaranteed in group work. (See B.2.a.)

SP-12: Confidentiality in Family Counseling. Counselors must not disclose information about one family member in counseling to another family member without prior consent. (See B.2.b.)

SP-13: Confidentiality of Records. Counselors must maintain appropriate confidentiality in creating, storing, accessing, transferring, and disposing of counseling records. (See B.4.b.)

SP-14: Permission to Record or Observe. Counselors must obtain prior consent from clients in order to electronically record or observe sessions. (See B.4.c.)

SP-15: Disclosure or Transfer of Records. Counselors must obtain client consent to disclose or transfer records to third parties, unless exceptions listed in SP-9 exist. (See B.4.e.)

SP-16: Data Disguise Required. Counselors must disguise the identity of the client when using data for training, research, or publication. (See B.5.a.)

Section C: Professional Responsibility

SP-17: Boundaries of Competence. Counselors must practice only within the boundaries of their competence. (See C.2.a.)

SP-18: Continuing Education. Counselors must engage in continuing education to maintain their professional competence. (See C.2.f.)

SP-19: Impairment of Professionals. Counselors must refrain from offering professional services when their personal problems or conflicts may cause harm to a client or others. (See C.2.g.)

SP-20: Accurate Advertising. Counselors must accurately represent their credentials and services when advertising. (See C.3.a.)

SP-21: Recruiting Through Employment. Counselors must not use their place of employment or institutional affiliation to recruit clients for their private practices. (See C.3.d.)

SP-22: Credentials Claimed. Counselors must claim or imply only professional credentials possessed and must correct any known misrepresentations of their credentials by others. (See C.4.a.)

SP-23: Sexual Harassment. Counselors must not engage in sexual harassment. (See C.5.b.)

SP-24: Unjustified Gains. Counselors must not use their professional positions to seek or receive unjustified personal gains, sexual favors, unfair advantage, or unearned goods or services. (See C.5.e.)

SP-25: Clients Served by Others. With the consent of the client, counselors must inform other mental health professionals serving the same client that a counseling relationship between the counselor and client exists. (See C.6.c.)

SP-26: Negative Employment Conditions. Counselors must alert their employers to institutional policy or conditions that may be potentially disruptive or damaging to the counselor's professional responsibilities, or that may limit their effectiveness or deny clients' rights. (See D.1.c.)

SP-27: Personnel Selection and Assignment. Counselors must select competent staff and must assign responsibilities compatible with staff skills and experiences. (See D.1.h.)

SP-28: Exploitive Relationships with Subordinates. Counselors must not engage in exploitive relationships with individuals over whom they have supervisory, evaluative, or instructional control or authority. (See D.1.k.)

Section D: Relationship with Other Professionals

SP-29: Accepting Fees from Agency Clients. Counselors must not accept fees or other remuneration for consultation with persons entitled to such services through the counselor's employing agency or institution. (See D.3.a.)

SP-30: Referral Fees. Counselors must not accept referral fees. (See D.3.b.)

Section E: Evaluation, Assessment, and Interpretation

SP-31: Limits of Competence. Counselors must perform only testing and assessment services for which they are competent. Counselors must not allow the use of psychological assessment techniques by unqualified persons under their supervision. (See E.2.a.)

SP-32: Appropriate Use of Assessment Instruments. Counselors must use assessment instruments in the manner for which they were intended. (See E.2.b.)

SP-33: Assessment Explanations to Clients. Counselors must provide explanations to clients prior to assessment about the nature and purposes of assessment and the specific uses of results. (See E.3.a.)

SP-34: Recipients of Test Results. Counselors must ensure that accurate and appropriate interpretations accompany any release of testing and assessment information. (See E.3.b.)

SP-35: Obsolete Tests and Outdated Test Results. Counselors must not base their assessment or intervention decisions or recommendations on data or test results that are obsolete or outdated for the current purpose. (See E.11.)

Section F: Teaching, Training, and Supervision

SP-36: Sexual Relationships with Students or Supervisees. Counselors must not engage in sexual relationships with their students and supervisees. (See F.1.c.)

SP-37: Credit for Contributions to Research. Counselors must give credit to students or supervisees for their contributions to research and scholarly projects. (See F.1.d.)

SP-38: Supervision Preparation. Counselors who offer clinical supervision services must be trained and prepared in supervision methods and techniques. (See F.1.f.)

SP-39: Evaluation Information. Counselors must clearly state to students and supervisees in advance of training, the levels of competency expected, appraisal methods, and timing of evaluations. Counselors must provide students and supervisees with periodic performance appraisal and evaluation feedback throughout the training program. (See F.2.c.)

SP-40: Peer Relationships in Training. Counselors must make every effort to ensure that the rights of peers are not violated when students and supervisees are assigned to lead counseling groups or provide clinical supervision. (See F.2.e.)

SP-41: Limitations of Students and Supervisees. Counselors must assist students and supervisees in securing remedial assistance, when needed, and must dismiss from the training program students and supervisees who are unable to provide competent service due to academic or personal limitations. (See F.3.a.)

SP-42: Self-Growth Experiences. Counselors who conduct experiences for students or supervisees that include self-growth or self disclosure must inform participants of counselors' ethical obligations to the profession and must not grade participants based on their nonacademic performance. (See F.3.b.)

SP-43: Standards for Students and Supervisees. Students and supervisees preparing to become counselors must adhere to the *Code of Ethics* and the *Standards of Practice* of counselors. (See F.3.e.)

Section G: Research and Publication

SP-44: Precautions to Avoid Injury in Research. Counselors must avoid causing physical, social, or psychological harm or injury to subjects in research. (See G.1.c.)

SP-45: Confidentiality of Research Information. Counselors must keep confidential information obtained about research participants. (See G.2.d.)

SP-46: Information Affecting Research Outcome. Counselors must report all variables and conditions known to the investigator that may have affected research data or outcomes. (See G.3.a.)

SP-47: Accurate Research Results. Counselors must not distort or misrepresent research data, nor fabricate or intentionally bias research results. (See G.3.b.)

SP-48: Publication Contributors. Counselors must give appropriate credit to those who have contributed to research. (See G.4.a. and G.4.b.)

Section H: Resolving Ethical Issues

SP-49: Ethical Behavior Expected. Counselors must take appropriate action when they possess reasonable cause that raises doubts as to whether counselors or other mental health professionals are acting in an ethical manner. (See H.2.a.)

SP-50: Unwarranted Complaints. Counselors must not initiate, participate in, or encourage the filing of ethics complaints that are unwarranted or intended to harm a mental health professional rather than to protect clients or the public. (See H.2.f.)

SP-51: Cooperation with Ethics Committees. Counselors must cooperate with investigations, proceedings, and requirements of the ACA Ethics Committee or ethics committees of other duly constituted associations or boards having jurisdiction over those charged with a violation. (See H.3.)

REFERENCES

The following documents are available to counselors as resources to guide them in their practices. These resources are not a part of the *Code of Ethics* and the *Standards of Practice.*

American Association for Counseling and Development/Association for Measurement and Evaluation in Counseling and Development. (1989). *The responsibilities of users of standardized tests (revised)*. Washington, DC: Author.

American Counseling Association. (1988) *American Counseling Association ethical standards.* Alexandria, VA: Author.

American Psychological Association. (1985). *Standards for educational and psychological testing (revised)*. Washington, DC: Author.

American Rehabilitation Counseling Association, Commission on Rehabilitation Counselor Certification, and National Rehabilitation Counseling Association. (1987). *Code of professional ethics for rehabilitation counselors.* Alexandria, VA: Author.

American School Counselor Association. (1992). *Ethical standards for school counselors.* Alexandria, VA: Author.

Joint Committee on Testing Practices. (1988). *Code of fair testing practices in education*. Washington, DC: Author.

National Board for Certified Counselors. (1989). *National Board for Certified Counselors code of ethics*. Alexandria, VA: Author.

Prediger, D. J. (Ed.). (1993, March). *Multicultural assessment standards*. Alexandria, VA: Association for Assessment in Counseling.

ETHICAL STANDARDS OF THE AMERICAN PSYCHOLOGICAL ASSOCIATION

◆

INTRODUCTION

The American Psychological Association's (APA's) Ethical Principles of Psychologists and Code of Conduct (hereinafter referred to as the Ethics Code) consists of an Introduction, a Preamble, six General Principles (A—F), and specific Ethical Standards. The Introduction discusses the intent, organization, procedural considerations, and scope of application of the Ethics Code. The Preamble and General Principles are *aspi-* *rational* goals to guide psychologists toward the highest ideals of psychology. Although the Preamble and General Principles are not themselves enforceable rules, they should be considered by psychologists in arriving at an ethical course of action and may be considered by ethics bodies in interpreting the Ethical Standards. The Ethical Standards set forth *enforceable* rules for conduct as psychologists. Most

This version of the APA Ethics Code was adopted by the American Psychological Association's Council of Representatives during its meeting, August 13 and 16, 1992, and is effective beginning December 1, 1992. Inquiries concerning the substance of interpretation of the APA Ethics Code should be addressed to the Director, Office of Ethics, American Psychological Association, 750 First Street, NE, Washington, DC 20002-4242.

This Code will be used to adjudicate complaints brought concerning alleged conduct occurring on or after the effective date. Complaints regarding conduct occurring prior to the effective date will be adjudicated on the basis of the version of the Code that was in effect at the time the conduct occurred, except that no provisions repealed in June 1989, will be enforced even if an earlier version contains the provision. The Ethics Code will undergo continuing review and study for further revisions; comments on the Code may be sent to the above address.

The APA has previously published its Ethical Standards as follows:

American Psychological Association. (1953). *Ethical standards of psychologists*. Washington, DC: Author.

American Psychological Association. (1958). Standards of ethical behavior for psychologists. *American Psychologist, 13*, 268–271.

American Psychological Association. (1963). Ethical standards of psychologists. *American Psychologist, 18*, 56–60.

American Psychological Association. (1968). Ethical standards of psychologists. *American Psychologist, 23*, 357–361.

American Psychological Association. (1977, March). Ethical standards of psychologists. *APA Monitor*, pp. 22–23.

American Psychological Association. (1979). *Ethical standards of psychologists*. Washington, DC: Author.

American Psychological Association. (1981). Ethical principles of psychologists. *American Psychologist, 36*, 633–638.

American Psychological Association. (1990). Ethical principles of psychologists (Amended June 2, 1989). *American Psychologist, 45*, 390–395.

Request copies of the APA's Ethical Principles of Psychologists and Code of Conduct from the APA Order Department, 750 First Street, NE, Washington, DC 20002-4242, or phone (202) 336-5510.

of the Ethical Standards are written broadly, in order to apply to psychologists in varied roles, although the application of an Ethical Standard may vary depending on the context. The Ethical Standards are not exhaustive. The fact that a given conduct is not specifically addressed by the Ethics Code does not mean that it is necessarily either ethical or unethical.

Membership in the APA commits members to adhere to the APA Ethics Code and to the rules and procedures used to implement it. Psychologists and students, whether or not they are APA members, should be aware that the Ethics Code may be applied to them by state psychology boards, courts, or other public bodies.

This Ethics Code applies only to psychologists' work-related activities, that is, activities that are part of the psychologists' scientific and professional functions or that are psychological in nature. It includes the clinical or counseling practice of psychology, research, teaching, supervision of trainees, development of assessment instruments, conducting assessments, educational counseling, organizational consulting, social intervention, administration, and other activities as well. These work-related activities can be distinguished from the purely private conduct of a psychologist, which ordinarily is not within the purview of the Ethics Code.

The Ethics Code is intended to provide standards of professional conduct that can be applied by the APA and by other bodies that choose to adopt them. Whether or not a psychologist has violated the Ethics Code does not by itself determine whether he or she is legally liable in a court action, whether a contract is enforceable, or whether other legal consequences occur. These results are based on legal rather than ethical rules. However, compliance with or violation of the Ethics Code may be admissible as evidence in some legal proceedings, depending on the circumstances.

In the process of making decisions regarding their professional behavior, psychologists must consider this Ethics Code, in addition to applicable laws and psychology board regulations. If the Ethics Code establishes a higher standard of conduct than is required by law, psychologists must meet the higher ethical standard. If the Ethics Code standard appears to conflict with the requirements of law, then psychologists make known their commitment to the Ethics Code and take steps to resolve the conflict in a responsible manner. If neither law nor the Ethics Code resolves an issue, psychologists should consider other professional materials[1] and the dictates of their own conscience, as well as seek consultation with others within the field when this is practical.

The procedures for filing, investigating, and resolving complaints of unethical conduct are described in the current Rules and Procedures of the APA Ethics Committee. The actions that APA may take for violations of the Ethics Code include actions such as reprimand, censure, termination of APA membership, and referral of the matter to other bodies. Complainants who seek remedies such as monetary damages in alleging ethical violations by a psychologist must resort to private negotiation, administrative bodies, or the courts. Actions that violate the Ethics Code may lead to the imposition of sanctions on a psychologist by bodies other than APA, including state psychological associations, other professional groups, psychology boards, other state or federal agencies, and payors for health services. In addition to actions for violation of the Ethics Code, the APA Bylaws provide that APA may take action against a member after his or her conviction of a felony, expulsion or suspension from an affiliated state psychological association, or suspension or loss of licensure.

---

[1] Professional materials that are most helpful in this regard are guidelines and standards that have been adopted or endorsed by professional psychological organizations. Such guidelines and standards, whether adopted by the American Psychological Association (APA) or its Divisions, are not enforceable as such by this Ethics Code, but are of educative value to psychologists, courts, and professional bodies. Such materials include, but are not limited to, the APA's *General Guidelines for Providers of Psychological Services* (1987), *Specialty Guidelines for the Delivery of Services by Clinical Psychologists, Industrial Organizational Psychologists, and School Psychologists* (1981), *Guidelines for Computer Based Tests and Interpretations* (1987), *Standards for Educational and Psychological Testing* (1985), *Ethical Principles in the Conduct of Research With Human Participants* (1982), *Guidelines for Ethical Conduct in the Care and Use of Animals* (1986), *Guidelines for Providers of Psychological Services to Ethnic, Linguistic, and Culturally Diverse Populations* (1990), and *Publication Manual of the American Psychological Association* (3rd ed., 1983). Materials not adopted by APA as a whole include the APA Division 41 (Forensic Psychology)/American Psychology—Law Society's *Specialty Guidelines for Forensic Psychologists* (1991).

PREAMBLE

Psychologists work to develop a valid and reliable body of scientific knowledge based on research. They may apply that knowledge to human behavior in a variety of contexts. In doing so, they perform many roles, such as researcher, educator, diagnostician, therapist, supervisor, consultant, administrator, social interventionist, and expert witness. Their goal is to broaden knowledge of behavior and, where appropriate, to apply it pragmatically to improve the condition of both the individual and society. Psychologists respect the central importance of freedom of inquiry and expression in research, teaching, and publication. They also strive to help the public in developing informed judgments and choices concerning human behavior. This Ethics Code provides a common set of values upon which psychologists build their professional and scientific work.

This Code is intended to provide both the general principles and the decision rules to cover most situations encountered by psychologists. It has as its primary goal the welfare and protection of the individuals and groups with whom psychologists work. It is the individual responsibility of each psychologist to aspire to the highest possible standards of conduct. Psychologists respect and protect human and civil rights, and do not knowingly participate in or condone unfair discriminatory practices.

The development of a dynamic set of ethical standards for a psychologist's work-related conduct requires a personal commitment to a lifelong effort to act ethically; to encourage ethical behavior by students, supervisees, employees, and colleagues, as appropriate; and to consult with others, as needed, concerning ethical problems. Each psychologist supplements, but does not violate, the Ethics Code's values and rules on the basis of guidance drawn from personal values, culture, and experience.

GENERAL PRINCIPLES
Principle A: Competence

Psychologists strive to maintain high standards of competence in their work. They recognize the boundaries of their particular competencies and the limitations of their expertise. They provide only those services and use only those techniques for which they are qualified by education, training, or experience. Psychologists are cognizant of the fact that the competencies required in serving, teaching, and/or studying groups of people vary with the distinctive characteristics of those groups. In those areas in which recognized professional standards do not yet exist, psychologists exercise careful judgment and take appropriate precautions to protect the welfare of those with whom they work. They maintain knowledge of relevant scientific and professional information related to the services they render, and they recognize the need for ongoing education. Psychologists make appropriate use of scientific, professional, technical, and administrative resources.

Principle B: Integrity

Psychologists seek to promote integrity in the science, teaching, and practice of psychology. In these activities psychologists are honest, fair, and respectful of others. In describing or reporting their qualifications, services, products, fees, research, or teaching, they do not make statements that are false, misleading, or deceptive. Psychologists strive to be aware of their own belief systems, values, needs, and limitations and the effect of these on their work. To the extent feasible, they attempt to clarify for relevant parties the roles they are performing and to function appropriately in accordance with those roles. Psychologists avoid improper and potentially harmful dual relationships.

Principle C: Professional and Scientific Responsibility

Psychologists uphold professional standards of conduct, clarify their professional roles and obligations, accept appropriate responsibility for their behavior, and adapt their methods to the needs of different populations. Psychologists consult with, refer to, or cooperate with other professionals and institutions to the extent needed to serve the best interests of their patients, clients, or other recipients of their services. Psychologists' moral standards and conduct are personal matters to the same degree as is true for any other person, except as psychologists' conduct may compromise their professional responsibilities or reduce the public's trust in psychology and psychologists. Psychologists are concerned about the ethical compliance of their colleagues' scientific and professional conduct. When appropriate, they consult with colleagues in order to prevent or avoid unethical conduct.

Principle D: Respect for People's Rights and Dignity

Psychologists accord appropriate respect to the fundamental rights, dignity, and worth of all people. They respect the rights of individuals to privacy, confidentiality, self-determination, and autonomy, mindful that legal and other obligations may lead to inconsistency and conflict with the exercise of these rights. Psychologists are aware of cultural, individual, and role differences, including those due to age, gender, race, ethnicity, national origin, religion, sexual orientation, disability, language, and socioeconomic status. Psychologists try to eliminate the effect on their work of biases based on those factors, and they do not knowingly participate in or condone unfair discriminatory practices.

Principle E: Concern for Others' Welfare

Psychologists seek to contribute to the welfare of those with whom they interact professionally. In their professional actions, psychologists weigh the welfare and rights of their patients or clients, students, supervisees, human research participants, and other affected persons, and the welfare of animal subjects of research. When conflicts occur among psychologists' obligations or concerns, they attempt to resolve these conflicts and to perform their roles in a responsible fashion that avoids or minimizes harm. Psychologists are sensitive to real and ascribed differences in power between themselves and others, and they do not exploit or mislead other people during or after professional relationships.

Principle F: Social Responsibility

Psychologists are aware of their professional and scientific responsibilities to the community and the society in which they work and live. They apply and make public their knowledge of psychology in order to contribute to human welfare. Psychologists are concerned about and work to mitigate the causes of human suffering. When undertaking research, they strive to advance human welfare and the science of psychology.

Psychologists try to avoid misuse of their work. Psychologists comply with the law and encourage the development of law and social policy that serve the interests of their patients and clients and the public. They are encouraged to contribute a portion of their professional time for little or no personal advantage.

ETHICAL STANDARDS
1. General Standards

These General Standards are potentially applicable to the professional and scientific activities of all psychologists.

1.01 Applicability of the Ethics Code

The activity of a psychologist subject to the Ethics Code may be reviewed under these Ethical Standards only if the activity is part of his or her work-related functions or the activity is psychological in nature. Personal activities having no connection to or effect on psychological roles are not subject to the Ethics Code.

1.02 Relationship of Ethics and Law

If psychologists' ethical responsibilities conflict with law, psychologists make known their commitment to the Ethics Code and take steps to resolve the conflict in a responsible manner.

1.03 Professional and Scientific Relationship

Psychologists provide diagnostic, therapeutic, teaching, research, supervisory, consultative, or other psychological services only in the context of a defined professional or scientific relationship or role. (See also Standards 2.01, Evaluation, Diagnosis, and Interventions in Professional Context, and 7.02, Forensic Assessments.)

1.04 Boundaries of Competence

a.   Psychologists provide services, teach, and conduct research only within the boundaries of their competence, based on their education, training, supervised experience, or appropriate professional experience.

b.   Psychologists provide services, teach, or conduct research in new areas or involving new techniques only after first undertaking appropriate study, training, supervision, and/or consultation from persons who are competent in those areas or techniques.

c. In those emerging areas in which generally recognized standards for preparatory training do not yet exist, psychologists nevertheless take reasonable steps to ensure the competence of their work and to protect patients, clients, students, research participants, and others from harm.

1.05 Maintaining Expertise

Psychologists who engage in assessment, therapy, teaching, research, organizational consulting, or other professional activities maintain a reasonable level of awareness of current scientific and professional information in their fields of activity, and undertake ongoing efforts to maintain competence in the skills they use.

1.06 Basis for Scientific and Professional Judgments

Psychologists rely on scientifically and professionally derived knowledge when making scientific or professional judgments or when engaging in scholarly or professional endeavors.

1.07 Describing the Nature and Results of Psychological Services

a. When psychologists provide assessment, evaluation, treatment, counseling, supervision, teaching, consultation, research, or other psychological services to an individual, a group, or an organization, they provide, using language that is reasonably understandable to the recipient of those services, appropriate information beforehand about the nature of such services and appropriate information later about results and conclusions. (See also Standard 2.09, Explaining Assessment Results.)

b. If psychologists will be precluded by law or by organizational roles from providing such information to particular individuals or groups, they so inform those individuals or groups at the outset of the service.

1.08 Human Differences

Where differences of age, gender, race, ethnicity, national origin, religion, sexual orientation, disability, language, or socioeconomic status significantly affect psychologists' work concerning particular individuals or groups, psychologists obtain the training, experience, consultation, or supervision necessary to ensure the competence of their services, or they make appropriate referrals.

1.09 Respecting Others

In their work-related activities, psychologists respect the rights of others to hold values, attitudes, and opinions that differ from their own.

1.10 Nondiscrimination

In their work-related activities, psychologists do not engage in unfair discrimination based on age, gender, race ethnicity, national origin, religion, sexual orientation, disability, socioeconomic status, or any basis proscribed by law.

1.11 Sexual Harassment

a. Psychologists do not engage in sexual harassment. Sexual harassment is sexual solicitation, physical advances, or verbal or nonverbal conduct that is sexual in nature, that occurs in connection with the psychologist's activities or roles as a psychologist, and that either: (1) is unwelcome, is offensive, or creates a hostile workplace environment, and the psychologist knows or is told this; or (2) is sufficiently severe or intense to be abusive to a reasonable person in the context. Sexual harassment can consist of a single intense or severe act or of multiple persistent or pervasive acts.

b. Psychologists accord sexual-harassment complainants and respondents dignity and respect. Psychologists do not participate in denying a person academic admittance or advancement, employment, tenure, or promotion, based solely upon their having made, or their being the subject of, sexual-harassment charges. This does not preclude taking action based upon the outcome of such proceedings or consideration of other appropriate information.

1.12 Other Harassment

Psychologists do not knowingly engage in behavior that is harassing or demeaning to persons with whom they interact in their work based on factors such as those persons' age, gender, race, ethnicity, national origin, religion, sexual orientation, disability, language, or socioeconomic status.

1.13 Personal Problems and Conflicts

a. Psychologists recognize that their personal problems and conflicts may interfere with their effectiveness. Accordingly, they refrain from undertaking an activity when they know or should know that their personal problems are likely to lead to harm to a patient, client, colleague, student, research participant, or other person to whom they may owe a professional or scientific obligation.
b. In addition, psychologists have an obligation to be alert to signs of, and to obtain assistance for, their personal problems at an early stage, in order to prevent significantly impaired performance.
c. When psychologists become aware of personal problems that may interfere with their performing work-related duties adequately, they take appropriate measures, such as obtaining professional consultation or assistance, and determine whether they should limit, suspend, or terminate their work-related duties.

1.14 Avoiding Harm

Psychologists take reasonable steps to avoid harming their patients or clients, research participants, students, and others with whom they work, and to minimize harm where it is foreseeable and unavoidable.

1.15 Misuse of Psychologists' Influence

Because psychologists' scientific and professional judgments and actions may affect the lives of others, they are alert to and guard against personal, financial, social, organizational, or political factors that might lead to misuse of their influence.

1.16 Misuse of Psychologists' Work

a. Psychologists do not participate in activities in which it appears likely that their skills or data will be misused by others, unless corrective mechanisms are available. (See also Standard 7.04, Truthfulness and Candor.)
b. If psychologists learn of misuse or misrepresentation of their work, they take reasonable steps to correct or minimize the misuse or misrepresentation.

1.17 Multiple Relationships

a. In many communities and situations, it may not be feasible or reasonable for psychologists to avoid social or other nonprofessional contacts with persons such as patients, clients, students, supervisees, or research participants. Psychologists must always be sensitive to the potential harmful effects of other contacts on their work and on those persons with whom they deal. A psychologist refrains from entering into or promising another personal, scientific, professional, financial, or other relationship with such persons if it appears likely that such a relationship reasonably might impair the psychologist's objectivity or otherwise interfere with the psychologist's effectively performing his or her functions as a psychologist, or might harm or exploit the other party.
b. Likewise, whenever feasible, a psychologist refrains from taking on professional or scientific obligations when preexisting relationships would create a risk of such harm.
c. If a psychologist finds that, due to unforeseen factors, a potentially harmful multiple relationship has arisen, the psychologist attempts to resolve it with due regard for the best interests of the affected person and maximal compliance with the Ethics Code.

1.18 Barter (With Patients or Clients)

Psychologists ordinarily refrain from accepting goods, services, or other nonmonetary remuneration from patients or clients in return for psychological services because such arrangements create inherent potential for conflicts, exploitation, and distortion of the professional relationship. A psychologist may participate in bartering *only* if (1) it is not clinically contraindicated, *and* (2) the relationship is not exploitative. (See also Standards 1.17, Multiple Relationships, and 1.25, Fees and Financial Arrangements.)

1.19 Exploitative Relationships

a. Psychologists do not exploit persons over whom they have supervisory, evaluative, or other authority such as students, supervisees, employees, research participants, and clients or patients. (See also Standards 4.05–4.07 regarding sexual involvement with clients or patients.)

b. Psychologists do not engage in sexual relationships with students or supervisees in training over whom the psychologist has evaluative or direct authority, because such relationships are so likely to impair judgment or be exploitative.

1.20 Consultations and Referrals

a. Psychologists arrange for appropriate consultations and referrals based principally on the best interests of their patients or clients, with appropriate consent, and subject to other relevant considerations, including applicable law and contractual obligations. (See also Standards 5.01, Discussing the Limits of Confidentiality, and 5.06, Consultations.)

b. When indicated and professionally appropriate, psychologists cooperate with other professionals in order to serve their patients or clients effectively and appropriately.

c. Psychologists' referral practices are consistent with law.

1.21 Third-Party Requests for Services

a. When a psychologist agrees to provide services to a person or entity at the request of a third party, the psychologist clarifies to the extent feasible, at the outset of the service, the nature of the relationship with each party. This clarification includes the role of the psychologist (such as therapist, organizational consultant, diagnostician, or expert witness), the probable uses of the services provided or the information obtained, and the fact that there may be limits to confidentiality.

b. If there is a foreseeable risk of the psychologist's being called upon to perform conflicting roles because of the involvement of a third party, the psychologist clarifies the nature and direction of his or her responsibilities, keeps all parties appropriately informed as matters develop, and resolves the situation in accordance with this Ethics Code.

1.22 Delegation to and Supervision of Subordinates

a. Psychologists delegate to their employees, supervisees, and research assistants only those responsibilities that such persons can reasonably be expected to perform competently, on the basis of their education, training, or experience, either independently or with the level of supervision being provided.

b. Psychologists provide proper training and supervision to their employees or supervisees and take reasonable steps to see that such persons perform services responsibly, competently, and ethically.

c. If institutional policies, procedures, or practices prevent fulfillment of this obligation, psychologists attempt to modify their role or to correct the situation to the extent feasible.

1.23 Documentation of Professional and Scientific Work

a. Psychologists appropriately document their professional and scientific work in order to facilitate provision of services later by them or by other professionals, to ensure accountability, and to meet requirements of institutions or the law.

b. When psychologists have reason to believe that records of their professional services will be used in legal proceedings involving recipients of or participants in their work, they have a responsibility to create and maintain documentation in the kind of detail and quality that would be consistent with reasonable scrutiny in an adjudicative forum. (See also Standard 7.01, Professionalism, under Forensic Activities.)

1.24 Records and Data

Psychologists create, maintain, disseminate, store, retain, and dispose of records and data relating to their research, practice, and other work in accordance with law and in a manner that permits compliance with the requirements of this Ethics Code. (See also Standard 5.04, Maintenance of Records.)

1.25 Fees and Financial Arrangements

a. As early as is feasible in a professional or scientific relationship, the psychologist and the patient, client, or other appropriate recipient of psychological services reach an agreement specifying the compensation and the billing arrangements.

b. Psychologists do not exploit recipients of services or payors with respect to fees.

c. Psychologists' fee practices are consistent with law.

d. Psychologists do not misrepresent their fees.

e. If limitations to services can be anticipated because of limitations in financing, this is discussed with the patient, client, or other appropriate recipient of services as early as is feasible. (See also Standard 4.08, Interruption of Services.)

f. If the patient, client, or other recipient of services does not pay for services as agreed, and if the psychologist wishes to use collection agencies or legal measures to collect the fees, the psychologist first informs the person that such measures will be taken and provides that person an opportunity to make prompt payment. (See also Standard 5.11, Withholding Records for Nonpayment.)

1.26 Accuracy in Reports to Payors and Funding Sources

In their reports to payors for services or sources of research funding, psychologists accurately state the nature of research or service provided, the fees or charges, and where applicable, the identity of the provider, the findings, and the diagnosis. (See also Standard 5.05, Disclosures.)

1.27 Referrals and Fees

When a psychologist pays, receives payment from, or divides fees with another professional other than in an employer, employee relationship, the payment to each is based on the services (clinical, consultative, administrative, or other) provided and is not based on the referral itself.

2. Evaluation, Assessment, or Intervention

2.01 Evaluation, Diagnosis, and Interventions in Professional Context

a. Psychologists perform evaluations, diagnostic services, or interventions only within the context of a defined professional relationship. (See also Standard 1.03, Professional and Scientific Relationship.)

b. Psychologists' assessments, recommendations, reports, and psychological diagnostic or evaluative statements are based on information and techniques (including personal interviews of the individual when appropriate) sufficient to provide appropriate substantiation for their findings. (See also Standard 7.02, Forensic Assessments.)

2.02 Competence and Appropriate Use of Assessments and Interventions

a. Psychologists who develop, administer, score, interpret, or use psychological assessment techniques, interviews, tests, or instruments do so in a manner and for purposes that are appropriate in light of the research on or evidence of the usefulness and proper application of the techniques.

b. Psychologists refrain from misuse of assessment techniques, interventions, results, and interpretations and take reasonable steps to prevent others from misusing the information these techniques provide. This includes refraining from releasing raw test results or raw data to persons, other than to patients or clients as appropriate, who are not qualified to use such information. (See also Standards 1.02, Relationship of Ethics and Law, and 1.04, Boundaries of Competence.)

2.03 Test Construction

Psychologists who develop and conduct research with tests and other assessment techniques use scientific procedures and current professional knowledge for test design, standardization, validation, reduction or elimination of bias, and recommendations for use.

2.04 Use of Assessment in General and With Special Populations

a. Psychologists who perform interventions or administer, score, interpret, or use assessment techniques are familiar with the reliability, validation, and related standardization or outcome studies of, and proper applications and uses of, the techniques they use.

b. Psychologists recognize limits to the certainty with which diagnoses, judgments, or predictions can be made about individuals.

c. Psychologists attempt to identify situations in which particular interventions or assessment techniques or norms may not be applicable or may require adjustment in administration or interpretation because of factors such as individuals' gender, age, race, ethnicity, national origin, religion, sexual orientation, disability, language, or socioeconomic status.

2.05 Interpreting Assessment Results

When interpreting assessment results, including automated interpretations, psychologists take into account the various test factors and characteristics of the person being assessed that might affect psychologists' judgments or reduce the accuracy of their interpretations. They indicate any significant reservations they have about the accuracy or limitations of their interpretations.

2.06 Unqualified Persons

Psychologists do not promote the use of psychological assessment techniques by unqualified persons. (See also Standard 1.22, Delegation to and Supervision of Subordinates.)

2.07 Obsolete Tests and Outdated Test Results

a. Psychologists do not base their assessment or intervention decisions or recommendations on data or test results that are outdated for the current purpose.
b. Similarly, psychologists do not base such decisions or recommendations on tests and measures that are obsolete and not useful for the current purpose.

2.08 Test Scoring and Interpretation Services

a. Psychologists who offer assessment or scoring procedures to other professionals accurately describe the purpose, norms, validity, reliability, and applications of the procedures and any special qualifications applicable to their use.
b. Psychologists select scoring and interpretation services (including automated services) on the basis of evidence of the validity of the program and procedures as well as on other appropriate considerations.

c. Psychologists retain appropriate responsibility for the appropriate application, interpretation, and use of assessment instruments, whether they score and interpret such tests themselves or use automated or other services.

2.09 Explaining Assessment Results

Unless the nature of the relationship is clearly explained to the person being assessed in advance and precludes provision of an explanation of results (such as in some organizational consulting, preemployment or security screenings, and forensic evaluations), psychologists ensure that an explanation of the results is provided using language that is reasonably understandable to the person assessed or to another legally authorized person on behalf of the client. Regardless of whether the scoring and interpretation are done by the psychologist, by assistants, or by automated or other outside services, psychologists take reasonable steps to ensure that appropriate explanations of results are given.

2.10 Maintaining Test Security

Psychologists make reasonable efforts to maintain the integrity and security of tests and other assessment techniques consistent with law, contractual obligations, and in a manner that permits compliance with the requirements of this Ethics Code. (See also Standard 1.02, Relationship of Ethics and Law.)

3. Advertising and Other Public Statements

3.01 Definition of Public Statements

Psychologists comply with this Ethics Code in public statements relating to their professional services, products, or publications or to the field of psychology. Public statements include but are not limited to paid or unpaid advertising, brochures, printed matter, directory listings, personal resumes or curricula vitae, interviews or comments for use in media, statements in legal proceedings, lectures and public oral presentations, and published materials.

3.02 Statements by Others

a. Psychologists who engage others to create or place public statements that promote their professional practice, products, or activities retain professional responsibility for such statements.

b. In addition, psychologists make reasonable efforts to prevent others whom they do not control (such as employers, publishers, sponsors, organizational clients, and representatives of the print or broadcast media) from making deceptive statements concerning psychologists' practice or professional or scientific activities.

c. If psychologists learn of deceptive statements about their work made by others, psychologists make reasonable efforts to correct such statements.

d. Psychologists do not compensate employees of press, radio, television, or other communication media in return for publicity in a news item.

e. A paid advertisement relating to the psychologist's activities must be identified as such, unless it is already apparent from the context.

3.03 Avoidance of False or Deceptive Statements

a. Psychologists do not make public statements that are false, deceptive, misleading, or fraudulent, either because of what they state, convey, or suggest or because of what they omit, concerning their research, practice, or other work activities or those of persons or organizations with which they are affiliated. As examples (and not in limitation) of this standard, psychologists do not make false or deceptive statements concerning (1) their training, experience, or competence; (2) their academic degrees; (3) their credentials; (4) their institutional or association affiliations; (5) their services; (6) the scientific or clinical basis for, or results or degree of success of, their services; (7) their fees; or (8) their publications or research findings. (See also Standards 6.15, Deception in Research, and 6.18, Providing Participants With Information About the Study.)

b. Psychologists claim as credentials for their psychological work, only degrees that (1) were earned from a regionally accredited educational institution or (2) were the basis for psychology licensure by the state in which they practice.

3.04 Media Presentations

When psychologists provide advice or comment by means of public lectures, demonstrations, radio or television programs, prerecorded tapes, printed articles, mailed material, or other media, they take reasonable precautions to ensure that (1) the statements are based on appropriate psychological literature and practice, (2) the statements are otherwise consistent with this Ethics Code, and (3) the recipients of the information are not encouraged to infer that a relationship has been established with them personally.

3.05 Testimonials

Psychologists do not solicit testimonials from current psychotherapy clients or patients or other persons who because of their particular circumstances are vulnerable to undue influence.

3.06 In-Person Solicitation

Psychologists do not engage, directly or through agents, in uninvited in-person solicitation of business from actual or potential psychotherapy patients or clients or other persons who because of their particular circumstances are vulnerable to undue influence. However, this does not preclude attempting to implement appropriate collateral contacts with significant others for the purpose of benefiting an already engaged therapy patient.

4. Therapy

4.01 Structuring the Relationship

a. Psychologists discuss with clients or patients as early as is feasible in the therapeutic relationship appropriate issues, such as the nature and anticipated course of therapy, fees, and confidentiality. (See also Standards 1.25, Fees and Financial Arrangements, and 5.01, Discussing the Limits of Confidentiality.)

b. When the psychologist's work with clients or patients will be supervised, the above discussion includes that fact, and the name of the supervisor, when the supervisor has legal responsibility for the case.

c. When the therapist is a student intern, the client or patient is informed of that fact.

d. Psychologists make reasonable efforts to answer patients' questions and to avoid apparent misunderstandings about therapy. Whenever possible, psychologists provide oral and/or written information, using language that is reasonably understandable to the patient or client.

4.02 Informed Consent to Therapy

a. Psychologists obtain appropriate informed consent to therapy or related procedures, using language that is reasonably understandable to participants. The content of informed consent will vary depending on many circumstances; however, informed consent generally implies that the person (1) has the capacity to consent, (2) has been informed of significant information concerning the procedure, (3) has freely and without undue influence expressed consent, and (4) consent has been appropriately documented.

b. When persons are legally incapable of giving informed consent, psychologists obtain informed permission from a legally authorized person, if such substitute consent is permitted by law.

c. In addition, psychologists (1) inform those persons who are legally incapable of giving informed consent about the proposed interventions in a manner commensurate with the persons' psychological capacities, (2) seek their assent to those interventions, and (3) consider such persons' preferences and best interests.

4.03 Couple and Family Relationships

a. When a psychologist agrees to provide services to several persons who have a relationship (such as husband and wife or parents and children), the psychologist attempts to clarify at the outset (1) which of the individuals are patients or clients and (2) the relationship the psychologist will have with each person. This clarification includes the role of the psychologist and the probable uses of the services provided or the information obtained. (See also Standard 5.01, Discussing the Limits of Confidentiality.)

b. As soon as it becomes apparent that the psychologist may be called on to perform potentially conflicting roles (such as marital counselor to husband and wife, and then witness for one party in a divorce proceeding), the psychologist attempts to clarify and adjust, or withdraw from, roles appropriately. (See also Standard 7.03, Clarification of Role, under Forensic Activities.)

4.04 Providing Mental Health Services to Those Served by Others

In deciding whether to offer or provide services to those already receiving mental health services elsewhere, psychologists carefully consider the treatment issues and the potential patient's or client's welfare. The psychologist discusses these issues with the patient or client, or another legally authorized person on behalf of the client, in order to minimize the risk of confusion and conflict, consults with the other service providers when appropriate, and proceeds with caution and sensitivity to the therapeutic issues.

4.05 Sexual Intimacies With Current Patients or Clients

Psychologists do not engage in sexual intimacies with current patients or clients.

4.06 Therapy With Former Sexual Partners

Psychologists do not accept as therapy patients or clients persons with whom they have engaged in sexual intimacies.

4.07 Sexual Intimacies With Former Therapy Patients

a. Psychologists do not engage in sexual intimacies with a former therapy patient or client for at least two years after cessation or termination of professional services.

b. Because sexual intimacies with a former therapy patient or client are so frequently harmful to the patient or client, and because such intimacies undermine public confidence in the psychology profession and thereby deter the public's use of needed services, psychologists do not engage in sexual intimacies with former therapy patients and clients even after a two-year interval except in the most unusual circumstances. The psychologist who engages in such activities after the two years following cessation or termination of treatment bears the burden of demonstrating that there has been no exploitation, in light of all relevant factors, including (1) the amount of time that has passed since therapy terminated, (2) the nature and duration of therapy, (3) the circumstances of termination, (4) the patient's or client's personal history, (5) the patient's or client's current mental status, (6) the likelihood of adverse impact on the patient or client and others, and (7) any statements or actions made by the therapist during the course of therapy suggesting or inviting the possibility of a post-termination sexual or romantic relationship with the patient or client. (See also Standard 1.17 Multiple Relationships.)

4.08 Interruption of Services

a. Psychologists make reasonable efforts to plan for facilitating care in the event that psychological services are interrupted by factors such as the psychologist's illness, death, unavailability, or relocation or by the client's relocation or financial limitations. (See also Standard 5.09, Preserving Records and Data.)

b. When entering into employment or contractual relationships, psychologists provide for orderly and appropriate resolution of responsibility for patient or client care in the event that the employment or contractual relationship ends, with paramount consideration given to the welfare of the patient or client.

4.09 Terminating the Professional Relationship

a. Psychologists do not abandon patients or clients. (See also Standard 1.25e, under Fees and Financial Arrangements.)

b. Psychologists terminate a professional relationship when it becomes reasonably clear that the patient or client no longer needs the service, is not benefiting, or is being harmed by continued service.

c. Prior to termination for whatever reason, except where precluded by the patient's or client's conduct, the psychologist discusses the patient's or client's views and needs, provides appropriate pretermination counseling, suggests alternative services providers as appropriate, and takes other reasonable steps to facilitate transfer of responsibility to another provider if the patient or client needs one immediately.

5. Privacy and Confidentiality

These Standards are potentially applicable to the professional and scientific activities of all psychologists.

5.01 Discussing the Limits of Confidentiality

a. Psychologists discuss with persons and organizations with whom they establish a scientific or professional relationship (including, to the extent feasible, minors and their legal representatives) (1) the relevant limitations on confidentiality, including limitations where applicable in group, marital, and family therapy or in organizational consulting, and (2) the foreseeable uses of the information generated through their services.

b. Unless it is not feasible or is contraindicated, the discussion of confidentiality occurs at the outset of the relationship and thereafter as new circumstances may warrant.

c. Permission for electronic recording of interviews is secured from clients and patients.

5.02 Maintaining Confidentiality

Psychologists have a primary obligation and take reasonable precautions to respect the confidentiality rights of those with whom they work or consult, recognizing that confidentiality may be established by law, institutional rules, or professional or scientific relationships. (See also Standard 6.26, Professional Reviewers.)

5.03 Minimizing Intrusions on Privacy

a. In order to minimize intrusions on privacy, psychologists include in written and oral reports, consultations, and the like, only information germane to the purpose for which the communication is made.

b. Psychologists discuss confidential information obtained in clinical or consulting relationships, or evaluative data concerning patients, individual or organizational clients, students, research participants, supervisees, and employees, only for appropriate scientific or professional purposes and only with persons clearly concerned with such matters.

5.04 Maintenance of Records

Psychologists maintain appropriate confidentiality in creating, storing, accessing, transferring, and disposing of records under their control, whether these are written, automated, or in any other medium. Psychologists maintain and dispose of records in accordance with law and in a manner that permits compliance with the requirements of this Ethics Code.

5.05 Disclosures

a. Psychologists disclose confidential information without the consent of the individual only as mandated by law, or where permitted by law for a valid purpose, such as (1) to provide needed professional services to the patient or the individual or organizational client, (2) to obtain appropriate professional consultations, (3) to protect the patient or client or others from harm, or (4) to obtain payment for services, in which instance disclosure is limited to the minimum that is necessary to achieve the purpose.

b. Psychologists also may disclose confidential information with the appropriate consent of the patient or the individual or organizational client (or of another legally authorized person on behalf of the patient or client), unless prohibited by law.

5.06 Consultations

When consulting with colleagues, (1) psychologists do not share confidential information that reasonably could lead to the identification of a patient, client, research participant, or other person or organization with whom they have a confidential relationship unless they have obtained the prior consent of the person or organization or the disclosure cannot be avoided, and (2) they share information only to the extent necessary to achieve the purposes of the consultation. (See also Standard 5.02, Maintaining Confidentiality.)

5.07 Confidential Information in Databases

a. If confidential information concerning recipients of psychological services is to be entered into databases or systems of records available to persons whose access has not been consented to by the recipient, then psychologists use coding or other techniques to avoid the inclusion of personal identifiers.

b. If a research protocol approved by an institutional review board or similar body requires the inclusion of personal identifiers, such identifiers are deleted before the information is made accessible to persons other than those of whom the subject was advised.

c. If such deletion is not feasible, then before psychologists transfer such data to others or review such data collected by others, they take reasonable steps to determine that appropriate consent of personally identifiable individuals has been obtained.

5.08 Use of Confidential Information for Didactic or Other Purposes

a. Psychologists do not disclose in their writings, lectures, or other public media, confidential, personally identifiable information concerning their patients, individual or organizational clients, students, research participants, or other recipients of their services that they obtained during the course of their work, unless the person or organization has consented in writing or unless there is other ethical or legal authorization for doing so.

b. Ordinarily, in such scientific and professional presentations, psychologists disguise confidential information concerning such persons or organizations so that they are not individually identifiable to others and so that discussions do not cause harm to subjects who might identify themselves.

5.09 Preserving Records and Data

A psychologist makes plans in advance so that confidentiality of records and data is protected in the event of the psychologist's death, incapacity, or withdrawal from the position or practice.

5.10 Ownership of Records and Data

Recognizing that ownership of records and data is governed by legal principles, psychologists take reasonable and lawful steps so that records and data remain available to the extent needed to serve the best interests of patients, individual or organizational clients, research participants, or appropriate others.

5.11 Withholding Records for Nonpayment

Psychologists may not withhold records under their control that are requested and imminently needed for a patient's or client's treatment solely because payment has not been received, except as otherwise provided by law.

6. Teaching, Training Supervision, Research, and Publishing

6.01 Design of Education and Training Programs

Psychologists who are responsible for education and training programs seek to ensure that the programs are competently designed, provide the proper experiences, and meet the requirements for licensure, certification, or other goals for which claims are made by the program.

6.02 Descriptions of Education and Training Programs

a. Psychologists responsible for education and training programs seek to ensure that there is a current and accurate description of the program content, training goals and objectives, and requirements that must be met for satisfactory completion of the program. This information must be made readily available to all interested parties.

b. Psychologists seek to ensure that statements concerning their course outlines are accurate and not misleading, particularly regarding the subject matter to be covered, bases for evaluating progress, and the nature of course experiences. (See also Standard 3.03, Avoidance of False or Deceptive Statements.)

c. To the degree to which they exercise control, psychologists responsible for announcements, catalogs, brochures, or advertisements describing workshops, seminars, or other non-degree-granting educational programs ensure that they accurately describe the audience for which the program is intended, the educational objectives, the presenters, and the fees involved.

6.03 Accuracy and Objectivity in Teaching

a. When engaged in teaching or training, psychologists present psychological information accurately and with a reasonable degree of objectivity.

b. When engaged in teaching or training, psychologists recognize the power they hold over students or supervisees and therefore make reasonable efforts to avoid engaging in conduct that is personally demeaning to students or supervisees. (See also Standards 1.09, Respecting Others, and 1.12, Other Harassment.)

6.04 Limitation on Teaching

Psychologists do not teach the use of techniques or procedures that require specialized training, licensure, or expertise, including but not limited to hypnosis, biofeedback, and projective techniques, to individuals who lack the prerequisite training, legal scope of practice, or expertise.

6.05 Assessing Student and Supervisee Performance

a. In academic and supervisory relationships, psychologists establish an appropriate process for providing feedback to students and supervisees.

b. Psychologists evaluate students and supervisees on the basis of their actual performance on relevant and established program requirements.

6.06 Planning Research

a. Psychologists design, conduct, and report research in accordance with recognized standards of scientific competence and ethical research.

b. Psychologists plan their research so as to minimize the possibility that results will be misleading.

c. In planning research, psychologists consider its ethical acceptability under the Ethics Code. If an ethical issue is unclear, psychologists seek to resolve the issue through consultation with institutional review boards, animal care and use committees, peer consultations, or other proper mechanisms.

d. Psychologists take reasonable steps to implement appropriate protections for the rights and welfare of human participants, other persons affected by the research, and the welfare of animal subjects.

6.07 Responsibility

a. Psychologists conduct research competently and with due concern for the dignity and welfare of the participants.

b. Psychologists are responsible for the ethical conduct of research conducted by them or by others under their supervision or control.

c. Researchers and assistants are permitted to perform only those tasks for which they are appropriately trained and prepared.

d. As part of the process of development and implementation of research projects, psychologists consult those with expertise concerning any special population under investigation or most likely to be affected.

6.08 Compliance With Law and Standards

Psychologists plan and conduct research in a manner consistent with federal and state law and regulations, as well as professional standards governing the conduct of research, and particularly those standards governing research with human participants and animal subjects.

6.09 Institutional Approval

Psychologists obtain from host institutions or organizations appropriate approval prior to conducting research, and they provide accurate information about their research proposals. They conduct the research in accordance with the approved research protocol.

6.10 Research Responsibilities

Prior to conducting research (except research involving only anonymous surveys, naturalistic observations, or similar research), psychologists enter into an agreement with participants that clarifies the nature of the research and the responsibilities of each party.

6.11 Informed Consent to Research

a. Psychologists use language that is reasonably understandable to research participants in obtaining their appropriate informed consent (except as provided in Standard 6.12, Dispensing With Informed Consent). Such informed consent is appropriately documented.

b. Using language that is reasonably understandable to participants, psychologists inform participants of the nature of the research; they inform participants that they are free to participate or to decline to participate or to withdraw from the research; they explain the foreseeable consequences of declining or withdrawing; they inform participants of significant factors that may be expected to influence their willingness to participate (such as risks, discomfort, adverse effects, or limitations on confidentiality, except as provided in Standard 6.15, Deception in Research);

and they explain other aspects about which the prospective participants inquire.

c. When psychologists conduct research with individuals such as students or subordinates, psychologists take special care to protect the prospective participants from adverse consequences of declining or withdrawing from participation.

d. When research participation is a course requirement or opportunity for extra credit, the prospective participant is given the choice of equitable alternative activities.

e. For persons who are legally incapable of giving informed consent, psychologists nevertheless (1) provide an appropriate explanation, (2) obtain the participant's assent, and (3) obtain appropriate permission from a legally authorized person, if such substitute consent is permitted by law.

6.12 Dispensing With Informed Consent

Before determining that planned research (such as research involving only anonymous questionnaires, naturalistic observations, or certain kinds of archival research) does not require the informed consent of research participants, psychologists consider applicable regulations and institutional review board requirements, and they consult with colleagues as appropriate.

6.13 Informed Consent in Research Filming or Recording

Psychologists obtain informed consent from research participants prior to filming or recording them in any form, unless the research involves simply naturalistic observations in public places and it is not anticipated that the recording will be used in a manner that could cause personal identification or harm.

6.14 Offering Inducements for Research, Participants

a. In offering professional services as an inducement to obtain research participants, psychologists make clear the nature of the services, as well as the risks, obligations, and limitations. (See also Standard 1.18, Barter [With Patients or Clients].)

b. Psychologists do not offer excessive or inappropriate financial or other inducements to obtain research participants, particularly when it might tend to coerce participation.

6.15 Deception in Research

a. Psychologists do not conduct a study involving deception unless they have determined that the use of deceptive techniques is justified by the study's prospective scientific, educational, or applied value and that equally effective alternative procedures that do not use deception are not feasible.

b. Psychologists never deceive research participants about significant aspects that would affect their willingness to participate, such as physical risks, discomfort, or unpleasant emotional experiences.

c. Any other deception that is an integral feature of the design and conduct of an experiment must be explained to participants as early as is feasible, preferably at the conclusion of their participation, but no later than at the conclusion of the research. (See also Standard 6.18, Providing Participants With Information About the Study.)

6.16 Sharing and Utilizing Data

Psychologists inform research participants of their anticipated sharing or further use of personally identifiable research data and of the possibility of unanticipated future uses.

6.17 Minimizing Invasiveness

In conducting research, psychologists interfere with the participants or milieu from which data are collected only in a manner that is warranted by an appropriate research design and that is consistent with psychologists' roles as scientific investigators.

6.18 Providing Participants With Information About the Study

a. Psychologists provide a prompt opportunity for participants to obtain appropriate information about the nature, results, and conclusions of the research, and psychologists attempt to correct any misconceptions that participants may have.

b. If scientific or humane values justify delaying or withholding this information, psychologists take reasonable measures to reduce the risk of harm.

6.19 Honoring Commitments

Psychologists take reasonable measures to honor all commitments they have made to research participants.

6.20 Care and Use of Animals in Research

a. Psychologists who conduct research involving animals treat them humanely.

b. Psychologists acquire, care for, use, and dispose of animals in compliance with current federal, state, and local laws and regulations, and with professional standards.

c. Psychologists trained in research methods and experienced in the care of laboratory animals supervise all procedures involving animals and are responsible for ensuring appropriate consideration of their comfort, health, and humane treatment.

d. Psychologists ensure that all individuals using animals under their supervision have received instruction in research methods and in the care, maintenance, and handling of the species being used, to the extent appropriate to their role.

e. Responsibilities and activities of individuals assisting in a research project are consistent with their respective competencies.

f. Psychologists make reasonable efforts to minimize the discomfort, infection, illness, and pain of animal subjects.

g. A procedure subjecting animals to pain, stress, or privation is used only when an alternative procedure is unavailable and the goal is justified by its prospective scientific, educational, or applied value.

h. Surgical procedures are performed under appropriate anesthesia; techniques to avoid infection and minimize pain are followed during and after surgery.

i. When it is appropriate that the animal's life be terminated, it is done rapidly, with an effort to minimize pain, and in accordance with accepted procedures.

6.21 Reporting of Results

a. Psychologists do not fabricate data or falsify results in their publications.

b. If psychologists discover significant errors in their published data, they take reasonable steps to correct such errors in a correction, retraction, erratum, or other appropriate publication means.

6.22 Plagiarism

Psychologists do not present substantial portions or elements of another's work or data as their own, even if the other work or data source is cited occasionally.

6.23 Publication Credit

a. Psychologists take responsibility and credit, including authorship credit, only for work they have actually performed or to which they have contributed.

b. Principal authorship and other publication credits accurately reflect the relative scientific or professional contributions of the individuals involved, regardless of their relative status. Mere possession of an institutional position, such as Department Chair, does not justify authorship credit. Minor contributions to the research or to the writing for publications are appropriately acknowledged, such as in footnotes or in an introductory statement.

c. A student is usually listed as principal author on any multiple-authored article that is substantially based on the student's dissertation or thesis.

6.24 Duplicate Publication of Data

Psychologists do not publish, as original data, data that have been previously published. This does not preclude republishing data when they are accompanied by proper acknowledgement.

6.25 Sharing Data

After research results are published, psychologists do not withhold the data on which their conclusions are based from other competent professionals who seek to verify the substantive claims through reanalysis and who intend to use such data only for that purpose, provided that the confidentiality of the participants can be protected and unless legal rights concerning proprietary data preclude their release.

6.26 Professional Reviewers

Psychologists who review material submitted for publication, grant, or other research proposal review respect the confidentiality of and the proprietary rights in such information of those who submitted it.

7. Forensic Activities

7.01 Professionalism

Psychologists who perform forensic functions, such as assessments, interviews, consultations, reports, or expert testimony, must comply with all other provisions of this Ethics Code to the extent that they apply to such activities. In addition, psychologists base their forensic work on appropriate knowledge of and competence in the areas underlying such work, including specialized knowledge concerning special populations. (See also Standards 1.06, Basis for Scientific and Professional Judgments; 1.08, Human Differences, 1.15, Misuse of Psychologists' Influence; and 1.23, Documentation of Professional and Scientific Work.)

7.02 Forensic Assessments

a. Psychologists' forensic assessments, recommendations, and reports are based on information and techniques (including personal interviews of the individual, when appropriate) sufficient to provide appropriate substantiation for their findings. (See also Standards 1.03, Professional and Scientific Relationship; 1.23, Documentation of Professional and Scientific Work; 2.01, Evaluation, Diagnosis, and Interventions in Professional Context; and 2.05, Interpreting Assessment Results.)

b. Except as noted in (c), below, psychologists provide written or oral forensic reports or testimony of the psychological characteristics of an individual only after they have conducted an examination of the individual adequate to support their statements or conclusions.

c. When, despite reasonable efforts, such an examination is not feasible, psychologists clarify the impact of their limited information on the reliability and validity of their reports and testimony, and they appropriately limit the nature and extent of their conclusions or recommendation.

7.03 Clarification of Role

In most circumstances, psychologists avoid performing multiple and potentially conflicting roles in forensic matters. When psychologists may be called on to serve in more than one role in a legal proceeding— for example, as consultant or expert for one party or for the court and as a fact witness—they clarify role expectations and the extent of confidentiality in advance to the extent feasible, and thereafter as changes occur, in order to avoid compromising their professional judgment and objectivity and in order to avoid misleading others regarding their role.

7.04 Truthfulness and Candor

a. In forensic testimony and reports, psychologists testify truthfully, honestly, and candidly and, consistent with applicable legal procedures, describe fairly the bases for their testimony and conclusions.
b. Whenever necessary to avoid misleading, psychologists acknowledge the limits of their data or conclusions.

7.05 Prior Relationships

A prior professional relationship with a party does not preclude psychologists from testifying as fact witnesses or from testifying to their services to the extent permitted by applicable law. Psychologists appropriately take into account ways in which the prior relationship might affect their professional objectivity or opinions and disclose the potential conflict to the relevant parties.

7.06 Compliance With Law and Rules

In performing forensic roles, psychologists are reasonably familiar with the rules governing their roles. Psychologists are aware of the occasionally competing demands placed upon them by these principles and the requirements of the court system, and attempt to resolve these conflicts by making known their commitment to this Ethics Code and taking steps to resolve the conflict in a responsible manner. (See also Standard 1.02, Relationship of Ethics and Law.)

8. Resolving Ethical Issues

8.01 Familiarity With Ethics Code

Psychologists have an obligation to be familiar with this Ethics Code, other applicable ethics codes, and their application to psychologists' work. Lack of awareness or misunderstanding of an ethical standard is not itself a defense to a charge of unethical conduct.

8.02 Confronting Ethical Issues

When a psychologist is uncertain whether a particular situation or course of action would violate this Ethics Code, the psychologist ordinarily consults with other psychologists knowledgeable about ethical issues, with state or national psychology ethics committees, or with other appropriate authorities in order to choose a proper response.

8.03 Conflicts Between Ethics and Organizational Demands

If the demands of an organization with which psychologists are affiliated conflict with this Ethics Code, psychologists clarify the nature of the conflict, make known their commitment to the Ethics Code, and to the extent feasible, seek to resolve the conflict in a way that permits the fullest adherence to the Ethics Code.

8.04 Information Resolution of Ethical Violations

When psychologists believe that there may have been an ethical violation by another psychologist, they attempt to resolve the issue by bringing it to the attention of that individual if an informal resolution appears appropriate and the intervention does not violate any confidentiality rights that may be involved.

8.05 Reporting Ethical Violations

If an apparent ethical violation is not appropriate for informal resolution under Standard 8.04 or is not resolved properly in that fashion, psychologists take further action appropriate to the situation, unless such action conflicts with confidentiality rights in ways that cannot be resolved. Such action might include referral to state or national committees on professional ethics or to state licensing boards.

8.06 Cooperating With Ethics Committees

Psychologists cooperate in ethics investigations, proceedings, and resulting requirements of the APA or any affiliated state psychological association to which they belong. In doing so, they make reasonable efforts to resolve any issues as to confidentiality. Failure to cooperate is itself an ethics violation.

8.07 Improper Complaints

Psychologists do not file or encourage the filing of ethics complaints that are frivolous and are intended to harm the respondent rather than to protect the public.

DIAGNOSTIC AND STATISTICAL MANUAL, FOURTH EDITION (DSM-IV) CLASSIFICATIONS

◆

NOS = Not Otherwise Specified.

An *x* appearing in a diagnostic code indicates that a specific code number is required.

An ellipsis (. . .) is used in the names of certain disorders to indicate that the name of a specific mental disorder or general medical condition should be inserted when recording the name (e.g., 293.0 Delirium Due to Hypothyroidism).

Numbers in parentheses are page numbers.

If criteria are currently met, one of the following severity specifiers may be noted after the diagnosis:

Mild

Moderate

Severe

If criteria are no longer met, one of the following specifiers may be noted:

In Partial Remission

In Full Remission

Prior History

Source: *Diagnostic and Statistical Manual of Mental Disorders* (4th ed.). © American Psychiatric Association, 1994. Reprinted with permission.

DISORDERS USUALLY FIRST DIAGNOSED IN INFANCY, CHILDHOOD, OR ADOLESCENCE (37)

Mental Retardation (39)

Note: These are coded on Axis II.

317	Mild Mental Retardation (41)	
318.0	Moderate Mental Retardation (41)	
318.1	Severe Mental Retardation (41)	
318.2	Profound Mental Retardation (41)	
319	Mental Retardation, Severity Unspecified (42)	

Learning Disorders (46)

315.00	Reading Disorder (48)
315.1	Mathematics Disorder (50)
315.2	Disorder of Written Expression (51)
315.9	Learning Disorder NOS (53)

Motor Skills Disorder

315.4	Developmental Coordination Disorder (53)

Communication Disorders (55)

315.31	Expressive Language Disorder (55)
315.31	Mixed Receptive-Expressive Language Disorder (58)
315.39	Phonological Disorder (61)
307.0	Stuttering (63)
307.9	Communication Disorder NOS (65)

Pervasive Developmental Disorders (65)

299.00	Autistic Disorder (66)
299.80	Rett's Disorder (71)

299.10   Childhood Disintegrative Disorder (73)
299.80   Asperger's Disorder (75)
299.80   Pervasive Developmental Disorder NOS (77)

Attention-Deficit and Disruptive Behavior Disorders (78)

314.xx   Attention-Deficit/Hyperactivity Disorder (78)
.01   Combined Type
.00   Predominantly Inattention Type
.01   Predominantly Hyperactive-Impulse Type
314.9   Attention-Deficit/Hyperactivity Disorder NOS (85)
312.8   Conduct Disorder (85)
         Specify type: Childhood-Onset Type/Adolescent-Onset Type
313.81   Oppositional Defiant Disorder (91)
312.9   Disruptive Behavior Disorder NOS (94)

Feeding and Eating Disorders of Infancy or Early Childhood (94)

307.52   Pica (95)
307.53   Rumination Disorder (96)
307.59   Feeding Disorder of Infancy or Early Childhood (98)

Tic Disorders (100)

307.23   Tourette's Disorder (101)
307.22   Chronic Motor or Vocal Tic Disorder (103)
307.21   Transient Tic Disorder (104)
         Specify if: Single Episode/Recurrent
307.20   Tic Disorder NOS (105)

Elimination Disorders (106)

—.—   Encopresis (106)
787.6   With Constipation and Overflow Incontinence
307.7   Without Constipation and Overflow Incontinence
307.6   Enuresis (Not Due to a General Medical Condition) (108)
         Specify type: Nocturnal Only/Diurnal Only/Nocturnal and Diurnal

Other Disorders of Infancy, Childhood, or Adolescence

309.21   Separation Anxiety Disorder (110)

         Specify if: Early Onset
313.23   Selective Mutism (114)
313.89   Reactive Attachment Disorder of Infancy or Early Childhood (116)
         Specify type: Inhibited Type/Disinhibited Type
307.3   Stereotypic Movement Disorder (118)
         Specify if: With Self-injurious Behavior
313.9   Disorder of Infancy, Childhood, or Adolescence NOS (121)

DELIRIUM, DEMENTIA, AND AMNESTIC AND OTHER COGNITIVE DISORDERS (123)

Delirium (124)

293.0   Delirium Due to . . . *[Indicate the General Medical Condition]* (127)
—.—   Substance Intoxication Delirium *(refer to Substance-Related Disorders for substance-specific codes)* (129)
—.—   Substance Withdrawal Delirium *(refer to Substance-Related Disorders for substance-specific codes)* (129)
—.—   Delirium Due to Multiple Etiologies *(code each of the specific etiologies)* (132)
780.09   Delirium NOS (133)

Dementia (133)

290.xx   Dementia of the Alzheimer's Type, With Early Onset *(also code 331.0 Alzheimer's disease on Axis III)* (139)
.10   Uncomplicated
.11   With Delirium
.12   With Delusions
.13   With Depressed Mood
         Specify if: With Behavioral Disturbance
290.xx   Dementia of the Alzheimer's Type, With Late Onset *(also code 331.0 Alzheimer's disease on Axis III)* (139)
.0   Uncomplicated
.3   With Delirium
.20   With Delusions
.21   With Depressed Mood
         Specify if: With Behavioral Disturbance
290.xx   Vascular Dementia (143)
.40   Uncomplicated
.41   With Delirium
.42   With Delusions

.43   With Depressed Mood
            Specify if: With Behavioral Disturbance
294.9   Dementia Due to HIV Disease *(also code
            043.1 HIV infection affecting central ner-
            vous system on Axis III)* (148)
294.1   Dementia Due to Head Trauma *(also code
            854.00 head injury on Axis III)* (148)
294.1   Dementia Due to Parkinson's Disease *(also
            code 332.0 Parkinson's disease on Axis III)*
            (148)
294.1   Dementia Due to Huntington's Disease
            *(also code 333.4 Huntington's disease on
            Axis III)* (149)
294.1   Dementia Due to Pick's Disease *(also code
            331.1 Pick's disease on Axis III)* (149)
294.1   Dementia Due to Creutzfeldt-Jakob Disease
            *(also code 046.1 Creutzfeldt-Jakob disease
            on Axis III)* (150)
294.1   Dementia Due . . . *[Indicate the General
            Medical Condition not listed above] (also
            code the general medical condition on
            Axis III)* (151)
—.—   Substance-Induced Persisting Dementia
            *(refer to Substance-Related Disorders for
            substance-specific codes)* (152)
—.—   Dementia Due to Multiple Etiologies *(code
            each of the specific etiologies)* (154)
294.8   Dementia NOS (155)

Amnestic Disorders (156)

294.0   Amnestic Disorder Due to . . . *[Indicate the
            General Medical Condition]* (158)
            Specify if: Transient/Chronic
—.—   Substance-Induced Persisting Amnestic Dis-
            order *(refer to Substance-Related Disorders
            for substance-specific codes)* (161)
294.8   Amnestic Disorder NOS (163)

Other Cognitive Disorders (163)

294.9   Cognitive Disorder NOS (163)

MENTAL DISORDERS DUE TO A GENERAL MEDICAL CONDITION NOT ELSEWHERE CLASSIFIED (16)

293.89   Catatonic Disorder Due to . . . *[Indicate the
            General Medical Condition]* (169)

310.1   Personality Change Due to . . . *[Indicate the
            General Medical Condition]* (171)
            Specify type: Labile Type/Disinhibited
            Type/Aggressive Type/Apathetic Type/Para-
            noid Type/Other Type/Combined
            Type/Unspecified Type
293.9   Mental Disorder Due to . . . *[Indicate the
            General Medical Condition]* (174)

SUBSTANCE-RELATED DISORDERS (175)

[a]*The following specifiers may be applied to Substance Dependence:*

With Physiological Dependence/Without
Physiological Dependence

Early Full Remission/Early Partial Remission

Sustained Full Remission/Sustained Partial Remission

On Agonist Therapy/In a Controlled Environment

*The following specifiers apply to Substance-Induced
Disorders as noted:*

[I]With Onset During Intoxication/[W]With Onset During
Withdrawal

Alcohol-Related Disorders (194)

Alcohol Use Disorders
303.90   Alcohol Dependence[a]
305.00   Alcohol Abuse (196)

Alcohol-Induced Disorders
303.00   Alcohol Intoxication (196)
291.8   Alcohol Withdrawal (197)
            Specify if: With Perceptual Disturbances
291.0   Alcohol Intoxication Delirium (129)
291.0   Alcohol Withdrawal Delirium (129)
291.2   Alcohol-Induced Persisting Dementia (152)
291.1   Alcohol-Induced Persisting Amnestic Disor-
            der (161)
291.x   Alcohol-Induced Psychotic Disorder (310)
.5   With Delusions[I,W]
.3   With Hallucinations[I,W]
291.8   Alcohol-Induced Mood Disorder[I,W] (370)
291.8   Alcohol-Induced Anxiety Disorder[I,W] (439)
291.8   Alcohol-Induced Sexual Dysfunction[I] (519)
291.8   Alcohol-Induced Sleep Disorder[I,W] (601)
291.9   Alcohol-Related Disorder NOS (204)

Amphetamine (or Amphetamine-like)— Related Disorders (204)

Amphetamine Use Disorders
304.40 Amphetamine Dependence[2] (206)
305.70 Amphetamine Abuse (206)

Amphetamine-Induced Disorders
292.89 Amphetamine Intoxication (207)
   Specify if: With Perceptual Disturbances
292.0   Amphetamine Withdrawal (208)
292.81 Amphetamine Intoxication Delirium (129)
292.xx Amphetamine-Induced Psychotic Disorder (310)
.11   With Delusions[I]
.12   With Hallucinations[I]
292.84 Amphetamine-Induced Mood Disorder[I,W] (370)
292.89 Amphetamine-Induced Anxiety Disorder[I] (439)
292.89 Amphetamine-Induced Sexual Dysfunction[I] (519)
292.89 Amphetamine-Induced Sleep Disorder[I,W] (601)
292.92 Amphetamine-Related Disorder NOS (211)

CAFFEINE-RELATED DISORDERS (212)

Caffeine-Induced Disorders
305.90 Caffeine Intoxication (212)
292.89 Caffeine-Induced Anxiety Disorder[I] (439)
292.89 Caffeine-Induced Sleep Disorder[I] (601)
292.9   Caffeine-Related Disorder NOS (215)

Cannabis-Related Disorders (215)

Cannabis Use Disorders
304.30 Cannabis Dependence[2] (216)
305.20 Cannabis Abuse (217)

Cannabis-Induced Disorders
292.89 Cannabis Intoxication (217)
   Specify if: With Perceptual Disturbances
292.81 Cannabis Intoxication Delirium (129)
292.xx Cannabis-Induced Psychotic Disorder (310)
.11   With Delusions[I]
.12   With Hallucinations[I]
292.89 Cannabis-Induced Anxiety Disorder[I] (439)
292.9   Cannabis-Related Disorder NOS (221)

Cocaine-Related Disorders (221)

Cocaine Use Disorders
304.20 Cocaine Dependence[2] (222)
305.60 Cocaine Abuse (223)

Cocaine-Induced Disorders
292.89 Cocaine Intoxication (223)
   Specify if: With Perceptual Disturbances
292.0   Cocaine Withdrawal (225)
292.81 Cocaine Intoxication Delirium (129)
292.xx Cocaine-Induced Psychotic Disorder (310)
.11   With Delusions[I]
.12   With Hallucinations[I]
292.84 Cocaine-Induced Mood Disorder[I,W] (370)
292.89 Cocaine-Induced Anxiety Disorder[I,W] (439)
292.89 Cocaine-Induced Sexual Dysfunction[I] (519)
292.89 Cocaine-Induced Sleep Disorder[I,W] (601)
292.9   Cocaine-Related Disorder NOS (229)

Hallucinogen-Related Disorders (229)

Hallucinogen Use Disorders
304.50 Hallucinogen Dependence[2] (230)
305.30 Hallucinogen Abuse (231)

Hallucinogen-Induced Disorders
292.89 Hallucinogen Intoxication (232)
292.89 Hallucinogen Persisting Perception Disorder (Flashbacks) (233)
292.81 Hallucinogen Intoxication Delirium (129)
292.xx Hallucinogen-Induced Psychotic Disorder (310)
.11   With Delusions[I]
.12   With Hallucinations[I]
292.84 Hallucinogen-Induced Mood Disorder[I] (370)
292.89 Hallucinogen-Induced Anxiety Disorder[I] (439)
292.9   Hallucinogen-Related Disorder NOS (236)

Inhalant-Related Disorders (236)

Inhalant Use Disorders
304.60 Inhalant Dependence[2] (238)
305.90 Inhalant Abuse (238)

Inhalant-Induced Disorders
292.89 Inhalant Intoxication (239)
292.81 Inhalant Intoxication Delirium (129)
292.82 Inhalant-Induced Persisting Dementia (152)
292.xx Inhalant-Induced Psychotic Disorder (310)
.11   With Delusions[I]
.12   With Hallucinations[I]
292.84 Inhalant-Induced Mood Disorder[I] (370)

292.89   Inhalant-Induced Anxiety Disorder[I] (439)

292.9   Inhalant-Related Disorder NOS (242)

Nicotine-Related Disorders (242)

Nicotine Use Disorder
305.10   Nicotine Dependence[2] (243)
Nicotine-Induced Disorder
292.0   Nicotine Withdrawal (244)

292.9   Nicotine-Related Disorder NOS (247)

Opioid-Related Disorders (247)

Opioid Use Disorders
304.00   Opioid Dependence[2] (248)
305.40   Opioid Abuse (249)
Opioid-Induced Disorders
292.89   Opioid Intoxication (249)
           Specify if: With Perceptual Disturbances
292.0   Opioid Withdrawal (250)
292.81   Opioid Intoxication Delirium (129)
292.xx   Opioid-Induced Psychotic Disorder (310)
.11   With Delusions[I]
.12   With Hallucinations[I]
292.84   Opioid-Induced Mood Disorder[I] (370)
292.89   Opioid-Induced Sexual Dysfunction[I] (519)
292.89   Opioid-Induced Sleep Disorder[I,W] (601)
292.9   Opioid-Related Disorder NOS (244)

Phencyclidine (or Phencyclidine-Like)-Related Disorders (255)

Phencyclidine Use Disorders
304.90   Phencyclidine Dependence[2] (256)
305.90   Phencyclidine Abuse (257)
Phencyclidine-Induced Disorders
292.89   Phencyclidine Intoxication (257)
           Specify if: With Perceptual Disturbances
292.81   Phencyclidine Intoxication Delirium (129)
292.xx   Phencyclidine-Induced Psychotic Disorder (310)
.11   With Delusions[I]
.12   With Hallucinations[I]
292.84   Phencyclidine-Induced Mood Disorder[I] (370)
292.89   Phencyclidine-Induced Anxiety Disorder[I] (439)
292.9   Phencyclidine-Related Disorder NOS (261)

Sedative-, Hypnotic-, or Anxiolytic-Related Disorders (261)

Sedative, Hypnotic, or Anxiolytic Use Disorders
304.10   Sedative, Hypnotic, or Anxiolytic Dependence[2] (262)
305.40   Sedative, Hypnotic, or Anxiolytic Abuse (263)
Sedative-, Hypnotic-, or Anxiolytic-Induced Disorders
292.89   Sedative, Hypnotic, or Anxiolytic Intoxication (263)
292.0   Sedative, Hypnotic, or Anxiolytic Withdrawal (264)
           Specify if: With Perceptual Disturbances
292.81   Sedative, Hypnotic, or Anxiolytic Intoxication Delirium (129)
292.81   Sedative, Hypnotic, or Anxiolytic Withdrawal Delirium (129)
292.82   Sedative-, Hypnotic-, or Anxiolytic-Induced Persisting Dementia (152)
292.83   Sedative-, Hypnotic-, or Anxiolytic-Induced Persisting Amnestic Disorder (161)
292.xx   Sedative-, Hypnotic-, or Anxiolytic-Induced Psychotic Disorder (310)
.11   With Delusions[I,W]
.12   With Hallucinations[I,W]
292.84   Sedative-, Hypnotic-, or Anxiolytic-Induced Mood Disorder[I,W] (370)
292.89   Sedative-, Hypnotic-, or Anxiolytic-Induced Anxiety Disorder[W] (439)
292.89   Sedative-, Hypnotic-, or Anxiolytic-Induced Sexual Dysfunction[I] (519)
292.89   Sedative-, Hypnotic-, or Anxiolytic-Induced Sleep Disorder[I,W] (601)
292.9   Sedative-, Hypnotic-, or Anxiolytic-Related Disorder NOS (269)

Polysubstance-Related Disorder

304.80   Polysubstance Dependence[2] (270)

Other (or Unknown) Substance-Related Disorders (270)

Other (or Unknown) Substance Use Disorders
304.90   Other (or Unknown) Substance Dependence[2] (176)
305.90   Other (or Unknown) Substance Abuse (182)

Other (or Unknown) Substance-Induced Disorders

292.89 Other (or Unknown) Substance Intoxication (183)
        Specify if: With Perceptual Disturbances
292.0   Other (or Unknown) Substance Withdrawal (184)
        Specify if: With Perceptual Disturbances
292.81 Other (or Unknown) Substance-Induced Delirium (129)
292.82 Other (or Unknown) Substance-Induced Persisting Dementia (152)
292.83 Other (or Unknown) Substance-Induced Persisting Amnestic Disorder (161)
292.xx Other (or Unknown) Substance-Induced Psychotic Disorder (310)
.11   With Delusions[I,W]
.12   With Hallucinations[I,W]
292.84 Other (or Unknown) Substance-Induced Mood Disorder[I,W] (370)
292.89 Other (or Unknown) Substance-Induced Anxiety Disorder[W] (439)
292.89 Other (or Unknown) Substance-Induced Sexual Dysfunction[I] (519)
292.89 Other (or Unknown) Substance-Induced Sleep Disorder[I,W] (601)
292.9   Other (or Unknown) Substance-Related Disorder NOS (272)

.20   Catatonic Type (288)
.90   Undifferentiated Type (289)
.60   Residual Type (289)
295.40 Schizophreniform Disorder (290)
        Specify if: Without Good Prognostic Features/With Good Prognostic Features
295.70 Schizoaffective Disorder (292)
        Specify type: Bipolar Type/Depressive Type
297.1   Delusional Disorder (296)
        Specify type: Erotomanic Type/Grandiose Type/Jealous Type/Persecutory Type/Somatic Type/Mixed Type/Unspecified Type
298.8   Brief Psychotic Disorder (302)
        Specify if: With marked Stressor(s)/Without Marked Stressor(s)/With Postpartum Onset
297.3   Shared Psychotic Disorder (305)
293.xx Psychotic Disorder Due to . . .
        [Indicate the General Medical Condition] (306)
.81   With Delusions
.82   With Hallucinations
—.—   Substance-Induced Psychotic Disorder *(refer to Substance-Related Disorders for substance-specific codes)* (310)
        specify if: With Onset During Intoxication/With Onset During Withdrawal
298.9   Psychotic Disorder NOS (315)

SCHIZOPHRENIA AND OTHER PSYCHOTIC DISORDERS (273)

295.xx Schizophrenia (274)

The following Classification of Longitudinal Course applies to all subtypes of Schizophrenia:

Episodic With Interepisode Residual Symptoms (*specify if:* With Prominent Negative Symptoms)/Episodic With No Interepisode Residual Symptoms

Continuous (*specify if:* With Prominent Negative Symptoms)

Single Episode in Partial Remission (*specify if:* With Prominent Negative Symptoms)/Single Episode in Full Remission

Other or Unspecified Pattern

.30   Paranoid Type (287)
.10   Disorganized Type (287)

MOOD DISORDERS (317)

Code current state of Major Depressive Disorder or Bipolar I Disorder in fifth digit:

1 = Mild

2 = Moderate

3 = Severe Without Psychotic Features

4 = Severe With Psychotic Features

Specify: Mood-Congruent Psychotic Features/Mood-Incongruent Psychotic Features

5 = In Partial Remission

6 = In Full Remission

0 = Unspecified

The following specifiers apply (for current or most recent episode) to Mood Disorders as noted:

[a]Severity/Psychotic/Remission Specifiers/[b]Chronic/[c]With Catatonic Features/[d]With

Melancholic Features/ᵉWith Atypical Features/ᶠWith Postpartum Onset

The following specifiers apply to Mood Disorders as noted:

ᵍWith or Without Full Interepisode Recovery/ʰWith Seasonal Pattern/ⁱWith Rapid Cycling

Depressive Disorders

296.xx	Major Depressive Disorder, (339)
.2x	Single Episode^{a,b,c,d,e,f}
.3x	Recurrent^{a,b,c,d,e,f,g,h}
300.4	Dysthymic Disorder (345)
	Specify if: Early Onset/Late Onset
	Specify: With Atypical Features
311	Depressive Disorder NOS (350)

Bipolar Disorders

296.xx	Bipolar I Disorder, (350)
.0x	Single Manic Episode^{a,c,f}
	Specify if: Mixed
.40	Most Recent Episode Hypomanic^{g,h,i}
.4x	Most Recent Episode Manic^{a,c,f,g,h,i}
.6x	Most Recent Episode Mixed^{a,c,f,g,h,i}
.5x	Most Recent Episode Depressed^{a,b,c,d,e,f,g,h,i}
.7	Most Recent Episode Unspecified^{g,h,i}
296.89	Bipolar II Disorder^{a,b,c,d,e,f,g,h,i} (359)
	Specify (current or most recent episode): Hypomanic/Depressed
391.13	Cyclothymic Disorder (363)
296.80	Bipolar Disorder NOS (366)
293.83	Mood Disorder Due to . . .*[Indicate the General Medical Condition]* (366)
	Specify type: With Depressive Features/With Major Depressive-Like Episode/With Manic Features/With Mixed Features
—.—	Substance-Induced Mood Disorder *(refer to Substance-Related Disorders for substance-specific codes)* (370)
	Specify type: With Depressive Features/With Manic Features/With Mixed Features
	Specify if: With Onset During Intoxication/With Onset During Withdrawal
296.90	Mood Disorder NOS (375)

ANXIETY DISORDERS (393)

300.01	Panic Disorder Without Agoraphobia (397)
300.21	Panic Disorder With Agoraphobia (397)
300.22	Agoraphobia Without History of Panic Disorder (403)
300.29	Specific Phobia (405)
	Specify type: Animal Type/Natural Environment Type/Blood-Injection-Injury Type/Situational Type/Other Type
300.23	Social Phobia (411)
	Specify if: Generalized
300.3	Obsessive-Compulsive Disorder (417)
	Specify if: With Poor Insight
309.81	Posttraumatic Stress Disorder (424)
	Specify if: Acute/Chronic
	Specify if: With Delayed Onset
308.3	Acute Stress Disorder (429)
300.02	Generalized Anxiety Disorder (432)
293.89	Anxiety Disorder Due to . . .*[Indicate the General Medical Condition]* (436)
	Specify if: With Generalized Anxiety/With Panic Attacks/With Obsessive-Compulsive Symptoms
—.—	Substance-Induced Anxiety Disorder *(refer to Substance-Related Disorders for substance-specific codes)* (439)
	Specify if: With Generalized Anxiety/With Panic Attacks/With Obsessive-Compulsive Symptoms/With Phobic Symptoms
	Specify if: With Onset During Intoxication/With Onset During Withdrawal
300.0	Anxiety Disorder NOS (444)

SOMATOFORM DISORDERS (445)

300.81	Somatization Disorder (446)
300.81	Undifferentiated Somatoform Disorder (450)
300.11	Conversion Disorder (452)
	Specify type: With Motor Symptom or Deficit/With Sensory Symptom or Deficit/With Seizures or Convulsions/With Mixed Presentation
307.xx	Pain Disorder (458)
.80	Associated With Psychological Factors
.89	Associated With Both Psychological Factors and a General Medical Condition
	Specify if: Acute/Chronic
300.7	Hypochondriasis (462)

Specify if: With Poor Insight

300.7   Body Dysmorphic Disorder (466)

300.81   Somatoform Disorder NOS (468)

FACTITIOUS DISORDERS (471)

300.xx   Factitious Disorder (471)

.16   With Predominantly Psychological Signs and Symptoms

.19   With Predominantly Physical Signs and Symptoms

.19   With Combined Psychological and Physical Signs and Symptoms

300.19   Factitious Disorder NOS (475)

DISSOCIATIVE DISORDERS (477)

300.12   Dissociative Amnesia (478)

300.13   Dissociative Fugue (481)

300.14   Dissociative Identity Disorder (484)

300.6   Depersonalization Disorder (488)

300.15   Dissociative Disorder NOS (490)

SEXUAL AND GENDER IDENTITY DISORDERS (493)

Sexual Dysfunctions (493)

The following specifiers apply to all primary Sexual Dysfunctions:

Lifelong Type/Acquired Type

Generalized Type/Situational Type

Due to Psychological Factors/Due to Combined Factors

Sexual Desire Disorder

302.71   Hypoactive Sexual Desire Disorder (496)

302.79   Sexual Aversion Disorder (499)

Sexual Arousal Disorders

302.72   Female Sexual Arousal Disorder (500)

302.72   Male Erectile Disorder (502)

Orgasmic Disorders

302.73   Female Orgasmic Disorder (505)

302.74   Male Orgasmic Disorder (507)

302.75   Premature Ejaculation (509)

Sexual Pain Disorders

302.76   Dyspareunia (Not Due to a General Medical Condition) (511)

306.51   Vaginismus (Not Due to a General Medical Condition) (513)

Sexual Dysfunction Due to a General Medical Condition (515)

625.8   Female Hypoactive Sexual Desire Disorder Due to . . . *[Indicate the General Medical Condition]* (515)

608.89   Male Hypoactive Sexual Desire Disorder Due to . . . *[Indicate the General Medical Condition]* (515)

607.84   Male Erectile Disorder Due to . . . *[Indicate the General Medical Condition]* (515)

625.0   Female Dyspareunia Due to . . . *[Indicate the General Medical Condition]* (515)

608.89   Male Dyspareunia Due to . . . *[Indicate the General Medical Condition]* (515)

625.8   Other Female Sexual Dysfunction Due to . . . *[Indicate the General Medical Condition]* (515)

608.89   Other Male Sexual Dysfunction Due to . . . *[Indicate the General Medical Condition]* (515)

—.—   Substance-Induced Sexual Dysfunction *(refer to Substance-Related Disorders for substance-specific codes)* (519)

Specify if: With Impaired Desire/With Impaired Arousal/With Impaired Orgasm/With Sexual Pain

Specify if: With Onset During Intoxication

302.70   Sexual Dysfunction NOS (522)

Paraphilias (522)

302.4   Exhibitionism (525)

302.81   Fetishism (526)

302.89   Frotteurism (527)

302.2   Pedophilia (527)

Specify if: Sexually Attracted to Males/Sexually Attracted to Females/Sexually Attracted to Both

Specify if: Limited to Incest

Specify type: Exclusive Type/Nonexclusive Type

302.83   Sexual Masochism (529)

302.84   Sexual Sadism (530)

302.3   Transvestic Fetishism (530)

Specify if: With Gender Dysphoria

302.82   Voyeurism (532)

302.9   Paraphilia NOS (532)

GENDER IDENTITY DISORDERS (532)

302.xx   Gender Identity Disorder (532)
.6   in Children
.85   in Adolescents or Adults
          Specify if: Sexually Attracted to Males/Sexually Attracted to Females/Sexually Attracted to Both/Sexually Attracted to Neither
302.6   Gender Identity Disorder NOS (538)
302.9   Sexual Disorder NOS (538)

EATING DISORDERS (539)

307.1   Anorexia Nervosa (539)
          Specify type: Restricting Type; Binge-Eating/Purging Type
307.51   Bulimia Nervosa (545)
          Specify type: Purging Type/Nonpurging Type
307.50   Eating Disorder NOS (550)

SLEEP DISORDERS (551)

Primary Sleep Disorders (553)

Dyssomnias (553)
307.42   Primary Insomnia (533)
307.44   Primary Hypersomnia (557)
          Specify if: Recurrent
347   Narcolepsy (562)
780.59   Breathing-Related Sleep Disorder (573)
307.45   Circadian Rhythm Sleep Disorder (573)
          Specify type: Delayed Sleep Phase Type/Jet Lag Type/Shift Work Type/Unspecified Type
307.47   Dyssomnia NOS (579)

Parasomnias (579)
307.47   Nightmare Disorder (580)
307.46   Sleep Terror Disorder (583)
307.46   Sleepwalking Disorder (587)
307.47   Parasomnia NOS (592)

Sleep Disorders Related to Another Mental Disorder (592)

307.42   Insomnia Related to . . . *[Indicate the Axis I or Axis II Disorder]* (592)
307.44   Hypersomnia Related to . . . *[Indicate the Axis I or Axis II Disorder]* (592)

Other Sleep Disorders

780.xx   Sleep Disorder Due to . . . *[Indicate the General Medical Condition]* (597)

.52   Insomnia Type
.54   Hypersomnia Type
.59   Parasomnia Type
.59   Mixed Type
—.—   Substance-Induced Sleep Disorder *(refer to Substance-Related Disorders for substance-specific codes)* (601)
          Specify type: Insomnia Type/Hypersomnia Type/Parasomnia Type/Mixed Type
          Specify if: With Onset During Intoxication/With Onset During Withdrawal

IMPULSE-CONTROL DISORDERS NOT ELSEWHERE CLASSIFIED (609)

312.34   Intermittent Explosive Disorder (609)
312.32   Kleptomania (612)
312.33   Pyromania (614)
312.31   Pathological Gambling (615)
312.39   Trichotillomania (618)
312.30   Impulse-Control Disorder NOS (621)

ADJUSTMENT DISORDERS (623)

309.xx   Adjustment Disorder (623)
.0   With Depressed Mood
.24   With Anxiety
.28   With Mixed Anxiety and Depressed Mood
.3   With Disturbance of Conduct
.4   With Mixed Disturbance of Emotions and Conduct
.9   Unspecified
          Specify if: Acute/Chronic

PERSONALITY DISORDERS (629)

Note: These are coded on Axis II.
301.0   Paranoid Personality Disorder (634)
301.20   Schizoid Personality Disorder (638)
301.22   Schizotypal Personality Disorder (641)
301.7   Antisocial Personality Disorder (645)
301.83   Borderline Personality Disorder (650)
301.50   Histrionic Personality Disorder (655)
301.81   Narcissistic Personality Disorder (658)
301.82   Avoidant Personality Disorder (662)
301.6   Dependent Personality Disorder (665)
301.4   Obsessive-Compulsive Personality Disorder (669)
301.9   Personality Disorder NOS (673)

OTHER CONDITIONS THAT MAY BE A FOCUS OF CLINICAL ATTENTION (675)

Psychological Factors Affecting Medical Condition (675)

316   . . . *[Specified Psychological Factor] Affecting . . . [Indicate the General Medical Condition]* (675)
Choose name based on nature of factors:
Mental Disorder Affecting Medical Condition
Psychological Symptoms Affecting Medical Condition
Personality Traits or Coping Style Affecting Medical Condition
Maladaptive Health Behaviors Affecting Medical Condition
Stress-Related Physiological Response Affecting Medical Condition
Other or Unspecified Psychological Factors Affecting Medical Condition

Medication-Induced Movement Disorders (678)

332.1	Neuroleptic-Induced Parkinsonism (679)
333.92	Neuroleptic Malignant Syndrome (679)
333.7	Neuroleptic-Induced Acute Dystonia (679)
333.99	Neuroleptic-Induced Acute Akathisia (679)
333.82	Neuroleptic-Induced Tardive Dyskinesia (679)
333.1	Medication-Induced Postural Tremor (680)
333.90	Medication-Induced Movement Disorder NOS (680)

Other Medication-Induced Disorder

995.2   Adverse Effects of Medication NOS (680)

Relational Problems (680)

V61.9	Relational Problem Related to a Mental Disorder or General Medical Condition (681)
V61.20	Parent-Child Relational Problem (681)
V61.1	Partner Relational Problem (681)
V61.8	Sibling Relational Problem (681)
V62.81	Relational Problem NOS (681)

Problems Related to Abuse or Neglect (682)

V62.21   Physical Abuse of Child (682)
       (code 995.5 if focus of attention is on victim)
V62.21   Sexual Abuse of Child (682)
       (code 995.5 if focus of attention is on victim)
V62.21   Neglect of Child (682)
       (code 995.5 if focus of attention is on victim)
V61.1   Physical Abuse of Adult (682)
       (code 995.81 if focus of attention is on victim)
V61.1   Sexual Abuse of Adult (682)
       (code 995.81 if focus of attention is on victim)

Additional Conditions That May Be a Focus of Clinical Attention (683)

V15.81	Noncompliance With Treatment (683)
V65.2	Malingering (683)
V71.01	Adult Antisocial Behavior (683)
V71.02	Child or Adolescent Antisocial Behavior (684)
V62.89	Borderline Intellectual Functioning (684)
	Note: This is coded on Axis II.
780.9	Age-Related Cognitive Decline (684)
V62.82	Bereavement (684)
V62.3	Academic Problem (685)
V62.2	Occupational Problem (685)
313.82	Identity Problem (685)
V62.89	Religious or Spiritual Problem (685)
V62.4	Acculturation Problem (685)
V62.89	Phase of Life Problem (685)

ADDITIONAL CODES

300.9	Unspecified Mental Disorder (nonpsychotic) (687)
V71.09	No Diagnosis or Condition on Axis I (687)
799.9	Diagnosis or Condition Deferred on Axis I (687)
V71.09	No Diagnosis on Axis II (687)
799.9	Diagnosis Deferred on Axis II (687)

MULTIAXIAL SYSTEM

Axis I	Clinical Disorders
	Other Conditions That May Be a Focus of Clinical Attention
Axis II	Personality Disorders
	Mental Retardation
Axis III	General Medical Conditions
Axis IV	Psychosocial and Environmental Problems
Axis V	Global Assessment of Functioning

COUNSELING-RELATED ORGANIZATIONS

American Association for Marriage and Family Therapy
www.AAMFT.org
1133 Fifteenth Street, N.W., Suite 300
Washington, DC 20005-2710
(202) 452-0109

American Counseling Association
www.counseling.org
5999 Stevenson Avenue
Alexandria, VA 22304
(703) 823-9800

American Psychological Association
www.APA.org
Division 17/Counseling Psychology
750 First Street, N.E.
Washington, DC 20002-4242
(202) 336-5500

Chi Sigma Iota
www.csi-net.org
School of Education
250 Ferguson Building
University of North Carolina–Greensboro
Greensboro, NC 27412
(336) 334-4035

Council for Accreditation of Counseling and Related
    Educational Programs (CACREP)
www.counseling.org/CACREP/main.htm
5999 Stevenson Avenue
Alexandria, VA 22304-3302
(800) 347-5547, ext. 301

ERIC/CASS
www.uncg.edu/~ericcas2/
201 Ferguson Building
University of North Carolina–Greensboro
Greensboro, NC 27412
(336) 334-4114

National Board for Certified Counselors, Inc.
www.nbcc.org
3 Terrace Way, Suite D
Greensboro, NC 27403-3660
(336) 547-0607

NAME INDEX

SUBJECT INDEX

ABOUT THE AUTHOR

Samuel T. Gladding is a professor of counselor education and director of Counselor Education at Wake Forest University in Winston-Salem, North Carolina. His leadership in the field of counseling includes service as president of the Association for Specialists in Group Work, President of Chi Sigma Iota (counseling academic and professional honor society international), president of the Association for Counselor Education and Supervision, president of the Southern Association for Counselor Education and Supervision, and vice president of the Association for Humanistic Education and Development.

He is the former editor of the *Journal for Specialists in Group Work* and the ASGW newsletter, *Together.* He is also the author of more than 100 professional publications, including three videotapes. His most recent Merrill/Prentice Hall books are *Group Work: A Counseling Specialty* (3rd ed., 1999), *Family Therapy: History, Theory and Process* (2nd ed., 1998), and *Community and Agency Counseling* (1997).

Gladding's previous academic appointments have been at the University of Alabama at Birmingham, Fairfield University, Connecticut, and Rockingham Community College, Wentworth, North Carolina. He is the former director of children's services at the Rockingham County Mental Health Center, also in Wentworth, North Carolina. Gladding received his degrees from Wake Forest, Yale, and the University of North Carolina-Greensboro. He is a national certified counselor (NCC), a certified clinical mental health counselor (CCMHC), and a licensed professional counselor (North Carolina). He is a former member of the Alabama Board of Examiners in Counseling.

Gladding is married to the former Claire Tillson and is the father of three children: Benjamin, Nathaniel, and Timothy. Outside of counseling, he enjoys swimming, tennis, jogging, music, and humor. You can visit him at his Web site at www.wfu.edu/~stg or e-mail him at stg@wfu.edu.